Letters of Samuel Taylor Coleridge

Complete

Volumes I & II

Samuel Taylor Coleridge

Edited by Ernest Hartley Coleridge

TABLE OF CONTENTS

CHAPTER I. STUDENT LIFE, 1785-1794.

I.	Thomas Poole, February, 1797. (Biographia Literaria, 1847, ii. 313)
II.	Thomas Poole, March, 1797. (Biographia Literaria, 1847, ii. 315)
III.	Thomas Poole, October 9, 1797. (Biographia Literaria, 1847, ii. 319)
IV.	Thomas Poole, October 16, 1797. (Biographia Literaria, 1847, ii. 322)
V.	Thomas Poole, February 19, 1798. (Biographia Literaria, 1847, ii. 326)
VI.	Mrs. Coleridge, Senior, February 4, 1785. (Illustrated London News, April 1, 1893)
VII.	Rev. George Coleridge, undated, before 1790. (Illustrated London News, April 1, 1893)
VIII.	Rev. George Coleridge, October 16, 1791. (Illustrated London News, April 8, 1893)
IX.	Rev. George Coleridge, January 24, 1792
X.	Mrs. Evans, February 13, 1792
XI.	Mary Evans, February 13, 1792
XII.	Anne Evans, February 19, 1792
XIII.	Mrs. Evans, February 22 [1792]
XIV.	Mary Evans, February 22 [1792]
XV.	Rev. George Coleridge, April [1792]. (Illustrated London News, April 8, 1893)
XVI.	Mrs. Evans, February 5, 1793
XVII.	Mary Evans, February 7, 1793. (Illustrated London News, April 8, 1893)
XVIII.	Anne Evans, February 10, 1793
XIX.	Rev. George Coleridge, July 28, 1793
XX.	Rev. George Coleridge [Postmark, August 5, 1793]
XXI.	G. L. Tuckett, February 6 [1794], (Illustrated London News, April 15, 1893)
XXII.	Rev. George Coleridge, February 8, 1794
XXIII.	Rev. George Coleridge, February 11, 1794
XXIV.	Capt. James Coleridge, February 20, 1794. (Brandl's Life of Coleridge, 1887, p. 65)
XXV.	Rev. George Coleridge, March 12, 1794. (Illustrated London News, April 15, 1893)
XXVI.	Rev. George Coleridge, March 21, 1794
XXVII.	Rev. George Coleridge, end of March, 1794
XXVIII.	Rev. George Coleridge, March 27, 1794
XXIX.	Rev. George Coleridge, March 30, 1794
XXX.	Rev. George Coleridge, April 7, 1794
XXXI.	Rev. George Coleridge, May 1, 1794
XXXII.	Robert Southey, July 6, 1794. (Sixteen lines published, Southey's Life and Correspondence, 1849, i. 212)
XXXIII.	Robert Southey, July 15, 1794. (Portions published in Letter to H. Martin, July 22, 1794, Biographia Literaria, 1847, ii. 338)

XXXIV.	Robert Southey, September 18, 1794. (Eighteen lines published, Southey's Life and Correspondence, 1849, i. 218)
XXXV.	Robert Southey, September 19, 1794
XXXVI.	Robert Southey, September 26, 1794
XXXVII.	Robert Southey, October 21, 1794
XXXVIII.	Robert Southey, November, 1794
XXXIX.	Robert Southey, Autumn, 1794. (Illustrated London News, April 15, 1893
XL.	Rev. George Coleridge, November 6, 1794
XLI.	Robert Southey, December 11, 1794
XLII.	Robert Southey, December 17, 1794
XLIII.	Robert Southey, December, 1794. (Eighteen lines published, Southey's Life and Correspondence, 1849, i. 227)
XLIV.	Mary Evans, (?) December, 1794. (Samuel Taylor Coleridge, A Narrative, 1894, p. 38)
XLV.	Mary Evans, December 24, 1794. (Samuel Taylor Coleridge, A Narrative, 1894, p. 40)
XLVI.	Robert Southey, December, 1794

CHAPTER II. EARLY PUBLIC LIFE, 1795-1796.

XLVII.	Joseph Cottle, Spring, 1795. (Early Recollections, 1837, i. 16)
XLVIII.	Joseph Cottle, July 31, 1795. (Early Recollections, 1837, i. 52)
XLIX.	Joseph Cottle, 1795. (Early Recollections, 1837, i. 55)
L.	Robert Southey, October, 1795
LI.	Thomas Poole, October 7, 1795. (Biographia Literaria, 1847, ii. 347)
LII.	Robert Southey, November 13, 1795
LIII.	Josiah Wade, January 27, 1796. (Biographia Literaria, 1847, ii. 350)
LIV.	Joseph Cottle, February 22, 1796. (Early Recollections, 1837, i. 141; Biographia Literaria, 1847, ii. 356)
LV.	Thomas Poole, March 30, 1796. (Biographia Literaria, 1847, ii. 357)
LVI.	Thomas Poole, May 12, 1796. (Biographia Literaria, 1847, ii. 366; Thomas Poole and his Friends, 1887, i. 144)
LVII.	John Thelwall, May 13, 1796
LVIII.	Thomas Poole, May 29, 1796. (Biographia Literaria, 1847, ii. 368)
LIX.	John Thelwall, June 22, 1796
LX.	Thomas Poole, September 24, 1796. (Biographia Literaria, 1847, ii. 373; Thomas Poole and his Friends, 1887, i. 155)
LXI.	Charles Lamb [September 28, 1796]. (Gillman's Life of Coleridge, 1838, pp. 338-340)
LXII.	Thomas Poole, November 5, 1796. (Biographia Literaria, 1847, ii. 379; Thomas Poole and his Friends, 1887, i. 175)
LXIII.	Thomas Poole, November 7, 1796
LXIV.	John Thelwall, November 19 [1796]. (Twenty-six lines published, Samuel Taylor Coleridge, A Narrative, 1894, p. 58)
LXV.	Thomas Poole, December 11, 1796. (Thomas Poole and his Friends, 1887, i. 182)

LXVI.	Thomas Poole, December 12, 1796. (Thomas Poole and his Friends, 1887, i. 184)
LXVII.	Thomas Poole, December 13, 1796. (Thomas Poole and his Friends, 1887, i. 186)
LXVIII.	John Thelwall, December 17, 1796
LXIX.	Thomas Poole [? December 18, 1796]. (Thomas Poole and his Friends, 1887, i. 195)
LXX.	John Thelwall, December 31, 1796

CHAPTER III. THE STOWEY PERIOD, 1797-1798.

LXXI.	Rev. J. P. Estlin [1797]. (Privately printed, Philobiblon Society)
LXXII.	John Thelwall, February 6, 1797
LXXIII.	Joseph Cottle, June, 1797. (Early Recollections, 1837, i. 250)
LXXIV.	Robert Southey, July, 1797
LXXV.	John Thelwall [October 16], 1797
LXXVI.	John Thelwall [Autumn, 1797]
LXXVII.	John Thelwall [Autumn, 1797]
LXXVIII.	William Wordsworth, January, 1798. (Ten lines published, Life of Wordsworth, 1889, i. 128)
LXXIX.	Joseph Cottle, March 8, 1798. (Part published incorrectly, Early Recollections, 1837, i. 251)
LXXX.	Rev. George Coleridge, April, 1798
LXXXI.	Rev. J. P. Estlin, May [? 1798]. (Privately printed, Philobiblon Society)
LXXXII.	Rev. J. P. Estlin, May 14, 1798. (Privately printed, Philobiblon Society)
LXXXIII.	Thomas Poole, May 14, 1798. (Thirty-one lines published, Thomas Poole and his Friends, 1887, i. 268)
LXXXIV.	Thomas Poole [May 20, 1798]. (Eleven lines published, Thomas Poole and his Friends, 1887, i. 269)
LXXXV.	Charles Lamb [spring of 1798]

CHAPTER IV. A VISIT TO GERMANY, 1798-1799.

LXXXVI.	Thomas Poole, September 15, 1798. (Thomas Poole and his Friends, 1887, i. 273)
LXXXVII.	Mrs. S. T. Coleridge, September 19, 1798
LXXXVIII.	Mrs. S. T. Coleridge, October 20, 1798
LXXXIX.	Mrs. S. T. Coleridge, November 26, 1798
XC.	Mrs. S. T. Coleridge, December 2, 1798
XCI.	Rev. Mr. Roskilly, December 3, 1798
XCII.	Thomas Poole, January 4, 1799
XCIII.	Mrs. S. T. Coleridge, January 14, 179
XCIV.	Mrs. S. T. Coleridge, March 12, 1799. (Illustrated London News, April 29, 1893)
XCV.	Thomas Poole, April 6, 1799
XCVI.	Mrs. S. T. Coleridge, April 8, 1799. (Thirty lines published, Thomas Poole and his Friends, 1887, i. 295)
XCVII.	Mrs. S. T. Coleridge, April 23, 1799

XCVIII.	Thomas Poole, May 6, 1799. (Thomas Poole and his Friends, 1887, i. 297)

CHAPTER V. FROM SOUTH TO NORTH, 1799-1800.

XCIX.	Robert Southey, July 29, 1799
C.	Thomas Poole, September 16, 1799
CI.	Robert Southey, October 15, 1799
CII.	Robert Southey, November 10, 1799
CIII.	Robert Southey, December 9 [1799]
CIV.	Robert Southey [December 24], 1799
CV.	Robert Southey, January 25, 1800
CVI.	Robert Southey [early in 1800]
CVII.	Robert Southey [Postmark, February 18], 1800
CVIII.	Robert Southey [early in 1800]
CIX.	Robert Southey, February 28, 1800

CHAPTER VI. A LAKE POET, 1800-1803.

CX.	Thomas Poole, August 14, 1800. (Illustrated London News, May 27, 1893)
CXI.	Sir H. Davy, October 9, 1800. (Fragmentary Remains, 1858, p. 80)
CXII.	Sir H. Davy, October 18, 1800. (Fragmentary Remains, 1858, p. 79)
CXIII.	Sir H. Davy, December 2, 1800. (Fragmentary Remains, 1858, p. 83)
CXIV.	Thomas Poole, December 5, 1800. (Eight lines published, Thomas Poole and his Friends, 1887, ii. 21)
CXV.	Sir H. Davy, February 3, 1801. (Fragmentary Remains, 1858, p. 86)
CXVI.	Thomas Poole, March 16, 1801
CXVII.	Thomas Poole, March 23, 1801
CXVIII.	Robert Southey [May 6, 1801]
CXIX.	Robert Southey, July 22, 1801
CXX.	Robert Southey, July 25, 1801
CXXI.	Robert Southey, August 1, 1801
CXXII.	Thomas Poole, September 19, 1801. (Thomas Poole and his Friends, 1887, ii. 65)
CXXIII.	Robert Southey, December 31, 1801
CXXIV.	Mrs. S. T. Coleridge [February 24, 1802]
CXXV.	W. Sotheby, July 13, 1802
CXXVI.	W. Sotheby, July 19, 1802
CXXVII.	Robert Southey, July 29, 1802
CXXVIII.	Robert Southey, August 9, 1802
CXXIX.	W. Sotheby, August 26, 1802
CXXX.	W. Sotheby, September 10, 1802
CXXXI.	W. Sotheby, September 27, 1802
CXXXII.	Mrs. S. T. Coleridge, November 16, 1802
CXXXIII.	Rev. J. P. Estlin, December 7, 1802. (Privately printed, Philobiblon Society)
CXXXIV.	Robert Southey, December 25, 1802

CXXXV.	Thomas Wedgwood, January 9, 1803
CXXXVI.	Mrs. S. T. Coleridge, April 4, 1803
CXXXVII.	Robert Southey, July 2, 1803
CXXXVIII.	Robert Southey, July, 1803
CXXXIX.	Robert Southey, August 7, 1803
CXL.	Mrs. S. T. Coleridge, September 1, 1803
CXLI.	Robert Southey, September 10, 1803
CXLII.	Robert Southey, September 13, 1803
CXLIII.	Matthew Coates, December 5, 1803

CHAPTER VII. A LONG ABSENCE, 1804-1806.

CXLIV.	Richard Sharp, January 15, 1804. (Life of Wordsworth, 1889, ii. 9)
CXLV.	Thomas Poole, January 15, 1804. (Forty lines published, Thomas Poole and his Friends, 1887, ii. 122)
CXLVI.	Thomas Poole [January 26, 1804]
CXLVII.	The Wordsworth Family, February 8, 1804. (Life of Wordsworth, 1889, ii. 12)
CXLVIII.	Mrs. S. T. Coleridge, February 19, 1804
CXLIX.	Robert Southey, February 20, 1804
CL.	Mrs. S. T. Coleridge, April 1, 1804
CLI.	Robert Southey, April 16, 1804
CLII.	Daniel Stuart, April 21, 1804. (Privately printed, Letters from the Lake Poets, p. 33)
CLIII.	Mrs. S. T. Coleridge, June, 1804
CLIV.	Daniel Stuart, October 22, 1804. (Privately printed, Letters from the Lake Poets, p. 45)
CLV.	Robert Southey, February 2, 1805
CLVI.	Daniel Stuart, April 20, 1805. (Privately printed, Letters from the Lake Poets, p. 46)
CLVII.	Mrs. S. T. Coleridge, July 21, 1805
CLVIII.	Washington Allston, June 17, 1806. (Scribner's Magazine, January, 1892)
CLIX.	Daniel Stuart, August 18, 1806. (Privately printed, Letters from the Lake Poets, p. 54)

CHAPTER VIII. HOME AND NO HOME, 1806-1807.

CLX.	Daniel Stuart, September 15, 1806. (Privately printed, Letters from the Lake Poets, p. 60)
CLXI.	Mrs. S. T. Coleridge, September 16 [1806]
CLXII.	Mrs. S. T. Coleridge, December 25, 1806
CLXIII.	Hartley Coleridge, April 3, 1807
CLXIV.	Sir H. Davy, September 11, 1807. (Fragmentary Remains, 1858, p. 99)

CHAPTER IX. A PUBLIC LECTURER, 1807-1808.

CLXV.	The Morgan Family [November 23, 1807]
CLXVI.	Robert Southey [December 14, 1807]
CLXVII.	Mrs. Morgan, January 25, 1808

| CLXVIII. | Francis Jeffrey, May 23, 1808 |
| CLXIX. | Francis Jeffrey, July 20, 1808 |

CHAPTER X. GRASMERE AND THE FRIEND, 1808-1810.

CLXX.	Daniel Stuart [December 9, 1808]. (Privately printed, Letters from the Lake Poets, p. 93)
CLXXI.	Francis Jeffrey, December 14, 1808. (Illustrated London News, June 10, 1893)
CLXXII.	Thomas Wilkinson, December 31, 1808. (Friends' Quarterly Magazine, June, 1893)
CLXXIII.	Thomas Poole, February 3, 1809. (Fifteen lines published, Thomas Poole and his Friends, 1887, ii. 228)
CLXXIV.	Daniel Stuart, March 31, 1809. (Privately printed, Letters from the Lake Poets, p. 136)
CLXXV.	Daniel Stuart, June 13, 1809. (Privately printed, Letters from the Lake Poets, p. 165)
CLXXVI.	Thomas Poole, October 9, 1809. (Thomas Poole and his Friends, 1887, ii. 233)
CLXXVII.	Robert Southey, December, 1809
CLXXVIII.	Thomas Poole, January 28, 1810

CHAPTER XI. A JOURNALIST, A LECTURER, A PLAYWRIGHT, 1810-1813.

CLXXIX.	Mrs. S. T. Coleridge, Spring, 1810
CLXXX.	The Morgans, December 21, 1810
CLXXXI.	W. Godwin, March 15, 1811. (William Godwin, by C. Kegan Paul, ii. 222)
CLXXXII.	Daniel Stuart, June 4, 1811. (Gentleman's Magazine, 1838)
CLXXXIII.	Sir G. Beaumont, December 7, 1811. (Memorials of Coleorton, 1887, ii. 158)
CLXXXIV.	J. J. Morgan, February 28, 1812
CLXXXV.	Mrs. S. T. Coleridge, April 21, 1812
CLXXXVI.	Mrs. S. T. Coleridge, April 24, 1812
CLXXXVII.	Charles Lamb, May 2, 1812
CLXXXVIII.	William Wordsworth, May 4, 1812
CLXXXIX.	Daniel Stuart, May 8, 1812. (Privately printed, Letters from the Lake Poets, p. 211)
CXC.	William Wordsworth, May 11, 1812. (Life of Wordsworth, 1889, ii. 180)
CXCI.	Robert Southey [May 12, 1812]
CXCII.	William Wordsworth, December 7, 1812. (Life of Wordsworth, 1889, ii. 181)
CXCIII.	Mrs. S. T. Coleridge [January 20, 1813]
CXCIV.	Robert Southey, February 8, 1813. (Illustrated London News, June 24, 1894)
CXCV.	Thomas Poole, February 13, 1813. (Six lines published, Thomas Poole and his Friends, 1887, ii. 244)

CHAPTER XII. A MELANCHOLY EXILE, 1813-1815.

CXCVI.	Daniel Stuart, September 25, 1813. (Privately printed, Letters from the Lake Poets, p. 219).
CXCVII.	Joseph Cottle, April 26, 1814. (Early Recollections, 1837, ii. 155)
CXCVIII.	Joseph Cottle, May 27, 1814. (Early Recollections, 1837, ii. 165)
CXCIX.	Charles Mathews, May 30, 1814. (Memoir of C. Mathews, 1838, ii. 257)
CC.	Josiah Wade, June 26, 1814. (Early Recollections, 1837, ii. 185)
CCI.	John Murray, August 23, 1814. (Memoir of John Murray, 1890, i. 297)
CCII.	Daniel Stuart, September 12, 1814. (Privately printed, Letters from the Lake Poets, p. 221)
CCIII.	Daniel Stuart, October 30, 1814. (Privately printed, Letters from the Lake Poets, p. 248)
CCIV.	John Kenyon, November 3 [1814]
CCV.	Lady Beaumont, April 3, 1815. (Memorials of Coleorton, 1887, ii. 175)
CCVI.	William Wordsworth, May 30, 1815. (Life of Wordsworth, 1889, ii. 255)
CCVII.	Rev. W. Money, 1815

CHAPTER XIII. NEW LIFE AND NEW FRIENDS, 1816-1821.

CCVIII.	James Gillman [April 13, 1816]. (Life of Coleridge, 1838, p. 273)
CCIX.	Daniel Stuart, May 8, 1816. (Privately printed, Letters from the Lake Poets, p. 255)
CCX.	Daniel Stuart, May 13, 1816. (Privately printed, Letters from the Lake Poets, p. 262)
CCXI.	John Murray, February 27, 1817
CCXII.	Robert Southey [May, 1817]
CCXIII.	H. C. Robinson, June, 1817. (Diary of H. C. Robinson, 1869, ii. 57)
CCXIV.	Thomas Poole [July 22, 1817]. (Thomas Poole and his Friends, 1887, ii. 255)
CCXV.	Rev. H. F. Cary, October 29, 1817
CCXVI.	Rev. H. F. Cary, November 6, 1817
CCXVII.	Joseph Henry Green, November 14, 1817
CCXVIII.	Joseph Henry Green [December 13, 1817]
CCXIX.	Charles Augustus Tulk, 1818
CCXX.	Joseph Henry Green, May 2, 1818
CCXXI.	Mrs. Gillman, July 19, 1818
CCXXII.	W. Collins, A. R. A., December, 1818. (Memoirs of W. Collins, 1848, i. 146)
CCXXIII.	Thomas Allsop, December 2, 1818. (Letters, Conversations, and Recollections of S. T. Coleridge, 1836, i. 5)
CCXXIV.	Joseph Henry Green, January 16, 1819
CCXXV.	James Gillman, August 20, 1819
CCXXVI.	Mrs. Aders [?], October 28, 1819
CCXXVII.	Joseph Henry Green [January 14, 1820]
CCXXVIII.	Joseph Henry Green, May 25, 1820
CCXXIX.	Charles Augustus Tulk, February 12, 1821

CHAPTER XIV. THE PHILOSOPHER AND DIVINE, 1822-1832.

CCXXX.	John Murray, January 18, 1822
CCXXXI.	James Gillman, October 28, 1822. (Life of Coleridge, 1838, p. 344)
CCXXXII.	Miss Brent, July 7, 1823
CCXXXIII.	Rev. Edward Coleridge, July 23, 1823
CCXXXIV.	Joseph Henry Green, February 15, 1824
CCXXXV.	Joseph Henry Green, May 19, 1824
CCXXXVI.	James Gillman, November 2, 1824
CCXXXVII.	Rev. H. F. Cary, December 14, 1824
CCXXXVIII.	William Wordsworth [? 1825]. (Fifteen lines published, Life of Wordsworth, 1889, ii. 305)
CCXXXIX.	John Taylor Coleridge, April 8, 1825
CCXL.	Rev. Edward Coleridge, May 19, 1825
CCXLI.	Daniel Stuart, July 9, 1825. (Privately printed, Letters from the Lake Poets, p. 286)
CCXLII.	James Gillman, October 10, 1825
CCXLIII.	Rev. Edward Coleridge, December 9, 1825
CCXLIV.	Mrs. Gillman, May 3, 1827 745
CCXLV.	Rev. George May Coleridge, January 14, 1828
CCXLVI.	George Dyer, June 6, 1828. (The Mirror, xxxviii. 1841, p. 282)
CCXLVII.	George Cattermole, August 14, 1828
CCXLVIII.	Joseph Henry Green, June 1, 1830
CCXLIX.	Thomas Poole, 1830
CCL.	Mrs. Gillman, 1830
CCLI.	Joseph Henry Green, December 15, 1831
CCLII.	H. N. Coleridge, February 24, 1832
CCLIII.	Miss Lawrence, March 22, 1832
CCLIV.	Rev. H. F. Cary, April 22, 1832. (Memoir of H. F. Cary, 1847, ii. 194)
CCLV.	John Peirse Kennard, August 13, 1832

CHAPTER XV. THE BEGINNING OF THE END, 1833-1834.

CCLVI.	Joseph Henry Green, April 8, 1833
CCLVII.	Mrs. Aders [1833]
CCLVIII.	John Sterling, October 30, 1833
CCLIX.	Miss Eliza Nixon, July 9, 1834
CCLX.	Adam Steinmetz Kennard, July 13, 1834. (Early Recollections, 1837, ii. 193)

INTRODUCTION

Hitherto no attempt has been made to publish a collection of Coleridge's Letters. A few specimens were published in his lifetime, both in his own works and in magazines, and, shortly after his death in 1834, a large number appeared in print. Allsop's "Letters, Conversations, and Recollections of S. T. Coleridge," which was issued in 1836, contains forty-five letters or parts of letters; Cottle in his "Early Recollections" (1837) prints, for the most part incorrectly, and in piecemeal, some sixty in all, and Gillman, in his "Life of Coleridge" (1838), contributes, among others, some letters addressed to himself, and one, of the greatest interest, to Charles Lamb. In 1847, a series of early letters to Thomas Poole appeared for the first time in the Biographical Supplement to the "Biographia Literaria," and in 1848, when Cottle reprinted his "Early Recollections," under the title of "Reminiscences of Coleridge and Southey," he included sixteen letters to Thomas and Josiah Wedgwood. In Southey's posthumous "Life of Dr. Bell," five letters of Coleridge lie imbedded, and in "Southey's Life and Correspondence" (1849-50), four of his letters find an appropriate place. An interesting series was published in 1858 in the "Fragmentary Remains of Sir H. Davy," edited by his brother, Dr. Davy; and in the "Diary of H. C. Robinson," published in 1869, a few letters from Coleridge are interspersed. In 1870, the late Mr. W. Mark W. Call printed in the "Westminster Review" eleven letters from Coleridge to Dr. Brabant of Devizes, dated 1815 and 1816; and a series of early letters to Godwin, 1800-1811 (some of which had appeared in "Macmillan's Magazine" in 1864), was included by Mr. Kegan Paul in his "William Godwin" (1876). In 1874, a correspondence between Coleridge (1816-1818) and his publishers, Gale & Curtis, was contributed to "Lippincott's Magazine," and in 1878, a few letters to Matilda Betham were published in "Fraser's Magazine." During the last six years the vast store which still remained unpublished has been drawn upon for various memoirs and biographies. The following works containing new letters are given in order of publication: Herr Brandl's "Samuel T. Coleridge and the English Romantic School," 1887; "Memorials of Coleorton," edited by Professor Knight, 1887; "Thomas Poole and his Friends," by Mrs. H. Sandford, 1888; "Life of Wordsworth," by Professor Knight, 1889; "Memoirs of John Murray," by Samuel Smiles, LL. D., 1891; "De Quincey Memorials," by Alex. Japp, LL. D., 1891; "Life of Washington Allston," 1893.

Notwithstanding these heavy draughts, more than half of the letters which have come under my notice remain unpublished. Of more than forty which Coleridge wrote to his wife, only one has been published. Of ninety letters to Southey which are extant, barely a tenth have seen the light. Of nineteen addressed to W. Sotheby, poet and patron of poets, fourteen to Lamb's friend John Rickman, and four to Coleridge's old college friend, Archdeacon Wrangham, none have been published. Of more than forty letters addressed to the Morgan family, which belong for the most part to the least known period of Coleridge's life,—the years which intervened between his residence in Grasmere and his final settlement at Highgate,—only two or three, preserved in the MSS. Department of the British Museum, have been published. Of numerous letters written in later life to his friend and amanuensis, Joseph Henry Green; to Charles Augustus Tulk, M. P. for Sudbury; to his friends and hosts, the Gillmans; to Cary, the translator of Dante, only a few have found their way into print. Of more than forty to his brother, the Rev. George Coleridge, which were accidentally discovered in 1876, only five have been printed. Of some fourscore letters addressed to his nephews, William Hart Coleridge, John Taylor Coleridge, Henry Nelson Coleridge, Edward Coleridge, and to his son Derwent, all but two, or at most three, remain in manuscript. Of the youthful letters to the Evans family, one letter has recently appeared in the "Illustrated London News," and of the many addressed to John Thelwall, but one was printed in the same series.

The letters to Poole, of which more than a hundred have been preserved, those addressed to his Bristol friend, Josiah Wade, and the letters to Wordsworth, which, though few in number, are of great length, have been largely used for biographical purposes, but much, of the highest interest, remains unpublished. Of smaller groups of letters, published and unpublished, I make no detailed mention, but in the latter category are two to Charles Lamb, one to John Sterling, five to George Cattermole, one to John Kenyon, and many others to more obscure correspondents. Some important letters to Lord Jeffrey, to John Murray, to De Quincey, to Hugh James Rose, and to J. H. B. Williams, have, in the last few years, been placed in my hands for transcription.

A series of letters written between the years 1796 and 1814 to the Rev. John Prior Estlin, minister of the Unitarian Chapel at Lewin's Mead, Bristol, was printed some years ago for the Philobiblon Society, with an introduction by Mr. Henry A. Bright. One other series of letters has also been printed for private circulation. In 1889, the late Miss Stuart placed in my hands transcriptions of eighty-seven letters addressed by Coleridge to her father, Daniel Stuart, editor of "The Morning Post" and "Courier," and these, together with letters from Wordsworth and Southey, were printed in a single volume bearing the title, "Letters from the Lake Poets." Miss Stuart contributed a short account of her father's life, and also a reminiscence of Coleridge, headed "A Farewell."

Coleridge's biographers, both of the past and present generations, have met with a generous response to their appeal for letters to be placed in their hands for reference and for publication, but it is probable that many are in existence which have been withheld, sometimes no doubt intentionally, but more often from inadvertence. From his boyhood the poet was a voluminous if an irregular correspondent, and many letters which he is known to have addressed to his earliest friends—to Middleton, to Robert Allen, to Valentine and Sam Le Grice, to Charles Lloyd, to his Stowey neighbour, John Cruikshank, to Dr. Beddoes, and others—may yet be forthcoming. It is certain that he corresponded with Mrs. Clarkson, but if any letters have been preserved they have not come under my notice. It is strange, too, that among the letters of the Highgate period, which were sent to Henry Nelson Coleridge for transcription, none to John Hookham Frere, to Blanco White, or to Edward Irving appear to have been forthcoming.

The foregoing summary of published and unpublished letters, though necessarily imperfect, will enable the reader to form some idea of the mass of material from which the present selection has been made. A complete edition of Coleridge's Letters must await the "coming of the milder day," a renewed long-suffering on the part of his old enemy, the "literary public." In the meanwhile, a selection from some of the more important is here offered in the belief that many, if not all, will find a place in permanent literature. The letters are arranged in chronological order, and are intended rather to illustrate the story of the writer's life than to embody his critical opinions, or to record the development of his philosophical and theological speculations. But letters of a purely literary character have not been excluded, and in selecting or rejecting a letter, the sole criterion has been, Is it interesting? is it readable?

In letter-writing perfection of style is its own recommendation, and long after the substance of a letter has lost its savour, the form retains its original or, it may be, an added charm. Or if the author be the founder of a sect or a school, his writings, in whatever form, are received by the initiated with unquestioning and insatiable delight. But Coleridge's letters lack style. The fastidious critic who touched and retouched his exquisite lyrics, and always for the better, was at no pains to polish his letters. He writes to his friends as if he were talking to them, and he lets his periods take care of themselves. Nor is there any longer a school of reverent disciples to receive what the master gives and because he gives it. His influence as a teacher has passed into other channels, and he is no longer regarded as the oracular sage "questionable" concerning all mysteries. But as a poet, as a great literary critic, and as a "master of sentences," he holds his own and appeals to the general ear; and though, since his death, in 1834, a second generation has all but passed away, an unwonted interest in the man himself survives and must always survive. For not only, as Wordsworth declared, was he "a wonderful man," but the story of his life was a strange one, and as he tells it, we "cannot choose but hear." Coleridge, often to his own detriment, "wore his heart on his sleeve," and, now to one friend, now to another, sometimes to two or three friends on the same day, he would seek to unburthen himself of his hopes and fears, his thoughts and fancies, his bodily sufferings, and the keener pangs of the soul. It is, to quote his own words, these "profound touches of the human heart" which command our interest in Coleridge's Letters, and invest them with their peculiar charm.

At what period after death, and to what extent the private letters of a celebrated person should be given to the world, must always remain an open question both of taste and of morals. So far as Coleridge is concerned, the question was decided long age. Within a few years of his death, letters of the most private and even painful character were published without the sanction and in spite of the repeated remonstrances of his literary executor, and of all who had a right to be heard on the subject. Thenceforth, as the published writings of his immediate descendants testify, a fuller and therefore a fairer revelation was steadily contemplated. Letters collected for this purpose find a place in the present volume, but the selection has been made without reference to previous works or to any final presentation of the material at the editor's disposal.

My acknowledgments are due to many still living, and to others who have passed away, for their generous permission to print unpublished letters, which remained in their possession or had passed into their hands.

For the continued use of the long series of letters which Poole entrusted to Coleridge's literary executor in 1836, I have to thank Mrs. Henry Sandford and the Bishop of Gibraltar. For those addressed to the Evans family I am indebted to Mr. Alfred Morrison of Fonthill. The letters to Thelwall were placed in my hands by the late Mr. F. W. Cosens, who afforded me every facility for their transcription. For those to Wordsworth my thanks are due to the poet's grandsons, Mr. William and Mr. Gordon Wordsworth. Those addressed to the Gillmans I owe to the great kindness of their granddaughter, Mrs. Henry Watson, who placed in my hands all the materials at her disposal. For the right to publish the letters to H. F. Cary I am indebted to my friend the Rev. Offley Cary, the grandson of the translator of Dante. My acknowledgments are further due to the late Mr. John Murray for the right to republish letters which appeared in the "Memoirs of John Murray," and two others which were not included in that work; and to Mrs. Watt, the daughter of John Hunter of Craigcrook, for letters addressed to Lord Jeffrey. From the late Lord Houghton I received permission to publish the letters to the Rev. J. P. Estlin, which were privately printed for the Philobiblon Society. I have already mentioned my obligations to the late Miss Stuart of Harley Street.

For the use of letters addressed to his father and grandfather, and for constant and unwearying advice and assistance in this work I am indebted, more than I can well express, to the late Lord Coleridge. Alas! I can only record my gratitude.

To Mr. William Rennell Coleridge of Salston, Ottery St. Mary, my especial thanks are due for the interesting collection of unpublished letters, many of them relating to the "Army Episode," which the poet wrote to his brother, the Rev. George Coleridge.

I have also to thank Miss Edith Coleridge for the use of letters addressed to her father, Henry Nelson Coleridge; my cousin, Mrs. Thomas W. Martyn of Torquay, for Coleridge's letter to his mother, the earliest known to exist; and Mr. Arthur Duke Coleridge for one of the latest he ever wrote, that to Mrs. Aders.

During the preparation of this work I have received valuable assistance from men of letters and others. I trust that I may be permitted to mention the names of Mr. Leslie Stephen, Professor Knight, Mrs. Henry Sandford, Dr. Garnett of the British Museum, Professor Emile Legouis of Lyons, Mrs. Henry Watson, the Librarians of the Oxford and Cambridge Club, and of the Kensington Public Library, and Mrs. George Boyce of Chertsey.

Of my friend, Mr. Dykes Campbell, I can only say that he has spared neither time nor trouble in my behalf. Not only during the progress of the work has he been ready to give me the benefit of his unrivalled knowledge of the correspondence and history of Coleridge and of his contemporaries, but he has largely assisted me in seeing the work through the press. For the selection of the letters, or for the composition or accuracy of the notes, he must not be held in any way responsible; but without his aid, and without his counsel, much, which I hope has been accomplished, could never have been attempted at all. Of the invaluable assistance which I have received from his published works, the numerous references to his edition of Coleridge's "Poetical Works" (Macmillan, 1893), and his "Samuel Taylor Coleridge, A Narrative" (1894), are sufficient evidence. Of my gratitude he needs no assurance.

ERNEST HARTLEY COLERIDGE.

PRINCIPAL EVENTS IN THE LIFE OF S. T. COLERIDGE

Born, October 21, 1772.

Death of his father, October 4, 1781.

Entered at Christ's Hospital, July 18, 1782.

Elected a "Grecian," 1788.

Discharged from Christ's Hospital, September 7, 1791.

Went into residence at Jesus College, Cambridge, October, 1791.

Enlisted in King's Regiment of Light Dragoons, December 2, 1793.

Discharged from the army, April 10, 1794.

Visit to Oxford and introduction to Southey, June, 1794.

Proposal to emigrate to America—Pantisocracy—Autumn, 1794.

Final departure from Cambridge, December, 1794.

Settled at Bristol as public lecturer, January, 1795.

Married to Sarah Fricker, October 4, 1795.

Publication of "Conciones ad Populum," Clevedon, November 16, 1795.

Pantisocrats dissolve—Rupture with Southey—November, 1795.

Publication of first edition of Poems, April, 1796.

Issue of "The Watchman," March 1-May 13, 1796.

Birth of Hartley Coleridge, September 19, 1796.

Settled at Nether-Stowey, December 31, 1796.

Publication of second edition of Poems, June, 1797.

Settlement of Wordsworth at Alfoxden, July 14, 1797.

The "Ancient Mariner" begun, November 13, 1797.

First part of "Christabel," begun, 1797.

Acceptance of annuity of £150 from J. and T. Wedgwood, January, 1798.

Went to Germany, September 16, 1798.

Returned from Germany, July, 1799.

First visit to Lake Country, October-November, 1799.

Began to write for "Morning Post," December, 1799.

Translation of Schiller's "Wallenstein," Spring, 1800.

Settled at Greta Hall, Keswick, July 24, 1800.

Birth of Derwent Coleridge, September 14, 1800.

Wrote second part of "Christabel," Autumn, 1800.

Began study of German metaphysics, 1801.

Birth of Sara Coleridge, December 23, 1802.

Publication of third edition of Poems, Summer, 1803.

Set out on Scotch tour, August 14, 1803.

Settlement of Southey at Greta Hall, September, 1803.

Sailed for Malta in the Speedwell, April 9, 1804.

Arrived at Malta, May 18, 1804.

First tour in Sicily, August-November, 1804.

Left Malta for Syracuse, September 21, 1805.

Residence in Rome, January-May, 1806.

Returned to England, August, 1806.

Visit to Wordsworth at Coleorton, December 21, 1806.

Met De Quincey at Bridgwater, July, 1807.

First lecture at Royal Institution, January 12, 1808.

Settled at Allan Bank, Grasmere, September, 1808.

First number of "The Friend," June 1, 1809.

Last number of "The Friend," March 15, 1810.

Left Greta Hall for London, October 10, 1810.

Settled at Hammersmith with the Morgans, November 3, 1810.

First lecture at London Philosophical Society, November 18, 1811.

Last visit to Greta Hall, February-March, 1812.

First lecture at Willis's Rooms, May 12, 1812.

First lecture at Surrey Institution, November 3, 1812.

Production of "Remorse" at Drury Lane, January 23, 1813.

Left London for Bristol, October, 1813.

First course of Bristol lectures, October-November, 1813.

Second course of Bristol lectures, December 30, 1813.

Third course of Bristol lectures, April, 1814.

Residence with Josiah Wade at Bristol, Summer, 1814.

Rejoined the Morgans at Ashley, September, 1814.

Accompanied the Morgans to Calne, November, 1814.

Settles with Mr. Gillman at Highgate, April 16, 1816.

Publication of "Christabel," June, 1816.

Publication of the "Statesman's Manual," December, 1816.

Publication of second "Lay Sermon," 1817.

Publication of "Biographia Literaria" and "Sibylline Leaves," 1817.

First acquaintance with Joseph Henry Green, 1817.

Publication of "Zapolya," Autumn, 1817.

First lecture at "Flower-de-Luce Court," January 27, 1818.

Publication of "Essay on Method," January, 1818.

Revised edition of "The Friend," Spring, 1818.

Introduction to Thomas Allsop, 1818.

First lecture on "History of Philosophy," December 14, 1818.

First lecture on "Shakespeare" (last course), December 17, 1818.

Last public lecture, "History of Philosophy," March 29, 1819.

Nominated "Royal Associate" of Royal Society of Literature, May, 1824.

Read paper to Royal Society on "Prometheus of Æschylus," May 15, 1825.

Publication of "Aids to Reflection," May-June, 1825.

Publication of "Poetical Works," in three volumes, 1828.

Tour on the Rhine with Wordsworth, June-July, 1828.

Revised issue of "Poetical Works," in three volumes, 1829.

Marriage of Sara Coleridge to Henry Nelson Coleridge, September 3, 1829.

Publication of "Church and State," 1830.

Visit to Cambridge, June, 1833.

Death, July 25, 1834.

PRINCIPAL AUTHORITIES REFERRED TO IN THESE VOLUMES

1. The Complete Works of Samuel Taylor Coleridge. New York: Harper and Brothers, 7 vols. 1853.

2. Biographia Literaria [etc.]. By S. T. Coleridge. Second edition, prepared for publication in part by the late H. N. Coleridge: completed and published by his widow. 2 vols. 1847.

3. Essays on His Own Times. By Samuel Taylor Coleridge. Edited by his daughter. London: William Pickering. 3 vols. 1850.

4. The Table Talk and Omniana of Samuel Taylor Coleridge. Edited by T. Ashe. George Bell and Sons. 1884.

5. Letters, Conversations, and Recollections of S. T. Coleridge. [Edited by Thomas Allsop. First edition published anonymously.] Moxon. 2 vols. 1836.

6. The Life of S. T. Coleridge, by James Gillman. In 2 vols. (Vol. I. only was published.) 1838.

7. Memorials of Coleorton: being Letters from Coleridge, Wordsworth and his sister, Southey, and Sir Walter Scott, to Sir George and Lady Beaumont of Coleorton, Leicestershire, 1803-1834. Edited by William Knight, University of St. Andrews. 2 vols. Edinburgh. 1887.

8. Unpublished Letters from S. T. Coleridge to the Rev. John Prior Estlin. Communicated by Henry A. Bright (to the Philobiblon Society). n. d.

9. Letters from the Lake Poets—S. T. Coleridge, William Wordsworth, Robert Southey—to Daniel Stuart, editor of The Morning Post and The Courier. 1800-1838. Printed for private circulation. 1889. [Edited by Mr. Ernest Hartley Coleridge, in whom the copyright of the letters of S. T. Coleridge is vested.]

10. The Poetical Works of Samuel Taylor Coleridge. Edited, with a Biographical Introduction, by James Dykes Campbell. London and New York: Macmillan and Co. 1893.

11. Samuel Taylor Coleridge. A Narrative of the Events of His Life. By James Dykes Campbell. London and New York: Macmillan and Co. 1894.

12. Early Recollections: chiefly relating to the late S. T. Coleridge, during his long residence in Bristol. 2 vols. By Joseph Cottle. 1837.

13. Reminiscences of S. T. Coleridge and R. Southey. By Joseph Cottle. 1847.

14. Fragmentary Remains, literary and scientific, of Sir Humphry Davy, Bart. Edited by his brother, John Davy, M. D. 1838.

15. The Autobiography of Leigh Hunt. London. 1860.

16. Diary, Reminiscences, and Correspondence of Henry Crabb Robinson. Selected and Edited by Thomas Sadler, Ph.D. London. 1869.

17. A Group of Englishmen (1795-1815): being records of the younger Wedgwoods and their Friends. By Eliza Meteyard. 1871.

18. Memoir and Letters of Sara Coleridge [Mrs. H. N. Coleridge]. Edited by her daughter. 2 vols. 1873.

19. Samuel Taylor Coleridge and the English Romantic School. By Alois Brandl. English Edition by Lady Eastlake. London. 1887.

20. The Letters of Charles Lamb. Edited by Alfred Ainger. 2 vols. 1888.

21. Thomas Poole and his Friends. By Mrs. Henry Sandford. 2 vols. 1888.

22. The Life and Correspondence of R. Southey. Edited by his son, the Rev. Charles Cuthbert Southey. 6 vols. 1849-50.

23. Selections from the Letters of R. Southey. Edited by his son-in-law, John Wood Warter, B. D. 4 vols. 1856.

24. The Poetical Works of Robert Southey, Esq., LL.D. 9 vols. London. 1837.

25. Memoirs of William Wordsworth. By Christopher Wordsworth, D. D., Canon of Westminster [afterwards Bishop of Lincoln]. 2 vols. 1851.

26. The Life of William Wordsworth. By William Knight, LL.D. 3 vols. 1889.

27. The Complete Poetical Works of William Wordsworth. With an Introduction by John Morley. London and New York: Macmillan and Co. 1889.

LETTERS OF SAMUEL TAYLOR COLERIDGE

CHAPTER I
STUDENT LIFE
1785-1794

The five autobiographical letters addressed to Thomas Poole were written at Nether Stowey, at irregular intervals during the years 1797-98. They are included in the first chapter of the "Biographical Supplement" to the "Biographia Literaria." The larger portion of this so-called Biographical Supplement was prepared for the press by Henry Nelson Coleridge, and consists of the opening chapters of a proposed "biographical sketch," and a selection from the correspondence of S. T. Coleridge. His widow, Sara Coleridge, when she brought out the second edition of the "Biographia Literaria" in 1847, published this fragment and added some matter of her own. This edition has never been reprinted in England, but is included in the American edition of Coleridge's Works, which was issued by Harper & Brothers in 1853.

The letters may be compared with an autobiographical note dated March 9, 1832, which was written at Gillman's request, and forms part of the first chapter of his "Life of Coleridge."[1] The text of the present issue of the autobiographical letters is taken from the original MSS., and differs in many important particulars from that of 1847.

I. TO THOMAS POOLE.

Monday, February, 1797.

My dear Poole,—I could inform the dullest author how he might write an interesting book. Let him relate the events of his own life with honesty, not disguising the feelings that accompanied them. I never yet read even a Methodist's Experience in the "Gospel Magazine" without receiving instruction and amusement; and I should almost despair of that man who could peruse the Life of John Woolman[2] without an amelioration of heart. As to my Life, it has all the charms of variety,—high life and low life, vices and virtues, great folly and some wisdom. However, what I am depends on what I have been; and you, my best Friend! have a right to the narration. To me the task will be a useful one. It will renew and deepen my reflections on the past; and it will perhaps make you behold with no unforgiving or impatient eye those weaknesses and defects in my character, which so many untoward circumstances have concurred to plant there.

My family on my mother's side can be traced up, I know not how far. The Bowdons inherited a small farm in the Exmoor country, in the reign of Elizabeth, as I have been told, and, to my own knowledge, they have inherited nothing better since that time. On my father's side I can rise no higher than my grandfather, who was born in the Hundred of Coleridge[3] in the county of Devon, christened, educated, and apprenticed to the parish. He afterwards became a respectable woollen-draper in the town of South Molton.[4] (I have mentioned these particulars, as the time may come in which it will be useful to be able to prove myself a genuine sans-culotte, my veins uncontaminated with one drop of gentility.) My father received a better education than the others of his family, in consequence of his own exertions, not of his superior advantages. When he was not quite sixteen years old, my grandfather became bankrupt, and by a series of misfortunes was reduced to extreme poverty. My father received the half of his last crown and his blessing, and walked off to seek his fortune. After he had proceeded a few miles, he sat him down on the side of the road, so overwhelmed with painful thoughts that he wept audibly. A gentleman passed by, who knew him, and, inquiring into his distresses, took my father with him, and settled him in a neighbouring town as a schoolmaster. His school increased and he got money and knowledge: for he commenced a severe and ardent student. Here, too, he married his first wife, by whom he had three daughters, all now alive. While his first wife lived, having scraped up money enough at the age of twenty[5] he walked to Cambridge, entered at Sidney College, distinguished himself for Hebrew and Mathematics, and might have had a fellowship if he had not been married. He returned—his wife died. Judge Buller's father gave him the living of Ottery St. Mary, and put the present judge to school with him. He married my mother, by whom he had ten children, of whom I am the youngest, born October 20, 1772.

These sketches I received from my mother and aunt, but I am utterly unable to fill them up by any particularity of times, or places, or names. Here I shall conclude my first letter, because I cannot pledge myself for the accuracy of the accounts, and I will not therefore mingle them with those for the accuracy of which in the minutest parts I shall hold myself amenable to the Tribunal of Truth. You must regard this letter as the first chapter of an history which is devoted to dim traditions of times too remote to be pierced by the eye of investigation.

Yours affectionately,
S. T. Coleridge.

II. TO THE SAME.

Sunday, March, 1797.

My dear Poole,—My father (Vicar of, and Schoolmaster at, Ottery St. Mary, Devon) was a profound mathematician, and well versed in the Latin, Greek, and Oriental Languages. He published, or rather attempted to publish, several works; 1st, Miscellaneous Dissertations arising from the 17th and 18th Chapters of the Book of Judges; 2d, Sententiæ excerptæ, for the use of his own school; and 3d, his best work, a Critical Latin Grammar; in the preface to which he proposes a bold innovation in the names of the cases. My father's new nomenclature was not likely to become popular, although it must be allowed to be both sonorous and expressive. Exempli gratiâ, he calls the ablative the quippe-quare-quale-quia-quidditive case! My father made the world his confidant with respect to his learning and ingenuity, and the world seems to have kept the secret very faithfully. His various works, uncut, unthumbed, have been preserved free from all pollution. This piece of good luck promises to be hereditary; for all my compositions have the same amiable home-studying propensity. The truth is, my father was not a first-rate genius; he was, however, a first-rate Christian. I need not detain you with his character. In learning, good-heartedness, absentness of mind, and excessive ignorance of the world, he was a perfect Parson Adams.

My mother was an admirable economist, and managed exclusively. My eldest brother's name was John. He went over to the East Indies in the Company's service; he was a successful officer and a brave one, I have heard. He died of a consumption there about eight years ago. My second brother was called William. He went to Pembroke College, Oxford, and afterwards was assistant to Mr. Newcome's School, at Hackney. He died of a putrid fever the year before my father's death, and just as he was on the eve of marriage with Miss Jane Hart, the eldest daughter of a very wealthy citizen of Exeter. My third brother, James, has been in the army since the age of sixteen, has married a woman of fortune, and now lives at Ottery St. Mary, a respectable man. My brother Edward, the wit of the family, went to Pembroke College, and afterwards to Salisbury, as assistant to Dr. Skinner. He married a woman twenty years older than his mother. She is dead and he now lives at Ottery St. Mary. My fifth brother, George, was educated at Pembroke College, Oxford, and from there went to Mr. Newcome's, Hackney, on the death of William. He stayed there fourteen years, when the living of Ottery St. Mary[6] was given him. There he has now a fine school, and has lately married Miss Jane Hart, who with beauty and wealth had remained a faithful widow to the memory of William for sixteen years. My brother George is a man of reflective mind and elegant genius. He possesses learning in a greater degree than any of the family, excepting myself. His manners are grave and hued over with a tender sadness. In his moral character he approaches every way nearer to perfection than any man I ever yet knew; indeed, he is worth the whole family in a lump. My sixth brother, Luke (indeed, the seventh, for one brother, the second, died in his infancy, and I had forgot to mention him), was bred as a medical man. He married Miss Sara Hart, and died at the age of twenty-two, leaving one child, a lovely boy, still alive. My brother Luke was a man of uncommon genius, a severe student, and a good man. The eighth child was a sister, Anne.[7] She died a little after my brother Luke, aged twenty-one;

Rest, gentle Shade! and wait thy Maker's will;
Then rise unchang'd, and be an Angel still!
The ninth child was called Francis. He went out as a midshipman, under Admiral Graves. His ship lay on the Bengal coast, and he accidentally met his brother John, who took him to land, and procured him a commission in the Army. He died from the effects of a delirious fever brought on by his excessive exertions at the siege of Seringapatam, at which his conduct had been so gallant, that Lord Cornwallis paid him a high compliment in the presence of the army, and presented him with a valuable gold watch, which my mother now has. All my brothers are remarkably handsome; but they were as inferior to Francis as I am to them. He went by the name of "the handsome Coleridge." The tenth and last child was S. T. Coleridge, the subject of these epistles, born (as I told you in my last) October 20,[8] 1772.

From October 20, 1772, to October 20, 1773. Christened Samuel Taylor Coleridge—my godfather's name being Samuel Taylor, Esq. I had another godfather (his name was Evans), and two godmothers, both called "Monday."[9] From October 20, 1773, to October 20, 1774. In this year I was carelessly left by my nurse, ran to the fire, and pulled out a live coal—burnt myself dreadfully. While my hand was being dressed by a Mr. Young, I spoke for the first time (so my mother informs me) and said, "nasty Doctor Young!" The snatching at fire, and the circumstance of my first words expressing hatred to professional men—are they at all ominous? This year I went to school. My schoolmistress, the very image of Shenstone's, was named Old Dame Key. She was nearly related to Sir Joshua Reynolds.

From October 20, 1774, to October 20, 1775. I was inoculated; which I mention because I distinctly remember it, and that my eyes were bound; at which I manifested so much obstinate indignation, that at last they removed the bandage, and unaffrighted I looked at the lancet, and suffered the scratch. At the close of the year I could read a chapter in the Bible.

Here I shall end, because the remaining years of my life all assisted to form my particular mind;—the three first years had nothing in them that seems to relate to it.

(Signature cut out.)

III. TO THE SAME.

October 9, 1797.

My dearest Poole,—From March to October—a long silence! But [as] it is possible that I may have been preparing materials for future letters,[10] the time cannot be considered as altogether subtracted from you.

From October, 1775, to October, 1778. These three years I continued at the Reading School, because I was too little to be trusted among my father's schoolboys. After breakfast I had a halfpenny given me, with which I bought three cakes at the baker's close by the school of my old mistress; and these were my dinner on every day except Saturday and Sunday, when I used to dine at home, and wallowed in a beef and pudding dinner. I am remarkably fond of beans and bacon; and this fondness I attribute to my father having given me a penny for having eat a large quantity of beans on Saturday. For the other boys did not like them, and as it was an economic food, my father thought that my attachment and penchant for it ought to be encouraged. My father was very fond of me, and I was my mother's darling: in consequence I was very miserable. For Molly, who had nursed my brother Francis, and was immoderately fond of him, hated me because my mother took more notice of me than of Frank, and Frank hated me because my mother gave me now and then a bit of cake, when he had none,—quite forgetting that for one bit of cake which I had and he had not, he had twenty sops in the pan, and pieces of bread and butter with sugar on them from Molly, from whom I received only thumps and ill names.

So I became fretful and timorous, and a tell-tale; and the schoolboys drove me from play, and were always tormenting me, and hence I took no pleasure in boyish sports, but read incessantly. My father's sister kept an everything shop at Crediton, and there I read through all the gilt-cover little books[11] that could be had at that time, and likewise all the uncovered tales of Tom Hickathrift, Jack the Giant-killer, etc., etc., etc., etc. And I used to lie by the wall and mope, and my spirits used to come upon me suddenly; and in a flood of them I was accustomed to race up and down the churchyard, and act over all I had been reading, on the docks, the nettles, and the rank grass. At six years old I remember to have read Belisarius, Robinson Crusoe, and Philip Quarles; and then I found the Arabian Nights' Entertainments, one tale of which (the tale of a man who was compelled to seek for a pure virgin) made so deep an impression on me (I had read it in the evening while my mother was mending stockings), that I was haunted by spectres, whenever I was in the dark: and I distinctly remember the anxious and fearful eagerness with which I used to watch the window in which the books lay, and whenever the sun lay upon them, I would seize it, carry it by the wall, and bask and read. My father found out the effect which these books had produced, and burnt them.

So I became a dreamer, and acquired an indisposition to all bodily activity; and I was fretful, and inordinately passionate, and as I could not play at anything, and was slothful, I was despised and hated by the boys; and because I could read and spell and had, I may truly say, a memory and understanding forced into almost an unnatural ripeness, I was flattered and wondered at by all the old women. And so I became very vain, and despised most of the boys that were at all near my own age, and before I was eight years old I was a character. Sensibility, imagination, vanity, sloth, and feelings of deep and bitter contempt for all who traversed the orbit of my understanding, were even then prominent and manifest.

From October, 1778, to 1779. That which I began to be from three to six I continued from six to nine. In this year [1778] I was admitted into the Grammar School, and soon outstripped all of my age. I had a dangerous putrid fever this year. My brother George lay ill of the same fever in the next room. My poor brother Francis, I remember, stole up in spite of orders to the contrary, and sat by my bedside and read Pope's Homer to me. Frank had a violent love of beating me; but whenever that was superseded by any humour or circumstances, he was always very fond of me, and used to regard me with a strange mixture of admiration and contempt. Strange it was not, for he hated books, and loved climbing, fighting, playing and robbing orchards, to distraction.

My mother relates a story of me, which I repeat here, because it must be regarded as my first piece of wit. During my fever, I asked why Lady Northcote (our neighbour) did not come and see me. My mother said she was afraid of catching the fever. I was piqued, and answered, "Ah, Mamma! the four Angels round my bed an't afraid of catching it!" I suppose you know the prayer:—

"Matthew! Mark! Luke and John!
God bless the bed which I lie on.
Four angels round me spread,
Two at my foot, and two at my head."
This prayer I said nightly, and most firmly believed the truth of it. Frequently have I (half-awake and half-asleep, my body diseased and fevered by my imagination), seen armies of ugly things bursting in upon me, and these four angels keeping them off. In my next I shall carry on my life to my father's death.

God bless you, my dear Poole, and your affectionate

S. T. Coleridge.

IV. TO THE SAME.

October 16, 1797.

Dear Poole,—From October, 1779, to October, 1781. I had asked my mother one evening to cut my cheese entire, so that I might toast it. This was no easy matter, it being a crumbly cheese. My mother, however, did it. I went into the garden for something or other, and in the mean time my brother Frank minced my cheese "to disappoint the favorite." I returned, saw the exploit, and in an agony of passion flew at Frank. He pretended to have been seriously hurt by my blow, flung himself on the ground, and there lay with outstretched limbs. I hung over him moaning, and in a great fright; he leaped up, and with a horse-laugh gave me a severe blow in the face. I seized a knife, and was running at him, when my mother came in and took me by the arm. I expected a flogging, and struggling from her I ran away to a hill at the bottom of which the Otter flows, about one mile from Ottery. There I stayed; my rage died away, but my obstinacy vanquished my fears, and taking out a little shilling book which had, at the end, morning and evening prayers, I very devoutly repeated them—thinking at the same time with inward and gloomy satisfaction how miserable my mother must be! I distinctly remember my feelings when I saw a Mr. Vaughan pass over the bridge, at about a furlong's distance, and how I watched the calves in the fields[12] beyond the river. It grew dark and I fell asleep. It was towards the latter end of October, and it proved a dreadful stormy night. I felt the cold in my sleep, and dreamt that I was pulling the blanket over me, and actually pulled over me a dry thorn bush which lay on the hill. In my sleep I had rolled from the top of the hill to within three yards of the river, which flowed by the unfenced edge at the bottom. I awoke several times, and finding myself wet and stiff and cold, closed my eyes again that I might forget it.

In the mean time my mother waited about half an hour, expecting my return when the sulks had evaporated. I not returning, she sent into the churchyard and round the town. Not found! Several men and all the boys were sent to ramble about and seek me. In vain! My mother was almost distracted; and at ten o'clock at night I was cried by the crier in Ottery, and in two villages near it, with a reward offered for me. No one went to bed; indeed, I believe half the town were up all the night. To return to myself. About five in the morning, or a little after, I was broad awake, and attempted to get up and walk; but I could not move. I saw the shepherds and workmen at a distance, and cried, but so faintly that it was impossible to hear me thirty yards off. And there I might have lain and died; for I was now almost given over, the ponds and even the river, near where I was lying, having been dragged. But by good luck, Sir Stafford Northcote,[13] who had been out all night, resolved to make one other trial, and came so near that he heard me crying. He carried me in his arms for near a quarter of a mile, when we met my father and Sir Stafford's servants. I remember and never shall forget my father's face as he looked upon me while I lay in the servant's arms—so calm, and the tears stealing down his face; for I was the child of his old age. My mother, as you may suppose, was outrageous with joy. [Meantime] in rushed a young lady, crying out, "I hope you'll whip him, Mrs. Coleridge!" This woman still lives in Ottery; and neither philosophy or religion have been able to conquer the antipathy which I feel towards her whenever I see her. I was put to bed and recovered in a day or so, but I was certainly injured. For I was weakly and subject to the ague for many years after.

My father (who had so little of parental ambition in him, that he had destined his children to be blacksmiths, etc., and had accomplished his intention but for my mother's pride and spirit of aggrandizing her family)—my father had, however, resolved that I should be a parson. I read every book that came in my way without distinction; and my father was fond of me, and used to take me on his knee and hold long conversations with me. I remember that at eight years old I walked with him one winter evening from a farmer's house, a mile from Ottery, and he told me the names of the stars and how Jupiter was a thousand times larger than our world, and that the other twinkling stars were suns that had worlds rolling round them; and when I came home he shewed me how they rolled round. I heard him with a profound delight and admiration: but without the least mixture of wonder or incredulity. For from my early reading of fairy tales and genii, etc., etc., my mind had been habituated to the Vast, and I never regarded my senses in any way as the criteria of my belief. I regulated all my creeds by my conceptions, not by my sight, even at that age. Should children be permitted to read romances, and relations of giants and magicians and genii? I know all that has been said against it; but I have formed my faith in the affirmative. I know no other way of giving the mind a love of the Great and the Whole. Those who have been led to the same truths step by step, through the constant testimony of their senses, seem to me to want a sense which I possess. They contemplate nothing but parts, and all parts are necessarily little. And the universe to them is but a mass of little things. It is true, that the mind may become credulous and prone to superstition by the former method; but are not the experimentalists credulous even to madness in believing any absurdity, rather than believe the grandest truths, if they have not the testimony of their own senses in their favour? I have known some who have been rationally educated, as it is styled. They were marked by a microscopic acuteness, but when they looked at great things, all became a blank and they saw nothing, and denied (very illogically) that anything could be seen, and uniformly put the negation of a power for the possession of a power, and called the want of imagination judgment and the never being moved to rapture philosophy!

Towards the latter end of September, 1781, my father went to Plymouth with my brother Francis, who was to go as midshipman under Admiral Graves, who was a friend of my father's. My father settled my brother, and returned October 4, 1781. He arrived at Exeter about six o'clock, and was pressed to take a bed there at the Harts', but he refused, and, to avoid their entreaties, he told them, that he had never been superstitious, but that the night before he had had a dream which had made a deep impression. He dreamt that Death had appeared to him as he is commonly painted, and touched him with his dart. Well, he returned home, and all his family, I excepted, were up. He told my mother his dream;[14] but he was in high health and good spirits, and there was a bowl of punch made, and my father gave a long and particular account of his travel, and that he had placed Frank under a religious captain, etc. At length he went to bed, very well and in high spirits. A short time after he had lain down he complained of a pain in his bowels. My mother got him some peppermint water, and, after a pause, he said, "I am much better now, my dear!" and lay down again. In a minute my mother heard a noise in his throat, and spoke to him, but he did not answer; and she spoke repeatedly in vain. Her shriek awaked me, and I said, "Papa is dead!" I did not know of my father's return, but I knew that he was expected. How I came to think of his death I cannot tell; but so it was. Dead he was. Some said it was the gout in the heart;—probably it was a fit of apoplexy. He was an Israelite without guile, simple, generous, and taking some Scripture texts in their literal sense, he was conscientiously indifferent to the good and the evil of this world.

God love you and

S. T. Coleridge.

V. TO THE SAME.

February 19, 1798.

From October, 1781, to October, 1782.

After the death of my father, we of course changed houses, and I remained with my mother till the spring of 1782, and was a day-scholar to Parson Warren, my father's successor. He was not very deep, I believe; and I used to delight my mother by relating little instances of his deficiency in grammar knowledge,—every detraction from his merits seemed an oblation to the memory of my father, especially as Parson Warren did certainly pulpitize much better. Somewhere I think about April, 1782, Judge Buller, who had been educated by my father, sent for me, having procured a Christ's Hospital Presentation. I accordingly went to London, and was received by my mother's brother, Mr. Bowdon, a tobacconist and (at the same time) clerk to an underwriter. My uncle lived at the corner of the Stock Exchange and carried on his shop by means of a confidential servant, who, I suppose, fleeced him most unmercifully. He was a widower and had one daughter who lived with a Miss Cabriere, an old maid of great sensibilities and a taste for literature. Betsy Bowdon had obtained an unlimited influence over her mind, which she still retains. Mrs. Holt (for this is her name now) was not the kindest of daughters—but, indeed, my poor uncle would have wearied the patience and affection of an Euphrasia. He received me with great affection, and I stayed ten weeks at his house, during which time I went occasionally to Judge Buller's. My uncle was very proud of me, and used to carry me from coffee-house to coffee-house and tavern to tavern, where I drank and talked and disputed, as if I had been a man. Nothing was more common than for a large party to exclaim in my hearing that I was a prodigy, etc., etc., etc., so that while I remained at my uncle's I was most completely spoiled and pampered, both mind and body.

At length the time came, and I donned the blue coat[15] and yellow stockings and was sent down into Hertford, a town twenty miles from London, where there are about three hundred of the younger Blue-Coat boys. At Hertford I was very happy, on the whole, for I had plenty to eat and drink, and pudding and vegetables almost every day. I stayed there six weeks, and then was drafted up to the great school at London, where I arrived in September, 1782, and was placed in the second ward, then called Jefferies' Ward, and in the under Grammar School. There are twelve wards or dormitories of unequal sizes, beside the sick ward, in the great school, and they contained all together seven hundred boys, of whom I think nearly one third were the sons of clergymen. There are five schools,—a mathematical, a grammar, a drawing, a reading and a writing school,—all very large buildings. When a boy is admitted, if he reads very badly, he is either sent to Hertford or the reading school. (N. B. Boys are admissible from seven to twelve years old.) If he learns to read tolerably well before nine, he is drafted into the Lower Grammar School; if not, into the Writing School, as having given proof of unfitness for classical attainments. If before he is eleven he climbs up to the first form of the Lower Grammar School, he is drafted into the head Grammar School; if not, at eleven years old, he is sent into the Writing School, where he continues till fourteen or fifteen, and is then either apprenticed and articled as clerk, or whatever else his turn of mind or of fortune shall have provided for him. Two or three times a year the Mathematical Master beats up for recruits for the King's boys, as they are called; and all who like the Navy are drafted into the Mathematical and Drawing Schools, where they continue till sixteen or seventeen, and go out as midshipmen and schoolmasters in the Navy. The boys, who are drafted into the Head Grammar School remain there till thirteen, and then, if not chosen for the University, go into the Writing School.

Each dormitory has a nurse, or matron, and there is a head matron to superintend all these nurses. The boys were, when I was admitted, under excessive subordination to each other, according to rank in school; and every ward was governed by four Monitors (appointed by the Steward, who was the supreme Governor out of school,—our temporal lord), and by four Markers, who wore silver medals and were appointed by the Head Grammar Master, who was our supreme spiritual lord. The same boys were commonly both monitors and markers. We read in classes on Sundays to our Markers, and were catechized by them, and under their sole authority during prayers, etc. All other authority was in the monitors; but, as I said, the same boys were ordinarily both the one and the other. Our diet was very scanty.[16] Every morning, a bit of dry bread and some bad small beer. Every evening, a larger piece of bread and cheese or butter, whichever we liked. For dinner,—on Sunday, boiled beef and broth; Monday, bread and butter, and milk and water; on Tuesday, roast mutton; Wednesday, bread and butter, and rice milk; Thursday, boiled beef and broth; Saturday, bread and butter, and pease-porritch. Our food was portioned; and, excepting on Wednesdays, I never had a belly full. Our appetites were damped, never satisfied; and we had no vegetables.

S. T. Coleridge.

VI. TO HIS MOTHER.

February 4, 1785 [London, Christ's Hospital].

Dear Mother,[17]—I received your letter with pleasure on the second instant, and should have had it sooner, but that we had not a holiday before last Tuesday, when my brother delivered it me. I also with gratitude received the two handkerchiefs and the half-a-crown from Mr. Badcock, to whom I would be glad if you would give my thanks. I shall be more careful of the somme, as I now consider that were it not for my kind friends I should be as destitute of many little necessaries as some of my schoolfellows are; and Thank God and my relations for them! My brother Luke saw Mr. James Sorrel, who gave my brother a half-a-crown from Mrs. Smerdon, but mentioned not a word of the plumb cake, and said he would call again. Return my most respectful thanks to Mrs. Smerdon for her kind favour. My aunt was so kind as to accommodate me with a box. I suppose my sister Anna's beauty has many admirers. My brother Luke says that Burke's Art of Speaking would be of great use to me. If Master Sam and Harry Badcock are not gone out of (Ottery), give my kindest love to them. Give my compliments to Mr. Blake and Miss Atkinson, Mr. and Mrs. Smerdon, Mr. and Mrs. Clapp, and all other friends in the country. My uncle, aunt, and cousins join with myself and Brother in love to my sisters, and hope they are well, as I, your dutiful son,

S. Coleridge, am at present.

P. S. Give my kind love to Molly.

VII. TO THE REV. GEORGE COLERIDGE.

Undated, from Christ's Hospital, before 1790.

Dear Brother,—You will excuse me for reminding you that, as our holidays commence next week, and I shall go out a good deal, a good pair of breeches will be no inconsiderable accession to my appearance. For though my present pair are excellent for the purposes of drawing mathematical figures on them, and though a walking thought, sonnet, or epigram would appear on them in very splendid type, yet they are not altogether so well adapted for a female eye—not to mention that I should have the charge of vanity brought against me for wearing a looking-glass. I hope you have got rid of your cold—and I am your affectionate brother,

Samuel Taylor Coleridge.

P. S. Can you let me have them time enough for re-adaptation before Whitsunday? I mean that they may be made up for me before that time.

VIII. TO THE SAME.

October 16, 1791.

Dear Brother,—Here I am, videlicet, Jesus College. I had a tolerable journey, went by a night coach packed up with five more, one of whom had a long, broad, red-hot face, four feet by three. I very luckily found Middleton at Pembroke College, who (after breakfast, etc.) conducted me to Jesus. Dr. Pearce is in Cornwall and not expected to return to Cambridge till the summer, and what is still more extraordinary (and, n. b., rather shameful) neither of the tutors are here. I keep (as the phrase is) in an absent member's rooms till one of the aforesaid duetto return to appoint me my own. Neither Lectures, Chapel, or anything is begun. The College is very thin, and Middleton has not the least acquaintance with any of Jesus except a very blackguardly fellow whose physiog. I did not like. So I sit down to dinner in the Hall in silence, except the noise of suction which accompanies my eating, and rise up ditto. I then walk to Pembroke and sit with my friend Middleton. Pray let me hear from you. Le Grice will send a parcel in two or three days.

Believe me, with sincere affection and gratitude, yours ever,

S. T. Coleridge.

IX. TO THE SAME.

January 24, 1792.

Dear Brother,—Happy am I, that the country air and exercise have operated with due effect on your health and spirits—and happy, too, that I can inform you, that my own corporealities are in a state of better health, than I ever recollect them to be. This indeed I owe in great measure to the care of Mrs. Evans,[18 with whom I spent a fortnight at Christmas: the relaxation from study coöperating with the cheerfulness and attention, which I met there, proved very potently medicinal. I have indeed experienced from her a tenderness scarcely inferior to the solicitude of maternal affection. I wish, my dear brother, that some time, when you walk into town, you would call at Villiers Street, and take a dinner or dish of tea there. Mrs. Evans has repeatedly expressed her wish, and I too have made a half promise that you would. I assure you, you will find them not only a very amiable, but a very sensible family.

I send a parcel to Le Grice on Friday morning, which (you may depend on it as a certainty) will contain your sermon. I hope you will like it.

I am sincerely concerned at the state of Mr. Sparrow's health. Are his complaints consumptive? Present my respects to him and Mrs. Sparrow.

When the Scholarship falls, I do not know. It must be in the course of two or three months. I do not relax in my exertions, neither do I find it any impediment to my mental acquirements that prudence has obliged me to relinquish the mediæ pallescere nocti. We are examined as Rustats,[19] on the Thursday in Easter Week. The examination for my year is "the last book of Homer and Horace's De Arte Poetica." The Master (i. e. Dr. Pearce) told me that he would do me a service by pushing my examination as deep as he possibly could. If ever hogs-lard is pleasing, it is when our superiors trowel it on. Mr. Frend's company[20] is by no means invidious. On the contrary, Pearce himself is very intimate with him. No!

Though I am not an Alderman, I have yet prudence enough to respect that gluttony of faith waggishly yclept orthodoxy.

Philanthropy generally keeps pace with health—my acquaintance becomes more general. I am intimate with an undergraduate of our College, his name Caldwell,[21] who is pursuing the same line of study (nearly) as myself. Though a man of fortune, he is prudent; nor does he lay claim to that right, which wealth confers on its possessor, of being a fool. Middleton is fourth senior optimate—an honourable place, but by no means so high as the whole University expected, or (I believe) his merits deserved. He desires his love to Stevens:[22] to which you will add mine.

At what time am I to receive my pecuniary assistance? Quarterly or half yearly? The Hospital issue their money half yearly, and we receive the products of our scholarship at once, a little after Easter. Whatever additional supply you and my brother may have thought necessary would be therefore more conducive to my comfort, if I received it quarterly—as there are a number of little things which require us to have some ready money in our pockets—particularly if we happen to be unwell. But this as well as everything of the pecuniary kind I leave entirely ad arbitrium tuum.

I have written my mother, of whose health I am rejoiced to hear. God send that she may long continue to recede from old age, while she advances towards it! Pray write me very soon.

Yours with gratitude and affection,
S. T. Coleridge.

X. TO MRS. EVANS.

February 13, 1792.

My very Dear,—What word shall I add sufficiently expressive of the warmth which I feel? You covet to be near my heart. Believe me, that you and my sister have the very first row in the front box of my heart's little theatre—and—God knows! you are not crowded. There, my dear spectators! you shall see what you shall see—Farce, Comedy, and Tragedy—my laughter, my cheerfulness, and my melancholy. A thousand figures pass before you, shifting in perpetual succession; these are my joys and my sorrows, my hopes and my fears, my good tempers and my peevishness: you will, however, observe two that remain unalterably fixed, and these are love and gratitude. In short, my dear Mrs. Evans, my whole heart shall be laid open like any sheep's heart; my virtues, if I have any, shall not be more exposed to your view than my weaknesses. Indeed, I am of opinion that foibles are the cement of affection, and that, however we may admire a perfect character, we are seldom inclined to love and praise those whom we cannot sometimes blame. Come, ladies! will you take your seats in this play-house? Fool that I am! Are you not already there? Believe me, you are!

I am extremely anxious to be informed concerning your health. Have you not felt the kindly influence of this more than vernal weather, as well as the good effects of your own recommended regularity? I would I could transmit you a little of my superfluous good health! I am indeed at present most wonderfully well, and if I continue so, I may soon be mistaken for one of your very children: at least, in clearness of complexion and rosiness of cheek I am no contemptible likeness of them, though that ugly arrangement of features with which nature has distinguished me will, I fear, long stand in the way of such honorable assimilation. You accuse me of evading the bet, and imagine that my silence proceeded from a consciousness of the charge. But you are mistaken. I not only read your letter first, but, on my sincerity! I felt no inclination to do otherwise; and I am confident, that if Mary had happened to have stood by me and had seen me take up her letter in preference to her mother's, with all that ease and energy which she can so gracefully exert upon proper occasions, she would have lifted up her beautiful little leg, and kicked me round the room. Had Anne indeed favoured me with a few lines, I confess I should have seized hold of them before either of your letters; but then this would have arisen from my love of novelty, and not from any deficiency in filial respect. So much for your bet!

You can scarcely conceive what uneasiness poor Tom's accident has occasioned me; in everything that relates to him I feel solicitude truly fraternal. Be particular concerning him in your next. I was going to write him an half-angry letter for the long intermission of his correspondence; but I must change it to a consolatory one. You mention not a word of Bessy. Think you I do not love her?

And so, my dear Mrs. Evans, you are to take your Welsh journey in May? Now may the Goddess of Health, the rosy-cheeked goddess that blows the breeze from the Cambrian mountains, renovate that dear old lady, and make her young again! I always loved that old lady's looks. Yet do not flatter yourselves, that you shall take this journey tête-à-tête. You will have an unseen companion at your side, one who will attend you in your jaunt, who will be present at your arrival; one whose heart will melt with unutterable tenderness at your maternal transports, who will climb the Welsh hills with you, who will feel himself happy in knowing you to be so. In short, as St. Paul says, though absent in body, I shall be present in mind. Disappointment? You must not, you shall not be disappointed; and if a poetical invocation can help you to drive off that ugly foe to happiness here it is for you.

TO DISAPPOINTMENT.

Hence! thou fiend of gloomy sway,
Thou lov'st on withering blast to ride
O'er fond Illusion's air-built pride.
Sullen Spirit! Hence! Away!

Where Avarice lurks in sordid cell,
Or mad Ambition builds the dream,
Or Pleasure plots th' unholy scheme
There with Guilt and Folly dwell!

But oh! when Hope on Wisdom's wing
Prophetic whispers pure delight,
Be distant far thy cank'rous blight,
Demon of envenom'd sting.

Then haste thee, Nymph of balmy gales!
Thy poet's prayer, sweet May! attend!
Oh! place my parent and my friend
'Mid her lovely native vales.

Peace, that lists the woodlark's strains,
Health, that breathes divinest treasures,

Laughing Hours, and Social Pleasures
Wait my friend in Cambria's plains.

Affection there with mingled ray
Shall pour at once the raptures high
Of filial and maternal Joy;
Haste thee then, delightful May!

And oh! may Spring's fair flowerets fade,
May Summer cease her limbs to lave
In cooling stream, may Autumn grave
Yellow o'er the corn-cloath'd glade;

Ere, from sweet retirement torn,
She seek again the crowded mart:
Nor thou, my selfish, selfish heart
Dare her slow return to mourn!

In what part of the country is my dear Anne to be? Mary must and shall be with you. I want to know all your summer residences, that I may be on that very spot with all of you. It is not improbable that I may steal down from Cambridge about the beginning of April just to look at you, that when I see you again in autumn I may know how many years younger the Welsh air has made you. If I shall go into Devonshire on the 21st of May, unless my good fortune in a particular affair should detain me till the 4th of June.

I lately received the thanks of the College for a declamation[23] I spoke in public; indeed, I meet with the most pointed marks of respect, which, as I neither flatter nor fiddle, I suppose to be sincere. I write these things not from vanity, but because I know they will please you.

I intend to leave off suppers, and two or three other little unnecessaries, and in conjunction with Caldwell hire a garden for the summer. It will be nice exercise—your advice. La! it will be so charming to walk out in one's own garding, and sit and drink tea in an arbour, and pick pretty nosegays. To plant and transplant, and be dirty and amused! Then to look with contempt on your Londoners with your mock gardens and your smoky windows, making a beggarly show of withered flowers stuck in pint pots, and quart pots menacing the heads of the passengers below.

Now suppose I conclude something in the manner with which Mary concludes all her letters to me, "Believe me your sincere friend," and dutiful humble servant to command!

Now I do hate that way of concluding a letter. 'Tis as dry as a stick, as stiff as a poker, and as cold as a cucumber. It is not half so good as my old

God bless you
and
Your affectionately grateful
S. T. Coleridge.

XI. TO MARY EVANS.

February 13, 11 o'clock.

Ten of the most talkative young ladies now in London!

Now by the most accurate calculation of the specific quantities of sounds, a female tongue, when it exerts itself to the utmost, equals the noise of eighteen sign-posts, which the wind swings backwards and forwards in full creak. If then one equals eighteen, ten must equal one hundred and eighty; consequently, the circle at Jermyn Street unitedly must have produced a noise equal to that of one hundred and eighty old crazy sign-posts, inharmoniously agitated as aforesaid. Well! to be sure, there are few disagreeables for which the pleasure of Mary and Anne Evans' company would not amply compensate; but faith! I feel myself half inclined to thank God that I was fifty-two miles off during this clattering clapperation of tongues. Do you keep ale at Jermyn Street? If so, I hope it is not soured.

Such, my dear Mary, were the reflections that instantly suggested themselves to me on reading the former part of your letter. Believe me, however, that my gratitude keeps pace with my sense of your exertions, as I can most feelingly conceive the difficulty of writing amid that second edition of Babel with additions. That your health is restored gives me sincere delight. May the giver of all pleasure and pain preserve it so! I am likewise glad to hear that your hand is re-whiten'd, though I cannot help smiling at a certain young lady's effrontery in having boxed a young gentleman's ears till her own hand became black and blue, and attributing those unseemly marks to the poor unfortunate object of her resentment. You are at liberty, certainly, to say what you please.

It has been confidently affirmed by most excellent judges (tho' the best may be mistaken) that I have grown very handsome lately. Pray that I may have grace not to be vain. Yet, ah! who can read the stories of Pamela, or Joseph Andrews, or Susannah and the three Elders, and not perceive what a dangerous snare beauty is? Beauty is like the grass, that groweth up in the morning and is withered before night. Mary! Anne! Do not be vain of your beauty!!!!!

I keep a cat. Amid the strange collection of strange animals with which I am surrounded, I think it necessary to have some meek well-looking being, that I may keep my social affections alive. Puss, like her master, is a very gentle brute, and I behave to her with all possible politeness. Indeed, a cat is a very worthy animal. To be sure, I have known some very malicious cats in my lifetime, but then they were old—and besides, they had not nearly so many legs as you, my sweet Pussy. I wish, Puss! I could break you of that indecorous habit of turning your back front to the fire. It is not frosty weather now.

N. B.—If ever, Mary, you should feel yourself inclined to visit me at Cambridge, pray do not suffer the consideration of my having a cat to deter you. Indeed, I will keep her chained up all the while you stay.

I was in company the other day with a very dashing literary lady. After my departure, a friend of mine asked her her opinion of me. She answered: "The best I can say of him is, that he is a very gentle bear." What think you of this character?

What a lovely anticipation of spring the last three or four days have afforded. Nature has not been very profuse of her ornaments to the country about Cambridge; yet the clear rivulet that runs through the grove adjacent to our College, and the numberless little birds (particularly robins) that are singing away, and above all, the little lambs, each by the side of its mother, recall the most pleasing ideas of pastoral simplicity, and almost soothe one's soul into congenial innocence. Amid these delightful scenes, of which the uncommon flow of health I at present possess permits me the full enjoyment, I should not deign to think of London, were it not for a little family, whom I trust I need not name. What bird of the air whispers me that you too will soon enjoy the same and more delightful pleasures in a much more delightful country? What we strongly wish we are very apt to believe. At present, my presentiments on that head amount to confidence.

Last Sunday, Middleton and I set off at one o'clock on a ramble. We sauntered on, chatting and contemplating, till to our great surprise we came to a village seven miles from Cambridge. And here at a farmhouse we drank tea. The rusticity of the habitation and the inhabitants was charming; we had cream to our tea, which though not brought in a lordly dish, Sisera would have jumped at. Being here informed that we could return to Cambridge another way, over a common, for the sake of diversifying our walk, we chose this road, "if road it might be called, where road was none," though we were not unapprized of its difficulties. The fine weather deceived us. We forgot that it was a summer day in warmth only, and not in length; but we were soon reminded of it. For on the pathless solitude of this common, the night overtook us—we must have been four miles distant from Cambridge—the night, though calm, was as dark as the place was dreary: here steering our course by our imperfect conceptions of the point in which we conjectured Cambridge to lie, we wandered on "with cautious steps and slow." We feared the bog, the stump, and the fen: we feared the ghosts of the night—at least, those material and knock-me-down ghosts, the apprehension of which causes you, Mary (valorous girl that you are!), always to peep under your bed of a night. As we were thus creeping forward like the two children in the wood, we spy'd something white moving across the common. This we made up to, though contrary to our supposed destination. It proved to be a man with a white bundle. We enquired our way, and luckily he was going to Cambridge. He informed us that we had gone half a mile out of our way, and that in five minutes more we must have arrived at a deep quagmire grassed over. What an escape! The man was as glad of our company as we of his—for, it seemed, the poor fellow was afraid of Jack o' Lanthorns—the superstition of this county attributing a kind of fascination to those wandering vapours, so that whoever fixes his eyes on them is forced by some irresistible impulse to follow them. He entertained us with many a dreadful tale. By nine o'clock we arrived at Cambridge, betired and bemudded. I never recollect to have been so much fatigued.

Do you spell the word scarsely? When Momus, the fault-finding God, endeavoured to discover some imperfection in Venus, he could only censure the creaking of her slipper. I, too, Momuslike, can only fall foul on a single s. Yet will not my dear Mary be angry with me, or think the remark trivial, when she considers that half a grain is of consequence in the weight of a diamond.

I had entertained hopes that you would really have sent me a piece of sticking plaister, which would have been very convenient at that time, I having cut my finger. I had to buy sticking plaister, etc. What is the use of a man's knowing you girls, if he cannot chouse you out of such little things as that? Do not your fingers, Mary, feel an odd kind of titillation to be about my ears for my impudence?

On Saturday night, as I was sitting by myself all alone, I heard a creaking sound, something like the noise which a crazy chair would make, if pressed by the tremendous weight of Mr. Barlow's extremities. I cast my eyes around, and what should I behold but a Ghost rising out of the floor! A deadly paleness instantly overspread my body, which retained no other symptom of life but its violent trembling. My hair (as is usual in frights of this nature) stood upright by many degrees stiffer than the oaks of the mountains, yea, stiffer than Mr. ———; yet was it rendered oily-pliant by the profuse perspiration that burst from every pore. This spirit advanced with a book in his hand, and having first dissipated my terrors, said as follows: "I am the Ghost of Gray. There lives a young lady" (then he mentioned your name), "of whose judgment I entertain so high an opinion, that her approbation of my works would make the turf lie lighter on me; present her with this book, and transmit it to her as soon as possible, adding my love to her. And, as for you, O young man!" (now he addressed himself to me) "write no more verses. In the first place your poetry is vile stuff; and secondly" (here he sighed almost to bursting), "all poets go to —ll; we are so intolerably addicted to the vice of lying!" He vanished, and convinced me of the truth of his last dismal account by the sulphurous stink which he left behind him.

His first mandate I have obeyed, and, I hope you will receive safe your ghostly admirer's present. But so far have I been from obeying his second injunction, that I never had the scribble-mania stronger on me than for these last three or four days: nay, not content with suffering it myself, I must pester those I love best with the blessed effects of my disorder.

Besides two things, which you will find in the next sheet, I cannot forbear filling the remainder of this sheet with an Odeling, though I know and approve your aversion to mere prettiness, and though my tiny love ode possesses no other property in the world. Let then its shortness recommend it to your perusal—by the by, the only thing in which it resembles you, for wit, sense, elegance, or beauty it has none.

AN ODE IN THE MANNER OF ANACREON.[24]

As late in wreaths gay flowers I bound,
Beneath some roses Love I found,
And by his little frolic pinion
As quick as thought I seiz'd the minion,
Then in my cup the prisoner threw,
And drank him in its sparkling dew:
And sure I feel my angry guest
Flutt'ring his wings within my breast!
Are you quite asleep, dear Mary? Sleep on; but when you awake, read the following productions, and then, I'll be bound, you will sleep again sounder than ever.

A WISH WRITTEN IN JESUS WOOD, FEBRUARY 10, 1792.[25]

Lo! through the dusky silence of the groves,
Thro' vales irriguous, and thro' green retreats,
With languid murmur creeps the placid stream
And works its secret way.

Awhile meand'ring round its native fields,
It rolls the playful wave and winds its flight:
Then downward flowing with awaken'd speed
Embosoms in the Deep!

Thus thro' its silent tenor may my Life
Smooth its meek stream by sordid wealth unclogg'd,
Alike unconscious of forensic storms,
And Glory's blood-stain'd palm!

And when dark Age shall close Life's little day,

Satiate of sport, and weary of its toils,
E'en thus may slumb'rous Death my decent limbs
Compose with icy hand!

A LOVER'S COMPLAINT TO HIS MISTRESS
WHO DESERTED HIM IN QUEST OF A MORE WEALTHY
HUSBAND IN THE EAST INDIES.[26]

The dubious light sad glimmers o'er the sky:
'Tis silence all. By lonely anguish torn,
With wandering feet to gloomy groves I fly,
And wakeful Love still tracks my course forlorn.

And will you, cruel Julia? will you go?
And trust you to the Ocean's dark dismay?
Shall the wide, wat'ry world between us flow?
And winds unpitying snatch my Hopes away?

Thus could you sport with my too easy heart?
Yet tremble, lest not unaveng'd I grieve!
The winds may learn your own delusive art,
And faithless Ocean smile—but to deceive!
I have written too long a letter. Give me a hint, and I will avoid a repetition of the offence.

It's a compensation for the above-written rhymes (which if you ever condescend to read a second time, pray let it be by the light of their own flames) in my next letter I will send some delicious poetry lately published by the exquisite Bowles.

To-morrow morning I fill the rest of this sheet with a letter to Anne. And now, good-night, dear sister! and peaceful slumbers await us both!

S. T. Coleridge.

XII. TO ANNE EVANS.

February 19, 1792.

Dear Anne,—To be sure I felt myself rather disappointed at my not receiving a few lines from you; but I am nevertheless greatly rejoiced at your amicable dispositions towards me. Please to accept two kisses, as the seals of reconciliation—you will find them on the word "Anne" at the beginning of the letter—at least, there I left them. I must, however, give you warning, that the next time you are affronted with Brother Coly, and show your resentment by that most cruel of all punishments, silence, I shall address a letter to you as long and as sorrowful as Jeremiah's Lamentations, and somewhat in the style of your sister's favourite lover, beginning with,—

TO THE IRASCIBLE MISS.

Dear Miss, &c.

My dear Anne, you are my Valentine. I dreamt of you this morning, and I have seen no female in the whole course of the day, except an old bedmaker belonging to the College, and I don't count her one, as the bristle of her beard makes me suspect her to be of the masculine gender. Some one of the genii must have conveyed your image to me so opportunely, nor will you think this impossible, if you will read the little volumes which contain their exploits, and crave the honour of your acceptance.

If I could draw, I would have sent a pretty heart stuck through with arrows, with some such sweet posy underneath it as this:—

"The rose is red, the violet blue;
The pink is sweet, and so are you."
But as the Gods have not made me a drawer (of anything but corks), you must accept the will for the deed.

You never wrote or desired your sister to write concerning the bodily health of the Barlowites, though you know my affection for that family. Do not forget this in your next.

Is Mr. Caleb Barlow recovered of the rheumatism? The quiet ugliness of Cambridge supplies me with very few communicables in the news way. The most important is, that Mr. Tim Grubskin, of this town, citizen, is dead. Poor man! he loved fish too well. A violent commotion in his bowels carried him off. They say he made a very good end. There is his epitaph:—

"A loving friend and tender parent dear,
Just in all actions, and he the Lord did fear,
Hoping, that, when the day of Resurrection come,
He shall arise in glory like the Sun."
It was composed by a Mr. Thistlewait, the town crier, and is much admired. We are all mortal!!

His wife carries on the business. It is whispered about the town that a match between her and Mr. Coe, the shoemaker, is not improbable. He certainly seems very assiduous in consoling her, but as to anything matrimonial I do not write it as a well authenticated fact.

I went the other evening to the concert, and spent the time there much to my heart's content in cursing Mr. Hague, who played on the violin most piggishly, and a Miss (I forget her name)—Miss Humstrum, who sung most sowishly. O the Billington! That I should be absent during the oratorios! The prince unable to conceal his pain! Oh! oh! oh! oh! oh! oh! oh! oh! oh!

To which house is Mrs. B. engaged this season?

The mutton and winter cabbage are confoundedly tough here, though very venerable for their old age. Were you ever at Cambridge, Anne? The river Cam is a handsome stream of a muddy complexion, somewhat like Miss Yates, to whom you will present my love (if you like).

In Cambridge there are sixteen colleges, that look like workhouses, and fourteen churches that look like little houses. The town is very fertile in alleys, and mud, and cats, and dogs, besides men, women, ravens, clergy, proctors, tutors, owls, and other two-legged cattle. It likewise—but here I must interrupt my description to hurry to Mr. Costobadie's lectures on Euclid, who is as mathematical an author, my dear Anne, as you would wish to read on a long summer's day. Addio! God bless you, ma chère soeur, and your affectionate frère,

S. T. Coleridge.

P. S. I add a postscript on purpose to communicate a joke to you. A party of us had been drinking wine together, and three or four freshmen were most deplorably intoxicated. (I have too great a respect for delicacy to say drunk.) As we were returning homewards, two of them fell into the gutter (or kennel). We ran to assist one of them, who very generously stuttered out, as he lay sprawling in the mud: "N-n-n-no—n-n-no!—save my f-fr-fr-friend there; n-never mind me, I can swim."

Won't you write me a long letter now, Anne?

P. S. Give my respectful compliments to Betty, and say that I enquired after her health with the most emphatic energy of impassioned avidity.

XIII. TO MRS EVANS.

February 22 [1792].

Dear Madam,—The incongruity of the dates in these letters you will immediately perceive. The truth is that I had written the foregoing heap of nothingness six or seven days ago, but I was prevented from sending it by a variety of disagreeable little impediments.

Mr. Massy must be arrived in Cambridge by this time; but to call on an utter stranger just arrived with so trivial a message as yours and his uncle's love to him, when I myself had been in Cambridge five or six weeks, would appear rather awkward, not to say ludicrous. If, however, I meet him at any wine party (which is by no means improbable) I shall take the opportunity of mentioning it en passant. As to Mr. M.'s debts, the most intimate friends in college are perfect strangers to each other's affairs; consequently it is little likely that I should procure any information of this kind.

I hope and trust that neither yourself nor my sisters have experienced any ill effects from this wonderful change of weather. A very slight cold is the only favour with which it has honoured me. I feel myself apprehensive for all of you, but more particularly for Anne, whose frame I think most susceptible of cold.

Yesterday a Frenchman came dancing into my room, of which he made but three steps, and presented me with a card. I had scarcely collected, by glancing my eye over it, that he was a tooth-monger, before he seized hold of my muzzle, and, baring my teeth (as they do a horse's, in order to know his age), he exclaimed, as if in violent agitation: "Mon Dieu! Monsieur, all your teeth will fall out in a day or two, unless you permit me the honour of scaling them!" This ineffable piece of assurance discovered such a genius for impudence, that I could not suffer it to go unrewarded. So, after a hearty laugh, I sat down, and let the rascal chouse me out of half a guinea by scraping my grinders—the more readily, indeed, as I recollected the great penchant which all your family have for delicate teeth.

So (I hear) Allen[27] will be most precipitately emancipated. Good luck have thou of thy emancipation, Bob-bee! Tell him from me that if he does not kick Richards'[28] fame out of doors by the superiority of his own, I will never forgive him.

If you will send me a box of Mr. Stringer's tooth powder, mamma! we will accept of it.

And now, Right Reverend Mother in God, let me claim your permission to subscribe myself with all observance and gratitude, your most obedient humble servant, and lowly slave,

Samuel Taylor Coleridge,

Reverend in the future tense, and scholar of Jesus College in the present time.

XIV. TO MARY EVANS.

Jesus College, Cambridge, February 22 [1792].

Dear Mary,—Writing long letters is not the fault into which I am most apt to fall, but whenever I do, by some inexplicable ill luck, my prolixity is always directed to those whom I would yet least of all wish to torment. You think, and think rightly, that I had no occasion to increase the preceding accumulations of wearisomeness, but I wished to inform you that I have sent the poem of Bowles, which I mentioned in a former sheet; though I dare say you would have discovered this without my information. If the pleasure which you receive from the perusal of it prove equal to that which I have received, it will make you some small return for the exertions of friendship, which you must have found necessary in order to travel through my long, long, long letter.

Though it may be a little effrontery to point out beauties, which would be obvious to a far less sensible heart than yours, yet I cannot forbear the self-indulgence of remarking to you the exquisite description of Hope in the third page and of Fortitude in the sixth; but the poem "On leaving a place of residence" appears to me to be almost superior to any of Bowles's compositions.

I hope that the Jermyn Street ledgers are well. How can they be otherwise in such lovely keeping?

Your Jessamine Pomatum, I trust, is as strong and as odorous as ever, and the roasted turkeys at Villiers Street honoured, as usual, with a thick crust of your Mille (what do you call it?) powder.

I had a variety of other interesting inquiries to make, but time and memory fail me.

Without a swanskin waistcoat, what is man? I have got a swanskin waistcoat,—a most attractive external.

Yours with sincerity of friendship,
Samuel Taylor C.

XV. TO THE REV. GEORGE COLERIDGE.

Monday night, April [1792].

Dear Brother,—You would have heard from me long since had I not been entangled in such various businesses as have occupied my whole time. Besides my ordinary business, which, as I look forward to a smart contest some time this year, is not an indolent one, I have been writing for all the prizes, namely, the Greek Ode, the Latin Ode, and the Epigrams. I have little or no expectation of success, as a Mr. Smith,[29] a man of immense genius, author of some papers in the "Microcosm," is among my numerous competitors. The prize medals will be adjudged about the beginning of June. If you can think of a good thought for the beginning of the Latin Ode upon the miseries of the W. India slaves, communicate. My Greek Ode[30] is, I think, my chef d'œuvre in poetical composition. I have sent you a sermon metamorphosed from an obscure publication by vamping, transposition, etc. If you like it, I can send you two more of the same kidney. Our examination as Rustats comes [off] on the Thursday in Easter week. After it a man of our college has offered to take me to town in his gig, and, if he can bring me back, I think I shall accept his offer, as the expense, at all events, will not be more than 12 shillings, and my very commons, and tea, etc., would amount to more than that in the week which I intend to stay in town. Almost all the men are out of college, and I am most villainously vapoured. I wrote the following the other day under the title of "A Fragment found in a Lecture-Room:"—

Where deep in mud Cam rolls his slumbrous stream,
And bog and desolation reign supreme;
Where all Bœotia clouds the misty brain,
The owl Mathesis pipes her loathsome strain.
Far, far aloof the frighted Muses fly,
Indignant Genius scowls and passes by:
The frolic Pleasures start amid their dance,
And Wit congealed stands fix'd in wintry trance.
But to the sounds with duteous haste repair
Cold Industry, and wary-footed Care;
And Dulness, dosing on a couch of lead,
Pleas'd with the song uplifts her heavy head,
The sympathetic numbers lists awhile,
Then yawns propitiously a frosty smile....
[Cætera desunt.]

This morning I went for the first time with a party on the river. The clumsy dog to whom we had entrusted the sail was fool enough to fasten it. A gust of wind embraced the opportunity of turning over the boat, and baptizing all that were in it. We swam to shore, and walked dripping home, like so many river gods. Thank God! I do not feel as if I should be the worse for it.

I was matriculated on Saturday.[31] Oath-taking is very healthy in spring, I should suppose. I am grown very fat. We have two men at our college, great cronies, their names Head and Bones; the first an unlicked cub of a Yorkshireman, the second a very fierce buck. I call them Raw Head and Bloody Bones.

As soon as you can make it convenient I should feel thankful if you could transmit me ten or five pounds, as I am at present cashless.

Pray, was the bible clerk's place accounted a disreputable one at Oxford in your time? Poor Allen, who is just settled there, complains of the great distance with which the men treat him. 'Tis a childish University! Thank God! I am at Cambridge. Pray let me hear from you soon, and whether your health has held out this long campaign. I hope, however, soon to see you, till when believe me, with gratitude and affection, yours ever,

S. T. Coleridge.

XVI. TO MRS. EVANS.

February 5, 1793.

My dear Mrs. Evans,—This is the third day of my resurrection from the couch, or rather, the sofa of sickness. About a fortnight ago, a quantity of matter took it into its head to form in my left gum, and was attended with such violent pain, inflammation, and swelling, that it threw me into a fever. However, God be praised, my gum has at last been opened, a villainous tooth extracted, and all is well. I am still very weak, as well I may, since for seven days together I was incapable of swallowing anything but spoon meat, so that in point of spirits I am but the dregs of my former self—a decaying flame agonizing in the snuff of a tallow candle—a kind of hobgoblin, clouted and bagged up in the most contemptible shreds, rags, and yellow relics of threadbare mortality. The event of our examination[32] was such as surpassed my expectations, and perfectly accorded with my wishes. After a very severe trial of six days' continuance, the number of the competitors was reduced from seventeen to four, and after a further process of ordeal we, the survivors, were declared equal each to the other, and the Scholarship, according to the will of its founder, awarded to the youngest of us, who was found to be a Mr. Butler of St. John's College. I am just two months older than he is, and though I would doubtless have rather had it myself, I am yet not at all sorry at his success; for he is sensible and unassuming, and besides, from his circumstances, such an accession to his annual income must have been very acceptable to him. So much for myself.

I am greatly rejoiced at your brother's recovery; in proportion, indeed, to the anxiety and fears I felt on your account during his illness. I recollected, my most dear Mrs. Evans, that you are frequently troubled with a strange forgetfulness of yourself, and too apt to go far beyond your strength, if by any means you may alleviate the sufferings of others. Ah! how different from the majority of others whom we courteously dignify with the name of human—a vile herd, who sit still in the severest distresses of their friends, and cry out, There is a lion in the way! animals, who walk with leaden sandals in the paths of charity, yet to gratify their own inclinations will run a mile in a breath. Oh! I do know a set of little, dirty, pimping, petty-fogging, ambidextrous fellows, who would set your house on fire, though it were but to roast an egg for themselves! Yet surely, considering it were a selfish view, the pleasures that arise from whispering peace to those who are in trouble, and healing the broken in heart, are far superior to all the unfeeling can enjoy.

I have inclosed a little work of that great and good man Archdeacon Paley; it is entitled Motives of Contentment, addressed to the poorer part of our fellow men. The twelfth page I particularly admire, and the twentieth. The reasoning has been of some service to me, who am of the race of the Grumbletonians. My dear friend Allen has a resource against most misfortunes in the natural gaiety of his temper, whereas my hypochondriac, gloomy spirit amid blessings too frequently warbles out the hoarse gruntings of discontent! Nor have all the lectures that divines and philosophers have given us for these three thousand years past, on the vanity of riches, and the cares of greatness, etc., prevented me from sincerely regretting that Nature had not put it into the head of some rich man to beget me for his first-born, whereas now I am likely to get bread just when I shall have no teeth left to chew it. Cheer up, my little one (thus I answer I)! better late than never. Hath literature been thy choice, and hast thou food and raiment? Be thankful, be amazed at thy good fortune! Art thou dissatisfied and desirous of other things? Go, and make twelve votes at an election; it shall do thee more service and procure thee greater preferment than to have made twelve commentaries on the twelve prophets. My dear Mrs. Evans! excuse the wanderings of my castle building imagination. I have not a thought which I conceal from you. I write to others, but my pen talks to you. Convey my softest affections to Betty, and believe me,

Your grateful and affectionate boy,
S. T. Coleridge.

XVII. TO MARY EVANS.

Jesus College, Cambridge, February 7, 1793.

I would to Heaven, my dear Miss Evans, that the god of wit, or news, or politics would whisper in my ear something that might be worth sending fifty-four miles—but alas! I am so closely blocked by an army of misfortunes that really there is no passage left open for mirth or anything else. Now, just to give you a few articles in the large inventory of my calamities. Imprimis, a gloomy, uncomfortable morning. Item, my head aches. Item, the Dean has set me a swinging imposition for missing morning chapel. Item, of the two only coats which I am worth in the world, both have holes in the elbows. Item, Mr. Newton, our mathematical lecturer, has recovered from an illness. But the story is rather a laughable one, so I must tell it you. Mr. Newton (a tall, thin man with a little, tiny, blushing face) is a great botanist. Last Sunday, as he was strolling out with a friend of his, some curious plant suddenly caught his eye. He turned round his head with great eagerness to call his companion to a participation of discovery, and unfortunately continuing to walk forward he fell into a pool, deep, muddy, and full of chickweed. I was lucky enough to meet him as he was entering the college gates on his return (a sight I would not have lost for the Indies), his best black clothes all green with duckweed, he shivering and dripping, in short a perfect river god. I went up to him (you must understand we hate each other most cordially) and sympathized with him in all the tenderness of condolence. The consequence of his misadventure was a violent cold attended with fever, which confined him to his room, prevented him from giving lectures, and freed me from the necessity of attending them; but this misfortune I supported with truly Christian fortitude. However, I constantly asked after his health with filial anxiety, and this morning, making my usual inquiries, I was informed, to my infinite astonishment and vexation, that he was perfectly recovered and intended to give lectures this very day!!! Verily, I swear that six of his duteous pupils—myself as their general—sallied forth to the apothecary's house with a fixed determination to thrash him for having performed so speedy a cure, but, luckily for himself, the rascal was not at home. But here comes my fiddling master, for (but this is a secret) I am learning to play on the violin. Twit, twat, twat, twit! "Pray, M. de la Penche, do you think I shall ever make anything of this violin? Do you think I have an ear for music?" "Un magnifique! Un superbe! Par honneur, sir, you be a ver great genius in de music. Good morning, monsieur!" This M. de la Penche is a better judge than I thought for.

This new whim of mine is partly a scheme of self-defence. Three neighbours have run music-mad lately—two of them fiddle-scrapers, the third a flute-tooter—and are perpetually annoying me with their vile performances, compared with which the gruntings of a whole herd of sows would be seraphic melody. Now I hope, by frequently playing myself, to render my ear callous. Besides, the evils of life are crowding upon me, and music is "the sweetest assuager of cares." It helps to relieve and soothe the mind, and is a sort of refuge from calamity, from slights and neglects and censures and insults and disappointments; from the warmth of real enemies and the coldness of pretended friends; from your well wishers (as they are justly called, in opposition, I suppose, to well doers), men whose inclinations to serve you always decrease in a most mathematical proportion as their opportunities to do it increase; from the

"Proud man's contumely, and the spurns
Which patient merit of th' unworthy takes;"
from grievances that are the growth of all times and places and not peculiar to this age, which authors call this critical age, and divines this sinful age, and politicians this age of revolutions. An acquaintance of mine calls it this learned age in due reverence to his own abilities, and like Monsieur Whatd'yecallhim, who used to pull off his hat when he spoke of himself. The poet laureate calls it "this golden age," and with good reason,—

For him the fountains with Canary flow,
And, best of fruit, spontaneous guineas grow.
Pope, in his "Dunciad," makes it this leaden age, but I choose to call it without an epithet, this age. Many things we must expect to meet with which it would be hard to bear, if a compensation were not found in honest endeavours to do well, in virtuous affections and connections, and in harmless and reasonable amusements. And why should not a man amuse himself sometimes? Vive la bagatelle!

I received a letter this morning from my friend Allen. He is up to his ears in business, and I sincerely congratulate him upon it—occupation, I am convinced, being the great secret of happiness. "Nothing makes the temper so fretful as indolence," said a young lady who, beneath the soft surface of feminine delicacy, possesses a mind acute by nature, and strengthened by habits of reflection. 'Pon my word, Miss Evans, I beg your pardon a thousand times for bepraising you to your face, but, really, I have written so long that I had forgot to whom I was writing.

Have you read Mr. Fox's letter to the Westminster electors? It is quite the political go at Cambridge, and has converted many souls to the Foxite faith.

Have you seen the Siddons this season? or the Jordan? An acquaintance of mine has a tragedy coming out early in the next season, the principal character of which Mrs. Siddons will act. He has importuned me to write the prologue and epilogue, but, conscious of my inability, I have excused myself with a jest, and told him I was too good a Christian to be accessory to the damnation of anything.

There is an old proverb of a river of words and a spoonful of sense, and I think this letter has been a pretty good proof of it. But as nonsense is better than blank paper, I will fill this side with a song I wrote lately. My friend, Charles Hague[33] the composer, will set it to wild music. I shall sing it, and accompany myself on the violin. Ça ira!

Cathloma, who reigned in the Highlands of Scotland about two hundred years after the birth of our Saviour, was defeated and killed in a war with a neighbouring prince, and Nina-Thoma his daughter (according to the custom of those times and that country) was imprisoned in a cave by the seaside. This is supposed to be her complaint:—

How long will ye round me be swelling,
O ye blue-tumbling waves of the sea?
Not always in caves was my dwelling,
Nor beneath the cold blast of the Tree;

Thro' the high sounding Hall of Cathloma
In the steps of my beauty I strayed,
The warriors beheld Nina-Thoma,
And they blessed the dark-tressed Maid!

By my Friends, by my Lovers discarded,
Like the Flower of the Rock now I waste,
That lifts its fair head unregarded,
And scatters its leaves on the blast.

A Ghost! by my cavern it darted!
In moonbeams the spirit was drest—
For lovely appear the Departed,
When they visit the dreams of my rest!

But dispersed by the tempest's commotion,
Fleet the shadowy forms of Delight;
Ah! cease, thou shrill blast of the Ocean!
To howl thro' my Cavern by night.[34]

Are you asleep, my dear Mary? I have administered rather a strong dose of opium; however, if in the course of your nap you should chance to dream that I am, with ardor of eternal friendship, your affectionate

S. T. Coleridge,

you will never have dreamt a truer dream in all your days.

XVIII. TO ANNE EVANS.

Jesus College, Cambridge, February 10, 1793.

My dear Anne,—A little before I had received your mamma's letter, a bird of the air had informed me of your illness—and sure never did owl or night-raven ("those mournful messengers of heavy things") pipe a more loathsome song. But I flatter myself that ere you have received this scrawl of mine, by care and attention you will have lured back the rosy-lipped fugitive, Health. I know of no misfortune so little susceptible of consolation as sickness: it is indeed easy to offer comfort, when we ourselves are well; then we can be full of grave saws upon the duty of resignation, etc.; but alas! when the sore visitations of pain come home, all our philosophy vanishes, and nothing remains to be seen. I speak of myself, but a mere sensitive animal, with little wisdom and no patience. Yet if anything can throw a melancholy smile over the pale, wan face of illness, it must be the sight and attentions of those we love. There are one or two beings, in this planet of ours, whom God has formed in so kindly a mould that I could almost consent to be ill in order to be nursed by them.

O turtle-eyed affection!
If thou be present—who can be distrest?
Pain seems to smile, and sorrow is at rest:
No more the thoughts in wild repinings roll,
And tender murmurs hush the soften'd soul.
But I will not proceed at this rate, for I am writing and thinking myself fast into the spleen, and feel very obligingly disposed to communicate the same doleful fit to you, my dear sister. Yet permit me to say, it is almost your own fault. You were half angry at my writing laughing nonsense to you, and see what you have got in exchange—pale-faced, solemn, stiff-starched stupidity. I must confess, indeed, that the latter is rather more in unison with my present feelings, which from one untoward freak of fortune or other are not of the most comfortable kind. Within this last month I have lost a brother[35] and a friend! But I struggle for cheerfulness—and sometimes, when the sun shines out, I succeed in the effort. This at least I endeavour, not to infect the cheerfulness of others, and not to write my vexations upon my forehead. I read a story lately of an old Greek philosopher, who once harangued so movingly on the miseries of life, that his audience went home and hanged themselves; but he himself (my author adds) lived many years afterwards in very sleek condition.

God love you, my dear Anne! and receive as from a brother the warmest affections of your

S. T. Coleridge.

XIX. TO THE REV. GEORGE COLERIDGE.

Wednesday morning, July 28, 1793.

My dear Brother,—I left Salisbury on Tuesday morning—should have stayed there longer, but that Ned, ignorant of my coming, had preëngaged himself on a journey to Portsmouth with Skinner. I left Ned well and merry, as likewise his wife, who, by all the Cupids, is a very worthy old lady.[36]

Monday afternoon, Ned, Tatum, and myself sat from four till ten drinking! and then arose as cool as three undressed cucumbers. Edward and I (O! the wonders of this life) disputed with great coolness and forbearance the whole time. We neither of us were convinced, though now and then Ned was convicted. Tatum umpire sat,

And by decision more embroiled the fray.
I found all well in Exeter, to which place I proceeded directly, as my mother might have been unprepared from the supposition I meant to stay longer in Salisbury. I shall dine with James to-day at brother Phillips'.[37]

My ideas are so discomposed by the jolting of the coach that I can write no more at present.

A piece of gallantry!

I presented a moss rose to a lady. Dick Hart[38] asked her if she was not afraid to put it in her bosom, as perhaps there might be love in it. I immediately wrote the following little ode or song or what you please to call it.[39] It is of the namby-pamby genus.

THE ROSE.

As late each flower that sweetest blows
I plucked, the Garden's pride!
Within the petals of a Rose
A sleeping Love I spied.

Around his brows a beaming wreath
Of many a lucent hue;
All purple glowed his cheek beneath,
Inebriate with dew.
I softly seized the unguarded Power,
Nor scared his balmy rest;
And placed him, caged within the flower,
On Angelina's breast.

But when unweeting of the guile
Awoke the prisoner sweet,
He struggled to escape awhile
And stamped his faery feet.

Ah! soon the soul-entrancing sight
Subdued the impatient boy!
He gazed! he thrilled with deep delight!
Then clapped his wings for joy.

"And O!" he cried, "of magic kind
What charms this Throne endear!
Some other Love let Venus find—
I'll fix my empire here."

An extempore! Ned during the dispute, thinking he had got me down, said, "Ah! Sam! you blush!" "Sir," answered I,

Ten thousand Blushes
Flutter round me drest like little Loves,
And veil my visage with their crimson wings.

There is no meaning in the lines, but we both agreed they were very pretty. If you see Mr. Hussy, you will not forget to present my respects to him, and to his accomplished daughter, who certes is a very sweet young lady.

God bless you and your grateful and affectionate

S. T. Coleridge.

XX. TO THE SAME.

[Postmark, August 5, 1793.]

My dear Brother,—Since my arrival in the country I have been anxiously expecting a letter from you, nor can I divine the reason of your silence. From the letter to my brother James, a few lines of which he read to me, I am fearful that your silence proceeds from displeasure. If so, what is left for me to do but to grieve? The past is not in my power. For the follies of which I may have been guilty, I have been greatly disgusted; and I trust the memory of them will operate to future consistency of conduct.

My mother is very well,—indeed, better for her illness. Her complexion and eye, the truest indications of health, are much clearer. Little William and his mother are well. My brother James is at Sidmouth. I was there yesterday. He, his wife, and children are well. Frederick is a charming child. Little James had a most providential escape the day before yesterday. As my brother was in the field contiguous to his place he heard two men scream, and turning round saw a horse leap over little James, and then kick at him. He ran up; found him unhurt. The men said that the horse was feeding with his tail toward the child, and looking round ran at him open-mouthed, pushed him down and leaped over him, and then kicked back at him. Their screaming, my brother supposes, prevented the horse from repeating the blow. Brother was greatly agitated, as you may suppose. I stayed at Tiverton about ten days, and got no small kudos among the young belles by complimentary effusions in the poetic way.

A specimen:—

CUPID TURNED CHYMIST.

Cupid, if storying Legends tell aright,
Once framed a rich Elixir of Delight.
A chalice o'er love-kindled flames he fix'd,
And in it Nectar and Ambrosia mix'd:
With these the magic dews which Evening brings,
Brush'd from the Idalian star by faery wings:
Each tender pledge of sacred Faith he join'd,
Each gentler Pleasure of th' unspotted mind—
Day-dreams, whose tints with sportive brightness glow,
And Hope, the blameless parasite of Woe.
The eyeless Chymist heard the process rise,
The steamy chalice bubbled up in sighs;
Sweet sounds transpired, as when the enamor'd dove
Pours the soft murmuring of responsive Love.
The finished work might Envy vainly blame,
And "Kisses" was the precious Compound's name.
With half the God his Cyprian Mother blest,
And breath'd on Nesbitt's lovelier lips the rest.
Do you know Fanny Nesbitt? She was my fellow-traveler in the Tiverton diligence from Exeter. [She is], I think, a very pretty girl. The orders for tea are: Imprimis, five pounds of ten shillings green; Item, four pounds of eight shillings green; in all nine pounds of tea.

God bless you and your obliged

S. T. Coleridge.

XXI. TO G. L. TUCKETT.[40]

Henley, Thursday night, February 6 [1794].

Dear Tuckett,—I have this moment received your long letter! The Tuesday before last, an accident of the Reading Fair, our regiment was disposed of for the week in and about the towns within ten miles of Reading, and, as it was not known before we set off to what places we would go, my letters were kept at the Reading post-office till our return. I was conveyed to Henley-upon-Thames, which place our regiment left last Tuesday; but I am ordered to remain on account of these dreadfully troublesome eruptions, and that I might nurse my comrade, who last Friday sickened of the confluent smallpox. So here I am, videlicet the Henley workhouse.[41] It is a little house of one apartment situated in the midst of a large garden, about a hundred yards from the house. It is four strides in length and three in breadth; has four windows, which look to all the winds. The almost total want of sleep, the putrid smell, and the fatiguing struggles with my poor comrade during his delirium are nearly too much for me in my present state. In return I enjoy external peace, and kind and respectful behaviour from the people of the workhouse. Tuckett, your motives must have been excellent ones; how could they be otherwise! As an agent, therefore, you are blameless, but your efforts in my behalf demand my gratitude—that my heart will pay you, into whatever depth of horror your mistaken activity may eventually have precipitated me. As an agent, you stand acquitted, but the action was morally base. In an hour of extreme anguish, under the most solemn imposition of secrecy, I entrusted my place and residence to the young men at Christ's Hospital; the intelligence which you extorted from their imbecility should have remained sacred with you. It lost not the obligation of secrecy by the transfer. But your motives justify you? To the eye of your friendship the divulging might have appeared necessary, but what shadow of necessity is there to excuse you in showing my letters—to stab the very heart of confidence. You have acted, Tuckett, so uniformly well that reproof must be new to you. I doubtless shall have offended you. I would to God that I, too, possessed the tender irritableness of unhandled sensibility. Mine is a sensibility gangrened with inward corruption and the keen searching of the air from without. Your gossip with the commanding officer seems so totally useless and unmotived that I almost find a difficulty in believing it.

A letter from my brother George! I feel a kind of pleasure that it is not directed—it lies unopened—am I not already sufficiently miserable? The anguish of those who love me, of him beneath the shadow of whose protection I grew up—does it not plant the pillow with thorns and make my dreams full of terrors? Yet I dare not burn the letter—it seems as if there were a horror in the action. One pang, however acute, is better than long-continued solicitude. My brother George possessed the cheering consolation of conscience—but I am talking I know not what—yet there is a pleasure, doubtless an exquisite pleasure, mingled up in the most painful of our virtuous emotions. Alas! my poor mother! What an intolerable weight of guilt is suspended over my head by a hair on one hand; and if I endure to live—the look ever downward—insult, pity, hell! God or Chaos, preserve me! What but infinite Wisdom or infinite Confusion can do it?

XXII. TO THE REV. GEORGE COLERIDGE.

February 8, 1794.

My more than brother! What shall I say? What shall I write to you? Shall I profess an abhorrence of my past conduct? Ah me! too well do I know its iniquity! But to abhor! this feeble and exhausted heart supplies not so strong an emotion. O my wayward soul! I have been a fool even to madness. What shall I dare to promise? My mind is illegible to myself. I am lost in the labyrinth, the trackless wilderness of my own bosom. Truly may I say, "I am wearied of being saved." My frame is chill and torpid. The ebb and flow of my hopes and fears has stagnated into recklessness. One wish only can I read distinctly in my heart, that it were possible for me to be forgotten as though I had never been! The shame and sorrow of those who loved me! The anguish of him who protected me from my childhood upwards, the sore travail of her who bore me! Intolerable images of horror! They haunt my sleep, they enfever my dreams! O that the shadow of Death were on my eyelids, that I were like the loathsome form by which I now sit! O that without guilt I might ask of my Maker annihilation! My brother, my brother! pray for me, comfort me, my brother! I am very wretched, and, though my complaint be bitter, my stroke is heavier than my groaning.

S. T. Coleridge.

XXIII. TO THE SAME.

Tuesday night, February 11, 1794.

I am indeed oppressed, oppressed with the greatness of your love! Mine eyes gush out with tears, my heart is sick and languid with the weight of unmerited kindness. I had intended to have given you a minute history of my thoughts and actions for the last two years of my life. A most severe and faithful history of the heart would it have been—the Omniscient knows it. But I am so universally unwell, and the hour so late, that I must defer it till to-morrow. To-night I shall have a bed in a separate room from my comrade, and, I trust, shall have repaired my strength by sleep ere the morning. For eight days and nights I have not had my clothes off. My comrade is not dead; there is every hope of his escaping death. Closely has he been pursued by the mighty hunter! Undoubtedly, my brother, I could wish to return to College; I know what I must suffer there, but deeply do I feel what I ought to suffer. Is my brother James still at Salisbury? I will write to him, to all.

Concerning my emancipation, it appears to me that my discharge can be easily procured by interest, with great difficulty by negotiation; but of this is not my brother James a more competent judge?

What my future life may produce I dare not anticipate. Pray for me, my brother. I will pray nightly to the Almighty dispenser of good and evil, that his chastisement may not have harrowed my heart in vain. Scepticism has mildewed my hope in the Saviour. I was far from disbelieving the truth of revealed religion, but still far from a steady faith—the "Comforter that should have relieved my soul" was far from me.

Farewell! to-morrow I will resume my pen. Mr. Boyer! indeed, indeed, my heart thanks him; how often in the petulance of satire, how ungratefully have I injured that man!

S. T. Coleridge.

XXIV. TO CAPTAIN JAMES COLERIDGE.

February 20, 1794.

In a mind which vice has not utterly divested of sensibility, few occurrences can inflict a more acute pang than the receiving proofs of tenderness and love where only resentment and reproach were expected and deserved. The gentle voice of conscience which had incessantly murmured within the soul then raises its tone and speaks with a tongue of thunder. My conduct towards you, and towards my other brothers, has displayed a strange combination of madness, ingratitude, and dishonesty. But you forgive me. May my Maker forgive me! May the time arrive when I shall have forgiven myself!

With regard to my emancipation, every inquiry I have made, every piece of intelligence I could collect, alike tend to assure me that it may be done by interest, but not by negotiation without an expense which I should tremble to write. Forty guineas were offered for a discharge the day after a young man was sworn in, and were refused. His friends made interest, and his discharge came down from the War Office. If, however, negotiation must be first attempted, it will be expedient to write to our colonel—his name is Gwynne—he holds the rank of general in the army. His address is General Gwynne, K. L. D., King's Mews, London.

My assumed name is Silas Tomkyn Comberbacke, 15th, or King's Regiment of Light Dragoons, G Troop. My number I do not know. It is of no import. The bounty I received was six guineas and a half; but a light horseman's bounty is a mere lure; it is expended for him in things which he must have had without a bounty—gaiters, a pair of leather breeches, stable jacket, and shell; horse cloth, surcingle, watering bridle, brushes, and the long etc. of military accoutrement. I enlisted the 2d of December, 1793, was attested and sworn the 4th. I am at present nurse to a sick man, and shall, I believe, stay at Henley another week. There will be a large draught from our regiment to complete our troops abroad. The men were picked out to-day. I suppose I am not one, being a very indocile equestrian. Farewell.

S. T. Coleridge.

Our regiment is at Reading, and Hounslow, and Maidenhead, and Kensington; our headquarters, Reading, Berks. The commanding officer there, Lieutenant Hopkinson, our adjutant.

To Captain James Coleridge, Tiverton, Devonshire.

XXV. TO THE REV. GEORGE COLERIDGE.

The Compasses, High Wycombe, March 12, 1794.

My dear Brother,—Accept my poor thanks for the day's enclosed, which I received safely. I explained the whole matter to the adjutant, who laughed and said I had been used scurvily; he deferred settling the bill till Thursday morning. A Captain Ogle,[42] of our regiment, who is returned from abroad, has taken great notice of me. When he visits the stables at night he always enters into conversation with me, and to-day, finding from the corporal's report that I was unwell, he sent me a couple of bottles of wine. These things demand my gratitude. I wrote last week—currente calamo—a declamation for my friend Allen on the comparative good and evil of novels. The credit which he got for it I should almost blush to tell you. All the fellows have got copies, and they meditate having it printed, and dispersing it through the University. The best part of it I built on a sentence in a last letter of yours, and indeed, I wrote most part of it feelingly.

I met yesterday, smoking in the recess, a chimney corner of the pot-house[43] at which I am quartered, a man of the greatest information and most original genius I ever lit upon. His philosophical theories of heaven and hell would have both amused you and given you hints for much speculation. He solemnly assured me that he believed himself divinely inspired. He slept in the same room with me, and kept me awake till three in the morning with his ontological disquisitions. Some of the ideas would have made, you shudder from their daring impiety, others would have astounded with their sublimity. My memory, tenacious and systematizing, would enable [me] to write an octavo from his conversation. "I find [says he] from the intellectual atmosphere that emanes from, and envelops you, that you are in a state of recipiency." He was deceived. I have little faith, yet am wonderfully fond of speculating on mystical schemes. Wisdom may be gathered from the maddest flights of imagination, as medicines were stumbled upon in the wild processes of alchemy. God bless you. Your ever grateful

S. T. Coleridge.

Tuesday evening.—I leave this place [High Wycombe] on Thursday, 10 o'clock, for Reading. A letter will arrive in time before I go.

XXVI. TO THE SAME.

Sunday night, March 21, 1794.

I have endeavoured to feel what I ought to feel. Affiliated to you from my childhood, what must be my present situation? But I know you, my dear brother; and I entertain a humble confidence that my efforts in well-doing shall in some measure repay you. There is a vis inertiæ in the human mind—I am convinced that a man once corrupted will ever remain so, unless some sudden revolution, some unexpected change of place or station, shall have utterly altered his connection. When these shocks of adversity have electrified his moral frame, he feels a convalescence of soul, and becomes like a being recently formed from the hands of nature.

The last letter I received from you at High Wycombe was that almost blank letter which enclosed the guinea. I have written to the postmaster. I have breeches and waistcoats at Cambridge, three or four shirts, and some neckcloths, and a few pairs of stockings; the clothes, which, rather from the order of the regiment than the impulse of my necessities, I parted with in Reading on my first arrival at the regiment, I disposed of for a mere trifle, comparatively, and at a small expense can recover them all but my coat and hat. They are gone irrevocably. My shirts, which I have with me, are, all but one, worn to rags—mere rags; their texture was ill-adapted to the labour of the stables.

Shall I confess to you my weakness, my more than brother? I am afraid to meet you. When I call to mind the toil and wearisomeness of your avocations, and think how you sacrifice your amusements and your health; when I recollect your habitual and self-forgetting economy, how generously severe, my soul sickens at its own guilt. A thousand reflections crowd in my mind; they are almost too much for me. Yet you, my brother, would comfort me, not reproach me, and extend the hand of forgiveness to one whose purposes were virtuous, though infirm, and whose energies vigorous, though desultory. Indeed, I long to see you, although I cannot help dreading it.

I mean to write to Dr. Pearce. The letter I will enclose to you. Perhaps it may not be proper to write, perhaps it may be necessary. You will best judge. The discharge should, I think, be sent down to the adjutant—yet I don't know; it would be more comfortable to me to receive my dismission in London, were it not for the appearing in these clothes.

By to-morrow I shall be enabled to tell the exact expenses of equipping, etc.

I must conclude abruptly. God bless you, and your ever grateful

S. T. Coleridge.

XXVII. TO THE SAME.

End of March, 1794.

My dear Brother,—I have been rather uneasy, that I have not heard from you since my departure from High Wycombe. Your letters are a comfort to me in the comfortless hour— they are manna in the wilderness. I should have written you long ere this, but in truth I have been blockaded by a whole army of petty vexations, bad quarters, etc., and within this week I have been thrown three times from my horse and run away with to the no small perturbation of my nervous system almost every day. I ride a horse, young, and as undisciplined as myself. After tumult and agitation of any kind the mind and all its affections seem to doze for a while, and we sit shivering with chilly feverishness wrapped up in the ragged and threadbare cloak of mere animal enjoyment.

On Sunday last I was surprised, or rather confounded, with a visit from Mr. Cornish, so confounded that for more than a minute I could not speak to him. He behaved with great delicacy and much apparent solicitude of friendship. He passed through Reading with his sister Lady Shore. I have received several letters from my friends at Cambridge, of most soothing contents. They write me, that with "undiminished esteem and increased affection, the Jesuites look forward to my return as to that of a lost brother!"

My present address is the White Hart, Reading, Berks.

Adieu, most dear brother!

S. T. Coleridge.

XXVIII. TO THE SAME.

March 27, 1794.

My dear Brother,—I find that I was too sanguine in my expectations of recovering all my clothes. My coat, which I had supposed gone, and all the stockings, viz., four pairs of almost new silk stockings, and two pairs of new silk and cotton, I can get again for twenty-three shillings. I have ordered, therefore, a pair of breeches, which will be nineteen shillings, a waistcoat at twelve shillings, a pair of shoes at seven shillings and four pence. Besides these I must have a hat, which will be eighteen shillings, and two neckcloths, which will be five or six shillings. These things I have ordered. My travelling expenses will be about half a guinea. Have I done wrong in ordering these things? Or did you mean me to do it by desiring me to arrange what was necessary for my personal appearance at Cambridge? I have so seldom acted right, that in every step I take of my own accord I tremble lest I should be wrong. I forgot in the above account to mention a flannel waistcoat; it will be six shillings. The military dress is almost oppressively warm, and so very ill as I am at present I think it imprudent to hazard cold. I will see you at London, or rather at Hackney. There will be two or three trifling expenses on my leaving the army; I know not their exact amount. The adjutant dismissed me from all duty yesterday. My head throbs so, and I am so sick at stomach that it is with difficulty I can write. One thing more I wished to mention. There are three books, which I parted with at Reading. The bookseller, whom I have occasionally obliged by composing advertisements for his newspaper, has offered them me at the same price he bought them. They are a very valuable edition of Casimir[44] by Barbou,[45] a Synesius[46] by Canterus and Bentley's Quarto Edition. They are worth thirty shillings, at least, and I sold them for fourteen. The two first I mean to translate. I have finished two or three Odes of Casimir, and shall on my return to College send them to Dodsley as a specimen of an intended translation. Barbou's edition is the only one that contains all the works of Casimir. God bless you. Your grateful

S. T. C.

XXIX. TO THE SAME.

Sunday night, March 30, 1794.

My dear Brother,—I received your enclosed. I am fearful, that as you advise me to go immediately to Cambridge after my discharge, that the utmost contrivances of economy will not enable [me] to make it adequate to all the expenses of my clothes and travelling. I shall go across the country on many accounts. The expense (I have examined) will be as nearly equal as well can be. The fare from Reading to High Wycombe on the outside is four shillings, from High Wycombe to Cambridge (for there is a coach that passes through Cambridge from Wycombe) I suppose about twelve shillings, perhaps a trifle more. I shall be two days and a half on the road, two nights. Can I calculate the expense at less than half a guinea, including all things? An additional guinea would perhaps be sufficient. Surely, my brother, I am not so utterly abandoned as not to feel the meaning and duty of economy. Oh me! I wish to God I were happy; but it would be strange indeed if I were so.

I long ago theoretically and in a less degree experimentally knew the necessity of faith in order to regulate virtue, nor did I even seriously disbelieve the existence of a future state. In short, my religious creed bore and, perhaps, bears a correspondence with my mind and heart. I had too much vanity to be altogether a Christian, too much tenderness of nature to be utterly an infidel. Fond of the dazzle of wit, fond of subtlety of argument, I could not read without some degree of pleasure the levities of Voltaire or the reasonings of Helvetius; but, tremblingly alive to the feelings of humanity, and susceptible to the charms of truth, my heart forced me to admire the "beauty of holiness" in the Gospel, forced me to love the Jesus, whom my reason (or perhaps my reasonings) would not permit me to worship,—my faith, therefore, was made up of the Evangelists and the deistic philosophy—a kind of religious twilight. I said "perhaps bears,"—yes! my brother, for who can say, "Now I'll be a Christian"? Faith is neither altogether voluntary; we cannot believe what we choose, but we can certainly cultivate such habits of thinking and acting as will give force and effective energy to the arguments on either side.

If I receive my discharge by Thursday, I will be, God pleased, in Cambridge on Sunday. Farewell, my brother! Believe me your severities only wound me as they awake the voice within to speak, ah! how more harshly! I feel gratitude and love towards you, even when I shrink and shiver.

Your affectionate
S. T. Coleridge.

XXX. TO THE SAME.

April 7, 1794.

My dear Brother,—The last three days I have spent at Bray, near Maidenhead, at the house of a gentleman who has behaved with particular attention to me. I accepted his invitation as it was in my power in some measure to repay his kindness by the revisal of a performance he is about to publish, and by writing him a dedication and preface. At my return I found two letters from you, the one containing the two guineas, which will be perfectly adequate to my expenses, and, my brother, what some part of your letter made me feel, I am ill able to express; but of this at another time. I have signed the certificate of my expenses, but not my discharge. The moment I receive it I shall set off for Cambridge immediately, most probably through London, as the gentleman, whose house I was at at Bray, has pressed me to take his horse, and accompany him on Wednesday morning, as he himself intends to ride to town that day. If my discharge comes down on Tuesday morning I shall embrace his offer, particularly as I shall be introduced to his bookseller, a thing of some consequence to my present views.

Clagget[47] has set four songs of mine most divinely, for two violins and a pianoforte. I have done him some services, and he wishes me to write a serious opera, which he will set, and have introduced. It is to be a joint work. I think of it. The rules for adaptable composition which he has given me are excellent, and I feel my powers greatly strengthened, owing, I believe, to my having read little or nothing for these last four months.

XXXI. TO THE SAME.

May 1, 1794.

My dear Brother,—I have been convened before the fellows.[48] Dr. Pearce behaved with great asperity, Mr. Plampin[49] with exceeding and most delicate kindness. My sentence is a reprimand (not a public one, but implied in the sentence), a month's confinement to the precincts of the College, and to translate the works of Demetrius Phalareus into English. It is a thin quarto of about ninety Greek pages. All the fellows tried to persuade the Master to greater leniency, but in vain. Without the least affectation I applaud his conduct, and think nothing of it. The confinement is nothing. I have the fields and grove of the College to walk in, and what can I wish more? What do I wish more? Nothing. The Demetrius is dry, and utterly untransferable to modern use, and yet from the Doctor's words I suspect that he wishes it to be a publication, as he has more than once sent to know how I go on, and pressed me to exert erudition in some notes, and to write a preface. Besides this, I have had a declamation to write in the routine of college business, and the Rustat examination, at which I got credit. I get up every morning at five o'clock.

Every one of my acquaintance I have dropped solemnly and forever, except those of my College with whom before my departure I had been least of all connected—who had always remonstrated against my imprudences, yet have treated me with almost fraternal affection, Mr. Caldwell particularly. I thought the most decent way of dropping acquaintances was to express my intention, openly and irrevocably.

I find I must either go out at a by-term or degrade to the Christmas after next; but more of this to-morrow. I have been engaged in finishing a Greek ode. I mean to write for all the prizes. I have had no time upon my hands. I shall aim at correctness and perspicuity, not genius. My last ode was so sublime that nobody could understand it. If I should be so very lucky as to win one of the prizes, I could comfortably ask the Doctor advice concerning the time of my degree. I will write to-morrow.

God bless you, my brother! my father!

S. T. Coleridge.

XXXII. TO ROBERT SOUTHEY.

Gloucester, Sunday morning, July 6, 1794.

S. T. Coleridge to R. Southey, Health and Republicanism to be! When you write, direct to me, "To be kept at the Post Office, Wrexham, Denbighshire, N. Wales." I mention this circumstance now, lest carried away by a flood of confluent ideas I should forget it. You are averse to gratitudinarian flourishes, else would I talk about hospitality, attentions, etc. However, as I must not thank you, I will thank my stars. Verily, Southey, I like not Oxford nor the inhabitants of it. I would say, thou art a nightingale among owls, but thou art so songless and heavy towards night that I will rather liken thee to the matin lark. Thy nest is in a blighted cornfield, where the sleepy poppy nods its red-cowled head, and the weak-eyed mole plies his dark work; but thy soaring is even unto heaven. Or let me add (for my appetite for similes is truly canine at this moment) that as the Italian nobles their new-fashioned doors, so thou dost make the adamantine gate of democracy turn on its golden hinges to most sweet music. Our journeying has been intolerably fatiguing from the heat and whiteness of the roads, and the unhedged country presents nothing but stone fences, dreary to the eye and scorching to the touch. But we shall soon be in Wales.

Gloucester is a nothing-to-be-said-about town. The women have almost all of them sharp noses.

………

It is wrong, Southey! for a little girl with a half-famished sickly baby in her arms to put her head in at the window of an inn—"Pray give me a bit of bread and meat!" from a party dining on lamb, green peas, and salad. Why? Because it is impertinent and obtrusive! "I am a gentleman! and wherefore the clamorous voice of woe intrude upon mine ear?" My companion is a man of cultivated, though not vigorous understanding; his feelings are all on the side of humanity; yet such are the unfeeling remarks, which the lingering remains of aristocracy occasionally prompt. When the pure system of pantisocracy shall have aspheterized—from ἀ, non, and σφέτερος, proprius (we really wanted such a word), instead of travelling along the circuitous, dusty, beaten highroad of diction, you thus cut across the soft, green, pathless field of novelty! Similes for ever! Hurrah! I have bought a little blank book, and portable ink horn; [and] as I journey onward, I ever and anon pluck the wild flowers of poesy, "inhale their odours awhile," then throw them away and think no more of them. I will not do so! Two lines of mine:—

And o'er the sky's unclouded blue
The sultry heat suffus'd a brassy hue.
The cockatrice is a foul dragon with a crown on its head. The Eastern nations believe it to be hatched by a viper on a cock's egg. Southey, dost thou not see wisdom in her Coan vest of allegory? The cockatrice is emblematic of monarchy, a monster generated by ingratitude or absurdity. When serpents sting, the only remedy is to kill the serpent, and besmear the wound with the fat. Would you desire better sympathy?

Description of heat from a poem I am manufacturing, the title: "Perspiration. A Travelling Eclogue."

The dust flies smothering, as on clatt'ring wheel
Loath'd aristocracy careers along;
The distant track quick vibrates to the eye,
And white and dazzling undulates with heat,
Where scorching to the unwary travellers' touch,
The stone fence flings its narrow slip of shade;
Or, where the worn sides of the chalky road
Yield their scant excavations (sultry grots!),
Emblem of languid patience, we behold
The fleecy files faint-ruminating lie.
Farewell, sturdy Republican! Write me concerning Burnett and thyself, and concerning etc., etc. My next shall be a more sober and chastened epistle; but, you see, I was in the humour for metaphors, and, to tell thee the truth, I have so often serious reasons to quarrel with my inclination, that I do not choose to contradict it for trifles. To Lovell, fraternity and civic remembrances! Hucks' compliments.

S. T. Coleridge.

Addressed to "Robert Southey. Miss Tyler's, Bristol."

XXXIII. TO THE SAME.

Wrexham, Sunday, July 15, 1794.[50]

Your letter, Southey! made me melancholy. Man is a bundle of habits, but of all habits the habit of despondence is the most pernicious to virtue and happiness. I once shipwrecked my frail bark on that rock; a friendly plank was vouchsafed me. Be you wise by my experience, and receive unhurt the flower, which I have climbed precipices to pluck. Consider the high advantages which you possess in so eminent a degree—health, strength of mind, and confirmed habits of strict morality. Beyond all doubt, by the creative powers of your genius, you might supply whatever the stern simplicity of republican wants could require. Is there no possibility of procuring the office of clerk in a compting-house? A month's application would qualify you for it. For God's sake, Southey! enter not into the church. Concerning Allen I say little, but I feel anguish at times. This earnestness of remonstrance! I will not offend you by asking your pardon for it. The following is a fact. A friend of Hucks' after long struggles between principle and interest, as it is improperly called, accepted a place under government. He took the oaths, shuddered, went home and threw himself in an agony out of a two-pair of stairs window! These dreams of despair are most soothing to the imagination. I well know it. We shroud ourselves in the mantle of distress, and tell our poor hearts, "This is happiness!" There is a dignity in all these solitary emotions that flatters the pride of our nature. Enough of sermonizing. As I was meditating on the capability of pleasure in a mind like yours, I unwarily fell into poetry:[51]—

'Tis thine with fairy forms to talk,
And thine the philosophic walk;
And what to thee the sweetest are—
The setting sun, the Evening Star—
The tints, that live along the sky,
The Moon, that meets thy raptured eye,
Where grateful oft the big drops start,
Dear silent pleasures of the Heart!
But if thou pour one votive lay,
For humble independence pray;
Whom (sages say) in days of yore
Meek Competence to Wisdom bore.
So shall thy little vessel glide
With a fair breeze adown the tide,
Till Death shall close thy tranquil eye
While Faith exclaims: "Thou shalt not die!"

"The heart-smile glowing on his aged cheek
Mild as decaying light of summer's eve,"
are lines eminently beautiful. The whole is pleasing. For a motto! Surely my memory has suffered an epileptic fit. A Greek motto would be pedantic. These lines will perhaps do:—

All mournful to the pensive sages' eye,[52]
The monuments of human glory lie;
Fall'n palaces crush'd by the ruthless haste
Of Time, and many an empire's silent waste—
....

But where a sight shall shuddering sorrow find
Sad as the ruins of the human mind,—
Bowles.
A better will soon occur to me. Poor Poland! They go on sadly there. Warmth of particular friendship does not imply absorption. The nearer you approach the sun, the more intense are his rays. Yet what distant corner of the system do they not cheer and vivify? The ardour of private attachments makes philanthropy a necessary habit of the soul. I love my friend. Such as he is, all mankind are or might be. The deduction is evident. Philanthropy (and indeed every other virtue) is a thing of concretion. Some home-born feeling is the centre of the ball, that rolling on through life collects and assimilates every congenial affection. What did you mean by H. has "my understanding"? I have puzzled myself in vain to discover the import of the sentence. The only sense it seemed to bear was so like mock-humility, that I scolded myself for the momentary supposition.[53] My heart is so heavy at present, that I will defer the finishing of this letter till to-morrow.

I saw a face in Wrexham Church this morning, which recalled "Thoughts full of bitterness and images" too dearly loved! now past and but "Remembered like sweet sounds of yesterday!" At Ross (sixteen miles from Gloucester) we took up our quarters at the King's Arms, once the house of Kyrle, the Man of Ross. I gave the window-shutter the following effusion:[54]—

Richer than Misers o'er their countless hoards,
Nobler than Kings, or king-polluted Lords,
Here dwelt the Man of Ross! O Traveller, hear!
Departed Merit claims the glistening tear.
Friend to the friendless, to the sick man health,
With generous joy he viewed his modest wealth;
He heard the widow's heaven-breathed prayer of praise,
He mark'd the sheltered orphan's tearful gaze;
And o'er the dowried maiden's glowing cheek
Bade bridal love suffuse its blushes meek.
If 'neath this roof thy wine-cheer'd moments pass,
Fill to the good man's name one grateful glass!
To higher zest shall Memory wake thy soul,
And Virtue mingle in the sparkling bowl.
But if, like me, thro' life's distressful scene,
Lonely and sad thy pilgrimage hath been,
And if thy breast with heart-sick anguish fraught,
Thou journeyest onward tempest-tost in thought,
Here cheat thy cares,—in generous visions melt,
And dream of Goodness thou hast never felt!
I will resume the pen to-morrow.

Monday, 11 o'clock. Well, praised be God! here I am. Videlicet, Ruthin, sixteen miles from Wrexham. At Wrexham Church I glanced upon the face of a Miss E. Evans, a young lady with [whom] I had been in habits of fraternal correspondence. She turned excessively pale; she thought it my ghost, I suppose. I retreated with all possible speed to our inn. There, as I was standing at the window, passed by Eliza Evans, and with her to my utter surprise her sister, Mary Evans, quam efflictim et perdite amabam. I apprehend she is come from London on a visit to her grandmother, with whom Eliza lives. I turned sick, and all but fainted away! The two sisters, as H. informs me, passed by the window anxiously several times afterwards; but I had retired.

Vivit, sed mihi non vivit—nova forte marita,
Ah dolor! alterius carâ, a cervice pependit.
Vos, malefida valete accensæ insomnia mentis,
Littora amata valete! Vale, ah! formosa Maria!
My fortitude would not have supported me, had I recognized her—I mean appeared to do it! I neither ate nor slept yesterday. But love is a local anguish; I am sixteen miles distant, and am not half so miserable. I must endeavour to forget it amid the terrible graces of the wild wood scenery that surround me. I never durst even in a whisper avow my passion, though I knew she loved me. Where were my fortunes? and why should I make her miserable! Almighty God bless her! Her image is in the sanctuary of my heart, and never can it be torn away but with the strings that grapple it to life. Southey! there are few men of whose delicacy I think so highly as to have written all this. I am glad I have so deemed of you. We are soothed by communications.

Denbigh (eight miles from Ruthin).

And now to give you some little account of our journey. From Oxford to Gloucester, to Ross, to Hereford, to Leominster, to Bishop's Castle, to Welsh Pool, to Llanfyllin, nothing occurred worthy notice except that at the last place I preached pantisocracy and aspheterism with so much success that two great huge fellows of butcher-like appearance danced about the room in enthusiastic agitation. And one of them of his own accord called for a large glass of brandy, and drank it off to this his own toast, "God save the King! And may he be the last." Southey! Such men may be of use. They would kill the golden calf secundum artem. From Llanfyllin we penetrated into the interior of the country to Llangunnog, a village most romantically situated. We dined there on hashed mutton, cucumber, bread and cheese, and beer, and had two pots of ale—the sum total of the expense being sixteen pence for both of us! From Llangunnog we walked over the mountains to Bala—most sublimely terrible! It was scorchingly hot. I applied my mouth ever and anon to the side of the rocks and sucked in draughts of water cold as ice, and clear as infant diamonds in their embryo dew! The rugged and stony clefts are stupendous, and in winter must form cataracts most astonishing. At this time of the year there is just water enough dashed down over them to "soothe, not disturb the pensive traveller's ear." I slept by the side of one an hour or more. As we descended the mountain, the sun was reflected in the river, that winded through the valley with insufferable brightness; it rivalled the sky. At Bala is nothing remarkable except a lake of eleven miles in circumference. At the inn I was sore afraid that I had caught the itch from a Welsh democrat, who was charmed with my sentiments: he grasped my hand with flesh-bruising ardor, and I trembled lest some disappointed citizens of the animalcular republic should have emigrated.

Shortly after, into the same room, came a well-dressed clergyman and four others, among whom (the landlady whispers me) was a justice of the peace and the doctor of the parish. I was asked for a gentleman. I gave General Washington. The parson said in a low voice, "Republicans!" After which, the medical man said, "Damn toasts! I gives a sentiment: May all republicans be guillotined!" Up starts the Welsh democrat. "May all fools be gulloteen'd—and then you will be the first." Thereon rogue, villain, traitor flew thick in each other's faces as a hailstorm. This is nothing in Wales. They make calling one another liars, etc., necessary vent-holes to the superfluous fumes of the temper. At last I endeavoured to articulate by observing that, whatever might be our opinions in politics, the appearance of a clergyman in the company assured me we were all Christians; "though," continued I, "it is rather difficult to reconcile the last sentiment with the spirit of Christianity." "Pho!" quoth the parson, "Christianity! Why, we are not at church now, are we? The gemman's sentiment was a very good one; it showed he was sincere in his principles." Welsh politics could not prevail over Welsh hospitality. They all, except the parson, shook me by the hand, and said I was an open-hearted, honest-speaking fellow, though I was a bit of a democrat.

From Bala we travelled onward to Llangollen, a most beautiful village in a most beautiful situation. On the road we met two Cantabs of my college, Brookes and Berdmore. These rival pedestrians—perfect Powells—were vigorously pursuing their tour in a post-chaise! We laughed famously. Their only excuse was that Berdmore had been ill. From Llangollen to Wrexham, from Wrexham to Ruthin, to Denbigh. At Denbigh is a ruined castle; it surpasses everything I could have conceived. I wandered there an hour and a half last evening (this is Tuesday morning). Two well-dressed young men were walking there. "Come," says one, "I'll play my flute; 'twill be romantic." "Bless thee for the thought, man of genius and sensibility!" I exclaimed, and preattuned my heartstring to tremulous emotion. He sat adown (the moon just peering) amid the awful part of the ruins, and the romantic youth struck up the affecting tune of "Mrs. Carey."[55] 'Tis fact, upon my honour.

God bless you, Southey! We shall be at Aberystwith[56] this day week. When will you come out to meet us? There you must direct your letter. Hucks' compliments. I anticipate much accession of republicanism from Lovell. I have positively done nothing but dream of the system of no property every step of the way since I left you, till last Sunday. Heigho!

Robert Southey, No. 8 Westcott Buildings, Bath.

XXXIV. TO THE SAME.

10 o'clock, Thursday morning, September 18, 1794.

Well, my dear Southey! I am at last arrived at Jesus. My God! how tumultuous are the movements of my heart. Since I quitted this room what and how important events have been evolved! America! Southey! Miss Fricker! Yes, Southey, you are right. Even Love is the creature of strong motive. I certainly love her. I think of her incessantly and with unspeakable tenderness,—with that inward melting away of soul that symptomatizes it.

Pantisocracy! Oh, I shall have such a scheme of it! My head, my heart, are all alive. I have drawn up my arguments in battle array; they shall have the tactician excellence of the mathematician with the enthusiasm of the poet. The head shall be the mass; the heart the fiery spirit that fills, informs, and agitates the whole. Harwood—pish! I say nothing of him.

SHAD GOES WITH US. HE IS MY BROTHER! I am longing to be with you. Make Edith my sister. Surely, Southey, we shall be frendotatoi meta frendous—most friendly where all are friends. She must, therefore, be more emphatically my sister.

Brookes and Berdmore, as I suspected, have spread my opinions in mangled forms at Cambridge. Caldwell, the most pantisocratic of aristocrats, has been laughing at me. Up I arose, terrible in reasoning. He fled from me, because "he could not answer for his own sanity, sitting so near a madman of genius." He told me that the strength of my imagination had intoxicated my reason, and that the acuteness of my reason had given a directing influence to my imagination. Four months ago the remark would not have been more elegant than just. Now it is nothing.

I like your sonnets exceedingly—the best of any I have yet seen.[57] "Though to the eye fair is the extended vale" should be "to the eye though fair the extended vale." I by no means disapprove of discord introduced to produce effect, nor is my ear so fastidious as to be angry with it where it could not have been avoided without weakening the sense. But discord for discord's sake is rather too licentious.

"Wild wind" has no other but alliterative beauty; it applies to a storm, not to the autumnal breeze that makes the trees rustle mournfully. Alter it to "That rustle to the sad wind moaningly."

"'Twas a long way and tedious," and the three last lines are marked beauties—unlaboured strains poured soothingly along from the feeling simplicity of heart. The next sonnet is altogether exquisite,—the circumstance common yet new to poetry, the moral accurate and full of soul.[58] "I never saw," etc., is most exquisite. I am almost ashamed to write the following, it is so inferior. Ashamed? No, Southey! God knows my heart! I am delighted to feel you superior to me in genius as in virtue.

No more my visionary soul shall dwell
On joys that were; no more endure to weigh
The shame and anguish of the evil day.
Wisely forgetful! O'er the ocean swell
Sublime of Hope, I seek the cottag'd dell
Where Virtue calm with careless step may stray,
And, dancing to the moonlight roundelay,
The wizard Passions weave an holy spell.
Eyes that have ach'd with sorrow! ye shall weep
Tears of doubt-mingled joy, like theirs who start
From precipices of distemper'd sleep,
On which the fierce-eyed fiends their revels keep,
And see the rising sun, and feel it dart
New rays of pleasance trembling to the heart.[59]

I have heard from Allen, and write the third letter to him. Yours is the second. Perhaps you would like two sonnets I have written to my Sally. When I have received an answer from Allen I will tell you the contents of his first letter.

My compliments to Heath.

I will write you a huge, big letter next week. At present I have to transact the tragedy business, to wait on the Master, to write to Mrs. Southey, Lovell, etc., etc.

God love you, and

S. T. Coleridge.

XXXV. TO THE SAME.

Friday morning, September 19, 1794.

My fire was blazing cheerfully—the tea-kettle even now boiled over on it. Now sudden sad it looks. But, see, it blazes up again as cheerily as ever. Such, dear Southey, was the effect of your this morning's letter on my heart. Angry, no! I esteem and confide in you the more; but it did make me sorrowful. I was blameless; it was therefore only a passing cloud empictured on the breast. Surely had I written to you the first letter you directed to me at Cambridge, I would not have believed that you could have received it without answering it. Still less that you could have given a momentary pain to her that loved you. If I could have imagined no rational excuse for you, I would have peopled the vacancy with events of impossibility!

On Wednesday, September 17, I arrived at Cambridge. Perhaps the very hour you were writing in the severity of offended friendship, was I pouring forth the heart to Sarah Fricker. I did not call on Caldwell; I saw no one. On the moment of my arrival I shut my door, and wrote to her. But why not before?

In the first place Miss F. did not authorize me to direct immediately to her. It was settled that through you in our weekly parcels were the letters to be conveyed. The moment I arrived at Cambridge, and all yesterday, was I writing letters to you, to your mother, to Lovell, etc., to complete a parcel.

In London I wrote twice to you, intending daily to go to Cambridge; of course I deferred the parcel till then. I was taken ill, very ill. I exhausted my finances, and ill as I was, I sat down and scrawled a few guineas' worth of nonsense for the booksellers, which Dyer disposed of for me. Languid, sick at heart, in the back room of an inn! Lofty conjunction of circumstances for me to write to Miss F. Besides, I told her I should write the moment I arrived at Cambridge. I have fulfilled the promise. Recollect, Southey, that when you mean to go to a place to-morrow, and to-morrow, and to-morrow, the time that intervenes is lost. Had I meant at first to stay in London, a fortnight should not have elapsed without my writing to her. If you are satisfied, tell Miss F. that you are so, but assign no reasons—I ought not to have been suspected.

The tragedy[60] will be printed in less than a week. I shall put my name, because it will sell at least a hundred copies in Cambridge. It would appear ridiculous to put two names to such a work. But, if you choose it, mention it and it shall be done. To every man who praises it, of course I give the true biography of it; to those who laugh at it, I laugh again, and I am too well known at Cambridge to be thought the less of, even though I had published James Jennings' Satire.

………

Southey! Precipitance is wrong. There may be too high a state of health, perhaps even virtue is liable to a plethora. I have been the slave of impulse, the child of imbecility. But my inconsistencies have given me a tarditude and reluctance to think ill of any one. Having been often suspected of wrong when I was altogether right, from fellow-feeling I judge not too hastily, and from appearances. Your undeviating simplicity of rectitude has made you rapid in decision. Having never erred, you feel more indignation at error than pity for it. There is phlogiston in your heart. Yet am I grateful for it. You would not have written so angrily but for the greatness of your esteem and affection. The more highly we have been wont to think of a character, the more pain and irritation we suffer from the discovery of its imperfections. My heart is very heavy, much more so than when I began to write.

Yours most fraternally.
S. T. Coleridge.

XXXVI. TO THE SAME.

Friday night, September 26, 1794.

My dear, dear Southey,—I am beyond measure distressed and agitated by your letter to Favell. On the evening of the Wednesday before last, I arrived in Cambridge; that night and the next day I dedicated to writing to you, to Miss F., etc. On the Friday I received your letter of phlogistic rebuke. I answered it immediately, wrote a second letter to Miss F., inclosed them in the aforesaid parcel, and sent them off by the mail directed to Mrs. Southey, No. 8 Westcott Buildings, Bath. They should have arrived on Sunday morning. Perhaps you have not heard from Bath; perhaps—damn perhapses! My God, my God! what a deal of pain you must have suffered before you wrote that letter to Favell. It is an Ipswich Fair time, and the Norwich company are theatricalizing. They are the first provincial actors in the kingdom. Much against my will, I am engaged to drink tea and go to the play with Miss Brunton[61] (Mrs. Merry's sister). The young lady, and indeed the whole family, have taken it into their heads to be very much attached to me, though I have known them only six days. The father (who is the manager and proprietor of the theatre) inclosed in a very polite note a free ticket for the season. The young lady is said to be the most literary of the beautiful, and the most beautiful of the literatæ. It may be so; my faculties and discernments are so completely jaundiced by vexation that the Virgin Mary and Mary Flanders, alias Moll, would appear in the same hues.

All last night, I was obliged to listen to the damned chatter of our mayor, a fellow that would certainly be a pantisocrat, were his head and heart as highly illuminated as his face. At present he is a High Churchman, and a Pittite, and is guilty (with a very large fortune) of so many rascalities in his public character, that he is obliged to drink three bottles of claret a day in order to acquire a stationary rubor, and prevent him from the trouble of running backwards and forwards for a blush once every five minutes. In the tropical latitudes of this fellow's nose was I obliged to fry. I wish you would write a lampoon upon him—in me it would be unchristian revenge.

Our tragedy is printed, all but the title-page. It will be complete by Saturday night.

God love you. I am in the queerest humour in the world, and am out of love with everybody.

S. T. Coleridge.

XXXVII. TO THE SAME.

October 21, 1794.

To you alone, Southey, I write the first part of this letter. To yourself confine it.

"Is this handwriting altogether erased from your memory? To whom am I addressing myself? For whom am I now violating the rules of female delicacy? Is it for the same Coleridge, whom I once regarded as a sister her best-beloved Brother? Or for one who will ridicule that advice from me, which he has rejected as offered by his family? I will hazard the attempt. I have no right, nor do I feel myself inclined to reproach you for the Past. God forbid! You have already suffered too much from self-accusation. But I conjure you, Coleridge, earnestly and solemnly conjure you to consider long and deeply, before you enter into any rash schemes. There is an Eagerness in your Nature, which is ever hurrying you in the sad Extreme. I have heard that you mean to leave England, and on a Plan so absurd and extravagant that were I for a moment to imagine it true, I should be obliged to listen with a more patient Ear to suggestions, which I have rejected a thousand times with scorn and anger. Yes! whatever Pain I might suffer, I should be forced to exclaim, 'O what a noble mind is here o'erthrown, Blasted with ecstacy.' You have a country, does it demand nothing of you? You have doting Friends! Will you break their Hearts! There is a God—Coleridge! Though I have been told (indeed I do not believe it) that you doubt of his existence and disbelieve a hereafter. No! you have too much sensibility to be an Infidel. You know I never was rigid in my opinions concerning Religion—and have always thought Faith to be only Reason applied to a particular subject. In short, I am the same Being as when you used to say, 'We thought in all things alike.' I often reflect on the happy hours we spent together and regret the Loss of your Society. I cannot easily forget those whom I once loved—nor can I easily form new Friendships. I find women in general vain—all of the same Trifle, and therefore little and envious, and (I am afraid) without sincerity; and of the other sex those who are offered and held up to my esteem are very prudent, and very worldly. If you value my peace of mind, you must on no account answer this letter, or take the least notice of it. I would not for the world any part of my Family should suspect that I have written to you. My mind is sadly tempered by being perpetually obliged to resist the solicitations of those whom I love. I need not explain myself. Farewell, Coleridge! I shall always feel that I have been your Sister."

No name was signed,—it was from Mary Evans. I received it about three weeks ago. I loved her, Southey, almost to madness. Her image was never absent from me for three years, for more than three years. My resolution has not faltered, but I want a comforter. I have done nothing, I have gone into company, I was constantly at the theatre here till they left us, I endeavoured to be perpetually with Miss Brunton, I even hoped that her exquisite beauty and uncommon accomplishments might have cured one passion by another. The latter I could easily have dissipated in her absence, and so have restored my affections to her whom I do not love, but whom by every tie of reason and honour I ought to love. I am resolved, but wretched! But time shall do much. You will easily believe that with such feelings I should have found it no easy task to write to ———. I should have detested myself, if after my first letter I had written coldly—how could I write as warmly? I was vexed too and alarmed by your letter concerning Mr. and Mrs. Roberts, Shad, and little Sally. I was wrong, very wrong, in the affair of Shad, and have given you reason to suppose that I should assent to the innovation. I will most assuredly go with you to America, on this plan, but remember, Southey, this is not our plan, nor can I defend it. "Shad's children will be educated as ours, and the education we shall give them will be such as to render them incapable of blushing at the want of it in their parents"—Perhaps! With this one word would every Lilliputian reasoner demolish the system. Wherever men can be vicious, some will be. The leading idea of pantisocracy is to make men necessarily virtuous by removing all motives to evil—all possible temptation. "Let them dine with us and be treated with as much equality as they would wish, but perform that part of labour for which their education has fitted them." Southey should not have written this sentence. My friend, my noble and high-souled friend should have said to his dependents, "Be my slaves, and ye shall be my equals;" to his wife and sister, "Resign the name of Ladyship and ye shall retain the thing." Again. Is every family to possess one of these unequal equals, these Helot Egalités? Or are the few you have mentioned, "with more toil than the peasantry of England undergo," to do for all of us "that part of labour which their education has fitted them for"? If your remarks on the other side are just, the inference is that the scheme of pantisocracy is impracticable, but I hope and believe that it is not a necessary inference. Your remark of the physical evil in the long infancy of men would indeed puzzle a Pangloss—puzzle him to account for the wish of a benevolent heart like yours to discover malignancy in its Creator. Surely every eye but an eye jaundiced by habit of peevish scepticism must have seen that the mothers' cares are repaid even to rapture by the mothers' endearments, and that the long helplessness of the babe is the means of our superiority in the filial and maternal affection and duties to the same feelings in the brute creation. It is likewise among other causes the means of society, that thing which makes them a little lower than the angels. If Mrs. S. and Mrs. F. go with us, they can at least prepare the food of simplicity for us. Let the married women do only what is absolutely convenient and customary for pregnant women or nurses. Let the husband do all the rest, and what will that all be? Washing with a machine and cleaning the house. One hour's addition to our daily labor, and pantisocracy in its most perfect sense is practicable. That the greater part of our female companions should have the task of maternal exertion at the same time is very improbable; but, though it were to happen, an infant is almost always sleeping, and during its slumbers the mother may in the same room perform the little offices of ironing clothes or making shirts. But the hearts of the women are not all with us. I do believe that Edith and Sarah are exceptions, but do even they know the bill of fare for the day, every duty that will be incumbent upon them?

All necessary knowledge in the branch of ethics is comprised in the word justice: that the good of the whole is the good of each individual, that, of course, it is each individual's duty to be just, because it is his interest. To perceive this and to assent to it as an abstract proposition is easy, but it requires the most wakeful attentions of the most reflective mind in all moments to bring it into practice. It is not enough that we have once swallowed it. The heart should have fed upon the truth, as insects on a leaf, till it be tinged with the colour, and show its food in every the minutest fibre. In the book of pantisocracy I hope to have comprised all that is good in Godwin, of whom and of whose book I will write more fully in my next letter (I think not so highly of him as you do, and I have read him with the greatest attention). This will be an advantage to the minds of our women.

What have been your feelings concerning the War with America, which is now inevitable? To go from Hamburg will not only be a heavy additional expense, but dangerous and uncertain, as nations at war are in the habit of examining neutral vessels to prevent the importation of arms and seize subjects of the hostile governments. It is said that one cause of the ministers having been so cool on the business is that it will prevent emigration, which it seems would be treasonable to a hostile country. Tell me all you think on these subjects. What think you of the difference in the prices of land as stated by Cowper from those given by the American agents? By all means read, ponder on Cowper, and when I hear your thoughts I will give you the result of my own.

Thou bleedest, my poor Heart! and thy distress
Doth Reason ponder with an anguished smile,
Probing thy sore wound sternly, tho' the while
Her eye be swollen and dim with heaviness.
Why didst thou listen to Hope's whisper bland?
Or, listening, why forget its healing tale,
When Jealousy with feverish fancies pale

Jarr'd thy fine fibres with a maniac's hand?
Faint was that Hope, and rayless. Yet 'twas fair
And sooth'd with many a dream the hour of rest:
Thou should'st have loved it most, when most opprest,
And nursed it with an agony of care,
E'en as a mother her sweet infant heir
That pale and sickly droops upon her breast![62]

When a man is unhappy he writes damned bad poetry, I find. My Imitations too depress my spirits—the task is arduous, and grows upon me. Instead of two octavo volumes, to do all I hoped to do two quartos would hardly be sufficient.

Of your poetry I will send you a minute critique, when I send you my proposed alterations. The sonnets are exquisite.[63] Banquo is not what it deserves to be. Towards the end it grows very flat, wants variety of imagery—you dwell too long on Mary, yet have made less of her than I expected. The other figures are not sufficiently distinct; indeed, the plan of the ode (after the first forty lines which are most truly sublime) is so evident an imitation of Gray's Descent of Odin, that I would rather adopt Shakespeare's mode of introducing the figures themselves, and making the description now the Witches' and now Fleance's. I detest monodramas, but I never wished to establish my judgment on the throne of critical despotism. Send me up the Elegy on the Exiled Patriots and the Scripture Sonnets. I have promised them to Flower.[64] The first will do good, and more good in a paper than in any other vehicle.

My thoughts are floating about in a most chaotic state. I had almost determined to go down to Bath, and stay two days, that I might say everything I wished. You mean to acquaint your aunt with the scheme? As she knows it, and knows that you know that she knows it, justice cannot require it, but if your own comfort makes it necessary, by all means do it, with all possible gentleness. She has loved you tenderly; be firm, therefore, as a rock, mild as the lamb. I sent a hundred "Robespierres" to Bath ten days ago and more.

Five hundred copies of "Robespierre" were printed. A hundred [went] to Bath; a hundred to Kearsley, in London; twenty-five to March, at Norwich; thirty I have sold privately (twenty-five of these thirty to Dyer, who found it inconvenient to take fifty). The rest are dispersed among the Cambridge booksellers; the delicacies of academic gentlemanship prevented me from disposing of more than the five propriâ personâ. Of course we only get ninepence for each copy from the booksellers. I expected that Mr. Field would have sent for fifty, but have heard nothing of it. I sent a copy to him, with my respects, and have made presents of six more. How they sell in London, I know not. All that are in Cambridge will sell—a great many are sold. I have been blamed for publishing it, considering the more important work I have offered to the public. N'importe. 'Tis thought a very aristocratic performance; you may suppose how hyper-democratic my character must have been. The expenses of paper, printing, and advertisements are nearly nine pounds. We ought to have charged one shilling and sixpence a copy.

I presented a copy to Miss Brunton with these verses in the blank leaf:[65]—

Much on my early youth I love to dwell,
Ere yet I bade that guardian dome farewell,
Where first beneath the echoing cloisters pale,
I heard of guilt and wondered at the tale!
Yet though the hours flew by on careless wing
Full heavily of Sorrow would I sing.

Aye, as the star of evening flung its beam
In broken radiance on the wavy stream,
My pensive soul amid the twilight gloom
Mourned with the breeze, O Lee Boo! o'er thy tomb.
Whene'er I wander'd, Pity still was near,
Breath'd from the heart, and glitter'd in the tear:
No knell, that toll'd, but fill'd my anguish'd eye,
"And suffering Nature wept that one should die!"
Thus to sad sympathies I sooth'd my breast,
Calm as the rainbow in the weeping West:
When slumb'ring Freedom rous'd by high Disdain
With giant fury burst her triple chain!
Fierce on her front the blasting Dog star glow'd;
Her banners, like a midnight meteor, flow'd;
Amid the yelling of the storm-rent skies
She came, and scatter'd battles from her eyes!
Then Exultation woke the patriot fire
And swept with wilder hand th' empassioned lyre;
Red from the Tyrants' wounds I shook the lance,
And strode in joy the reeking plains of France!
In ghastly horror lie th' oppressors low,
And my Heart akes tho' Mercy struck the blow!
With wearied thought I seek the amaranth Shade
Where peaceful Virtue weaves her myrtle braid.
And O! if Eyes, whose holy glances roll
The eloquent Messengers of the pure soul;
If Smiles more cunning and a gentler Mien,
Than the love-wilder'd Maniac's brain hath seen
Shaping celestial forms in vacant air,
If these demand the wond'ring Poets' care—
If Mirth and soften'd Sense, and Wit refin'd,
The blameless features of a lovely mind;
Then haply shall my trembling hand assign
No fading flowers to Beauty's saintly shrine.
Nor, Brunton! thou the blushing Wreath refuse,
Though harsh her notes, yet guileless is my Muse.
Unwont at Flattery's Voice to plume her wings.
A child of Nature, as she feels, she sings.
S. T. C.
Jes. Coll., Cambridge.

Till I dated this letter I never recollected that yesterday was my birthday—twenty-two years old.

I have heard from my brothers—from him particularly who has been friend, brother, father. 'Twas all remonstrance and anguish, and suggestions that I am deranged! Let me receive from you a letter of consolation; for, believe me, I am completely wretched.

Yours most affectionately, S. T. Coleridge.
XXXVIII. TO ROBERT SOUTHEY.

November, 1794.

My feeble and exhausted heart regards with a criminal indifference the introduction of servitude into our society; but my judgment is not asleep, nor can I suffer your reason, Southey, to be entangled in the web which your feelings have woven. Oxen and horses possess not intellectual appetites, nor the powers of acquiring them. We are therefore justified in employing their labour to our own benefit: mind hath a divine right of sovereignty over body. But who shall dare to transfer "from man to brute" to "from man to man"? To be employed in the toil of the field, while we are pursuing philosophical studies—can earldoms or emperorships boast so huge an inequality? Is there a human being of so torpid a nature as that placed in our society he would not feel it? A willing slave is the worst of slaves! His soul is a slave. Besides, I must own myself incapable of perceiving even the temporary convenience of the proposed innovation. The men do not want assistance, at least none that Shad can particularly give; and to the women, what assistance can little Sally, the wife of Shad, give more than any other of our married women? Is she to have no domestic cares of her own? No house? No husband to provide for? No children? Because Mr. and Mrs. Roberts are not likely to have children, I see less objection to their accompanying us. Indeed, indeed, Southey, I am fearful that Lushington's prophecy may not be altogether vain. "Your system, Coleridge, appears strong to the head and lovely to the heart; but depend upon it, you will never give your women sufficient strength of mind, liberality of heart, or vigilance of attention. They will spoil it."

I am extremely unwell; have run a nail into my heel, and before me stand "Embrocation for the throbbing of the head," "To be shaked up well that the ether may mix," "A wineglass full to be taken when faint." 'Sdeath! how I hate the labels of apothecary's bottles. Ill as I am, I must go out to supper. Farewell for a few hours.

'Tis past one o'clock in the morning. I sat down at twelve o'clock to read the "Robbers" of Schiller.[66] I had read, chill and trembling, when I came to the part where the Moor fixes a pistol over the robbers who are asleep. I could read no more. My God, Southey, who is this Schiller, this convulser of the heart? Did he write his tragedy amid the yelling of fiends? I should not like to be able to describe such characters. I tremble like an aspen leaf. Upon my soul, I write to you because I am frightened. I had better go to bed. Why have we ever called Milton sublime? that Count de Moor horrible wielder of heart-withering virtues? Satan is scarcely qualified to attend his execution as gallows chaplain.

Tuesday morning.—I have received your letter. Potter of Emanuel[67] drives me up to town in his phaeton on Saturday morning. I hope to be with you by Wednesday week. Potter is a "Son of Soul"—a poet of liberal sentiments in politics—yet (would you believe it?) possesses six thousand a year independent.

I feel grateful to you for your sympathy. There is a feverish distemperature of brain, during which some horrible phantom threatens our eyes in every corner, until, emboldened by terror, we rush on it, and then—why then we return, the heart indignant at its own palpitation! Even so will the greater part of our mental miseries vanish before an effort. Whatever of mind we will to do, we can do! What, then, palsies the will? The joy of grief. A mysterious pleasure broods with dusky wings over the tumultuous mind, "and the Spirit of God moveth on the darkness of the waters." She was very lovely, Southey! We formed each other's minds; our ideas were blended. Heaven bless her! I cannot forget her. Every day her memory sinks deeper into my heart.

Nutrito vulnere tabens
Impatiensque mei feror undique, solus et excors,

Et desideriis pascor!
I wish, Southey, in the stern severity of judgment, that the two mothers were not to go, and that the children stayed with them. Are you wounded by my want of feeling? No! how highly must I think of your rectitude of soul, that I should dare to say this to so affectionate a son! That Mrs. Fricker! We shall have her teaching the infants Christianity,—I mean, that mongrel whelp that goes under its name,—teaching them by stealth in some ague fit of superstition.

There is little danger of my being confined. Advice offered with respect from a brother; affected coldness, an assumed alienation mixed with involuntary bursts of anguish and disappointed affection; questions concerning the mode in which I would have it mentioned to my aged mother—these are the daggers which are plunged into my peace. Enough! I should rather be offering consolation to your sorrows than be wasting my feelings in egotistic complaints. "Verily my complaint is bitter, yet my stroke is heavier than my groaning."

God love you, my dear Southey!

S. T. Coleridge.

A friend of mine hath lately departed this life in a frenzy fever induced by anxiety. Poor fellow, a child of frailty like me! Yet he was amiable. I poured forth these incondite lines[68] in a moment of melancholy dissatisfaction:—

——! thy grave with aching eye I scan,
And inly groan for Heaven's poor outcast—Man!
'Tis tempest all, or gloom! In earliest youth
If gifted with th' Ithuriel lance of Truth
He force to start amid the feign'd caress
Vice, siren-hag, in native ugliness;
A brother's fate shall haply rouse the tear,
And on he goes in heaviness and fear!
But if his fond heart call to Pleasure's bower
Some pigmy Folly in a careless hour,
The faithless Guest quick stamps th' enchanted ground,
And mingled forms of Misery threaten round:
Heart-fretting Fear, with pallid look aghast,
That courts the future woe to hide the past;
Remorse, the poison'd arrow in his side,
And loud lewd Mirth to Anguish close allied;
Till Frenzy, frantic child of moping Pain,
Darts her hot lightning-flash athwart the brain!
Rest, injur'd Shade! shall Slander, squatting near,
Spit her cold venom in a dead man's ear?
'Twas thine to feel the sympathetic glow
In Merit's joy and Poverty's meek woe:
Thine all that cheer the moment as it flies,
The zoneless Cares and smiling Courtesies.
Nurs'd in thy heart the generous Virtues grew,
And in thy heart they wither'd! such chill dew
Wan Indolence on each young blossom shed;
And Vanity her filmy network spread,

With eye that prowl'd around in asking gaze,
And tongue that trafficked in the trade of praise!
Thy follies such the hard world mark'd them well.
Were they more wise, the proud who never fell?
Rest, injur'd Shade! the poor man's grateful prayer,
On heavenward wing, thy wounded soul shall bear!

As oft in Fancy's thought thy grave I pass,
And sit me down upon its recent grass,
With introverted eye I contemplate
Similitude of soul—perhaps of fate!
To me hath Heaven with liberal hand assign'd
Energic reason and a shaping mind,
The daring soul of Truth, the patriot's part,
And Pity's sigh, that breathes the gentle heart—
Sloth-jaundiced all! and from my graspless hand
Drop Friendship's precious pearls, like hour-glass sand.
I weep, yet stoop not! the faint anguish flows,
A dreamy pang in Morning's fev'rish doze!

Is that pil'd earth our Being's passless mound?
Tell me, cold Grave! is Death with poppies crown'd?
Tir'd Sentinel! with fitful starts I nod,
And fain would sleep, though pillow'd on a clod!

SONG.

When Youth his fairy reign began[69]
Ere Sorrow had proclaim'd me Man;
While Peace the present hour beguil'd,
And all the lovely Prospect smil'd;
Then, Mary, mid my lightsome glee
I heav'd the painless Sigh for thee!

And when, along the wilds of woe
My harass'd Heart was doom'd to know
The frantic burst of Outrage keen,
And the slow Pang that gnaws unseen;
Then shipwreck'd on Life's stormy sea
I heav'd an anguish'd Sigh for thee!

But soon Reflection's hand imprest
A stiller sadness on my breast;
And sickly Hope with waning eye
Was well content to droop and die:
I yielded to the stern decree,
Yet heav'd the languid Sigh for thee!

And though in distant climes to roam,
A wanderer from my native home,
I fain would woo a gentle Fair

To soothe the aching sense of care,
Thy Image may not banish'd be—
Still, Mary! still I sigh for thee!
S. T. C.
God love you.

XXXIX. TO THE SAME.

Autumn, 1794.

Last night, dear Southey, I received a special invitation from Dr. Edwards[70] (the great Grecian of Cambridge and heterodox divine) to drink tea and spend the evening. I there met a councillor whose name is Lushington, a democrat, and a man of the most powerful and Briarean intellect. I was challenged on the subject of pantisocracy, which is, indeed, the universal topic at the University. A discussion began and continued for six hours. In conclusion, Lushington and Edwards declared the system impregnable, supposing the assigned quantum of virtue and genius in the first individuals. I came home at one o'clock this morning in the honest consciousness of having exhibited closer argument in more elegant and appropriate language than I had ever conceived myself capable of. Then my heart smote me, for I saw your letter on the propriety of taking servants with us. I had answered that letter, and feel conviction that you will perceive the error into which the tenderness of your nature had led you. But other queries obtruded themselves on my understanding. The more perfect our system is, supposing the necessary premises, the more eager in anxiety am I that the necessary premises exist. O for that Lyncean eye that can discover in the acorn of Error the rooted and widely spreading oak of Misery! Quære: should not all who mean to become members of our community be incessantly meliorating their temper and elevating their understandings? Qu.: whether a very respectable quantity of acquired knowledge (History, Politics, above all, Metaphysics, without which no man can reason but with women and children) be not a prerequisite to the improvement, of the head and heart? Qu.: whether our Women have not been taught by us habitually to contemplate the littleness of individual comforts and a passion for the novelty of the scheme rather than a generous enthusiasm of Benevolence? Are they saturated with the Divinity of Truth sufficiently to be always wakeful? In the present state of their minds, whether it is not probable that the Mothers will tinge the minds of the infants with prejudication? The questions are meant merely as motives to you, Southey, to the strengthening the minds of the Women, and stimulating them to literary acquirements. But, Southey, there are Children going with us. Why did I never dare in my disputations with the unconvinced to hint at this circumstance? Was it not because I knew, even to certainty of conviction, that it is subversive of rational hopes of a permanent system? These children,—the little Frickers, for instance, and your brothers,—are they not already deeply tinged with the prejudices and errors of society? Have they not learned from their schoolfellows Fear and Selfishness, of which the necessary offsprings are Deceit and desultory Hatred? How are we to prevent them from infecting the minds of our children? By reforming their judgments? At so early an age, can they have felt the ill consequences of their errors in a manner sufficiently vivid to make this reformation practicable? How can we insure their silence concerning God, etc.? Is it possible they should enter into our motives for this silence? If not, we must produce their Obedience by Terror. Obedience? Terror? The repetition is sufficient. I need not inform you that they are as inadequate as inapplicable. I have told you, Southey, that I will accompany you on an imperfect system. But must our system be thus necessarily imperfect? I ask the question that I may know whether or not I should write the Book of Pantisocracy.

I received your letter of Oyez; it brought a smile on a countenance that for these three weeks has been cloudy and stern in its solitary hours. In company, wit and laughter are Duties. Slovenly? I could mention a lady of fashionable rank, and most fashionable ideas, who declared to Caldwell that I (S. T. Coleridge) was a man of the most courtly and polished manners, of the most gentlemanly address she had ever met with. But I will not crow! Slovenly, indeed!

XL. TO THE REV. GEORGE COLERIDGE.

Thursday, November 6, 1794.

My dear Brother,—Your letter of this morning gave me inexpressible consolation. I thought that I perceived in your last the cold and freezing features of alienated affection. Surely, said I, I have trifled with the spirit of love, and it has passed away from me! There is a vice of such powerful venom, that one grain of it will poison the overflowing goblet of a thousand virtues. This vice constitution seems to have implanted in me, and habit has made it almost Omnipotent. It is indolence![71] Hence, whatever web of friendship my presence may have woven, my absence has seldom failed to unravel. Anxieties that stimulate others infuse an additional narcotic into my mind. The appeal of duty to my judgment, and the pleadings of affection at my heart, have been heard indeed, and heard with deep regard. Ah! that they had been as constantly obeyed. But so it has been. Like some poor labourer, whose night's sleep has but imperfectly refreshed his overwearied frame, I have sate in drowsy uneasiness, and doing nothing have thought what a deal I had to do. But I trust that the kingdom of reason is at hand, and even now cometh!

How often and how unkindly are the ebullitions of youthful disputations mistaken for the result of fixed principles. People have resolved that I am a dηmocrat, and accordingly look at everything I do through the spectacles of prejudication. In the feverish distemperature of a bigoted aristocrat's brain, some phantom of Dηmocracy threatens him in every corner of my writings.

And Hébert's atheist crew, whose maddening hand
Hurl'd down the altars of the living God
With all the infidel intolerance.[72]

"Are these lines in character," observed a sensible friend of mine, "in a speech on the death of the man whom it just became the fashion to style 'The ambitious Theocrat'?" "I fear not," was my answer, "I gave way to my feelings." The first speech of Adelaide,[73] whose Automaton is this character? Who spoke through Le Gendre's mouth,[74] when he says, "Oh, what a precious name is Liberty To scare or cheat the simple into slaves"? But in several parts I have, it seems, in the strongest language boasted the impossibility of subduing France. Is not this sentiment highly characteristic? Is it forced into the mouths of the speakers? Could I have even omitted it without evident absurdity? But, granted that it is my own opinion, is it an anti-pacific one? I should have classed it among the anti-polemics. Again, are all who entertain and express this opinion dηmocrats? God forbid! They would be a formidable party indeed! I know many violent anti-reformists, who are as violent against the war on the ground that it may introduce that reform, which they (perhaps not unwisely) imagine would chant the dirge of our constitution. Solemnly, my brother, I tell you, I am not a dηmocrat. I see, evidently, that the present is not the highest state of society of which we are capable. And after a diligent, I may say an intense, study of Locke, Hartley, and others who have written most wisely on the nature of man, I appear to myself to see the point of possible perfection, at which the world may perhaps be destined to arrive. But how to lead mankind from one point to the other is a process of such infinite complexity, that in deep-felt humility I resign it to that Being "Who shaketh the Earth out of her place, and the pillars thereof tremble," "Who purifieth with Whirlwinds, and maketh the Pestilence his Besom," Who hath said, "that violence shall no more be heard of; the people shall not build and another inhabit; they shall not plant and another eat;" "the wolf and the lamb shall feed together." I have been asked what is the best conceivable mode of meliorating society. My answer has been this: "Slavery is an abomination to my feeling of the head and the heart. Did Jesus teach the abolition of it? No! He taught those principles of which the necessary effect was to abolish all slavery. He prepared the mind for the reception before he poured the blessing." You ask me what the friend of universal equality should do. I answer: "Talk not politics. Preach the Gospel!"

Yea, my brother! I have at all times in all places exerted my power in the defence of the Holy One of Nazareth against the learning of the historian, the libertinism of the wit, and (his worst enemy) the mystery of the bigot! But I am an infidel, because I cannot thrust my head into a mud gutter, and say, "How deep I am!" And I am a dηmocrat, because I will not join in the maledictions of the despotist—because I will bless all men and curse no one! I have been a fool even to madness; and I am, therefore, an excellent hit for calumny to aim her poisoned probabilities at! As the poor flutterer, who by hard struggling has escaped from the bird-limed thornbush, still bears the clammy incumbrance on his feet and wings, so I am doomed to carry about with me the sad mementos of past imprudence and anguish from which I have been imperfectly released.

Mr. Potter of Emanuel drives me up to town in his phaeton, on Saturday morning. Of course I shall see you on Sunday. Poor Smerdon! the reports concerning his literary plagiarism (as far as concerns my assistance) are falsehoods. I have felt much for him, and on the morning I received your letter I poured forth these incondite rhymes. Of course they are meant for a brother's eye.

Smerdon! thy grave with aching eye I scan, etc.[75]
God love you, dear brother, and your affectionate and grateful

S. T. Coleridge.

XLI. TO ROBERT SOUTHEY.

December 11, 1794.

My dear Southey,—I sit down to write to you, not that I have anything particular to say, but it is a relief, and forms a very respectable part in my theory of "Escapes from the Folly of Melancholy." I am so habituated to philosophizing that I cannot divest myself of it, even when my own wretchedness is the subject. I appear to myself like a sick physician, feeling the pang acutely, yet deriving a wonted pleasure from examining its progress and developing its causes.

Your poems and Bowles' are my only morning companions. "The Retrospect!"[76] Quod qui non prorsus amat et deperit, illum omnes et virtutes et veneres odere! It is a most lovely poem, and in the next edition of your works shall be a perfect one. The "Ode to Romance"[77] is the best of the odes. I dislike that to Lycon, excepting the last stanza, which is superlatively fine. The phrase of "let honest truth be vain" is obscure. Of your blank verse odes, "The Death of Mattathias"[78] is by far the best. That you should ever write another, Pulcher Apollo veta! Musæ prohibete venustæ! They are to poetry what dumb-bells are to music; they can be read only for exercise, or to make a man tired that he may be sleepy. The sonnets are wonderfully inferior to those which I possess of yours, of which that "To Valentine"[79] ("If long and lingering seem one little day The motley crew of travellers among"); that on "The Fire"[80] (not your last, a very so-so one); on "The Rainbow"[81] (particularly the four last lines), and two or three others, are all divine and fully equal to Bowles. Some parts of "Miss Rosamund"[82] are beautiful—the working scene, and that line with which the poem ought to have concluded, "And think who lies so cold and pale below." Of the "Pauper's Funeral,"[83] that part in which you have done me the honour to imitate me is by far the worst; the thought has been so much better expressed by Gray. On the whole (like many of yours), it wants compactness and totality; the same thought is repeated too frequently in different words. That all these faults may be remedied by compression, my editio purgata of the poem shall show you.

What! and not one to heave the pious sigh?
Not one whose sorrow-swoln and aching eye,
For social scenes, for life's endearments fled,
Shall drop a tear and dwell upon the dead?
Poor wretched Outcast! I will sigh for thee,
And sorrow for forlorn humanity!
Yes, I will sigh! but not that thou art come
To the stern Sabbath of the silent tomb:
For squalid Want and the black scorpion Care,
(Heart-withering fiends) shall never enter there.
I sorrow for the ills thy life has known,
As through the world's long pilgrimage, alone,
Haunted by Poverty and woe-begone,
Unloved, unfriended, thou didst journey on;
Thy youth in ignorance and labour past,
And thy old age all barrenness and blast!
Hard was thy fate, which, while it doom'd to woe,
Denied thee wisdom to support the blow;
And robb'd of all its energy thy mind,
Ere yet it cast thee on thy fellow-kind,
Abject of thought, the victim of distress,
To wander in the world's wide wilderness.
Poor Outcast! sleep in peace! The winter's storm
Blows bleak no more on thy unsheltered form!
Thy woes are past; thou restest in the tomb;—
I pause ... and ponder on the days to come.

Now! Is it not a beautiful poem? Of the sonnet, "No more the visionary soul shall dwell,"[84] I wrote the whole but the second and third lines. Of the "Old Man in the Snow,"[85] ten last lines entirely, and part of the four first. Those ten lines are, perhaps, the best I ever did write.

Lovell has no taste or simplicity of feeling. I remarked that when a man read Lovell's poems he mus cus (that is a rapid way of pronouncing "must curse"), but when he thought of Southey's, he'd "buy on!" For God's sake let us have no more Bions or Gracchus's. I abominate them! Southey is a name much more proper and handsome, and, I venture to prophesy, will be more famous. Your "Chapel Bell"[86] I love, and have made it, by a few alterations and the omission of one stanza (which, though beautiful quoad se, interrupted the run of the thought "I love to see the aged spirit soar"), a perfect poem. As it followed the "Exiled Patriots," I altered the second and fourth lines to, "So freedom taught, in high-voiced minstrel's weed;" "For cap and gown to leave the patriot's meed."

The last verse now runs thus:—

"But thou, Memorial of monastic gall!
What fancy sad or lightsome hast thou given?
Thy vision-scaring sounds alone recall
The prayer that trembles on a yawn to Heaven,
And this Dean's gape, and that Dean's nasal tone."
Would not this be a fine subject for a wild ode?

St. Withold footed thrice the Oulds,
He met the nightmare and her nine foals;
He bade her alight and her troth plight,
And, "Aroynt thee, Witch!" he said.
I shall set about one when I am in a humour to abandon myself to all the diableries that ever met the eye of a Fuseli!

Le Grice has jumbled together all the quaint stupidity he ever wrote, amounting to about thirty pages, and published it in a book about the size and dimensions of children's twopenny books. The dedication is pretty. He calls the publication "Tineum;"[87] for what reason or with what meaning would give Madame Sphinx a complete victory over Œdipus.

A wag has handed about, I hear, an obtuse angle of wit, under the name of "An Epigram." 'Tis almost as bad as the subject.

"A tiny man of tiny wit
A tiny book has published.
But not alas! one tiny bit
His tiny fame established."

TO BOWLES.[88]

My heart has thank'd thee, Bowles! for those soft strains,
That, on the still air floating, tremblingly
Woke in me Fancy, Love, and Sympathy!
For hence, not callous to a Brother's pains
Thro' Youth's gay prime and thornless paths I went;
And when the darker day of life began,
And I did roam, a thought-bewildered man!
Thy kindred Lays an healing solace lent,
Each lonely pang with dreamy joys combin'd,
And stole from vain Regret her scorpion stings;

While shadowy Pleasure, with mysterious wings,
Brooded the wavy and tumultuous mind,
Like that great Spirit, who with plastic sweep
Mov'd on the darkness of the formless Deep!

Of the following sonnet, the four last lines were written by Lamb, a man of uncommon genius. Have you seen his divine sonnet of "O! I could laugh to hear the winter winds," etc.?

SONNET.[89]

O gentle look, that didst my soul beguile,
Why hast thou left me? Still in some fond dream
Revisit my sad heart, auspicious smile!
As falls on closing flowers the lunar beam;
What time in sickly mood, at parting day
I lay me down and think of happier years;
Of joys, that glimmered in Hope's twilight ray,
Then left me darkling in a vale of tears.
O pleasant days of Hope—for ever flown!
Could I recall one!—But that thought is vain.
Availeth not Persuasion's sweetest tone
To lure the fleet-winged travellers back again:
Anon, they haste to everlasting night,
Nor can a giant's arm arrest them in their flight.

The four last lines are beautiful, but they have no particular meaning which "that thought is vain" does not convey. And I cannot write without a body of thought. Hence my poetry is crowded and sweats beneath a heavy burden of ideas and imagery! It has seldom ease. The little song ending with "I heav'd the painless sigh for thee!" is an exception, and, accordingly, I like it the best of all I ever wrote. My sonnets to eminent contemporaries are among the better things I have written. That to Erskine is a bad specimen. I have written ten, and mean to write six more. In "Fayette" I unwittingly (for I did not know it at the time) borrowed a thought from you.

I will conclude with a little song of mine,[90] which has no other merit than a pretty simplicity of silliness.

If while my passion I impart,
You deem my words untrue,
O place your hand upon my heart—
Feel how it throbs for you!

Ah no! reject the thoughtless claim
In pity to your Lover!
That thrilling touch would aid the flame
It wishes to discover!

I am a complete necessitarian, and understand the subject as well almost as Hartley himself, but I go farther than Hartley, and believe the corporeality of thought, namely, that it is motion. Boyer thrashed Favell most cruelly the day before yesterday, and I sent him the following note of consolation: "I condole with you on the unpleasant motions, to which a certain uncouth automaton has been mechanized; and am anxious to know the motives that impinged on its optic or auditory nerves so as to be communicated in such rude vibrations through the medullary substance of its brain, thence rolling their stormy surges into the capillaments of its tongue, and the muscles of its arm. The diseased violence of its thinking corporealities will, depend upon it, cure itself by exhaustion. In the mean time I trust that you have not been assimilated in degradation by losing the ataxy of your temper, and that necessity which dignified you by a sentience of the pain has not lowered you by the accession of anger or resentment."

God love you, Southey! My love to your mother!

S. T. Coleridge.

XLII. TO THE SAME.

Wednesday, December 17, 1794.

When I am unhappy a sigh or a groan does not feel sufficient to relieve the oppression of my heart. I give a long whistle. This by way of a detached truth.

"How infinitely more to be valued is integrity of heart than effulgence of intellect!" A noble sentiment, and would have come home to me, if for "integrity" you had substituted "energy." The skirmishes of sensibility are indeed contemptible when compared with the well-disciplined phalanx of right-onward feelings. O ye invincible soldiers of virtue, who arrange yourselves under the generalship of fixed principles, that you would throw up your fortifications around my heart! I pronounce this a very sensible, apostrophical, metaphorical rant.

I dined yesterday with Perry and Grey (the proprietor and editor of the "Morning Chronicle") at their house, and met Holcroft. He either misunderstood Lovell, or Lovell misunderstood him. I know not which, but it is very clear to me that neither of them understands nor enters into the views of our system. Holcroft opposes it violently and thinks it not virtuous. His arguments were such as Nugent and twenty others have used to us before him; they were nothing. There is a fierceness and dogmatism of conversation in Holcroft for which you receive little compensation either from the veracity of his information, the closeness of his reasoning, or the splendour of his language. He talks incessantly of metaphysics, of which he appears to me to know nothing, to have read nothing. He is ignorant as a scholar, and neglectful of the smaller humanities as a man. Compare him with Porson! My God! to hear Porson crush Godwin, Holcroft, etc. They absolutely tremble before him! I had the honour of working H. a little, and by my great coolness and command of impressive language certainly did him over. "Sir!" said he, "I never knew so much real wisdom and so much rank error meet in one mind before!" "Which," answered I, "means, I suppose, that in some things, sir, I agree with you, and in others I do not." He absolutely infests you with atheism; and his arguments are such that the nonentities of Nugent consolidate into oak or ironwood by comparison! As to his taste in poetry, he thinks lightly, or rather contemptuously, of Bowles' sonnets; the language flat and prosaic and inharmonious, and the sentiments only fit for girls! Come, come, Mr. Holcroft, as much unintelligible metaphysics and as much bad criticism as you please, but no blasphemy against the divinity of a Bowles! Porson idolizes the sonnets. However it happened, I am higher in his good graces than he in mine. If I am in town I dine with him and Godwin, etc., at his house on Sunday.

I am astonished at your preference of the "Elegy." I think it the worst thing you ever wrote.

"Qui Gratio non odit, amet tua carmina, Avaro!"[91]
Why, 'tis almost as bad as Lovell's "Farmhouse," and that would be at least a thousand fathoms deep in the dead sea of pessimism.

"The hard world scoff'd my woes, the chaste one's pride,
Mimic of virtue, mock'd my keen distress,
[92]And Vice alone would shelter wretchedness.
Even life is loathsome now," etc.

These two stanzas are exquisite, but the lovely thought of the "hot sun," etc., as pitiless as proud prosperity loses part of its beauty by the time being night. It is among the chief excellences of Bowles that his imagery appears almost always prompted by surrounding scenery.

Before you write a poem you should say to yourself, "What do I intend to be the character of this poem; which feature is to be predominant in it?" So you make it unique. But in this poem now Charlotte speaks and now the Poet. Assuredly the stanzas of Memory, "three worst of fiends," etc., and "gay fancy fond and frolic" are altogether poetical. You have repeated the same rhymes ungracefully, and the thought on which you harp so long recalls too forcibly the Εὕδεις βρέφος of Simonides. Unfortunately the "Adventurer" has made this sweet fragment an object of popular admiration. On the whole, I think it unworthy of your other "Botany Bay Eclogues," yet deem the two stanzas above selected superior almost to anything you ever wrote; quod est magna res dicere, a great thing to say.

SONNET.[93]

Though king-bred rage with lawless Tumult rude
Have driv'n our Priestley o'er the ocean swell;
Though Superstition and her wolfish brood
Bay his mild radiance, impotent and fell;
Calm in his halls of brightness he shall dwell!
For lo! Religion at his strong behest
Disdainful rouses from the Papal spell,
And flings to Earth her tinsel-glittering vest,
Her mitred state and cumbrous pomp unholy;
And Justice wakes to bid th' oppression wail,
That ground th' ensnared soul of patient Folly;
And from her dark retreat by Wisdom won,
Meek Nature slowly lifts her matron veil,
To smile with fondness on her gazing son!

SONNET.

O what a loud and fearful shriek was there,
As though a thousand souls one death-groan poured!
Great Kosciusko 'neath an hireling's sword
The warriors view'd! Hark! through the list'ning air
(When pauses the tir'd Cossack's barbarous yell
Of triumph) on the chill and midnight gale
Rises with frantic burst or sadder swell

The "Dirge of Murder'd Hope!" while Freedom pale
Bends in such anguish o'er her destined bier,
As if from eldest time some Spirit meek
Had gathered in a mystic urn each tear
That ever furrowed a sad Patriot's cheek,
And she had drench'd the sorrows of the bowl
Ev'n till she reel'd, intoxicate of soul!
Tell me which you like the best of the above two. I have written one to Godwin, but the mediocrity of the eight first lines is most miserably magazinish! I have plucked, therefore, these scentless road-flowers from the chaplet, and entreat thee, thou river god of Pieria, to weave into it the gorgeous water-lily from thy stream, or the far-smelling violets on thy bank. The last six lines are these:—

Nor will I not thy holy guidance bless
And hymn thee, Godwin! with an ardent lay;
For that thy voice, in Passion's stormy day,
When wild I roam'd the bleak Heath of Distress,
Bade the bright form of Justice meet my way,—
And told me that her name was Happiness.

Give me your minutest opinion concerning the following sonnet, whether or no I shall admit it into the number. The move of bepraising a man by enumerating the beauties of his polygraph is at least an original one; so much so that I fear it will be somewhat unintelligible to those whose brains are not τοῦ ἀμείνονος πηλοῦ. (You have read S.'s poetry and know that the fancy displayed in it is sweet and delicate to the highest degree.)

TO R. B. SHERIDAN, ESQ.

Some winged Genius, Sheridan! imbreath'd
His various influence on thy natal hour:
My fancy bodies forth the Guardian Power,
His temples with Hymettian flowerets wreath'd;
And sweet his voice, as when o'er Laura's bier
Sad music trembled through Vauclusa's glade;
Sweet, as at dawn the lovelorn serenade
That bears soft dreams to Slumber's listening ear!
Now patriot Zeal and Indignation high
Swell the full tones! and now his eye-beams dance
Meanings of Scorn and Wit's quaint revelry!
Th' Apostate by the brainless rout adored,
Writhes inly from the bosom-probing glance,
As erst that nobler Fiend beneath great Michael's sword!

I will give the second number as deeming that it possesses mind:—

As late I roamed through Fancy's shadowy vale,
With wetted cheek and in a mourner's guise,
I saw the sainted form of Freedom rise:
He spake:—not sadder moans th' autumnal gale—
"Great Son of Genius! sweet to me thy name,
Ere in an evil hour with altered voice
Thou badst Oppression's hireling crew rejoice,
Blasting with wizard spell my laurell'd fame.

Yet never, Burke! thou drank'st Corruption's bowl!
Thee stormy Pity and the cherish'd lure
Of Pomp and proud precipitance of soul
Urged on with wild'ring fires. Ah, spirit pure!
That Error's mist had left thy purged eye;
So might I clasp thee with a Mother's joy."

ADDRESS TO A YOUNG JACKASS AND ITS TETHERED MOTHER.[94]

Poor little foal of an oppressed race!
I love the languid patience of thy face:
And oft with friendly hand I give thee bread,
And clap thy ragged coat and pat thy head.
But what thy dulled spirit hath dismay'd,
That never thou dost sport upon the glade?
And (most unlike the nature of things young)
That still to earth thy moping head is hung?
Do thy prophetic tears anticipate,
Meek Child of Misery, thy future fate?
The starving meal and all the thousand aches
That "patient Merit of the Unworthy takes"?
Or is thy sad heart thrill'd with filial pain
To see thy wretched mother's lengthened chain?
And truly, very piteous is her lot,
Chained to a log upon a narrow spot,
Where the close-eaten grass is scarcely seen,
While sweet around her waves the tempting green!
Poor Ass! thy master should have learnt to show
Pity best taught by fellowship of Woe!
For much I fear me that He lives like thee
Half-famish'd in a land of Luxury!
How askingly its steps towards me bend!
It seems to say, "And have I then one friend?"
Innocent foal! thou poor, despis'd forlorn!
I hail thee Brother, spite of the fool's scorn!
And fain I'd take thee with me in the Dell
Of high-souled Pantisocracy to dwell;
Where Toil shall call the charmer Health his bride,
And Laughter tickle Plenty's ribless side!
How thou wouldst toss thy heels in gamesome play,
And frisk about, as lamb or kitten gay.
Yea, and more musically sweet to me
Thy dissonant harsh bray of joy would be,
Than Banti's warbled airs, that soothe to rest
The tumult of a scoundrel Monarch's breast!
How do you like it?

I took the liberty—Gracious God! pardon me for the aristocratic frigidity of that expression—I indulged my feelings by sending this among my Contemporary Sonnets:

Southey! Thy melodies steal o'er mine ear

Like far-off joyance, or the murmuring
Of wild bees in the sunny showers of Spring—
Sounds of such mingled import as may cheer
The lonely breast, yet rouse a mindful tear:
Waked by the song doth Hope-born Fancy fling
Rich showers of dewy fragrance from her wing,
Till sickly Passion's drooping Myrtles sear
Blossom anew! But O! more thrill'd I prize
Thy sadder strains, that bid in Memory's Dream
The faded forms of past Delight arise;
Then soft on Love's pale cheek the tearful gleam
Of Pleasure smiles as faint yet beauteous lies
The imaged Rainbow on a willowy stream.
God love you and your mother and Edith and Sara and Mary and little Eliza, etc., etc., etc., etc., etc., and

S. T. Coleridge.

[The following lines in Southey's handwriting are attached to this letter:—

What though oppression's blood-cemented force
Stands proudly threatening arrogant in state,
Not thine his savage priests to immolate
Or hurl the fabric on the encumber'd plain
As with a whirlwind's fury. It is thine
When dark Revenge masked in the form adored
Of Justice lifts on high the murderer's sword
To save the erring victims from her shrine.
To Godwin.]

XLIII. TO THE SAME.

Monday morning, December, 1794.

My dear Southey,—I will not say that you treat me coolly or mysteriously, yet assuredly you seem to look upon me as a man whom vanity, or some other inexplicable cause, has alienated from the system, or what could build so injurious a suspicion? Wherein, when roused to the recollection of my duty, have I shrunk from the performance of it? I hold my life and my feeble feelings as ready sacrifices to justice—καυκάω ὑπορᾶς γάρ. I dismiss a subject so painful to me as self-vindication; painful to me only as addressing you on whose esteem and affection I have rested with the whole weight of my soul.

Southey! I must tell you that you appear to me to write as a man who is aweary of the world because it accords not with his ideas of perfection. Your sentiments look like the sickly offspring of disgusted pride. It flies not away from the couches of imperfection because the patients are fretful and loathsome.

Why, my dear, very dear Southey, do you wrap yourself in the mantle of self-centring resolve, and refuse to us your bounden quota of intellect? Why do you say, "I, I, I will do so and so," instead of saying, as you were wont to do, "It is all our duty to do so and so, for such and such reasons"?

For God's sake, my dear fellow, tell me what we are to gain by taking a Welsh farm. Remember the principles and proposed consequences of pantisocracy, and reflect in what degree they are attainable by Coleridge, Southey, Lovell, Burnett, and Co., some five men going partners together? In the next place, supposing that we have proved the preponderating utility of our aspheterizing in Wales, let us by our speedy and united inquiries discover the sum of money necessary, whether such a farm with so very large a house is to be procured without launching our frail and unpiloted bark on a rough sea of anxieties. How much is necessary for the maintenance of so large a family—eighteen people for a year at least?

I have read my objections to Lovell. If he has not answered them altogether to my fullest conviction, he has however shown me the wretchedness that would fall on the majority of our party from any delay in so forcible a light, that if three hundred pounds be adequate to the commencement of the system (which I very much doubt), I am most willing to give up all my views and embark immediately with you.

If it be determined that we shall go to Wales (for which I now give my vote), in what time? Mrs. Lovell thinks it impossible that we should go in less than three months. If this be the case, I will accept of the reporter's place to the "Telegraph," live upon a guinea a week, and transmit the [? balance], finishing in the same time my "Imitations."

However, I will walk to Bath to-morrow morning and return in the evening.

Mr. and Mrs. Lovell, Sarah, Edith, all desire their best love to you, and are anxious concerning your health.

May God love you and your affectionate

S. T. Coleridge.

XLIV. TO MARY EVANS.

(?) December, 1794.

Too long has my heart been the torture house of suspense. After infinite struggles of irresolution, I will at last dare to request of you, Mary, that you will communicate to me whether or no you are engaged to Mr. ———. I conjure you not to consider this request as presumptuous indelicacy. Upon mine honour, I have made it with no other design or expectation than that of arming my fortitude by total hopelessness. Read this letter with benevolence—and consign it to oblivion.

For four years I have endeavoured to smother a very ardent attachment; in what degree I have succeeded you must know better than I can. With quick perceptions of moral beauty, it was impossible for me not to admire in you your sensibility regulated by judgment, your gaiety proceeding from a cheerful heart acting on the stores of a strong understanding. At first I voluntarily invited the recollection of these qualities into my mind. I made them the perpetual object of my reveries, yet I entertained no one sentiment beyond that of the immediate pleasure annexed to the thinking of you. At length it became a habit. I awoke from the delusion, and found that I had unwittingly harboured a passion which I felt neither the power nor the courage to subdue. My associations were irrevocably formed, and your image was blended with every idea. I thought of you incessantly; yet that spirit (if spirit there be that condescends to record the lonely beatings of my heart), that spirit knows that I thought of you with the purity of a brother. Happy were I, had it been with no more than a brother's ardour!

The man of dependent fortunes, while he fosters an attachment, commits an act of suicide on his happiness. I possessed no establishment. My views were very distant; I saw that you regarded me merely with the kindness of a sister. What expectations could I form? I formed no expectations. I was ever resolving to subdue the disquieting passion; still some inexplicable suggestion palsied my efforts, and I clung with desperate fondness to this phantom of love, its mysterious attractions and hopeless prospects. It was a faint and rayless hope![95] Yet it soothed my solitude with many a delightful day-dream. It was a faint and rayless hope! Yet I nursed it in my bosom with an agony of affection, even as a mother her sickly infant. But these are the poisoned luxuries of a diseased fancy. Indulge, Mary, this my first, my last request, and restore me to reality, however gloomy. Sad and full of heaviness will the intelligence be; my heart will die within me. I shall, however, receive it with steadier resignation from yourself, than were it announced to me (haply on your marriage day!) by a stranger. Indulge my request; I will not disturb your peace by even a look of discontent, still less will I offend your ear by the whine of selfish sensibility. In a few months I shall enter at the Temple and there seek forgetful calmness, where only it can be found, in incessant and useful activity.

Were you not possessed of a mind and of a heart above the usual lot of women, I should not have written you sentiments that would be unintelligible to three fourths of your sex. But our feelings are congenial, though our attachment is doomed not to be reciprocal. You will not deem so meanly of me as to believe that I shall regard Mr. —— with the jaundiced eye of disappointed passion. God forbid! He whom you honour with your affections becomes sacred to me. I shall love him for your sake; the time may perhaps come when I shall be philosopher enough not to envy him for his own.

S. T. Coleridge.

I return to Cambridge to-morrow morning.

Miss Evans, No. 17 Sackville Street, Piccadilly.

XLV. TO THE SAME.

December 24, 1794.

I have this moment received your letter, Mary Evans. Its firmness does honour to your understanding, its gentleness to your humanity. You condescend to accuse yourself—most unjustly! You have been altogether blameless. In my wildest day-dream of vanity, I never supposed that you entertained for me any other than a common friendship.

To love you, habit has made unalterable. This passion, however, divested as it now is of all shadow of hope, will lose its disquieting power. Far distant from you I shall journey through the vale of men in calmness. He cannot long be wretched, who dares be actively virtuous.

I have burnt your letters—forget mine; and that I have pained you, forgive me!

May God infinitely love you!

S. T. Coleridge.

XLVI. TO ROBERT SOUTHEY.

December, 1794.

I am calm, dear Southey! as an autumnal day, when the sky is covered with gray moveless clouds. To love her, habit has made unalterable. I had placed her in the sanctuary of my heart, nor can she be torn from thence but with the strings that grapple it to life. This passion, however, divested as it now is of all shadow of hope, seems to lose its disquieting power. Far distant, and never more to behold or hear of her, I shall sojourn in the vale of men, sad and in loneliness, yet not unhappy. He cannot be long wretched who dares be actively virtuous. I am well assured that she loves me as a favourite brother. When she was present, she was to me only as a very dear sister; it was in absence that I felt those gnawings of suspense, and that dreaminess of mind, which evidence an affection more restless, yet scarcely less pure than the fraternal. The struggle has been well nigh too much for me; but, praised be the All-Merciful! the feebleness of exhausted feelings has produced a calm, and my heart stagnates into peace.

Southey! my ideal standard of female excellence rises not above that woman. But all things work together for good. Had I been united to her, the excess of my affection would have effeminated my intellect. I should have fed on her looks as she entered into the room, I should have gazed on her footsteps when she went out from me.

To lose her! I can rise above that selfish pang. But to marry another. O Southey! bear with my weakness. Love makes all things pure and heavenly like itself,—but to marry a woman whom I do not love, to degrade her whom I call my wife by making her the instrument of low desire, and on the removal of a desultory appetite to be perhaps not displeased with her absence! Enough! These refinements are the wildering fires that lead me into vice. Mark you, Southey! I will do my duty.

I have this moment received your letter. My friend, you want but one quality of mind to be a perfect character. Your sensibilities are tempestuous; you feel indignation at weakness. Now Indignation is the handsome brother of Anger and Hatred. His looks are "lovely in terror," yet still remember who are his relations. I would ardently that you were a necessitarian, and (believing in an all-loving Omnipotence) an optimist. That puny imp of darkness yclept scepticism, how could it dare to approach the hallowed fires that burn so brightly on the altar of your heart?

Think you I wish to stay in town? I am all eagerness to leave it; and am resolved, whatever be the consequence, to be at Bath by Saturday. I thought of walking down.

I have written to Bristol and said I could not assign a particular time for my leaving town. I spoke indefinitely that I might not disappoint.

I am not, I presume, to attribute some verses addressed to S. T. C., in the "Morning Chronicle," to you. To whom? My dear Allen! wherein has he offended? He did never promise to form one of our party. But of all this when we meet. Would a pistol preserve integrity? So concentrate guilt? no very philosophical mode of preventing it. I will write of indifferent subjects. Your sonnet,[96] "Hold your mad hands!" is a noble burst of poetry; and—but my mind is weakened and I turn with selfishness of thought to those wilder songs that develop my lonely feelings. Sonnets are scarcely fit for the hard gaze of the public. I read, with heart and taste equally delighted, your prefatory sonnet.[97] I transcribe it, not so much to give you my corrections, as for the pleasure it gives me.

With wayworn feet, a pilgrim woe-begone,
Life's upland steep I journeyed many a day,
And hymning many a sad yet soothing lay,
Beguiled my wandering with the charms of song.
Lonely my heart and rugged was my way,
Yet often plucked I, as I passed along,
The wild and simple flowers of poesy:
And, as beseemed the wayward Fancy's child,
Entwined each random weed that pleased mine eye.
Accept the wreath, Beloved! it is wild
And rudely garlanded; yet scorn not thou
The humble offering, when the sad rue weaves
With gayer flowers its intermingled leaves,
And I have twin'd the myrtle for thy brow!

It is a lovely sonnet. Lamb likes it with tears in his eyes. His sister has lately been very unwell, confined to her bed, dangerously. She is all his comfort, he hers. They dote on each other. Her mind is elegantly stored; her heart feeling. Her illness preyed a good deal on his spirits, though he bore it with an apparent equanimity as beseemed him who, like me, is a Unitarian Christian, and an advocate for the automatism of man.

I was writing a poem, which when finished you shall see, and wished him to describe the character and doctrines of Jesus Christ for me; but his low spirits prevented him. The poem is in blank verse on the Nativity. I sent him these careless lines, which flowed from my pen extemporaneously:—

TO C. LAMB.[98]

Thus far my sterile brain hath framed the song
Elaborate and swelling: but the heart
Not owns it. From thy spirit-breathing power
I ask not now, my friend! the aiding verse,
Tedious to thee, and from thy anxious thought
Of dissonant mood. In fancy (well I know)
Thou creepest round a dear-loved Sister's bed
With noiseless step, and watchest the faint look,
Soothing each pang with fond solicitude,
And tenderest tones, medicinal of love.
I too a Sister had, an only Sister—
She loved me dearly, and I doted on her!

On her soft bosom I reposed my cares
And gained for every wound a healing scar.
To her I pour'd forth all my puny sorrows,
(As a sick Patient in his Nurse's arms),
And of the heart those hidden maladies
That shrink ashamed from even Friendship's eye.
O! I have woke at midnight and have wept
Because she was not! Cheerily, dear Charles!
Thou thy best friend shalt cherish many a year:
Such high presages feel I of warm hope!
For not uninterested, the dear Maid
I've view'd—her Soul affectionate yet wise,
Her polish'd wit as mild as lambent glories
That play around a holy infant's head.
He knows (the Spirit who in secret sees,
Of whose omniscient and all-spreading Love
Aught to implore were Impotence of mind)
That my mute thoughts are sad before his throne,
Prepar'd, when he his healing pay vouchsafes,
To pour forth thanksgiving with lifted heart,
And praise Him Gracious with a Brother's Joy!
Wynne is indeed a noble fellow. More when we meet.

Your
S. T. Coleridge.

CHAPTER II
EARLY PUBLIC LIFE
1795-1796

XLVII. TO JOSEPH COTTLE.

Spring, 1795.

My dear Sir,—Can you conveniently lend me five pounds, as we want a little more than four pounds to make up our lodging bill, which is indeed much higher than we expected; seven weeks and Burnett's lodging for twelve weeks, amounting to eleven pounds?

Yours affectionately,
S. T. Coleridge.

XLVIII. TO THE SAME.

July 31, 1795.

Dear Cottle,—By the thick smokes that precede the volcanic eruptions of Etna, Vesuvius, and Hecla, I feel an impulse to fumigate, at 25 College Street, one pair of stairs' room; yea, with our Oronoco, and, if thou wilt send me by the bearer four pipes, I will write a panegyrical epic poem upon thee, with as many books as there are letters in thy name. Moreover, if thou wilt send me "the copy-book," I hereby bind myself, by to-morrow morning, to write out enough copy for a sheet and a half.

God bless you.

S. T. C.

XLIX. TO THE SAME.

1795.

Dear Cottle,—Shall I trouble you (I being over the mouth and nose, in doing something of importance, at ———'s) to send your servant into the market and buy a pound of bacon, and two quarts of broad beans; and when he carries it down to College Street, to desire the maid to dress it for dinner, and tell her I shall be home by three o'clock? Will you come and drink tea with me? and I will endeavour to get the etc. ready for you.

Yours affectionately,
S. T. C.

L. TO ROBERT SOUTHEY.

October, 1795.

My dear Southey,—It would argue imbecility and a latent wickedness in myself, if for a moment I doubted concerning your purposes and final determination. I write, because it is possible that I may suggest some idea to you which should find a place in your answer to your uncle, and I write, because in a letter I can express myself more connectedly than in conversation.

The former part of Mr. Hill's reasonings is reducible to this. It may not be vicious to entertain pure and virtuous sentiments; their criminality is confined to the promulgation (if we believe democracy to be pure and virtuous, to us it is so). Southey! Pantisocracy is not the question: its realization is distant—perhaps a miraculous millennium. What you have seen, or think that you have seen of the human heart, may render the formation even of a pantisocratic seminary improbable to you, but this is not the question. Were £300 a year offered to you as a man of the world, as one indifferent to absolute equality, but still on the supposition that you were commonly honest, I suppose it possible that doubts might arise; your mother, your brother, your Edith, would all crowd upon you, and certain misery might be weighed against distant, and perhaps unattainable happiness. But the point is, whether or no you can perjure yourself. There are men who hold the necessity and moral optimism of our religious establishment. Its peculiar dogmas they may disapprove, but of innovation they see dreadful and unhealable consequence; and they will not quit the Church for a few follies and absurdities, any more than for the same reason they would desert a valued friend. Such men I do not condemn. Whatever I may deem of their reasoning, their hearts and consciences I include not in the anathema. But you disapprove of an establishment altogether; you believe it iniquitous, a mother of crimes. It is impossible that you could uphold it by assuming the badge of affiliation.

My prospects are not bright, but to the eye of reason as bright as when we first formed our plan; nor is there any opposite inducement offered, of which you were not then apprized, or had cause to expect. Domestic happiness is the greatest of things sublunary, and of things celestial it is impossible, perhaps, for unassisted man to believe anything greater; but it is not strange that those things, which, in a pure form of society, will constitute our first blessings, should in its present morbid state be our most perilous temptations. "He that doth not love mother or wife less than me, is not worthy of me!"

This have I written, Southey, altogether disinterestedly. Your desertion or adhesion will in no wise affect my feelings, opinions, or conduct, and in a very inconsiderable degree my fortunes! That Being who is "in will, in deed, Impulse of all to all," whichever be your determination, will make it ultimately the best.

God love you, my dear Southey!

S. T. Coleridge.

LI. TO THOMAS POOLE.

Wednesday evening, October 7, 1795.

My dear Sir,—God bless you; or rather, God be praised for that he has blessed you!

On Sunday morning I was married at St. Mary's Redcliff, poor Chatterton's church! The thought gave a tinge of melancholy to the solemn joy which I felt, united to the woman whom I love best of all created beings. We are settled, nay, quite domesticated, at Clevedon, our comfortable cot!

Mrs. Coleridge! I like to write the name. Well, as I was saying, Mrs. Coleridge desires her affectionate regards to you. I talked of you on my wedding night. God bless you! I hope that some ten years hence you will believe and know of my affection towards you what I will not now profess.

The prospect around is perhaps more various than any in the kingdom. Mine eye gluttonizes the sea, the distant islands, the opposite coast! I shall assuredly write rhymes, let the nine Muses prevent it if they can. Cruikshank, I find, is married to Miss Buclé. I am happy to hear it. He will surely, I hope, make a good husband to a woman, to whom he would be a villain who should make a bad one.

I have given up all thoughts of the magazine, for various reasons. Imprimis, I must be connected with R. Southey in it, which I could not be with comfort to my feelings. Secundo, It is a thing of monthly anxiety and quotidian bustle. Tertio, It would cost Cottle an hundred pounds in buying paper, etc.—all on an uncertainty. Quarto, To publish a magazine for one year would be nonsense, and if I pursue what I mean to pursue, my school plan, I could not publish it for more than a year. Quinto, Cottle has entered into an engagement to give me a guinea and a half for every hundred lines of poetry I write, which will be perfectly sufficient for my maintenance, I only amusing myself on mornings; and all my prose works he is eager to purchase. Sexto, In the course of half a year I mean to return to Cambridge (having previously taken my name off from the University control) and taking lodgings there for myself and wife, finish my great work of "Imitations," in two volumes. My former works may, I hope, prove somewhat of genius and of erudition. This will be better; it will show great industry and manly consistency; at the end of it I shall publish proposals for school, etc. Cottle has spent a day with me, and takes this letter to Bristol. My next will be long, and full of something. This is inanity and egotism. Pray let me hear from you, directing the letter to Mr. Cottle, who will forward it. My respectful and grateful remembrance to your mother, and believe me, dear Poole, your affectionate and mindful friend, shall I so soon dare to say? Believe me, my heart prompts it.

S. T. Coleridge.

LII. TO ROBERT SOUTHEY.[99]

Friday morning, November 13, 1795.

Southey, I have lost friends—friends who still cherish for me sentiments of high esteem and unextinguished tenderness. For the sum total of my misbehaviour, the Alpha and Omega of their accusations, is epistolary neglect. I never speak of them without affection, I never think of them without reverence. Not "to this catalogue," Southey, have I "added your name." You are lost to me, because you are lost to Virtue. As this will probably be the last time I shall have occasion to address you, I will begin at the beginning and regularly retrace your conduct and my own. In the month of June, 1794, I first became acquainted with your person and character. Before I quitted Oxford, we had struck out the leading features of a pantisocracy. While on my journey through Wales you invited me to Bristol with the full hopes of realising it. During my abode at Bristol the plan was matured, and I returned to Cambridge hot in the anticipation of that happy season when we should remove the selfish principle from ourselves, and prevent it in our children, by an abolition of property; or, in whatever respects this might be impracticable, by such similarity of property as would amount to a moral sameness, and answer all the purposes of abolition. Nor were you less zealous, and thought and expressed your opinion, that if any man embraced our system he must comparatively disregard "his father and mother and wife and children and brethren and sisters, yea, and his own life also, or he could not be our disciple." In one of your letters, alluding to your mother's low spirits and situation, you tell me that "I cannot suppose any individual feelings will have an undue weight with you," and in the same letter you observe (alas! your recent conduct has made it a prophecy!), "God forbid that the ebullience of schematism should be over. It is the Promethean fire that animates my soul, and when that is gone all will be darkness. I have devoted myself."

Previously to my departure from Jesus College, and during my melancholy detention in London, what convulsive struggles of feeling I underwent, and what sacrifices I made, you know. The liberal proposal from my family affected me no further than as it pained me to wound a revered brother by the positive and immediate refusal which duty compelled me to return. But there was a—I need not be particular; you remember what a fetter I burst, and that it snapt as if it had been a sinew of my heart. However, I returned to Bristol, and my addresses to Sara, which I at first paid from principle, not feeling, from feeling and from principle I renewed; and I met a reward more than proportionate to the greatness of the effort. I love and I am beloved, and I am happy!

Your letter to Lovell (two or three days after my arrival at Bristol), in answer to some objections of mine to the Welsh scheme, was the first thing that alarmed me. Instead of "It is our duty," "Such and such are the reasons," it was "I and I" and "will and will,"—sentences of gloomy and self-centering resolve. I wrote you a friendly reproof, and in my own mind attributed this unwonted style to your earnest desires of realising our plan, and the angry pain which you felt when any appeared to oppose or defer its execution. However, I came over to your opinions of the utility, and, in course, the duty of rehearsing our scheme in Wales, and, so, rejected the offer of being established in the Earl of Buchan's family. To this period of our connection I call your more particular attention and remembrance, as I shall revert to it at the close of my letter.

We commenced lecturing. Shortly after, you began to recede in your conversation from those broad principles in which pantisocracy originated. I opposed you with vehemence, for I well knew that no notion of morality or its motives could be without consequences. And once (it was just before we went to bed) you confessed to me that you had acted wrong. But you relapsed; your manner became cold and gloomy, and pleaded with increased pertinacity for the wisdom of making Self an undiverging Center. At Mr. Jardine's[100] your language was strong indeed. Recollect it. You had left the table, and we were standing at the window. Then darted into my mind the dread that you were meditating a separation. At Chepstow[101] your conduct renewed my suspicion, and I was greatly agitated, even to many tears. But in Peircefield Walks[102] you assured me that my suspicions were altogether unfounded, that our differences were merely speculative, and that you would certainly go into Wales. I was glad and satisfied. For my heart was never bent from you but by violent strength, and heaven knows how it leapt back to esteem and love you. But alas! a short time passed ere your departure from our first principles became too flagrant.

Remember when we went to Ashton[103] on the strawberry party. Your conversation with George Burnett on the day following he detailed to me. It scorched my throat. Your private resources were to remain your individual property, and everything to be separate except a farm of five or six acres. In short, we were to commence partners in a petty farming trade. This was the mouse of which the mountain Pantisocracy was at last safely delivered. I received the account with indignation and loathings of unutterable contempt. Such opinions were indeed unassailable,—the javelin of argument and the arrows of ridicule would have been equally misapplied; a straw would have wounded them mortally. I did not condescend to waste my intellect upon them; but in the most express terms I declared to George Burnett my opinion (and, Southey, next to my own existence, there is scarce any fact of which at this moment I entertain less doubt), to Burnett I declared it to be my opinion "that you had long laid a plot of separation, and were now developing it by proposing such a vile mutilation of our scheme as you must have been conscious I should reject decisively and with scorn." George Burnett was your most affectionate friend; I knew his unbounded veneration for you, his personal attachment; I knew likewise his gentle dislike of me. Yet him I bade be the judge. I bade him choose his associate. I would adopt the full system or depart. George, I presume, detailed of this my conversation what part he chose; from him, however, I received your sentiments, viz.: that you would go into Wales, or what place I liked. Thus your system of prudentials and your apostasy were not sudden; these constant nibblings had sloped your descent from virtue. "You received your uncle's letter," I said— "what answer have you returned?" For to think with almost superstitious veneration of you had been such a deep-rooted habit of my soul that even then I did not dream you could hesitate concerning so infamous a proposal. "None," you replied, "nor do I know what answer I shall return." You went to bed. George sat half-petrified, gaping at the pigmy virtue of his supposed giant. I performed the office of still-struggling friendship by writing you my free sentiments concerning the enormous guilt of that which your uncle's doughty sophistry recommended.

On the next morning I walked with you towards Bath; again I insisted on its criminality. You told me that you had "little notion of guilt," and that "you had a pretty sort of lullaby faith of your own." Finding you invulnerable in conscience, for the sake of mankind I did not, however, quit the field, but pressed you on the difficulties of your system. Your uncle's intimacy with the bishop, and the hush in which you would lie for the two years previous to your ordination, were the arguments (variously urged in a long and desultory conversation) by which you solved those difficulties. "But your 'Joan of Arc'—the sentiments in it are of the boldest order. What if the suspicions of the Bishop be raised, and he particularly questions you concerning your opinions of the Trinity and the Redemption?" "Oh," you replied, "I am pretty well up to their jargon, and shall answer them accordingly." In fine, you left me fully persuaded that you would enter into Holy Orders. And, after a week's interval or more, you desired George Burnett to act independently of you, and gave him an invitation to Oxford. Of course, we both concluded that the matter was absolutely determined. Southey! I am not besotted that I should not know, nor hypocrite enough not to tell you, that you were diverted from being a Priest only by the weight of infamy which you perceived coming towards you like a rush of waters.

Then with good reason I considered you as one fallen back into the ranks; as a man admirable for his abilities only, strict, indeed, in the lesser honesties, but, like the majority of men, unable to resist a strong temptation. Friend is a very sacred appellation. You were become an acquaintance, yet one for whom I felt no common tenderness. I could not forget what you had been. Your sun was set; your sky was clouded; but those clouds and that sky were yet tinged with the recent sun. As I considered you, so I treated you. I studiously avoided all particular subjects. I acquainted you with nothing relative to myself.

Literary topics engrossed our conversation. You were too quick-sighted not to perceive it. I received a letter from you. "You have withdrawn your confidence from me, Coleridge. Preserving still the face of friendship when we meet, you yet avoid me and carry on your plans in secrecy." If by "the face of friendship" you meant that kindliness which I show to all because I feel it for all, your statement was perfectly accurate. If you meant more, you contradict yourself; for you evidently perceived from my manners that you were a "weight upon me" in company—an intruder, unwished and unwelcome. I pained you by "cold civility, the shadow which friendship leaves behind him." Since that letter I altered my conduct no otherwise than by avoiding you more. I still generalised, and spoke not of myself, except my proposed literary works. In short, I spoke to you as I should have done to any other man of genius who had happened to be my acquaintance. Without the farce and tumult of a rupture I wished you to sink into that class. "Face to face you never changed your manners to me." And yet I pained you by "cold civility." Egregious contradiction! Doubtless I always treated you with urbanity, and meant to do so; but I locked up my heart from you, and you perceived it, and I intended you to perceive it. "I planned works in conjunction with you." Most certainly; the magazine which, long before this, you had planned equally with me, and, if it had been carried into execution, would of course have returned you a third share of the profits. What had you done that should make you an unfit literary associate to me? Nothing. My opinion of you as a man was altered, not as a writer. Our Muses had not quarrelled. I should have read your poetry with equal delight, and corrected it with equal zeal if correction it needed. "I received you on my return from Shurton with my usual shake of the hand." You gave me your hand, and dreadful must have been my feelings if I had refused to take it. Indeed, so long had I known you, so highly venerated, so dearly loved you, that my hand would have taken yours mechanically. But is shaking the hand a mark of friendship? Heaven forbid! I should then be a hypocrite many days in the week. It is assuredly the pledge of acquaintance, and nothing more. But after this did I not with most scrupulous care avoid you? You know I did.

In your former letters you say that I made use of these words to you: "You will be retrograde that you may spring the farther forward." You have misquoted, Southey! You had talked of rejoining pantisocracy in about fourteen years. I exploded this probability, but as I saw you determined to leave it, hoped and wished it might be so—hoped that we might run backwards only to leap forward. Not to mention that during that conversation I had taken the weight and pressing urgency of your motives as truths granted; but when, on examination, I found them a show and mockery of unreal things, doubtless, my opinion of you must have become far less respectful. You quoted likewise the last sentence of my letter to you, as a proof that I approved of your design; you knew that sentence to imply no more than the pious confidence of optimism—however wickedly you might act, God would make it ultimately the best. You knew this was the meaning of it—I could find twenty parallel passages in the lectures. Indeed, such expressions applied to bad actions had become a habit of my conversation. You had named, not unwittingly, Dr. Pangloss. And Heaven forbid that I should not now have faith that however foul your stream may run here, yet that it will filtrate and become pure in its subterraneous passage to the Ocean of Universal Redemption.

Thus far had I written when the necessities of literary occupation crowded upon me, and I met you in Redcliff, and, unsaluted and unsaluting, passed by the man to whom for almost a year I had told my last thoughts when I closed my eyes, and the first when I awoke. But "ere this I have felt sorrow!"

I shall proceed to answer your letters, and first excriminate myself, and then examine your conduct. You charge me with having industriously trumpeted your uncle's letter. When I mentioned my intended journey to Clevedon with Burnett, and was asked by my immediate friends why you were not with us, should I have been silent and implied something mysterious, or have told an open untruth and made myself your accomplice? I could do neither; I answered that you were quite undetermined, but had some thoughts of returning to Oxford. To Danvers, indeed, and to Cottle I spoke more particularly, for I knew their prudence and their love for you—and my heart was very full. But to Mrs. Morgan I did not mention it. She met me in the streets, and said: "So! Southey is going into the Church! 'Tis all concluded, 'tis in vain to deny it!" I answered: "You are mistaken; you must contradict; Southey has received a splendid offer, but he has not determined." This, I have some faint recollection, was my answer, but of this particular conversation my recollection is very faint. By what means she received the intelligence I know not; probably from Mrs. Richardson, who might have been told it by Mr. Wade. A considerable time after, the subject was renewed at Mrs. Morgan's, Burnett and my Sara being present. Mrs. M. told me that you had asserted to her, that with regard to the Church you had barely hesitated, that you might consider your uncle's arguments, that you had given up no one principle—and that I was more your friend than ever. I own I was roused to an agony of passion; nor was George Burnett undisturbed. Whatever I said that afternoon (and since that time I have but often repeated what I said, in gentler language) George Burnett did give his decided Amen to. And I said, Southey, that you had given up every principle—that confessedly you were going into the law, more opposite to your avowed principles, if possible, than even the Church—and that I had in my pocket a letter in which you charged me with having withdrawn my friendship; and as to your barely hesitating about your uncle's proposal, I was obliged in my own defence to relate all that passed between us, all on which I had founded a conviction so directly opposite.

I have, you say, distorted your conversation by "gross misrepresentation and wicked and calumnious falsehoods. It has been told me by Mrs. Morgan that I said: 'I have seen my error! I have been drunk with principle!'" Just over the bridge, at the bottom of the High Street, returning one night from Redcliff Hill, in answer to my pressing contrast of your then opinions of the selfish kind with what you had formerly professed, you said: "I was intoxicated with the novelty of a system!" That you said, "I have seen my error," I never asserted. It is doubtless implied in the sentence which you did say, but I never charged it to you as your expression. As to your reserving bank bills, etc., to yourself, the charge would have been so palpable a lie that I must have been madman as well as villain to have been guilty of it. If I had, George Burnett and Sara would have contradicted it. I said that your conduct in little things had appeared to me tinged with selfishness, and George Burnett attributed, and still does attribute, your defection to your unwillingness to share your expected annuity with us. As to the long catalogue of other lies, they not being particularised, I, of course, can say nothing about them. Tales may have been fetched and carried with embellishments calculated to improve them in everything but the truth. I spoke "the plain and simple truth" alone.

And now for your conduct and motives. My hand trembles when I think what a series of falsehood and duplicity I am about to bring before the conscience of a man who has dared to write me that "his conduct has been uniformly open." I must revert to your first letter, and here you say:—

"The plan you are going upon is not of sufficient importance to justify me to myself in abandoning a family, who have none to support them but me." The plan you are going upon! What plan was I meditating, save to retire into the country with George Burnett and yourself, and taking by degrees a small farm, there be learning to get my own bread by my bodily labour—and then to have all things in common—thus disciplining my body and mind for the successful practice of the same thing in America with more numerous associates? And even if this should never be the case, ourselves and our children would form a society sufficiently large. And was not this your own plan—the plan for the realising of which you invited me to Bristol; the plan for which I abandoned my friends, and every prospect, and every certainty, and the woman whom I loved to an excess which you in your warmest dream of fancy could never shadow out? When I returned from London, when you deemed pantisocracy a duty—duty unaltered by numbers—when you said, that, if others left it, you and George Burnett and your brother would stand firm to the post of virtue—what then were our circumstances? Saving Lovell, our number was the same, yourself and Burnett and I. Our prospects were only an uncertain hope of getting thirty shillings a week between us by writing for some London paper—for the remainder we were to rely on our agricultural exertions. And as to your family you stood precisely in the same situation as you now stand. You meant to take your mother with you, and your brother. And where, indeed, would have been the difficulty? She would have earned her maintenance by her management and savings—considering the matter even in this cold-hearted way. But when you broke from us our prospects were brightening; by the magazine or by poetry we might and should have got ten guineas a month.

But if you are acting right, I should be acting right in imitating you. What, then, would George Burnett do—he "whom you seduced

"With other promises and other vaunts
Than to repent, boasting you could subdue
Temptation!"
He cannot go into the Church, for you did "give him principles"! and I wish that you had indeed "learnt from him how infinitely more to be valued is integrity of heart than effulgence of intellect." Nor can he go into the law, for the same principles declare against it, and he is not calculated for it. And his father will not support any expense of consequence relative to his further education—for Law or Physic he could not take his degree in, or be called to, without sinking of many hundred pounds. What, Southey, was George Burnett to do?

Then, even if you had persisted in your design of taking Orders, your motives would have been weak and shadowy and vile; but when you changed your ground for the Law they were annihilated. No man dreams of getting bread in the Law, till six or eight years after his first entrance at the Temple. And how very few even then? Before this time your brothers would have been put out, and the money which you must of necessity have sunk in a wicked profession would have given your brother an education, and provided a premium fit for the first compting-house in the world. But I hear that you have again changed your ground. You do not now mean to study the Law, but to maintain yourself by your writings and on your promised annuity, which, you told Mrs. Morgan, would be more than a hundred a year. Could you not have done the same with us? I neither have nor could deign to have a hundred a year. Yet by my own exertions I will struggle hard to maintain myself, and my wife, and my wife's mother and my associate. Or what if you dedicated this hundred a year to your family? Would you not be precisely as I am? Is not George Burnett accurate when he undoubtedly ascribes your conduct to an unparticipating propensity—to a total want of the boasted flocci-nauci-nihili-pilificating sense? O selfish, money-loving man! What principle have you not given up? Though death had been the consequence, I would have spat in that man's face and called him liar, who should have spoken that last sentence concerning you nine months ago. For blindly did I esteem you. O God! that such a mind should fall in love with that low, dirty, gutter-grubbing trull, Worldly Prudence!

Curse on all pride! 'Tis a harlot that buckrams herself up in virtue only that she may fetch a higher price. 'Tis a rock where virtue may be planted, but cannot strike root.

Last of all, perceiving that your motives vanished at the first ray of examination, and that those accounts of your mother and family which had drawn easy tears down wrinkled cheeks had no effect on keener minds, your last resource has been to calumniate me. If there be in nature a situation perilous to honesty, it is this, when a man has not heart to be, yet lusts to seem virtuous. My indolence you assigned to Lovell as the reason for your quitting pantisocracy. Supposing it true, it might indeed be a reason for rejecting me from the system. But how does this affect pantisocracy, that you should reject it? And what has Burnett done, that he should not be a worthy associate? He who leaned on you with all his head and with all his heart; he who gave his all for pantisocracy, and expected that pantisocracy would be at least bread and cheese to him. But neither is the charge a true one. My own lectures I wrote for myself, eleven in number, excepting a very few pages which most reluctantly you eked out for me. And such pages! I would not have suffered them to have stood in a lecture of yours. To your lectures I dedicated my whole mind and heart, and wrote one half in quantity; but in quality you must be conscious that all the tug of brain was mine, and that your share was little more than transcription. I wrote with vast exertion of all my intellect the parts in the "Joan of Arc," and I corrected that and other poems with greater interest than I should have felt for my own. Then my own poems, and the recomposing of my lectures, besides a sermon, and the correction of some poems for a friend. I could have written them in half the time and with less expense of thought. I write not these things boastfully, but to excriminate myself. The truth is, you sat down and wrote; I used to saunter about and think what I should write. And we ought to appreciate our comparative industry by the quantum of mental exertion, not the particular mode of it—by the number of thoughts collected, not by the number of lines through which these thoughts are diffused. But I will suppose myself guilty of the charge. How would an honest man have reasoned in your letter and how acted? Thus: "Here is a man who has abandoned all for what I believe to be virtue. But he professed himself an imperfect being when he offered himself an associate to me. He confessed that all his valuable qualities were 'sloth-jaundiced,' and in his letters is a bitter self-accuser. This man did not deceive me. I accepted of him in the hopes of curing him, but I half despair of it. How shall I act? I will tell him fully and firmly, that much as I love him I love pantisocracy more, and if in a certain time I do not see this disqualifying propensity subdued, I must and will reject him." Such would have been an honest man's reasoning, such his conduct. Did you act so? Did you even mention to me, "face to face," my indolence as a motive for your recent conduct? Did you ever mention it in Peircefield Walks? and some time after, that night when you scattered some heart-chilling sentiments, and in great agitation I did ask you solemnly whether you disapproved of anything in my conduct, and you answered, "Nothing. I like you better now than at the commencement of our friendship!" an answer which so startled Sara, that she affronted you into angry silence by exclaiming, "What a story!" George Burnett, I believe, was present. This happened after all our lectures, after every one of those proofs of indolence on which you must found your charge. A charge which with what indignation did you receive when brought against me by Lovell! Yet then there was some shew for it. I had been criminally indolent. But since then I have exerted myself more than I could have supposed myself capable. Enough! I heard for the first time on Thursday that you were to set off for Lisbon on Saturday morning. It gives me great pain on many accounts, but principally that those moments which should be sacred to your affections may be disturbed by this long letter.

Southey, as far as happiness will be conducive to your virtue, which alone is final happiness, may you possess it! You have left a large void in my heart. I know no man big enough to fill it. Others I may love equally, and esteem equally, and some perhaps I may admire as much. But never do I expect to meet another man, who will make me unite attachment for his person with reverence for his heart and admiration of his genius. I did not only venerate you for your own virtues, I prized you as the sheet-anchor of mine; and even as a poet my vanity knew no keener gratification than your praise. But these things are passed by like as when a hungry man dreams, and lo! he feasteth, but he awakes and his soul is empty.

May God Almighty bless and preserve you! and may you live to know and feel and acknowledge that unless we accustom ourselves to meditate adoringly on Him, the source of all virtue, no virtue can be permanent.

Be assured that G. Burnett still loves you better than he can love any other man, and Sara would have you accept her love and blessing; accept it as the future husband of her best loved sister. Farewell!

S. T. Coleridge.

LIII. TO JOSIAH WADE.[104]

Nottingham, Wednesday morning, January 27, 1796.

My dear Friend,—You will perceive by this letter that I have changed my route. From Birmingham, which I quitted on Friday last (four o'clock in the morning), I proceeded to Derby, stayed there till Monday morning, and am now at Nottingham. From Nottingham I go to Sheffield; from Sheffield to Manchester; from Manchester to Liverpool; from Liverpool to London; from London to Bristol. Ah, what a weary way! My poor crazy ark has been tossed to and fro on an ocean of business, and I long for the Mount Ararat on which it is to rest. At Birmingham I was extremely unwell.... Business succeeded very well there; about an hundred subscribers, I think. At Derby tolerably well. Mr. Strutt (the successor to Sir Richard Arkwright) tells me I may count on forty or fifty in Derby and round about.

Derby is full of curiosities, the cotton, the silk mills, Wright,[105] the painter, and Dr. Darwin, the everything, except the Christian![106] Dr. Darwin possesses, perhaps, a greater range of knowledge than any other man in Europe, and is the most inventive of philosophical men. He thinks in a new train on all subjects except religion. He bantered me on the subject of religion. I heard all his arguments, and told him that it was infinitely consoling to me, to find that the arguments which so great a man adduced against the existence of a God and the evidences of revealed religion were such as had startled me at fifteen, but had become the objects of my smile at twenty. Not one new objection—not even an ingenious one. He boasted that he had never read one book in defence of such stuff, but he had read all the works of infidels! What should you think, Mr. Wade, of a man, who, having abused and ridiculed you, should openly declare that he had heard all that your enemies had to say against you, but had scorned to enquire the truth from any of your own friends? Would you think him an honest man? I am sure you would not. Yet of such are all the infidels with whom I have met. They talk of a subject infinitely important, yet are proud to confess themselves profoundly ignorant of it. Dr. Darwin would have been ashamed to have rejected Hutton's theory of the earth[107] without having minutely examined it; yet what is it to us how the earth was made, a thing impossible to be known, and useless if known? This system the doctor did not reject without having severely studied it; but all at once he makes up his mind on such important subjects, as whether we be the outcasts of a blind idiot called Nature, or the children of an all-wise and infinitely good God; whether we spend a few miserable years on this earth, and then sink into a clod of the valley, or only endure the anxieties of mortal life in order to fit us for the enjoyment of immortal happiness. These subjects are unworthy a philosopher's investigation. He deems that there is a certain self-evidence in infidelity, and becomes an atheist by intuition. Well did St. Paul say: "Ye have an evil heart of unbelief." I had an introductory letter from Mr. Strutt to a Mr. Fellowes of Nottingham. On Monday evening when I arrived I found there was a public dinner in honour of Mr. Fox's birthday, and that Mr. Fellowes was present. It was a piece of famous good luck, and I seized it, waited on Mr. Fellowes, and was introduced to the company. On the right hand of the president whom should I see but an old College acquaintance? He hallooed out: "Coleridge, by God!" Mr. Wright, the president of the day, was his relation—a man of immense fortune. I dined at his house yesterday, and underwent the intolerable slavery of a dinner of three courses. We sat down at four o'clock, and it was six before the cloth was removed.

What lovely children Mr. Barr at Worcester has! After church, in the evening, they sat round and sang hymns so sweetly that they overwhelmed me. It was with great difficulty I abstained from weeping aloud—and the infant in Mrs. Barr's arms leaned forwards, and stretched his little arms, and stared and smiled. It seemed a picture of Heaven, where the different orders of the blessed join different voices in one melodious allelujah; and the baby looked like a young spirit just that moment arrived in Heaven, startling at the seraphic songs, and seized at once with wonder and rapture.

My kindest remembrances to Mrs. Wade, and believe me, with gratitude and unfeigned friendship, your

S. T. Coleridge.

LIV. TO JOSEPH COTTLE.

Redcliff Hill, February 22, 1796.

My dear Sir,—It is my duty and business to thank God for all his dispensations, and to believe them the best possible; but, indeed, I think I should have been more thankful, if he had made me a journeyman shoemaker, instead of an author by trade. I have left my friends; I have left plenty; I have left that ease which would have secured a literary immortality, and have enabled me to give the public works conceived in moments of inspiration, and polished with leisurely solicitude; and alas! for what have I left them? for — — who deserted me in the hour of distress, and for a scheme of virtue impracticable and romantic! So I am forced to write for bread; write the flights of poetic enthusiasm, when every minute I am hearing a groan from my wife. Groans, and complaints, and sickness! The present hour I am in a quick-set hedge of embarrassment, and whichever way I turn a thorn runs into me! The future is cloud and thick darkness! Poverty, perhaps, and the thin faces of them that want bread, looking up to me! Nor is this all. My happiest moments for composition are broken in upon by the reflection that I must make haste. I am too late! I am already months behind! I have received my pay beforehand! Oh, wayward and desultory spirit of genius! Ill canst thou brook a taskmaster! The tenderest touch from the hand of obligation wounds thee like a scourge of scorpions.

I have been composing in the fields this morning, and came home to write down the first rude sheet of my preface, when I heard that your man had brought a note from you. I have not seen it, but I guess its contents. I am writing as fast as I can. Depend on it you shall not be out of pocket for me! I feel what I owe you, and independently of this I love you as a friend; indeed, so much, that I regret, seriously regret, that you have been my copyholder.

If I have written petulantly, forgive me. God knows I am sore all over. God bless you, and believe me that, setting gratitude aside, I love and esteem you, and have your interest at heart full as much as my own.

S. T. Coleridge.

LV. TO THOMAS POOLE.

March 30, 1796.

My dear Poole,—For the neglect in the transmission of "The Watchman," you must blame George Burnett, who undertook the business. I however will myself see it sent this week with the preceding numbers. I am greatly obliged to you for your communication (on the Slave Trade in No. V.); it appears in this number, and I am anxious to receive more from you, and likewise to know what you dislike in "The Watchman," and what you like; but particularly the former. You have not given me your opinion of "The Plot Discovered."[108]

Since last you saw me I have been well nigh distracted. The repeated and most injurious blunders of my printer out-of-doors, and Mrs. Coleridge's increasing danger at home, added to the gloomy prospect of so many mouths to open and shut like puppets, as I move the string in the eating and drinking way—but why complain to you? Misery is an article with which every market is so glutted, that it can answer no one's purpose to export it. Alas! Alas! oh! ah! oh! oh! etc.

I have received many abusive letters, post-paid, thanks to the friendly malignants! But I am perfectly callous to disapprobation, except when it tends to lessen profit. There, indeed, I am all one tremble of sensibility, marriage having taught me the wonderful uses of that vulgar commodity, yclept bread. "The Watchman" succeeds so as to yield a bread-and-cheesish profit. Mrs. Coleridge is recovering apace, and deeply regrets that she was deprived of seeing [you]. We are in our new house, where there is a bed at your service whenever you will please to delight us with a visit. Surely in spring you might force a few days into a sojourning with me.

Dear Poole, you have borne yourself towards me most kindly with respect to my epistolary ingratitude. But I know that you forbade yourself to feel resentment towards me because you had previously made my neglect ingratitude. A generous temper endures a great deal from one whom it has obliged deeply.

My poems are finished. I will send you two copies the moment they are published. In the third number of "The Watchman" there are a few lines entitled "The Hour when we shall meet again," "Dim hour that sleeps on pillowy clouds afar," which I think you will like. I have received two or three letters from different anonymi, requesting me to give more poetry. One of them writes:—

"Sir! I detest your principles; your prose I think very so-so; but your poetry is so exquisitely beautiful, so gorgeously sublime, that I take in your 'Watchman' solely on account of it. In justice therefore to me and some others of my stamp, I intreat you to give us more verse and less democratic scurrility. Your admirer,—not esteemer."

Have you read over Dr. Lardner on the Logos? It is, I think, scarcely possible to read it and not be convinced.

I find that "The Watchman" comes more easy to me, so that I shall begin about my Christian Lectures. I will immediately order for you, unless you immediately countermand it, Count Rumford's Essays; in No. V. of "The Watchman" you will see why. I have enclosed Dr. Beddoes's late pamphlets, neither of them as yet published. The doctor sent them to me. I can get no one but the doctor to agree with me in my opinion that Burke's "Letter to a Noble Lord"[109] is as contemptible in style as in matter—it is sad stuff.

My dutiful love to your excellent mother, whom, believe me, I think of frequently and with a pang of affection. God bless you. I'll try and venture to scribble a line and a half every time the man goes with "The Watchman" to you.

N. B. The "Essay on Fasting"[110] I am ashamed of; but it is one of my misfortunes that I am obliged to publish extempore as well as compose. God bless you,

and S. T. Coleridge.

LVI. TO THE SAME.

12th May, 1796.

Poole! The Spirit, who counts the throbbings of the solitary heart, knows that what my feelings ought to be, such they are. If it were in my power to give you anything which I have not already given, I should be oppressed by the letter now before me.[111] But no! I feel myself rich in being poor; and because I have nothing to bestow, I know how much I have bestowed. Perhaps I shall not make myself intelligible; but the strong and unmixed affection which I bear to you seems to exclude all emotions of gratitude, and renders even the principle of esteem latent and inert. Its presence is not perceptible, though its absence could not be endured.

Concerning the scheme itself, I am undetermined. Not that I am ashamed to receive—God forbid! I will make every possible exertion; my industry shall be at least commensurate with my learning and talents;—if these do not procure for me and mine the necessary comforts of life, I can receive as I would bestow, and, in either case—receiving or bestowing—be equally grateful to my Almighty Benefactor. I am undetermined, therefore—not because I receive with pain and reluctance, but—because I suspect that you attribute to others your own enthusiasm of benevolence; as if the sun should say, "With how rich a purple those opposite windows are burning!" But with God's permission I shall talk with you on this subject. By the last page of No. X. you will perceive that I have this day dropped "The Watchman." On Monday morning I will go per caravan to Bridgewater, where, if you have a horse of tolerable meekness unemployed, you will let him meet me.

I should blame you for the exaggerated terms in which you have spoken of me in the Proposal, did I not perceive the motive. You wished to make it appear an offering—not a favour—and in excess of delicacy have, I fear, fallen into some grossness of flattery.

God bless you, my dear, very dear Friend. The widow[112] is calm, and amused with her beautiful infant. We are all become more religious than we were. God be ever praised for all things! Mrs. Coleridge begs her kind love to you. To your dear mother my filial respects.

S. T. Coleridge.

LVII. TO JOHN THELWALL.

May 13, 1796.

My dear Thelwall,—You have given me the affection of a brother, and I repay you in kind. Your letters demand my friendship and deserve my esteem; the zeal with which you have attacked my supposed delusions proves that you are deeply interested for me, and interested even to agitation for what you believe to be truth. You deem that I have treated "systems and opinions with the furious prejudices of the conventicle, and the illiberal dogmatism of the cynic;" that I have "layed about me on this side and on that with the sledge hammer of abuse." I have, you think, imitated the "old sect in politics and morals" in their "outrageous violence," and have sunk into the "clownish fierceness of intolerant prejudice." I have "branded" the presumptuous children of scepticism "with vile epithets and hunted them down with abuse." "These be hard words, Citizen! and I will be bold to say they are not to be justified" by the unfortunate page which has occasioned them. The only passage in it which appears offensive (I am not now inquiring concerning the truth or falsehood of this or the remaining passages) is the following: "You have studied Mr. G.'s Essay on Politi[cal] Jus[tice]—but to think filial affection folly, gratitude a crime, marriage injustice, and the promiscuous intercourse of the sexes right and wise, may class you among the despisers of vulgar prejudices, but cannot increase the probability that you are a patriot. But you act up to your principles—so much the worse. Your principles are villainous ones. I would not entrust my wife or sister to you; think you I would entrust my country?" My dear Thelwall! how are these opinions connected with the conventicle more than with the Stoa, the Lyceum, or the grove of Academus? I do not perceive that to attack adultery is more characteristic of Christian prejudices than of the prejudices of the disciples of Aristotle, Zeno, or Socrates. In truth, the offensive sentence, "Your principles are villainous," was suggested by the Peripatetic Sage who divides bad men into two classes. The first he calls "wet or intemperate sinners"—men who are hurried into vice by their appetites, but acknowledge their actions to be vicious; these are reclaimable. The second class he names dry villains—men who are not only vicious but who (the steams from the polluted heart rising up and gathering round the head) have brought themselves and others to believe that vice is virtue. We mean these men when we say men of bad principles—guilt is out of the question. I am a necessarian, and of course deny the possibility of it. However, a letter is not the place for reasoning. In some form or other, or by some channel or other, I shall publish my critique on the New Philosophy, and, I trust, shall demean myself not ungently, and disappoint your auguries.... "But, you cannot be a patriot unless you are a Christian." Yes, Thelwall, the disciples of Lord Shaftesbury and Rousseau as well as of Jesus—but the man who suffers not his hopes to wander beyond the objects of sense will in general be sensual, and I again assert that a sensualist is not likely to be a patriot. Have I tried these opinions by the double test of argument and example? I think so. The first would be too

81

large a field, the second some following sentences of your letter forced me to.... Gerrald[113] you insinuate is an atheist. Was he so, when he offered those solemn prayers to God Almighty at the Scotch conventicle, and was this sincerity? But Dr. Darwin and (I suppose from his actions) Gerrald think sincerity a folly and therefore vicious. Your atheistic brethren square their moral systems exactly according to their inclinations. Gerrald and Dr. Darwin are polite and good-natured men, and willing to attain at good by attainable roads. They deem insincerity a necessary virtue in the present imperfect state of our nature. Godwin, whose very heart is cankered by the love of singularity, and who feels no disinclination to wound by abrupt harshness, pleads for absolute sincerity, because such a system gives him a frequent opportunity of indulging his misanthropy. Poor Williams,[114] the Welsh bard (a very meek man), brought the tear into my eye by a simple narration of the manner in which Godwin insulted him under the pretence of reproof, and Thomas Walker of Manchester told me that his indignation and contempt were never more powerfully excited than by an unfeeling and insolent speech of the said Godwin to the poor Welsh bard. Scott told me some shocking stories of Godwin. His base and anonymous attack on you is enough for me. At that time I had prepared a letter to him, which I was about to have sent to the "Morning Chronicle," and I convinced Dr. Beddoes by passages from the "Tribune" of the calumnious nature of the attack. I was once and only once in company with Godwin. He appeared to me to possess neither the strength of intellect that discovers truth, nor the powers of imagination that decorate falsehood; he talked sophisms in jejune language. I like Holcroft a thousand times better, and think him a man of much greater ability. Fierce, hot, petulant, the very high priest of atheism, he hates God "with all his heart, with all his mind, with all his soul, and with all his strength." Every man not an atheist is only not a fool. "Dr. Priestley? there is a petitesse in his mind. Hartley? pshaw! Godwin, sir, is a thousand times a better metaphysician!" But this intolerance is founded on benevolence. (I had almost forgotten that horrible story about his son.)

....

On the subject of using sugar, etc., I will write you a long and serious letter. This grieves me more than you [imagine]. I hope I shall be able by severe and unadorned reasoning to convince you you are wrong.

Your remarks on my poems are, I think, just in general; there is a rage and affectation of double epithets. "Unshuddered, unaghasted" is, indeed, truly ridiculous. But why so violent against metaphysics in poetry? Is not Akenside's a metaphysical poem? Perhaps you do not like Akenside? Well, but I do, and so do a great many others. Why pass an act of uniformity against poets? I received a letter from a very sensible friend abusing love verses; another blaming the introduction of politics, "as wider from true poetry than the equator from the poles." "Some for each" is my motto. That poetry pleases which interests. My religious poetry interests the religious, who read it with rapture. Why? Because it awakes in them all the associations connected with a love of future existence, etc. A very dear friend of mine,[115] who is, in my opinion, the best poet of the age (I will send you his poem when published), thinks that the lines from 364 to 375 and from 403 to 428 the best in the volume,—indeed, worth all the rest. And this man is a republican, and, at least, a semi-atheist. Why do you object to "shadowy of truth"? It is, I acknowledge, a Grecism, but, I think, an elegant one. Your remarks on the della-crusca place of emphasis are just in part. Where we wish to point out the thing, and the quality is mentioned merely as a decoration, this mode of emphasis is indeed absurd; therefore, I very patiently give up to critical vengeance "high tree," "sore wounds," and "rough rock;" but when you wish to dwell chiefly on the quality rather than the thing, then this mode is proper, and, indeed, is used in common conversation. Who says good man? Therefore, "big soul," "cold earth," "dark womb," and "flamy child" are all right, and introduce a variety into the versification, [which is] an advantage where you can attain it without any sacrifice of sense. As to harmony, it is all association. Milton is harmonious to me, and I absolutely nauseate Darwin's poems.

Yours affectionately,
S. T. Coleridge.

John Thelwall,
Beaufort Buildings, Strand, London.

LVIII. TO THOMAS POOLE.

May 29, 1796.

My dear Poole,—This said caravan does not leave Bridgewater till nine. In the market place stands the hustings. I mounted it, and, pacing the boards, mused on bribery, false swearing, and other foibles of election times. I have wandered, too, by the river Parret, which looks as filthy as if all the parrots of the House of Commons had been washing their consciences therein. Dear gutter of Stowey![116] Were I transported to Italian plains, and lay by the side of the streamlet that murmured through an orange grove, I would think of thee, dear gutter of Stowey, and wish that I were poring on thee!

So much by way of rant. I have eaten three eggs, swallowed sundries of tea and bread and butter, purely for the purpose of amusing myself! I have seen the horse fed. When at Cross, where I shall dine, I shall think of your happy dinner, celebrated under the auspices of humble independence, supported by brotherly love! I am writing, you understand, for no worldly purpose but that of avoiding anxious thoughts. Apropos of honey-pie, Caligula or Elagabalus (I forget which) had a dish of nightingales' tongues served up. What think you of the stings of bees? God bless you! My filial love to your mother, and fraternity to your sister. Tell Ellen Cruikshank that in my next parcel to you I will send my Haleswood poem to her. Heaven protect her and you and Sara and your mother and, like a bad shilling passed off between a handful of guineas,

Your affectionate friend and brother,
S. T. Coleridge.

P. S.—Don't forget to send by Milton [carrier] my old clothes, and linen that once was clean, etcetera. A pretty periphrasis that!

LIX. TO JOHN THELWALL.

Wednesday, June 22, 1796.

Dear Thelwall,—That I have not written you has been an act of self-denial, not indolence. I heard that you were electioneering, and would not be the occasion that any of your thoughts should diverge from that focus.

I wish very much to see you. Have you given up the idea of spending a few weeks or month at Bristol? You might be making way in your review of Burke's life and writings, and give us once or twice a week a lecture, which I doubt not would be crowded. We have a large and every way excellent library, to which I could make you a temporary subscriber, that is, I would get a subscription ticket transferred to you.

You are certainly well calculated for the review you meditate. Your answer to Burke is, I will not say, the best, for that would be no praise; it is certainly the only good one, and it is a very good one. In style and in reflectiveness it is, I think, your chef d'œuvre. Yet the "Peripatetic"[117]—for which accept my thanks—pleased me more because it let me into your heart; the poetry is frequently sweet and possesses the fire of feeling, but not enough (I think) of the light of fancy. I am sorry that you should entertain so degrading an opinion of me as to imagine that I industriously collected anecdotes unfavourable to the characters of great men. No, Thelwall, but I cannot shut my ears, and I have never given a moment's belief to any one of those stories unless when they were related to me at different times by professed democrats. My vice is of the opposite class, a precipitance in praise; witness my panegyric on Gerrald and that black gentleman Margarot in the "Conciones," and my foolish verses to Godwin in the "Morning Chronicle."[118] At the same time, Thelwall, do not suppose that I admit your palliations. Doubtless I could fill a book with slanderous stories of professed Christians, but those very men would allow they were acting contrary to Christianity; but, I am afraid, an atheistic bad man manufactures his system of principles with an eye to his peculiar propensities, and makes his actions the criterion of what is virtuous, not virtue the criterion of his actions. Where the disposition is not amiable, an acute understanding I deem no blessing. To the last sentence in your letter I subscribe fully and with all my inmost affections. "He who thinks and feels will be virtuous; and he who is absorbed in self will be vicious, whatever maybe his speculative opinions." Believe me, Thelwall, it is not his atheism that has prejudiced me against Godwin, but Godwin who has, perhaps, prejudiced me against atheism. Let me see you—I already know a deist, and Calvinists, and Moravians whom I love and reverence—and I shall leap forwards to realise my principles by feeling love and honour for an atheist. By the bye, are you an atheist? For I was told that Hutton was an atheist, and procured his three massy quartos on the principle of knowledge in the hopes of finding some arguments in favor of atheism, but lo! I discovered him to be a profoundly pious deist,—"independent of fortune, satisfied with himself, pleased with his species, confident in his Creator."

God bless you, my dear Thelwall! Believe me with high esteem and anticipated tenderness,

Yours sincerely,
S. T. Coleridge.

P. S. We have a hundred lovely scenes about Bristol, which would make you exclaim, O admirable Nature! and me, O Gracious God!

LX. TO THOMAS POOLE.

Saturday, September 24, 1796.

My dear, very dear Poole,—The heart thoroughly penetrated with the flame of virtuous friendship is in a state of glory; but lest it should be exalted above measure there is given it a thorn in the flesh. I mean that when the friendship of any person forms an essential part of a man's happiness, he will at times be pestered by the little jealousies and solicitudes of imbecile humanity. Since we last parted I have been gloomily dreaming that you did not leave me so affectionately as you were wont to do. Pardon this littleness of heart, and do not think the worse of me for it. Indeed, my soul seems so mantled and wrapped around by your love and esteem, that even a dream of losing but the smallest fragment of it makes me shiver, as though some tender part of my nature were left uncovered in nakedness.

Last week I received a letter from Lloyd, informing me that his parents had given their joyful concurrence to his residence with me; but that, if it were possible that I could be absent for three or four days, his father wished particularly to see me. I consulted Mrs. Coleridge, who advised me to go.... Accordingly on Saturday night I went by the mail to Birmingham and was introduced to the father, who is a mild man, very liberal in his ideas, and in religion an allegorizing Quaker. I mean that all the apparently irrational path of his sect he allegorizes into significations, which for the most part you or I might assent to. We became well acquainted, and he expressed himself "thankful to heaven that his son was about to be with me." He said he would write to me concerning money matters after his son had been some time under my roof.

On Tuesday morning I was surprised by a letter from Mr. Maurice, our medical attendant, informing me that Mrs. Coleridge was delivered on Monday, September 19, 1796, half past two in the morning, of a SON, and that both she and the child were uncommonly well. I was quite annihilated with the suddenness of the information, and retired to my own room to address myself to my Maker, but I could only offer up to Him the silence of stupefied feelings. I hastened home, and Charles Lloyd returned with me. When I first saw the child,[119] I did not feel that thrill and overflowing of affection which I expected. I looked on it with a melancholy gaze; my mind was intensely contemplative and my heart only sad. But when two hours after I saw it at the bosom of its mother, on her arm, and her eye tearful and watching its little features, then I was thrilled and melted, and gave it the kiss of a father.... The baby seems strong, and the old nurse has over-persuaded my wife to discover a likeness of me in its face—no great compliment to me, for, in truth, I have seen handsomer babies in my lifetime. Its name is David Hartley Coleridge. I hope that ere he be a man, if God destines him for continuance in this life, his head will be convinced of, and his heart saturated with, the truths so ably supported by that great master of Christian Philosophy.

Charles Lloyd wins upon me hourly; his heart is uncommonly pure, his affection delicate, and his benevolence enlivened but not sicklied by sensibility. He is assuredly a man of great genius; but it must be in tête-à-tête with one whom he loves and esteems that his colloquial powers open; and this arises not from reserve or want of simplicity, but from having been placed in situations where for years together he met with no congenial minds, and where the contrariety of his thoughts and notions to the thoughts and notions of those around him induced the necessity of habitually suppressing his feelings. His joy and gratitude to Heaven for the circumstance of his domestication with me I can scarcely describe to you; and I believe that his fixed plans are of being always with me. His father told me that if he saw that his son had formed habits of severe economy he should not insist upon his adopting any profession; as then his fair share of his (the father's) wealth would be sufficient for him.

My dearest Poole, can you conveniently receive us in the course of a week? We can both sleep in one bed, which we do now. And I have much, very much to say to you and consult with you about, for my heart is heavy respecting Derby,[120] and my feelings are so dim and huddled that though I can, I am sure, communicate them to you by my looks and broken sentences, I scarce know how to convey them in a letter. And Charles Lloyd wishes much to know you personally. I shall write on the other side of the paper two of Charles Lloyd's sonnets, which he wrote in one evening at Birmingham. The latter of them alludes to the conviction of the truth of Christianity, which he had received from me, for he had been, if not a deist, yet quite a sceptic.

Let me hear from you by post immediately; and give my kind love to that young man with the soul-beaming face,[121] which I recollect much better than I do his name.

God bless you, my dear friend.

Believe me, with deep affection, your
S. T. Coleridge.

LXI. TO CHARLES LAMB.[122]

[September 28, 1796.]

Your letter, my friend, struck me with a mighty horror. It rushed upon me and stupefied my feelings. You bid me write you a religious letter. I am not a man who would attempt to insult the greatness of your anguish by any other consolation. Heaven knows that in the easiest fortunes there is much dissatisfaction and weariness of spirit; much that calls for the exercise of patience and resignation; but in storms like these, that shake the dwelling and make the heart tremble, there is no middle way between despair and the yielding up of the whole spirit unto the guidance of faith. And surely it is a matter of joy that your faith in Jesus has been preserved; the Comforter that should relieve you is not far from you. But as you are a Christian, in the name of that Saviour, who was filled with bitterness and made drunken with wormwood, I conjure you to have recourse in frequent prayer to "his God and your God;" the God of mercies, and father of all comfort. Your poor father is, I hope, almost senseless of the calamity; the unconscious instrument of Divine Providence knows it not, and your mother is in heaven. It is sweet to be roused from a frightful dream by the song of birds and the gladsome rays of the morning. Ah, how infinitely more sweet to be awakened from the blackness and amazement of a sudden horror by the glories of God manifest and the hallelujahs of angels.

As to what regards yourself, I approve altogether of your abandoning what you justly call vanities. I look upon you as a man called by sorrow and anguish and a strange desolation of hopes into quietness, and a soul set apart and made peculiar to God! We cannot arrive at any portion of heavenly bliss without in some measure imitating Christ; and they arrive at the largest inheritance who imitate the most difficult parts of his character, and, bowed down and crushed underfoot, cry in fulness of faith, "Father, thy will be done."

I wish above measure to have you for a little while here; no visitants shall blow on the nakedness of your feelings; you shall be quiet, and your spirit may be healed. I see no possible objection, unless your father's helplessness prevent you, and unless you are necessary to him. If this be not the case, I charge you write me that you will come.

I charge you, my dearest friend, not to dare to encourage gloom or despair. You are a temporary sharer in human miseries that you may be an eternal partaker of the Divine nature. I charge you, if by any means it be possible, come to me.

I remain your affectionate
S. T. Coleridge.

LXII. TO THOMAS POOLE.

Saturday night, November 5, 1796.

Thanks, my heart's warm thanks to you, my beloved friend, for your tender letter! Indeed, I did not deserve so kind a one; but by this time you have received my last.

To live in a beautiful country, and to enure myself as much as possible to the labour of the field, have been for this year past my dream of the day, my sigh at midnight. But to enjoy these blessings near you, to see you daily, to tell you all my thoughts in their first birth, and to hear yours, to be mingling identities with you as it were,—the vision-wearing fancy has indeed often pictured such things, but hope never dared whisper a promise. Disappointment! Disappointment! dash not from my trembling hand the bowl which almost touches my lips. Envy me not this immortal draught, and I will forgive thee all thy persecutions. Forgive thee! Impious! I will bless thee, black-vested minister of optimism, stern pioneer of happiness! Thou hast been "the cloud" before me from the day that I left the flesh-pots of Egypt, and was led through the way of a wilderness—the cloud that hast been guiding me to a land flowing with milk and honey—the milk of innocence, the honey of friendship!

I wanted such a letter as yours, for I am very unwell. On Wednesday night I was seized with an intolerable pain from my right temple to the tip of my right shoulder, including my right eye, cheek, jaw, and that side of the throat. I was nearly frantic, and ran about the house naked, endeavouring by every means to excite sensations in different parts of my body, and so to weaken the enemy by creating division. It continued from one in the morning till half past five, and left me pale and fainting. It came on fitfully, but not so violently, several times on Thursday, and began severer threats towards night; but I took between sixty and seventy drops of laudanum,[123] and sopped the Cerberus, just as his mouth began to open. On Friday it only niggled, as if the chief had departed from a conquered place, and merely left a small garrison behind, or as if he had evacuated the Corsica,[124] and a few straggling pains only remained. But this morning he returned in full force, and his name is Legion. Giant-fiend of a hundred hands, with a shower of arrowy death-pangs he transpierced me, and then he became a wolf, and lay a-gnawing at my bones! I am not mad, most noble Festus, but in sober sadness I have suffered this day more bodily pain than I had before a conception of. My right cheek has certainly been placed with admirable exactness under the focus of some invisible burning-glass, which concentrated all the rays of a Tartarean sun. My medical attendant decides it to be altogether nervous, and that it originates either in severe application, or excessive anxiety. My beloved Poole! in excessive anxiety, I believe it might originate. I have a blister under my right ear, and I take twenty-five drops of laudanum every five hours, the ease and spirits gained by which have enabled me to write you this flighty but not exaggerated account. With a gloomy wantonness of imagination I had been coquetting with the hideous possibles of disappointment. I drank fears like wormwood, yea, made myself drunken with bitterness; for my ever-shaping and distrustful mind still mingled gall-drops, till out of the cup of hope I almost poisoned myself with despair.

Your letter is dated November 2d; I wrote to you November 1st. Your sister was married on that day; and on that day several times I felt my heart overflowed with such tenderness for her as made me repeatedly ejaculate prayers in her behalf. Such things are strange. It may be superstitious to think about such correspondences; but it is a superstition which softens the heart and leads to no evil. We will call on your dear sister as soon as I am quite well, and in the mean time I will write a few lines to her.

I am anxious beyond measure to be in the country as soon as possible. I would it were possible to get a temporary residence till Adscombe is ready for us. I would that it could be that we could have three rooms in Bill Poole's large house for the winter. Will you try to look out for a fit servant for us—simple of heart, physiognomically handsome, and scientific in vaccimulgence? That last word is a new one, but soft in sound and full of expression. Vaccimulgence! I am pleased with the word. Write to me all things about yourself. Where I cannot advise I can condole and communicate, which doubles joy, halves sorrow.

Tell me whether you think it at all possible to make any terms with William Poole. You know I would not wish to touch with the edge of the nail of my great toe the line which should be but half a barley-corn out of the niche of the most trembling delicacy. I will write Cruikshank to-morrow, if God permit me.

God bless and protect you, friend, brother, beloved!

S. T. Coleridge.

Sara's best love, and Lloyd's. David Hartley is well, saving that he is sometimes inspired by the god Æolus, and like Isaiah, "his bowels sound like an harp." My filial love to your dear mother. Love to Ward. Little Tommy, I often think of thee.

LXIII. TO THE SAME.

Monday night, November 7, 1796.

My dearest Poole,—I wrote you on Saturday night under the immediate inspiration of laudanum, and wrote you a flighty letter, but yet one most accurately descriptive both of facts and feelings. Since then my pains have been lessening, and the greater part of this day I have enjoyed perfect ease, only I am totally inappetent of food, and languid, even to an inward perishing.

I wrote John Cruikshank this morning, and this moment I have received a letter from him. My letter written before the receipt of his contains everything I would write in answer to it, and I do not like to write to him superfluously, lest I should break in on his domestic terrors and solitary broodings with regard to Anna Cruikshank.[125] May the Father and lover of the meek preserve that meek woman, and give her a safe and joyful deliverance!

I wrote this morning a short note of congratulatory kindness to your sister, and shall be eager to call on her, when Legion has been thoroughly exorcised from my temple and cheeks. Tell Cruikshank that I have received his letter, and thank him for it.

A few lines in your last letter betokened, I thought, a wounded spirit. Let me know the particulars, my beloved friend. I shall forget and lose my own anxieties while I am healing yours with cheerings of sympathy.

I met with the following sonnet in some very dull poems, among which it shone like a solitary star when the night is dark, and one little space of blue uninvaded by the floating blackness, or, if a terrestrial simile be required, like a red carbuncle on a negro's nose. From the languor and exhaustion to which pain and my frequent doses of laudanum have reduced me, it suited the feeble temper of [my] mind, and I have transcribed it on the other page. I amused myself the other day (having some paper at the printer's which I could employ no other way) in selecting twenty-eight sonnets,[126] to bind up with Bowles's. I charge sixpence for them, and have sent you five to dispose of. I have only printed two hundred, as my paper held out to no more; and dispose of them privately, just enough to pay the printing. The essay which I have written at the beginning I like.... I have likewise sent you Burke's pamphlet which was given to me; it has all his excellences without any of his faults. This parcel I send to-morrow morning, enclosed in a parcel to Bill Poole of Thurston.

God love you, my affectionate brother, and your affectionate

S. T. Coleridge.

SONNET.

With passive joy the moment I survey
When welcome Death shall set my spirit free.
My soul! the prospect brings no fear to thee,
But soothing Fancy rises to pourtray
The dear and parting words my Friends will say:
With secret Pride their heaving Breast I see,
And count the sorrows that will flow for me.
And now I hear my lingering knell decay
And mark the Hearse! Methinks, with moisten'd eye,
Clara beholds the sad Procession move
That bears me to the Resting-place of Care,
And sighs, "Poor youth! thy Bosom well could love,
And well thy Numbers picture Love's despair."
Vain Dreams! yet such as make it sweet to die.

LXIV. TO JOHN THELWALL.

Saturday, November 19, [1796].
Oxford Street, Bristol.

My dear Thelwall,—Ah me! literary adventure is but bread and cheese by chance. I keenly sympathise with you. Sympathy, the only poor consolation I can offer you. Can no plan be suggested?... Of course you have read the "Joan of Arc."[127] Homer is the poet for the warrior, Milton for the religionist, Tasso for women, Robert Southey for the patriot. The first and fourth books of the "Joan of Arc" are to me more interesting than the same number of lines in any poem whatever. But you and I, my dear Thelwall, hold different creeds in poetry as well as religion. N'importe! By the bye, of your works I have now all, except your "Essay on Animal Vitality" which I never had, and your Poems, which I bought on their first publication, and lost them. From these poems I should have supposed our poetical tastes more nearly alike than, I find, they are. The poem on the Sols [?] flashes genius through Strophe I, Antistrophe I, and Epode I. The rest I do not perhaps understand, only I love these two lines:—

"Yet sure the verse that shews the friendly mind
To Friendship's ear not harshly flows."
Your larger narrative affected me greatly. It is admirably written, and displays strong sense animated by feeling, and illumined by imagination, and neither in the thoughts nor rhythm does it encroach on poetry.

There have been two poems of mine in the new "Monthly Magazine,"[128] with my name; indeed, I make it a scruple of conscience never to publish anything, however trifling, without it. Did you like them? The first was written at the desire of a beautiful little aristocrat; consider it therefore as a lady's poem. Bowles (the bard of my idolatry) has written a poem lately without plan or meaning, but the component parts are divine. It is entitled "Hope, an Allegorical Sketch." I will copy two of the stanzas, which must be peculiarly interesting to you, virtuous high-treasonist, and your friends the democrats.

"But see, as one awaked from deadly trance,
With hollow and dim eyes, and stony stare,
Captivity with faltering step advance!
Dripping and knotted was her coal-black hair:
For she had long been hid, as in the grave;
No sounds the silence of her prison broke,
Nor one companion had she in her cave
Save Terror's dismal shape, that no word spoke,
But to a stony coffin on the floor
With lean and hideous finger pointed evermore.

"The lark's shrill song, the early village chime,
The upland echo of the winding horn,
The far-heard clock that spoke the passing time,
Had never pierced her solitude forlorn:
At length released from the deep dungeon's gloom
She feels the fragrance of the vernal gale,
She sees more sweet the living landscape bloom,
And while she listens to Hope's tender tale,
She thinks her long-lost friends shall bless her sight,
And almost faints for joy amidst the broad daylight."
The last line is exquisite.

Your portrait of yourself interested me. As to me, my face, unless when animated by immediate eloquence, expresses great sloth, and great, indeed, almost idiotic good-nature. 'Tis a mere carcass of a face;[129] fat, flabby, and expressive chiefly of inexpression. Yet I am told that my eyes, eyebrows, and forehead are physiognomically good; but of this the deponent knoweth not. As to my shape, 'tis a good shape enough if measured, but my gait is awkward, and the walk of the whole man indicates indolence capable of energies. I am, and ever have been, a great reader, and have read almost everything—a library cormorant. I am deep in all out of the way books, whether of the monkish times, or of the puritanical era. I have read and digested most of the historical writers; but I do not like history. Metaphysics and poetry and "facts of mind," that is, accounts of all the strange phantasms that ever possessed "your philosophy;" dreamers, from Thoth the Egyptian to Taylor the English pagan, are my darling studies. In short, I seldom read except to amuse myself, and I am almost always reading. Of useful knowledge, I am a so-so chemist, and I love chemistry. All else is blank; but I will be (please God) an horticulturalist and a farmer. I compose very little, and I absolutely hate composition, and such is my dislike that even a sense of duty is sometimes too weak to overpower it.

I cannot breathe through my nose, so my mouth, with sensual thick lips, is almost always open. In conversation I am impassioned, and oppose what I deem error with an eagerness which is often mistaken for personal asperity; but I am ever so swallowed up in the thing that I perfectly forget my opponent. Such am I. I am just going to read Dupuis' twelve octavos,[130] which I have got from London. I shall read only one octavo a week, for I cannot speak French at all and I read it slowly.

My wife is well and desires to be remembered to you and your Stella and little ones. N. B. Stella (among the Romans) was a man's name. All the classics are against you; but our Swift, I suppose, is authority for this unsexing.

Write on the receipt of this, and believe me as ever, with affectionate esteem,

Your sincere friend,
S. T. Coleridge.

P. S. I have enclosed a five-guinea note. The five shillings over please to lay out for me thus. In White's (of Fleet Street or the Strand, I forget which—O! the Strand I believe, but I don't know which), well, in White's catalogue are the following books:—

4674. Iamblichus,[131] Proclus, Porphyrius, etc., one shilling and sixpence, one little volume.

4686. Juliani Opera, three shillings: which two books you will be so kind as to purchase for me, and send down with the twenty-five pamphlets. But if they should unfortunately be sold, in the same catalogue are:—

2109. Juliani Opera, 12s. 6d.

676. Iamblichus de Mysteriis, 10s. 6d.

2681. Sidonius Apollinaris, 6s.

And in the catalogue of Robson, the bookseller in New Bond Street, Plotini Opera, a Ficino, £1.1.0, making altogether £2.10.0.

If you can get the two former little books, costing only four and sixpence, I will rest content with them; if they are gone, be so kind as to purchase for me the others I mentioned to you, amounting to two pounds, ten shillings; and, as in the course of next week I shall send a small parcel of books and manuscripts to my very dear Charles Lamb of the India House, I shall be enabled to convey the money to you in a letter, which he will leave at your house. I make no apology for this commission, because I feel (to use a vulgar phrase) that I would do as much for you. P. P. S. Can you buy them time enough to send down with your pamphlets? If not, make a parcel per se. I hope your hurts from the fall are not serious; you have given a proof now that you are no Ippokrite, but I forgot that you are not a Greekist, and perchance you hate puns; but, in Greek, Krites signifies a judge and hippos a horse. Hippocrite, therefore, may mean a judge of horses. My dear fellow, I laugh more and talk more nonsense in a week than [most] other people do in a year. Farewell.

John Thelwall,
Beaufort Buildings, Strand, London.

LXV. TO THOMAS POOLE.[132]

Sunday morning, December 11, 1796.

My beloved Poole,—The sight of your villainous hand-scrawl was a great comfort to me. How have you been diverted in London? What of the theatres? And how found you your old friends? I dined with Mr. King yesterday week. He is quantum suff: a pleasant man, and (my wife says) very handsome. Hymen lies in the arms of Hygeia, if one may judge by your sister; she looks remarkably well! But has she not caught some complaint in the head? Some scurfy disorder? For her hair was filled with an odious white Dandruff. ("N. B. Nothing but powder," Mrs. King.) About myself, I have so much to say that I really can say nothing. I mean to work very hard—as Cook, Butler, Scullion, Shoe-cleaner, occasional Nurse, Gardener, Hind, Pig-protector, Chaplain, Secretary, Poet, Reviewer, and omnium-botherum shilling-Scavenger. In other words, I shall keep no servant, and will cultivate my land-acre and my wise-acres, as well as I can. The motives which led to this determination are numerous and weighty; I have thought much and calmly, and calculated time and money with unexceptionable accuracy; and at length determined not to take the charge of Charles Lloyd's mind on me. Poor fellow! he still hopes to live with me—is now at Birmingham. I wish that little cottage by the roadside were gettable? That with about two or three rooms—it would quite do for us, as we shall occupy only two rooms. I will write more fully on the receipt of yours. God love you and

S. T. Coleridge.

LXVI. TO THE SAME.

December 12, 1796.

You tell me, my dear Poole, that my residence near you would give you great pleasure, and I am sure that if you had any objections on your own account to my settling near Stowey you would have mentioned them to me. Relying on this, I assure you that a disappointment would try my philosophy. Your letter did indeed give me unexpected and most acute pain. I will make the cottage do. We want but three rooms. If Cruikshank have promised more than his circumstances enable him to perform, I am sure that I can get the other purchased by my friends in Bristol. I mean, the place at Adscombe. I wrote him pressingly on this head some ten days ago; but he has returned me no answer. Lloyd has obtained his father's permission and will return to me. He is willing to be his own servant. As to Acton, 'tis out of the question. In Bristol I have Cottle and Estlin (for Mr. Wade is going away) willing and eager to serve me; but how they can serve me more effectually at Acton than at Stowey, I cannot divine. If I live at Stowey, you indeed can serve me effectually, by assisting me in the acquirement of agricultural practice. If you can instruct me to manage an acre and a half of land, and to raise in it, with my own hands, all kinds of vegetables and grain, enough for myself and my wife and sufficient to feed a pig or two with the refuse, I hope that you will have served me most effectually by placing me out of the necessity of being served. I receive about forty guineas yearly from the "Critical Review" and the new "Monthly Magazine." It is hard if by my greater works I do not get twenty more. I know how little the human mind requires when it is tranquil, and in proportion as I should find it difficult to simplify my wants it becomes my duty to simplify them. For there must be a vice in my nature, which woe be to me if I do not cure. The less meat I eat the more healthy I am; and strong liquors of any kind always and perceptibly injure me. Sixteen shillings would cover all the weekly expenses of my wife, infant, and myself. This I say from my wife's own calculation.

But whence this sudden revolution in your opinions, my dear Poole? You saw the cottage that was to be our temporary residence, and thought we might be happy in it, and now you hurry to tell me that we shall not even be comfortable in it. You tell me I shall be "too far from my friends," that is, Cottle and Estlin, for I have no other in Bristol. In the name of Heaven, what can Cottle or Estlin [do] for me? They do nothing who do not teach me how to be independent of any except the Almighty Dispenser of sickness and health. And "too far from the press." With the printing of the review and the magazine I have no concern; and, if I publish any work on my own account, I will send a fair and faultless copy, and Cottle promises to correct the press for me. Mr. King's family may be very worthy sort of people, for aught I know; but assuredly I can employ my time wiselier than to gabble with my tongue to beings with whom neither my head nor heart can commune. My habits and feelings have suffered a total alteration. I hate company except of my dearest friends, and systematically avoid it; and when in it keep silence as far as social humanity will permit me. Lloyd's father, in a letter to me yesterday, enquired how I should live without any companions. I answered him not an hour before I received your letter:—

"I shall have six companions: My Sara, my babe, my own shaping and disquisitive mind, my books, my beloved friend Thomas Poole, and lastly, Nature looking at me with a thousand looks of beauty, and speaking to me in a thousand melodies of love. If I were capable of being tired with all these, I should then detect a vice in my nature, and would fly to habitual solitude to eradicate it."

Yes, my friend, while I opened your letter my heart was glowing with enthusiasm towards you. How little did I expect that I should find you earnestly and vehemently persuading me to prefer Acton to Stowey, and in return for the loss of your society recommending Mr. King's family as "very pleasant neighbours." Neighbours! Can mere juxtaposition form a neighbourhood? As well should the louse in my head call himself my friend, and the flea in my bosom style herself my love!

On Wednesday week we must leave our house, so that if you continue to dissuade me from settling near Stowey I scarcely know what I shall do. Surely, my beloved friend, there must be some reason which you have not yet told me, which urged you to send this hasty and heart-chilling letter. I suspect that something has passed between your sister and dear mother (in whose illness I sincerely sympathise with you).

I have never considered my settlement at Stowey in any other relation than its advantages to myself, and they would be great indeed. My objects (assuredly wise ones) were to learn agriculture (and where should I get instructed except at Stowey?) and to be where I can communicate in a literary way. I must conclude. I pray you let me hear from you immediately. God bless you and

S. T. Coleridge.

LXVII. TO THE SAME.

Monday night.

I wrote the former letter immediately on receipt of yours, in the first flutter of agitation. The tumult of my spirits has now subsided, but the Damp struck into my very heart; and there I feel it. O my God! my God! where am I to find rest? Disappointment follows disappointment, and Hope seems given me merely to prevent my becoming callous to Misery. Now I know not where to turn myself. I was on my way to the City Library, and wrote an answer to it there. Since I have returned I have been poring into a book, as a shew for not looking at my wife and the baby. By God, I dare not look at them. Acton! The very name makes me grind my teeth! What am I to do there?

"You will have a good garden; you may, I doubt not, have ground." But am I not ignorant as a child of everything that concerns the garden and the ground? and shall I have one human being there who will instruct me? The House too—what should I do with it? We want but two rooms, or three at the furthest. And the country around is intolerably flat. I would as soon live on the banks of a Dutch canal! And no one human being near me for whom I should, or could, care a rush! No one walk where the beauties of nature might endear solitude to me! There is one Ghost that I am afraid of; with that I should be perpetually haunted in this same cursed Acton—the hideous Ghost of departed Hope. O Poole! how could you make such a proposal to me? I have compelled myself to reperuse your letter, if by any means I may be able to penetrate into your motives. I find three reasons assigned for my not settling at Stowey. The first, the distance from my friends and the Press. This I answered in the former letter. As to my friends, what can they do for me? And as to the Press, even if Cottle had not promised to correct it for me, yet I might as well be fifty miles from it as twelve, for any purpose of correcting. Secondly, the expense of moving. Well, but I must move to Acton, and what will the difference be? Perhaps three guineas.... I would give three guineas that you had not assigned this reason. Thirdly, the wretchedness of that cottage, which alone we can get. But surely, in the house which I saw, two rooms may be found, which, by a little green list and a carpet, and a slight alteration in the fireplace, may be made to exclude the cold: and this is all we want. Besides, it will be but for a while. If Cruikshank cannot buy and repair Adscombe, I have no doubt that my friends here and at Birmingham would, some of them, purchase it. So much for the reasons: but these cannot be the real reasons. I was with you for a week, and then we talked over the whole scheme, and you approved of it, and I gave up Derby. More than nine weeks have elapsed since then, and you saw and examined the cottage, and you knew every other of these reasons, if reasons they can be called. Surely, surely, my friend, something has occurred which you have not mentioned to me. Your mother has manifested a strong dislike to our living near you—or something or other; for the reasons you have assigned tell me nothing except that there are reasons which you have not assigned.

Pardon, if I write vehemently. I meant to have written calmly; but bitterness of soul came upon me. Mrs. Coleridge has observed the workings of my face while I have been writing, and is entreating to know what is the matter. I dread to show her your letter. I dread it. My God! my God! What if she should dare to think that my most beloved friend has grown cold towards me!

Tuesday morning, 11 o'clock.—After an unquiet and almost sleepless night, I resume my pen. As the sentiments over leaf came into my heart, I will not suppress them. I would keep a letter by me which I wrote to a mere acquaintance, lest anything unwise should be found in it; but my friend ought to know not only what my sentiments are, but what my feelings were.

I am, indeed, perplexed and cast down. My first plan, you know, was this—My family was to have consisted of Charles Lloyd, my wife and wife's mother, my infant, the servant, and myself.

My means of maintaining them—Eighty pounds a year from Charles Lloyd, and forty from the Review and Magazine. My time was to have been divided into four parts: 1. Three hours after breakfast to studies with C. L. 2. The remaining hours till dinner to our garden. 3. From after dinner till tea, to letter-writing and domestic quietness. 4. From tea till prayer-time to the reviews, magazines, and other literary labours.

In this plan I calculated nothing on my garden but amusement. In the mean time I heard from Birmingham that Lloyd's father had declared that he should insist on his son's returning to him at the close of a twelvemonth. What am I to do then? I shall be again afloat on the wide sea, unpiloted and unprovisioned. I determined to devote my whole day to the acquirement of practical horticulture, to part with Lloyd immediately, and live without a servant. Lloyd intreated me to give up the Review and Magazine, and devote the evenings to him, but this would be to give up a permanent for a temporary situation, and after subtracting £40 from C. Ll.'s £80 in return for the Review business, and then calculating the expense of a servant, a less severe mode of general living, and Lloyd's own board and lodging, the remaining £40 would make but a poor figure. And what was I to do at the end of a twelvemonth? In the mean time Mrs. Fricker's son could not be got out as an apprentice—he was too young, and premiumless, and no one would take him; and the old lady herself manifested a great aversion to leaving Bristol. I recurred therefore to my first promise of allowing her £20 a year; but all her furniture must of course be returned, and enough only remains to furnish one bedroom and a kitchen-parlour.

If Charles Lloyd and the servant went with me I must have bought new furniture to the amount of £40 or £50, which, if not Impossibility in person, was Impossibility's first cousin. We determined to live by ourselves. We arranged our time, money, and employments. We found it not only practicable but easy; and Mrs. Coleridge entered with enthusiasm into the scheme.

To Mrs. Coleridge the nursing and sewing only would have belonged; the rest I took upon myself, and since our resolution have been learning the practice. With only two rooms and two people—their wants severely simple—no great labour can there be in their waiting upon themselves. Our washing we should put out. I should have devoted my whole head, heart, and body to my acre and a half of garden land, and my evenings to literature. Mr. and Mrs. Estlin approved, admired, and applauded the scheme, and thought it not only highly virtuous, but highly prudent. In the course of a year and a half, I doubt not that I should feel myself independent, for my bodily strength would have increased, and I should have been weaned from animal food, so as never to touch it but once a week; and there can be no shadow of a doubt that an acre and a half of land, divided properly, and managed properly, would maintain a small family in everything but clothes and rent. What had I to ask of my friends? Not money; for a temporary relief of my want is nothing, removes no gnawing of anxiety, and debases the dignity of man. Not their interest. What could their interest (supposing they had any) do for me? I can accept no place in state, church, or dissenting meeting. Nothing remains possible but a school, or writer to a newspaper, or my present plan. I could not love the man who advised me to keep a school, or write for a newspaper. He must have a hard heart. What then could I ask of my friends? What of Mr. Wade? Nothing. What of Mr. Cottle? Nothing.... What of Thomas Poole? O! a great deal. Instruction, daily advice, society—everything necessary to my feelings and the realization of my innocent independence. You know it would be impossible for me to learn everything myself. To pass across my garden once or twice a day, for five minutes, to set me right, and cheer me with the sight of a friend's face, would be more to me than hundreds. Your letter was not a kind one. One week only and I must leave my house, and yet in one week you advise me to alter the plan which I had been three months framing, and in which you must have known by the letters I wrote you, during my illness, that I was interested even to an excess and violence of Hope. And to abandon this plan for darkness and a renewal of anxieties which might be fatal to me! Not one word have you mentioned how I am to live, or even exist, supposing I were to go to Acton. Surely, surely, you do not advise me to lean with the whole weight of my necessities on the Press? Ghosts indeed! I should be haunted with ghosts enough—the ghosts of Otway and Chatterton, and the phantasms of a wife broken-hearted, and a hunger-bitten baby! O Thomas Poole! Thomas Poole! if you did but know what a Father and a Husband must feel who toils with his brain for uncertain bread! I dare not think of it. The evil face of Frenzy looks at me. The husbandman puts his seed in the ground, and the goodness, power, and wisdom of God have pledged themselves that he shall have bread, and health, and quietness in return for industry, and simplicity of wants and innocence. The author scatters his seed—with aching head, and wasted health, and all the heart-leapings of anxiety; and the follies, the vices, and the fickleness of man promise him printers' bills and the Debtors' Side of Newgate as full and sufficient payment.

Charles Lloyd is at Birmingham. I hear from him daily. In his yesterday's letter he says: "My dearest friend, everything seems clearing around me. My friends enter fully into my views. They seem altogether to have abandoned any ambitious views on my account. My health has been very good since I left you; and I own I look forward with more pleasure than ever to a permanent connection with you. Hitherto I could only look forward to the pleasures of a year. All beyond was dark and uncertain. My father now completely acquiesces in my abandoning the prospect of any profession or trade. If God grant me health, there now remains no obstacle to a completion of my most sanguine wishes." Charles Lloyd will furnish his own room, and feels it his duty to be in all things his own servant. He will put up a press-bed, so that one room will be his bedchamber and parlour; and I shall settle with him the hours and seasons of our being together, and the hours and seasons of our being apart. But I shall rely on him for nothing except his own maintenance.

As to the poems, they are Cottle's property, not mine. There is no obstacle from me—no new poems intended to be put in the volume, except the "Visions of the Maid of Orleans."... But literature, though I shall never abandon it, will always be a secondary object with me. My poetic vanity and my political furor have been exhaled; and I would rather be an expert, self-maintaining gardener than a Milton, if I could not unite both.

My friend, wherein I have written impetuously, pardon me! and consider what I have suffered, and still am suffering, in consequence of your letter....

Finally, my Friend! if your opinion of me and your attachment to me remain unaltered, and if you have assigned the true reasons which urged you to dissuade me from a settlement at Stowey, and if indeed (provided such settlement were consistent with my good and happiness), it would give you unmixed pleasure, I adhere to Stowey, and consider the time from last evening as a distempered dream. But if any circumstances have occurred that have lessened your love or esteem or confidence; or if there be objections to my settling in Stowey on your own account, or any other objections than what you have urged, I doubt not you will declare them openly and unreservedly to me, in your answer to this, which I shall expect with a total incapability of doing or thinking of anything, till I have received it. Indeed, indeed, I am very miserable. God bless you and your affectionate

S. T. Coleridge.

Tuesday, December 13, 1796.

LXVIII. TO JOHN THELWALL.

December 17, 1796.

My dear Thelwall,—I should have written you long ere this, had not the settlement of my affairs previous to my leaving Bristol and the organization of my new plan occupied me with bulky anxieties that almost excluded everything but self from my thoughts. And, besides, my health has been very bad, and remains so. A nervous affection from my right temple to the extremity of my right shoulder almost distracted me, and made the frequent use of laudanum absolutely necessary. And, since I have subdued this, a rheumatic complaint in the back of my head and shoulders, accompanied with sore throat and depression of the animal spirits, has convinced me that a man may change bad lodgers without bettering himself. I write these things, not so much to apologise for my silence, or for the pleasure of complaining, as that you may know the reason why I have not given you a "strict account" how I have disposed of your books. This I will shortly do, with all the veracity which that solemn incantation, "upon your honour," must necessarily have conjured up.

Your second and third part promise great things. I have counted the subjects, and by a nice calculation find that eighteen Scotch doctors would write fifty-four quarto volumes, each choosing his thesis out of your syllabus. May you do good by them, and moreover enable yourself to do more good, I should say, to continue to do good. My farm will be a garden of one acre and a half, in which I mean to raise vegetables and corn enough for myself and wife, and feed a couple of snouted and grunting cousins from the refuse. My evenings I shall devote to literature; and, by reviews, the magazine, and the other shilling-scavenger employments, shall probably gain forty pounds a year; which economy and self-denial, gold-beaters, shall hammer till it cover my annual expenses. Now, in favour of this scheme, I shall say nothing, for the more vehement my ratiocinations were, previous to the experiment, the more ridiculous my failure would appear; and if the scheme deserve the said ratiocinations I shall live down all your objections. I doubt not that the time will come when all our utilities will be directed in one simple path. That time, however, is not come; and imperious circumstances point out to each one his particular road. Much good may be done in all. I am not fit for public life; yet the light shall stream to a far distance from my cottage window. Meantime, do you uplift the torch dreadlessly, and show to mankind the face of that idol which they have worshipped in darkness! And now, my dear fellow, for a little sparring about poetry. My first sonnet[133] is obscure; but you ought to distinguish between obscurity residing in the uncommonness of the thought, and that which proceeds from thoughts unconnected and language not adapted to the expression of them. Where you do find out the meaning of my poetry, can you (in general, I mean) alter the language so as to make it more perspicuous—the thought remaining the same? By "dreamy semblance" I did mean semblance of some unknown past, like to a dream, and not "a semblance presented in a dream." I meant to express that ofttimes, for a second or two, it flashed upon my mind that the then company, conversation, and everything, had occurred before with all the precise circumstances; so as to make reality appear a semblance, and the present like a dream in sleep. Now this thought is obscure; because few persons have experienced the same feeling. Yet several have; and they were proportionably delighted with the lines, as expressing some strange sensations, which they themselves had never ventured to communicate, much less had ever seen developed in poetry. The lines I have altered to,—

Oft o'er my brain does that strange rapture roll
Which makes the present (while its brief fit last)
Seem a mere semblance of some unknown past,
Mixed with such feelings as distress the soul
When dreaming that she dreams.[134]

Next as to "mystical." Now that the thinking part of man, that is, the soul, existed previously to its appearance in its present body may be very wild philosophy, but it is very intelligible poetry; inasmuch as "soul" is an orthodox word in all our poets, they meaning by "soul" a being inhabiting our body, and playing upon it, like a musician enclosed in an organ whose keys were placed inwards. Now this opinion I do not hold; not that I am a materialist, but because I am a Berkleyan. Yet as you, who are not a Christian, wished you were, that we might meet in heaven, so I, who did not believe in this descending and incarcerated soul, yet said if my baby had died before I had seen him I should have struggled to believe it. Bless me! a commentary of thirty-five lines in defence of a sonnet! and I do not like the sonnet much myself. In some (indeed, in many of my poems) there is a garishness and swell of diction which I hope that my poems in future, if I write any, will be clean of, but seldom, I think, any conceits. In the second edition, now printing, I have swept the book with the expurgation-besom to a fine tune, having omitted nearly one third. As to Bowles, I affirm that the manner of his accentuation in the words "brōad dāylīght" (three long syllables) is a beauty, as it admirably expresses the captive's dwelling on the sight of noon with rapture and a kind of wonder.

The common sun, the air, the skies
To him are opening paradise.
Gray.

But supposing my defence not tenable; yet how a blunder in metre stamps a man Italian or Della Cruscan I cannot perceive. As to my own poetry, I do confess that it frequently, both in thought and language, deviates from "nature and simplicity." But that Bowles, the most tender, and, with the exception of Burns, the only always natural in our language, that he should not escape the charge of Della Cruscanism,—this cuts the skin and surface of my heart. "Poetry to have its highest relish must be impassioned." True. But, firstly, poetry ought not always to have its highest relish; and, secondly, judging of the cause from its effect, poetry, though treating on lofty and abstract truths, ought to be deemed impassioned by him who reads it with impassioned feelings. Now Collins's "Ode on the Poetical Character,"—that part of it, I should say, beginning with "The band (as faery legends say) Was wove on that creating day,"—has inspired and whirled me along with greater agitations of enthusiasm than any the most impassioned scene in Schiller or Shakespeare, using "impassioned" in its confined sense, for writing in which the human passions of pity, fear, anger, revenge, jealousy, or love are brought into view with their workings. Yet I consider the latter poetry as more valuable, because it gives more general pleasure, and I judge of all things by their utility. I feel strongly and I think strongly, but I seldom feel without thinking or think without feeling. Hence, though my poetry has in general a hue of tenderness or passion over it, yet it seldom exhibits unmixed and simple tenderness or passion. My philosophical opinions are blended with or deduced from my feelings, and this, I think, peculiarises my style of writing, and, like everything else, it is sometimes a beauty and sometimes a fault. But do not let us introduce an Act of Uniformity against Poets. I have room enough in my brain to admire, aye, and almost equally, the head and fancy of Akenside, and the heart and fancy of Bowles, the solemn lordliness of Milton, and the divine chit-chat of Cowper.[135] And whatever a man's excellence is, that will be likewise his fault.

There were some verses of yours in the last "Monthly Magazine" with which I was much pleased—calm good sense combined with feeling, and conveyed in harmonious verse and a chaste and pleasing imagery. I wish much, very much, to see your other poem. As to your Poems which you informed me in the accompanying letter that you had sent in the same parcel with the pamphlets, whether or no your verses had more than their proper number of feet I cannot say; but certain it is, that somehow or other they marched off. No "Poems by John Thelwall" could I find. When I charged you with anti-religious bigotry, I did not allude to your pamphlet, but to passages in your letters to me, and to a circumstance which Southey, I think, once mentioned, that you had asserted that the name of God ought never to be produced in poetry.[136] Which, to be sure, was carrying hatred to your Creator very far indeed.

My dear Thelwall! "It is the principal felicity of life and the chief glory of manhood to speak out fully on all subjects." I will avail myself of it. I will express all my feelings, but will previously take care to make my feelings benevolent. Contempt is hatred without fear; anger, hatred accompanied with apprehension. But because hatred is always evil, contempt must be always evil, and a good man ought to speak contemptuously of nothing. I am sure a wise man will not of opinions which have been held by men, in other respects at least, confessed of more powerful intellect than himself. 'Tis an assumption of infallibility; for if a man were wakefully mindful that what he now thinks foolish he may himself hereafter think wise, it is not in nature that he should despise those who now believe what it is possible he may himself hereafter believe; and if he deny the possibility he must on that point deem himself infallible and immutable. Now, in your letter of yesterday, you speak with contempt of two things: old age and the Christian religion; though religion was believed by Newton, Locke, and Hartley, after intense investigation, which in each had been preceded by unbelief. This does not prove its truth, but it should save its followers from contempt, even though through the infirmities of mortality they should have lost their teeth. I call that man a bigot, Thelwall, whose intemperate zeal, for or against any opinions, leads him to contradict himself in the space of half a dozen lines. Now this you appear to me to have done. I will write fully to you now, because I shall never renew the subject. I shall not be idle in defence of the religion I profess, and my books will be the place, not my letters. You say the Christian is a mean religion. Now the religion which Christ taught is simply, first, that there is an omnipresent Father of infinite power, wisdom, and goodness, in whom we all of us move and have our being; and, secondly, that when we appear to men to die we do not utterly perish, but after this life shall continue to enjoy or suffer the consequences and natural effects of the habits we have formed here, whether good or evil. This is the Christian religion, and all of the Christian religion. That there is no fancy in it I readily grant, but that it is mean and deficient in mind and energy it were impossible for me to admit, unless I admitted that there could be no dignity, intellect, or force in anything but atheism. But though it appeal not itself to the fancy, the truths which it teaches admit the highest exercise of it. Are the "innumerable multitude of angels and archangels" less splendid beings than the countless gods and goddesses of Rome and Greece? And can you seriously think that Mercury from Jove equals in poetic sublimity "the mighty angel that came down from heaven, whose face was as it were the sun and his feet as pillars of fire: who set his right foot on the sea, and his left foot on the earth. And he sent forth a loud voice; and when he had sent it forth, seven thunders uttered their voices: and when the seven thunders had uttered their voices, the mighty Angel[137] lifted up his hand to heaven, and sware by Him that liveth for ever and ever that Time was no more"? Is not Milton a sublimer poet than Homer or Virgil? Are not his personages more sublimely clothed, and do you not know that there is not perhaps one page in Milton's Paradise Lost in which he has not borrowed his imagery from the Scriptures? I allow and rejoice that Christ appealed only to the understanding and the affections; but I affirm that after reading Isaiah, or St. Paul's "Epistle to the Hebrews," Homer and Virgil are disgustingly tame to me, and Milton himself barely tolerable. You and I are very differently organized if you think that the following (putting serious belief out of the question) is a mean flight of impassioned eloquence in which the Apostle marks the difference between the Mosaic and Christian Dispensation: "For ye are not come unto the mount that might be touched" (that is, a material and earthly place) "and that burned with fire, nor unto blackness, and tempest, and the sound of a trumpet, and the voice of words; which voice they that heard entreated that the word should not be spoken to them any more. But ye are come unto Mount Sion, and unto the city of the living God, to an innumerable company of angels, to God the Judge of all, and to the spirits of just men made perfect."[138] You may prefer to all this the quarrels of Jupiter and Juno, the whimpering of wounded Venus, and the jokes of the celestials on the lameness of Vulcan. Be it so (the difference in our tastes it would not be difficult to account for from the different feelings which we have associated with these ideas); I shall continue with Milton to say that

"Zion Hill
Delights me more, and Siloa's brook that flow'd
Fast by the oracle of God!"
"Visions fit for slobberers!" If infidelity do not lead to sensuality, which in every case except yours I have observed it to do, it always takes away all respect for those who become unpleasant from the infirmities of disease or decaying nature. Exempli gratiâ, "the aged are slobberers."[139] The only vision which Christianity holds forth is indeed peculiarly adapted to these slobberers. Yes, to these lowly and despised and perishing slobberers it proclaims that their "corruptible shall put on incorruption, and their mortal put on immortality."

"Morals to the Magdalen and Botany Bay." Now, Thelwall, I presume that to preach morals to the virtuous is not quite so requisite as to preach them to the vicious. "The sick need a physician." Are morals which would make a prostitute a wife and a sister, which would restore her to inward peace and purity; are morals which would make drunkards sober, the ferocious benevolent, and thieves honest, mean morals? Is it a despicable trait in our religion, that its professed object is to heal the broken-hearted and give wisdom to the poor man? It preaches repentance. What repentance? Tears and sorrow and a repetition of the same crimes? No, a "repentance unto good works;" a repentance that completely does away all superstitious terrors by teaching that the past is nothing in itself, that, if the mind is good, that it was bad imports nothing. "It is a religion for democrats." It certainly teaches in the most explicit terms the rights of man, his right to wisdom, his right to an equal share in all the blessings of nature; it commands its disciples to go everywhere, and everywhere to preach these rights; it commands them never to use the arm of flesh, to be perfectly non-resistant; yet to hold the promulgation of truth to be a law above law, and in the performance of this office to defy "wickedness in high places," and cheerfully to endure ignominy, and wretchedness, and torments, and death, rather than intermit the performance of it; yet, while enduring ignominy, and wretchedness, and torments, and death, to feel nothing but sorrow, and pity, and love for those who inflicted them; wishing their oppressors to be altogether such as they, "excepting these bonds." Here is truth in theory and in practice, a union of energetic action and more energetic suffering. For activity amuses; but he who can endure calmly must possess the seeds of true greatness. For all his animal spirits will of necessity fail him; and he has only his mind to trust to. These doubtless are morals for all the lovers of mankind, who wish to act as well as speculate; and that you should allow this, and yet, not three lines before call the same morals mean, appears to me a gross self-contradiction symptomatic of bigotry. I write freely, Thelwall; for, though personally unknown, I really love you, and can count but few human beings whose hand I would welcome with a more hearty grasp of friendship. I suspect, Thelwall, that you never read your Testament, since your understanding was matured, without carelessness, and previous contempt, and a somewhat like hatred. Christianity regards morality as a process. It finds a man vicious and unsusceptible of noble motives and gradually leads him, at least desires to lead him, to the height of disinterested virtue; till, in relation and proportion to his faculties and power, he is perfect "even as our Father in heaven is perfect." There is no resting-place for morality. Now I will make one other appeal, and have done forever with the subject. There is a passage in Scripture which comprises the whole process, and each component part, of Christian morals. Previously let me explain the word faith. By faith I understand, first, a deduction from experiments in favour of the existence of something not experienced, and, secondly, the motives which attend such a deduction. Now motives, being selfish, are only the beginning and the foundation, necessary and of first-rate importance, yet made of vile materials, and hidden beneath the splendid superstructure.

"Now giving all diligence, add to your faith fortitude, and to fortitude knowledge, and to knowledge purity, and to purity patience,[140] and to patience godliness,[141] and to godliness brotherly-kindness, and to brotherly-kindness universal love."[142]

I hope, whatever you may think of godliness, you will like the note on it. I need not tell you, that godliness is God-likeness, and is paraphrased by Peter "that ye may be partakers of the divine nature," that is, act from a love of order and happiness, not from any self-respecting motive; from the excellency into which you have exalted your nature, not from the keenness of mere prudence. "Add to your faith fortitude, and to fortitude knowledge, and to knowledge purity, and to purity patience, and to patience godliness, and to godliness brotherly-kindness, and to brotherly-kindness universal love." Now, Thelwall, putting faith out of the question (which, by the bye, is not mentioned as a virtue, but as the leader to them), can you mention a virtue which is not here enjoined? and supposing the precepts embodied in the practice of any one human being, would not perfection be personified? I write these things not with any expectation of making you a Christian. I should smile at my own folly, if I conceived it even in a friendly day-dream.

………

"The ardour of undisciplined benevolence seduces us into malignity," and, while you accustom yourself to speak so contemptuously of doctrines you do not accede to, and persons with whom you do not accord, I must doubt whether even your brotherly-kindness might not be made more perfect. That is surely fit for a man which his mind after sincere examination approves, which animates his conduct, soothes his sorrows, and heightens his pleasures. Every good and earnest Christian declares that all this is true of the visions (as you please to style them, God knows why) of Christianity. Every earnest Christian, therefore, is on a level with slobberers. Do not charge me with dwelling on one expression. These expressions are always indicative of the habit of feeling. You possess fortitude and purity, and a large portion of brotherly-kindness and universal love; drink with unquenchable thirst of the two latter virtues, and acquire patience; and then, Thelwall, should your system be true, all that can be said is that (if both our systems should be found to increase our own and our fellow-creatures' happiness), "Here lie and did lie the all of John Thelwall and S. T. Coleridge. They were both humane, and happy, but the former was the more knowing;" and if my system should prove true, we, I doubt not, shall both meet in the kingdom of heaven, and I, with transport in my eye, shall say, "I told you so, my dear fellow." But seriously, the faulty habit of feeling, which I have endeavoured to point out in you, I have detected in at least as great degree in my own practice, and am struggling to subdue it. I rejoice that the bankrupt honesty of the public has paid even the small dividend you mentioned. As to your second part, I will write you about it in a day or two, when I give you an account how I have disposed of your first. My dear little baby! and my wife thinks that he already begins to flutter the callow wings of his intellect. Oh, the wise heart and foolish head of a mother! Kiss your little girl for me, and tell her if I knew her I would love her; and then I hope in your next letter you will convey her love to me and my Sara. Your dear boy, I trust, will return with rosy cheeks. Don't you suspect, Thelwall, that the little atheist Madam Stella has an abominable Christian kind of heart? My Sara is much interested about her; and I should not wonder if they were to be sworn sister-seraphs in the heavenly Jerusalem. Give my love to her.

I have sent you some loose sheets which Charles Lloyd and I printed together, intending to make a volume, but I gave it up and cancelled them.[143] Item, Joan of Arc, with only the passage of my writing cut out for the printers, as I am printing it in my second edition, with very great alterations and an addition of four hundred lines, so as to make it a complete and independent poem, entitled, "The Progress of Liberty," or "The Visions of the Maid of Orleans." Item, a sheet of sonnets[144] collected by me for the use of a few friends, who paid the printing. There you will see my opinion of sonnets. Item, Poem by C. Lloyd[145] on the death of one of your "slobberers," a very venerable old lady, and a Quaker. The book is dressed like a rich Quaker, in costly raiment but unornamented. The loss of her almost killed my poor young friend; for he doted on her from his infancy. Item, a poem of mine on Burns[146] which was printed to be dispersed among friends. It was addressed to Charles Lamb. Item, (Shall I give it thee, blasphemer? No! I won't, but) to thy Stella I do present the poems of my youth for a keepsake. Of this parcel I do entreat thy acceptance. I have another Joan of Arc, so you have a right to the one enclosed. Postscript. Item, a humorous "Droll" on S. Ireland, of which I have likewise another. Item, a strange poem written by an astrologer here, who was a man of fine genius, which, at intervals, he still discovers. But, ah me! Madness smote with her hand and stamped with her feet and swore that he should be hers, and hers he is. He is a man of fluent eloquence and general knowledge, gentle in his manners, warm in his affections; but unfortunately he has received a few rays of supernatural light through a crack in his upper story. I express myself unfeelingly; but indeed my heart always aches when I think of him. Item, some verses of Robert Southey to a college cat.[147] And, finally, the following lines by thy affectionate friend,

S. T. Coleridge.

TO A YOUNG MAN
WHO ABANDONED HIMSELF TO A CAUSELESS
AND INDOLENT MELANCHOLY.[148]

Hence that fantastic wantonness of woe,
O youth to partial Fortune vainly dear!

To plunder'd Want's half-sheltered hovel go,
Go, and some hunger-bitten infant hear
Moan haply in a dying mother's ear.

Or seek some widow's grave; whose dearer part
Was slaughtered, where o'er his uncoffin'd limbs
The flocking flesh-birds scream'd! Then, while thy heart
Groans, and thine eyes a fiercer sorrow dims,
Know (and the truth shall kindle thy young mind),
What Nature makes thee mourn she bids thee heal.
O abject! if, to sickly dreams resign'd,
All effortless thou leave Earth's common weal
A prey to the thron'd Murderess of Mankind!
After the first five lines these two followed:—

Or when the cold and dismal fog-damps brood
O'er the rank church-yard with sere elm-leaves strew'd,
Pace round some widow's grave, etc.
These they rightly omitted. I love sonnets; but upon my honour I do not love my sonnets.

N. B.—Direct your letters, S. T. Coleridge, Mr. Cottle's, High Street, Bristol.

LXIX. TO THOMAS POOLE.

Sunday morning [? December 18, 1796.]

My dear Poole,—I wrote to you with improper impetuosity; but I had been dwelling so long on the circumstance of living near you, that my mind was thrown by your letter into the feelings of those distressful dreams[149] where we imagine ourselves falling from precipices. I seemed falling from the summit of my fondest desires, whirled from the height just as I had reached it.

We shall want none of the Woman's furniture; we have enough for ourselves. What with boxes of books, and chests of drawers, and kitchen furniture, and chairs, and our bed and bed-linen, etc., we shall have enough to fill a small waggon, and to-day I shall make enquiry among my trading acquaintance, whether it would be cheaper to hire a waggon to take them straight to Stowey, than to put them in the Bridgwater waggon. Taking in the double trouble and expense of putting them in the drays to carry them to the public waggon, and then seeing them packed again, and again to be unpacked and packed at Bridgwater, I much question whether our goods would be good for anything. I am very poorly, not to say ill. My face monstrously swollen—my recondite eye sits distent quaintly, behind the flesh-hill, and looks as little as a tomtit's. And I have a sore throat that prevents my eating aught but spoon-meat without great pain. And I have a rheumatic complaint in the back part of my head and shoulders. Now all this demands a small portion of Christian patience, taking in our present circumstances. My apothecary says it will be madness for me to walk to Stowey on Tuesday, as, in the furious zeal of a new convert to economy, I had resolved to do. My wife will stay a week or fortnight after me; I think it not improbable that the weather may break up by that time. However, if I do not get worse, I will be with you by Wednesday or Thursday at the furthest, so as to be there before the waggon. Is there any grate in the house? I should think we might Rumfordize one of the chimneys. I shall bring down with me a dozen yards of green list. I can endure cold, but not a cold room. If we can but contrive to make two rooms warm and wholesome, we will laugh in the faces of gloom and ill-lookingness.

I shall lose the post if I say a word more. You thoroughly and in every nook and corner of your heart forgive me for my letters? Indeed, indeed, Poole, I know no one whom I esteem more—no one friend whom I love so much. But bear with my infirmities! God bless you, and your grateful and affectionate

S. T. Coleridge.

LXX. TO JOHN THELWALL.

December 31, 1796.

Enough, my dear Thelwall, of theology. In my book on Godwin, I compare the two systems, his and Jesus', and that book I am sure you will read with attention. I entirely accord with your opinion of Southey's "Joan." The ninth book is execrable, and the poem, though it frequently reach the sentimental, does not display the poetical-sublime. In language at once natural, perspicuous, and dignified in manly pathos, in soothing and sonnet-like description, and, above all, in character and dramatic dialogue, Southey is unrivalled; but as certainly he does not possess opulence of imaginative lofty-paced harmony, or that toil of thinking which is necessary in order to plan a whole. Dismissing mock humility, and hanging your mind as a looking-glass over my idea-pot, so as to image on the said mind all the bubbles that boil in the said idea-pot (there's a damned long-winded metaphor for you), I think that an admirable poet might be made by amalgamating him and me. I think too much for a poet, he too little for a great poet. But he abjures feeling. Now (as you say) they must go together. Between ourselves the enthusiasm of friendship is not with S. and me. We quarrelled and the quarrel lasted for a twelvemonth. We are now reconciled; but the cause of the difference was solemn, and "the blasted oak puts not forth its buds anew." We are acquaintances, and feel kindliness towards each other, but I do not esteem or love Southey, as I must esteem and love the man whom I dared call by the holy name of friend: and vice versâ Southey of me. I say no more. It is a painful subject, and do you say nothing. I mention this for obvious reasons, but let it go no farther. It is a painful subject. Southey's direction at present is R. Southey, No. 8 West-gate Buildings, Bath, but he leaves Bath for London in the course of a week. You imagine that I know Bowles personally. I never saw him but once, and when I was a boy and in Salisbury market-place.

The passage in your letter respecting your mother affected me greatly. Well, true or false, heaven is a less gloomy idea than annihilation. Dr. Beddoes and Dr. Darwin think that Life is utterly inexplicable, writing as materialists. You, I understand, have adopted the idea that it is the result of organised matter acted on by external stimuli. As likely as any other system, but you assume the thing to be proved. The "capability of being stimulated into sensation" ... is my definition of animal life. Monro believes in a plastic, immaterial nature, all-pervading.

And what if all of animated nature
Be but organic harps diversely framed,
That tremble into thought, as o'er them sweeps

Plastic and vast, etc.
(By the bye, that is the favourite of my poems; do you like it?) Hunter says that the blood is the life, which is saying nothing at all; for, if the blood were life, it could never be otherwise than life, and to say it is alive is saying nothing; and Ferriar believes in a soul, like an orthodox churchman. So much for physicians and surgeons! Now as to the metaphysicians. Plato says it is harmony. He might as well have said a fiddlestick's end; but I love Plato, his dear, gorgeous nonsense; and I, though last not least, I do not know what to think about it. On the whole, I have rather made up my mind that I am a mere apparition, a naked spirit, and that life is, I myself I; which is a mighty clear account of it. Now I have written all this, not to express my ignorance (that is an accidental effect, not the final cause), but to shew you that I want to see your essay on "Animal Vitality," of which Bowles the surgeon spoke in high terms. Yet he believes in a body and a soul. Any book may be left at Robinson's for me, "to be put into the next parcel, to be sent to 'Joseph Cottle, bookseller, Bristol.'" Have you received an "Ode"[150] of mine from Parsons? In your next letter tell me what you think of the scattered poems I sent you. Send me any poems, and I will be minute in criticism. For, O Thelwall, even a long-winded abuse is more consolatory to an author's feelings than a short-breathed, asthma-lunged panegyric. Joking apart, I would to God we could sit by a fireside and joke vivâ voce, face to face—Stella and Sara, Jack Thelwall and I. As I once wrote to my dear friend, T. Poole, "repeating—

'Such verse as Bowles, heart-honour'd poet, sang,
That wakes the Tear, yet steals away the Pang,
Then, or with Berkeley or with Hobbes romance it,
Dissecting Truth with metaphysic lancet.
Or, drawn from up those dark unfathom'd wells,
In wiser folly clink the Cap and Bells.
How many tales we told! what jokes we made!
Conundrum, Crambo, Rebus, or Charade;
Ænigmas that had driven the Theban[151] mad,
And Puns, then best when exquisitely bad;
And I, if aught of archer vein I hit
With my own laughter stifled my own wit.'"[152]

CHAPTER III
THE STOWEY PERIOD
1797-1798

LXXI. TO REV. J. P. ESTLIN.

[Stowey, 1797.]

My dear Friend,—I was indeed greatly rejoiced at the first sight of a letter from you; but its contents were painful. Dear, dear Mrs. Estlin! Sara burst into an agony of tears that she had been so ill. Indeed, indeed, we hover about her, and think and talk of her, with many an interjection of prayer. I do not wonder that you have acquired a distaste to London—your associations must be painful indeed. But God be praised! you shall look back on those sufferings as the vexations of a dream! Our friend, T. Poole, particularly requests me to mention how deeply he condoles with you in Mrs. Estlin's illness, how fervently he thanks God for her recovery. I assure you he was extremely affected. We are all remarkably well, and the child grows fat and strong. Our house is better than we expected—there is a comfortable bedroom and sitting-room for C. Lloyd, and another for us, a room for Nanny, a kitchen, and outhouse. Before our door a clear brook runs of very soft water; and in the back yard is a nice well of fine spring water. We have a very pretty garden, and large enough to find us vegetables and employment, and I am already an expert gardener, and both my hands can exhibit a callum as testimonials of their industry. We have likewise a sweet orchard, and at the end of it T. Poole made a gate, which leads into his garden, and from thence either through the tan yard into his house, or else through his orchard over a fine meadow into the garden of a Mrs. Cruikshank, an old acquaintance, who married on the same day as I, and has got a little girl a little younger than David Hartley. Mrs. Cruikshank is a sweet little woman, of the same size as my Sara, and they are extremely cordial. T. Poole's mother behaves to us as a kind and tender mother. She is very fond indeed of my wife, so that, you see, I ought to be happy, and, thank God, I am so....

LXXII. TO JOHN THELWALL.

Stowey near Bridgewater, Somerset.
February 6, 1797.

I thank you, my dear Thelwall, for the parcel, and your letters. Of the contents I shall speak in the order of their importance. First, then, of your scheme of a school, I approve it; and fervently wish, that you may find it more easy of accomplishment than my fears suggest. But try, by all means, try. Have hopes without expectations to hazard disappointment. Most of our patriots are tavern and parlour patriots, that will not avow their principles by any decisive action; and of the few who would wish to do so, the larger part are unable, from their children's expectancies on rich relations, etc., etc. May these remain enough for your Stella to employ herself on! Try, by all means, try. For your comfort, for your progressiveness in literary excellence, in the name of everything that is happy, and in the name of everything that is miserable, I would have you do anything honest rather than lean with the whole weight of your necessities on the Press. Get bread and cheese, clothing and housing independently of it; and you may then safely trust to it for beef and strong beer. You will find a country life a happy one; and you might live comfortably with an hundred a year. Fifty pounds you might, I doubt not, gain by reviewing and furnishing miscellanies for the different magazines; you might safely speculate on twenty pounds a year or more from your compositions published separately—50 + 20 = £70; and by severe economy, a little garden labour, and a pigstye, this would do. And, if the education scheme did not succeed, and I could get engaged by any one of the Reviews and the new "Monthly Magazine," I would try it, and begin to farm by little and slow degrees. You perceive that by the Press I mean merely writing without a certainty. The other is as secure as anything else could be to you. With health and spirits it would stand; and without health and spirits every other mode of maintenance, as well as reviewing, would be impracticable. You are going to Derby! I shall be with you in spirit. Derby is no common place; but where you will find citizens enough to fill your lecture-room puzzles me. Dr. Darwin will no doubt excite your respectful curiosity. On the whole, I think, he is the first literary character in Europe, and the most original-minded man. Mrs. Crompton is an angel; and Dr. Crompton a truly honest and benevolent man, possessing good sense and a large portion of humour. I never think of him without respect and tenderness; never (for, thank Heaven! I abominate Godwinism) without gratitude. William Strutt[153] is a man of stern aspect, but strong, very strong abilities. Joseph Strutt every way amiable. He deserves his wife—which is saying a great deal—for she is a sweet-minded woman, and one that you would be apt to recollect whenever you met or used the words lovely, handsome, beautiful, etc. "While smiling Loves the shaft display, And lift the playful torch elate." Perhaps you may be so fortunate as to meet with a Mrs. Evans whose seat is at Darley, about a mile from Derby. Blessings descend on her! emotions crowd on me at the sight of her name. We spent five weeks at her house, a sunny spot in our life. My Sara sits and thinks and thinks of her and bursts into tears, and when I turn to her says, "I was thinking, my dear, of Mrs. Evans and Bessy" (that is, her daughter). I mention this to you, because things are characterized by their effects. She is no common being who could create so warm and lasting an interest in our hearts; for we are no common people. Indeed, indeed, Thelwall, she is without exception the greatest woman I have been fortunate enough to meet with in my brief pilgrimage through life.

At Nottingham you will surely be more likely to obtain audiences; and, I doubt not, you will find a hospitable reception there. I was treated by many families with kindliness, by some with a zeal of affection. Write me if you go and when you go. Now for your pamphlet. It is well written, and the doctrine sound, although sometimes, I think, deduced falsely. For instance (p. iii.): It is true that all a man's children, "however begotten, whether in marriage or out," are his heirs in nature, and ought to be so in true policy; but, instead of tacitly allowing that I meant by it to encourage what Mr. B.[154] and the priests would call licentiousness (and which surely, Thelwall, in the present state of society you must allow to be injustice, inasmuch as it deprives the woman of her respectability in the opinions of her neighbours), I would have shown that such a law would of all others operate most powerfully in favour of marriage; by which word I mean not the effect of spells uttered by conjurers, but permanent cohabitation useful to society as the best conceivable means (in the present state of society, at least) of ensuring nurture and systematic education to infants and children. We are but frail beings at present, and want such motives to the practice of our duties. Unchastity may be no vice,—I think it is,—but it may be no vice, abstractly speaking; yet from a variety of causes unchaste women are almost without exception careless mothers. Wife is a solemn name to me because of its influence on the more solemn duties of mother. Such passages (p. 30 is another of them) are offensive. They are mere assertions, and of course can convince no person who thinks differently; and they give pain and irritate. I write so frequently to you on this subject, because I have reason to know that passages of this order did give very general offence in your first part, and have operated to retard the sale of the second. If they had been arguments or necessarily connected with your main argument, I am not the man, Thelwall, who would oppose the filth of prudentials merely to have it swept away by the indignant torrent of your honesty. But as I said before, they are mere assertions; and certainly their truth is not self-evident. With the exception of these passages, the pamphlet is the best I have read since the commencement of the war; warm, not fiery, well-seasoned without being dry, the periods harmonious yet avoiding metrical harmony, and the ornaments so dispersed as to set off the features of truth without turning the attention on themselves. I account for its slow sale partly from your having compared yourself to Christ in the first (which gave great offence, to my knowledge, although very foolishly, I confess), and partly from the sore and fatigued state of men's minds, which disqualifies them for works of principle that exert the intellect without agitating the passions. But it has not been reviewed yet, has it? I read your narrative and was almost sorry I had read it, for I had become much interested, and the abrupt "no more" jarred me. I never heard before of your variance with Horne Tooke. Of the poems, the two Odes are the best. Of the two Odes, the last, I think; it is in the best style of Akenside's best Odes. Several of the sonnets are pleasing, and whenever I was pleased I paused, and imaged you in my mind in your captivity.... My Ode[155] by this time you are conscious that you have praised too highly. With the exception of "I unpartaking of the evil thing," which line I do not think injudiciously weak, I accede to all your remarks, and shall alter accordingly. Your remark that the line on the Empress had more of Juvenal than Pindar flashed itself on my mind. I had admired the line before, but I became immediately of your opinion, and that criticism has convinced me that your nerves are exquisite electrometers[156] of taste. You forgot to point out to me that the whole childbirth of Nature is at once ludicrous and disgusting, an epigram smart yet bombastic. The review of Bryant's pamphlet is good—the sauce is better than the fish. Speaking of Lewis's death, surely you forget that the legislature of France were to act by laws and not by general morals; and that they violated the law which they themselves had made. I will take in the "Corresponding Society Magazine." That good man, James Losh, has just published an admirable treatise translated from the French of Benjamin Constant,[157] entitled, "Consideration on the Strength of the Present Government of France." "Woe to that country when crimes are punished by crimes, and where men murder in the name of justice." I apply this to the death of the mistaken but well-meaning Lewis.[158] I never go to Bristol. From seven till half past eight I work in my garden; from breakfast till twelve I read and compose, then read again, feed the pigs, poultry, etc., till two o'clock; after dinner work again till tea; from tea till supper, review. So jogs the day, and I am happy. I have society—my friend T. Poole, and as many acquaintances as I can dispense with. There are a number of very pretty young women in Stowey, all musical, and I am an immense favourite: for I pun, conundrumize, listen, and dance. The last is a recent acquirement. We are very happy, and my little David Hartley grows a sweet boy and has high health; he laughs at us till he makes us weep for very fondness. You would smile to see my eye rolling up to the ceiling in a lyric fury, and on my knee a diaper pinned to warm. I send and receive to and from Bristol every week, and will transcribe that part of your last letter and send it to Reed.

I raise potatoes and all manner of vegetables, have an orchard, and shall raise corn with the spade, enough for my family. We have two pigs, and ducks and geese. A cow would not answer the keep: for we have whatever milk we want from T. Poole. God bless you and your affectionate

S. T. Coleridge.

LXXIII. TO JOSEPH COTTLE.[159]

June, 1797.

My dear Cottle,—I am sojourning for a few days at Racedown, the mansion of our friend Wordsworth, who has received Fox's "Achmed." He returns you his acknowledgments, and presents his kindliest respects to you. I shall be home by Friday—not to-morrow—but the next Friday. If the "Ode on the Departing Year" be not reprinted, please to omit the lines from "When shall scepter'd slaughter cease," to "For still does Madness roam on Guilt's bleak dizzy height," inclusive.[160] The first epode is to end at the words "murderer's fate." Wordsworth admires my tragedy, which gives me great hopes. Wordsworth has written a tragedy himself. I speak with heartfelt sincerity, and (I think) unblinded judgment, when I tell you that I feel myself a little man by his side, and yet do not think myself the less man than I formerly thought myself. His drama is absolutely wonderful. You know I do not commonly speak in such abrupt and unmingled phrases, and therefore will the more readily believe me. There are in the piece those profound touches of the human heart which I find three or four times in "The Robbers" of Schiller, and often in Shakespeare, but in Wordsworth there are no inequalities. T. Poole's opinion of Wordsworth is that he is the greatest man he ever knew; I coincide.

It is not impossible, that in the course of two or three months I may see you. God bless you, and

S. T. Coleridge.

Thursday.—Of course, with the lines you omit the notes that relate to them.

Mr. Cottle, Bookseller, High Street, Bristol.

LXXIV. TO ROBERT SOUTHEY.

July, 1797.

Dear Southey,—You are acting kindly in your exertions for Chatterton's sister; but I doubt the success. Chatterton's or Rowley's poems were never popular. The very circumstance which made them so much talked of, their ancientness, prevented them from being generally read, in the degree, I mean, that Goldsmith's poems or even Rogers' thing upon memory has been. The sale was never very great. Secondly, the London Edition and the Cambridge Edition, which are now both of them the property of London booksellers, are still in hand, and these booksellers will "hardly exert their interest for a rival." Thirdly, these are bad times. Fourthly, all who are sincerely zealous for Chatterton, or who from knowledge of her are interested in poor Mrs. Newton, will come forwards first, and if others should drop in but slowly, Mrs. Newton will either receive no benefit at all from those her friends, or one so long procrastinated, from the necessity of waiting for the complement of subscribers, that it may at last come too late. For these reasons I am almost inclined to think a subscription simply would be better. It is unpleasant to cast a damp on anything; but that benevolence alone is likely to be beneficent which calculates. If, however, you continue to entertain higher hopes than I, believe me, I will shake off my sloth, and use my best muscles in gaining subscribers. I will certainly write a preliminary essay, and I will attempt to write a poem on the life and death of Chatterton, but the Monody must not be reprinted. Neither this nor the Pixies' Parlour would have been in the second edition, but for dear Cottle's solicitous importunity. Excepting the last eighteen lines of the Monody, which, though deficient in chasteness and severity of diction, breathe a pleasing spirit of romantic feeling, there are not five lines in either poem which might not have been written by a man who had lived and died in the self-same St. Giles' cellar, in which he had been first suckled by a drab with milk and gin. The Pixies is the least disgusting, because the subject leads you to expect nothing, but on a life and death so full of heart-going realities as poor Chatterton's, to find such shadowy nobodies as cherub-winged Death, Trees of Hope, bare-bosomed Affection and simpering Peace, makes one's blood circulate like ipecacuanha. But so it is. A young man by strong feelings is impelled to write on a particular subject, and this is all his feelings do for him. They set him upon the business and then they leave him. He has such a high idea of what poetry ought to be, that he cannot conceive that such things as his natural emotions may be allowed to find a place in it; his learning therefore, his fancy, or rather conceit, and all his powers of buckram are put on the stretch. It appears to me that strong feeling is not so requisite to an author's being profoundly pathetic as taste and good sense.

Poor old Whag! his mother died of a dish of clotted cream, which my mother sent her as a present.

I rejoice that your poems are all sold. In the ballad of "Mary the Maid of the Inn," you have properly enough made the diction colloquial, but "engages the eye," applied to a gibbet, strikes me as slipshoppish from the unfortunate meaning of the word "engaging." Your praise of my Dedication[161] gave me great pleasure. From the ninth to the fourteenth the five lines are flat and prosish, and the versification ever and anon has too much of the rhyme couplet cadence, and the metaphor[162] on the diverse sorts of friendship is hunted down, but the poem is dear to me, and in point of taste I place it next to "Low was our pretty Cot," which I think the best of my poems.

I am as much a Pangloss as ever, only less contemptuous than I used to be, when I argue how unwise it is to feel contempt for anything.

I had been on a visit to Wordsworth's at Racedown, near Crewkerne, and I brought him and his sister back with me, and here I have settled them. By a combination of curious circumstances a gentleman's seat, with a park and woods, elegantly and completely furnished, with nine lodging rooms, three parlours, and a hall, in the most beautiful and romantic situation by the seaside, four miles from Stowey,—this we have got for Wordsworth at the rent of twenty-three pounds a year, taxes included! The park and woods are his for all purposes he wants them, and the large gardens are altogether and entirely his. Wordsworth is a very great man, the only man to whom at all times and in all modes of excellence I feel myself inferior, the only one, I mean, whom I have yet met with, for the London literati appear to me to be very much like little potatoes, that is, no great things, a compost of nullity and dullity.

Charles Lamb has been with me for a week.[163] He left me Friday morning. The second day after Wordsworth came to me, dear Sara accidentally emptied a skillet of boiling milk on my foot, which confined me during the whole time of C. Lamb's stay and still prevents me from all walks longer than a furlong. While Wordsworth, his sister, and Charles Lamb were out one evening, sitting in the arbour of T. Poole's garden[164] which communicates with mine I wrote these lines, with which I am pleased. (I heard from C. Lamb of Favell and Le Grice.[165] Poor Allen! I knew nothing of it.[166] As to Rough,[167] he is a wonderful fellow; and when I returned from the army, cut me for a month, till he saw that other people were as much attached as before.)

Well, they are gone, and here must I remain,
Lam'd by the scathe of fire, lonely and faint,
This lime-tree bower my prison! They, meantime
My Friends,[168] whom I may never meet again,
On springy[169] heath, along the hill-top edge
Wander delighted, and look down, perchance,
On that same rifted Dell, where many an ash
Twists its wild limbs beside the ferny[170] rock
Whose plumy ferns forever nod and drip,
Spray'd by the waterfall. But chiefly thou
My gentle-hearted Charles! thou who had pin'd
And hunger'd after Nature many a year,
In the great City pent, winning thy way
With sad yet bowed soul, through evil and pain
And strange calamity! Ah! slowly sink
Behind the western ridge, thou glorious Sun!
Shine in the slant heaven of the sinking orb,
Ye purple heath-flowers! richlier burn, ye clouds
Live in the yellow Light, ye distant groves!
Struck with joy's deepest calm, and gazing round
On[171] the wide view, may gaze till all doth seem
Less gross than bodily; a living thing
That acts upon the mind, and with such hues
As clothe the Almighty Spirit, when He makes
Spirits perceive His presence!
A delight
Comes sudden on my heart, and I am glad
As I myself were there! nor in the bower
Want I sweet sounds or pleasing shapes. I watch'd
The sunshine of each broad transparent leaf
Broke by the shadows of the leaf or stem,
Which hung above it: and that walnut-tree
Was richly ting'd, and a deep radiance lay
Full on the ancient ivy, which usurps
Those fronting elms, and now with blackest mass
Makes their dark foliage gleam a lighter hue
Through the late twilight: and though the rapid bat
Wheels silent by, and not a swallow titters,
Yet still the solitary humble bee
Sings in the bean-flower! Henceforth I shall know
That Nature ne'er deserts the wise and pure;
No scene so narrow, but may well employ
Each faculty of sense, and keep the heart
Awake to Love and Beauty! and sometimes
'Tis well to be bereav'd of promised good,
That we may lift the soul and contemplate
With lively joy the joys we cannot share.
My Sister and my Friends! when the last rook
Beat its straight path along the dusky air

Homewards, I bless'd it! deeming its black wing
Cross'd like a speck the blaze of setting day
While ye stood gazing; or when all was still,
Flew creaking o'er your heads, and had a charm
For you, my Sister and my Friends, to whom
No sound is dissonant which tells of Life.
I would make a shift by some means or other to visit you, if I thought that you and Edith Southey would return with me. I think—indeed, I am almost certain—that I could get a one-horse chaise free of all expense. I have driven back Miss Wordsworth over forty miles of execrable roads, and have been always very cautious, and am now no inexpert whip. And Wordsworth, at whose house I now am for change of air, has commissioned me to offer you a suite of rooms at this place, which is called "All-foxen;" and so divine and wild is the country that I am sure it would increase your stock of images, and three weeks' absence from Christchurch will endear it to you; and Edith Southey and Sara may not have another opportunity of seeing one another, and Wordsworth is very solicitous to know you, and Miss Wordsworth is a most exquisite young woman in her mind and heart. I pray you write me immediately, directing Stowey, near Bridgewater, as before.

God bless you and your affectionate

S. T. Coleridge.

LXXV. TO JOHN THELWALL.

Saturday morning [October 16], 1797.

My dear Thelwall,—I have just received your letter, having been absent a day or two, and have already, before I write to you, written to Dr. Beddoes. I would to Heaven it were in my power to serve you; but alas! I have neither money or influence, and I suppose that at last I must become a Unitarian minister, as a less evil than starvation. For I get nothing by literature.... You have my wishes and, what is very liberal in me for such an atheist reprobate, my prayers. I can at times feel strongly the beauties you describe, in themselves and for themselves; but more frequently all things appear little, all the knowledge that can be acquired child's play; the universe itself! what but an immense heap of little things? I can contemplate nothing but parts, and parts are all little! My mind feels as if it ached to behold and know something great, something one and indivisible. And it is only in the faith of that that rocks or waterfalls, mountains or caverns, give me the sense of sublimity or majesty! But in this faith all things counterfeit infinity.

"Struck with the deepest calm of joy,"[172] I stand
Silent, with swimming sense; and gazing round
On the wide landscape, gaze till all doth seem
Less gross than bodily, a living Thing
Which acts upon the mind and with such hues
As clothe th' Almighty Spirit, where He makes
Spirits perceive His presence!...
It is but seldom that I raise and spiritualize my intellect to this height; and at other times I adopt the Brahmin creed, and say, "It is better to sit than to stand, it is better to lie than to sit, it is better to sleep than to wake, but Death is the best of all!" I should much wish, like the Indian Vishnu, to float about along an infinite ocean cradled in the flower of the Lotus,

and wake once in a million years for a few minutes just to know that I was going to sleep a million years more. I have put this feeling in the mouth of Alhadra, my Moorish Woman. She is going by moonlight to the house of Velez, where the band turn off to wreak their vengeance on Francesco, but

She moved steadily on,
Unswerving from the path of her resolve.
A Moorish priest, who has been with her and then left her to seek the men, had just mentioned the owl, "Its note comes dreariest in the fall of the year." This dwells on her mind, and she bursts into this soliloquy:—

The[173] hanging woods, that touch'd by autumn seem'd
As they were blossoming hues of fire and gold,—
The hanging woods, most lovely, in decay,
The many clouds, the sea, the rock, the sands,
Lay in the silent moonshine; and the owl,
(Strange! very strange!) the scritch owl only waked,
Sole voice, sole eye of all that world of beauty!
Why such a thing am I? Where are these men?
I need the sympathy of human faces
To beat away this deep contempt for all things,
Which quenches my revenge. Oh! would to Alla
The raven and the sea-mew were appointed
To bring me food, or rather that my soul
Could drink in life from universal air!
It were a lot divine in some small skiff,
Along some ocean's boundless solitude,
To float for ever with a careless course,
And think myself the only being alive!

I do not wonder that your poem procured you kisses and hospitality. It is indeed a very sweet one, and I have not only admired your genius more, but I have loved you better since I have read it. Your sonnet (as you call it, and, being a freeborn Briton, who shall prevent you from calling twenty-five blank verse lines a sonnet, if you have taken a bloody resolution so to do)—your sonnet I am much pleased with; but the epithet "downy" is probably more applicable to Susan's upper lip than to her bosom, and a mother is so holy and divine a being that I cannot endure any corporealizing epithets to be applied to her or any body of her—besides, damn epithets! The last line and a half I suppose to be miswritten. What can be the meaning of "Or scarce one leaf to cheer," etc.? "Cornelian virtues"—pedantry! The "melancholy fiend," villainous in itself, and inaccurate; it ought to be the "fiend that makes melancholy." I should have written it thus (or perhaps something better), "but with matron cares drives away heaviness;" and in your similes, etc., etc., a little compression would make it a beautiful poem. Study compression!

I presume you mean decorum by Harum Dick. An affected fellow at Bridgwater called truces "trusses." I told him I admired his pronunciation, for that lately they had been found "to suspend ruptures without curing them."

There appeared in the "Courier" the day before yesterday a very sensible vindication of the conduct of the Directory. Did you see it?

Your news respecting Mrs. E. did not surprise me. I saw it even from the first week I was at Darley. As to the other event, our non-settlement at Darley, I suspect, had little or nothing to do with it—but the cause of our non-settlement there might perhaps—O God! O God! I wish (but what is the use of wishing?)—I wish that Walter Evans may have talent enough to appreciate Mrs. Evans, but I suspect his intellect is not tall enough even to measure hers.

Hartley is well, and will not walk or run, having discovered the art of crawling with wonderful ease and rapidity. Wordsworth and his sister are well. I want to see your wife. God bless her!...

Oh, my Tragedy! it is finished, transcribed, and to be sent off to-day; but I have no hope of its success, or even of its being acted.

God bless, etc.,

S. T. Coleridge.

Mr. John Thelwall, Derby.

LXXVI. TO THE SAME.

Saturday morning, Bridgwater.
[Autumn, 1797.]

My dear Thelwall,—Yesterday morning I miss'd the coach, and was ill and could not walk. This morning the coach was completely full, but I was not ill, and so did walk; and here I am, footsore very, and weary somewhat. With regard to the business, I mentioned it at Howell's; but I perceive he is absolutely powerless. Chubb I would have called on, but there are the Assizes, and I find he is surrounded in his own house by a mob of visitors whom it is scarcely possible for him to leave, long enough at least for the conversation I want with him. I will write him to-morrow morning, and shall have an answer the same day, which I will transmit to you on Monday, but you cannot receive it till Tuesday night. If, therefore, you leave Swansea before that time, or, in case of accident, before Wednesday night, leave directions with the postmaster to have your letter forwarded.

I go for Stowey immediately, which will make my walk forty-one miles. The Howells desire to be remembered to you kindly.

I am sad at heart about you on many accounts, but chiefly anxious for this present business. The aristocrats seem to persecute even Wordsworth.[174] But we will at least not yield without a struggle; and if I cannot get you near me, it shall not be for want of a trial on my part. But perhaps I am passing the worn-out spirits of a fag-walk for the real aspect of the business.

God love you, and believe me affectionately your friend,

S. T. Coleridge.

Mr. Thelwall,
To be left at the Post Office, Swansea, Glamorganshire.

LXXVII. TO THE SAME.

[Autumn, 1797.]

Dear Thelwall,—This is the first hour that I could write to you anything decisive. I have received an answer from Chubb, intimating that he will undertake the office of procuring you a cottage, provided it was thought right that you should settle here; but this (that is the whole difficulty) he left for T. Poole and me to settle, and he acquainted Poole with this determination. Consequently, the whole returns to its former situation; and the hope which I had entertained, that you could have settled without any the remotest interference of Poole, has vanished. To such interference on his part there are insuperable difficulties: the whole malignity of the aristocrats will converge to him as to the one point; his tranquillity will be perpetually interrupted, his business and his credit hampered and distressed by vexatious calumnies, the ties of relationship weakened, perhaps broken; and, lastly, his poor old mother made miserable—the pain of the stone aggravated by domestic calamity and quarrels betwixt her son and those neighbours with whom and herself there have been peace and love for these fifty years. Very great odium T. Poole incurred by bringing me here. My peaceable manners and known attachment to Christianity had almost worn it away when Wordsworth came, and he, likewise by T. Poole's agency, settled here. You cannot conceive the tumult, calumnies, and apparatus of threatened persecutions which this event has occasioned round about us. If you, too, should come, I am afraid that even riots, and dangerous riots, might be the consequence. Either of us separately would perhaps be tolerated, but all three together, what can it be less than plot and damned conspiracy—a school for the propagation of Demagogy and Atheism? And it deserves examination, whether or no as moralists we should be justified in hazarding the certain evil of calling forth malignant passions for the contingent good, that might result from our living in the same neighbourhood? Add to which, that in point of the public interest, we must take into the balance the Stowey Benefit Club. Of the present utility of this T. Poole thinks highly; of its possible utility, very, very highly indeed; but the interests, nay, perhaps the existence of this club, is interwoven with his character as a peaceable and undesigning man; certainly, any future and greater excellence which he hopes to realize in and through the society will vanish like a dream of the morning. If, therefore, you can get the land and cottage near Bath of which you spoke to me, I would advise it on many accounts; but if you still see the arguments on the other side in a stronger light than those which I have stated, come, but not yet. Come in two or three months—take lodgings at Bridgwater—familiarise the people to your name and appearance, and, when the monstrosity of the thing is gone off, and the people shall have begun to consider you as a man whose mouth won't eat them, and whose pocket is better adapted for a bundle of sonnets than the transportation or ambush place of a French army, then you may take a house; but indeed (I say it with a very sad but a very clear conviction), at present I see that much evil and little good would result from your settling here.

I am unwell. This business has, indeed, preyed much on my spirits, and I have suffered for you more than I hope and trust you will suffer yourself.

God love you and yours.

S. T. Coleridge.

Mr. Thelwall,
To be left at the Post Office, Swansea, Glamorganshire.

LXXVIII. TO WILLIAM WORDSWORTH.

Tuesday morning, January, 1798.

My dear Wordsworth,—You know, of course, that I have accepted the magnificent liberality of Josiah and Thomas Wedgwood.[175] I accepted it on the presumption that I had talents, honesty, and propensities to perseverant effort. If I have hoped wisely concerning myself, I have acted justly. But dismissing severer thoughts, believe me, my dear fellow! that of the pleasant ideas which accompanied this unexpected event, it was not the least pleasant, nor did it pass through my mind the last in the procession, that I should at least be able to trace the spring and early summer at Alfoxden with you, and that wherever your after residence may be, it is probable that you will be within the reach of my tether, lengthened as it now is. The country round Shrewsbury is rather tame. My imagination has clothed it with all its summer attributes; but I still can see in it no possibility beyond that of beauty. The Society here were sufficiently eager to have me as their minister, and, I think, would have behaved kindly and respectfully, but I perceive clearly that without great courage and perseverance in the use of the monosyllabic No! I should have been plunged in a very Maelstrom of visiting—whirled round, and round, and round, never changing yet always moving. Visiting with all its pomp and vanities is the mania of the place; and many of the congregation are both rich and expensive. I met a young man, a Cambridge undergraduate. Talking of plays, etc., he told me that an acquaintance of his was printing a translation of one of Kotzebue's tragedies, entitled, "Benyowski."[176] The name startled me, and upon examination I found that the story of my "Siberian Exiles" has been already dramatized. If Kotzebue has exhibited no greater genius in it than in his negro slaves, I shall consider this as an unlucky circumstance; but the young man speaks enthusiastically of its merits. I have just read the "Castle Spectre," and shall bring it home with me. I will begin with its defects, in order that my "But" may have a charitable transition. 1. Language; 2. Character; 3. Passion; 4. Sentiment; 5. Conduct. (1.) Of styles, some are pleasing durably and on reflection, some only in transition, and some are not pleasing at all; and to this latter class belongs the "Castle Spectre."[177] There are no felicities in the humorous passages; and in the serious ones it is Schiller Lewis-ized, that is, a flat, flabby, unimaginative bombast oddly sprinkled with colloquialisms. (2.) No character at all. The author in a postscript lays claim to novelty in one of his characters, that of Hassan. Now Hassan is a negro, who had a warm and benevolent heart; but having been kidnapped from his country and barbarously used by the Christians, becomes a misanthrope. This is all!! (3.) Passion—horror! agonizing pangs of conscience! Dreams full of hell, serpents, and skeletons; starts and attempted murders, etc., but positively, not one line that marks even a superficial knowledge of human feelings could I discover. (4.) Sentiments are moral and humorous. There is a book called the "Frisky Songster," at the end of which are two chapters: the first containing frisky toasts and sentiments, the second, "Moral Toasts," and from these chapters I suspect Mr. Lewis has stolen all his sentimentality, moral and humorous. A very fat friar, renowned for gluttony and lubricity, furnishes abundance of jokes (all of them abdominal vel si quid infra), jokes that would have stunk, had they been fresh, and alas! they have the very sæva mephitis of antiquity on them. But (5.) the Conduct of the Piece is, I think, good; except that the first act is wholly taken up with explanation and narration. This play proves how accurately you conjectured concerning theatric merit. The merit of the "Castle Spectre" consists wholly in its situations. These are all borrowed and all absolutely pantomimical; but they are admirably managed for stage effect. There is not much bustle, but situations for ever. The whole plot, machinery, and incident are borrowed. The play is a mere patchwork of plagiarisms; but they are very well worked up, and for stage effect make an excellent whole. There is a pretty little ballad-song introduced, and Lewis, I think has great and peculiar excellence in these compositions. The simplicity and naturalness is his own, and not imitated; for it is made to subsist in congruity with a language perfectly modern, the language of his own times, in the same way that the language of the writer of "Sir Cauline" was the language of his times. This, I think, a rare merit: at least, I find, I cannot attain this innocent nakedness, except by assumption. I resemble the Duchess of Kingston, who masqueraded in the character of "Eve before the Fall," in flesh-coloured Silk. This play struck me with utter hopelessness. It would [be easy] to produce these situations, but not in a play so [constructed] as to admit the permanent and closest beauties of style, passion, and character. To admit pantomimic tricks, the plot itself must be pantomimic. Harlequin cannot be had unaccompanied by the Fool.

I hope to be with you by the middle of next week. I must stay over next Sunday, as Mr. Row is obliged to go to Bristol to seek a house. He and his family are honest, sensible, pleasant people. My kind love to Dorothy, and believe me, with affectionate esteem, yours sincerely,

S. T. Coleridge.[178]

LXXIX. TO JOSEPH COTTLE.

Stowey, March 8, 1798.

My dear Cottle,—I have been confined to my bed for some days through a fever occasioned by the stump of a tooth.... I thank you, my dear friend, for your late kindness, and in a few weeks will either repay you in money or by verses, as you like. With regard to Lloyd's verses, it is curious that I should be applied to to be "persuaded to resign, and in hope that I might" consent to give up a number of poems which were published at the earnest request of the author, who assured me that the circumstance was "of no trivial import to his happiness." Times change and people change; but let us keep our souls in quietness! I have no objection to any disposal of C. Lloyd's poems, except that of their being republished with mine. The motto which I had prefixed, "Duplex," etc.,[179] from Groscollius, has placed me in a ridiculous situation; but it was a foolish and presumptuous start of affectionateness, and I am not unwilling to incur punishments due to my folly. By past experiences we build up our moral being. How comes it that I have never heard from dear Mr. Estlin, my fatherly and brotherly friend? This idea haunted me through my sleepless nights, till my sides were sore in turning from one to the other, as if I were hoping to turn from the idea. The Giant Wordsworth—God love him! Even when I speak in the terms of admiration due to his intellect, I fear lest those terms should keep out of sight the amiableness of his manners.... He has written more than 1,200 lines of a blank verse, superior, I hesitate not to aver, to anything in our language which any way resembles it. Poole (whom I feel so consolidated with myself that I seem to have no occasion to speak of him out of myself) thinks of it as likely to benefit mankind much more than anything Wordsworth has yet written. With regard to my poems, I shall prefix the "Maid of Orleans," 1,000 lines, and three blank verse poems, making all three about 200, and I shall utterly leave out perhaps a larger quantity of lines; and I should think it would answer to you in a pecuniary way to print the third edition humbly and cheaply. My alterations in the "Religious Musings" will be considerable, and will lengthen the poem. Oh, Poole desires you not to mention his house to any one unless you hear from him again, as since I have been writing a thought has struck us of letting it to an inhabitant of the village, which we should prefer, as we should be certain that his manners would be severe, inasmuch as he would be a Stow-ic.

God bless you and

S. T. C.

LXXX. TO THE REV. GEORGE COLERIDGE.

April, 1798.

My dear Brother,—An illness, which confined me to my bed, prevented me from returning an immediate answer to your kind and interesting letter. My indisposition originated in the stump of a tooth over which some matter had formed; this affected my eye, my eye my stomach, my stomach my head, and the consequence was a general fever, and the sum of pain was considerably increased by the vain attempts of our surgeon to extract the offending member. Laudanum gave me repose, not sleep; but you, I believe, know how divine that repose is, what a spot of enchantment, a green spot of fountain and flowers and trees in the very heart of a waste of sands! God be praised, the matter has been absorbed; and I am now recovering apace, and enjoy that newness of sensation from the fields, the air, and the sun which makes convalescence almost repay one for disease. I collect from your letter that our opinions and feelings on political subjects are more nearly alike than you imagine them to be. Equally with you (and perhaps with a deeper conviction, for my belief is founded on actual experience), equally with you I deprecate the moral and intellectual habits of those men, both in England and France, who have modestly assumed to themselves the exclusive title of Philosophers and Friends of Freedom. I think them at least as distant from greatness as from goodness. If I know my own opinions, they are utterly untainted with French metaphysics, French politics, French ethics, and French theology. As to the Rulers of France, I see in their views, speeches, and actions nothing that distinguishes them to their advantage from other animals of the same species. History has taught me that rulers are much the same in all ages, and under all forms of government; they are as bad as they dare to be. The vanity of ruin and the curse of blindness have clung to them like an hereditary leprosy. Of the French Revolution I can give my thoughts most adequately in the words of Scripture: "A great and strong wind rent the mountains, and brake in pieces the rocks before the Lord; but the Lord was not in the wind; and after the wind an earthquake; and after the earthquake a fire; and the Lord was not in the fire;" and now (believing that no calamities are permitted but as the means of good) I wrap my face in my mantle and wait, with a subdued and patient thought, expecting to hear "the still small voice" which is of God. In America (I have received my information from unquestionable authority) the morals and domestic habits of the people are daily deteriorating; and one good consequence which I expect from revolution is that individuals will see the necessity of individual effort; that they will act as good Christians, rather than as citizens and electors; and so by degrees will purge off that error, which to me appears as wild and more pernicious than the πάγχρυσον and panacea of the alchemists, the error of attributing to governments a talismanic influence over our virtues and our happiness, as if governments were not rather effects than causes. It is true that all effects react and become causes, and so it must be in some degree with governments; but there are other agents which act more powerfully because by a nigher and more continuous agency, and it remains true that governments are more the effect than the cause of that which we are. Do not therefore, my brother, consider me as an enemy to government and its rulers, or as one who says they are evil. I do not say so. In my opinion it were a species of blasphemy! Shall a nation of drunkards presume to babble against sickness and the headache? I regard governments as I regard the abscesses produced by certain fevers—they are necessary consequences of the disease, and by their pain they increase the disease; but yet they are in the wisdom and goodness of Nature, and not only are they physically necessary as effects, but also as causes they are morally necessary in order to prevent the utter dissolution of the patient. But what should we think of a man who expected an absolute cure from an ulcer that only prevented his dying. Of guilt I say nothing, but I believe most steadfastly in original sin; that from our mothers' wombs our understandings are darkened; and even where our understandings are in the light, that our organization is depraved and our volitions imperfect; and we sometimes see the good without wishing to attain it, and oftener wish it without the energy that wills and performs. And for this inherent depravity I believe that the spirit of the Gospel is the sole cure; but permit me to add, that I look for the spirit of the Gospel "neither in the mountain, nor at Jerusalem."

You think, my brother, that there can be but two parties at present, for the Government and against the Government. It may be so. I am of no party. It is true I think the present Ministry weak and unprincipled men; but I would not with a safe conscience vote for their removal; I could point out no substitutes. I think very seldom on the subject; but as far as I have thought, I am inclined to consider the aristocrats as the most respectable of our three factions, because they are more decorous. The Opposition and the Democrats are not only vicious, they wear the filthy garments of vice.

He that takes
Deep in his soft credulity the stamp
Design'd by loud declaimers on the part
Of liberty, themselves the slaves of lust,
Incurs derision for his easy faith
And lack of knowledge, and with cause enough:
For when was public virtue to be found
Where private was not? Can he love the whole
Who loves no part? He be a nation's friend,
Who is, in truth, the friend of no man there?
Can he be strenuous in his country's cause
Who slights the charities, for whose dear sake
That country, if at all, must be belov'd?
Cowper.[180]
I am prepared to suffer without discontent the consequences of my follies and mistakes; and unable to conceive how that which I am of Good could have been without that which I have been of evil, it is withheld from me to regret anything. I therefore consent to be deemed a Democrat and a Seditionist. A man's character follows him long after he has ceased to deserve it; but I have snapped my squeaking baby-trumpet of sedition, and the fragments lie scattered in the lumber-room of penitence. I wish to be a good man and a Christian, but I am no Whig, no Reformist, no Republican, and because of the multitude of fiery and undisciplined spirits that lie in wait against the public quiet under these titles, because of them I chiefly accuse the present ministers, to whose folly I attribute, in a great measure, their increased and increasing numbers. You think differently, and if I were called upon by you to prove my assertions, although I imagine I could make them appear plausible, yet I should feel the insufficiency of my data. The Ministers may have had in their possession facts which alter the whole state of the argument, and make my syllogisms fall as

flat as a baby's card-house. And feeling this, my brother! I have for some time past withdrawn myself totally from the consideration of immediate causes, which are infinitely complex and uncertain, to muse on fundamental and general causes the "causæ causarum." I devote myself to such works as encroach not on the anti-social passions—in poetry, to elevate the imagination and set the affections in right tune by the beauty of the inanimate impregnated as with a living soul by the presence of life—in prose to the seeking with patience and a slow, very slow mind, "Quid sumus, et quidnam victuri gignimus,"—what our faculties are and what they are capable of becoming. I love fields and woods and mountains with almost a visionary fondness. And because I have found benevolence and quietness growing within me as that fondness has increased, therefore I should wish to be the means of implanting it in others, and to destroy the bad passions not by combating them but by keeping them in inaction.

Not useless do I deem
These shadowy sympathies with things that hold
An inarticulate Language; for the Man—
Once taught to love such objects as excite
No morbid passions, no disquietude,
No vengeance, and no hatred—needs must feel
The joy of that pure principle of love
So deeply, that, unsatisfied with aught
Less pure and exquisite, he cannot choose
But seek for objects of a kindred love
In fellow-nature and a kindred joy.
Accordingly he by degrees perceives
His feelings of aversion softened down;
A holy tenderness pervade his frame!
His sanity of reason not impair'd,
Say, rather, that his thoughts now flowing clear
From a clear fountain flowing, he looks round,
He seeks for good; and finds the good he seeks.
Wordsworth.[181]

I have laid down for myself two maxims, and, what is more I am in the habit of regulating myself by them. With regard to others, I never controvert opinions except after some intimacy, and when alone with the person, and at the happy time when we both seem awake to our own fallibility, and then I rather state my reasons than argue against his. In general conversation to find out the opinions common to us, or at least the subjects on which difference of opinion creates no uneasiness, such as novels, poetry, natural scenery, local anecdotes, and (in a serious mood and with serious men) the general evidences of our religion. With regard to myself, it is my habit, on whatever subject I think, to endeavour to discover all the good that has resulted from it, that does result, or that can result. To this I bind down my mind, and after long meditation in this tract slowly and gradually make up my opinions on the quantity and nature of the evil. I consider this as the most important rule for the regulation of the intellect and the affections, as the only means of preventing the passions from turning reason into a hired advocate. I thank you for your kindness, and propose in a short time to walk down to you: but my wife must forego the thought, as she is within five or six weeks of lying-in. She and my child, whose name is David Hartley, are remarkably well. You will give my duty to my mother, and love to my brothers, to Mrs. S. and G. Coleridge.

Excuse my desultory style and illegible scrawl, for I have written you a long letter, you see, and am in truth too weary to write a fair copy of it, or rearrange my ideas, and I am anxious you should know me as I am.

God bless you, from your affectionate brother,

S. T. Coleridge.

LXXXI. TO REV. J. P. ESTLIN.[182]

May [? 1798].

My dear Friend,—I write from Cross, to which place I accompanied Mr. Wordsworth, who will give you this letter. We visited Cheddar, but his main business was to bring back poor Lloyd, whose infirmities have been made the instruments of another man's darker passions. But Lloyd (as we found by a letter that met us in the road) is off for Birmingham. Wordsworth proceeds, lest possibly Lloyd may not be gone, and likewise to see his own Bristol friends, as he is so near them. I have now known him a year and some months, and my admiration, I might say my awe, of his intellectual powers has increased even to this hour, and (what is of more importance) he is a tried good man. On one subject we are habitually silent; we found our data dissimilar, and never renewed the subject. It is his practice and almost his nature to convey all the truth he knows without any attack on what he supposes falsehood, if that falsehood be interwoven with virtues or happiness. He loves and venerates Christ and Christianity. I wish he did more, but it were wrong indeed if an incoincidence with one of our wishes altered our respect and affection to a man of whom we are, as it were, instructed by one great Master to say that not being against us he is for us. His genius is most apparent in poetry, and rarely, except to me in tête-à-tête, breaks forth in conversational eloquence. My best and most affectionate wishes attend Mrs. Estlin and your little ones, and believe me, with filial and fraternal friendship, your grateful

S. T. Coleridge.

Rev. J. P. Estlin,
St. Michael's Hill, Bristol.

LXXXII. TO THE SAME.

Monday, May 14, 1798.

My dear Friend,—I ought to have written to you before; and have done very wrong in not writing. But I have had many sorrows and some that bite deep; calumny and ingratitude from men who have been fostered in the bosom of my confidence! I pray God that I may sanctify these events by forgiveness and a peaceful spirit full of love. This morning, half-past one, my wife was safely delivered of a fine boy;[183] she had a remarkably good time, better if possible than her last, and both she and the child are as well as can be. By the by, it is only three in the morning now. I walked in to Taunton and back again, and performed the divine services for Dr. Toulmin. I suppose you must have heard that his daughter, in a melancholy derangement, suffered herself to be swallowed up by the tide on the sea-coast between Sidmouth and Bere. These events cut cruelly into the hearts of old men; but the good Dr. Toulmin bears it like the true practical Christian,—there is indeed a tear in his eye, but that eye is lifted up to the Heavenly Father. I have been too neglectful of practical religion—I mean, actual and stated prayer, and a regular perusal of scripture as a morning and evening duty. May God grant me grace to amend this error, for it is a grievous one! Conscious of frailty I almost wish (I say it confidentially to you) that I had become a stated minister, for indeed I find true joy after a sincere prayer; but for want of habit my mind wanders, and I cannot pray as often as I ought. Thanksgiving is pleasant in the performance; but prayer and distinct confession I find most serviceable to my spiritual health when I can do it. But though all my doubts are done away, though Christianity is my passion, it is too much my intellectual passion, and therefore will do me but little good in the hour of temptation and calamity.

My love to Mrs. E. and the dear little ones, and ever, O ever, believe me, with true affection and gratitude,

Your filial friend,
S. T. Coleridge.

LXXXIII. TO THOMAS POOLE.

Monday, May 14, 1798.
Morning, 10 o'clock.

My dearest Friend,—I have been sitting many minutes with my pen in my hand, full of prayers and wishes for you, and the house of affliction in which you have so trying a part to sustain—but I know not what to write. May God support you! May he restore your brother—but above all, I pray that he will make us able to cry out with a fervent sincerity: Thy will be done! I have had lately some sorrows that have cut more deeply into my heart than they ought to have done, and I have found religion, and commonplace religion too, my restorer and my comfort, giving me gentleness and calmness and dignity! Again and again, may God be with you, my best, dear friend! and believe me, my Poole! dearer, to my understanding and affections unitedly, than all else in the world!

It is almost painful and a thing of fear to tell you that I have another boy; it will bring upon your mind the too affecting circumstance of poor Mrs. Richard Poole! The prayers which I have offered for her have been a relief to my own mind; I would that they could have been a consolation to her. Scripture seems to teach us that our fervent prayers are not without efficacy, even for others; and though my reason is perplexed, yet my internal feelings impel me to a humble faith, that it is possible and consistent with the divine attributes.

Poor Dr. Toulmin! he bears his calamity like one in whom a faith through Jesus is the Habit of the whole man, of his affections still more than of his convictions. The loss of a dear child in so frightful a way cuts cruelly with an old man, but though there is a tear and an anguish in his eye, that eye is raised to heaven.

Sara was safely delivered at half past one this morning—the boy is already almost as large as Hartley. She had an astonishingly good time, better if possible than her last; and excepting her weakness, is as well as ever. The child is strong and shapely, and has the paternal beauty in his upper lip. God be praised for all things.

Your affectionate and entire friend,
S. T. Coleridge.

LXXXIV. TO THE SAME.

Sunday evening [May 20, 1798].

My dearest Poole,—I was all day yesterday in a distressing perplexity whether or no it would be wise or consolatory for me to call at your house, or whether I should write to your mother, as a Christian friend, or whether it would not be better to wait for the exhaustion of that grief which must have its way.

So many unpleasant and shocking circumstances have happened to me in my immediate knowledge within the last fortnight, that I am in a nervous state, and the most trifling thing makes me weep. Poor Richard! May Providence heal the wounds which it hath seen good to inflict!

Do you wish me to see you to-day? Shall I call on you? Shall I stay with you? or had I better leave you uninterrupted? In all your sorrows as in your joys, I am, indeed, my dearest Poole, a true and faithful sharer!

May God bless and comfort you all!

S. T. Coleridge.

LXXXV. TO CHARLES LAMB.[184]

[Spring of 1798.]

Dear Lamb,—Lloyd has informed me through Miss Wordsworth that you intend no longer to correspond with me. This has given me little pain; not that I do not love and esteem you, but on the contrary because I am confident that your intentions are pure. You are performing what you deem a duty, and humanly speaking have that merit which can be derived from the performance of a painful duty. Painful, for you would not without struggles abandon me in behalf of a man[185] who, wholly ignorant of all but your name, became attached to you in consequence of my attachment, caught his from my enthusiasm, and learned to love you at my fireside, when often while I have been sitting and talking of your sorrows and afflictions I have stopped my conversations and lifted up wet eyes and prayed for you. No! I am confident that although you do not think as a wise man, you feel as a good man.

From you I have received little pain, because for you I suffer little alarm. I cannot say this for your friend; it appears to me evident that his feelings are vitiated, and that his ideas are in their combination merely the creatures of those feelings. I have received letters from him, and the best and kindest wish which, as a Christian, I can offer in return is that he may feel remorse.

Some brief resentments rose in my mind, but they did not remain there; for I began to think almost immediately, and my resentments vanished. There has resulted only a sort of fantastic scepticism concerning my own consciousness of my own rectitude. As dreams have impressed on him the sense of reality, my sense of reality may be but a dream. From his letters it is plain that he has mistaken the heat and bustle and swell of self-justification for the approbation of his conscience. I am certain that this is not the case with me, but the human heart is so wily and inventive that possibly it may be cheating me, who am an older warrior, with some newer stratagem. When I wrote to you that my Sonnet to Simplicity[186] was not composed with reference to Southey, you answered me (I believe these were the words): "It was a lie too gross for the grossest ignorance to believe;" and I was not angry with you, because the assertion which the grossest ignorance would believe a lie the Omniscient knew to be truth. This, however, makes me cautious not too hastily to affirm the falsehood of an assertion of Lloyd's that in Edmund Oliver's[187] love-fit, leaving college, and going into the army he had no sort of allusion to or recollection of my love-fit, leaving college, and going into the army, and that he never thought of my person in the description of Oliver's person in the first letter of the second volume. This cannot appear stranger to me than my assertion did to you, and therefore I will suspend my absolute faith.

I wrote to you not that I wish to hear from you, but that I wish you to write to Lloyd and press upon him the propriety, nay the necessity, of his giving me a meeting either tête-à-tête or in the presence of all whose esteem I value. This I owe to my own character; I owe it to him if by any means he may even yet be extricated. He assigned as reasons for his rupture my vices; and he is either right or wrong. If right, it is fit that others should know it and follow his example; if wrong, he has acted very wrong. At present, I may expect everything from his heated mind rather than continence of language, and his assertions will be the more readily believed on account of his former enthusiastic attachment, though with wise men this would cast a hue of suspicion over the whole affair; but the number of wise men in the kingdom would not puzzle a savage's arithmetic—you may tell them in every [community] on your fingers. I have been unfortunate in my connections. Both you and Lloyd became acquainted with me when your minds were far from being in a composed or natural state, and you clothed my image with a suit of notions and feelings which could belong to nothing human. You are restored to comparative saneness, and are merely wondering what is become of the Coleridge with whom you were so passionately in love; Charles Lloyd's mind has only changed his disease, and he is now arraying his ci-devant Angel in a flaming San Benito—the whole ground of the garment a dark brimstone and plenty of little devils flourished out in black. Oh, me! Lamb, "even in laughter the heart is sad!" My kindness, my affectionateness, he deems wheedling; but, if after reading all my letters to yourself and to him, you can suppose him wise in his treatment and correct in his accusations of me, you think worse of human nature than poor human nature, bad as it is, deserves to be thought of.

God bless you and
S. T. Coleridge.

CHAPTER IV
A VISIT TO GERMANY
1798-1799

The letters which Coleridge wrote from Germany were, with few exceptions, addressed either to his wife or to Poole. They have never been published in full, but during his life and since his death various extracts have appeared in print. The earlier letters descriptive of his voyage, his two visits to Hamburg, his interviews with Klopstock, and his settlement at Ratzeburg were published as "Satyrane's Letters," first in November-December, 1809, in Nos. 14, 16, and 18 of "The Friend," and again, in 1817, in the "Biographia Literaria" (ii. 183-253). Two extracts from letters to his wife, dated respectively January 14 and April 8, 1799, appeared in No. 19 of "The Friend," December 28, 1809, as "Christmas Indoors in North Germany," and "Christmas Out of Doors." In 1828, Coleridge placed a selection of unpublished letters from Germany in the hands of the late S. C. Hall, who printed portions of two (dated "Clausthal, May 17, 1799") in the "Amulet" of 1829, under the title of "Fragments of a Journal of a Tour over the Brocken, by S. T. Coleridge." The same extract is included in Gillman's "Life of Coleridge," pp. 125, 138.

After Coleridge's death, Mr. Hall published in the "New Monthly Magazine" (1835, No. 45, pp. 211-226) the three last letters from Germany, dated May 17, 18, and 19, which include the "Tour over the Brocken." Selections from Coleridge's letters to Poole of April 8 and May 6, 1799, were published by Mrs. Sandford in "Thomas Poole and his Friends" (i. 295-299), and four letters from Poole to Coleridge are included in the same volume (pp. 277-294). A hitherto unpublished letter from Coleridge to his wife, dated January 14, 1799, appeared in "The Illustrated London News," April 29, 1893. For further particulars relative to Coleridge's life in Germany, see Carlyon's "Early Years," etc., 1856, i. 26-198, passim, and Brandl's "Life of Coleridge," 1887, pp. 230-252.

LXXXVI. TO THOMAS POOLE.

September 15, 1798.

My very dear Poole,—We have arrived at Yarmouth just in time to be hurried into the packet—and four or five letters of recommendation have been taken away from me, owing to their being wafered. Wedgwood's luckily were not.

I am at the point of leaving my native country for the first time—a country which God Almighty knows is dear to me above all things for the love I bear to you. Of many friends whom I love and esteem, my head and heart have ever chosen you as the friend—as the one being in whom is involved the full and whole meaning of that sacred title. God love you, my dear Poole! and your faithful and most affectionate

S. T. Coleridge.

P. S. We may be only two days, we may be a fortnight going. The same of the packet that returns. So do not let my poor Sara be alarmed if she do not hear from me. I will write alternately to you and her, twice every week during my absence. May God preserve us, and make us continue to be joy, and comfort, and wisdom, and virtue to each other, my dear, dear Poole!

LXXXVII. TO HIS WIFE.

Hamburg, September 19, 1798.

Over what place does the moon hang to your eye, my dearest Sara? To me it hangs over the left bank of the Elbe, and a long trembling road of moonlight reaches from thence up to the stern of our vessel, and there it ends. We have dropped anchor in the middle of the stream, thirty miles from Cuxhaven, where we arrived this morning at eleven o'clock, after an unusually fine passage of only forty-eight hours. The Captain agreed to take all the passengers up to Hamburg for ten guineas; my share amounted only to half a guinea. We shall be there, if no fogs intervene, to-morrow morning. Chester was ill the whole voyage; Wordsworth shockingly ill; his sister worst of all, and I neither sick nor giddy, but gay as a lark. The sea rolled rather high, but the motion was pleasant to me. The stink of a sea cabin in a packet (what with the bilge-water, and what from the crowd of sick passengers) is horrible. I remained chiefly on deck. We left Yarmouth Sunday morning, September 16, at eleven o'clock. Chester and Wordsworth ill immediately. Our passengers were: ‡Wordsworth, ✻Chester, S. T. Coleridge, a Dane, second Dane, third Dane, a Prussian, a Hanoverian and ✻his servant, a German tailor and his ✻wife, a French ‡emigrant and ✻French servant, ✻two English gentlemen, and ‡a Jew. All these with the prefix ✻ were sick, those marked ‡ horribly sick. The view of Yarmouth from the sea is interesting; besides, it was English ground that was flying away from me. When we lost sight of land, the moment that we quite lost sight of it and the heavens all round me rested upon the waters, my dear babes came upon me like a flash of lightning; I saw their faces[188] so distinctly! This day enriched me with characters, and I passed it merrily. Each of those characters I will delineate to you in my journal, which you and Poole alternately will receive regularly as soon as I arrive at any settled place, which will be in a week. Till then I can do little more than give you notice of my safety and my faithful affection to you (but the journal will commence from the day of my arrival at London, and give every day's occurrence, etc.). I have it written, but I have neither paper or time to transcribe it. I trust nothing to memory. The Ocean is a noble thing by night; a beautiful white cloud of foam at momentary intervals roars and rushes by the side of the vessel, and stars of flame dance and sparkle and go out in it, and every now and then light detachments of foam dart away from the vessel's side with their galaxies of stars and scour out of sight like a Tartar troop over a wilderness. What these stars are I cannot say; the sailors say they are fish spawn, which is phosphorescent. The noisy passengers swear in all their languages, with drunken hiccups, that I shall write no more, and I must join them. Indeed, they present a rich feast for a dramatist. My kind love to Mrs. Poole (with what wings of swiftness would I fly home if I could find something in Germany to do her good!). Remember me affectionately to Ward, and my love to the Chesters (Bessy, Susan, and Julia) and to Cruickshank, etc., etc., Ellen and Mary when you see them, and to Lavinia Poole and Harriet and Sophy, and be sure to give my kind love to Nanny. I associate so much of Hartley's infancy with her, so many of his figures, looks, words, and antics with her form, that I shall never cease to think of her, poor girl! without interest. Tell my best good friend, my dear Poole! that all his manuscripts, with Wordsworth's Tragedy, are safe in Josiah Wedgwood's hands; and they will be returned to him together. Good-night, my dear, dear Sara!—"every night when I go to bed, and every morning when I rise," I will think with yearning love of you and of my blessed babies! Once more, my dear Sara! good-night.

Wednesday afternoon, four o'clock.—We are safe in Hamburg—an ugly city that stinks in every corner, house, and room worse than cabins, sea-sickness, or bilge-water! The hotels are all crowded. With great difficulty we have procured a very filthy room at a large expense; but we shall move to-morrow. We get very excellent claret for a trifle—a guinea sells at present for more than twenty-three shillings here. But for all particulars I must refer your patience to my journal, and I must get some proper paper—I shall have to pay a shilling or eighteenpence with every letter. N. B. Johnson the bookseller, without any poems sold to him, but purely out of affection conceived for me, and as part of anything I might do for him, gave me an order on Remnant at Hamburg for thirty pounds. The "Epea Pteroenta," an Essay on Population, and a "History of Paraguay," will come down for me directed to Poole, and for Poole's reading. Likewise I have desired Johnson to print in quarto[189] a little poem of mine, one of which quartos must be sent to my brother, Rev. G. C., Ottery St. Mary, carriage paid. Did you receive my letter directed in a different hand, with the 30l. banknote? The "Morning Post" and Magazine will come to you as before. If not regularly, Stuart desires that you will write to him. I pray you, my dear love! read Edgeworth's "Essay on Education"—read it heart and soul, and if you approve of the mode, teach Hartley his letters. I am very desirous that you should teach him to read; and they point out some easy modes. J. Wedgwood informed me that the Edgeworths were most miserable when children; and yet the father in his book is ever vapouring about their happiness. However, there are very good things in the work—and some nonsense.

Kiss my Hartley and Bercoo baby brodder (kiss them for their dear father, whose heart will never be absent from them many hours together). My dear Sara! I think of you with affection and a desire to be home, and in the full and noblest sense of the word, and after the antique principles of Religion, unsophisticated by Philosophy, will be, I trust, your husband faithful unto death,

S. T. Coleridge.

Wednesday night, eleven o'clock.—The sky and colours of the clouds are quite English, just as if I were coming out of T. Poole's homeward with you in my arm.

LXXXVIII. TO THE SAME.

[Ratzeburg], October 20, 1798.

... But I must check these feelings and write more collectedly. I am well, my dear Love! very well, and my situation is in all respects comfortable. My room is large and healthy; the house commands an enchanting prospect. The pastor is worthy and a learned man—a widower with eight children, five of whom are at home. The German language is spoken here in the utmost purity. The children often stand round my sofa and chatter away; and the little one of all corrects my pronunciation with a pretty pert lisp and self-sufficient tone, while the others laugh with no little joyance. The Gentry and Nobility here pay me almost an adulatory attention. There is a very beautiful little woman—less, I think, than you—a Countess Kilmansig;[190] her father is our Lord Howe's cousin. She is the wife of a very handsome man, and has two fine little children. I have quite won her heart by a German poem which I wrote. It is that sonnet, "Charles! my slow heart was only sad when first," and considerably dilated with new images, and much superior in the German to its former dress. It has excited no small wonder here for its purity and harmony. I mention this as a proof of my progress in the language—indeed, it has surprised myself; but I want to be home, and I work hard, very hard, to shorten the time of absence. The little Countess said to me, "Oh! Englishmen be always sehr gut fathers and husbands. I hope dat you will come and lofe my little babies, and I will sing to you and play on the guitar and the pianoforte; and my dear huspan he sprachs sehr gut English, and he lofes England better than all the world." (Sehr gut is very good; sprach, speaks or talks.) She is a sweet little woman, and, what is very rare in Germany, she has perfectly white, regular, French teeth. I could give you many instances of the ridiculous partiality, or rather madness, for the English. One of the first things which strikes an Englishman is the German cards. They are very different from ours; the court cards have two heads, a very convenient thing, as it prevents the necessity of turning the cards and betraying your hand, and are smaller and cost only a penny; yet the envelope in which they are sold has "Wahrlich Englische Karten," that is, genuine English cards. I bought some sticking-plaister yesterday; it cost twopence a very large piece, but it was three-halfpence farthing too dear—for indeed it looked like a nasty rag of black silk which cat or mouse dung had stained and spotted—but this was "Königl. Pat. Engl. Im. Pflaster," that is, Royal Patent English Ornament Plaister. They affect to write English over their doors. One house has "English Lodgement and Caffee Hous!" But the most amusing of all is an advertisement of a quack medicine of the same class with Dr. Solomon's and Brody's, for the spirits and all weakness of mind and body. What, think you? "A wonderful and secret Essence extracted with patience and God's blessing from the English Oaks, and from that part thereof which the heroic sailors of that Great Nation call the Heart of Oak. This invaluable and infallible Medicine has been godlily extracted therefrom by the slow processes of the Sun and magnetical Influences of the Planets and fixed Stars." This is a literal translation. At the concert, when I entered, the band played "Britannia rule the waves," and at the dinner which was given in honour of Nelson's victory, twenty-one guns were fired by order of the military Governor, and between each firing the military band played an English tune. I never saw such enthusiasm, or heard such tumultuous shouting, as when the Governor gave as a toast, "The Great Nation." By this name they always designate England, in opposition to the same title self-assumed by France. The military Governor is a pleasant man, and both he and the Amtmann (i. e. the civil regent) are particularly attentive to me. I am quite domesticated in the house of the latter; his first wife was an English woman, and his partiality for England is without bounds. God bless you, my Love! Write me a very, very long letter; write me all that can cheer me; all that will make my eyes swim and my heart melt with tenderness! Your faithful and affectionate husband,

S. T. Coleridge.

P. S. A dinner lasts not uncommonly three hours!

LXXXIX. TO THE SAME.

Ratzeburg, November 26, 1798.

Another and another and yet another post day; and still Chester greets me with, "No letters from England!" A knell, that strikes out regularly four times a week. How is this, my Love? Why do you not write to me? Do you think to shorten my absence by making it insupportable to me? Or perhaps you anticipate that if I received a letter I should idly turn away from my German to dream of you—of you and my beloved babies! Oh, yes! I should indeed dream of you for hours and hours; of you, and of beloved Poole, and of the infant that sucks at your breast, and of my dear, dear Hartley. You would be present, you would be with me in the air that I breathe; and I should cease to see you only when the tears rolled out of my eyes, and this naked, undomestic room became again visible. But oh, with what leaping and exhilarated faculties should I return to the objects and realities of my mission. But now—nay, I cannot describe to you the gloominess of thought, the burthen and sickness of heart, which I experience every post day. Through the whole remaining day I am incapable of everything but anxious imaginations, of sore and fretful feelings. The Hamburg newspapers arrive here four times a week; and almost every newspaper commences with, "Schreiben aus London—They write from London." This day's, with schreiben aus London, vom November 13. But I am certain that you have written more than once; and I stumble about in dark and idle conjectures, how and by what means it can have happened that I have not received your letters. I recommence my journal, but with feelings that approach to disgust—for in very truth I have nothing interesting to relate.

XC. TO THE SAME.

December 2, 1798.

Sunday Evening.—God, the Infinite, be praised that my babes are alive. His mercy will forgive me that late and all too slowly I raised up my heart in thanksgiving. At first and for a time I wept as passionately as if they had been dead; and for the whole day the weight was heavy upon me, relieved only by fits of weeping. I had long expected, I had passionately expected, a letter; I received it, and my frame trembled. I saw your hand, and all feelings of mind and body crowded together. Had the news been cheerful and only "We are as you left us," I must have wept to have delivered myself of the stress and tumult of my animal sensibility. But when I read the danger and the agony—My dear Sara! my love! my wife!—God bless you and preserve us. I am well; but a stye, or something of that kind, has come upon and enormously swelled my eyelids, so that it is painful and improper for me to read or write. In a few days it will now disappear, and I will write at length (now it forces me to cease). To-morrow I will write a line or two on the other side of the page to Mr. Roskilly.

I received your letter Friday, November 31. I cannot well account for the slowness. Oh, my babies! Absence makes it painful to be a father.

My life, believe and know that I pant to be home and with you.

S. T. Coleridge.

December 3.—My eyes are painful, but there is no doubt but they will be well in two or three days. I have taken physic, eat very little flesh, and drink only water, but it grieves me that I cannot read. I need not have troubled my poor eyes with a superfluous love to my dear Poole.

XCI. TO THE REV. MR. ROSKILLY.[191]

Ratzeburg, Germany, December 3, 1798.

My dear Sir,—There is an honest heart out of Great Britain that enters into your good fortune with a sincere and lively joy. May you enjoy life and health—all else you have,—a good wife, a good conscience, a good temper, sweet children, and competence! The first glass of wine I drink shall be a bumper—not to you, no! but to the Bishop of Gloucester! God bless him!

Sincerely your friend,
S. T. Coleridge.

XCII. TO THOMAS POOLE.

January 4, 1799—Morning, 11 o'clock.

My friend, my dear friend! Two hours have past since I received your letter. It was so frightfully long since I received one!! My body is weak and faint with the beating of my heart. But everything affects me more than it ought to do in a foreign country. I cried myself blind about Berkeley, when I ought to have been on my knees in the joy of thanksgiving. The waywardness of the pacquets is wonderful. On December the seventh Chester received a letter from his sister dated November 27. Yours is dated November 22, and I received it only this morning. I am quite well, calm and industrious. I now read German as English,—that is, without any mental translation as I read. I likewise understand all that is said to me, and a good deal of what they say to each other. On very trivial and on metaphysical subjects I can talk tolerably—so, so!—but in that conversation, which is between both, I bungle most ridiculously. I owe it to my industry that I can read old German, and even the old low German, better than most of even the educated natives. It has greatly enlarged my knowledge of the English language. It is a great bar to the amelioration of Germany, that through at least half of it, and that half composed almost wholly of Protestant States, from whence alone amelioration can proceed, the agriculturists and a great part of the artizans talk a language as different from the language of the higher classes (in which all books are written) as the Latin is from the Greek. The differences are greater than the affinities, and the affinities are darkened by the differences of pronunciation and spelling. I have written twice to Mr. Josiah Wedgwood,[192] and in a few days will follow a most voluminous letter, or rather series of letters, which will comprise a history of the bauers or peasants collected, not so much from books as from oral communications from the Amtmann here—(an Amtmann is a sort of perpetual Lord Mayor, uniting in himself Judge and Justice of Peace over the bauers of a certain district). I have enjoyed great advantages in this place, but I have paid dear for them. Including all expenses, I have not lived at less than two pounds a week. Wordsworth (from whom I receive long and affectionate letters) has enjoyed scarcely one advantage, but his expenses have been considerably less than they were in England. Here I shall stay till the last week in January, when I shall proceed to Göttingen, where, all expenses included, I can live for 15 shillings a week. For these last two months I have drunk nothing but water, and I eat but little animal food. At Göttingen I shall hire lodging for two months, buy my own cold beef at an eating-house, and dine in my chamber, which I can have at a dollar a week. And here at Göttingen I must endeavour to unite the advantages of advancing in German and doing something to repay myself. My dear Poole! I am afraid that, supposing I return in the first week of May, my whole expenses[193] from Stowey to Stowey, including books and clothes, will not have been less than 90 pounds! and if I buy ten pounds' worth more of books it will have been a hundred. I despair not but with intense application and regular use of time, to which I have now almost accustomed myself, that by three months' residence at Göttingen I shall have on paper at least all the materials if not the whole structure of a work that will repay me. The work I have planned, and I have imperiously excluded all waverings about other works. That is the disease of my mind—it is comprehensive in its conceptions, and wastes itself in the contemplations of the many things which it might do. I am aware of the disease, and for the next three months (if I cannot cure it) I will at least suspend its operation. This book is a life of Lessing, and interweaved with it a true state of German literature in its rise and present state. I have already written a little life from three different biographies, divided it into years, and at Göttingen I will read his works regularly according to the years in which they were written, and the controversies, religious and literary, which they occasioned. But of this say nothing to any one. The journey to Germany has certainly done me good. My habits are less irregular and my mind more in my own power. But I have much still to do! I did, indeed, receive great joy from Roskilly's good fortune, and in a little note to my dear Sara I joined a note of congratulation to Roskilly. O Poole! you are a noble heart as ever God made! Poor ———! he is passing through a fiery discipline, and I would fain believe that it will end in his peace and utility. Wordsworth is divided in his mind,— unquietly divided between the neighbourhood of Stowey and the North of England. He cannot think of settling at a distance from me, and I have told him that I cannot leave the vicinity of Stowey. His chief objection to Stowey is the want of books. The Bristol Library is a hum, and will do us little service; and he thinks that he can procure a house near Sir Gilford Lawson's by the Lakes, and have free access to his immense library. I think it better once in a year to walk to Cambridge, in the summer vacation—perhaps I may be able to get rooms for nothing, and there for a couple of months read like a Turk on a given plan, and return home with a mass of materials which, with dear, independent Poetry, will fully employ the remaining year. But this is idle prating about a future. But indeed, it is time to be looking out for a house for me—it is not possible I can be either comfortable or useful in so small a house as that in Lime Street. If Woodlands can be gotten at a reasonable price, I would have it. I will now finish my long-neglected journal.

Sara, I suppose, is at Bristol—on Monday I shall write to her. The frost here has been uncommonly severe. For two days it was 20 degrees under the freezing point. Wordsworth has left Goslar, and is on his road into higher Saxony to cruise for a pleasanter place; he has made but little progress in the language. I am interrupted, and if I do not conclude shall lose the post. Give my kind love to your dear mother. Oh, that I could but find her comfortable on my return. To Ward remember me affectionately—likewise remember to James Cole; and my grateful remembrances to Mrs. Cole for her kindness during my wife's domestic troubles. To Harriet, Sophia, and Lavinia Poole—to the Chesters—to Mary and Ellen Cruickshank—in short, to all to whom it will give pleasure remember me affectionately.

My dear, dear Poole, God bless us!

S. T. Coleridge.

P. S. The Amtmann, who is almost an Englishman and an idolizer of our nation, desires to be kindly remembered to you. He told me yesterday that he had dreamt of you the night before.

XCIII. TO HIS WIFE.

Ratzeburg, Monday, January 14, 1799.

My dearest Love,—Since the wind changed, and it became possible for me to have letters, I lost all my tranquillity. Last evening I was absent in company, and when I returned to solitude, restless in every fibre, a novel which I attempted to read seemed to interest me so extravagantly that I threw it down, and when it was out of my hands I knew nothing of what I had been reading. This morning I awoke long before light, feverish and unquiet. I was certain in my mind that I should have a letter from you, but before it arrived my restlessness and the irregular pulsation of my heart had quite wearied me down, and I held the letter in my hand like as if I was stupid, without attempting to open it. "Why don't you read the letter?" said Chester, and I read it. Ah, little Berkeley—I have misgivings, but my duty is rather to comfort you, my dear, dear Sara! I am so exhausted that I could sleep. I am well, but my spirits have left me. I am completely homesick, I must walk half an hour, for my mind is too scattered to continue writing. I entreat and entreat you, Sara! take care of yourself. If you are well, I think I could frame my thoughts so that I should not sink under other losses. You do right in writing me the truth. Poole is kind, but you do right, my dear! In a sense of reality there is always comfort. The workings of one's imagination ever go beyond the worst that nature afflicts us with; they have the terror of a superstitious circumstance. I express myself unintelligibly. Enough that you write me always the whole truth. Direct your next letter thus: An den Herrn Coleridge, à la Poste Restante, Göttingen, Germany. If God permit I shall be there before this day three weeks, and I hope on May-day to be once more at Stowey. My motives for going to Göttingen I have written to Poole. I hear as often from Wordsworth as letters can go backward and forward in a country where fifty miles in a day and night is expeditious travelling! He seems to have employed more time in writing English than in studying German. No wonder! for he might as well have been in England as at Goslar, in the situation which he chose and with his unseeking manners. He has now left it, and is on his journey to Nordhausen. His taking his sister with him was a wrong step; it is next but impossible for any but married women, or in the suit of married women, to be introduced to any company in Germany. Sister here is considered as only a name for mistress. Still, however, male acquaintance he might have had, and had I been at Goslar I would have had them; but W., God love him! seems to have lost his spirits and almost his inclination for it. In the mean time his expenses have been almost less than they [would have been] in England; mine have been very great, but I do not despair of returning to England with somewhat to pay the whole. O God! I do languish to be at home.

I will endeavour to give you some idea of Ratzeburg, but I am a wretched describer. First you must imagine a lake, running from south to north about nine miles in length, and of very various breadths—the broadest part may be, perhaps, two or three miles, the narrowest scarce more than half a mile. About a mile from the southernmost point of the lake, that is, from the beginning of the lake, is the island-town of Ratzeburg.

- is Ratzeburg; is our house on the hill; from the bottom of the hill there lies on the lake a slip of land, scarcely two stone-throws wide, at the end of which is a little bridge with a superb military gate, and this bridge joins Ratzeburg to the slip of land—you pass through Ratzeburg up a little hill, and down the hill, and this brings you to another bridge, narrow, but of an immense length, which communicates with the other shore.

The water to the south of Ratzeburg is called the little lake and the other the large lake, though they are but one piece of water. This little lake is very beautiful, the shores just often enough green and bare to give the proper effect to the magnificent groves which mostly fringe them. The views vary almost every ten steps, such and so beautiful are the turnings and windings of the shore—they unite beauty and magnitude, and can be but expressed by feminine grandeur! At the north of the great lake, and peering over, you see the seven church-towers of Lubec, which is twelve or fourteen miles from Ratzeburg. Yet you see them as distinctly as if they were not three miles from you. The worse thing is that Ratzeburg is built entirely of bricks and tiles, and is therefore all red—a clump of brick-dust red—it gives you a strong idea of perfect neatness, but it is not beautiful.[194] In the beginning or middle of October, I forget which, we went to Lubec in a boat. For about two miles the shores of the lake are exquisitely beautiful, the woods now running into the water, now retiring in all angles. After this the left shore retreats,—the lake acquires its utmost breadth, and ceases to be beautiful. At the end of the lake is the river, about as large as the river at Bristol, but winding in infinite serpentines through a dead flat, with willows and reeds, till you reach Lubec, an old fantastic town. We visited the churches at Lubec—they were crowded with gaudy gilded figures, and a profusion of pictures, among which were always the portraits of the popular pastors who had served the church. The pastors here wear white ruffs exactly like the pictures of Queen Elizabeth. There were in the Lubec churches a very large attendance, but almost all women. The genteeler people dressed precisely as the English; but behind every lady sat her maid,—the caps with gold and silver combs. Altogether, a Lubec church is an amusing sight. In the evening I wished myself a painter, just to draw a German Party at cards. One man's long pipe rested on the table, by the fish-dish; another who was shuffling, and of course had both hands employed, held his pipe in his teeth, and it hung down between his thighs even to his ankles, and the distortion which the attitude and effort occasioned made him a most ludicrous phiz.... [If it] had been possible I would have loitered a week in those churches, and found incessant amusement. Every picture, every legend cut out in gilded wood-work, was a history of the manners and feelings of the ages in which such works were admired and executed.

As the sun both rises and sets over the little lake by us, both rising and setting present most lovely spectacles.[195] In October Ratzeburg used at sunset to appear completely beautiful. A deep red light spread over all, in complete harmony with the red town, the brown-red woods, and the yellow-red reeds on the skirts of the lake and on the slip of land. A few boats, paddled by single persons, used generally to be floating up and down in the rich light. But when first the ice fell on the lake, and the whole lake was frozen one large piece of thick transparent glass—O my God! what sublime scenery I have beheld. Of a morning I have seen the little lake covered with mist; when the sun peeped over the hills the mist broke in the middle, and at last stood as the waters of the Red Sea are said to have done when the Israelites passed; and between these two walls of mist the sunlight burst upon the ice in a straight road of golden fire, all across the lake, intolerably bright, and the walls of mist partaking of the light in a multitude of colours. About a month ago the vehemence of the wind had shattered the ice; part of it, quite shattered, was driven to shore and had frozen anew; this was of a deep blue, and represented an agitated sea—the water that ran up between the great islands of ice shone of a yellow-green (it was at sunset), and all the scattered islands of smooth ice were blood, intensely bright blood; on some of the largest islands the fishermen were pulling out their immense nets through the holes made in the ice for this purpose, and the fishermen, the net-poles, and the huge nets made a part of the glory! O my God! how I wished you to be with me! In skating there are three pleasing circumstances—firstly, the infinitely subtle particles of ice which the skate cuts up, and which creep and run before the skater like a low mist, and in sunrise or sunset become coloured; second, the shadow of the skater in the water seen through the transparent ice; and thirdly, the melancholy undulating sound from the skate, not without variety; and, when very many are skating together, the sounds give an impulse to the icy trees, and the woods all round the lake tinkle. It is a pleasant amusement to sit in an ice stool (as they are called) and be driven along by two skaters, faster than most horses can gallop. As to the customs here, they are nearly the same as in England, except that [the men] never sit after dinner [and only] drink at dinner, which often lasts three or four hours, and in noble families is divided into three gangs, that is, walks. When you have sat about an hour, you rise up, each lady takes a gentleman's arm, and you walk about for a quarter of an hour—in the mean time another course is put upon the table; and, this in great dinners, is repeated three times. A man here seldom sees his wife till dinner,—they take their coffee in separate rooms, and never eat at breakfast; only as soon as they are up they take their coffee, and about eleven o'clock eat a bit of bread and butter with the coffee. The men at least take a pipe. Indeed, a pipe at breakfast is a great addition to the comfort of life. I shall [smoke at] no other time in England. Here I smoke four times a day—1 at breakfast, 1 half an hour before dinner, 1 in the afternoon at tea, and 1 just before bed-time—but I shall give it all up, unless, as before observed, you should happen to like the smoke of a pipe at breakfast. Once when I first came here I smoked a pipe immediately after dinner; the pastor expressed his surprise: I expressed mine that he could smoke before breakfast. "O Herr Gott!" (that is, Lord God) quoth he, "it is delightful; it invigorates the frame and it clears out the mouth so." A common amusement at the German Universities is for a number of young men to smoke out a candle! that is, to fill a room with tobacco smoke till the candle goes out. Pipes are quite the rage—a pipe of a particular kind, that has been smoked for a year or so, will sell here for twenty guineas—the same pipe when new costs four or five. They are called Meerschaum.

God bless you, my dear Love! I will soon write again.

S. T. Coleridge.

Postscript. Perhaps you are in Bristol. However, I had better direct it to Stowey. My love to Martha and your mother and your other sisters. Once more, my dearest Love, God love and preserve us through this long absence! O my dear Babies! my Babies!

XCIV. TO THE SAME.

Bei dem Radermacher Gohring, in der Bergstrasse, Göttingen,
March 12, 1799. Sunday Night.

My dearest Love,—It has been a frightfully long time since we have heard from each other. I have not written, simply because my letters could have gone no further than Cuxhaven, and would have stayed there to the [no] small hazard of their being lost. Even now the mouth of the Elbe is so much choked with ice that the English Pacquets cannot set off. Why need I say how anxious this long interval of silence has made me! I have thought and thought of you, and pictured you and the little ones so often and so often that my imagination is tired down, flat and powerless, and I languish after home for hours together in vacancy, my feelings almost wholly unqualified by thoughts. I have at times experienced such an extinction of light in my mind—I have been so forsaken by all the forms and colourings of existence, as if the organs of life had been dried up; as if only simply Being remained, blind and stagnant. After I have recovered from this strange state and reflected upon it, I have thought of a man who should lose his companion in a desart of sand, where his weary Halloos drop down in the air without an echo. I am deeply convinced that if I were to remain a few years among objects for whom I had no affection I should wholly lose the powers of intellect. Love is the vital air of my genius, and I have not seen one human being in Germany whom I can conceive it possible for me to love, no, not one; in my mind they are an unlovely race, these Germans.

We left Ratzeburg, Feb. 6, in the Stage Coach. This was not the coldest night of the century, because the night following was two degrees colder—the oldest man living remembers not such a night as Thursday, Feb. 7. This whole winter I have heard incessant complaints of the unusual cold, but I have felt very little of it. But that night! My God! Now I know what the pain of cold is, and what the danger. The pious care of the German Governments that none of their loving subjects should be suffocated is admirable! On Friday morning when the light dawned, the Coach looked like a shapeless idol of suspicion with an hundred eyes, for there were at least so many holes in it. And as to rapidity! We left Ratzeburg at 7 o'clock Wednesday evening, and arrived at Lüneburg—i. e., 35 English miles—at 3 o'clock on Thursday afternoon. This is a fair specimen! In England I used to laugh at the "flying waggons;" but, compared with a German Post Coach, the metaphor is perfectly justifiable, and for the future I shall never meet a flying waggon without thinking respectfully of its speed. The whole country from Ratzeburg almost to Einbeck—i. e., 155 English miles—is a flat, objectless, hungry heath, bearing no marks of cultivation, except close by the towns, and the only remarks which suggested themselves to me were that it was cold—very cold—shocking cold—never felt it so cold in my life! Hanover is 115 miles from Ratzeburg. We arrived there Saturday evening.

The Herr von Döring, a nobleman who resides at Ratzeburg, gave me letters to his brother-in-law at Hanover, and by the manner in which he received me I found that they were not ordinary letters of recommendation. He pressed me exceedingly to stay a week in Hanover, but I refused, and left it on Monday noon. In the mean time, however, he had introduced me to all the great people and presented me "as an English gentleman of first-rate character and talents" to Baron Steinburg, the Minister of State, and to Von Brandes, the Secretary of State and Governor of Göttingen University. The first was amazingly perpendicular, but civil and polite, and gave me letters to Heyne, the head Librarian, and, in truth, the real Governor of Göttingen. Brandes likewise gave me letters to Heyne and Blumenbach, who are his brothers-in-law. Baron Steinburg offered to present me to the Prince (Adolphus), who is now in Hanover; but I deferred the honour till my return. I shall make Poole laugh when I return with the visiting-card which the Baron left at my inn.

The two things worth seeing in Hanover are (1) the conduit representing Mount Parnassus, with statues of Apollo, the Muses, and a great many others; flying horses, rhinoceroses, and elephants, etc.; and (2) a bust of Leibnitz—the first for its excessive absurdity, ugliness, and indecency—(absolutely I could write the most humorous octavo volume containing the description of it with a commentary)—the second—i. e. the bust of Leibnitz—impressed on my soul a sensation which has ennobled it. It is the face of a god! and Leibnitz was almost more than a man in the wonderful capaciousness of his judgment and imagination! Well, we left Hanover on Monday noon, after having paid a most extravagant bill. We lived with Spartan frugality, and paid with Persian pomp! But I was an Englishman, and visited by half a dozen noblemen and the Minister of State. The landlord could not dream of affronting me by anything like a reasonable charge! On the road we stopped with the postillion always, and our expenses were nothing. Chester and I made a very hearty dinner of cold beef, etc., and both together paid only fourpence, and for coffee and biscuits only threepence each. In short, a man may travel cheap in Germany, but he must avoid great towns and not be visited by Ministers of State.

In a village some four miles from Einbeck we stopped about 4 o'clock in the morning. It was pitch dark, and the postillion led us into a room where there was not a ray of light—we could not see our hand—but it felt extremely warm. At length and suddenly the lamp came, and we saw ourselves in a room thirteen strides in length, strew'd with straw, and lying by the side of each other on the straw twelve Jews. I assure you it was curious. Their dogs lay at their feet. There was one very beautiful boy among them, fast asleep, with the softest conceivable opening of the mouth, with the white beard of his grandfather upon his cheek—a fair, rosy cheek.

This day I called with my letters on the Professor Heyne, a little, hopping, over-civil sort of a thing, who talks very fast and with fragments of coughing between every ten words. However, he behaved very courteously to me. The next day I took out my matricula, and commenced student of the University of Göttingen. Heyne has honoured me so far that he has given me the right, which properly only professors have, of sending to the Library for an indefinite number of books in my own name.

On Saturday evening I went to the concert. Here the other Englishmen introduced themselves. After the concert Hamilton, a Cambridge man, took me as his guest to the Saturday Club, where what is called the first class of students meet and sup once a week. Here were all the nobility and three Englishmen. Such an evening I never passed before— roaring, kissing, embracing, fighting, smashing bottles and glasses against the wall, singing— in short, such a scene of uproar I never witnessed before, no, not even at Cambridge. I drank nothing, but all except two of the Englishmen were drunk, and the party broke up a little after one o'clock in the morning. I thought of what I had been at Cambridge and of what I was, of the wild bacchanalian sympathy with which I had formerly joined similar parties, and of my total inability now to do aught but meditate, and the feeling of the deep alteration in my moral being gave the scene a melancholy interest to me.

We are quite well. Chester will write soon to his family; in the mean time he sends duty, love, and remembrance to all to whom they are due. I have drunk no wine or fermented liquor for more than three months, in consequence of which I am apt to be wakeful; but then I never feel any oppression after dinner, and my spirits are much more equable, blessings which I esteem inestimable! My dear Hartley—my Berkeley—how intensely do I long for you! My Sara, O my dear Sara! To Poole, God bless him! to dear Mrs. Poole and Ward, kindest love, and to all love and remembrance.

S. T. Coleridge.

XCV. TO THOMAS POOLE.

April 6, 1799.

My dearest Poole,—Your two letters, dated January 24 and March 15,[196] followed close on each other. I was still enjoying "the livelier impulse and the dance of thought" which the first had given me when I received the second. At the time, in which I read Sara's lively account of the miseries which herself and the infant had undergone, all was over and well— there was nothing to think of—only a mass of pain was brought suddenly and closely within the sphere of my perception, and I was made to suffer it over again. For this bodily frame is an imitative thing, and touched by the imagination gives the hour which is past as faithfully as a repeating watch. But Death—the death of an infant—of one's own infant! I read your letter in calmness, and walked out into the open fields, oppressed, not by my feelings, but by the riddles which the thought so easily proposes, and solves—never! A parent—in the strict and exclusive sense a parent!—to me it is a fable wholly without meaning except in the moral which it suggests—a fable of which the moral is God. Be it so—my dear, dear friend! Oh let it be so! La Nature (says Pascal) "La Nature confond les

Pyrrhoniens, et la Raison confond les Dogmatistes. Nous avons une impuissance à prouver invincible à tout le Dogmatisme. Nous avons une idée de la verité invincible à tout le Pyrrhonisme." I find it wise and human to believe, even on slight evidence, opinions, the contrary of which cannot be proved, and which promote our happiness without hampering our intellect. My baby has not lived in vain—this life has been to him what it is to all of us—education and development! Fling yourself forward into your immortality only a few thousand years, and how small will not the difference between one year old and sixty years appear! Consciousness!—it is no otherwise necessary to our conceptions of future continuance than as connecting the present link of our being with the one immediately preceding it; and that degree of consciousness, that small portion of memory, it would not only be arrogant, but in the highest degree absurd, to deny even to a much younger infant. 'Tis a strange assertion that the essence of identity lies in recollective consciousness. 'Twere scarcely less ridiculous to affirm that the eight miles from Stowey to Bridgwater consist in the eight milestones. Death in a doting old age falls upon my feelings ever as a more hopeless phenomenon than death in infancy; but nothing is hopeless. What if the vital force which I sent from my arm into the stone as I flung it in the air and skimmed it upon the water—what if even that did not perish! It was life!—it was a particle of being!—it was power! and how could it perish? Life, Power, Being! Organization may and probably is their effect—their cause it cannot be! I have indulged very curious fancies concerning that force, that swarm of motive powers which I sent out of my body into that stone, and which, one by one, left the untractable or already possessed mass, and—but the German Ocean lies between us. It is all too far to send you such fancies as these! Grief, indeed,—

Doth love to dally with fantastic thoughts,
And smiling like a sickly Moralist,
Finds some resemblance to her own concern
In the straws of chance, and things inanimate.[197]

But I cannot truly say that I grieve—I am perplexed—I am sad—and a little thing—a very trifle—would make me weep—but for the death of the baby I have not wept! Oh this strange, strange, strange scene-shifter Death!—that giddies one with insecurity and so unsubstantiates the living things that one has grasped and handled! Some months ago Wordsworth transmitted me a most sublime epitaph. Whether it had any reality I cannot say. Most probably, in some gloomier moment he had fancied the moment in which his sister might die.

EPITAPH.

A slumber did my spirit seal,
I had no human fears;
She seemed a thing that could not feel
The touch of earthly years.
No motion has she now, no force,
She neither hears nor sees:
Mov'd round in Earth's diurnal course
With rocks, and stones, and trees!

XCVI. TO HIS WIFE.

Göttingen, in der Wondestrasse, April 8, 1799.

It is one of the discomforts of my absence, my dearest Love! that we feel the same calamities at different times—I would fain write words of consolation to you; yet I know that I shall only fan into new activity the pang which was growing dead and dull in your heart. Dear little Being! he had existed to me for so many months only in dreams and reveries, but in them existed and still exists so livelily, so like a real thing, that although I know of his death, yet when I am alone and have been long silent, it seems to me as if I did not understand it. Methinks there is something awful in the thought, what an unknown being one's own infant is to one—a fit of sound—a flash of light—a summer gust that is as it were created in the bosom of the calm air, that rises up we know not how, and goes we know not whither! But we say well; it goes! it is gone! and only in states of society in which the revealing voice of our most inward and abiding nature is no longer listened to (when we sport and juggle with abstract phrases, instead of representing our feelings and ideas), only then we say it ceases! I will not believe that it ceases—in this moving, stirring, and harmonious universe—I cannot believe it! Can cold and darkness come from the sun? where the sun is not, there is cold and darkness! But the living God is everywhere, and works everywhere—and where is there room for death? To look back on the life of my baby, how short it seems! but consider it referently to nonexistence, and what a manifold and majestic Thing does it not become? What a multitude of admirable actions, what a multitude of habits of actions it learnt even before it saw the light! and who shall count or conceive the infinity of its thoughts and feelings, its hopes, and fears, and joys, and pains, and desires, and presentiments, from the moment of its birth to the moment when the glass, through which we saw him darkly, was broken—and he became suddenly invisible to us? Out of the Mount that might not be touched, and that burnt with fire, out of darkness, and blackness, and tempest, and with his own Voice, which they who heard entreated that they might not hear it again, the most high God forbade us to use his name vainly. And shall we who are Christians, shall we believe that he himself uses his own power vainly? That like a child he builds palaces of mud and clay in the common road, and then he destroys them, as weary of his pastime, or leaves them to be trod under by the hoof of Accident? That God works by general laws are to me words without meaning or worse than meaningless—ignorance, and imbecility, and limitation must wish in generals. What and who are these horrible shadows necessity and general law, to which God himself must offer sacrifices—hecatombs of sacrifices? I feel a deep conviction that these shadows exist not—they are only the dreams of reasoning pride, that would fain find solutions for all difficulties without faith—that would make the discoveries which lie thick sown in the path of the eternal Future unnecessary; and so conceiting that there is sufficiency and completeness in the narrow present, weakens the presentiment of our wide and ever widening immortality. God works in each for all—most true—but more comprehensively true is it, that he works in all for each. I confess that the more I think, the more I am discontented with the doctrines of Priestley. He builds the whole and sole hope of future existence on the words and miracles of Jesus—yet doubts or denies the future existence of infants—only because according to his own system of materialism he has not discovered how they can be made conscious. But Jesus has declared that all who are in the grave shall arise—and that those who should arise to perceptible progression must be ever as the infant which He held in his arms and blessed. And although the Man Jesus had never appeared in the world, yet I am Quaker enough to believe, that in the heart of every man the Christ would have revealed himself, the Power of the Word, that was even in the wilderness. To me who am absent this faith is a real consolation,—and the few, the slow, the quiet tears which I shed, are the accompaniments of high and solemn thought, not the workings of pain or sorrow. When I return indeed, and see the vacancy that has been made—when nowhere anything corresponds to the form which will perhaps for ever dwell on my mind, then it is possible that a keener pang will come upon me. Yet I trust, my love! I trust, my dear Sara! that this event which has forced us to think of the death of what is most dear to us, as at all times probable, will in many and various ways be good for us. To have shared—nay, I should say—to have divided with any human being any one deep sensation of joy or of sorrow, sinks deep the foundations of a lasting love. When in moments of fretfulness and imbecility I am disposed to anger or reproach, it will, I trust, be always a restoring thought—"We have wept over the same little one,—and with whom I am angry? With her who so patiently and unweariedly sustained my poor and sickly infant through his long pains—with her, who, if I too should be called away, would stay in the deep anguish over my death-pillow! who would never forget me!" Ah, my poor Berkeley! A few weeks ago an Englishman desired me to write an epitaph on an infant who had died before its christening. While I wrote it, my heart with a deep misgiving turned my thoughts homewards.

ON AN INFANT, WHO DIED BEFORE ITS CHRISTENING.

Be rather than be call'd a Child of God!
Death whisper'd. With assenting Nod
Its head upon the Mother's breast
The baby bow'd, and went without demur,
Of the kingdom of the blest
Possessor, not Inheritor.

It refers to the second question in the Church Catechism. We are well, my dear Sara. I hope to be home at the end of ten or eleven weeks. If you should be in Bristol, you will probably be shewn by Mr. Estlin three letters which I have written to him altogether—and one to Mr. Wade. Mr. Estlin will permit you to take the letters to Stowey that Poole may see them, and Poole will return them. I have no doubt but I shall repay myself by the work which I am writing, to such an amount, that I shall have spent out of my income only fifty pounds at the end of August. My love to your sisters—and love and duty to your mother. God bless you, my love! and shield us from deeper afflictions, or make us resigned unto them (and perhaps the latter blessedness is greater than the former).

Your affectionate and faithful husband,
S. T. Coleridge.

XCVII. TO THE SAME.

April 23, 1799.

My dear Sara,—Surely it is unnecessary for me to say how infinitely I languish to be in my native country, and with how many struggles I have remained even so long in Germany! I received your affecting letter, dated Easter Sunday; and, had I followed my impulses, I should have packed up and gone with Wordsworth and his sister, who passed through (and only passed through) this place two or three days ago. If they burn with such impatience to return to their native country, they who are all to each other, what must I feel with everything pleasant and everything valuable and everything dear to me at a distance—here, where I may truly say my only amusement is—to labour! But it is, in the strictest sense of the word, impossible to collect what I have to collect in less than six weeks from this day; yet I read and transcribe from eight to ten hours every day. Nothing could support me but the knowledge that if I return now we shall be embarrassed and in debt; and the moral certainty that having done what I am doing we shall be more than cleared—not to add that so large a work with so great a quantity and variety of information from sources so scattered and so little known, even in Germany, will of course establish my character for industry and erudition certainly; and, I would fain hope, for reflection and genius. This day in June I hope and trust that I shall be in England. Oh that the vessel could but land at Shurton Bars! Not that I should wish to see you and Poole immediately on my landing. No!—the sight, the touch of my native country, were sufficient for one whole feeling, the most deep unmingled emotion—but then and after a lonely walk of three miles—then, first of all, whom I knew, to see you and my Friend! It lessens the delight of the thought of my return that I must get at you through a tribe of acquaintances, damping the freshness of one's joy! My poor little baby! At this time I see the corner of the room where his cradle stood—and his cradle too—and I cannot help seeing him in the cradle. Little lamb! and the snow would not melt on his limbs! I have some faint recollections that he had that difficulty of breathing once before I left England—or was it Hartley? "A child, a child is born, and the fond heart dances; and yet the childless are the most happy." At Christmas[198] I saw a custom which pleased and interested me here. The children make little presents to their parents, and to one another, and the parents to the children. For three or four months before Christmas the girls are all busy, and the boys save up their pocket-money, to make or purchase these presents. What the present is to be is cautiously kept secret, and the girls have a world of contrivances to conceal it, such as working when they are at a visit, and the others are not with them, and getting up in the morning long before light, etc. Then on the evening before Christmas Day, one of the parlours is lighted up by the children, into which the parents must not go. A great yew bough is fastened on the table at a little distance from the wall, a multitude of little tapers are fastened in the bough, but not so as to burn it, till they are nearly burnt out, and coloured paper, etc., hangs and flutters from the twigs. Under this bough the children lay out in great neatness the presents they mean for their parents, still concealing in their pockets what they intend for each other. Then the parents are introduced, and each presents his little gift—and then they bring out the others, and present them to each other with kisses and embraces. Where I saw the scene there were eight or nine children of different ages; and the eldest daughter and the mother wept aloud for joy and tenderness, and the tears ran down the cheek of the father, and he clasped all his children so tight to his heart, as if he did it to stifle the sob that was rising within him. I was very much affected, and the shadow of the bough on the wall, and arching over on the ceiling, made a pretty picture—and then the raptures of the very little ones, when at last the twigs and thread-leaves began to catch fire and snap! Oh that was a delight for them! On the next day in the great parlour the parents lay out on the tables the presents for the children; a scene of more sober joy succeeds, as, on this day, after an old custom, the mother says privately to each of her daughters, and the father to each of his sons, that which he has observed most praiseworthy, and that which he has observed most faulty in their conduct. Formerly, and still in all the little towns and villages through the whole of North Germany, these presents were sent by all the parents of the village to some one fellow, who, in high buskins, a white robe, a mask, and an enormous flax wig, personates Knecht Rupert, that is, the servant Rupert. On Christmas night he goes round to every house and says that Jesus Christ his Master sent him there; the parents and older children receive him with great pomp of reverence, while the little ones are most terribly frightened. He then enquires for the children, and according to the character which he hears from the parent he gives them the intended presents, as if they came out of Heaven from Jesus Christ; or, if they should have been bad children, he gives the parents a rod, and, in the name of his Master Jesus, recommends them to use it frequently. About eight or nine years old, the children are let into the secret; and it is curious, how faithfully they all keep it. There are a multitude of strange superstitions among the bauers;—these still survive in spite of the efforts of the Clergy, who in the north of Germany, that is, in the Hanoverian, Saxon, and Prussian dominions, are almost all Deists. But they make little or no impressions on the bauers, who are wonderfully religious and fantastically superstitious, but not in the least priest-rid. But in the Catholic countries of Germany the difference is vast indeed! I met lately an intelligent and calm-minded man who had spent a considerable time at Marburg in the Bishopric of Paderborn in Westphalia. He told me that bead-prayers to the Holy Virgin are universal, and universally, too, are magical powers attributed to one particular formula of words which are absolutely jargons; at least, the words are to be found in no known language. The peasants believe it, however, to be a prayer to the Virgin, and happy is the man among them who is made confident by a priest that he can repeat it perfectly; for heaven knows what terrible calamity might not happen if any one should venture to repeat it and blunder. Vows and pilgrimages to particular images are still common among the bauers. If any one dies before the performance of his vow, they believe that he hovers between heaven and earth, and at times hobgoblins his relations till they perform it for him. Particular saints are believed to be eminently favourable to particular prayers, and he assured me solemnly that a little before he left Marburg a lady of Marburg had prayed and given money to have the public prayers at St. Erasmus's Chapel to St. Erasmus—for what, think you?—that the baby, with which she was then pregnant, might be a boy with light hair and rosy cheeks. When their cows, pigs, or horses are sick they take them to the Dominican monks, who transcribe texts out of the holy books, and perform exorcisms. When men or women are sick they give largely to the Convent, who on good conditions dress them in Church robes, and lay a particular and highly venerated Crucifix on their breast, and perform a multitude of antic ceremonies. In general, my informer confessed that they cured the persons, which he seemed to think extraordinary, but which I think very natural. Yearly on St. Blasius's Day unusual multitudes go to receive the Lord's Supper; and while they are receiving it the monks hold a Blasius's Taper (as it is called) before the forehead of the kneeling person, and then pray to St. Blasius to drive away all headaches for the ensuing year. Their wishes are often expressed in this form: "Mary, Mother of God, make her Son do so and so." Yet with all this, from every information which I can collect (and I have had many opportunities of collecting various accounts), the peasants in the Catholic countries of Germany, but especially in Austria, are far better off, and a far happier and livelier race, than those in the Protestant lands.... I fill up the sheet with scattered customs put down in the order in which I happened to see them. The peasant children, wherever I have been, are dressed warm and tight, but very ugly; the dress looks a frock coat, some of coarse blue cloth, some of plaid, buttoned behind—the row of buttons running down the back, and the seamless, buttonless fore-part has an odd look. When the peasants marry, if the girl is of a good character, the clergyman gives her a Virgin Crown (a tawdry, ugly thing made of gold and silver tinsel, like the royal crowns in shape). This they wear with cropped, powdered, and pomatumed hair—in short, the bride looks ugliness personified. While I was at Ratzeburg a girl came to beg the pastor to let her be married in this crown, and she had had two bastards! The pastor refused, of course. I wondered that a reputable farmer should marry her; but the pastor told me that where a female bauer is the heiress, her having had a bastard does not much stand in her way; and yet, though little or no infamy attaches to it, the number of bastards is but small—two in seventy has been the average of Ratzeburg among the peasants. By the bye, the bells in Germany are not rung as ours, with ropes, but two men stand, one on each side of the bell, and each pushes the bell away from him with his foot. In the churches, what is a baptismal font in our churches is a great Angel with a bason in his hand; he draws up and down with a chain like a lamp. In a particular part of the ceremony down comes the great stone Angel with the bason, presenting it to the pastor, who, having taken quant. suff., up flies my Angel to his old place in the ceiling—you cannot conceive how droll it looked. The graves in the little village churchyards are in square or parallelogrammic wooden cases—they look like boxes without lids—and thorns and briars are woven over them, as is done in some parts of England. Perhaps you recollect that beautiful passage in Jeremy Taylor's Holy Dying, "and the Summer brings briers to bud on our graves." The shepherds with iron soled boots walk before the sheep, as in the East—you know our Saviour says—"My Sheep follow me." So it is here. The dog and the shepherd walk first, the shepherd with his romantic fur, and generally knitting a pair of white worsted gloves—he walks on and his dog by him, and then follow the sheep winding along the roads in a beautiful stream! In the fields I observed a multitude of poles with bands and trusses of straw tied round the higher part and the top—on enquiry we found that they were put there for the owls to perch upon. And the owls? They catch the field mice, who do amazing damage in the light soil all throughout the north of Germany. The gallows near Göttingen, like that near Ratzeburg, is three great stone pillars, square, like huge tall chimneys, and connected with each other at the top by three iron bars with hooks to them—and near them is a wooden pillar with a wheel on the top of it on which the head is exposed, if the person instead of being hung is beheaded. I was frightened at first to see such a multitude of bones and skeletons of sheep, oxen, and horses, and bones as I imagined of men for many, many yards all round the gallows. I found that in Germany the hangman is by the laws of the Empire infamous—these hangmen form a caste, and their families marry with each other, etc.—and that all dead cattle, who have died, belong to them, and are carried by the owners to the gallows and left there. When their cattle are bewitched, or otherwise desperately sick, the peasants take them and tie them to the gallows—drowned dogs and kittens, etc., are thrown there—in short, the grass grows rank, and yet the bones overtop it (the fancy of human bones must, I suppose, have arisen in my ignorance of comparative anatomy). God bless you, my Love! I will write again speedily. When I was at Ratzeburg I wrote one wintry night in bed, but never sent you, three stanzas which, I dare say, you will think very silly, and so they are: and yet they were not written without a yearning, yearning, yearning Inside—for my yearning affects more than my heart. I feel it all within me.

I.

If I had but two little wings,
And were a little feath'ry bird,
To you I'd fly, my dear!
But thoughts like these are idle things—
And I stay here.

II.

But in my sleep to you I fly:
I'm always with you in my sleep—
The World is all one's own.
But then one wakes—And where am I?—
All, all alone!

III.

Sleep stays not, though a monarch bids:
So I love to wake ere break of day:
For though my sleep be gone,
Yet while 'tis dark, one shuts one's lids,
And still dreams on![199]
If Mrs. Southey be with you, remember me with all kindness and thankfulness for their attention to you and Hartley. To dear Mrs. Poole give my filial love. My love to Ward. Why should I write the name of Tom Poole, except for the pleasure of writing it? It grieves me to the heart that Nanny is not with you—I cannot bear changes—Death makes enough!

God bless you, my dear, dear wife, and believe me with eagerness to clasp you to my heart, your ever faithful husband,

S. T. Coleridge.

XCVIII. TO THOMAS POOLE.

May 6, 1799, Monday morn.

My dear Poole, my dear Poole!—I am homesick. Society is a burden to me; and I find relief only in labour. So I read and transcribe from morning till night, and never in my life have I worked so hard as this last month, for indeed I must sail over an ocean of matter with almost spiritual speed, to do what I have to do in the time in which I will do it or leave it undone! O my God, how I long to be at home! My whole Being so yearns after you, that when I think of the moment of our meeting, I catch the fashion of German joy, rush into your arms, and embrace you. Methinks my hand would swell if the whole force of my feeling were crowded there. Now the Spring comes, the vital sap of my affections rises as in a tree! And what a gloomy Spring! But a few days ago all the new buds were covered with snow; and everything yet looks so brown and wintry, that yesterday the roses (which the ladies carried on the ramparts, their promenade), beautiful as they were, so little harmonized with the general face of nature, that they looked to me like silk and made roses. But these leafless Spring Woods! Oh, how I long to hear you whistle to the Rippers![200] There are a multitude of nightingales here (poor things! they sang in the snow). I thought of my own[201] verses on the nightingale, only because I thought of Hartley, my only Child. Dear lamb! I hope he won't be dead before I get home. There are moments in which I have such a power of life within me, such a conceit of it, I mean, that I lay the blame of my child's death to my absence. Not intellectually; but I have a strange sort of sensation, as if, while I was present, none could die whom I entirely loved, and doubtless it was no absurd idea of yours that there may be unions and connections out of the visible world.

Wordsworth and his sister passed through here, as I have informed you. I walked on with them five English miles, and spent a day with them. They were melancholy and hypped. W. was affected to tears at the thought of not being near me—wished me of course to live in the North of England near Sir Frederick Vane's great library.[202] I told him that, independent of the expense of removing, and the impropriety of taking Mrs. Coleridge to a place where she would have no acquaintance, two insurmountable objections, the library was no inducement to me—for I wanted old books chiefly, such as could be procured anywhere better than in a gentleman's new fashionable collection. Finally I told him plainly that you had been the man in whom first and in whom alone I had felt an anchor! With all my other connections I felt a dim sense of insecurity and uncertainty, terribly incompatible. W. was affected to tears, very much affected; but he deemed the vicinity of a library absolutely necessary to his health, nay to his existence. It is painful to me, too, to think of not living near him; for he is a good and kind man, and the only one whom in all things I feel my superior—and you will believe me when I say that I have few feelings more pleasurable than to find myself, in intellectual faculties, an inferior.

But my resolve is fixed, not to leave you till you leave me! I still think that Wordsworth will be disappointed in his expectation of relief from reading without society; and I think it highly probable that where I live, there he will live; unless he should find in the North any person or persons, who can feel and understand him, and reciprocate and react on him. My many weaknesses are of some advantage to me; they unite me more with the great mass of my fellow-beings—but dear Wordsworth appears to me to have hurtfully segregated and isolated his being. Doubtless his delights are more deep and sublime; but he has likewise more hours that prey upon the flesh and blood. With regard to Hancock's house, if I can get no place within a mile or two of Stowey I must try to get that; but I confess I like it not—not to say that it is not altogether pleasant to live directly opposite to a person who had behaved so rudely to Mrs. Coleridge. But these are in the eye of reason trifles, and if no other house can be got—in my eye, too, they shall be trifles.

………

O Poole! I am homesick. Yesterday, or rather yesternight, I dittied the following horrible ditty; but my poor Muse is quite gone—perhaps she may return and meet me at Stowey.

'Tis sweet to him who all the week
Through city-crowds must push his way,
To stroll alone through fields and woods,
And hallow thus the Sabbath-day.

And sweet it is, in summer bower,
Sincere, affectionate, and gay,
One's own dear children feasting round,
To celebrate one's marriage day.

But what is all to his delight,
Who having long been doomed to roam,
Throws off the bundle from his back,
Before the door of his own home?

Home-sickness is no baby pang—
This feel I hourly more and more:
There's only musick in thy wings,
Thou breeze that play'st on Albion's Shore.[203]

The Professors here are exceedingly kind to all the Englishmen, but to me they pay the most flattering attentions, especially Blumenbach and Eichhorn. Nothing can be conceived more delightful than Blumenbach's lectures, and, in conversation, he is, indeed, a most interesting man. The learned Orientalist Tychsen[204] has given me instruction in the Gothic and Theotuscan languages, which I can now read pretty well; and hope in the course of a year to be thoroughly acquainted with all the languages of the North, both German and Celtic. I find being learned is a mighty easy thing, compared with any study else. My God! a miserable poet must he be, and a despicable metaphysician, whose acquirements have not cost him more trouble and reflection than all the learning of Tooke, Porson, and Parr united. With the advantage of a great library, learning is nothing—methinks, merely a sad excuse for being idle. Yet a man gets reputation by it, and reputation gets money; and for reputation I don't care a damn, but money—yes—money I must get by all honest ways. Therefore at the end of two or three years, if God grant me life, expect to see me come out with some horribly learned book, full of manuscript quotations from Laplandish and Patagonian authors, possibly, on the striking resemblance of the Sweogothian and Sanscrit languages, and so on! N. B. Whether a sort of parchment might not be made of old shoes; and whether apples should not be grafted on oak saplings, as the fruit would be the same as now, but the wood far more valuable? Two ideas of mine.—To extract aqua fortis from cucumbers is a discovery not yet made, but sugar from bete, oh! all Germany is mad about it. I have seen the sugar sent to Blumenbach from Achard[205] the great chemist, and it is good enough. They say that an hundred pounds weight of bete will make twelve pounds of sugar, and that there is no expense in the preparation. It is the Beta altissima, belongs to the Beta vulgaris, and in Germany is called Runkelrübe. Its leaves resemble those of the common red bete. It is in shape like a clumsy nine pin and about the size of a middling turnip. The flesh is white but has rings of a reddish cast. I will bring over a quantity of the seed.

....

A stupid letter!—I believe my late proficiency in learning has somewhat stupified me, but live in hopes of one better worth postage. In the last week of June, I trust, you will see me. Chester is well and desires love and duty to his family. To your dear Mother and to Ward give my kind love, and to all who ask after me.

My dear Poole! don't let little Hartley die before I come home. That's silly—true—and I burst into tears as I wrote it. Yours

S. T. Coleridge.

CHAPTER V
FROM SOUTH TO NORTH
1799-1800

XCIX. TO ROBERT SOUTHEY.

Nether Stowey, July 29, 1799.

I am doubtful, Southey, whether the circumstances which impel me to write to you ought not to keep me silent, and, if it were only a feeling of delicacy, I should remain silent, for it is good to do all things in faith. But I have been absent, Southey! ten months, and if you knew that domestic affection was hard upon me, and that my own health was declining, would you not have shootings within you of an affection which ("though fallen, though changed") has played too important a part in the event of our lives and the formation of our character, ever to be forgotten? I am perplexed what to write, or how to state the object of my writing. Any participation in each other's moral being I do not wish, simply because I know enough of the mind of man to know that [it] is impossible. But, Southey, we have similar talents, sentiments nearly similar, and kindred pursuits; we have likewise, in more than one instance, common objects of our esteem and love. I pray and intreat you, if we should meet at any time, let us not withhold from each other the outward expressions of daily kindliness; and if it be no longer in your power to soften your opinions, make your feelings at least more tolerant towards me—(a debt of humility which assuredly we all of us owe to our most feeble, imperfect, and self-deceiving nature). We are few of us good enough to know our own hearts, and as to the hearts of others, let us struggle to hope that they are better than we think them, and resign the rest to our common Maker. God bless you and yours.

S. T. Coleridge.

[Southey's answer to this appeal has not been preserved, but its tenor was that Coleridge had slandered him to others. In his reply Coleridge "avers on his honour as a man and a gentleman" that he never charged Southey with "aught but deep and implacable enmity towards himself," and that his authorities for this accusation were those on whom Southey relied, that is, doubtless, Lloyd and Lamb. He appeals to Poole, the "repository" of his every thought, and to Wordsworth, "with whom he had been for more than one whole year almost daily and frequently for weeks together," to bear him out in this statement. A letter from Poole to Southey dated August 8, and forwarded to Minehead by "special messenger," bears ample testimony to Coleridge's disavowal. "Without entering into particulars," he writes, "I will say generally, that in the many conversations I have had with Coleridge concerning yourself, he has never discovered the least personal enmity against, but, on the contrary, the strongest affection for you stifled only by the untoward events of your separation." Poole's intervention was successful, and once again the cottage opened its doors to a distinguished guest. The Southeys remained as visitors at Stowey until, in company with their host, they set out for Devonshire.]

C. TO THOMAS POOLE.

Exeter, Southey's Lodgings, Mr. Tucker's, Fore Street Hill,
September 16, 1799.[206]

My dear Poole,—Here I am just returned from a little tour[207] of five days, having seen rocks and waterfalls, and a pretty river or two; some wide landscapes, and a multitude of ash-tree dells, and the blue waters of the "roaring sea," as little Hartley says, who on Friday fell down stairs and injured his arm. 'Tis swelled and sprained, but, God be praised, not broken. The views of Totness and Dartmouth are among the most impressive things I have ever seen; but in general what of Devonshire I have lately seen is tame to Quantock, Porlock, Culbone, and Linton. So much for the country! Now as to the inhabitants thereof, they are bigots, unalphabeted in the first feelings of liberality; of course in all they speak and all they do not speak, they give good reasons for the opinions which they hold, viz. they hold the propriety of slavery, an opinion which, being generally assented to by Englishmen, makes Pitt and Paul the first among the moral fitnesses of things. I have three brothers, that is to say, relations by gore. Two are parsons and one is a colonel. George and the colonel, good men as times go—very good men—but alas! we have neither tastes nor feelings in common. This I wisely learnt from their conversation, and did not suffer them to learn it from mine. What occasion for it? Hunger and thirst—roast fowls, mealy potatoes, pies, and clouted cream! bless the inventors of them! An honest philosopher may find therewith preoccupation for his mouth, keeping his heart and brain, the latter in his scull, the former in the pericardium some five or six inches from the roots of his tongue! Church and King! Why I drink Church and King, mere cutaneous scabs of loyalty which only ape the king's evil, but affect not the interior of one's health. Mendicant sores! it requires some little caution to keep them open, but they heal of their own accord. Who (such a friend as I am to the system of fraternity) could refuse such a toast at the table of a clergyman and a colonel, his brother? So, my dear Poole! I live in peace. Of the other party, I have dined with a Mr. Northmore, a pupil of Wakefield, who possesses a fine house half a mile from Exeter. In his boyhood he was at my father's school.... But Southey and self called upon him as authors—he having edited a Tryphiodorus and part of Plutarch, and being a notorious anti-ministerialist and free-thinker. He welcomed us as he ought, and we met at dinner Hucks (at whose house I dine Wednesday), the man who toured with me in Wales and afterwards published his "Tour," Kendall, a poet, who really looks like a man of genius, pale and gnostic, has the merit of being a Jacobin or so, but is a shallowist—and finally a Mr. Banfill, a man of sense, information, and various literature, and most perfectly a gentleman—in short a pleasant man. At his house we dine to-morrow. Northmore himself is an honest, vehement sort of a fellow who splutters out all his opinions like a fiz-gig, made of gunpowder not thoroughly dry, sudden and explosive, yet ever with a certain adhesive blubberliness of elocution. Shallow! shallow! A man who can read Greek well, but shallow! Yet honest, too, and who ardently wishes the well-being of his fellowmen, and believes that without more liberty and more equality this well-being is not possible. He possesses a most noble library. The victory at Novi![208] If I were a good caricaturist I would sketch off Suwarrow in a car of conquest drawn by huge crabs!! With what retrograde majesty the vehicle advances! He may truly say he came off with éclat, that is, a claw! I shall be back at Stowey in less than three weeks....

We hope your dear mother remains well. Give my filial love to her. God bless her! I beg my kind love to Ward. God bless you and

S. T. Coleridge.

Monday night.

CI. TO ROBERT SOUTHEY.

Stowey, Tuesday evening, October 15, 1799.

It is fashionable among our philosophizers to assert the existence of a surplus of misery in the world, which, in my opinion, is no proof that either systematic thinking or unaffected self-observation is fashionable among them. But Hume wrote, and the French imitated him, and we the French, and the French us; and so philosophisms fly to and fro, in series of imitated imitations—shadows of shadows of shadows of a farthing-candle placed between two looking-glasses. For in truth, my dear Southey! I am harassed with the rheumatism in my head and shoulders, not without arm-and-thigh-twitches—but when the pain intermits it leaves my sensitive frame so sensitive! My enjoyments are so deep, of the fire, of the candle, of the thought I am thinking, of the old folio I am reading, and the silence of the silent house is so most and very delightful, that upon my soul! the rheumatism is no such bad thing as people make for. And yet I have, and do suffer from it, in much pain and sleeplessness and often sick at stomach through indigestion of the food, which I eat from compulsion. Since I received your former letter, I have spent a few days at Upcott;[209] but was too unwell to be comfortable, so I returned yesterday. Poor Tom![210] he has an adventurous calling. I have so wholly forgotten my geography that I don't know where Ferrol is, whether in France or Spain. Your dear mother must be very anxious indeed. If he return safe, it will have been good. God grant he may!

Massena![211] and what say you of the resurrection and glorification of the Saviour of the East after his trials in the wilderness? (I am afraid that this is a piece of blasphemy; but it was in simple verity such an infusion of animal spirits into me.) Buonaparte! Buonaparte! dear, dear, dear Buonaparte! It would be no bad fun to hear the clerk of the Privy Council read this paragraph before Pitt, etc. "You ill-looking frog-voiced reptile! mind you lay the proper emphasis on the third dear, or I'll split your clerkship's skull for you!" Poole ordered a paper. He has found out, he says, why the newspapers had become so indifferent to him. Inventive Genius! He begs his kind remembrances to you. In consequence of the news he burns like Greek Fire, under all the wets and waters of this health-and-harvest destroying weather. He flames while his barley smokes. "See!" he says, "how it grows out again, ruining the prospects of those who had cut it down!" You are harvest-man enough, I suppose, to understand the metaphor. Jackson[212] is, I believe, out of all doubt a bad man. Why is it, if it be, and I fear it is, why is it that the studies of music and painting are so unfavourable to the human heart? Painters have been commonly very clever men, which is not so generally the case with musicians, but both alike are almost uniformly debauchees. It is superfluous to say how much your account of Bampfylde[213] interested me. Predisposition to madness gave him a cast of originality, and he had a species of taste which only genius could give; but his genius does not appear a powerful or ebullient faculty (nearer to Lamb's than to the Gebir-man [Landor], so I judge from the few specimens I have seen). If you think otherwise, you are right I doubt not. I shall be glad to give Mr. and Mrs. Keenan[214] the right hand of welcome with looks and tones in fit accompaniment. For the wife of a man of genius who sympathises effectively with her husband in his habits and feelings is a rara avis with me; though a vast majority of her own sex and too many of ours will scout her for a rara piscis. If I am well enough, Sara and I go to Bristol in a few days. I hope they will not come in the mean time. It is singularly unpleasant to me that I cannot renew our late acquaintances in Exeter without creating very serious uneasinesses at

Ottery, Northmore is so preëminently an offensive character to the aristocrats. He sent Paine's books as a present to a clergyman of my brother's acquaintance, a Mr. Markes. This was silly enough....

I will set about "Christabel" with all speed; but I do not think it a fit opening poem. What I think would be a fit opener, and what I would humbly lay before you as the best plan of the next Anthologia, I will communicate shortly in another letter entirely on this subject. Mohammed I will not forsake; but my money-book I must write first. In the last, or at least in a late "Monthly Magazine" was an Essay on a Jesuitic conspiracy and about the Russians. There was so much genius in it that I suspected William Taylor for the author; but the style was so nauseously affected, so absurdly pedantic, that I was half-angry with myself for the suspicion. Have you seen Bishop Prettyman's book? I hear it is a curiosity. You remember Scott the attorney, who held such a disquisition on my simile of property resembling matter rather than blood? and eke of St. John? and you remember, too, that I shewed him in my face that there was no room for him in my heart? Well, sir! this man has taken a most deadly hatred to me, and how do you think he revenges himself? He imagines that I write for the "Morning Post," and he goes regularly to the coffee-houses, calls for the paper, and reading it he observes aloud, "What damn'd stuff of poetry is always crammed in this paper! such damn'd silly nonsense! I wonder what coxcomb it is that writes it! I wish the paper was kicked out of the coffee-house." Now, but for Cruikshank, I could play Scott a precious trick by sending to Stuart, "The Angry Attorney, a True Tale," and I know more than enough of Scott's most singular parti-coloured rascalities to make a most humorous and biting satire of it.

I have heard of a young Quaker who went to the Lobby, with a monstrous military cock-hat on his head, with a scarlet coat and up to his mouth in flower'd muslin, swearing too most bloodily—all "that he might not be unlike other people!" A Quaker's son getting himself christen'd to avoid being remarkable is as improbable a lie as ever self-delusion permitted the heart to impose on the understanding, or the understanding to invent without the consent of the heart. But so it is. Soon after Lloyd's arrival at Cambridge I understand Christopher Wordsworth wrote his uncle, Mr. Cookson,[215] that Lloyd was going to read Greek with him. Cookson wrote back recommending caution, and whether or no an intimacy with so marked a character might not be prejudicial to his academical interests. (This is his usual mild manner.) Christopher Wordsworth returned for answer that Lloyd was by no means a democrat, and as a proof of it, transcribed the most favourable passages from the "Edmund Oliver," and here the affair ended. You remember Lloyd's own account of this story, of course, more accurately than I, and can therefore best judge how far my suspicions of falsehood and exaggeration were well-founded. My dear Southey! the having a bad heart and not having a good one are different things. That Charles Lloyd has a bad heart, I do not even think; but I venture to say, and that openly, that he has not a good one. He is unfit to be any man's friend, and to all but a very guarded man he is a perilous acquaintance. Your conduct towards him, while it is wise, will, I doubt not, be gentle. Of confidence he is not worthy; but social kindness and communicativeness purely intellectual can do you no harm, and may be the means of benefiting his character essentially. Aut ama me quia sum Dei, aut ut sim Dei, said St. Augustin, and in the laxer sense of the word "Ama" there is wisdom in the expression notwithstanding its wit. Besides, it is the way of peace. From Bristol perhaps I go to London, but I will write you where I am. Yours affectionately,

S. T. Coleridge.

I have great affection for Lamb, but I have likewise a perfect Lloyd-and-Lambophobia! Independent of the irritation attending an epistolary controversy with them, their prose comes so damn'd dear! Lloyd especially writes with a woman's fluency in a large rambling hand, most dull though profuse of feeling. I received from them in last quarter letters so many, that with the postage I might have bought Birch's Milton.—Sara will write soon. Our love to Edith and your mother.

CII. TO THE SAME.

Keswick,[216] Sunday, November 10, 1799.

My dear Southey,—I am anxious lest so long silence should seem unaffectionate, or I would not, having so little to say, write to you from such a distant corner of the kingdom. I was called up to the North by alarming accounts of Wordsworth's health, which, thank God! are but little more than alarms. Since I have visited the Lakes and in a pecuniary way have made the trip answer to me. From hence I go to London, having had (by accident here) a sort of offer made to me of a pleasant kind, which, if it turn out well, will enable me and Sara to reside in London for the next four or five months—a thing I wish extremely on many and important accounts. So much for myself. In my last letter I said I would give you my reasons for thinking "Christabel," were it finished, and finished as spiritedly as it commences, yet still an improper opening poem. My reason is it cannot be expected to please all. Those who dislike it will deem it extravagant ravings, and go on through the rest of the collection with the feeling of disgust, and it is not impossible that were it liked by any it would still not harmonise with the real-life poems that follow. It ought, I think, to be the last. The first ought me judice to be a poem in couplets, didactic or satirical, such a one as the lovers of genuine poetry would call sensible and entertaining, such as the ignoramuses and Pope-admirers would deem genuine poetry. I had planned such a one, and, but for the absolute necessity of scribbling prose, I should have written it. The great and master fault of the last "Anthology" was the want of arrangement. It is called a collection, and meant to be continued annually; yet was distinguished in nothing from any other single volume of poems equally good. Yours ought to have been a cabinet with proper compartments, and papers in them, whereas it was only the papers. Some such arrangement as this should have been adopted: First. Satirical and Didactic. 2. Lyrical. 3. Narrative. 4. Levities.

"Sic positi quoniam suaves miscetis odores,
Neve inter vites corylum sere"—
is, I am convinced, excellent advice of Master Virgil's. N. B. A good motto! 'Tis from Virgil's seventh Eclogue.

"Populus Alcidæ gratissima, vitis Iaccho,
Formosæ myrtus Veneri, sua laurea Phœbo;
Phyllis amat corylos."
But still, my dear Southey! it goes grievously against the grain with me, that you should be editing anthologies. I would to Heaven that you could afford to write nothing, or at least to publish nothing, till the completion and publication of the "Madoc." I feel as certain, as my mind dare feel on any subject, that it would lift you with a spring into a reputation that would give immediate sale to your after compositions and a license of writing more at ease. Whereas "Thalaba" would gain you (for a time at least) more ridiculers than admirers, and the "Madoc" might in consequence be welcomed with an ecce iterum. Do, do, my dear Southey! publish the "Madoc" quam citissime, not hastily, but yet speedily. I will instantly

publish an Essay on Epic Poetry in reference to it. I have been reading the Æneid, and there you will be all victorious, excepting the importance of Æneas and his connection with events existing in Virgil's time. This cannot be said of "Madoc." There are other faults in the construction of your poem, but nothing compared to those in the Æneid. Homer I shall read too.

(No signature.)

CIII. TO THE SAME.

December 9, [1799].

My dear Southey,—I pray you in your next give me the particulars of your health. I hear accounts so contradictory that I know only enough to be a good deal frightened. You will surely think it your duty to suspend all intellectual exertion; as to money, you will get it easily enough. You may easily make twice the money you receive from Stuart by the use of the scissors; for your name is prodigiously high among the London publishers. I would to God your health permitted you to come to London. You might have lodgings in the same house with us. And this I am certain of, that not even Kingsdown is a more healthy or airy place. I have enough for us to do that would be mere child's work to us, and in which the women might assist us essentially, by the doing of which we might easily get a hundred and fifty pounds each before the first of April. This I speak, not from guess but from absolute conditions with booksellers. The principal work to which I allude would be likewise a great source of amusement and profit to us in the execution, and assuredly we should be a mutual comfort to each other. This I should press on you were not Davy at Bristol, but he is indeed an admirable young man; not only must he be of comfort to you, but in whom can you place such reliance as a medical man? But for Davy, I should advise your coming to London; the difference of expense for three months could not be above fifty pounds. I do not see how it could be half as much. But I pray you write me all particulars, how you have been, how you are, and what you think the particular nature of your disease.

Now for poor George.[217] Assuredly I am ready and willing to become his bondsman for five hundred pounds if, on the whole, you think the scheme a good one. I see enough of the boy to be fully convinced of his goodness and well-intentionedness; of his present or probable talents I know little. To remain all his life an under clerk, as many have done, and earn fifty pounds a year in his old age with a trembling hand—alas! that were a dreary prospect. No creature under the sun is so helpless, so unfitted, I should think, for any other mode of life as a clerk, a mere clerk. Yet still many have begun so and risen into wealth and importance, and it is not impossible that before his term closed we might be able, if nought better offered, perhaps to procure him a place in a public office. We might between us keep him neat in clothes from our own wardrobes, I should think, and I am ready to allow five guineas this year, in addition to Mr. Savary's twelve pounds. More I am not justified to promise. Yet still I think it matter of much reflection with you. The commercial prospects of this country are, in my opinion, gloomy; our present commerce is enormous: that it must diminish after a peace is certain, and should any accident injure the West India trade, and give to France a paramountship in the American affections, that diminution would be vast indeed, and, of course, great would be the number of clerks, etc., wholly out of employment. This is no visionary speculation; for we are consulting concerning a life, for probably fifty years. I should have given a more intense conviction to the goodness of the former scheme of apprenticing him to a printer, and would make every exertion to raise my share of the money wanting. However, all this is talk at random. I leave it to you to decide. What does Charles Danvers think? He has been very kind to George. But to whom is he not kind, that body—blood—bone—muscle—nerve—heart and head—good man! I lay final stress on his opinion in almost everything except verses; those I know more about than he does—"God bless him, to use a vulgar phrase." This is a quotation from Godwin, who used these words in conversation with me and Davy. The pedantry of atheism tickled me hugely. Godwin is no great things in intellect; but in heart and manner he is all the better for having been the husband of Mary Wollstonecraft. Why did not George Dyer (who, by the bye, has written a silly milk-and-water life of you,[218] in which your talents for pastoral and rural imagery are extolled, and in which you are asserted to be a republican), why did not George Dyer send to the "Anthology" that poem in the last "Monthly Magazine?" It is so very far superior to anything I have ever seen of his, and might have made some atonement for his former transgressions. God love him, he is a very good man; but he ought not to degrade himself by writing lives of living characters for Phillips; and all his friends make wry faces, peeping out of the pillory of his advertisemental notes. I hold to my former opinion concerning the arrangement of the "Anthology," and the booksellers with whom I have talked coincide with me. On this I am decided, that all the light pieces should be put together under one title with a motto[219] thus: "Nos hæc novimus esse nihil—Phillis amat Corylos." I am afraid that I have scarce poetic enthusiasm enough to finish "Christabel;" but the poem, with which Davy is so much delighted, I probably may finish time enough. I shall probably not publish my letters, and if I do so, I shall most certainly not publish any verses in them. Of course, I expect to see them in the "Anthology." As to title, I should wish a fictitious one or none; were I sure that I could finish the poem I spoke of. I do not know how to get the conclusion of Mrs. Robinson's poem for you. Perhaps it were better omitted, and I mean to put the thoughts of that concert poem into smoother metre. Our "Devil's Thoughts" have been admired far and wide, most enthusiastically admired. I wish to have my name in the collection at all events; but I should better like it to better poems than these I have been hitherto able to give you. But I will write again on Saturday. Supposing that Johnson should mean to do nothing more with the "Fears in Solitude" and the two accompanying poems, would they be excluded from the plan of your "Anthology?" There were not above two hundred sold, and what is that to a newspaper circulation? Collins's Odes were thus reprinted in Dodsley's Collection. As to my future residence, I can say nothing—only this, that to be near you would be a strong motive with me for my wife's sake as well as myself. I think it not impossible that a number might be found to go with you and settle in a warmer climate. My kind love to your wife. Sara and Hartley arrived safe, and here they are, No. 21 Buckingham Street, Strand. God bless you, and your affectionate

S. T. Coleridge.

Thursday evening.

P. S. Mary Hayes[220] is writing the "Lives of Famous Women," and is now about your friend Joan. She begs you to tell her what books to consult, or to communicate something to her. This from Tobin, who sends his love.

CIV. TO THE SAME.

Tuesday night, 12 o'clock [December 24], 1799.

My dear Southey,—My Spinosism (if Spinosism it be, and i' faith 'tis very like it) disposed me to consider this big city as that part of the supreme One which the prophet Moses was allowed to see—I should be more disposed to pull off my shoes, beholding Him in a Bush, than while I am forcing my reason to believe that even in theatres He is, yea! even in the Opera House. Your "Thalaba" will beyond all doubt bring you two hundred pounds, if you will sell it at once; but do not print at a venture, under the notion of selling the edition. I assure you that Longman regretted the bargain he made with Cottle concerning the second edition of the "Joan of Arc," and is indisposed to similar negotiations; but most and very eager to have the property of your works at almost any price. If you have not heard it from Cottle, why, you may hear it from me, that is, the arrangement of Cottle's affairs in London. The whole and total copyright of your "Joan," and the first volume of your poems (exclusive of what Longman had before given), was taken by him at three hundred and seventy pounds. You are a strong swimmer, and have borne up poor Joey with all his leaden weights about him, his own and other people's! Nothing has answered to him but your works. By me he has lost somewhat—by Fox, Amos, and himself very much. I can sell your "Thalaba" quite as well in your absence as in your presence. I am employed from I-rise to I-set[221] (that is, from nine in the morning to twelve at night), a pure scribbler. My mornings to booksellers' compilations, after dinner to Stuart, who pays all my expenses here, let them be what they will; the earnings of the morning go to make up an hundred and fifty pounds for my year's expenditure; for, supposing all clear my year's (1800) allowance is anticipated. But this I can do by the first of April (at which time I leave London). For Stuart I write often his leading paragraphs on Secession, Peace, Essay on the new French Constitution,[222] Advice to Friends of Freedom, Critiques on Sir W. Anderson's Nose, Odes to Georgiana D. of D. (horribly misprinted), Christmas Carols, etc., etc.,—anything not bad in the paper, that is not yours, is mine. So if any verses there strike you as worthy the "Anthology," "do me the honour, sir!" However, in the course of a week I do mean to conduct a series of essays in that paper which may be of public utility. So much for myself, except that I long to be out of London; and that my Xstmas Carol is a quaint performance, and, in as strict a sense as is possible, an Impromptu, and, had I done all I had planned, that "Ode to the Duchess"[223] would have been a better thing than it is—it being somewhat dullish, etc. I have bought the "Beauties of the Anti-jacobin," and attorneys and counsellors advise me to prosecute, and offer to undertake it, so as that I shall have neither trouble or expense. They say it is a clear case, etc.[224] I will speak to Johnson about the "Fears in Solitude." If he gives them up they are yours. That dull ode has been printed often enough, and may now be allowed to "sink with dead swoop, and to the bottom go," to quote an admired author; but the two others will do with a little trimming.

My dear Southey! I have said nothing concerning that which most oppresses me. Immediately on my leaving London I fall to the "Life of Lessing;" till that is done, till I have given the Wedgwoods some proof that I am endeavouring to do well for my fellow-creatures, I cannot stir. That being done, I would accompany you, and see no impossibility of forming a pleasant little colony for a few years in Italy or the South of France. Peace will soon come. God love you, my dear Southey! I would write to Stuart, and give up his paper immediately. You should do nothing that did not absolutely please you. Be idle, be very idle! The habits of your mind are such that you will necessarily do much; but be as idle as you can.

Our love to dear Edith. If you see Mary, tell her that we have received our trunk. Hartley is quite well, and my talkativeness is his, without diminution on my side. 'Tis strange, but certainly many things go in the blood, beside gout and scrophula. Yesterday I dined at Longman's and met Pratt, and that honest piece of prolix dullity and nullity, young Towers, who desired to be remembered to you. To-morrow Sara and I dine at Mister Gobwin's, as

Hartley calls him, who gave the philosopher such a rap on the shins with a ninepin that Gobwin in huge pain lectured Sara on his boisterousness. I was not at home. Est modus in rebus. Moshes is somewhat too rough and noisy, but the cadaverous silence of Godwin's children is to me quite catacombish, and, thinking of Mary Wollstonecraft, I was oppressed by it the day Davy and I dined there.

God love you and

S. T. Coleridge.

CV. TO THE SAME.

Saturday, January 25, 1800.

My dear Southey,—No day passes in which I do not as it were yearn after you, but in truth my occupations have lately swoln above smothering point. I am over mouth and nostrils. I have inclosed a poem which Mrs. Robinson gave me for your "Anthology." She is a woman of undoubted genius. There was a poem of hers in this morning's paper which both in metre and matter pleased me much. She overloads everything; but I never knew a human being with so full a mind—bad, good, and indifferent, I grant you, but full and overflowing. This poem I asked for you, because I thought the metre stimulating and some of the stanzas really good. The first line of the twelfth would of itself redeem a worse poem.[225] I think you will agree with me, but should you not, yet still put it in, my dear fellow! for my sake, and out of respect to a woman-poet's feelings. Miss Hayes I have seen. Charles Lloyd's conduct has been atrocious beyond what you stated. Lamb himself confessed to me that during the time in which he kept up his ranting, sentimental correspondence with Miss Hayes, he frequently read her letters in company, as a subject for laughter, and then sate down and answered them quite à la Rousseau! Poor Lloyd! Every hour new-creates him; he is his own posterity in a perpetually flowing series, and his body unfortunately retaining an external identity, their mutual contradictions and disagreeings are united under one name, and of course are called lies, treachery, and rascality! I would not give him up, but that the same circumstances which have wrenched his morals prevent in him any salutary exercise of genius. And therefore he is not worth to the world that I should embroil and embrangle myself in his interests.

Of Miss Hayes' intellect I do not think so highly as you, or rather, to speak sincerely, I think not contemptuously but certainly despectively thereof. Yet I think you likely in this case to have judged better than I; for to hear a thing, ugly and petticoated, ex-syllogize a God with cold-blooded precision, and attempt to run religion through the body with an icicle, an icicle from a Scotch Hog-trough! I do not endure it; my eye beholds phantoms, and "nothing is, but what is not."

By your last I could not find whether or no you still are willing to execute the "History of the Levelling Principle." Let me hear. Tom Wedgwood is going to the Isle of St. Nevis. As to myself, Lessing out of the question; I must stay in England.... Dear Hartley is well, and in high force; he sported of his own accord a theologico-astronomical hypothesis. Having so perpetually heard of good boys being put up into the sky when they are dead, and being now beyond measure enamoured of the lamps in the streets, he said one night coming through the streets, "Stars are dead lamps, they be'nt naughty, they are put up in the sky."

Two or three weeks ago he was talking to himself while I was writing, and I took down his soliloquy. It would make a most original poem.

You say, I illuminize. I think that property will some time or other be modified by the predominance of intellect, even as rank and superstition are now modified by and subordinated to property, that much is to be hoped of the future; but first those particular modes of property which more particularly stop the diffusion must be done away, as injurious to property itself; these are priesthood and the too great patronage of Government. Therefore, if to act on the belief that all things are the process, and that inapplicable truths are moral falsehoods, be to illuminize, why then I illuminize! I know that I have been obliged to illuminize so late at night, or rather mornings, that eyes have smarted as if I had allum in eyes! I believe I have misspelt the word, and ought to have written Alum; that aside, 'tis a humorous pun!

Tell Davy that I will soon write. God love him! You and I, Southey! know a good and great man or two in this world of ours.

God love you, my dear Southey, and your affectionate

S. T. Coleridge.

My kind love to Edith. Let me hear from you, and do not be angry with me that I don't answer your letters regularly.

CVI. TO THE SAME.

(Early in 1800.)

My dear Southey,—I shall give up this Newspaper business; it is too, too fatiguing. I have attended the Debates twice, and the first time I was twenty-five hours in activity, and that of a very unpleasant kind; and the second time, from ten in the morning till four o'clock the next morning. I am sure that you will excuse my silence, though indeed after two such letters from you I cannot scarcely excuse it myself. First of the book business. I find a resistance which I did not expect to the anonymousness of the publication. Longman seems confident that a work on such a subject without a name would not do. Translations and perhaps Satires are, he says, the only works that booksellers now venture on without a name. He is very solicitous to have your "Thalaba," and wonders (most wonderful!) that you do not write a novel. That would be the thing! and truly, if by no more pains than a "St. Leon"[226] requires you could get four hundred pounds!! or half the money, I say so too! If we were together we might easily toss up a novel, to be published in the name of one of us, or two, if that were all, and then christen 'em by lots. As sure as ink flows in my pen, by help of an amanuensis I could write a volume a week—and Godwin got four hundred pounds! for it—think of that, Master Brooks. I hope that some time or other you will write a novel on that subject of yours! I mean the "Rise and Progress of a Laugher"—Le Grice in your eye—the effect of Laughing on taste, manners, morals, and happiness! But as to the Jacobin Book, I must wait till I hear from you. Phillips would be very glad to engage you to write a school book for him, the History of Poetry in all nations, about 400 pages; but this, too, must have your name. He would give sixty pounds. If poor dear Burnett were with you, he might do it under your eye and with your instructions as well as you or I could do it, but it is the name. Longman remarked acutely enough, "The booksellers scarcely pretend to judge the merits of the book, but we know the saleableness of the name! and as they continue to buy most books on the calculation of a first edition of a thousand copies, they are seldom much mistaken; for the name gives them the excuse for sending it to all the Gemmen in Great Britain and the Colonies, from whom they have standing orders for new books of reputation." This is the secret why books published by country booksellers, or by authors on their own account, so seldom succeed.

As to my schemes of residence, I am as unfixed as yourself, only that we are under the absolute necessity of fixing somewhere, and that somewhere will, I suppose, be Stowey. There are all my books and all our furniture. In May I am under a kind of engagement to go with Sara to Ottery. My family wish me to fix there, but that I must decline in the names of public liberty and individual free-agency. Elder brothers, not senior in intellect, and not sympathising in main opinions, are subjects of occasional visits; not temptations to a co-township. But if you go to Burton, Sara and I will waive the Ottery plan, if possible, and spend May and June with you, and perhaps July; but she must be settled in a house by the latter end of July, or the first week in August. Till we are with you, Sara means to spend five weeks with the Roskillies, and a week or two at Bristol, where I shall join her. She will leave London in three weeks at least, perhaps a fortnight; and I shall give up lodgings and billet myself free of expense at my friend Purkis's, at Brentford. This is my present plan. O my dear Southey! I would to God that your health did not enforce you to migrate—we might most assuredly continue to fix a residence somewhere, which might possess a sort of centrality. Alfoxden would make two houses sufficiently divided for unimpinging independence.

Tell Davy that I have not forgotten him, because without an epilepsy I cannot forget him; and if I wrote to him as often as I think of him, Lord have mercy on his pocket!

God bless you again and again.

S. T. Coleridge.

I pass this evening with Charlotte Smith at her house.

CVII. TO THE SAME.

[Postmark February 18], 1800.

My dear Southey,—What do you mean by the words, "it is indeed by expectation"? speaking of your state of health. I cannot bear to think of your going to a strange country without any one who loves and understands you. But we will talk of all this. I have not a moment's time, and my head aches. I was up till five o'clock this morning. My brain is so overworked that I could doze troublously and with cold limbs, so affected was my circulation. I shall do no more for Stuart. Read Pitt's speech[227] in the "Morning Post" of to-day (February 18, Tuesday). I reported the whole with notes so scanty, that—Mr. Pitt is much obliged to me. For, by Heaven, he never talked half as eloquently in his life-time. He is a stupid, insipid charlatan, that Pitt. Indeed, except Fox, I, you, or anybody might learn to speak better than any man in the House. For the next fortnight I expect to be so busy, that I shall go out of London a mile or so to be wholly uninterrupted. I do not understand the Beguin-nings[228] of Holland. Phillips is a good-for-nothing fellow, but what of that? He will give you sixty pounds, and advance half the money now for a book you can do in a fortnight, or three weeks at farthest. I would advise you not to give it up so hastily. Phillips eats no flesh. I observe, wittily enough, that whatever might be thought of innate ideas, there could be no doubt to a man who had seen Phillips of the existence of innate beef. Let my "Mad Ox" keep my name. "Fire and Famine" do just what you like with. I have no wish either way. The "Fears in Solitude," I fear, is not my property, and I have no encouragement to think it will be given up, but if I hear otherwise I will let you know speedily; in the mean time, do not rely on it. Your review-plan[229] cannot answer for this reason. It could exist only as long as the ononymous anti-anonymists remained in life, health, and the humour, and no publisher would undertake a periodical publication on so gossamery a tie. Besides, it really would not be right for any man to make so many people have strange and uncomfortable feelings towards him; which must be the case, however kind the reviews might be—and what but nonsense is published? The author of "Gebir" I cannot find out. There are none of his books in town. You have made a sect of Gebirites by your review, but it was not a fair, though a very kind review. I have sent a letter to Mrs. Fricker, which Sara directed to you. I hope it has come safe. Let me see, are there any other questions?

So, my dear Southey, God love you, and never, never cease to believe that I am affectionately yours,

S. T. Coleridge.

Love to Edith.

CVIII. TO THE SAME.

No. 21 Buckingham Street [early in 1800].

My dear Southey,—I will see Longman on Tuesday, at the farthest, but I pray you send me up what you have done, if you can, as I will read it to him, unless he will take my word for it. But we cannot expect that he will treat finally without seeing a considerable specimen. Send it by the coach, and be assured that it will be as safe as in your own escritoire, and I will remit it the very day Longman or any bookseller has treated for it satisfactorily. Less than two hundred pounds I would not take. Have you tried warm bathing in a high temperature? As to your travelling, your first business must, of course, be to settle. The Greek Islands[230] and Turkey in general are one continued Hounslow Heath, only that the highwaymen there have an awkward habit of murdering people. As to Poland and Hungary, the detestable roads and inns of them both, and the severity of the climate in the former, render travelling there little suited to your state of health. Oh! for peace and the South of France! What a detestable villainy is not the new Constitution.[231] I have written all that relates to it which has appeared in the "Morning Post;" and not without strength or elegance. But the French are children.[232] 'Tis an infirmity to hope or fear concerning them. I wish they had a king again, if it were only that Sieyès and Bonaparte might be hung. Guillotining is too republican a death for such reptiles! You'll write another quarter for Mr. Stuart? You will torture yourself for twelve or thirteen guineas? I pray you do not do so! You might get without the exertion, and with but little more expenditure of time, from fifty to an hundred pounds. Thus, for instance, bring together on your table, or skim over successively Brücker, Lardner's "History of Heretics," Russell's "Modern Europe," and Andrews' "History of England," and write a history of levellers and the levelling principle under some goodly title, neither praising or abusing them. Lacedæmon, Crete, and the attempts at agrarian laws in Rome—all these you have by heart.... Plato and Zeno are, I believe, nearly all that relates to the purpose in Brücker. Lardner's is a most amusing book to read. Write only a sheet of letter paper a day, which you can easily do in an hour, and in twelve weeks you will have produced (without any toil of brains, observing none but chronological arrangement, and giving you little more than the trouble of transcription) twenty-four sheets octavo. I will gladly write a philosophical introduction that shall enlighten without offending, and therein state the rise of property, etc. For this you might secure sixty or seventy guineas, and receive half the money on producing the first eight sheets, in a month from your first commencement of the work. Many other works occur to me, but I mention this because it might be doing great good, inasmuch as boys and youths would read it with far different impressions from their fathers and godfathers, and yet the latter find nothing alarming in the nature of the work, it being purely historical. If I am not deceived by the recency of their date, my "Ode to the Duchess" and my "Xmas Carol" will do for your "Anthology." I have therefore transcribed them for you. But I need not ask you, for God's sake, to use your own judgment without spare.

(No signature.)

CIX. TO THE SAME.

February 28, 1800.

It goes to my heart, my dear Southey! to sit down and write to you, knowing that I can scarcely fill half a side—the postage lies on my conscience. I am translating manuscript plays of Schiller.[233] They are poems, full of long speeches, in very polish'd blank verse. The theatre! the theatre! my dear Southey! it will never, never, never do! If you go to Portugal, your History thereof will do, but, for present money, novels or translations. I do not see that a book said by you in the preface to have been written merely as a book for young persons could injure your reputation more than Milton's "Accidence" injured his. I would do it, because you can do it so easily. It is not necessary that you should say much about French or German Literature. Do it so. Poetry of savage nations—Poetry of rudely civilized—Homer and the Hebrew Poetry, etc.—Poetry of civilized nations under Republics and Polytheism, State of Poetry under the Roman and Greek Empires—Revival of it in Italy, in Spain, and England—then go steadily on with England to the end, except one chapter about German Poetry to conclude with, which I can write for you.

In the "Morning Post" was a poem of fascinating metre by Mary Robinson; 'twas on Wednesday, Feb. 26, and entitled the "Haunted Beach."[234] I was so struck with it that I sent to her to desire that [it] might be preserved in the "Anthology." She was extremely flattered by the idea of its being there, as she idolizes you and your doings. So, if it be not too late, I pray you let it be in. If you should not have received that day's paper, write immediately that I may transcribe it. It falls off sadly to the last, wants tale and interest; but the images are new and very distinct—that "silvery carpet" is so just that it is unfortunate it should seem so bad, for it is really good; but the metre, ay! that woman has an ear. William Taylor, from whom I have received a couple of letters full of thought and information, says what astounded me, that double rhymes in our language have always a ludicrous association. Mercy on the man! where are his ears and feelings? His taste cannot be quite right, from this observation; but he is a famous fellow—that is not to be denied.

Sara is poorly still. Hartley rampant, and emperorizes with your pictures. Harry is a fine boy. Hartley told a gentleman, "Metinks you are like Southey," and he was not wholly unlike you—but the chick calling you simple "Southey," so pompously!

God love you and your Edith.

S. T. Coleridge.

CHAPTER VI
A LAKE POET
1800-1803

CX. TO THOMAS POOLE.

August 14, 1800.

My dear Poole,—Your two letters[235] I received exactly four days ago—some days they must have been lying at Ambleside before they were sent to Grasmere, and some days at Grasmere before they moved to Keswick.... It grieved me that you had felt so much from my silence. Believe me, I have been harassed with business, and shall remain so for the remainder of this year. Our house is a delightful residence, something less than half a mile from the lake of Keswick and something more than a furlong from the town. It commands both that lake and the lake of Bassenthwaite. Skiddaw is behind us; to the left, the right, and in front mountains of all shapes and sizes. The waterfall of Lodore is distinctly visible. In garden, etc., we are uncommonly well off, and our landlord, who resides next door in this twofold house, is already much attached to us. He is a quiet, sensible man, with as large a library as yours,—and perhaps rather larger,—well stored with encyclopædias, dictionaries, and histories, etc., all modern. The gentry of the country, titled and untitled, have all called or are about to call on me, and I shall have free access to the magnificent library of Sir Gilfrid Lawson. I wish you could come here in October after your harvesting, and stand godfather at the christening of my child. In October the country is in all its blaze of beauty.

We are well and the Wordsworths are well. The two volumes of the "Lyrical Ballads" will appear in about a fortnight or three weeks. Sara sends her best kind love to your mother. How much we rejoice in her health I need not say. Love to Ward, and to Chester, to whom I shall write as soon as I am at leisure. I was standing at the very top of Skiddaw, by a little shed of slate stones on which I had scribbled with a bit of slate my name among the other names. A lean-expression-faced man came up the hill, stood beside me a little while, then, on running over the names, exclaimed, "Coleridge! I lay my life that is the poet Coleridge!"

God bless you, and for God's sake never doubt that I am attached to you beyond all other men.

S. T. Coleridge.

CXI. TO SIR H. DAVY.

Thursday night, October 9, 1800.

My dear Davy,—I was right glad, glad with a stagger of the heart, to see your writing again. Many a moment have I had all my France and England curiosity suspended and lost, looking in the advertisement front column of the "Morning Post Gazeteer" for Mr. Davy's Galvanic habitudes of charcoal.—Upon my soul I believe there is not a letter in those words round which a world of imagery does not circumvolve; your room, the garden, the cold bath, the moonlight rocks, Barristed, Moore, and simple-looking Frere, and dreams of wonderful things attached to your name,—and Skiddaw, and Glaramara, and Eagle Crag, and you, and Wordsworth, and me, on the top of them! I pray you do write to me immediately, and tell me what you mean by the possibility of your assuming a new occupation. Have you been successful to the extent of your expectations in your late chemical inquiries?

As to myself, I am doing little worthy the relation. I write for Stuart in the "Morning Post," and I am compelled by the god Pecunia—which was one name of the supreme Jupiter—to give a volume of letters from Germany, which will be a decent lounge book, and not an atom more. The "Christabel" was running up to 1,300 lines,[236] and was so much admired by Wordsworth, that he thought it indelicate to print two volumes with his name, in which so much of another man's was included; and, which was of more consequence, the poem was in direct opposition to the very purpose for which the lyrical ballads were published, viz., an experiment to see how far those passions which alone give any value to extraordinary incidents were capable of interesting, in and for themselves, in the incidents of common life. We mean to publish the "Christabel," therefore, with a long blank-verse poem of Wordsworth's, entitled "The Pedlar."[237] I assure you I think very differently of "Christabel." I would rather have written "Ruth," and "Nature's Lady," than a million such poems. But why do I calumniate my own spirit by saying "I would rather"? God knows it is as delightful to me that they are written. I know that at present, and I hope that it will be so; my mind has disciplined itself into a willing exertion of its powers, without any reference to their comparative value.

I cannot speak favourably of W.'s health, but, indeed, he has not done common justice to Dr. Beddoes's kind prescriptions. I saw his countenance darken, and all his hopes vanish, when he saw the prescriptions—his scepticism concerning medicines! nay, it is not enough scepticism! Yet, now that peas and beans are over, I have hopes that he will in good earnest make a fair and full trial. I rejoice with sincere joy at Beddoes's recovery.

Wordsworth is fearful you have been much teased by the printers on his account, but you can sympathise with him. The works which I gird myself up to attack as soon as money concerns will permit me are the Life of Lessing, and the Essay on Poetry. The latter is still more at my heart than the former: its title would be an essay on the elements of poetry,—it would be in reality a disguised system of morals and politics. When you write,—and do write soon,—tell me how I can get your essay on the nitrous oxide. If you desired Johnson to have one sent to Lackington's, to be placed in Mr. Crosthwaite's monthly parcel for Keswick, I should receive it. Are your galvanic discoveries important? What do they lead to? All this is ultra-crepidation, but would to Heaven I had as much knowledge as I have sympathy!

My wife and children are well; the baby was dying some weeks ago, so the good people would have it baptized; his name is Derwent Coleridge,[238] so called from the river, for, fronting our house, the Greta runs into the Derwent. Had it been a girl the name should have been Greta. By the bye, Greta, or rather Grieta, is exactly the Cocytus of the Greeks. The word, literally rendered in modern English, is "the loud lamenter;" to griet in the Cambrian dialect, signifying to roar aloud for grief or pain, and it does roar with a vengeance! I will say nothing about spring—a thirsty man tries to think of anything but the stream when he knows it to be ten miles off! God bless you!

Your most affectionate
S. T. Coleridge.

CXII. TO THE SAME.

October 18, 1800.

My dear Davy,—Our mountains northward end in the mountain Carrock,—one huge, steep, enormous bulk of stones, desolately variegated with the heath plant; at its foot runs the river Calder, and a narrow vale between it and the mountain Bowscale, so narrow, that in its greatest width it is not more than a furlong. But that narrow vale is so green, so beautiful, there are moods in which a man might weep to look at it. On this mountain Carrock, at the summit of which are the remains of a vast Druid circle of stones, I was wandering, when a thick cloud came on, and wrapped me in such darkness that I could not see ten yards before me, and with the cloud a storm of wind and hail, the like of which I had never before seen and felt. At the very summit is a cone of stones, built by the shepherds, and called the Carrock Man. Such cones are on the tops of almost all our mountains, and they are all called men. At the bottom of the Carrock Man I seated myself for shelter, but the wind became so fearful and tyrannous, that I was apprehensive some of the stones might topple down upon me, so I groped my way farther down and came to three rocks, placed on this wise , each one supported by the other like a child's house of cards, and in the hollow and screen which they made I sate for a long while sheltered, as if I had been in my own study in which I am now writing: there I sate with a total feeling worshipping the power and "eternal link" of energy. The darkness vanished as by enchantment; far off, far, far off to the south, the mountains of Glaramara and Great Gable and their family appeared distinct, in deepest, sablest blue. I rose, and behind me was a rainbow bright as the brightest. I descended by the side of a torrent, and passed, or rather crawled (for I was forced to descend on all fours), by many a naked waterfall, till, fatigued and hungry (and with a finger almost broken, and which remains swelled to the size of two fingers), I reached the narrow vale, and the single house nestled in ash and sycamores. I entered to claim the universal hospitality of this country; but instead of the life and comfort usual in these lonely houses, I saw dirt, and every appearance of misery—a pale woman sitting by a peat fire. I asked her for bread and milk, and she sent a small child to fetch it, but did not rise herself. I eat very heartily of the black, sour bread, and drank a bowl of milk, and asked her to permit me to pay her. "Nay," says she, "we are not so scant as that— you are right welcome; but do you know any help for the rheumatics, for I have been so long ailing that I am almost fain to die?" So I advised her to eat a great deal of mustard, having seen in an advertisement something about essence of mustard curing the most obstinate cases of rheumatism. But do write me, and tell me some cure for the rheumatism; it is in her shoulders, and the small of her back chiefly. I wish much to go off with some bottles of stuff to the poor creature. I should walk the ten miles as ten yards. With love and honour, my dear Davy,

Yours,
S. T. Coleridge.

CXIII. TO THE SAME.

Greta Hall, Tuesday night, December 2, 1800.

My dear Davy,—By an accident I did not receive your letter till this evening. I would that you had added to the account of your indisposition the probable causes of it. It has left me anxious whether or no you have not exposed yourself to unwholesome influences in your chemical pursuits. There are few beings both of hope and performance, but few who combine the "are" and the "will be." For God's sake, therefore, my dear fellow, do not rip open the bird that lays the golden eggs. I have not received your book. I read yesterday a sort of medical review about it. I suppose Longman will send it to me when he sends down the "Lyrical Ballads" to Wordsworth. I am solicitous to read the latter part. Did there appear to you any remote analogy between the case I translated from the German Magazine and the effects produced by your gas? Did Carlisle[239] ever communicate to you, or has he in any way published his facts concerning pain which he mentioned when we were with him? It is a subject which exceedingly interests me. I want to read something by somebody expressly on pain, if only to give an arrangement to my own thoughts, though if it were well treated I have little doubt it would revolutionize them. For the last month I have been trembling on through sands and swamps of evil and bodily grievance. My eyes have been inflamed to a degree that rendered reading and writing scarcely possible; and, strange as it seems, the act of metre composition, as I lay in bed, perceptibly affected them, and my voluntary ideas were every minute passing, more or less transformed into vivid spectra. I had leeches repeatedly applied to my temples, and a blister behind my ear—and my eyes are now my own, but in the place where the blister was, six small but excruciating boils have appeared, and harass me almost beyond endurance. In the mean time my darling Hartley has been taken with a stomach illness, which has ended in the yellow jaundice; and this greatly alarms me. So much for the doleful! Amid all these changes, and humiliations, and fears, the sense of the Eternal abides in me, and preserves unsubdued my cheerful faith, that all I endure is full of blessings!

At times, indeed, I would fain be somewhat of a more tangible utility than I am; but so I suppose it is with all of us—one while cheerful, stirring, feeling in resistance nothing but a joy and a stimulus; another while drowsy, self-distrusting, prone to rest, loathing our own self-promises, withering our own hopes—our hopes, the vitality and cohesion of our being!

I purpose to have "Christabel" published by itself—this I publish with confidence—but my travels in Germany come from me now with mortal pangs. Nothing but the most pressing necessity could have induced me—and even now I hesitate and tremble. Be so good as to have all that is printed of "Christabel" sent to me per post.

Wordsworth has nearly finished the concluding poem. It is of a mild, unimposing character, but full of beauties to those short-necked men who have their hearts sufficiently near their heads—the relative distance of which (according to citizen Tourdes, the French translator of Spallanzani) determines the sagacity or stupidity of all bipeds and quadrupeds.

There is a deep blue cloud over the heavens; the lake, and the vale, and the mountains are all in darkness; only the summits of all the mountains in long ridges, covered with snow, are bright to a dazzling excess. A glorious scene! Hartley was in my arms the other evening, looking at the sky; he saw the moon glide into a large cloud. Shortly after, at another part of the cloud, several stars sailed in. Says he, "Pretty creatures! they are going in to see after their mother moon."

Remember me kindly to King. Write as often as you can; but above all things, my loved and honoured dear fellow, do not give up the idea of letting me and Skiddaw see you. God love you!

S. T. Coleridge.

Tobin writes me that Thompson[240] has made some lucrative discovery. Do you know aught about it? Have you seen T. Wedgwood since his return?

CXIV. TO THOMAS POOLE.

Greta Hall, Keswick, Saturday night, December 5, 1800.

My dearest Friend,—I have been prevented from answering your last letter entirely by the state of my eyes, and my wish to write more fully to you than their weakness would permit. For the last month and more I have indeed been a very crazy machine.... That consequence of this long-continued ill-health which I most regret is, that it has thrown me so sadly behindhand in the performance of my engagements with the bookseller, that I almost fear I shall not be able to raise money enough by Christmas to make it prudent for me to journey southward. I shall, however, try hard for it. My plan was to go to London, and make a faint trial whether or no I could get a sort of dramatic romance, which I had more than half finished, upon the stage, and from London to visit Stowey and Gunville. Dear little Hartley has been ill in a stomach complaint which ended in the yellow jaundice, and frightened me sorely, as you may well believe. But, praise be to God, he is recovered and begins to look like himself. He is a very extraordinary creature, and if he live will, I doubt not, prove a great genius. Derwent is a fat, pretty child, healthy and hungry. I deliberated long whether I should not call him Thomas Poole Coleridge, and at last gave up the idea only because your nephew is called Thomas Poole, and because if ever it should be my destiny once again to live near you, I believed that such a name would give pain to some branches of your family. You will scarcely exact a very severe account of what a man has been doing who has been obliged for days and days together to keep his bed. Yet I have not been altogether idle, having in my own conceit gained great light into several parts of the human mind which have hitherto remained either wholly unexplained or most falsely explained. To one resolution I am wholly made up, to wit, that as soon as I am a freeman in the world of money I will never write a line for the express purpose of money (but only as believing it good and useful, in some way or other). Although I am certain that I have been greatly improving both in knowledge and power in these last twelve months, yet still at times it presses upon me with a painful weight that I have not evidenced a more tangible utility. I have too much trifled with my reputation. You have conversed much with Davy; he is delighted with you. What do you think of him? Is he not a great man, think you?... I and my wife were beyond measure delighted by your account of your mother's health. Give our best, kindest loves to her. Charles Lloyd has settled at Ambleside, sixteen miles from Keswick. I shall not see him. If I cannot come, I will write you a very, very long letter, containing the most important of the many thoughts and feelings which I want to communicate to you, but hope to do it face to face.

Give my love to Ward, and to J. Chester. How is poor old Mr. Rich and his wife?

God have you ever in his keeping, making life tranquil to you. Believe me to be what I have been ever, and am, attached to you one degree more at least than to any other living man.

S. T. Coleridge.

CXV. TO SIR H. DAVY.

February 3, 1801.

My dear Davy,—I can scarcely reconcile it to my conscience to make you pay postage for another letter. Oh, what a fine unveiling of modern politics it would be if there were published a minute detail of all the sums received by government from the post establishment, and of all the outlets in which the sums so received flowed out again! and, on the other hand, all the domestic affections which had been stifled, all the intellectual progress that would have been, but is not, on account of the heavy tax, etc., etc. The letters of a nation ought to be paid for as an article of national expense. Well! but I did not take up this paper to flourish away in splenetic politics. A gentleman resident here, his name Calvert,[241] an idle, good-hearted, and ingenious man, has a great desire to commence fellow-student with me and Wordsworth in chemistry. He is an intimate friend of Wordsworth's, and he has proposed to W. to take a house which he (Calvert) has nearly built, called Windy Brow, in a delicious situation, scarce half a mile from Greta Hall, the residence of S. T. Coleridge, Esq., and so for him (Calvert) to live with them, that is, Wordsworth and his sister. In this case he means to build a little laboratory, etc. Wordsworth has not quite decided, but is strongly inclined to adopt the scheme, because he and his sister have before lived with Calvert on the same footing, and are much attached to him; because my health is so precarious and so much injured by wet, and his health, too, is like little potatoes, no great things, and therefore Grasmere (thirteen miles from Keswick) is too great a distance for us to enjoy each other's society without inconvenience, as much as it would be profitable for us both; and, likewise, because he feels it more necessary for him to have some intellectual pursuit less closely connected with deep passion than poetry, and is of course desirous, too, not to be so wholly ignorant of knowledge so exceedingly important. However, whether Wordsworth come or no, Calvert and I have determined to begin and go on. Calvert is a man of sense and some originality, and is, besides, what is well called a handy man. He is a good practical mechanic, etc., and is desirous to lay out any sum of money that is necessary. You know how long, how ardently I have wished to initiate myself in chemical science, both for its own sake and in no small degree likewise, my beloved friend, that I may be able to sympathise with all that you do and think. Sympathise blindly with it all I do even now, God knows! from the very middle of my heart's heart, but I would fain sympathise with you in the light of knowledge. This opportunity is exceedingly precious to me, as on my own account I could not afford the least additional expense, having been already, by long and successive illnesses, thrown behindhand so much that for the next four or five months I fear, let me work as hard as I can, I shall not be able to do what my heart within me burns to do, that is, to concentre my free mind to the affinities of the feelings with words and ideas under the title of "Concerning Poetry, and the nature of the Pleasures derived from it." I have faith that I do understand the subject, and I am sure that if I write what I ought to do on it, the work would supersede all the books of metaphysics, and all the books of morals too. To whom shall a young man utter his pride, if not to a young man whom he loves?

I beg you, therefore, my dear Davy, to write me a long letter when you are at leisure, informing me: Firstly, What books it will be well for me and Calvert to purchase. Secondly, Directions for a convenient little laboratory. Thirdly, To what amount apparatus would run in expense, and whether or no you would be so good as to superintend its making at Bristol. Fourthly, Give me your advice how to begin. And, fifthly, and lastly, and mostly, do send a drop of hope to my parched tongue, that you will, if you can, come and visit me in the spring. Indeed, indeed, you ought to see this country, this beautiful country, and then the joy you would send into me!

The shape of this paper will convince you with what eagerness I began this letter; I really did not see that it was not a sheet.

I have been thinking vigorously during my illness, so that I cannot say that my long, long wakeful nights have been all lost to me. The subject of my meditations has been the relations of thoughts to things; in the language of Hume, of ideas to impressions. I may be truly described in the words of Descartes: I have been "res cogitans, id est, dubitans, affirmans, negans, pauca intelligens, multa ignorans, volens, nolens, imaginans etiam, et sentiens." I please myself with believing that you will receive no small pleasure from the result of these broodings, although I expect in you (in some points) a determined opponent, but I say of my mind in this respect: "Manet imperterritus ille hostem magnanimum opperiens, et mole suâ stat." Every poor fellow has his proud hour sometimes, and this I suppose is mine.

I am better in every respect than I was, but am still very feeble. The weather has been woefully against me for the last fortnight, having rained here almost incessantly. I take quantities of bark, but the effect is (to express myself with the dignity of science) $x = 0000000$, and I shall not gather strength, or that little suffusion of bloom which belongs to my healthy state, till I can walk out.

God bless you, my dear Davy! and your ever affectionate friend,

S. T. Coleridge.

P. S. An electrical machine, and a number of little knickknacks connected with it, Mr. Calvert has.—Write.

CXVI. TO THOMAS POOLE.

Monday, March 16, 1801.

My dear Friend,—The interval since my last letter has been filled up by me in the most intense study. If I do not greatly delude myself, I have not only completely extricated the notions of time and space, but have overthrown the doctrine of association, as taught by Hartley, and with it all the irreligious metaphysics of modern infidels—especially the doctrine of necessity. This I have done; but I trust that I am about to do more—namely, that I shall be able to evolve all the five senses, that is, to deduce them from one sense, and to state their growth and the causes of their difference, and in this evolvement to solve the process of life and consciousness. I write this to you only, and I pray you, mention what I have written to no one. At Wordsworth's advice, or rather fervent entreaty, I have intermitted the pursuit. The intensity of thought, and the number of minute experiments with light and figure, have made me so nervous and feverish that I cannot sleep as long as I ought and have been used to do; and the sleep which I have is made up of ideas so connected, and so little different from the operations of reason, that it does not afford me the due refreshment. I shall therefore take a week's respite, and make "Christabel" ready for the press; which I shall publish by itself, in order to get rid of all my engagements with Longman. My German Book I have suffered to remain suspended chiefly because the thoughts which had employed my sleepless nights during my illness were imperious over me; and though poverty was staring me in the face, yet I dared behold my image miniatured in the pupil of her hollow eye, so steadily did I look her in the face; for it seemed to me a suicide of my very soul to divert my attention from truths so important, which came to me almost as a revelation. Likewise, I cannot express to you, dear Friend of my heart! the loathing which I once or twice felt when I attempted to write, merely for the bookseller, without any sense of the moral utility of what I was writing. I shall therefore, as I said, immediately publish my "Christabel," with two essays annexed to it, on the "Preternatural" and on "Metre."—This done, I shall propose to Longman, instead of my Travels (which, though nearly done, I am exceedingly anxious not to publish, because it brings me forward in a personal way, as a man who relates little adventures of himself to amuse people, and thereby exposes me to sarcasm and the malignity of anonymous critics, and is, besides, beneath me, ...) I shall propose to Longman to accept instead of these Travels a work on the originality and merits of Locke, Hobbes, and Hume, which work I mean as a pioneer to my greater work, and as exhibiting a proof that I have not formed opinions without an attentive perusal of the works of my predecessors, from Aristotle to Kant.

I am confident that I can prove that the reputation of these three men has been wholly unmerited, and I have in what I have already written traced the whole history of the causes that effected this reputation entirely to Wordsworth's satisfaction.

You have seen, I hope, the "Lyrical Ballads." In the divine poem called "Michael," by an infamous blunder[242] of the printer, near twenty lines are omitted in page 210, which makes it nearly unintelligible. Wordsworth means to write to you and to send them together with a list of the numerous errata. The character of the "Lyrical Ballads" is very great, and will increase daily. They have extolled them in the "British Critic." Ask Chester (to whom I shall write in a week or so concerning his German books) for Greenough's address, and be so kind as to send it immediately. Indeed, I hope for a long letter from you, your opinion of the L. B., the preface, etc. You know, I presume, that Davy is appointed Director of the Laboratory, and Professor at the Royal Institution? I received a very affectionate letter from him on the occasion. Love to all. We are all well, except, perhaps, myself. Write! God love you and

S. T. Coleridge.

CXVII. TO THE SAME.

Monday, March 23, 1801.

My dear Friend,—I received your kind letter of the 14th. I was agreeably disappointed in finding that you had been interested in the letter respecting Locke. Those which follow are abundantly more entertaining and important; but I have no one to transcribe them. Nay, three letters are written which have not been sent to Mr. Wedgwood,[243] because I have no one to transcribe them for me, and I do not wish to be without copies. Of that letter which you have I have no copy. It is somewhat unpleasant to me that Mr. Wedgwood has never answered my letter requesting his opinion of the utility of such a work, nor acknowledged the receipt of the long letter containing the evidences that the whole of Locke's system, as far as it was a system, and with the exclusion of those parts only which have been given up as absurdities by his warmest admirers, preëxisted in the writings of Descartes, in a far more pure, elegant, and delightful form. Be not afraid that I shall join the party of the Little-ists. I believe that I shall delight you by the detection of their artifices. Now Mr. Locke was the founder of this sect, himself a perfect Little-ist.

My opinion is thus: that deep thinking is attainable only by a man of deep feeling, and that all truth is a species of revelation. The more I understand of Sir Isaac Newton's works, the more boldly I dare utter to my own mind, and therefore to you, that I believe the souls of five hundred Sir Isaac Newtons would go to the making up of a Shakespeare or a Milton. But if it please the Almighty to grant me health, hope, and a steady mind (always the three clauses of my hourly prayers), before my thirtieth year I will thoroughly understand the whole of Newton's works. At present I must content myself with endeavouring to make myself entire master of his easier work, that on Optics. I am exceedingly delighted with the beauty and neatness of his experiments, and with the accuracy of his immediate deductions from them; but the opinions founded on these deductions, and indeed his whole theory is, I am persuaded, so exceedingly superficial as without impropriety to be deemed false. Newton was a mere materialist. Mind, in his system, is always passive,—a lazy Looker-on on an external world. If the mind be not passive, if it be indeed made in God's Image, and that, too, in the sublimest sense, the Image of the Creator, there is ground for suspicion that any system built on the passiveness of the mind must be false, as a system. I need not observe, my dear friend, how unutterably silly and contemptible these opinions would be if written to any but to another self. I assure you, solemnly assure you, that you and Wordsworth are the only men on earth to whom I would have uttered a word on this subject.

It is a rule, by which I hope to direct all my literary efforts, to let my opinions and my proofs go together. It is insolent to differ from the public opinion in opinion, if it be only opinion. It is sticking up little i by itself, i against the whole alphabet. But one word with meaning in it is worth the whole alphabet together. Such is a sound argument, an incontrovertible fact.

Oh, for a Lodge in a land where human life was an end to which labour was only a means, instead of being, as it is here, a mere means of carrying on labour. I am oppressed at times with a true heart-gnawing melancholy when I contemplate the state of my poor oppressed country. God knows, it is as much as I can do to put meat and bread on my own table, and hourly some poor starving wretch comes to my door to put in his claim for part of it. It fills me with indignation to hear the croaking account which the English emigrants send home of America. "The society so bad, the manners so vulgar, the servants so insolent!" Why, then, do they not seek out one another and make a society? It is arrant ingratitude to talk so of a land in which there is no poverty but as a consequence of absolute idleness; and to talk of it, too, with abuse comparatively with England, with a place where the laborious poor are dying with grass in their bellies. It is idle to talk of the seasons, as if that country must not needs be miserably governed in which an unfavourable season introduces a famine. No! no! dear Poole, it is our pestilent commerce, our unnatural crowding together of men in cities, and our government by rich men, that are bringing about the manifestations of offended Deity. I am assured that such is the depravity of the public mind, that no literary man can find bread in England except by mis-employing and debasing his talents; that nothing of real excellence would be either felt or understood. The annuity which I hold, perhaps by a very precarious tenure, will shortly from the decreasing value of money become less than one half what it was when first allowed to me. If I were allowed to retain it, I would go and settle near Priestley, in America. I shall, no doubt, get a certain price for the two or three works which I shall next publish, but I foresee they will not sell. The booksellers, finding this, will treat me as an unsuccessful author, that is, they will employ me only as an anonymous translator at a guinea a sheet. I have no doubt that I could make £500 a year if I liked. But then I must forego all desire of truth and excellence. I say I would go to America if Wordsworth would go with me, and we could persuade two or three farmers of this country, who are exceedingly attached to us, to accompany us. I would go, if the difficulty of procuring sustenance in this country remain in the state and degree in which it is at present; not on any romantic scheme, but merely because society has become a matter of great indifference to me. I grow daily more and more attached to solitude; but it is a matter of the utmost importance to be removed from seeing and suffering want.

God love you, my dear friend.

S. T. Coleridge.

CXVIII. TO ROBERT SOUTHEY.

Greta Hall, Keswick, [May 6, 1801].

My dear Southey,—I wrote you a very, very gloomy letter; and I have taken blame to myself for inflicting so much pain on you without any adequate motive. Not that I exaggerated anything, as far as the immediate present is concerned; but had I been in better health and a more genial state of sensation, I should assuredly have looked out upon a more cheerful future. Since I wrote you, I have had another and more severe fit of illness, which has left me weak, very weak, but with so calm a mind that I am determined to believe that this fit was bonâ fide the last. Whether I shall be able to pass the next winter in this country is doubtful; nor is it possible I should know till the fall of the leaf. At all events, you will (I hope and trust, and if need were, entreat) spend as much of the summer and autumn with us as will be in your power, and if our healths should permit it, I am confident there will be no other solid objection to our living together in the same house, divided. We have ample room,—room enough, and more than enough, and I am willing to believe that the blessed dreams we dreamt some six years ago may be auguries of something really noble which we may yet perform together.

We wait impatiently, anxiously, for a letter announcing your arrival. Indeed, the article Falmouth has taken precedence of the Leading Paragraph with me for the last three weeks. Our best love to Edith. Derwent is the boast of the county; the little river god is as beautiful as if he had been the child of Venus Anaduomene previous to her emersion. Dear Hartley! we are at times alarmed by the state of his health, but at present he is well. If I were to lose him, I am afraid it would exceedingly deaden my affection for any other children I may have.

A little child, a limber elf
Singing, dancing to itself;
A faery thing with red round cheeks
That always finds, and never seeks,
Doth make a vision to the sight,5
Which fills a father's eyes with light!
And pleasures flow in so thick and fast
Upon his heart that he at last
Must needs express his love's excess
In words of wrong and bitterness.10
Perhaps it is pretty to force together
Thoughts so all unlike each other;
To mutter and mock a broken charm;

To dally with wrong that does no harm.
Perhaps 'tis tender, too, and pretty,15
At each wild word to feel within
A sweet recoil of love and pity;
And what if in a world of sin
(Oh sorrow and shame! should this be true)
Such giddiness of heart and brain20
Comes seldom, save from rage and pain,
So talks as it's most used to do.[244]
A very metaphysical account of fathers calling their children rogues, rascals, and little varlets, etc.

God bless you, my dear Southey! I need not say, Write.

S. T. Coleridge.

P. S. We shall have peas, beans, turnips (with boiled leg of mutton), cauliflowers, French beans, etc., etc., endless! We have a noble garden.

CXIX. TO THE SAME.

Wednesday, July 22, 1801.

My dear Southey,—Yesterday evening I met a boy on an ass, winding down as picturisk a glen as eye ever looked at, he and his beast no mean part of the picture. I had taken a liking to the little blackguard at a distance, and I could have downright hugged him when he gave me a letter in your handwriting. Well, God be praised! I shall surely see you once more, somewhere or other. If it be really impracticable for you to come to me, I will doubtless do anything rather than not see you, though, in simple truth, travelling in chaises, or coaches even, for one day is sure to lay me up for a week. But do, do, for heaven's sake, come and go the shortest way, however dreary it be; for there is enough to be seen when you get to our house. If you did but know what a flutter the old moveable at my left breast has been in since I read your letter. I have not had such a fillip for many months. My dear Edith; how glad you were to see old Bristol again!

I am again climbing up that rock of convalescence from which I have been so often washed off and hurried[back; but I have been so unusually well these last two days that I should begin to look the damsel Hope full in the face, instead of sheep's-eyeing her, were it not that the weather has been so unusually hot, and that is my joy. Yes, sir! we will go to Constantinople; but as it rains there, which my gout loves as the devil does holy water, the Grand Turk shall shew the exceeding attachment he will no doubt form towards us by appointing us his viceroys in Egypt. I will be Supreme Bey of that showerless district, and you shall be my supervisor. But for God's sake make haste and come to me, and let us talk of the sands of Arabia while we are floating in our lazy boat on Keswick Lake, with our eyes on massy Skiddaw, so green and high. Perhaps Davy might accompany you. Davy will remain unvitiated; his deepest and most recollectable delights have been in solitude, and the next to those with one or two whom he loved. He is placed, no doubt, in a perilous desert of good things; but he is connected with the present race of men by a very awful tie, that of being able to confer immediate benefit on them; and the cold-blooded, venom-toothed snake that winds around him shall be only his coat of arms, as God of Healing.

I exceedingly long to see "Thalaba," and perhaps still more to read "Madoc" over again. I never heard of any third edition of my poems. I think you must have confused it with the L. B. Longman could not surely be so uncouthly ill-mannered as not to write to me to know if I wished to make any corrections or additions. If I am well enough, I mean to alter, with a devilish sweep of revolution, my Tragedy, and publish it in a little volume by itself, with a new name, as a poem. But I have no heart for poetry. Alas! alas! how should I? who have passed nine months with giddy head, sick stomach, and swoln knees. My dear Southey! it is said that long sickness makes us all grow selfish, by the necessity which it imposes of continuously thinking about ourselves. But long and sleepless nights are a fine antidote.

Oh, how I have dreamt about you! Times that have been, and never can return, have been with me on my bed of pain, and how I yearned towards you in those moments. I myself can know only by feeling it over again. But come "strengthen the weak hands, and confirm the feeble knees. Then shall the lame man leap as a hart, and sorrow and sighing shall flee away."

I am here, in the vicinity of Durham, for the purpose of reading from the Dean and Chapter's Library an ancient of whom you may have heard, Duns Scotus! I mean to set the poor old Gemman on his feet again; and in order to wake him out of his present lethargy, I am burning Locke, Hume, and Hobbes under his nose. They stink worse than feather or assafœtida. Poor Joseph! [Cottle] he has scribbled away both head and heart. What an affecting essay I could write on that man's character! Had he gone in his quiet way on a little pony, looking about him with a sheep's-eye cast now and then at a short poem, I do verily think from many parts of the "Malvern Hill," that he would at last have become a poet better than many who have had much fame, but he would be an Epic, and so

"Victorious o'er the Danes, I Alfred, preach,
Of my own forces, Chaplain-General!"
... Write immediately, directing Mr. Coleridge, Mr. George Hutchinson's,[245] Bishop's Middleham, Rushiford, Durham, and tell me when you set off, and I will contrive and meet you at Liverpool, where, if you are jaded with the journey, we can stay a day or two at Dr. Crompton's, and chat a bit with Roscoe and Curry,[246] whom you will like as men far, far better than as writers. O Edith; how happy Sara will be, and little Hartley, who uses the air of the breezes as skipping-ropes, and fat Derwent, so beautiful, and so proud of his three teeth, that there's no bearing of him!

God bless you, dear Southey, and

S. T. Coleridge.

P. S. Remember me kindly to Danvers and Mrs. Danvers.

[Care of] Mrs. Danvers,
Kingsdown Parade, Bristol.

CXX. TO THE SAME.

Durham, Saturday, July 25, 1801.

My dear Southey,—I do loathe cities, that's certain. I am in Durham, at an inn,—and that, too, I do not like, and have dined with a large parcel of priests all belonging to the cathedral, thoroughly ignorant and hard-hearted. I have had no small trouble in gaining permission to have a few books sent to me eight miles from the place, which nobody has ever read in the memory of man. Now you will think what follows a lie, and it is not. I asked a stupid haughty fool, who is the Librarian of the Dean and Chapter's Library in this city, if it had Leibnitz. He answered, "We have no Museum in this Library for natural curiosities; but there is a Mathematical Instrument setter in the town, who shews such animalcula through a glass of great magnifying powers." Heaven and earth! he understood the word "live nits." Well, I return early to-morrow to Middleham; to a quiet good family that love me dearly—a young farmer and his sister, and he makes very droll verses in the northern dialects and in the metre of Burns, and is a great humourist, and the woman is so very good a woman that I have seldom indeed seen the like of her. Death! that everywhere there should be one or two good and excellent people like these, and that they should not have the power given 'em ... to whirl away the rest to Hell!

I do not approve the Palermo and Constantinople scheme, to be secretary to a fellow that would poison you for being a poet, while he is only a lame verse-maker. But verily, dear Southey! it will not suit you to be under any man's control, or biddances. What if you were a consul? 'Twould fix you to one place, as bad as if you were a parson. It won't do. Now mark my scheme! St. Nevis is the most lovely as well as the most healthy island in the W. Indies. Pinney's[247] estate is there, and he has a country-house situated in a most heavenly way, a very large mansion. Now between you and me I have reason to believe that not only this house is at my service, but many advantages in a family way that would go one half to lessen the expenses of living there, and perhaps Pinney would appoint us sinecure negro-drivers, at a hundred a year each, or some other snug and reputable office, and, perhaps, too, we might get some office in which there is quite nothing to do under the Governor. Now I and my family, and you and Edith, and Wordsworth and his sister might all go there, and make the Island more illustrious than Cos or Lesbos! A heavenly climate, a heavenly country, and a good house. The seashore so near us, dells and rocks and streams. Do now think of this. But say nothing about it on account of old Pinney. Wordsworth would certainly go if I went. By the living God, it is my opinion that we should not leave three such men behind us. N. B. I have every reason to believe Keswick (and Cumberland and Westmoreland in general) full as dry a climate as Bristol. Our rains fall more certainly in certain months, but we have fewer rainy days, taking the year through. As to cold, I do not believe the difference perceptible by the human body. But I feel that there is no relief for me in any part of England. Very hot weather brings me about in an instant, and I relapse as soon as it coldens.

You say nothing of your voyage homeward, or the circumstances that preceded it. This, however, I far rather hear from your mouth than your letters. Come! and come quickly. My love to Edith, and remember me kindly to Mary and Martha and Eliza and Mrs. Fricker. My kind respects to Charles and Mrs. Danvers. Is Davy with you? If he is, I am sure he speaks affectionately of me. God bless you! Write.

S. T. Coleridge.

CXXI. TO THE SAME.

Scarborough, August 1, 1801.

My dear Southey,—On my return from Durham (I foolishly walked back), I was taken ill, and my left knee swelled "pregnant with agony," as Mr. Dodsley says in one of his poems. Dr. Fenwick[248] has earnestly persuaded me to try horse-exercise and warm sea-bathing, and I took the opportunity of riding with Sara Hutchinson to her brother Tom, who lives near the place, where I can ride to and fro, and bathe with no other expense there than that of the bath. The fit comes on me either at nine at night, or two in the morning. In the former case it continues nine hours, in the latter five. I am often literally sick with pain. In the daytime, however, I am well, surprisingly so indeed, considering how very little sleep I am able to snatch. Your letter was sent after me, and arrived here this morning, and but that my letter can reach you on the 5th of this month, I would immediately set off again, though I arrived here only last night. But I am unwilling not to try the baths for one week. If, therefore, you have not made the immediate preparation you may stay one week longer at Bristol. But if you have, you must look at the lake, and play with my babies three or four days, though this grieves me. I do not like it. I want to be with you, and to meet you even to the very verge of the Lake Country. I would far rather that you would stay a week at Grasmere (which is on the road, fourteen miles from Keswick), with Wordsworth, than go on to Keswick, and I not there. Oh, how you will love Grasmere!

All I ever wish of you with regard to wintering at Keswick is to stay with me till you find the climate injurious. When I read that cheerful sentence, "We will climb Skiddaw this year and scale Etna the next," with a right piteous and humorous smile did I ogle my poor knee, which at this present moment is larger than the thickest part of my thigh.

A little Quaker girl (the daughter of the great Quaker mathematician Slee, a friend of anti-negro-trade Clarkson, who has a house at the foot of Ulleswater, which Slee Wordsworth dined with, a pretty parenthesis!), this little girl, four years old, happened after a very hearty meal to eructate, while Wordsworth was there. Her mother looked at her, and the little creature immediately and formally observed: "Yan belks when yan's fu, and when yan's empty." That is, "One belches when one's full and when one's empty." Since that time this is a favourite piece of slang at Grasmere and Greta Hall, whenever we talk of poor Joey, George Dyer, and other perseverants in the noble trade of scribbleism.

Wrangham,[249] who lives near here, one of your anthology friends, has married again, a lady of a neat £700 a year. His living by the Inclosure [Act] will be something better than £600, besides what little fortune he had with his last wife, who died in the first year. His present wife's cousin observed, "Mr. W. is a lucky man: his present lady is very weakly and delicate." I like the idea of a man's speculating in sickly wives. It would be no bad character for a farce.

That letter £ was a kind-hearted, honest, well-spoken citizen. The three strokes which did for him were, as I take it, (1), the Ictus Cardiacus, which devitalized his moral heart; (2ondly) the stroke of the apoplexy in his head; and (thirdly) a stroke of the palsy in his right hand, which produces a terrible shaking and impotence in the very attempt to reach his breeches pocket. O dear Southey! what incalculable blessings, worthy of thanksgiving in Heaven, do we not owe to our being and having been poor! No man's heart can wholly stand up against property. My love to Edith.

S. T. Coleridge.

CXXII. TO THOMAS POOLE.

Keswick, September 19, 1801.

By a letter from Davy I have learnt, Poole, that your mother is with the Blessed. I have given her the tears and the pang which belong to her departure, and now she will remain to me forever, what she had long been—a dear and venerable image, often gazed at by me in imagination, and always with affection and filial piety. She was the only being whom I ever felt in the relation of Mother; and she is with God! We are all with God!

What shall I say to you! I can only offer a prayer of thanksgiving for you, that you are one who has habitually connected the act of thought with that of feeling; and that your natural sorrow is so mingled up with a sense of the omnipresence of the Good Agent, that I cannot wish it to be other than what I know it is. The frail and the too painful will gradually pass away from you, and there will abide in your spirit a great and sacred accession to those solemn Remembrances and faithful Hopes in which, and by which, the Almighty lays deep the foundations of our continuous Life, and distinguishes us from the Brutes that perish. As all things pass away, and those habits are broken up which constituted our own and particular Self, our nature by a moral instinct cherishes the desire of an unchangeable Something, and thereby awakens or stirs up anew the passion to promote permanent good, and facilitates that grand business of our existence—still further, and further still, to generalise our affections, till Existence itself is swallowed up in Being, and we are in Christ even as He is in the Father.

It is among the advantages of these events that they learn us to associate a keen and deep feeling with all the old good phrases, all the reverend sayings of comfort and sympathy, that belong, as it were, to the whole human race. I felt this, dear Poole! as I was about to write my old

God bless you, and love you for ever and ever!

Your affectionate friend,
S. T. Coleridge.

Would it not be well if you were to change the scene awhile! Come to me, Poole! No—no—no. You have none that love you so well as I. I write with tears that prevent my seeing what I am writing.

CXXIII. TO ROBERT SOUTHEY.

Nether Stowey, Bridgewater, December 31, 1801.

Dear Southey,—On Xmas Day I breakfasted with Davy, with the intention of dining with you; but I returned very unwell, and in very truth in so utter a dejection of spirits as both made it improper for me to go anywhither, and a most unfit man to be with you. I left London on Saturday morning, 4 o'clock, and for three hours was in such a storm as I was never before out in, for I was atop of the coach—rain, and hail, and violent wind, with vivid flashes of lightning, that seemed almost to alternate with the flash-like re-emersions of the waning moon, from the ever-shattered, ever-closing clouds. However, I was armed cap-a-pie in a complete panoply, namely, in a huge, most huge, roquelaure, which had cost the government seven guineas, and was provided for the emigrants in the Quiberon expedition, one of whom, falling sick, stayed behind and parted with his cloak to Mr. Howel,[250] who lent it me. I dipped my head down, shoved it up—and it proved a complete tent to me. I was as dry as if I had been sitting by the fire. I arrived at Bath at eleven o'clock at night, and spent the next day with Warren, who has gotten a very sweet woman to wife and a most beautiful house and situation at Whitcomb on the Hill over the bridge. On Monday afternoon I arrived at Stowey. I am a good deal better; but my bowels are by no means de-revolutionized. So much for me. I do not know what I am to say to you of your dear mother. Life passes away from us in all modes and ways, in our friends, in ourselves. We all "die daily." Heaven knows that many and many a time I have regarded my talents and requirements as a porter's burthen, imposing on me the capital duty of going on to the end of the journey, when I would gladly lie down by the side of the road, and become the country for a mighty nation of maggots. For what is life, gangrened, as it is with me, in its very vitals, domestic tranquillity? These things being so, I confess that I feel for you, but not for the event, as for the event only by an act of thought, and not by any immediate shock from the like feeling within myself. When I return to town I can scarcely tell. I have not yet made up my mind whether or no I shall move Devonward. My relations wish to see me, and I wish to avoid the uneasy feeling I shall have, if I remain so near them without gratifying the wish. No very brotherly mood of mind, I must confess—but it is, nine tenths of it at least, a work of their own doing. Poole desires to be remembered to you. Remember me to your wife and Mrs. Lovell.

God bless you and

S. T. Coleridge.

CXXIV. TO HIS WIFE.

King Street, Covent Garden, [February 24, 1802.]

My dear Love,—I am sure it will make you happy to hear that both my health and spirits have greatly improved, and I have small doubts that a residence of two years in a mild and even climate will, with God's blessing, give me a new lease in a better constitution. You may be well assured that I shall do nothing rashly, but our journey thither I shall defray by letters to Poole and the Wedgwoods, or more probably addressed to Mawman, the bookseller, who will honour my drafts in return. Of course I shall not go till I have earned all the money necessary for the journey that I can. The plan will be this, unless you can think of any better. Wordsworth will marry soon after my return, and he, Mary, and Dorothy will be our companions and neighbours. Southey means, if it is in his power, to pass into Spain that way. About July we shall all set sail from Liverpool to Bordeaux. Wordsworth has not yet settled whether he shall be married from Gallow Hill or at Grasmere. But they will of course make a point that either Sarah shall be with Mary or Mary with Sarah previous to so long a parting. If it be decided that Sarah is to come to Grasmere, I shall return by York, which will be but a few miles out of the way, and bring her. At all events, I shall stay a few days at Derby,—for whom, think you, should I meet in Davy's lecture-room but Joseph Strutt? He behaved most affectionately to me, and pressed me with great earnestness to pass through Darley (which is on the road to Derby) and stay a few days at his house among my old friends. I assure you I was much affected by his kind and affectionate invitation (though I felt a little awkward, not knowing whom I might venture to ask after). I could not bring out the word "Mrs. Evans," and so said, "Your sister, sir? I hope she is well!"

On Sunday I dined at Sir William Rush's, and on Monday likewise, and went with them to Mrs. Billington's Benefit. 'Twas the "Beggar's Opera;" it was perfection! I seem to have acquired a new sense by hearing her. I wished you to have been there. I assure you I am quite a man of fashion; so many titled acquaintances and handsome carriages stopping at my door, and fine cards. And then I am such an exquisite judge of music and painting, and pass criticisms on furniture and chandeliers, and pay such very handsome compliments to all women of fashion, that I do verily believe that if I were to stay three months in town and have tolerable health and spirits, I should be a Thing in vogue,—the very tonish poet and Jemmy-Jessamy-fine-talker in town. If you were only to see the tender smiles that I occasionally receive from the Honourable Mrs. Damer! you would scratch her eyes out for jealousy! And then there's the sweet (N. B. musky) Lady Charlotte ——! Nay, but I won't tell you her name,—you might perhaps take it into your head to write an anonymous letter to her, and distrust our little innocent amour.

Oh that I were at Keswick with my darlings! My Hartley and my fat Derwent! God bless you, my dear Sarah! I shall return in love and cheerfulness, and therefore in pleasurable convalescence, if not in health. We shall try to get poor dear little Robert into Christ's Hospital; that wretch of a Quaker will do nothing. The skulking rogue! just to lay hold of the time when Mrs. Lovell was on a visit to Southey; there was such low cunning in the thought.

Remember me most kindly to Mr. and Mrs. Wilkinson, and tell Mr. Jackson that I have not shaken a hand since I quitted him with more esteem and glad feeling than I shall soon, I trust, shake his with. God bless you, and your affectionate and faithful husband (notwithstanding the Honourable Mrs. D. and Lady Charlotte!),

S. T. Coleridge.

CXXV. TO W. SOTHEBY.

Greta Hall, Keswick, Tuesday, July 13, 1802.

My dear Sir,—I had written you a letter and was about to have walked to the post with it when I received yours from Luff.[251] It gave me such lively pleasure that I threw my letter into the fire, for it related chiefly to the "Erste Schiffer" of Gesner, and I could not endure that my first letter to you should begin with a subject so little interesting to my heart or understanding. I trust that you are before this at the end of your journey, and that Mrs. and Miss Sotheby have so completely recovered themselves as to have almost forgotten all the fatigue except such instances of it as it may be pleasant to them to remember. Why need I say how often I have thought of you since your departure, and with what hope and pleasurable emotion? I will acknowledge to you that your very, very kind letter was not only a pleasure to me, but a relief to my mind; for, after I had left you on the road between Ambleside and Grasmere, I was dejected by the apprehension that I had been unpardonably loquacious, and had oppressed you, and still more Mrs. Sotheby, with my many words so impetuously uttered! But in simple truth, you were yourselves, in part, the innocent causes of it. For the meeting with you, the manner of the meeting, your kind attentions to me, the deep and healthful delight which every impressive and beautiful object seemed to pour out upon you; kindred opinions, kindred pursuits, kindred feelings in persons whose habits, and, as it were, walk of life, have been so different from my own,—these and more than these, which I would but cannot say, all flowed in upon me with unusually strong impulses of pleasure,—and pleasure in a body and soul such as I happen to possess "intoxicates more than strong wine." However, I promise to be a much more subdued creature when you next meet me, for I had but just recovered from a state of extreme dejection, brought on in part by ill health, partly by other circumstances; and solitude and solitary musings do of themselves impregnate our thoughts, perhaps, with more life and sensation than will leave the balance quite even. But you, my dear sir! looked at a brother poet with a brother's eyes. Oh that you were now in my study and saw, what is now before the window at which I am writing,—that rich mulberry-purple which a floating cloud has thrown on the lake, and that quiet boat making its way through it to the shore!

We have had little else but rain and squally weather since you left us till within the last three days. But showery weather is no evil to us; and even that most oppressive of all weathers, hot, small drizzle, exhibits the mountains the best of any. It produced such new combinations of ridges in the Lodore and Borrowdale mountains on Saturday morning that I declare, had I been blindfolded and so brought to the prospect, I should scarcely have known them again. It was a dream such as lovers have,—a wild and transfiguring, yet enchantingly lovely dream, of an object lying by the side of the sleeper. Wordsworth, who has walked through Switzerland, declared that he never saw anything superior, perhaps nothing equal, in the Alps.

The latter part of your letter made me truly happy. Uriel himself should not be half as welcome; and indeed he, I must admit, was never any great favourite of mine. I always thought him a bantling of zoneless Italian muses, which Milton heard cry at the door of his imagination and took in out of charity. However, come as you may, carus mihi expectatusque venies.[252] De cœteris rebus si quid agendum est, et quicquid sit agendum, ut quam rectissime agantur omni meâ curâ, operâ, diligentiâ, gratiâ providebo.[253]

On my return to Keswick, I reperused the "Erste Schiffer" with great attention, and the result was an increasing disinclination to the business of translating it; though my fancy was not a little flattered by the idea of seeing my rhymes in such a gay livery.—As poor Giordano Bruno[254] says in his strange, yet noble poem, "De Immenso et Innumerabili,"—

"Quam Garymedeo cultu, graphiceque venustus!
Narcissis referam, peramarunt me quoque Nymphæ."
But the poem was too silly. The first conception is noble, so very good that I am spiteful enough to hope that I shall discover it not to have been original in Gesner,—he has so abominably maltreated it. First, the story is very inartificially constructed. We should have been let into the existence of the girl by her mother, through the young man, and after his appearance. This, however, is comparatively a trifle. But the machinery is so superlatively contemptible and commonplace; as if a young man could not dream of a tale which had deeply impressed him without Cupid, or have a fair wind all the way to an island without Æolus. Æolus himself is a god devoted and dedicated, I should have thought, to the Muse of Travestie. His speech in Gesner is not deficient in fancy, but it is a girlish fancy, and the god of the wind, exceedingly disquieted with animal love, makes a very ridiculous figure in my imagination. Besides, it was ill taste to introduce Cupid and Æolus at a time which we

positively know to have been anterior to the invention and establishment of the Grecian Mythology; and the speech of Æolus reminds me perpetually of little engravings from the cut stones of the ancients,—seals, and whatever else they call them. Again, the girl's yearnings and conversations with him are something between the nursery and the Veneris volgivagæ templa, et libidinem spirat et subsusurrat, dum innocentiæ loquillam, et virginiæ cogitationis dulciter offensantis luctamina simulat.

It is not the thought that a lonely girl could have; but exactly such as a boarding-school miss, whose imagination, to say no worse, had been somewhat stirred and heated by the perusal of French or German pastorals, would suppose her to say. But this is, indeed, general in the German and French poets. It is easy to clothe imaginary beings with our own thoughts and feelings; but to send ourselves out of ourselves, to think ourselves into the thoughts and feelings of beings in circumstances wholly and strangely different from our own, hic labor hoc opus; and who has achieved it? Perhaps only Shakespeare. Metaphysics is a word that you, my dear sir, are no great friend to, but yet you will agree with me that a great poet must be implicité, if not explicité, a profound metaphysician. He may not have it in logical coherence in his brain and tongue, but he must have the ear of a wild Arab listening in the silent desert, the eye of a North American Indian tracing the footsteps of an enemy upon the leaves that strew the forest, the touch of a blind man feeling the face of a darling child. And do not think me a bigot if I say that I have read no French or German writer who appears to me to have a heart sufficiently pure and simple to be capable of this or anything like it. I could say a great deal more in abuse of poor Gesner's poems, but I have said more than I fear will be creditable in your opinion to my good nature. I must, though, tell you the malicious motto which I have written in the first part of Klopstock's "Messias:"—

"Tale tuum carmen nobis, divine poeta!
Quale sopor!"
Only I would have the words divine poeta translated "verse-making divine." I have read a great deal of German; but I do dearly, dearly, dearly love my own countrymen of old times, and those of my contemporaries who write in their spirit.

William Wordsworth and his sister left me yesterday on their way to Yorkshire. They walked yesterday to the foot of Ulleswater, from thence they go to Penrith, and take the coach. I accompanied them as far as the seventh milestone. Among the last things which he said to me was, "Do not forget to remember me to Mr. Sotheby with whatever affectionate terms so slight an intercourse may permit; and how glad we shall all be to see him again!"

I was much pleased with your description of Wordsworth's character as it appeared to you. It is in a few words, in half a dozen strokes, like one of Mortimer's[255] figures, a fine portrait. The word "homogeneous" gave me great pleasure, as most accurately and happily expressing him. I must set you right with regard to my perfect coincidence with his poetic creed. It is most certain that the heads of our mutual conversations, etc., and the passages, were indeed partly taken from note of mine; for it was at first intended that the preface should be written by me. And it is likewise true that I warmly accord with Wordsworth in his abhorrence of these poetic licenses, as they are called, which are indeed mere tricks of convenience and laziness. Ex. gr. Drayton has these lines:—

"Ouse having Ouleney past, as she were waxed mad
From her first stayder course immediately doth gad,
And in meandered gyres doth whirl herself about,
That, this way, here and there, backward in and out.

And like a wanton girl oft doubling in her gait
In labyrinthian turns and twinings intricate," etc.[256]
The first poets, observing such a stream as this, would say with truth and beauty, "it strays;" and now every stream shall stray, wherever it prattles on its pebbled way, instead of its bed or channel. And I have taken the instance from a poet from whom as few instances of this vile, commonplace, trashy style could be taken as from any writer [namely], from Bowles' execrable translation[257] of that lovely poem of Dean Ogle's (vol. ii. p. 27). I am confident that Bowles good-naturedly translated it in a hurry, merely to give him an excuse for printing the admirable original. In my opinion, every phrase, every metaphor, every personification, should have its justifying clause in some passion, either of the poet's mind or of the characters described by the poet. But metre itself implies a passion, that is, a state of excitement both in the poet's mind, and is expected, in part, of the reader; and, though I stated this to Wordsworth, and he has in some sort stated it in his preface, yet he has not done justice to it, nor has he, in my opinion, sufficiently answered it. In my opinion, poetry justifies as poetry, independent of any other passion, some new combinations of language and commands the omission of many others allowable in other compositions. Now Wordsworth, me saltem judice, has in his system not sufficiently admitted the former, and in his practice has too frequently sinned against the latter. Indeed, we have had lately some little controversy on the subject, and we begin to suspect that there is somewhere or other a radical difference in our opinions. Dulce est inter amicos rarissimâ dissensione condere plurimas consentiones, saith St. Augustine, who said more good things than any saint or sinner that I ever read in Latin.

Bless me! what a letter! And I have yet to make a request to you. I have read your Georgics at a friend's house in the neighbourhood, and in sending for the book, I find that it belonged to a book-club, and has been returned. If you have a copy interleaved, or could procure one for me and will send it to me per coach, with a copy of your original poems, I will return them to you with many thanks in the autumn, and will endeavour to improve my own taste by writing on the blank leaves my feelings both of the original and your translation. Your poems I want for another purpose, of which hereafter.

Mrs. Coleridge and my children are well. She desires to be respectfully remembered to Mrs. and Miss Sotheby. Tell Miss Sotheby that I will endeavour to send her soon the completion of the "Dark Ladie," as she was good-natured enough to be pleased with the first part.

Let me hear from you soon, my dear sir! and believe me with heartfelt wishes for you and yours, in every-day phrase, but, indeed, indeed, not with every-day feeling.

Yours most sincerely,
S. T. Coleridge.

I long to lead Mrs. Sotheby to a scene that has the grandeur without the toil or danger of Scale Force. It is called the White Water Dash.[258]

CXXVI. TO THE SAME.

Keswick, July 19, 1802.

My dear Sir,—I trouble you with another letter to inform you that I have finished the First Book[259] of the "Erste Schiffer." It consists of 530 lines; the Second Book will be a hundred lines less. I can transcribe both legibly in three single-sheet letters; you will only be so good as to inform me whither and whether I am to send them. If they are likely to be of any use to Tomkins he is welcome to them; if not, I shall send them to the "Morning Post." I have given a faithful translation in blank verse. To have decorated Gesner would have been, indeed, "to spice the spices;" to have lopped and pruned somewhat would have only produced incongruity; to have done it sufficiently would have been to have published a poem of my own, not Gesner's. I have aimed at nothing more than purity and elegance of English, a keeping and harmony in the colour of the style, a smoothness without monotony in the versification. If I have succeeded, as I trust I have, in these respects, my translation will be just so much better than the original as metre is better than prose, in their judgment, at least, who prefer blank verse to prose. I was probably too severe on the morals of the poem, uncharitable perhaps. But I am a downright Englishman, and tolerate downright grossness more patiently than this coy and distant dallying with the appetites. "Die pflanzen entstehen aus dem saamen, gewisse thiere gehen aus dem hervor andre so, andre anders, ich hab es alles bemerkt, was hab ich zu thun." Now I apprehend it will occur to nineteen readers out of twenty, that a maiden so very curious, so exceedingly inflamed and harassed by a difficulty, and so subtle in the discovery of even comparatively distant analogies, would necessarily have seen the difference of sex in her flocks and herds, and the marital as well as maternal character could not have escaped her. Now I avow that the grossness and vulgar plain sense of Theocritus' shepherd lads, bad as it is, is in my opinion less objectionable than Gesner's refinement, which necessarily leads the imagination to ideas without expressing them. Shaped and clothed, the mind of a pure being would turn away from them from natural delicacy of taste, but in that shadowy half-being, that state of nascent existence in the twilight of imagination and just on the vestibule of consciousness, they are far more incendiary, stir up a more lasting commotion, and leave a deeper stain. The suppression and obscurity arrays a simple truth in a veil of something like guilt, that is altogether meretricious, as opposed to the matronly majesty of our Scripture, for instance; and the conceptions as they recede from distinctness of idea approximate to the nature of feeling, and gain thereby a closer and more immediate affinity with the appetites. But, independently of this, the whole passage, consisting of precisely one fourth of the whole poem, has not the least influence on the action of the poem, and it is scarcely too much to say that it has nothing to do with the main subject, except indeed it be pleaded that Love is induced by compassion for this maiden to make a young man dream of her, which young man had been, without any influence of the said Cupid, deeply interested in the story, and, therefore, did not need the interference of Cupid at all; any more than he did the assistance of Æolus for a fair wind all the way to an island that was within sight of shore.

I translated the poem, partly because I could not endure to appear irresolute and capricious to you in the first undertaking which I had connected in any way with your person; in an undertaking which I connect with our journey from Keswick to Grasmere, the carriage in which were your son, your daughter, and your wife (all of whom may God Almighty bless! a prayer not the less fervent, my dear sir! for being a little out of place here); and, partly, too, because I wished to force myself out of metaphysical trains of thought, which, when I wished to write a poem, beat up game of far other kind. Instead of a covey of poetic partridges with whirring wings of music, or wild ducks shaping their rapid flight in forms always regular (a still better image of verse), up came a metaphysical bustard, urging its slow, heavy, laborious, earth-skimming flight over dreary and level wastes. To have done with poetical prose (which is a very vile Olio), sickness and some other and worse afflictions first forced me into downright metaphysics. For I believe that by nature I have more of the poet in me. In a poem written during that dejection, to Wordsworth, and the greater part of a private nature, I thus expressed the thought in language more forcible than harmonious:[260]—

Yes, dearest poet, yes!
There was a time when tho' my path was rough,
The joy within me dallied with distress,
And all misfortunes were but as the stuff
Whence fancy made me dreams of happiness:
For Hope grew round me, like the climbing vine,
And fruit, and foliage, not my own, seemed mine.
But now afflictions bow me down to earth:
Nor care I, that they rob me of my mirth,
But oh! each visitation
Suspends what nature gave me at my birth,
My shaping spirit of Imagination.
....

For not to think of what I needs must feel,
But to be still and patient, all I can;
And haply by abstruse research to steal
From my own nature all the natural man—
This was my sole resource, my wisest plan:
And that which suits a part infects the whole,
And now is almost grown the temper of my soul.

Thank heaven! my better mind has returned to me, and I trust I shall go on rejoicing. As I have nothing better to fill the blank space of this sheet with, I will transcribe the introduction of that poem to you, that being of a sufficiently general nature to be interesting to you. The first lines allude to a stanza in the Ballad of Sir Patrick Spence: "Late, late yestreen I saw the new moon with the old one in her arms, and I fear, I fear, my master dear, there will be a deadly storm."

Letter, written Sunday evening, April 4.

Well! if the Bard was weatherwise, who made
The dear old Ballad of Sir Patrick Spence,
This night, so tranquil now, will not go hence
Unrous'd by winds, that ply a busier trade
Than that, which moulds yon clouds in lazy flakes,
Or the dull sobbing draft, that drones and rakes
Upon the strings of this Eolian lute,
Which better far were mute.
For lo! the New Moon, winter-bright!
And overspread with phantom light
(With swimming phantom light o'erspread,
But rimmed and circled with a silver thread)
I see the Old Moon in her lap foretelling
The coming on of rain and squally blast!
And O! that even now the gust were swelling,
And the slant night-shower driving loud and fast.
....

A grief without a pang, void, dark, and drear!
A stifling, drowsy, unimpassioned grief,
That finds no natural outlet, no relief,
In word, or sigh, or tear!
This, William, well thou know'st,

Is that sore evil which I dread the most,
And oftnest suffer. In this heartless mood,
To other thoughts by yonder throstle woo'd,
That pipes within the larch-tree, not unseen,
The larch, that pushes out in tassels green
Its bundled leafits, woo'd to mild delights,
By all the tender sounds and gentle sights
Of this sweet primrose-month, and vainly woo'd!
O dearest Poet, in this heartless mood,
All this long eve, so balmy and serene,
Have I been gazing on the Western sky,
And its peculiar tint of yellow-green:
And still I gaze—and with how blank an eye!
And those thin clouds above, in flakes and bars,
That give away their motion to the stars;
Those stars, that glide behind them, or between,
Now sparkling, now bedimmed, but always seen;
Yon crescent moon, as fix'd as if it grew
In its own cloudless, starless lake of blue,
A boat becalm'd! thy own sweet sky-canoe![261]
I see them all, so exquisitely fair!
I see, not feel! how beautiful they are!
My genial spirits fail;
And what can these avail,
To lift the smoth'ring weight from off my breast?
It were a vain endeavour,
Though I should gaze for ever
On that green light that lingers in the west;
I may not hope from outward forms to win
The passion and the life, whose fountains are within.
....

O Wordsworth! we receive but what we give,
And in our life alone does Nature live;
Ours is her wedding garment, ours her shroud!
And would we aught behold, of higher worth,
Than that inanimate, cold world, allow'd
To the poor, loveless, ever-anxious crowd,
Ah! from the soul itself must issue forth,
A light, a glory, a fair luminous cloud
Enveloping the earth!
And from the soul itself must there be sent
A sweet and powerful voice, of its own birth,
Of all sweet sounds the life and element!
O pure of heart! thou need'st not ask of me
What this strong music in the soul may be?
What and wherein it doth exist,
This light, this glory, this fair luminous mist,
This beautiful and beauty-making Power.
Joy, blameless poet! Joy that ne'er was given
Save to the pure, and in their purest hour,
Joy, William, is the spirit and the power
That wedding Nature to us gives in dower,

A new Earth and new Heaven,
Undream'd of by the sensual and proud—
We, we ourselves rejoice!
And thence comes all that charms or ear or sight,
All melodies an echo of that voice!
All colours a suffusion from that light!
Calm, steadfast spirit, guided from above,
O Wordsworth! friend of my devoutest choice,
Great son of genius! full of light and love,
Thus, thus, dost thou rejoice.
To thee do all things live, from pole to pole,
Their life the eddying of thy living Soul!
Brother and friend of my devoutest choice,
Thus mayst thou ever, ever more rejoice!
. . . .

I have selected from the poem, which was a very long one and truly written only for the solace of sweet song, all that could be interesting or even pleasing to you, except, indeed, perhaps I may annex as a fragment a few lines on the "Æolian Lute," it having been introduced in its dronings in the first stanza. I have used Yule for Christmas.

Nay, wherefore did I let it haunt my mind,
This dark, distressful dream?
I turn from it and listen to the wind
Which long has rav'd unnotic'd! What a scream
Of agony by torture lengthened out,
That lute sent out! O thou wild storm without,
Bare crag, or Mountain Tairn, or blasted tree,
Or pine-grove whither woodman never clomb,
Or lonely house, long held the witches' home,
Methinks were fitter instruments for thee
Mad Lutanist! that, in this month of showers,
Of dark-brown gardens, and of peeping flowers,
Mak'st devil's Yule, with worse than wintry song,
The blossoms, buds, and timorous leaves among!
Thou Actor, perfect in all tragic sounds!
Thou mighty Poet, even to frenzy bold!
What tell'st thou now about?
'Tis of the rushing of an host in rout,
With many groans from men, with smarting wounds—
At once they groan with pain, and shudder with the cold!
But hush! there is a pause of deeper silence!
Again! but all that noise, as of a rushing crowd,
With groans, and tremulous shudderings—all is over!
And it has other sounds, less fearful and less loud—
A tale of less affright,
And tempered with delight,
As thou thyself had'st fram'd the tender lay—
'Tis of a little child,
Upon a heath wild,
Not far from home, but she has lost her way—
And now moans low in utter grief and fear;

And now screams loud, and hopes to make her mother hear.
....

My dear sir! ought I to make an apology for troubling you with such a long, verse-cramm'd letter? Oh, that instead of it, I could but send to you the image now before my eyes, over Bassenthwaite. The sun is setting in a glorious, rich, brassy light, on the top of Skiddaw, and one third adown it is a huge, enormous mountain of cloud, with the outlines of a mountain. This is of a starchy grey, but floating past along it, and upon it, are various patches of sack-like clouds, bags and woolsacks, of a shade lighter than the brassy light. Of the clouds that hide the setting sun,—a fine yellow-red, somewhat more than sandy light, and these, the farthest from the sun, are suffused with the darkness of a stormy colour. Marvellous creatures! how they pass along! Remember me with most respectful kindness to Mrs. and Miss Sotheby, and the Captains Sotheby.

Truly yours,
S. T. Coleridge.

CXXVII. TO ROBERT SOUTHEY.[262]

Greta Hall, Keswick, July 29, 1802.

My dear Southey,—Nothing has given me half the pleasure, these many, many months, as last week did Edith's heralding to us of a minor Robert; for that it will be a boy, one always takes for granted. From the bottom of my heart I say it, I never knew a man that better deserved to be a father by right of virtues that eminently belonged to him, than yourself; but beside this I have cheering hopes that Edith will be born again, and be a healthy woman. When I said, nothing had given me half the pleasure, I spoke truly, and yet said more than you are perhaps aware of, for, by Lord Lonsdale's death, there are excellent reasons for believing that the Wordsworths will gain £5,000, the share of which (and no doubt Dorothy will have more than a mere share) will render William Wordsworth and his sister quite independent. They are now in Yorkshire, and he returns in about a month one of us.... Estlin's Sermons, I fear, are mere moral discourses. If so, there is but small chance of their sale. But if he had published a volume of sermons, of the same kind with those which he has published singly, i. e. apologetical and ecclesiastico-historical, I am almost confident, they would have a respectable circulation. To publish single sermons is almost always a foolish thing, like single sheet quarto poems. Estlin's sermon on the Sabbath really surprised me. It was well written in style, I mean, and the reasoning throughout is not only sound, but has a cast of novelty in it. A superior sermon altogether it appeared to me. I am myself a little theological, and if any bookseller will take the risque, I shall in a few weeks, possibly, send to the press a small volume under the title of "Letters to the British Critic concerning Granville Sharp's Remarks on the uses of the Definitive article in the Greek Text of the New Testament, and the Revd C. Wordsworth's Six Letters, to G. Sharp Esqr, in confirmation of the same, together with a Review of the Controversy between Horsley and Priestley respecting the faith of the Primitive Christians." This is no mere dream, like my "Hymns to the Elements," for I have written more than half the work. I purpose afterwards to publish a book concerning Tythes and Church Establishment, for I conceit that I can throw great light on the subject. You are not apt to be much surprised at any change in my mind, active as it is, but it will perhaps please you to know that I am become very fond of History, and that I have read much with very great attention. I exceedingly like the job of Amadis de Gaul. I wish you may half as well like the job, in which I shall very shortly appear. Of its sale I have no doubt; but of its prudence? There's the rub. "Concerning Poetry and the characteristic merits of the Poets, our contemporaries." One volume Essays, the second Selections.—The Essays are on Bloomfield, Burns, Bowles, Cowper, Campbell, Darwin, Hayley, Rogers, C. Smith, Southey, Woolcot, Wordsworth—the Selections from every one who has written at all, any being above the rank of mere scribblers—Pye and his Dative Case Plural, Pybus, Cottle, etc., etc. The object is not to examine what is good in each writer, but what has ipso facto pleased, and to what faculties, or passions, or habits of the mind they may be supposed to have given pleasure. Of course Darwin and Wordsworth having given each a defence of their mode of poetry, and a disquisition on the nature and essence of poetry in general, I shall necessarily be led rather deeper, and these I shall treat of either first or last. But I will apprise you of one thing, that although Wordsworth's Preface is half a child of my own brain, and arose out of conversations so frequent that, with few exceptions, we could scarcely either of us, perhaps, positively say which first started any particular thought (I am speaking of the Preface as it stood in the second volume), yet I am far from going all lengths with Wordsworth. He has written lately a number of Poems (thirty-two in all), some of them of considerable length (the longest one hundred and sixty lines), the greater number of these, to my feelings, very excellent compositions, but here and there a daring humbleness of language and versification, and a strict adherence to matter of fact, even to prolixity, that startled me. His alterations, likewise, in "Ruth" perplexed me, and I have thought and thought again, and have not had my doubts solved by Wordsworth. On the contrary, I rather suspect that somewhere or other there is a radical difference in our theoretical opinions respecting poetry; this I shall endeavour to go to the bottom of, and, acting the arbitrator between the old school and the new school, hope to lay down some plain and perspicuous, though not superficial canons of criticism respecting poetry. What an admirable definition Milton gives, quite in an "obiter" way, when he says of poetry, that it is "simple, sensuous, passionate!" It truly comprises the whole that can be said on the subject. In the new edition of the L. Ballads there is a valuable appendix, which I am sure you must like, and in the Preface itself considerable additions; one on the dignity and nature of the office and character of a Poet, that is very grand, and of a sort of Verulamian power and majesty, but it is, in parts (and this is the fault, me judice, of all the latter half of that Preface), obscure beyond any necessity, and the extreme elaboration and almost constrainedness of the diction contrasted (to my feelings) somewhat harshly with the general style of the Poems, to which the Preface is an introduction. Sara (why, dear Southey! will you write it always Sarah? Sara, methinks, is associated with times that you and I cannot and do not wish ever to forget), Sara, said, with some acuteness, that she wished all that part of the Preface to have been in blank verse, and vice versâ, etc. However, I need not say, that any diversity of opinion on the subject between you and myself, or Wordsworth and myself, can only be small, taken in a practical point of view.

I rejoice that your History marches on so victoriously. It is a noble subject, and I have the fullest confidence of your success in it. The influence of the Catholic Religion—the influence of national glory on the individual morals of a people, especially in the downfall of the nobility of Portugal,—the strange fact (which seems to be admitted as with one voice by all travellers) of the vileness of the Portuguese nobles compared with the Spanish, and of the superiority of the Portuguese commonalty to the same class in Spain; the effects of colonization on a small and not very fruitful country; the effects important, and too often forgotten of absolute accidents, such as the particular character of a race of Princes on a nation—Oh what awful subjects these are! I long to hear you read a few chapters to me. But I conjure you do not let "Madoc" go to sleep. Oh that without words I could cause you to know all that I think, all that I feel, all that I hope concerning that Poem! As to myself, all my poetic genius (if ever I really possessed any genius, and it was not rather a mere general aptitude of talent, and quickness in imitation) is gone, and I have been fool enough to suffer deeply in my mind, regretting the loss, which I attribute to my long and exceedingly severe metaphysical investigations, and these partly to ill-health, and partly to private afflictions which rendered any subjects, immediately connected with feeling, a source of pain and disquiet to me.

There was a Time when tho' my Path was rough,
I had a heart that dallied with distress;
And all misfortunes were but as the stuff
Whence Fancy made me dreams of Happiness;
For Hope grew round me like the climbing Vine,
And Fruits and Foliage, not my own, seemed mine!
But now afflictions bow me down to earth,
Nor car'd I that they robb'd me of my mirth.
But oh! each visitation
Suspends what Nature gave me at my Birth,
My shaping Spirit of Imagination!
Here follow a dozen lines that would give you no pleasure, and then what follows:—
For not to think of what I needs must feel,
But to be still and patient, all I can;
And haply by abstruse Research to steal
From my own Nature all the Natural Man,
This was my sole Resource, my wisest Plan!
And that which suits a part, infects the whole,
And now is almost grown the Temper of my Soul.
Having written these lines, I rejoice for you as well as for myself, that I am able to inform you, that now for a long time there has been more love and concord in my house than I have known for years before. I had made up my mind to a very awful step, though the struggles of my mind were so violent, that my sleep became the valley of the shadows of Death and my health was in a state truly alarming. It did alarm Mrs. Coleridge. The thought of separation wounded her pride,—she was fully persuaded that deprived of the society of my children and living abroad without any friends I should pine away, and the fears of widowhood came upon her, and though these feelings were wholly selfish, yet they made her serious, and that was a great point gained. For Mrs. Coleridge's mind has very little that is bad in it; it is an innocent mind; but it is light and unimpressible, warm in anger, cold in sympathy, and in all disputes uniformly projects itself forth to recriminate, instead of turning itself inward with a silent self-questioning. Our virtues and our vices are exact antitheses. I so attentively watch my own nature that my worst self-delusion is a complete self-knowledge so mixed with intellectual complacency, that my quickness to see and readiness to acknowledge my faults is too often frustrated by the small pain which the sight of them gives me, and the consequent slowness to amend them. Mrs. C. is so stung with the very first thought of being in the wrong, because she never endures to look at her own mind in all its faulty parts, but shelters herself from painful self-inquiry by angry recrimination. Never, I suppose, did the stern match-maker bring together two minds so utterly contrariant in their primary and organical constitution. Alas! I have suffered more, I think, from the amiable propensities of my nature than from my worst faults and most erroneous habits, and I have suffered much from both. But, as I said, Mrs. Coleridge was made serious, and for the first time since our marriage she felt and acted as beseemed a wife and a mother to a husband and the father of her children. She promised to set about an alteration in her external manners and looks and language, and to fight against her inveterate habits of puny thwarting and unintermitting dyspathy, this immediately, and to do her best endeavours to cherish other feelings. I, on my part, promised to be more

attentive to all her feelings of pride, etc., etc., and to try to correct my habits of impetuous censure. We have both kept our promises, and she has found herself so much more happy than she had been for years before, that I have the most confident hopes that this happy revolution in our domestic affairs will be permanent, and that this external conformity will gradually generate a greater inward likeness of thoughts and attachments than has hitherto existed between us. Believe me, if you were here, it would give you a deep delight to observe the difference of our minutely conduct towards each other, from that which, I fear, could not but have disturbed your comfort when you were here last. Enough. But I am sure you have not felt it tedious.

So Corry[263] and you are off? I suspected it, but Edith never mentioned an iota of the business to her sister. It is well. It was not your destiny. Wherever you are, God bless you! My health is weak enough, but it is so far amended that it is far less dependent on the influences of the weather. The mountains are better friends in this respect. Would that I could flatter myself that the same would be the case with you. The only objection on my part is now,—God be praised!—done away. The services and benefits I should receive from your society and the spur of your example would be incalculable. The house consists—the first floor (or rather ground floor) of a kitchen and a back kitchen, a large parlour and two nice small parlours; the second floor of three bedrooms, one a large one, and one large drawing-room; the third floor or floors of three bedrooms—in all twelve rooms. Besides these, Mr. Jackson offers to make that nice outhouse or workshop either two rooms or one noble large one for a study if I wish it. If it suited you, you might have one kitchen, or (if Edith and Sara thought it would answer) we might have the two kitchens in common. You might have, I say, the whole ground floor, consisting of two sweet wing-rooms, commanding that loveliest view of Borrowdale, and the great parlour; and supposing we each were forced to have two servants, a nursemaid and a housemaid, the two housemaids would sleep together in one of the upper rooms, and the nursemaids have each a room to herself, and the long room on the ground floor must be yours and Edith's room, and if Mary be with you, the other hers. We should have the whole second floor, consisting of the drawing-room, which would be Mrs. Coleridge's parlour, two bedrooms, which (as I am so often ill, and when ill cannot rest at all, unless I have a bed to myself) is absolutely necessary for me, and one room for you if occasion should be, or any friend of yours or mine. The highest room in the house is a very large one intended for two, but suffered to remain one by my desire. It would be a capital healthy nursery. The outhouse would become my study, and I have a couch-bed on which I am now sitting (in bed) and writing to you. It is now in the study; of course it would be removed to the outhouse when that became my study, and would be a second spare bed. I have no doubt but that Mr. Jackson would willingly let us retain my present study, which might be your library and study room. My dear Southey, I merely state these things to you. All our lot on earth is compromise. Blessings obtained by blessings foregone, or by evils undergone. I should be glad, no doubt, if you thought that your health and happiness would find a home under the same roof with me; and I am sure you will not accuse me as indelicate or obtrusive in mentioning things as they are; but if you decline it altogether, I shall know that you have good reasons for doing so, and be perfectly satisfied, for if it detracted from your comfort it could, of course, be nothing but the contrary of all advantage to me. You would have access to four or five libraries: Sir W. Lawson's, a most magnificent one, but chiefly in Natural History, Travels, etc.; Carlton House (I am a prodigious favourite of Mrs. Wallis, the owner and resident, mother of the Privy Counsellor Wallis); Carlisle, Dean and Chapter; the Library at Hawkshead School, and another (of what value I know not) at St. Bees, whither I mean to walk to-morrow to spend five or six days for bathing. It is four miles from Whitehaven by the seaside. Mrs. Coleridge is but poorly, children well. Love to Edith and May, and to whom I am at all interested. God love you. If you let me hear from you, it is among my firmest resolves—God ha' mercy on 'em!—to be a regular correspondent of yours.

S. T. Coleridge.

P. S. Mrs. C. must have one room on the ground floor, but this is only putting one of your rooms on the second floor.

CXXVIII. TO THE SAME.

Monday night, August 9, 1802.

My dear Southey,—Derwent can say his letters, and if you could but see his darling mouth when he shouts out Q! This is a digression.

On Sunday, August 1st,[264] after morning church, I left Greta Hall, crossed the fields to Portinscale, went through Newlands, where "Great Robinson looks down upon Marden's Bower," and drank tea at Buttermere, crossed the mountains to Ennerdale, and slept at a farm-house a little below the foot of the lake, spent the greater part of the next day mountaineering, and went in the evening through Egremont to St. Bees, and slept there; returned next day to Egremont, and slept there; went by the sea-coast as far as Gosforth, then turned off and went up Wasdale, and slept at T. Tyson's at the head of the vale. Thursday morning crossed the mountains and ascended Scafell, which is more than a hundred yards higher than either Helvellyn or Skiddaw; spent the whole day among clouds, and one of them a frightening thunder-cloud; slipped down into Eskdale, and there slept, and spent a good part of the next day; proceeded that evening to Devock Lake, and slept at Ulpha Kirk; on Saturday passed through the Dunnerdale Mountains to Broughton Vale, Tarver Vale, and in upon Coniston. On Sunday I surveyed the lake, etc., of Coniston, and proceeded to Bratha, and slept at Lloyd's house; this morning walked from Bratha to Grasmere, and from Grasmere to Greta Hall, where I now am, quite sweet and ablute, and have not even now read through your letter, which I will answer by the night's post, and therefore must defer all account of my very interesting tour, saying only that of all earthly things which I have beheld, the view of Scafell and from Scafell (both views from its own summit) is the most heart-exciting.

And now for business. The rent of the whole house, including taxes and the furniture we have, will not be under forty, and not above forty-two, pounds a year. You will have half the house and half the furniture, and of course your share will be either twenty pounds or twenty guineas. As to furniture, the house certainly will not be wholly, that is, completely furnished by Jackson. Two rooms we must somehow or other furnish between us, but not immediately; you may pass the winter without it, and it is hard if we cannot raise thirty pounds in the course of the winter between us. And whatever we buy may be disposed of any Saturday, to a moral certainty, at its full value, or Mr. Jackson, who is uncommonly desirous that you should come, will take it. But we can get on for the winter well enough.

Your books may come all the way from Bristol either to Whitehaven, Maryport, or Workington; sometimes directly, always by means of Liverpool. In the latter case, they must be sent to Whitehaven, from whence waggons come to Keswick twice a week. You will have twenty or thirty shillings to lay out in tin and crockery, and you must bring with you, or buy here (which you may do at eight months' credit), knives and forks, etc., and all your linen, from the diaper subvestments of the young jacobin[265] to diaper table clothes, sheets, napkins, etc. But these, I suppose, you already have.

What else I have to say I cannot tell, and indeed shall be too late for the post. But I will write soon again. I was exceedingly amused with the Cottelism; but I have not time to speak of this or of other parts of your letter. I believe that I can execute the criticisms with no offence to Hayley, and in a manner highly satisfactory to the admirers of the poet Bloomfield, and to the friends of the man Bloomfield. But there are certainly other objections of great weight.

Sara is well, and the children pretty well. Hartley is almost ill with transport at my Scafell expedition. That child is a poet, spite of the forehead, "villainously low," which his mother smuggled into his face. Derwent is more beautiful than ever, but very backward with his tongue, although he can say all his letters.—N. B. Not out of the book. God bless you and yours!

S. T. Coleridge.

If you are able to determine, you will of course let me know it without waiting for a second letter from me; as if you determine in the affirmative[266] of the scheme, it will be a great motive with Jackson, indeed, a most infallible one, to get immediately to work so as to have the whole perfectly furnished six weeks at least before your arrival. Another reason for your writing immediately is, that we may lay you in a stock of coals during the summer, which is a saving of some pounds; when I say determine, of course I mean such determination as the thousand contingencies, black and white, permit a wise man to make, and which would be enough for me to act on.

Sara will write to Edith soon.

I have just received a letter from Poole; but I have found so many letters that I have opened yours only.

CXXIX. TO W. SOTHEBY.

Thursday, August 26, 1802.

My dear Sir,—I was absent on a little excursion when your letter arrived, and since my return I have been waiting and making every enquiry in the hopes of announcing the receipt of your "Orestes" and its companions, with my sincere thanks for your kindness. But I can hear nothing of them. Mr. Lamb,[267] however, goes to Penrith next week, and will make strict scrutiny. I am not to find the "Welsh Tour" among them; and yet I think I am correct in referring the ode "Netley Abbey" to that collection,—a poem which I believe I can very nearly repeat by heart, though it must have been four or five years since I last read it. I well remember that, after reading your "Welsh Tour," Southey observed to me that you, I, and himself had all done ourselves harm by suffering an admiration of Bowles to bubble up too often on the surface of our poems. In perusing the second volume of Bowles, which I owe to your kindness, I met a line of my own which gave me great pleasure, from the thought what a pride and joy I should have had at the time of writing it if I had supposed it possible that Bowles would have adopted it. The line is,—

Had melancholy mus'd herself to sleep.[268]
I wrote the lines at nineteen, and published them many years ago in the "Morning Post" as a fragment, and as they are but twelve lines, I will transcribe them:—

Upon a mouldering abbey's broadest wall,
Where ruining ivies prop the ruins steep—
Her folded arms wrapping her tatter'd pall
Had Melancholy mused herself to sleep.
The fern was press'd beneath her hair,
The dark green Adder's Tongue was there;
And still as came the flagging sea gales weak,
Her long lank leaf bow'd fluttering o'er her cheek.

Her pallid cheek was flush'd; her eager look
Beam'd eloquent in slumber! Inly wrought,
Imperfect sounds her moving lips forsook,
And her bent forehead work'd with troubled thought.

I met these lines yesterday by accident, and ill as they are written there seemed to me a force and distinctness of image in them that were buds of promise in a schoolboy performance, though I am giving them perhaps more than their deserts in thus assuring them a reading from you. I have finished the "First Navigator," and Mr. Tomkins[269] may have it whenever he wishes. It would be gratifying to me if you would look it over and alter anything you like. My whole wish and purpose is to serve Mr. Tomkins, and you are not only much more in the habit of writing verse than I am, but must needs have a better tact of what will offend that class of readers into whose hands a showy publication is likely to fall. I do not mean, my dear sir, to impose on you ten minutes' thought, but often currente oculo a better phrase or position of words will suggest itself. As to the ten pounds, it is more than the thing is worth, either in German or English. Mr. Tomkins will better give the true value of it by kindly accepting what is given with kindness. Two or three copies presented in my name, one to each of the two or three friends of mine who are likely to be pleased with a fine book,—this is the utmost I desire or will receive. I shall for the ensuing quarter send occasional verses, etc., to the "Morning Post," under the signature Ἔστησε, and I mention this to you because I have some intention of translating Voss's "Idylls" in English hexameter, with a little prefatory essay on modern hexameters. I have discovered that the poetical parts of the Bible and the best parts of Ossian are little more than slovenly hexameters, and the rhythmical prose of Gesner is still more so, and reads exactly like that metre in Boethius' and Seneca's tragedies, which consists of the latter half of the hexameter. The thing is worth an experiment, and I wish it to be considered merely as an experiment. I need not say that the greater number of the verses signed Ἔστησε be such as were never meant for anything else but the peritura charta of the "Morning Post."

I had written thus far when your letter of the 16th arrived, franked on the 23d from Weymouth, with a polite apology from Mr. Bedingfell (if I have rightly deciphered the name) for its detention. I am vexed I did not write immediately on my return home, but I waited, day after day, in hopes of the "Orestes," etc. It is an old proverb that "extremes meet," and I have often regretted that I had not noted down as they incurred the interesting instances in which the proverb is verified. The newest subject, though brought from the planets (or asteroids) Ceres and Pallas, could not excite my curiosity more than "Orestes." I will write immediately to Mr. Clarkson, who resides at the foot of Ulleswater, and beg him to walk into Penrith, and ask at all the inns if any parcel have arrived; if not, I will myself write to Mr. Faulder and inform him of the failure. There is a subject of great merit in the ancient mythology hitherto untouched—I believe so, at least. But for the mode of the death, which mingles the ludicrous and terrible, but which might be easily altered, it is one of the finest subjects for tragedy that I am acquainted with. Medea, after the murder of her children [having] fled to the court of the old King Pelias, was regarded with superstitious horror, and shunned or insulted by the daughters of Pelias, till, hearing of her miraculous restoration of Æson, they conceived the idea of recalling by her means the youth of their own father. She avails herself of their credulity, and so works them up by pretended magical rites that they consent to kill their father in his sleep and throw him into the magic cauldron. Which done, Medea leaves them with bitter taunts of triumph. The daughters are called Asteropæa, Autonoe, and Alcestis. Ovid alludes briefly to this story in the couplet,—

"Quid referam Peliæ natas pietate nocentes,
Cæsaque virgineâ membra paterna manu?"
Ovid, Epist. XII. 129, 130.

What a thing to have seen a tragedy raised on this fable by Milton, in rivalry of the "Macbeth" of Shakespeare! The character of Medea, wandering and fierce, and invested with impunity by the strangeness and excess of her guilt, and truly an injured woman on the other hand and possessed of supernatural powers! The same story is told in a very different way by some authors, and out of their narrations matter might be culled that would very well coincide with and fill up the main incidents—her imposing the sacred image of Diana on the priesthood of Iolcus, and persuading them to join with her in inducing the daughters of Pelias to kill their father; the daughters under the persuasion that their father's youth would be restored, the priests under the faith that the goddess required the death of the old king, and that the safety of the country depended on it. In this way Medea might be suffered to escape under the direct protection of the priesthood, who may afterwards discover the delusion. The moral of the piece would be a very fine one.

Wordsworth wrote a very animated account of his difficulties and his joyous meeting with you, which he calls the happy rencontre or fortunate rainstorm. Oh! that you had been with me during a thunder-storm[270] on Thursday, August the 3d! I was sheltered (in the phrase of the country, lownded) in a sort of natural porch on the summit of Sca Fell, the central mountain of our Giants, said to be higher than Skiddaw or Helvellyn, and in chasm, naked crag, bursting springs, and waterfall the most interesting, without a rival. When the cloud passed away, to my right and left, and behind me, stood a great national convention of mountains which our ancestors most descriptively called Copland, that is, the Land of Heads. Before me the mountains died away down to the sea in eleven parallel ridges; close under my feet, as it were, were three vales: Wastdale, with its lake; Miterdale and Eskdale, with the rivers Irt, Mite, and Esk seen from their very fountains to their fall into the sea at Ravenglass Bay, which, with these rivers, form to the eye a perfect trident.

Turning round, I looked through Borrowdale out upon the Derwentwater and the Vale of Keswick, even to my own house, where my own children were. Indeed, I had altogether a most interesting walk through Newlands to Buttermere, over the fells to Ennerdale, to St. Bees; up Wastdale to Sca Fell, down Eskdale to Devock Lake, Ulpha Kirk, Broughton Mills, Tarver, Coniston, Windermere, Grasmere, Keswick. If it would entertain you, I would transcribe my notes and send them you by the first opportunity. I have scarce left room for my best wishes to Mrs. and Miss Sotheby, and affectionate wishes for your happiness and all who constitute it.

With unfeigned esteem, dear sir,

Yours, etc.,

S. T. Coleridge.

P. S. I am ashamed to send you a scrawl so like in form to a servant wench's first letter. You will see that the first half was written before I received your last letter.

CXXX. TO THE SAME.

Greta Hall, Keswick, September 10, 1802.

My dear Sir,—The books have not yet arrived, and I am wholly unable to account for the delay. I suspect that the cause of it may be Mr. Faulder's mistake in sending them by the Carlisle waggon. A person is going to Carlisle on Monday from this place, and will make diligent inquiry, and, if he succeed, still I cannot have them in less than a week, as they must return to Penrith and there wait for the next Tuesday's carrier. I ought, perhaps, to be ashamed of my weakness, but I must confess I have been downright vexed by the business. Every cart, every return-chaise from Penrith has renewed my hopes, till I began to play tricks with my own impatience, and say, "Well, I take it for granted that I shan't get them for these seven days," etc.,—with other of those half-lies that fear begets on hope. You have imposed a pleasing task on me in requesting the minutiæ of my opinions concerning your "Orestes." Whatever these opinions may be, the disclosure of them will be a sort of map of my mind, as a poet and reasoner, and my curiosity is strongly excited. I feel you a man of genius in the choice of the subject. It is my faith that the genus irritabile is a phrase applicable only to bad poets. Men of great genius have, indeed, as an essential of their composition, great sensibility, but they have likewise great confidence in their own powers, and fear must always precede anger in the human mind. I can with truth say that, from those I love, mere general praise of anything I have written is as far from giving me pleasure as mere general censure; in anything, I mean, to which I have devoted much time or effort. "Be minute, and assign your reasons often, and your first impressions always, and then blame or praise. I care not which, I shall be gratified." These are my sentiments, and I assuredly believe that they are the sentiments of all who have indeed felt a true call to the ministry of song. Of course, I, too, will act on the golden rule of doing to others what I wish others to do unto me. But, while I think of it, let me say that I should be much concerned if you applied this to the "First Navigator." It would absolutely mortify me if you did more than look over it, and when a correction suggested itself to you, take your pen and make it, and let the copy go to Tomkins. What they have been, I shall know when I see the thing in print; for it must please the present times if it please any, and you have been far more in the fashionable world than I, and must needs have a finer and surer tact of that which will offend or disgust in the higher circles of life. Yet it is not what I should have advised Tomkins to do, and that is one reason why I cannot and will not accept more than a brace of copies from him. I do not like to be associated in a man's mind with his losses. If he have the translation gratis, he must take it on his own judgment; but when a man pays for a thing, and he loses by it, the idea will creep in, spite of himself, that the failure was in part owing to the badness of the translation. While I was translating the "Wallenstein," I told Longman it would never answer; when I had finished it I wrote to him and foretold that it would be waste paper on his shelves, and the dullness charitably laid upon my shoulders. Longman lost two hundred and fifty pounds by the work, fifty pounds of which had been paid to me,—poor pay, Heaven knows! for a thick octavo volume of blank verse; and yet I am sure that Longman never thinks of me but "Wallenstein" and the ghosts of his departed guineas dance an ugly waltz round my idea. This would not disturb me a tittle, if I thought well of the work myself. I should feel a confidence that it would win its way at last;

but this is not the case with Gesner's "Der erste Schiffer." It may as well lie here till Tomkins wants it. Let him only give me a week's notice, and I will transmit it to you with a large margin. Bowles's stanzas on "Navigation"[271] are among the best in that second volume, but the whole volume is wofully inferior to its predecessor. There reigns through all the blank verse poems such a perpetual trick of moralizing everything, which is very well, occasionally, but never to see or describe any interesting appearance in nature without connecting it, by dim analogies, with the moral world proves faintness of impression. Nature has her proper interest, and he will know what it is who believes and feels that everything has a life of its own, and that we are all One Life. A poet's heart and intellect should be combined, intimately combined and unified with the great appearances of nature, and not merely held in solution and loose mixture with them, in the shape of formal similes. I do not mean to exclude these formal similes; there are moods of mind in which they are natural, pleasing moods of mind, and such as a poet will often have, and sometimes express; but they are not his highest and most appropriate moods. They are "sermoni propriora," which I once translated "properer for a sermon." The truth is, Bowles has indeed the sensibility of a poet, but he has not the passion of a great poet. His latter writings all want native passion. Milton here and there supplies him with an appearance of it, but he has no native passion because he is not a thinker, and has probably weakened his intellect by the haunting fear of becoming extravagant. Young, somewhere in one of his prose works, remarks that there is as profound a logic in the most daring and dithyrambic parts of Pindar as in the "Organon" of Aristotle. The remark is a valuable one.

Poetic feelings, like the flexuous boughs
Of mighty oaks! yield homage to the gale,
Toss in the strong winds, drive before the gust,
Themselves one giddy storm of fluttering leaves;
Yet, all the while, self-limited, remain
Equally near the fix'd and parent trunk
Of truth in nature—in the howling blast,
As in the calm that stills the aspen grove.[272]
That this is deep in our nature, I felt when I was on Scafell. I involuntarily poured forth a hymn[273] in the manner of the Psalms, though afterwards I thought the ideas, etc., disproportionate to our humble mountains.... You will soon see it in the "Morning Post," and I should be glad to know whether and how far it pleased you. It has struck me with great force lately that the Psalms afford a most complete answer to those who state the Jehovah of the Jews, as a personal and national God, and the Jews as differing from the Greeks only in calling the minor Gods Cherubim and Seraphim, and confining the word "God" only to their Jupiter. It must occur to every reader that the Greeks in their religious poems address always the Numina Loci, the Genii, the Dryads, the Naiads, etc., etc. All natural objects were dead, mere hollow statues, but there was a Godkin or Goddessling included in each. In the Hebrew poetry you find nothing of this poor stuff, as poor in genuine imagination as it is mean in intellect. At best, it is but fancy, or the aggregating faculty of the mind, not imagination or the modifying and coadunating faculty. This the Hebrew poets appear to me to have possessed beyond all others, and next to them the English. In the Hebrew poets each thing has a life of its own, and yet they are all our life. In God they move and live and have their being; not had, as the cold system of Newtonian Theology represents, but have. Great pleasure indeed, my dear sir, did I receive from the latter part of your letter. If there be any two subjects which have in the very depths of my nature interested me, it has been the Hebrew and Christian Theology, and the Theology of Plato. Last winter I read the Parmenides and the Timæus with great care, and oh, that you were here—even in this howling rainstorm that dashes itself against my windows—on the other side of my blazing fire, in that great armchair there! I guess we should encroach on

the morning ere we parted. How little the commentators of Milton have availed themselves of the writings of Plato, Milton's darling! But alas, commentators only hunt out verbal parallelisms—numen abest. I was much impressed with this in all the many notes on that beautiful passage in "Comus" from l. 629 to 641. All the puzzle is to find out what plant Hæmony is; which they discover to be the English spleenwort, and decked out as a mere play and licence of poetic fancy with all the strange properties suited to the purpose of the drama. They thought little of Milton's platonizing spirit, who wrote nothing without an interior meaning. "Where more is meant than meets the ear," is true of himself beyond all writers. He was so great a man that he seems to have considered fiction as profane unless where it is consecrated by being emblematic of some truth. What an unthinking and ignorant man we must have supposed Milton to be, if, without any hidden meaning, he had described it as growing in such abundance that the dull swain treads on it daily, and yet as never flowering. Such blunders Milton of all others was least likely to commit. Do look at the passage. Apply it as an allegory of Christianity, or, to speak more precisely, of the Redemption by the Cross, every syllable is full of light! "A small unsightly root."—"To the Greeks folly, to the Jews a stumbling-block"—"The leaf was darkish and had prickles on it"—"If in this life only we have hope, we are of all men the most miserable," and a score of other texts. "But in another country, as he said, Bore a bright golden flower"—"The exceeding weight of glory prepared for us hereafter"—"But not in this soil; Unknown and like esteemed and the dull swain Treads on it daily with his clouted shoon"—The promises of Redemption offered daily and hourly, and to all, but accepted scarcely by any—"He called it Hæmony." Now what is Hæmony? αἷμα οἶνος, Blood-wine. "And he took the wine and blessed it and said, 'This is my Blood,'"—the great symbol of the Death on the Cross. There is a general ridicule cast on all allegorising of poets. Read Milton's prose works, and observe whether he was one of those who joined in this ridicule. There is a very curious passage in Josephus [De Bello Jud. 6, 7, cap. 25 (vi. § 3)] which is, in its literal meaning, more wild and fantastically absurd than the passage in Milton; so much so, that Lardner quotes it in exultation and says triumphantly, "Can any man who reads it think it any disparagement to the Christian Religion that it was not embraced by a man who would believe such stuff as this? God forbid that it should affect Christianity, that it is not believed by the learned of this world!" But the passage in Josephus, I have no doubt, is wholly allegorical.

Ἔστησε signifies "He hath stood,"[274] which, in these times of apostasy from the principles of freedom or of religion in this country, and from both by the same persons in France, is no unmeaning signature, if subscribed with humility, and in the remembrance of "Let him that stands take heed lest he fall!" However, it is, in truth, no more than S. T. C. written in Greek—Es tee see.

Pocklington will not sell his house, but he is ill, and perhaps it may be to be sold, but it is sunless all winter.

God bless you, and
S. T. Coleridge.

CXXXI. TO THE SAME.

Greta Hall, Keswick, Tuesday, September 27, 1802.

My dear Sir,—The river is full, and Lodore is full, and silver-fillets come out of clouds and glitter in every ravine of all the mountains; and the hail lies like snow, upon their tops, and the impetuous gusts from Borrowdale snatch the water up high, and continually at the bottom of the lake it is not distinguishable from snow slanting before the wind—and under this seeming snow-drift the sunshine gleams, and over all the nether half of the Lake it is bright and dazzles, a cauldron of melted silver boiling! It is in very truth a sunny, misty, cloudy, dazzling, howling, omniform day, and I have been looking at as pretty a sight as a father's eyes could well see—Hartley and little Derwent running in the green where the gusts blow most madly, both with their hair floating and tossing, a miniature of the agitated trees, below which they were playing, inebriate both with the pleasure—Hartley whirling round for joy, Derwent eddying, half-willingly, half by the force of the gust,—driven backward, struggling forward, and shouting his little hymn of joy. I can write thus to you, my dear sir, with a confident spirit; for when I received your letter on the 22nd, and had read the "family history," I laid down the sheet upon my desk, and sate for half an hour thinking of you, dreaming of you, till the tear grown cold upon my cheek awoke me from my reverie. May you live long, long, thus blessed in your family, and often, often may you all sit around one fireside. Oh happy should I be now and then to sit among you—your pilot and guide in some of your summer walks!

"Frigidus ut sylvis Aquilo si increverit, aut si
Hiberni pluviis dependent nubibus imbres,
Nos habeat domus, et multo Lar luceat igne.
Ante focum mihi parvus erit, qui ludat, Iulus,
Blanditias ferat, et nondum constantia verba;
Ipse legam magni tecum monumenta Platonis!"

Or, what would be still better, I could talk to you (and, if you were here now, to an accompaniment of winds that would well suit the subject) instead of writing to you concerning your "Orestes." When we talk we are our own living commentary, and there are so many running notes of look, tone, and gesture, that there is small danger of being misunderstood, and less danger of being imperfectly understood—in writing; but no! it is foolish to abuse a good substitute because it is not all that the original is,—so I will do my best and, believe me, I consider this letter which I am about to write as merely an exercise of my own judgment—a something that may make you better acquainted, perhaps, with the architecture and furniture of my mind, though it will probably convey to you little or nothing that had not occurred to you before respecting your own tragedy. One thing I beg solicitously of you, that, if anywhere I appear to speak positively, you will acquit me of any correspondent feeling. I hope that it is not a frequent feeling with me in any case, and, that if it appear so, I am belied by my own warmth of manner. In the present instance it is impossible. I have been too deeply impressed by the work, and I am now about to give you, not criticisms nor decisions, but a history of my impressions, and, for the greater part, of my first impressions, and if anywhere there seem anything like a tone of warmth or dogmatism, do, my dear sir, be kind enough to regard it as no more than a way of conveying to you the whole of my meaning; or, for I am writing too seriously, as the dexterous toss, necessary to turn an idea out of its pudding-bag, round and unbroken.

[No signature.]

Several pages of minute criticisms on Sotheby's "Orestes" form part of the original transcript of the letter.

CXXXII. TO HIS WIFE.

St. Clear, Caermarthen, Tuesday, November 16, 1802.

My dear Love,—I write to you from the New Passage, Saturday morning, November 13. We had a favourable passage, dined on the other side, and proceeded in a post-chaise to Usk, and from thence to Abergavenny, where we supped and slept and breakfasted—a vile supper, vile beds, and vile breakfast. From Abergavenny to Brecon, through the vale of Usk, I believe, nineteen miles of most delightful country. It is not indeed comparable with the meanest part of our Lake Country, but hills, vale, and river, cottages and woods are nobly blended, and, thank Heaven, I seldom permit my past greater pleasures to lessen my enjoyment of present charms. Of the things which this nineteen miles has in common with our whole vale of Keswick (which is about nineteen miles long), I may say that the two vales and the two rivers are equal to each other, that the Keswick vale beats the Welsh one all hollow in cottages, but is as much surpassed by it in woods and timber trees. I am persuaded that every tree in the south of England has three times the number of leaves that a tree of the same sort and size has in Cumberland or Westmoreland, and there is an incomparably larger number of very large trees. Even the Scotch firs luxuriate into beauty and pluminess, and the larches are magnificent creatures indeed, in S. Wales. I must not deceive you, however, with all the advantages. S. Wales, if you came into it with the very pictures of Keswick, Ulleswater, Grasmere, etc., in your fancy, and were determined to hold them, and S. Wales together with all its richer fields, woods, and ancient trees, would needs appear flat and tame as ditchwater. I have no firmer persuasion than this, that there is no place in our island (and, saving Switzerland, none in Europe perhaps), which really equals the vale of Keswick, including Borrowdale, Newlands, and Bassenthwaite. O Heaven! that it had but a more genial climate! It is now going on for the eighteenth week since they have had any rain here, more than a few casual refreshing showers, and we have monopolized the rain of the whole kingdom. From Brecon to Trecastle—a churchyard, two or three miles from Brecon, is belted by a circle of the largest and noblest yews I ever saw—in a belt, to wit; they are not so large as the yew in Borrowdale or that in Lorton, but so many, so large and noble, I never saw before—and quite glowing with those heavenly-coloured, silky-pink-scarlet berries. From Trecastle to Llandovery, where we found a nice inn, an excellent supper, and good beds. From Llandovery to Llandilo—from Llandilo to Caermarthen, a large town all whitewashed—the roofs of the houses all whitewashed! a great town in a confectioner's shop, on Twelfth-cake-Day, or a huge snowpiece at a distance. It is nobly situated along a hill among hills, at the head of a very extensive vale. From Caermarthen after dinner to St. Clear, a little hamlet nine miles from Caermarthen, three miles from the sea (the nearest seaport being Llangan, pronounced Larne, on Caermarthen Bay—look in the map), and not quite a hundred miles from Bristol. The country immediately round is exceedingly bleak and dreary—just the sort of country that there is around Shurton, etc. But the inn, the Blue Boar, is the most comfortable little public-house I was ever in. Miss S. Wedgwood left us this morning (we arrived here at half past four yesterday evening) for Crescelly, Mr. Allen's seat (the Mrs. Wedgwood's father), fifteen miles from this place, and T. Wedgwood is gone out cock-shooting, in high glee and spirits. He is very much better than I expected to have found him—he says, the thought of my coming, and my really coming so immediately, has sent a new life into him. He will be out all the mornings. The evenings we chat, discuss, or I read to him. To me he is a delightful and instructive companion. He possesses the finest, the subtlest mind and taste I have ever yet met with. His mind resembles that miniature in my "Three Graves:"[275]—

A small blue sun! and it has got
A perfect glory too!

Ten thousand hairs of colour'd light,
Make up a glory gay and bright,
Round that small orb so blue!

I continue in excellent health, compared with my state at Keswick.... I have now left off beer too, and will persevere in it. I take no tea; in the morning coffee, with a teaspoonful of ginger in the last cup; in the afternoon a large cup of ginger-tea, and I take ginger at twelve o'clock at noon, and a glass after supper. I find not the least inconvenience from any quantity, however large. I dare say I take a large table-spoonful in the course of the twenty-four hours, and once in the twenty-four hours (but not always at the same time) I take half a grain of purified opium, equal to twelve drops of laudanum, which is not more than an eighth part of what I took at Keswick, exclusively of beer, brandy, and tea, which last is undoubtedly a pernicious thing—all which I have left off, and will give this regimen a fair, complete trial of one month, with no other deviation than that I shall sometimes lessen the opiate, and sometimes miss a day. But I am fully convinced, and so is T. Wedgwood, that to a person with such a stomach and bowels as mine, if any stimulus is needful, opium in the small quantities I now take it is incomparably better in every respect than beer, wine, spirits, or any fermented liquor, nay, far less pernicious than even tea. It is my particular wish that Hartley and Derwent should have as little tea as possible, and always very weak, with more than half milk. Read this sentence to Mary, and to Mrs. Wilson. I should think that ginger-tea, with a good deal of milk in it, would be an excellent thing for Hartley. A teaspoonful piled up of ginger would make a potful of tea, that would serve him for two days. And let him drink it half milk. I dare say that he would like it very well, for it is pleasant with sugar, and tell him that his dear father takes it instead of tea, and believes that it will make his dear Hartley grow. The whole kingdom is getting ginger-mad. My dear love! I have said nothing of Italy, for I am as much in the dark as when I left Keswick, indeed much more. For I now doubt very much whether we shall go or no. Against our going you must place T. W.'s improved state of health, and his exceeding dislike to continental travelling, and horror of the sea, and his exceeding attachment to his family; for our going, you must place his past experience, the transiency of his enjoyments, the craving after change, and the effect of a cold winter, especially if it should come on wet or sleety. His determinations are made so rapidly, that two or three days of wet weather with a raw cold air might have such an effect on his spirits, that he might go off immediately to Naples, or perhaps for Teneriffe, which latter place he is always talking about. Look out for it in the Encyclopædia. Again, these latter causes make it not impossible that the pleasure he has in me as a companion may languish. I must subscribe myself in haste,

Your dear husband,
S. T. Coleridge.

The mail is waiting.

CXXXIII. TO THE REV. J. P. ESTLIN.

Crescelly, near Narbarth, Pembrokeshire,
December 7, 1802.

My dear Friend,—I took the liberty of desiring Mrs. Coleridge to direct a letter for me to you, fully expecting to have seen you; but I passed rapidly through Bristol, and left it with Mr. Wedgwood immediately—I literally had no time to see any one. I hope, however, to see you on my return, for I wish very much to have some hours' conversation with you on a subject that will not cease to interest either of us while we live at least, and I trust that is a synonym of "for ever!"... Have you seen my different essays in the "Morning Post"?[276]— the comparison of Imperial Rome and France, the "Once a Jacobin, always a Jacobin," and the two letters to Mr. Fox? Are my politics yours?

Have you heard lately from America? A gentleman informed me that the progress of religious Deism in the middle Provinces is exceedingly rapid, that there are numerous congregations of Deists, etc., etc. Would to Heaven this were the case in France! Surely, religious Deism is infinitely nearer the religion of our Saviour than the gross idolatry of Popery, or the more decorous, but not less genuine, idolatry of a vast majority of Protestants. If there be meaning in words, it appears to me that the Quakers and Unitarians are the only Christians, altogether pure from Idolatry, and even of these I am sometimes jealous, that some of the Unitarians make too much an Idol of their one God. Even the worship of one God becomes Idolatry in my convictions, when, instead of the Eternal and Omnipresent, in whom we live and move and have our Being, we set up a distinct Jehovah, tricked out in the anthropomorphic attributes of Time and successive Thoughts, and think of him as a Person, from whom we had our Being. The tendency to Idolatry seems to me to lie at the root of all our human vices—it is our original Sin. When we dismiss three Persons in the Deity, only by subtracting two, we talk more intelligibly, but, I fear, do not feel more religiously—for God is a Spirit, and must be worshipped in spirit.

O my dear sir! it is long since we have seen each other—believe me, my esteem and grateful affection for you and Mrs. Estlin has suffered no abatement or intermission—nor can I persuade myself that my opinions, fully stated and fully understood, would appear to you to differ essentially from your own. My creed is very simple—my confession of Faith very brief. I approve altogether and embrace entirely the Religion of the Quakers, but exceedingly dislike the sect, and their own notions of their own Religion. By Quakerism I understand the opinions of George Fox rather than those of Barclay—who was the St. Paul of Quakerism.—I pray for you and yours!

S. T. Coleridge.

CXXXIV. TO ROBERT SOUTHEY.

Christmas Day, 1802.

My dear Southey,—I arrived at Keswick with T. Wedgwood on Friday afternoon, that is to say, yesterday, and had the comfort to find that Sara was safely brought to bed, the morning before, that is on Thursday, half-past six, of a healthy Girl. I had never thought of a girl as a possible event; the words child and man-child were perfect synonyms in my feelings. However, I bore the sex with great fortitude, and she shall be called Sara. Both Mrs. Coleridge and the Coleridgiella are as well as can be. I left the little one sucking at a great rate. Derwent and Hartley are both well.

I was at Cote[277] in the beginning of November, and of course had calculated on seeing you, and, above all, on seeing little Edith's physiognomy, among the certain things of my expedition, but I had no sooner arrived at Cote than I was forced to quit it, T. Wedgwood having engaged to go into Wales with his sister. I arrived at Cote in the afternoon, and till late evening did not know or conjecture that we were to go off early in the next morning. I do not say this for you,—you must know how earnestly I yearn to see you,—but for Mr. Estlin, who expressed himself wounded by the circumstance. When you see him, therefore, be so good as to mention this to him. I was much affected by Mrs. Coleridge's account of your health and eyes. God have mercy on us! We are all sick, all mad, all slaves! It is a theory of mine that virtue and genius are diseases of the hypochondriacal and scrofulous genera, and exist in a peculiar state of the nerves and diseased digestion, analogous to the beautiful diseases that colour and variegate certain trees. However, I add, by way of comfort, that it is my faith that the virtue and genius produce the disease, not the disease the virtue, etc., though when present it fosters them. Heaven knows, there are fellows who have more vices than scabs, and scabs countless, with fewer ideas than plaisters. As to my own health it is very indifferent. I am exceedingly temperate in everything, abstain wholly from wine, spirits, or fermented liquors, almost wholly from tea, abjure all fermentable and vegetable food, bread excepted, and use that sparingly; live almost entirely on eggs, fish, flesh, and fowl, and thus contrive not to be ill. But well I am not, and in this climate never shall be. A deeply ingrained though mild scrofula is diffused through me, and is a very Proteus. I am fully determined to try Teneriffe or Gran Canaria, influenced to prefer them to Madeira solely by the superior cheapness of living. The climate and country are heavenly, the inhabitants Papishes, all of whom I would burn with fire and faggot, for what didn't they do to us Christians under bloody Queen Mary? Oh the Devil sulphur-roast them! I would have no mercy on them, unless they drowned all their priests, and then, spite of the itch (which they have in an inveterate degree, rich and poor, gentle and simple, old and young, male and female), would shake hands with them ungloved.

By way of one impudent half line in this meek and mild letter—will you go with me? "I" and "you" mean mine and yours, of course. Remember you are to give me Thomas Aquinas and Scotus Erigena.

God bless you and

S. T. Coleridge.

I can have the best letters and recommendation. My love and their sisters to Mary and Edith, and if you see Mrs. Fricker, be so good as to tell her that she will hear from me or Sara in the course of ten days.

CXXXV. TO THOMAS WEDGWOOD.

[The text of this letter, which was first published in Cottle's "Reminiscences," 1849, p. 450, has been collated with that of the original.]

Keswick, January 9, 1803.

My dear Wedgwood,—I send you two letters, one from your dear sister, the second from Sharp, by which you will see at what short notice I must be off, if I go to the Canaries. If your last plan continue in full force in your mind, of course I have not even the phantom of a wish thitherward struggling, but if aught have happened to you, in the things without, or in the world within, to induce you to change the plan in itself, or the plan relatively to me, I think I could raise the money, at all events, and go and see. But I would a thousand-fold rather go with you whithersoever you go. I shall be anxious to hear how you have gone on since I left you. Should you decide in favour of a better climate somewhere or other, the best scheme I can think of is that in some part of Italy or Sicily which we both liked. I would look out for two houses. Wordsworth and his family would take the one, and I the other, and then you might have a home either with me, or, if you thought of Mr. and Mrs. Luff, under this modification, one of your own; and in either case you would have neighbours, and so return to England when the homesickness pressed heavy upon you, and back to Italy when it was abated, and the climate of England began to poison your comforts. So you would have abroad, in a genial climate, certain comforts of society among simple and enlightened men and women; and I should be an alleviation of the pang which you will necessarily feel, always, as often as you quit your own family.

I know no better plan: for travelling in search of objects is, at best, a dreary business, and whatever excitement it might have had, you must have exhausted it. God bless you, my dear friend. I write with dim eyes, for indeed, indeed, my heart is very full of affectionate sorrowful thoughts toward you.

I found Mrs. Coleridge not so well as I expected, but she is better to-day—and I, myself, write with difficulty, with all the fingers but one of my right hand very much swollen. Before I was half up Kirkstone the storm had wetted me through and through, and before I reached the top it was so wild and outrageous, that it would have been unmanly to have suffered the poor woman (guide) to continue pushing on, up against such a torrent of wind and rain; so I dismounted and sent her home with the storm to her back. I am no novice in mountain mischiefs, but such a storm as this was I never witnessed, combining the intensity of the cold with the violence of the wind and rain. The rain-drops were pelted or, rather, slung against my face by the gusts, just like splinters of flint, and I felt as if every drop cut my flesh. My hands were all shrivelled up like a washerwoman's, and so benumbed that I was obliged to carry my stick under my arm. Oh, it was a wild business! Such hurry-skurry of clouds, such volleys of sound! In spite of the wet and the cold, I should have had some pleasure in it but for two vexations: first, an almost intolerable pain came into my right eye, a smarting and burning pain; and secondly, in consequence of riding with such cold water under my seat, extremely uneasy and burthensome feelings attacked my groin, so that, what with the pain from the one, and the alarm from the other, I had no enjoyment at all!

Just at the brow of the hill I met a man dismounted, who could not sit on horseback. He seemed quite scared by the uproar, and said to me, with much feeling, "Oh, sir, it is a perilous buffeting, but it is worse for you than for me, for I have it at my back." However I got safely over, and, immediately, all was calm and breathless, as if it was some mighty fountain just on the summit of Kirkstone, that shot forth its volcano of air, and precipitated huge streams of invisible lava down the road to Patterdale.

I went on to Grasmere. I was not at all unwell when I arrived there, though wet of course to the skin. My right eye had nothing the matter with it, either to the sight of others, or to my own feelings, but I had a bad night, with distressful dreams, chiefly about my eye; and awaking often in the dark I thought it was the effect of mere recollection, but it appeared in the morning that my right eye was bloodshot, and the lid swollen. That morning, however, I walked home, and before I reached Keswick my eye was quite well, but I felt unwell all over. Yesterday I continued unusually unwell all over me till eight o'clock in the evening. I took no laudanum or opium, but at eight o'clock, unable to bear the stomach uneasiness and aching of my limbs, I took two large teaspoonsfull of ether in a wine-glass of camphorated gum water, and a third teaspoonfull at ten o'clock, and I received complete relief,—my body calmed, my sleep placid,—but when I awoke in the morning my right hand, with three of the fingers, was swollen and inflamed.... This has been a very rough attack, but though I am much weakened by it, and look sickly and haggard, yet I am not out of heart. Such a bout, such a "perilous buffeting," was enough to have hurt the health of a strong man. Few constitutions can bear to be long wet through in intense cold. I fear it will tire you to death to read this prolix scrawled story, but my health, I know, interests you. Do continue to send me a few lines by the market people on Friday—I shall receive it on Tuesday morning.

Affectionately, dear friend, yours ever,
S. T. Coleridge.

[Addressed "T. Wedgwood, Esq., C. Luff's Esq., Glenridding, Ulleswater."]

CXXXVI. TO HIS WIFE.

[London], Monday, April 4, 1803.

My dear Sara,—I have taken my place for Wednesday night, and, barring accidents, shall arrive at Penrith on Friday noon. If Friday be a fine morning, that is, if it do not rain, you will get Mr. Jackson to send a lad with a horse or pony to Penruddock. The boy ought to be at Penruddock by twelve o'clock that his horse may bait and have a feed of corn. But if it be rain, there is no choice but that I must take a chaise. At all events, if it please God, I shall be with you by Friday, five o'clock, at the latest. You had better dine early. I shall take an egg or two at Penrith and drink tea at home. For more than a fortnight we have had burning July weather. The effect on my health was manifest, but Lamb objected, very sensibly, "How do you know what part may not be owing to the excitement of bustle and company?" On Friday night I was unwell and restless, and uneasy in limbs and stomach, though I had been extremely regular. I told Lamb on Saturday morning that I guessed the weather had changed. But there was no mark of it; it was hotter than ever. On Saturday evening my right knee and both my ankles swelled and were very painful; and within an hour after there came a storm of wind and rain. It continued raining the whole night. Yesterday it was a fine day, but cold; to-day the same, but I am a great deal better, and the swelling in my ankle is gone down and that in my right knee much decreased. Lamb observed that he was glad he had seen all this with his own eyes; he now knew that my illness was truly linked with the weather, and no whim or restlessness of disposition in me. It is curious, but I have found that the weather-glass changed on Friday night, the very hour that I found myself unwell. I will try to bring down something for Hartley, though toys are so outrageously dear, and I so short of money, that I shall be puzzled.

To-day I dine again with Sotheby. He had informed me that ten gentlemen who have met me at his house desired him to solicit me to finish the "Christabel," and to permit them to publish it for me; and they engaged that it should be in paper, printing, and decorations the most magnificent thing that had hitherto appeared. Of course I declined it. The lovely lady shan't come to that pass! Many times rather would I have it printed at Soulby's on the true ballad paper. However, it was civil, and Sotheby is very civil to me.

I had purposed not to speak of Mary Lamb, but I had better write it than tell it. The Thursday before last she met at Rickman's a Mr. Babb, an old friend and admirer of her mother. The next day she smiled in an ominous way; on Sunday she told her brother that she was getting bad, with great agony. On Tuesday morning she laid hold of me with violent agitation and talked wildly about George Dyer. I told Charles there was not a moment to lose; and I did not lose a moment, but went for a hackney-coach and took her to the private mad-house at Hugsden. She was quite calm, and said it was the best to do so. But she wept bitterly two or three times, yet all in a calm way. Charles is cut to the heart. You will send this note to Grasmere or the contents of it, though, if I have time, I shall probably write myself to them to-day or to-morrow.

Yours affectionately,
S. T. Coleridge.

CXXXVII. TO ROBERT SOUTHEY.

Keswick, Wednesday, July 2, 1803.

My dear Southey,—You have had much illness as well as I, but I thank God for you, you have never been equally diseased in voluntary power with me. I knew a lady who was seized with a sort of asthma which she knew would be instantly relieved by a dose of ether. She had the full use of her limbs, and was not an arm's-length from the bell, yet could not command voluntary power sufficient to pull it, and might have died but for the accidental coming in of her daughter. From such as these the doctrines of materialism and mechanical necessity have been deduced; and it is some small argument against the truth of these doctrines that I have perhaps had a more various experience, a more intuitive knowledge of such facts than most men, and yet I do not believe these doctrines. My health is middling. If this hot weather continue, I hope to go on endurably, and oh, for peace! for I forbode a miserable winter in this country. Indeed, I am rather induced to determine on wintering in Madeira, rather than staying at home. I have enclosed ten pounds for Mrs. Fricker. Tell her I wish it were in my power to increase this poor half year's mite; but ill health keeps me poor. Bella is with us, and seems likely to recover. I have not seen the "Edinburgh Review." The truth is that Edinburgh is a place of literary gossip, and even I have had my portion of puff there, and of course my portion of hatred and envy. One man puffs me up—he has seen and talked with me; another hears him, goes and reads my poems, written when almost a boy, and candidly and logically hates me, because he does not admire my poems, in the proportion in which one of his acquaintance had admired me. It is difficult to say whether these reviewers do you harm or good.

You read me at Bristol a very interesting piece of casuistry from Father Somebody, the author, I believe, of the "Theatre Critic," respecting a double infant. If you do not immediately want it, or if my using it in a book of logic, with proper acknowledgment, will not interfere with your use of it, I should be extremely obliged to you if you would send it me without delay. I rejoice to hear of the progress of your History. The only thing I dread is the division of the European and Colonial History. In style you have only to beware of short, biblical, and pointed periods. Your general style is delightfully natural and yet striking.

You may expect certain explosions in the "Morning Post," Coleridge versus Fox, in about a week. It grieved me to hear (for I have a sort of affection for the man) from Sharp, that Fox had not read my two letters, but had heard of them, and that they were mine, and had expressed himself more wounded by the circumstance than anything that had happened since Burke's business. Sharp told this to Wordsworth, and told Wordsworth that he had been so affected by Fox's manner, that he himself had declined reading the two letters. Yet Sharp himself thinks my opinions right and true; but Fox is not to be attacked, and why? Because he is an amiable man; and not by me, because he had thought highly of me, etc., etc. O Christ! this is a pretty age in the article morality! When I cease to love Truth best of all things, and Liberty the next best, may I cease to live: nay, it is my creed that I should thereby cease to live, for as far as anything can be called probable in a subject so dark, it seems to me most probable that our immortality is to be a work of our own hands.

All the children are well, and love to hear Bella talk of Margaret. Love to Edith and to Mary and

S. T. Coleridge.

I have received great delight and instruction from Scotus Erigena. He is clearly the modern founder of the school of Pantheism; indeed he expressly defines the divine nature as quæ fit et facit, et creat et creatur; and repeatedly declares creation to be manifestation, the epiphany of philosophers. The eloquence with which he writes astonished me, but he had read more Greek than Latin, and was a Platonist rather than an Aristotelian. There is a good deal of omne meus oculus in the notion of the dark ages, etc., taken intensively; in extension it might be true. They had wells: we are flooded ankle high: and what comes of it but grass rank or rotten? Our age eats from that poison-tree of knowledge yclept "Too-Much and Too-Little." Have you read Paley's last book?[278] Have you it to review? I could make a dashing review of it.

CXXXVIII. TO THE SAME.

Keswick, July, 1803.

My dear Southey,—... I write now to propose a scheme,[279] or rather a rude outline of a scheme, of your grand work. What harm can a proposal do? If it be no pain to you to reject it, it will be none to me to have it rejected. I would have the work entitled Bibliotheca Britannica, or an History of British Literature, bibliographical, biographical, and critical. The two last volumes I would have to be a chronological catalogue of all noticeable or extant books; the others, be the number six or eight, to consist entirely of separate treatises, each giving a critical biblio-biographical history of some one subject. I will, with great pleasure, join you in learning Welsh and Erse; and you, I, Turner, and Owen,[280] might dedicate ourselves for the first half-year to a complete history of all Welsh, Saxon, and Erse books that are not translations that are the native growth of Britain. If the Spanish neutrality continues, I will go in October or November to Biscay, and throw light on the Basque.

Let the next volume contain the history of English poetry and poets, in which I would include all prose truly poetical. The first half of the second volume should be dedicated to great single names, Chaucer and Spenser, Shakespeare, Milton and Taylor, Dryden and Pope; the poetry of witty logic,—Swift, Fielding, Richardson, Sterne; I write par hasard, but I mean to say all great names as have either formed epochs in our taste, or such, at least, as are representative; and the great object to be in each instance to determine, first, the true merits and demerits of the books; secondly, what of these belong to the age—what to the author quasi peculium. The second half of the second volume should be a history of poetry and romances, everywhere interspersed with biography, but more flowing, more consecutive, more bibliographical, chronological, and complete. The third volume I would have dedicated to English prose, considered as to style, as to eloquence, as to general impressiveness; a history of styles and manners, their causes, their birth-places and parentage, their analysis....

These three volumes would be so generally interesting, so exceedingly entertaining, that you might bid fair for a sale of the work at large. Then let the fourth volume take up the history of metaphysics, theology, medicine, alchemy, common canon, and Roman law, from Alfred to Henry VII.; in other words, a history of the dark ages in Great Britain: the fifth volume—carry on metaphysics and ethics to the present day in the first half; the second half, comprise the theology of all the reformers. In the fourth volume there would be a grand article on the philosophy of the theology of the Roman Catholic religion; in this (fifth volume), under different names,—Hooker, Baxter, Biddle, and Fox,—the spirit of the theology of all the other parts of Christianity. The sixth and seventh volumes must comprise all the articles you can get, on all the separate arts and sciences that have been treated of in books since the Reformation; and, by this time, the book, if it answered at all, would have gained so high a reputation that you need not fear having whom you liked to write the different articles—medicine, surgery, chemistry, etc., etc., navigation, travellers, voyagers, etc., etc. If I go into Scotland, shall I engage Walter Scott to write the history of Scottish poets? Tell me, however, what you think of the plan. It would have one prodigious advantage: whatever accident stopped the work, would only prevent the future good, not mar the past; each volume would be a great and valuable work per se. Then each volume would awaken a new interest, a new set of readers, who would buy the past volumes of course; then it would allow you ample time and opportunities for the slavery of the catalogue volumes, which should be at the same time an index to the work, which would be in very truth a pandect of knowledge, alive and swarming with human life, feeling, incident. By the bye, what a strange abuse has been made of the word encyclopædia! It signifies properly, grammar, logic, rhetoric, and ethics, and metaphysics, which last, explaining the ultimate principle of grammar—log.—rhet., and eth.—formed a circle of knowledge.... To call a huge unconnected miscellany of the omne scibile, in an arrangement determined by the accident of initial letters, an encyclopædia is the impudent ignorance of your Presbyterian book-makers. Good night!

God bless you!
S. T. C.

CXXXIX. TO THE SAME.

Keswick, Sunday, August 7, 1803.

(Read the last lines first; I send you this letter merely to show you how anxious I have been about your work.)

My dear Southey,—The last three days I have been fighting up against a restless wish to write to you. I am afraid lest I should infect you with my fears rather than furnish you with any new arguments, give you impulses rather than motives, and prick you with spurs that had been dipped in the vaccine matter of my own cowardliness. While I wrote that last sentence, I had a vivid recollection, indeed an ocular spectrum, of our room in College Street, a curious instance of association. You remember how incessantly in that room I used to be compounding these half-verbal, half-visual metaphors. It argues, I am persuaded, a particular state of general feeling, and I hold that association depends in a much greater degree on the recurrence of resembling states of feeling than on trains of ideas, that the recollection of early childhood in latest old age depends on and is explicable by this, and if this be true, Hartley's system totters. If I were asked how it is that very old people remember visually only the events of early childhood, and remember the intervening spaces either not at all or only verbally, I should think it a perfectly philosophical answer that old age remembers childhood by becoming "a second childhood!" This explanation will derive some additional value if you would look into Hartley's solution of the phenomena—how flat, how wretched! Believe me, Southey! a metaphysical solution, that does not instantly tell you something in the heart is grievously to be suspected as apocryphal. I almost think that ideas never recall ideas, as far as they are ideas, any more than leaves in a forest create each other's motion. The breeze it is that runs through them—it is the soul, the state of feeling. If I had said no one idea ever recalls another, I am confident that I could support the assertion. And this is a digression.—My dear Southey, again and again I say, that whatever your plan may be, I will contrive to work for you with equal zeal if not with equal pleasure. But the arguments against your plan weigh upon me the more heavily, the more I reflect; and it could not be otherwise than that I should feel a confirmation of them from Wordsworth's complete coincidence—I having requested his deliberate opinion without having communicated an iota of my own. You seem to me, dear friend, to hold the dearness of a scarce work for a proof that the work would have a general sale, if not scarce. Nothing can be more fallacious than this. Burton's Anatomy used to sell for a guinea to two guineas. It was republished. Has it paid the expense of reprinting? Scarcely. Literary history informs us that most of those great continental bibliographies, etc., were published by the munificence of princes, or nobles, or great monasteries. A book from having had little or no sale, except among great libraries, may become so scarce that the number of competitors for it, though few, may be proportionally very great. I have observed that great works are nowadays bought, not for curiosity or the amor proprius, but under the notion that they contain all the knowledge a man may ever want, and if he has it on his shelf why there it is, as snug as if it were in his brain. This has carried off the encyclopædia, and will continue to do so. I have weighed most patiently what you said respecting the persons and classes likely to purchase a catalogue of all British books. I have endeavoured to make some rude calculation of their numbers according to your own numeration table, and it falls very short of an adequate number. Your scheme appears to be in short faulty, (1) because, everywhere, the generally uninteresting, the catalogue part will overlay the interesting parts; (2) because the first volume will have nothing in it tempting or deeply valuable, for there is not time or room for it; (3) because it is impossible that any one of the volumes can be executed as well as they would otherwise be from the to-and-fro, now here, now there motion of the mind, and employment of the industry. Oh how I wish to be talking, not writing, for my mind is so full that my thoughts stifle and jam each other. And I have presented them as shapeless jellies, so that I am ashamed of what I have written—it so imperfectly expresses what I meant to have said. My advice certainly would be, that at all events you should make some classification. Let all the law books form a catalogue per se, and so forth; otherwise it is not a book of reference, without an index half as large as the work itself. I see no well-founded objection to the plan which I first sent. The two main advantages are that, stop where you will, you are in harbour, you sail in an archipelago so thickly clustered, (that) at each island you take in a completely new cargo, and the former cargo is in safe housage; and (2dly) that each labourer working by the piece, and not by the day, can give an undivided attention in some instances for three or four years, and bring to the work the whole weight of his interest and reputation.... An encyclopædia appears to me a worthless monster. What surgeon, or physician, professed student of pure or mixed mathematics, what chemist or architect, would go to an encyclopædia for his books? If valuable treatises exist on these subjects in an encyclopædia, they are out of their place—an equal hardship on the general reader, who pays for whole volumes which he cannot read, and on the professed student of that particular subject, who must buy a great work which he does not want in order to possess a valuable treatise, which he might otherwise have had for six or seven shillings. You omit those things only from your encyclopædia which are excrescences—each volume will set up the reader, give him at once connected trains of thought and facts, and a delightful miscellany for lounge-reading. Your treatises will be long in exact proportion to their general interest. Think what a strange confusion it will make, if you speak of each book, according to its date, passing from an Epic Poem to a treatise on the treatment of sore legs? Nobody can become an enthusiast in favour of the work.... A great change of weather has come on, heavy rain and wind, and I have been very ill, and still I am in uncomfortable restless health. I am not even certain whether I shall not be forced to put off my Scotch tour; but if I go, I go on Tuesday. I shall not send off this letter till this is decided.

God bless you and

S. T. C.

CXL. TO HIS WIFE.

Friday afternoon, 4 o'clock, Sept. (1), [1803].

My dear Sara,—I write from the Ferry of Ballater.... This is the first post since the day I left Glasgow. We went thence to Dumbarton (look at Stoddart's tour, where there is a very good view of Dumbarton Rock and Tower), thence to Loch Lomond, and a single house called Luss—horrible inhospitality and a fiend of a landlady! Thence eight miles up the Lake to E. Tarbet, where the lake is so like Ulleswater that I could scarcely see the difference; crossed over the lake and by a desolate moorland walked to another lake, Loch Katrine, up to a place called Trossachs, the Borrowdale of Scotland, and the only thing which really beats us. You must conceive the Lake of Keswick pushing itself up a mile or two into Borrowdale, winding round Castle Crag, and in and out among all the nooks and promontories, and you must imagine all the mountains more detachedly built up, a general dislocation; every rock its own precipice, with trees young and old. This will give you some faint idea of the place, of which the character is extreme intricacy of effect produced by very simple means. One rocky, high island, four or five promontories, and a Castle Crag, just like that in the gorge of Borrowdale, but not so large. It rained all the way, all the long, long day. We slept in a hay-loft,—that is, Wordsworth, I, and a young man who came in at the Trossachs and joined us. Dorothy had a bed in the hovel, which was varnished so rich with peat smoke an apartment of highly polished [oak] would have been poor to it—it would have wanted the metallic lustre of the smoke-varnished rafters. This was [the pleasantest] evening I had spent since my tour; for Wordsworth's hypochondriacal feelings keep him silent and self-centred. The next day it still was rain and rain; the ferry-boat was out for the preaching, and we stayed all day in the ferry wet to the skin. Oh, such a wretched hovel! But two Highland lassies,[281] who kept house in the absence of the ferryman and his wife, were very kind, and one of them was beautiful as a vision, and put both Dorothy and me in mind of the Highland girl in William's "Peter Bell."[282] We returned to E. Tarbet, I with the rheumatism in my head. And now William proposed to me to leave them and make my way on foot to Loch Katrine, the Trossachs, whence it is only twenty miles to Stirling, where the coach runs through to Edinburgh. He and Dorothy resolved to fight it out. I eagerly caught at the proposal; for the sitting in an open carriage in the rain is death to me, and somehow or other I had not been quite comfortable. So on Monday I accompanied them to Arrochar, on purpose to see the Cobbler which had impressed me so much in Mr. Wilkinson's drawings; and there I parted with them, having previously sent on all my things to Edinburgh by a Glasgow carrier who happened to be at E. Tarbet. The worst thing was the money. They took twenty-nine guineas, and I six—all our remaining cash. I returned to E. Tarbet; slept there that night; the next day walked to the very head of Loch Lomond to Glen Falloch, where I slept at a cottage-inn, two degrees below John Stanley's (but the good people were very kind),—meaning from hence to go over the mountains to the head of Loch Katrine again; but hearing from the gude man of the house that it was 40 miles to Glencoe (of which I had formed an idea from Wilkinson's drawings), and having found myself so happy alone (such blessing is there in perfect liberty!) I walked off. I have walked forty-five miles since then, and, except during the last mile, I am sure I may say I have not met with ten houses. For eighteen miles there are but two habitations! and all that way I met no sheep, no cattle, only one goat! All through moorlands with huge mountains, some craggy and bare, but the most green, with deep pinky channels worn by torrents. Glencoe interested me, but rather disappointed me. There was no superincumbency of crag, and the crags not so bare or precipitous as I had expected. I am now going to cross the ferry for Fort William, for I have resolved to eke out my cash by all sorts of self-denial, and to walk along the whole line of the Forts. I am unfortunately shoeless; there is no town where I can get a pair, and I have no money to spare to buy them, so I expect to enter Perth barefooted. I burnt my shoes in drying them at the boatman's hovel on Loch Katrine, and I have by this means hurt my heel. Likewise my left leg is a little inflamed, and the rheumatism in the right of my head afflicts me sorely when I begin to grow warm in my bed, chiefly my right eye, ear, cheek, and the three teeth; but, nevertheless, I am enjoying myself, having Nature with solitude and liberty—the liberty natural and solitary, the solitude natural and free! But you must contrive somehow or other to borrow ten pounds, or, if that cannot be, five pounds, for me, and send it without delay, directed to me at the Post Office, Perth. I guess I shall be there in seven days or eight at the furthest; and your letter will be two days getting thither (counting the day you put it into the office at Keswick as nothing); so you must calculate, and if this letter does not reach you in time, that is, within five days from the date hereof, you must then direct to Edinburgh. I will make five pounds do (you must borrow of Mr. Jackson), and I must beg my way for the last three or four days! It is useless repining, but if I had set off myself in the Mail for Glasgow or Stirling, and so gone by foot, as I am now doing, I should have saved twenty-five pounds; but then Wordsworth would have lost it.

I have said nothing of you or my dear children. God bless us all! I have but one untried misery to go through, the loss of Hartley or Derwent, ay, or dear little Sara! In my health I am middling. While I can walk twenty-four miles a day, with the excitement of new objects, I can support myself; but still my sleep and dreams are distressful, and I am hopeless. I take no opiates ... nor have I any temptation; for since my disorder has taken this asthmatic turn opiates produce none but positively unpl[easant effects].

[No signature.]

Mrs. Coleridge,
Greta Hall, Keswick, Cumberland, S. Britain.

CXLI. TO ROBERT SOUTHEY.

[Edinburgh], Sunday night, 9 o'clock, September 10, 1803.

My dearest Southey,—I arrived here half an hour ago, and have only read your letters—scarce read them.—O dear friend! it is idle to talk of what I feel—I am stunned at present by this beginning to write, making a beginning of living feeling within me. Whatever comfort I can be to you I will—I have no aversions, no dislikes that interfere with you—whatever is necessary or proper for you becomes ipso facto agreeable to me. I will not stay a day in Edinburgh—or only one to hunt out my clothes. I cannot chitchat with Scotchmen while you are at Keswick, childless![283] Bless you, my dear Southey! I will knit myself far closer to you than I have hitherto done, and my children shall be yours till it please God to send you another.

I have been a wild journey, taken up for a spy and clapped into Fort Augustus, and I am afraid they may [have] frightened poor Sara by sending her off a scrap of a letter I was writing to her. I have walked 263 miles in eight days, so I must have strength somewhere, but my spirits are dreadful, owing entirely to the horrors of every night—I truly dread to sleep. It is no shadow with me, but substantial misery foot-thick, that makes me sit by my bedside of a morning and cry.—I have abandoned all opiates, except ether be one.... And when you see me drink a glass of spirit-and-water, except by prescription of a physician, you shall despise me,—but still I cannot get quiet rest.

When on my bed my limbs I lay,
It hath not been my use to pray
With moving lips or bended knees;
But silently, by slow degrees,
My spirit I to Love compose,5
In humble trust my eyelids close,
With reverential resignation,
No wish conceiv'd, no thought exprest,
Only a Sense of supplication,
A Sense o'er all my soul imprest10
That I am weak, yet not unblest,
Since round me, in me, everywhere
Eternal strength and Goodness are!—

But yester-night I pray'd aloud
In anguish and in agony,15
Awaking from the fiendish crowd
Of shapes and thoughts that tortur'd me!
Desire with loathing strangely mixt,
On wild or hateful objects fixt.
Sense of revenge, the powerless will,20
Still baffled and consuming still;
Sense of intolerable wrong,
And men whom I despis'd made strong!
Vain glorious threats, unmanly vaunting,
Bad men my boasts and fury taunting;25
Rage, sensual passion, mad'ning Brawl,
And shame and terror over all!
Deeds to be hid that were not hid,

Which all confus'd I might not know,
Whether I suffer'd or I did:30
For all was Horror, Guilt, and Woe,
My own or others still the same,
Life-stifling Fear, soul-stifling Shame!

Thus two nights pass'd: the night's dismay
Sadden'd and stunn'd the boding day.35
I fear'd to sleep: Sleep seemed to be
Disease's worst malignity.
The third night, when my own loud scream
Had freed me from the fiendish dream,
O'ercome by sufferings dark and wild,40
I wept as I had been a child;
And having thus by Tears subdued
My Trouble to a milder mood,
Such punishments, I thought, were due
To Natures, deepliest stain'd with Sin;45
Still to be stirring up anew
The self-created Hell within,
The Horror of the crimes to view,
To know and loathe, yet wish to do!
With such let fiends make mockery—50
But I—Oh, wherefore this on me?
Frail is my soul, yea, strengthless wholly,
Unequal, restless, melancholy;
But free from Hate and sensual Folly!
To live belov'd is all I need,55
And whom I love, I love indeed,
And etc., etc., etc., etc.[284]

I do not know how I came to scribble down these verses to you—my heart was aching, my head all confused—but they are, doggerel as they may be, a true portrait of my nights. What to do, I am at a loss; for it is hard thus to be withered, having the faculties and attainments which I have. We will soon meet, and I will do all I can to console poor Edith.—O dear, dear Southey! my head is sadly confused. After a rapid walk of thirty-three miles your letters have had the effect of perfect intoxication in my head and eyes. Change! change! change! O God of Eternity! When shall we be at rest in thee?

S. T. Coleridge.

CXLII. TO THE SAME.

Edinburgh, Tuesday morning, September 13, 1803.

My dear Southey,—I wrote you a strange letter, I fear. But, in truth, yours affected my wretched stomach, and my head, in such a way that I wrote mechanically in the wake of the first vivid idea. No conveyance left or leaves this place for Carlisle earlier than to-morrow morning, for which I have taken my place. If the coachman do not turn Panaceist, and cure all my ills by breaking my neck, I shall be at Carlisle on Wednesday, midnight, and whether I shall go on in the coach to Penrith, and walk from thence, or walk off from Carlisle at once, depends on two circumstances, first, whether the coach goes on with no other than a common bait to Penrith, and secondly, whether, if it should not do so, I can trust my clothes, etc., to the coachman safely, to be left at Penrith. There is but eight miles difference in the walk, and eight or nine shillings difference in the expense. At all events, I trust that I shall be with you on Thursday by dinner time, if you dine at half-past two or three o'clock. God bless you! I will go and call on Elmsley.[285] What a wonderful city Edinburgh[286] is! What alternation of height and depth! A city looked at in the polish'd back of a Brobdingnag spoon held lengthways, so enormously stretched-up are the houses! When I first looked down on it, as the coach drove up on the higher street, I cannot express what I felt—such a section of wasps' nests striking you with a sort of bastard sublimity from the enormity and infinity of its littleness—the infinity swelling out the mind, the enormity striking it with wonder. I think I have seen an old plate of Montserrat that struck me with the same feeling, and I am sure I have seen huge quarries of lime and free stone in which the shafts or strata stood perpendicularly instead of horizontally with the same high thin slices and corresponding interstices. I climbed last night to the crags just below Arthur's Seat—itself a rude triangle-shaped-base cliff, and looked down on the whole city and firth—the sun then setting behind the magnificent rock, crested by the castle. The firth was full of ships, and I counted fifty-four heads of mountains, of which at least forty-four were cones or pyramids. The smoke was rising from ten thousand houses, each smoke from some one family. It was an affecting sight to me! I stood gazing at the setting sun, so tranquil to a passing look, and so restless and vibrating to one who looked stedfast; and then, all at once, turning my eyes down upon the city, it and all its smokes and figures became all at once dipped in the brightest blue-purple: such a sight that I almost grieved when my eyes recovered their natural tone! Meantime, Arthur's Crag, close behind me, was in dark blood-like crimson, and the sharpshooters were behind exercising minutely, and had chosen that place on account of the fine thunder echo which, indeed, it would be scarcely possible for the ear to distinguish from thunder. The passing a day or two, quite unknown, in a strange city, does a man's heart good. He rises "a sadder and a wiser man."

I had not read that part in your second requesting me to call on Elmsley, else perhaps I should have been talking instead of learning and feeling.

Walter Scott is at Lasswade, five or six miles from Edinburgh. His house in Edinburgh is divinely situated. It looks up a street, a new magnificent street, full upon the rock and the castle, with its zigzag walls like painters' lightning—the other way down upon cultivated fields, a fine expanse of water, either a lake or not to be distinguished from one, and low pleasing hills beyond—the country well wooded and cheerful. "I' faith," I exclaimed, "the monks formerly, but the poets now, know where to fix their habitations." There are about four things worth going into Scotland for,[287] to one who has been in Cumberland and Westmoreland: First, the views of all the islands at the foot of Loch Lomond from the top of the highest island called Inch devanna (sic); secondly, the Trossachs at the foot of Loch Katrine; third, the chamber and ante-chamber of the Falls of Foyers (the fall itself is very fine, and so, after rain, is White-Water Dash, seven miles below Keswick and very like it); and how little difference a height makes, you know as well as I. No fall of itself, perhaps, can be worth giving a long journey to see, to him who has seen any fall of water, but the pool and whole rent of the mountain is truly magnificent. Fourthly and lastly, the City of Edinburgh. Perhaps I might add Glencoe. It is at all events a good make-weight and very well worth going to see, if a man be a Tory and hate the memory of William the Third, which I am very willing to do; for the more of these fellows dead and living one hates, the less spleen and gall there remains for those with whom one is likely to have anything to do in real life....

I am tolerably well, meaning the day. My last night was not such a noisy night of horrors as three nights out of four are with me.[288] O God! when a man blesses the loud screams of agony that awake him night after night, night after night, and when a man's repeated night screams have made him a nuisance in his own house, it is better to die than to live. I have a joy in life that passeth all understanding; but it is not in its present Epiphany and Incarnation. Bodily torture! All who have been with me can bear witness that I can bear it like an Indian. It is constitutional with me to sit still, and look earnestly upon it and ask it what it is? Yea, often and often, the seeds of Rabelaisism germinating in me, I have laughed aloud at my own poor metaphysical soul. But these burrs by day of the will and the reason, these total eclipses by night! Oh, it is hard to bear them. I am complaining bitterly to others, I should be administrating comfort; but even this is one way of comfort. There are states of mind in which even distraction is still a diversion; we must none of us brood; we are not made to be brooders.

God bless you, dear friend, and

S. T. Coleridge.

Mrs. C. will get clean flannels ready for me.

CXLIII. TO MATTHEW COATES.[289]

Greta Hall, Keswick, December 5, 1803.

Dear Sir,—After a time of sufferings, great as mere bodily sufferings can well be conceived to be, and which the horrors of my sleep and night screams (so loud and so frequent as to make me almost a nuisance in my own house) seemed to carry beyond mere body, counterfeiting as it were the tortures of guilt, and what we are told of the punishment of a spiritual world, I am at length a convalescent, but dreading such another bout as much as I dare dread a thing which has no immediate connection with my conscience. My left hand is swollen and inflamed, and the least attempt to bend the fingers very painful, though not half as much so as I could wish; for if I could but fix this Jack-o'-lanthorn of a disease in my hand or foot, I should expect complete recovery in a year or two! But though I have no hope of this, I have a persuasion strong as fate, that from twelve to eighteen months' residence in a genial climate would send me back to dear old England a sample of the first resurrection. Mr. Wordsworth, who has seen me in all my illnesses for nearly four years, and noticed this strange dependence on the state of my moral feelings and the state of the atmosphere conjointly, is decidedly of the same opinion. Accordingly, after many sore struggles of mind from reluctance to quit my children for so long a time, I have arranged my affairs fully and finally, and hope to set sail for Madeira in the first vessel that clears out from Liverpool for that place. Robert Southey, who lives with us, informed me that Mrs. Matthew Coates had a near relative (a brother, I believe) in that island, the Dr. Adams[290] who wrote a very nice little pamphlet on Madeira, relative to the different sorts of consumption, and which I have now on my desk. I need not say that it would be a great comfort to me to be introduced to him by a letter from you or Mrs. Coates, entreating him to put me in a way of living as cheaply as possible. I have no appetites, passions, or vanities which lead to expense; it is now absolute habit to me, indeed, to consider my eating and drinking as a course of medicine. In books only am I intemperate—they have been both bane and blessing to me. For the last three years I have not read less than eight hours a day whenever I have been well enough to be out of bed, or even to sit up in it. Quiet, therefore, a comfortable bed and bedroom, and still better than that, the comfort of kind faces, English tongues, and English hearts now and then,—this is the sum total of my wants, as it is a thing which I need. I am far too contented with solitude. The same fullness of mind, the same crowding of thoughts and constitutional vivacity of feeling which makes me sometimes the first fiddle, and too often a watchman's rattle in society, renders me likewise independent of its excitements. However, I am wondrously calmed down since you saw me—perhaps through this unremitting disease, affliction, and self-discipline.

Mrs. Coleridge desires me to remember her with respectful regards to Mrs. Coates, and to enquire into the history of your little family. I have three children, Hartley, seven years old, Derwent, three years, and Sara, one year on the 23d of this month. Hartley is considered a genius by Wordsworth and Southey; indeed by every one who has seen much of him. But what is of much more consequence and much less doubtful, he has the sweetest temper and most awakened moral feelings of any child I ever saw. He is very backward in his book-learning, cannot write at all, and a very lame reader. We have never been anxious about it, taking it for granted that loving me, and seeing how I love books, he would come to it of his own accord, and so it has proved, for in the last month he has made more progress than in all his former life. Having learnt everything almost from the mouths of people whom he loves, he has connected with his words and notions a passion and a feeling which would appear strange to those who had seen no children but such as had been taught almost everything in books. Derwent is a large, fat, beautiful child, quite the pride of the village, as Hartley is the darling. Southey says wickedly that "all Hartley's guts are in his brains, and all Derwent's brains are in his guts." Verily the constitutional differences in the children are great indeed. From earliest infancy Hartley was absent, a mere dreamer at his meals, put the food into his mouth by one effort, and made a second effort to remember it was there and swallow it. With little Derwent it is a time of rapture and jubilee, and any story that has not pie or cake in it comes very flat to him. Yet he is but a baby. Our girl is a darling little thing, with large blue eyes, a quiet creature that, as I have often said, seems to bask in a sunshine as mild as moonlight, of her own happiness. Oh! bless them! Next to the Bible, Shakespeare, and Milton, they are the three books from which I have learned the most, and the most important and with the greatest delight.

I have been thus prolix about me and mine purposely, to induce you to tell me something of yourself and yours.

Believe me, I have never ceased to think of you with respect and a sort of yearning. You were the first man from whom I heard that article of my faith enunciated which is the nearest to my heart,—the pure fountain of all my moral and religious feelings and comforts,—I mean the absolute Impersonality of the Deity.

I remain, my dear sir, with unfeigned esteem and with good wishes, ever yours,

S. T. Coleridge.

FOOTNOTES:

[1] Pickering, 1838.

[2] The Journal of John Woolman, the Quaker abolitionist, was published in Philadelphia in 1774, and in London in 1775. From a letter of Charles Lamb, dated January 5, 1797, we may conclude that Charles Lloyd had, in the first instance, drawn Coleridge's attention to the writings of John Woolman. Compare, too, Essays of Elia, "A Quakers' Meeting." "Get the writings of John Woolman by heart; and love the early Quakers." Letters of Charles Lamb, 1888, i. 61; Prose Works, 1836, ii. 106.

[3] I have been unable to trace any connection between the family of Coleridge and the Parish or Hundred of Coleridge in North Devon. Coldridges or Coleridges have been settled for more than two hundred years in Doddiscombsleigh, Ashton, and other villages of the Upper Teign, and to the southwest of Exeter the name is not uncommon. It is probable that at some period before the days of parish registers, strangers from Coleridge who had settled farther south were named after their birthplace.

[4] Probably a mistake for Crediton. It was at Crediton that John Coleridge, the poet's father, was born (Feb. 21, 1718) and educated; and here, if anywhere, it must have been that the elder John Coleridge "became a respectable woollen-draper."

[5] John Coleridge, the younger, was in his thirty-first year when he was matriculated as sizar at Sidney Sussex College, Cambridge, March 18, 1748. He is entered in the college books as filius Johannis textoris. On the 13th of June, 1749, he was appointed to the mastership of Squire's Endowed Grammar School at South Molton. It is strange that Coleridge forgot or failed to record this incident in his father's life. His mother came from the neighbourhood, and several of his father's scholars, among them Francis Buller, afterwards the well-known judge, followed him from South Molton to Ottery St. Mary.

[6] George Coleridge was Chaplain Priest, and Master of the King's School, but never Vicar of Ottery St. Mary.

[7] Anne ("Nancy") Coleridge died in her twenty-fifth year. Her illness and early death form the subject of two of Coleridge's early sonnets. Poetical Works of Samuel Taylor Coleridge, Macmillan, 1893, p. 13. See, also, "Lines to a Friend," p. 37, and "Frost at Midnight," p. 127.

[8] A mistake for October 21st.

[9] Compare some doggerel verses "On Mrs. Monday's Beard" which Coleridge wrote on a copy of Southey's Omniana, under the heading of "Beards" (Omniana, 1812, ii. 54). Southey records the legend of a female saint, St. Vuilgefortis, who in answer to her prayers was rewarded with a beard as a mark of divine favour. The story is told in some Latin elegiacs from the Annus Sacer Poeticus of the Jesuit Sautel which Southey quotes at length. Coleridge comments thus, "Pereant qui ante nos nostra dixere! What! can nothing be one's own? This is the more vexatious, for at the age of eighteen I lost a legacy of Fifty pounds for the following Epigram on my Godmother's Beard, which she had the barbarity to revenge by striking me out of her Will."

The epigram is not worth quoting, but it is curious to observe that, even when scribbling for his own amusement, and without any view to publication, Coleridge could not resist the temptation of devising an "apologetic preface."

The verses, etc., are printed in Table Talk and Omniana, Bell, 1888, p. 391. The editor, the late Thomas Ashe, transcribed them from Gillman's copy of the Omniana, now in the British Museum. I have followed a transcript of the marginal note made by Mrs. H. N. Coleridge before the volume was cut in binding. Her version supplies one or two omissions.

[10] The meaning is that the events which had taken place between March and October, 1797, the composition, for instance, of his tragedy, Osorio, the visit of Charles Lamb to the cottage at Nether Stowey, the settling of Wordsworth and his sister Dorothy at Alfoxden, would hereafter be recorded in his autobiography. He had failed to complete the record of the past, only because he had been too much occupied with the present.

[11] He records his timorous passion for fairy stories in a note to The Friend (ed. 1850, i. 192). Another version of the same story is to be found in some MS. notes (taken by J. Tomalin) of the Lectures of 1811, the only record of this and other lectures:—

Lecture 5th, 1811. "Give me," cried Coleridge, with enthusiasm, "the works which delighted my youth! Give me the History of St. George, and the Seven Champions of Christendom, which at every leisure moment I used to hide myself in a corner to read! Give me the Arabian Nights' Entertainments, which I used to watch, till the sun shining on the bookcase approached, and, glowing full upon it, gave me the courage to take it from the shelf. I heard of no little Billies, and sought no praise for giving to beggars, and I trust that my heart is not the worse, or the less inclined to feel sympathy for all men, because I first learnt the powers of my nature, and to reverence that nature—for who can feel and reverence the nature of man and not feel deeply for the affliction of others possessing like powers and like nature?" Tomalin's Shorthand Report of Lecture V.

[12] Compare a MS. note dated July 19, 1803. "Intensely hot day, left off a waistcoat, and for yarn wore silk stockings. Before nine o'clock had unpleasant chillness, heard a noise which I thought Derwent's in sleep; listened and found it was a calf bellowing. Instantly came on my mind that night I slept out at Ottery, and the calf in the field across the river whose lowing so deeply impressed me. Chill and child and calf lowing."

[13] Sir Stafford, the seventh baronet, grandfather of the first Lord Iddesleigh, was at that time a youth of eighteen. His name occurs among the list of scholars who were subscribers to the second edition of the Critical Latin Grammar.

[14] Compare a MS. note dated March 5, 1818. "Memory counterfeited by present impressions. One great cause of the coincidence of dreams with the event—ἡ μήτηρ ἐμή."

[15] The date of admission to Hertford was July 18, 1782. Eight weeks later, September 12, he was sent up to London to the great school.

[16] Compare the autobiographical note of 1832. "I was in a continual low fever. My whole being was, with eyes closed to every object of present sense, to crumple myself up in a sunny corner and read, read, read; fixing myself on Robinson Crusoe's Island, finding a mountain of plumb cake, and eating a room for myself, and then eating it into the shapes of

tables and chairs—hunger and fancy." Lamb in his Christ's Hospital Five and Thirty Years Ago, and Leigh Hunt in his Autobiography, are in the same tale as to the insufficient and ill-cooked meals of their Bluecoat days. Life of Coleridge, by James Gillman, 1838, p. 20; Lamb's Prose Works, 1836, ii. 27; Autobiography of Leigh Hunt, 1860, p. 60.

[17] Coleridge's "letters home" were almost invariably addressed to his brother George. It may be gathered from his correspondence that at rare intervals he wrote to his mother as well, but, contrary to her usual practice, she did not, with this one exception, preserve his letters. It was, indeed, a sorrowful consequence of his "long exile" at Christ's Hospital, that he seems to have passed out of his mother's ken, that absence led to something like indifference on both sides.

[18] Compare the autobiographical note of 1832 as quoted by Gillman. About this time he became acquainted with a widow lady, "whose son," says he, "I, as upper boy, had protected, and who therefore looked up to me, and taught me what it was to have a mother. I loved her as such. She had three daughters, and of course I fell in love with the eldest." Life of Coleridge, p. 28.

[19] Scholarship of Jesus College, Cambridge, for sons of clergymen.

[20] At this time Frend was still a Fellow of Jesus College. Five years had elapsed since he had resigned from conscientious motives the living of Madingley in Cambridgeshire, but it was not until after the publication of his pamphlet Peace and Union, in 1793, that the authorities took alarm. He was deprived of his Fellowship, April 17, and banished from the University, May 30, 1793. Coleridge's demeanour in the Senate House on the occasion of Frend's trial before the Vice-Chancellor forms the subject of various contradictory anecdotes. See Life of Coleridge, 1838, p. 55; Reminiscences of Cambridge, Henry Gunning, 1855, i. 272-275.

[21] The Rev. George Caldwell was afterwards Fellow and Tutor of Jesus College. His name occurs among the list of subscribers to the original issue of The Friend. Letters of the Lake Poets, 1889, p. 452.

[22] "First Grecian of my time was Launcelot Pepys Stevens [Stephens], kindest of boys and men, since the Co-Grammar Master, and inseparable companion of Dr. T[rollop]e." Lamb's Prose Works, 1835, ii. 45. He was at this time Senior-Assistant Master at Newcome's Academy at Clapton near Hackney, and a colleague of George Coleridge. The school, which belonged to three generations of Newcomes, was of high repute as a private academy, and commanded the services of clever young schoolmasters as assistants or ushers. Mr. Sparrow, whose name is mentioned in the letter, was headmaster.

[23] A Latin essay on Posthumous Fame, described as a declamation and stated to have been composed by S. T. Coleridge, March, 1792, is preserved at Jesus College, Cambridge. Some extracts were printed in the College magazine, The Chanticleer, Lent Term, 1886.

[24] Poetical Works, p. 19.

[25] Ibid. p. 19.

[26] Poetical Works, p. 20.

[27] Robert Allen, Coleridge's earliest friend, and almost his exact contemporary (born October 18, 1772), was admitted to University College, Oxford, as an exhibitioner, in the spring of 1792. He entertained Coleridge and his compagnon de voyage, Joseph Hucks, on the occasion of the memorable visit to Oxford in June, 1794, and introduced them to his friend, Robert Southey of Balliol. He is mentioned in letters of Lamb to Coleridge, June 10, 1796, and October 11, 1802. In both instances his name is connected with that of Stoddart, and it is probable that it was through Allen that Coleridge and Stoddart became acquainted. For anecdotes concerning Allen, see Lamb's Essay, "Christ's Hospital," etc., Prose Works, 1836, ii. 47, and Leigh Hunt's Autobiography, 1860, p. 74. See, also, Letters to Allsop, 1864, p. 170.

[28] George Richards, a contemporary of Stephens, and, though somewhat senior, of Middleton, was a University prize-man and Fellow of Oriel. He was "author," says Lamb, "of the 'Aboriginal Britons,' the most spirited of Oxford prize poems." In after life he made his mark as a clergyman, as Bampton Lecturer (in 1800), and as Vicar of St. Martin-in-the-Fields. He was appointed Governor of Christ's Hospital in 1822, and founded an annual prize, the "Richards' Gold Medal," for the best copy of Latin hexameters. Christ's Hospital. List of Exhibitioners, from 1566-1885, compiled by A. M. Lockhart.

[29] Robert Percy (Bobus) Smith, 1770-1845, the younger brother of Sydney Smith, was Browne Medalist in 1791. His Eton and Cambridge prize poems, in Lucretian metre, are among the most finished specimens of modern Latinity. The principal contributors to the Microcosm were George Canning, John and Robert Smith, Hookham Frere, and Charles Ellis. Gentleman's Magazine, N. S., xxiii. 440.

[30] For complete text of the Greek Sapphic Ode, "On the Slave Trade," which obtained the Browne gold medal for 1792, see Appendix B, p. 476, to Coleridge's Poetical Works, Macmillan, 1893. See, also, Mr. Dykes Campbell's note on the style and composition of the ode, p. 653. I possess a transcript of the Ode, taken, I believe, by Sara Coleridge in 1823, on the occasion of her visit to Ottery St. Mary. The following note is appended:—

"Upon the receipt of the above poem, Mr. George Coleridge, being vastly pleased by the composition, thinking it would be a sort of compliment to the superior genius of his brother the author, composed the following lines:—

IBI HÆC INCONDITA SOLUS.

Say Holy Genius—Heaven-descended Beam,
Why interdicted is the sacred Fire
That flows spontaneous from thy golden Lyre?
Why Genius like the emanative Ray
That issuing from the dazzling Fount of Light
Wakes all creative Nature into Day,
Art thou not all-diffusive, all benign?
Thy partial hand I blame. For Pity oft
In Supplication's Vest—a weeping child
That meets me pensive on the barren wild,
And pours into my soul Compassion soft,
The never-dying strain commands to flow—
Man sure is vain, nor sacred Genius hears,
Now speak in melody—now weep in Tears.
G. C."

[31] He was matriculated as pensioner March 31, 1792. He had been in residence since September, 1791.

[32] For the Craven Scholarship. In an article contributed to the Gentleman's Magazine of December, 1834, portions of which are printed in Gillman's Life of Coleridge, C. V. Le Grice, a co-Grecian with Coleridge and Allen, gives the names of the four competitors. The successful candidate was Samuel Butler, afterwards Head Master of Shrewsbury and Bishop of Lichfield. Life of Coleridge, 1838, p. 50.

[33] Musical glee composer, 1769-1821. Biographical Dictionary.

[34] Poetical Works, p. 20.

[35] Francis Syndercombe Coleridge, who died shortly after the fall of Seringapatam, February 6, 1792.

[36] Edward Coleridge, the Vicar of Ottery's fourth son, was then assistant master in Dr. Skinner's school at Salisbury. His marriage with an elderly widow who was supposed to have a large income was a source of perennial amusement to his family. Some years after her death he married his first cousin, Anne Bowdon.

[37] The husband of Coleridge's half sister Elizabeth, the youngest of the vicar's first family, "who alone was bred up with us after my birth, and who alone of the three I was wont to think of as a sister." See Autobiographical Notes of 1832. Life of Coleridge, 1838, p. 9.

[38] The brother of Mrs. Luke and of Mrs. George Coleridge.

[39] A note to the Poems of Samuel Taylor Coleridge, Moxon, 1852, gives a somewhat different version of the origin of this poem, first printed in the edition of 1796 as Effusion 27, and of the lines included in Letter XX., there headed "Cupid turned Chymist," but afterwards known as "Kisses."

[40] G. L. Tuckett, to whom this letter was addressed, was the first to disclose to Coleridge's family the unwelcome fact that he had enlisted in the army. He seems to have guessed that the runaway would take his old schoolfellows into his confidence, and that they might be induced to reveal the secret. He was, I presume, a college acquaintance,— possibly an old Blue, who had left the University and was reading for the bar. In an unpublished letter from Robert Allen to Coleridge, dated February, 1796, there is an amusing reference to this kindly Deus ex Machina. "I called upon Tuckett, who thus prophesied: 'You know how subject Coleridge is to fits of idleness. Now, I'll lay any wager, Allen, that after three or four numbers (of the Watchman) the sheets will contain nothing but parliamentary debates, and Coleridge will add a note at the bottom of the page: "I should think myself deficient in my duty to the Public if I did not give these interesting debates at full length."'"

[41] It would seem that there were alleviations to the misery and discomfort of this direful experience. In a MS. note dated January, 1805, he recalls as a suitable incident for a projected work, The Soother in Absence, the "Domus quadrata hortensis, at Henley-on-Thames," and "the beautiful girl" who, it would seem, soothed the captivity of the forlorn trooper.

[42] In the various and varying reminiscences of his soldier days, which fell "from Coleridge's own mouth," and were repeated by his delighted and credulous hearers, this officer plays an important part. Whatever foundation of fact there may be for the touching anecdote that the Latin sentence, "Eheu! quam infortunii miserrimum est fuisse felicem," scribbled on the walls of the stable at Reading, caught the attention of Captain Ogle, "himself a scholar," and led to Comberbacke's detection, he was not, as the poet Bowles and Miss Mitford maintained, the sole instrument in procuring the discharge. He may have exerted himself privately, but his name does not occur in the formal correspondence which passed between Coleridge's brothers and the military authorities.

[43] The Compasses, now The Chequers, High Wycombe, where Coleridge was billeted just a hundred years ago, appears to have preserved its original aspect.

[44] See Notes to Poetical Works of Coleridge (1893), p. 568. The "intended translation" was advertised in the Cambridge Intelligencer for June 14 and June 16, 1794: "Proposals for publishing by subscription Imitations from the Modern Latin Poets, with a Critical and Biographical Essay on the Restoration of Literature. By S. T. Coleridge, of Jesus College, Cambridge....

"In the course of the Work will be introduced a copious selection from the Lyrics of Casimir, and a new Translation of the Basia of Secundus."

One ode, "Ad Lyram," was printed in The Watchman, No. 11, March 9, 1796, p. 49.

[45] The Barbou Casimir, published at Paris in 1759.

[46] Compare the note to chapter xii. of the Biographia Literaria: "In the Biographical Sketch of my Literary Life I may be excused if I mention here that I had translated the eight Hymns of Synesius from the Greek into English Anacreontics before my fifteenth year." The edition referred to may be that published at Basle in 1567. Interprete G. Cantero. Bentley's Quarto Edition was probably the Quarto Edition of Horace, published in 1711.

[47] Charles Clagget, a musical composer and inventor of musical instruments, flourished towards the close of the eighteenth century. I have been unable to ascertain whether the songs in question were ever published. Dictionary of Music and Musicians, edited by George Grove, D. C. L., 1879, article "Clagget," i. 359.

[48] The entry in the College Register of Jesus College is brief and to the point: "1794 Apr.: Coleridge admonitus est per magistrum in præsentiâ sociorum."

[49] A letter to George Coleridge dated April 16, 1794, and signed J. Plampin, has been preserved. The pains and penalties to which Coleridge had subjected himself are stated in full, but the kindly nature of the writer is shown in the concluding sentence: "I am happy in adding that I thought your brother's conduct on his return extremely proper; and I beg to assure you that it will give me much pleasure to see him take such an advantage of his experience as his own good sense will dictate."

[50] A week later, July 22, in a letter addressed to H. Martin, of Jesus College, to whom, in the following September, he dedicated "The Fall of Robespierre," Coleridge repeated almost verbatim large portions of this lettre de voyage. The incident of the sentiment and the Welsh clergyman takes a somewhat different shape, and both versions differ from the report of the same occurrence contained in Hucks' account of the tour, which was

published in the following year. Coleridge's letters from foreign parts were written with a view to literary effect, and often with the half-formed intention of sending them to the "booksellers." They are to be compared with "letters from our own correspondent," and in respect of picturesque adventure, dramatic dialogue, and so forth, must be judged solely by a literary standard. Biographia Literaria, 1847, ii. 338-343; J. Hucks' Tour in North Wales, 1795, p. 25.

[51] The lines are from "Happiness," an early poem first published in 1834. See Poetical Works, p. 17. See, too, Editor's Note, p. 564.

[52] Quoted from a poem by Bowles entitled, "Verses inscribed to His Grace the Duke of Leeds, and other Promoters of the Philanthropic Society." Southey adopted the last two lines of the quotation as a motto for his "Botany Bay Eclogues." Poetical Works of Milman, Bowles, etc., Paris, 1829, p. 117; Southey's Poetical Works, 1837, ii. 71.

[53] Southey, we may suppose, had contrasted Hucks with Coleridge. "H. is on my level, not yours."

[54] Poetical Works, p. 33. See, too, Editor's Note, p. 570.

[55] Hucks records the incident in much the same words, but gives the name of the tune as "Corporal Casey."

[56] The letter to Martin gives further particulars of the tour, including the ascent of Penmaen Mawr in company with Brookes and Berdmore. Compare Table Talk for May 31, 1830: "I took the thought of grinning for joy in that poem (The Ancient Mariner) from my companion's remark to me, when we had climbed to the top of Plinlimmon, and were nearly dead with thirst. We could not speak from the constriction till we found a little puddle under a stone. He said to me, 'You grinned like an idiot.' He had done the same." The parching thirst of the pedestrians, and their excessive joy at the discovery of a spring of water, are recorded by Hucks. Tour in North Wales, 1795, p. 62.

[57] Southey's Poetical Works, 1837, ii. 93.

[58] Southey's Poetical Works, 1837, ii. 94.

[59] See Letter XLI. p. 110, note 1.

[60] "A tragedy, of which the first act was written by S. T. Coleridge." See footnote to quotation from "The Fall of Robespierre," which occurs in the text of "An Address on the Present War." Conciones ad Populum, 1795, p. 66.

[61] One of six sisters, daughters of John Brunton of Norwich. Elizabeth, the eldest of the family, was married in 1791 to Robert Merry the dramatist, the founder of the so-called Della Cruscan school of poetry. Louisa Brunton, the youngest sister, afterwards Countess of Craven, made her first appearance at Covent Garden Theatre on October 5, 1803, and at most could not have been more than twelve or thirteen years of age in the autumn of 1794. Coleridge's Miss Brunton, to whom he sent a poem on the French Revolution, that is, "The Fall of Robespierre," must have been an intermediate sister less known to fame. It is curious to note that "The Right Hon. Lady Craven" was a subscriber to the original issue of The Friend in 1809. National Dictionary of Biography, articles "Craven" and "Merry." Letters of the Lake Poets, 1885, p. 455.

[62] This sonnet, afterwards headed, "On a Discovery made too late," was "first printed in Poems, 1796, as Effusion XIX., but in the Contents it was called, 'To my own Heart.'" Poetical Works, p. 34. See, too, Editor's Note, p. 571.

[63] "The Race of Banquo." Southey's Poetical Works, 1837, ii. 155.

[64] The Editor of the Cambridge Intelligencer.

[65] "To a Young Lady, with a Poem on the French Revolution." Poetical Works, p. 6.

[66] Compare "Sonnet to the Author of The Robbers." Poetical Works, p. 34.

[67] The date of this letter is fixed by that of Thursday, November 6, to George Coleridge. Both letters speak of a journey to town with Potter of Emanuel, but in writing to his brother he says nothing of a projected visit to Bath. There is no hint in either letter that he had made up his mind to leave the University for good and all. In a letter to Southey dated December 17, he says that "they are making a row about him at Jesus," and in a letter to Mary Evans, which must have been written a day or two later, he says, "I return to Cambridge to-morrow." From the date of the letter to George Coleridge of November 6 to December 11 there is a break in the correspondence with Southey, but from a statement in Letter XLIII. it appears plain that a visit was paid to the West in December, 1794. But whether he returned to Cambridge November 8, and for how long, is uncertain.

[68] "Lines on a Friend who died of a Frenzy Fever," etc. Poetical Works, p. 35. A copy of the same poem was sent on November 6 to George Coleridge.

[69] "The Sigh." Poetical Works, p. 29.

[70] Probably Thomas Edwards, LL. D., a Fellow of Jesus College, Cambridge, editor of Plutarch, De Educatione Liberorum, with notes, 1791, and author of "A Discourse on the Limits and Importance of Free Inquiry in Matters of Religion," 1792. Natural Dictionary of Biography, xvii. 130.

[71] Compare "Lines on a Friend," etc., which accompanied this letter.

To me hath Heaven with liberal hand assigned
Energic reason and a shaping mind,
. . . .
Sloth-jaundiced all! and from my graspless hand
Drop Friendship's precious pearls, like hour-glass sand.
Poetical Works, p. 35.

[72] The lines occur in Barrère's speech, which concludes the third act of the "Fall of Robespierre." Poetical Works, p. 225.

[73] "Fall of Robespierre," Act I. l. 198.

O this new freedom! at how dear a price
We've bought the seeming good! The peaceful virtues
And every blandishment of private life,
The father's care, the mother's fond endearment

All sacrificed to Liberty's wild riot.
Poetical Works, p. 215.

[74] See "Fall of Robespierre," Act I. 1. 40. Poetical Works, p. 212.

[75] For full text of the "Lines on a Friend who died of a Frenzy Fever," see Letter XXXVIII. See, too, Poetical Works, p. 35.

[76] Southey's Poetical Works, 1837, ii. 263.

[77] See Poems by Robert Lovell, and Robert Southey of Balliol College. Bath. Printed by A. Cruttwell, 1795, p. 17. "Ode to Lycon," p. 77.

The last stanza runs thus:—

Wilt thou float careless down the stream of time,
In sadness borne to dull oblivious shore,
Or shake off grief, and "build the lofty rhyme,"
And live till time shall be no more?
If thy light bark have met the storms,
If threatening cloud the sky deforms,
Let honest truth be vain; look back on me,
Have I been "sailing on a Summer sea"?
Have only zephyrs fill'd my swelling sails,
As smooth the gentle vessel glides along?
Lycon! I met unscar'd the wintry gales,
And sooth'd the dangers with the song:
So shall the vessel sail sublime,
And reach the port of fame adown the stream of time.
Bion [i. e. R. S.].
Compare the following unpublished letter from Southey to Miss Sarah Fricker:—

October 18, 1794.

"Amid the pelting of the pitiless storm" did I, Robert Southey, the Apostle of Pantisocracy, depart from the city of Bristol, my natal place—at the hour of five in a wet windy evening on the 17th of October, 1794, wrapped up in my father's old great coat and my own cogitations. Like old Lear I did not call the elements unkind,—and on I passed, musing on the lamentable effects of pride and prejudice—retracing all the events of my past life—and looking forward to the days to come with pleasure.

Three miles from Bristol, an old man of sixty, most royally drunk, laid hold of my arm, and begged we might join company, as he was going to Bath. I consented, for he wanted assistance, and dragged this foul animal through the dirt, wind, and rain!...

Think of me, with a mind so fully occupied, leading this man nine miles, and had I not led him he would have lain down under a hedge and probably perished.

I reached not Bath till nine o'clock, when the rain pelted me most unmercifully in the face. I rejoiced that my friends at Bath knew not where I was, and was once vexed at thinking that you would hear it drive against the window and be sorry for the way-worn traveller. Here I am, well, and satisfied with my own conduct....

My clothes are arrived. "I will never see his face again [writes Miss Tyler], and, if he writes, will return his letters unopened;" to comment on this would be useless. I feel that strong conviction of rectitude which would make me smile on the rack.... The crisis is over—things are as they should be; my mother vexes herself much, yet feels she is right. Hostilities are commenced with America! so we must go to some neutral fort—Hambro' or Venice.

Your sister is well, and sends her love to all; on Wednesday I hope to see you. Till then farewell,

Robert Southey.

Bath, Sunday morning.

Compare, also, letter to Thomas Southey, dated October 19, 1794. Southey's Life and Correspondence, i. 222.

[78] Poems, 1795, p. 123.

[79] See Southey's Poetical Works, 1837, ii. 91:—

"If heavily creep on one little day,
The medley crew of travellers among."
[80] Poems, 1795, p. 67.

[81] Poetical Works, 1837, ii. 92.

[82] "Rosamund to Henry; written after she had taken the veil." Poems, 1795, p. 85.

[83] Poetical Works, 1837, ii. 216. Southey appears to have accepted Coleridge's emendations. The variations between the text of the "Pauper's Funeral" and the editio purgata of the letter are slight and unimportant.

[84] In a letter from Southey to his brother Thomas, dated October 21, 1794, this sonnet "on the subject of our emigration" is attributed to Favell, a convert to pantisocracy who was still at Christ's Hospital. The first eight lines are included in the "Monody on Chatterton." See Poetical Works, p. 63, and Editor's Note, p. 563.

[85] Printed as Effusion XVI. in Poems, 1796. It was afterwards headed "Charity." In the preface he acknowledges that he was "indebted to Mr. Favell for the rough sketch." See Poetical Works, p. 45, and Editor's Note, p. 576.

[86] Southey's Poetical Works, ii. 143. In this instance Coleridge's corrections were not adopted.

[87] Published in 1794.

[88] First version, printed in Morning Chronicle, December 26, 1794. See Poetical Works, p. 40.

[89] First printed as Effusion XIV. in Poems, 1796. Of the four lines said to have been written by Lamb, Coleridge discarded lines 13 and 14, and substituted a favourite couplet,

which occurs in more than one of his early poems. See Poetical Works, p. 23, and Editor's Note, p. 566.

[90] Imitated from the Welsh. See Poetical Works, p. 33.

[91] A parody of "Qui Bavium non odit, amet tua carmina, Mævi." Virgil, Ecl. iii. 90. Gratio and Avaro were signatures adopted by Southey and Lovell in their joint volume of poems published at Bristol in 1795.

[92] Implied in the second line.

[93] Of the six sonnets included in this letter, those to Burke, Priestley, and Kosciusko had already appeared in the Morning Chronicle on the 9th, 11th, and 16th of December, 1794. The sonnets to Godwin, Southey, and Sheridan were published on the 10th, 14th, and 29th of January, 1795. See Poetical Works, pp. 38, 39, 41, 42.

[94] First published in the Morning Chronicle, December 30, 1794. An earlier draft, dated October 24, 1794, was headed "Monologue to a Young Jackass in Jesus Piece. Its Mother near it, chained to a Log." See Poetical Works, Appendix C, p. 477, and Editor's Note, p. 573.

[95] Compare the last six lines of a sonnet, "On a Discovery made too late," sent in a letter to Southey, dated October 21, 1794. (Letter XXXVII.) See Poetical Works, p. 34, and Editor's Note, p. 571.

[96] The first of six sonnets on the Slave Trade. Southey's Poetical Works, 1837, ii. 55.

[97] Prefixed as a dedication to Juvenile and Minor Poems. It is addressed to Edith Southey, and dated Bristol, 1796. Southey's Poetical Works, 1837, vol. ii. The text of 1837 differs considerably from the earlier version. Possibly in transcribing Coleridge altered the original to suit his own taste.

[98] To a Friend [Charles Lamb], together with an Unfinished Poem ["Religious Musings"]. Poetical Works, p. 37.

[99] This farewell letter of apology and remonstrance was not sent by post, but must have reached Southey's hand on the 13th of November, the eve of his wedding day. The original MS. is written on small foolscap. A first draft, or copy, of the letter was sent to Coleridge's friend, Josiah Wade.

[100] The Rev. David Jardine, Unitarian minister at Bath. Cottle lays the scene of the "inaugural sermons" on the corn laws and hair powder tax, which Coleridge delivered in a blue coat and white waistcoat, in Mr. Jardine's chapel at Bath. Early Recollections, i. 179.

[101] If we may believe Cottle, the dispute began by Southey attacking Coleridge for his non-appearance at a lecture which he had undertaken to deliver in his stead. The scene of the quarrel is laid at Chepstow, on the first day of the memorable excursion to Tintern Abbey, which Cottle had planned to "gratify his two young friends." Southey had been "dragged," much against the grain, into this "detestable party of pleasure," and was, no doubt, rendered doubly sore by his partner's delinquency. See Early Recollections, i. 40, 41. See, also, letter from Southey to Bedford, dated May 28, 1795. Life and Correspondence, i. 239.

[102] At Chepstow.

[103] A village three miles W. S. W. of Bristol.

[104] During the course of his tour (January-February, 1796) to procure subscribers for the Watchman, Coleridge wrote seven times to Josiah Wade. Portions of these letters have been published in Cottle's Early Recollections, i. 164-176, and in the "Biographical Supplement" to the Biographia Literaria, ii. 349-354. It is probable that Wade supplied funds for the journey, and that Coleridge felt himself bound to give an account of his progress and success.

[105] Joseph Wright, A. R. A., known as Wright of Derby, 1736-1797. Two of his most celebrated pictures were The Head of Ulleswater, and The Dead Soldier. An excellent specimen of Wright's work, An Experiment with the Air Pump, was presented to the National Gallery in 1863.

[106] Compare Biographia Literaria, ch. i. "During my first Cambridge vacation I assisted a friend in a contribution for a literary society in Devonshire, and in that I remember to have compared Darwin's works to the Russian palace of ice, glittering, cold, and transitory." Coleridge's Works, Harper & Bros., 1853, iii. 155.

[107] Dr. James Hutton, the author of the Plutonian theory. His Theory of the Earth was published at Edinburgh in 1795.

[108] The title of this pamphlet, which was published shortly after the Conciones ad Populum, was "The Plot Discovered; or, an Address to the People against Ministerial Treason. By S. T. Coleridge. Bristol, 1795." It had an outer wrapper with this half-title: "A Protest against Certain Wills. Bristol: Printed for the Author, November 28, 1795." It is reprinted in Essays on His Own Times, i. 56-98.

[109] The review of "Burke's Letter to a Noble Lord," which appeared in the first number of The Watchman, is reprinted in Essays on His Own Times, i. 107-119.

[110] Ibid. 120-126.

[111] The occasion of this "burst of affectionate feeling" was a communication from Poole that seven or eight friends had undertaken to subscribe a sum of £35 or £40 to be paid annually to the "author of the monody on the death of Chatterton," as "a trifling mark of their esteem, gratitude, and affection." The subscriptions were paid in 1796-97, but afterwards discontinued on the receipt of the Wedgwood annuity. See Thomas Poole and his Friends, i. 142.

[112] Mrs. Robert Lovell, whose husband had been carried off by a fever about two years after his marriage with my aunt.—S. C.

[113] Compare Conciones ad Populum, 1795, p. 22. "Such is Joseph Gerrald! Withering in the sickly and tainted gales of a prison, his healthful soul looks down from the citadel of his integrity on his impotent persecutors. I saw him in the foul and naked room of a jail; his cheek was sallow with confinement, his body was emaciated; yet his eye spake the invincible purpose of his soul, and he still sounded with rapture the successes of Freedom, forgetful of his own lingering martyrdom."

Together with four others, Gerrald was tried for sedition at Edinburgh in March, 1794. He delivered an eloquent speech in his own defence, but with the other prisoners was convicted and sentenced to be transported for fifteen years. "In April Gerrald was removed to London, and committed to Newgate, where Godwin and his other friends were allowed to visit him.... In May, 1795, he was suddenly taken from his prison and placed on board the hulks, and soon afterwards sailed. He survived his arrival in New South Wales only five months. A few hours before he died, he said to the friends around him, 'I die in the best of causes, and, as you witness, without repining.'" Mrs. Shelley's Notes, as quoted by Mr. C. Kegan Paul in his William Godwin, i. 125. See, too, "the very noble letter" (January 23, 1794) addressed by Godwin to Gerrald relative to his defence. Ibid. i. 125. Lords Cockburn and Jeffrey considered the conviction of these men a gross miscarriage of justice, and in 1844 a monument was erected at the foot of the Calton Hill, Edinburgh, to their memory.

[114] Edward Williams (Iolo Morgangw), 1747-1826. His poems in two volumes were published by subscription in 1794. Coleridge possessed a copy presented to him "by the author," and on the last page of the second volume he has scrawled a single but characteristic marginal note. It is affixed to a translation of one of the "Poetic Triades." "The three principal considerations of poetical description: what is obvious, what instantly engages the affections, and what is strikingly characteristic." The comment is as follows: "I suppose, rather what we recollect to have frequently seen in nature, though not in the description of it."

[115] The allusion must be to Wordsworth, but there is a difficulty as to dates. In a MS. note to the second edition of his poems (1797) Coleridge distinctly states that he had no personal acquaintance with Wordsworth as early as March, 1796. Again, in a letter (Letter LXXXI.) to Estlin dated "May [? 1797]," but certainly written in May, 1798, Coleridge says that he has known Wordsworth for a year and some months. On the other hand, there is Mrs. Wordsworth's report of her husband's "impression" that he first met Coleridge, Southey, Sara, and Edith Fricker "in a lodging in Bristol in 1795,"—an imperfect recollection very difficult to reconcile with other known facts. Secondly, there is Sara Coleridge's statement that "Mr. Coleridge and Mr. Wordsworth first met in the house of Mr. Pinney," in the spring or summer of 1795; and, thirdly, it would appear from a letter of Lamb to Coleridge, which belongs to the summer of 1796, that "the personal acquaintance" with Wordsworth had already begun. The probable conclusion is that there was a first meeting in 1795, and occasional intercourse in 1796, but that intimacy and friendship date from the visit to Racedown in June, 1797. Coleridge quotes Wordsworth in his "Lines from Shurton Bars," dated September, 1795, but the first trace of Wordsworth's influence on style and thought appears in "This Lime-Tree Bower my Prison," July, 1797. In May, 1796, Wordsworth could only have been "his very dear friend" sensu poetico. Life of W. Wordsworth, i. 111; Biographical Supplement to Biographia Literaria, chapter ii.; Letters of Charles Lamb, Macmillan, 1888, i. 6.

[116] On the side of the road, opposite to Poole's house in Castle Street, Nether Stowey, is a straight gutter through which a stream passes. See Thomas Poole and his Friends, i. 147.

[117] The Peripatetic, or Sketches of the Heart, of Nature, and of Society, a miscellany of prose and verse issued by John Thelwall, in 1793.

[118] January 10, 1795. See Poetical Works, p. 41, and Editor's Note, p. 575. Margarot, a West Indian, was one of those tried and transported with Gerrald.

[119] See Poetical Works, p. 66.

[120] Early in the autumn of 1796, a proposal had been made to Coleridge that he should start a day school in Derby. Poole dissuaded him from accepting this offer, or rather, perhaps, Coleridge succeeded in procuring Poole's disapproval of a plan which he himself dreaded and disliked.

[121] Thomas Ward, at first the articled clerk, and afterwards partner in business and in good works, of Thomas Poole. He it was who transcribed in "Poole's Copying Book" Coleridge's letters from Germany, and much of his correspondence besides. See Thomas Poole and his Friends, i. 159, 160, 304, 305, etc.

[122] This letter, first printed in Gillman's Life, pp. 338-340, and since reprinted in the notes to Canon Ainger's edition of Lamb's Letters (i. 314, 315), was written in response to a request of Charles Lamb in his letter of September 27, 1796, announcing the "terrible calamities" which had befallen his family. "Write me," said Lamb, "as religious a letter as possible." In his next letter, October 3, he says, "Your letter is an inestimable treasure." But a few weeks later, October 24, he takes exception to the sentence, "You are a temporary sharer in human miseries that you may be an eternal partaker of the Divine nature." Lamb thought that the expression savoured too much of theological subtlety, and outstepped the modesty of weak and suffering humanity. Coleridge's "religious letter" came from his heart, but he was a born preacher, and naturally clothes his thoughts in rhetorical language. I have seen a note written by him within a few hours of his death, when he could scarcely direct his pen. It breathes the tenderest loving-kindness, but the expressions are elaborate and formal. It was only in poetry that he attained to simplicity.

[123] Coleridge must have resorted occasionally to opiates long before this. In an unpublished letter to his brother George, dated November 21, 1791, he says, "Opium never used to have any disagreeable effects on me." Most likely it was given to him at Christ's Hospital, when he was suffering from rheumatic fever. In the sonnet on "Pain," which belongs to the summer of 1790, he speaks of "frequent pangs," of "seas of pain," and in the natural course of things opiates would have been prescribed by the doctors. Testimony of this nature appears at first sight to be inconsistent with statements made by Coleridge in later life to the effect that he began to take opium in the second year of his residence at Keswick, in consequence of rheumatic pains brought on by the damp climate. It was, however, the first commencement of the secret and habitual resort to narcotics which weighed on memory and conscience, and there is abundant evidence that it was not till the late spring of 1801 that he could be said to be under the dominion of opium. To these earlier indulgences in the "accursed drug," which probably left no "disagreeable effects," and of which, it is to be remarked, he speaks openly, he seems to have attached but little significance.

Since the above note was written, Mr. W. Aldis Wright has printed in the Academy, February 24, 1894, an extract from an unpublished letter from Coleridge to the Rev. Mr. Edwards of Birmingham, recently found in the Library of Trinity College, Cambridge. It is dated Bristol, "12 March, 1795" (read "1796"), and runs as follows:—

"Since I last wrote you, I have been tottering on the verge of madness—my mind overbalanced on the e contra side of happiness—the blunders of my associate [in the editing of the Watchman, G. Burnett], etc., etc., abroad, and, at home, Mrs. Coleridge dangerously ill.... Such has been my situation for the last fortnight—I have been obliged to take laudanum almost every night."

[124] The news of the evacuation of Corsica by the British troops, which took place on October 21, 1796, must have reached Coleridge a few days before the date of this letter. Corsica was ceded to the British, June 18, 1794. A declaration of war on the part of Spain (August 19, 1796) and a threatened invasion of Ireland compelled the home government to withdraw their troops from Corsica. In a footnote to chapter xxv. of his Life of Napoleon Bonaparte, Sir Walter Scott quotes from Napoleon's memoirs compiled at St. Helena the "odd observation" that "the crown of Corsica must, on the temporary annexation of the island to Great Britain, have been surprised at finding itself appertaining to the successor of Fingal." Sir Walter's patriotism constrained him to add the following comment: "Not more, we should think, than the diadem of France and the iron crown of Lombardy marvelled at meeting on the brow of a Corsican soldier of fortune."

In the Biographia Literaria, 1847, ii. 380, the word is misprinted Corrica, but there is no doubt as to the reading of the MS. letter, or to the allusion to contemporary history.

[125] It was to this lady that the lines "On the Christening of a Friend's Child" were addressed. Poetical Works, p. 83.

[126] See Letter LXVIII., p. 206, note.

[127] The preface to the quarto edition of Southey's Joan of Arc is dated Bristol, November, 1795, but the volume did not appear till the following spring. Coleridge's contribution to Book II. was omitted from the second (1797) and subsequent editions. It was afterwards republished, with additions, in Sibylline Leaves (1817) as "The Destiny of Nations."

[128] The lines "On a late Connubial Rupture" were printed in the Monthly Magazine for September, 1796. The well-known poem beginning "Low was our pretty Cot" appeared in the following number. It was headed, "Reflections on entering into active Life. A Poem which affects not to be Poetry."

[129] Compare the following lines from an early transcript of "Happiness" now in my possession:—

"Ah! doubly blest if Love supply
Lustre to the now heavy eye,
And with unwonted spirit grace
That fat vacuity of face."
The transcriber adds in a footnote, "The author was at this time, at seventeen, remarkable for a plump face."

The "Reminiscences of an Octogenarian" (The Rev. Leapidge Smith), contributed to the Leisure Hour, convey a different impression: "In person he was a tall, dark, handsome young man, with long, black, flowing hair; eyes not merely dark, but black, and keenly penetrating; a fine forehead, a deep-toned, harmonious voice; a manner never to be forgotten, full of life, vivacity, and kindness; dignified in person and, added to all these, exhibiting the elements of his future greatness."—Leisure Hour, 1870, p. 651.

[130] Origine de tous les Cultes, ou Religion universelle.

[131] Thelwall executed his commission. The Iamblichus and the Julian were afterwards presented by Coleridge to his son Derwent. They are still in the possession of the family.

[132] The three letters to Poole, dated December 11, 12, and 13, relative to Coleridge's residence at Stowey, were published for the first time in Thomas Poole and his Friends. The long letter of expostulation, dated December 13, which is in fact a continuation of that dated December 12, is endorsed by Poole: "An angry letter, but the breach was soon healed." Either on Coleridge's account or his own it was among the few papers retained by Poole when, to quote Mrs. Sandford, "in 1836 he placed the greater number of the letters which he had received from S. T. Coleridge at the disposal of his literary executors for biographical purposes." Thomas Poole and his Friends, i. 182-193. Mrs. Sandford has kindly permitted me to reprint it in extenso.

[133] "Sonnet composed on a journey homeward, the author having received intelligence of the birth of a son. September 20, 1796."

The opening lines, as quoted in the letter, differ from those published in 1797, and again from a copy of the same sonnet sent in a letter to Poole, dated November 1, 1796. See Poetical Works, p. 66, and Editor's Note, p. 582.

[134] Coleridge's Poetical Works, p. 66.

[135] Compare Lamb's letter to Coleridge, December 5, 1796. "I am glad you love Cowper. I could forgive a man for not enjoying Milton, but I would not call that man my friend who should be offended with the 'divine chit-chat of Cowper.'" Compare, too, letter of December 10, 1796, in which the origin of the phrase is attributed to Coleridge. Letters of Charles Lamb, i. 52, 54. See, too, Canon Ainger's note, i. 316.

[136] "Southey misrepresented me. My maxim was and is that the name of God should not be introduced into Love Sonnets." MS. Note by John Thelwall.

[137] Revelation x. 1-6. Some words and sentences of the original are omitted, either for the sake of brevity, or to heighten the dramatic effect.

[138] Hebrews xii. 18, 19, 22, 23.

[139] "In reading over this after an interval of twenty-three years I was wondering what I could have said that looked like contempt of age. May not slobberers have referred not to age but to the drivelling of decayed intellect, which is surely an ill guide in matters of understanding and consequently of faith?" MS. Note by John Thelwall, 1819.

[140] Patience—permit me as a definition of the word to quote one sentence from my first Address, p. 20. "Accustomed to regard all the affairs of man as a process, they never hurry and they never pause." In his not possessing this virtue, all the horrible excesses of Robespierre did, I believe, originate.—MS. note to text of letter by S. T. Coleridge.

[141] Godliness—the belief, the habitual and efficient belief, that we are always in the presence of our universal Parent. I will translate literally a passage [the passage is from Voss's Luise. I am enabled by the courtesy of Dr. Garnett, of the British Museum, to give an exact reference: Luise, ein ländliches Gedicht in drei Idyllen, von Johann Heinrich Voss, Königsberg, mdccxcv. Erste Idylle, pp. 41-45, lines 303-339.—E. H. C.] from a German hexameter poem. It is the speech of a country clergyman on the birthday of his daughter.

The latter part fully expresses the spirit of godliness, and its connection with brotherly-kindness. (Pardon the harshness of the language, for it is translated totidem verbis.)

"Yes! my beloved daughter, I am cheerful, cheerful as the birds singing in the wood here, or the squirrel that hops among the airy branches around its young in their nest. To-day it is eighteen years since God gave me my beloved, now my only child, so intelligent, so pious, and so dutiful. How the time flies away! Eighteen years to come—how far the space extends itself before us! and how does it vanish when we look back upon it! It was but yesterday, it seems to me, that as I was plucking flowers here, and offering praise, on a sudden the joyful message came, 'A daughter is born to us.' Much since that time has the Almighty imparted to us of good and evil. But the evil itself was good; for his loving-kindness is infinite. Do you recollect [to his wife] as it once had rained after a long drought, and I (Louisa in my arms) was walking with thee in the freshness of the garden, how the child snatched at the rainbow, and kissed me, and said: 'Papa! there it rains flowers from heaven! Does the blessed God strew these that we children may gather them up?' 'Yes!' I answered, 'full-blowing and heavenly blessings does the Father strew who stretched out the bow of his favour; flowers and fruits that we may gather them with thankfulness and joy. Whenever I think of that great Father then my heart lifts itself up and swells with active impulse towards all his children, our brothers who inhabit the earth around us; differing indeed from one another in powers and understanding, yet all dear children of the same parent, nourished by the same Spirit of animation, and ere long to fall asleep, and again to wake in the common morning of the Resurrection; all who have loved their fellow-creatures, all shall rejoice with Peter, and Moses, and Confucius, and Homer, and Zoroaster, with Socrates who died for truth, and also with the noble Mendelssohn who teaches that the divine one was never crucified.'"

Mendelssohn is a German Jew by parentage, and deist by election. He has written some of the most acute books possible in favour of natural immortality, and Germany deems him her profoundest metaphysician, with the exception of the most unintelligible Immanuel Kant.—MS. note to text of letter by S. T. Coleridge.

[142] 2 Peter i. 5-7.

[143] They were criticised by Lamb in his letter to Coleridge Dec. 10, 1796 (xxxi. of Canon Ainger's edition), but in a passage first printed in the Atlantic Monthly for February, 1891. The explanatory notes there printed were founded on a misconception, but the matter is cleared up in the Athenæum for June 13, 1891, in the article, "A Letter of Charles Lamb."

[144] The reference is to a pamphlet of sixteen pages containing twenty-eight sonnets by Coleridge, Southey, Lloyd, Lamb, and others, which was printed for private circulation towards the close of 1796, and distributed among a few friends. Of this selection of sonnets, which was made "for the purpose of binding them up with the sonnets of the Rev. W. L. Bowles," the sole surviving copy is now in the Dyce Collection of the South Kensington Museum. On the fly-leaf, in Coleridge's handwriting, is a "presentation note" to Mrs. Thelwall. For a full account of this curious and interesting volume, see Coleridge's Poetical and Dramatic Works, 4 vols., 1877-1880, ii. 377-379; also, Poetical Works (1893), 542-544.

[145] A folio edition of "Poems on the Death of Priscilla Farmer, by her grandson Charles Lloyd," was printed at Bristol in 1796. The volume was prefaced by Coleridge's sonnet, "The piteous sobs which choke the virgin's breast," and contained Lamb's "Grandame." As Mr. Dykes Campbell has pointed out, it is to this "magnificent folio" that Charles Lamb

alludes in his letter of December 10, 1796 (incorrectly dated 1797), when he speaks of "my granny so gaily decked," and records "the odd coincidence of two young men in one age carolling their grandmothers." Poetical Works, note 99, p. 583.

[146] "To a friend (C. Lamb) who had declared his intention of writing no more poetry." Poetical Works, p. 69. See, too, Editor's Note, p. 583.

[147] Printed in the Annual Anthology for 1799.

[148] These lines, which were published with the enlarged title "To a Young Man of Fortune who had abandoned himself to an indolent and causeless melancholy," may have been addressed to Charles Lloyd.

The last line, "A prey to the throned murderess of mankind," was afterwards changed to "A prey to tyrants, murderers of mankind." The reference is, doubtless, to Catherine of Russia. Her death had taken place a month before the date of this letter, but possibly when Coleridge wrote the lines the news had not reached England. It is not a little strange that Coleridge should write and print so stern and uncompromising a rebuke to his intimate and disciple before there had been time for coolness and alienation on either side. Very possibly the reproof was aimed in the first instance against himself, and afterwards he permitted it to apply to Lloyd.

[149] Compare the line, "From precipices of distressful sleep," which occurs in the sonnet, "No more my visionary soul shall dwell," which is attributed to Favell in a letter of Southey's to his brother Thomas, dated October 24, 1795. Southey's Life and Correspondence, i. 224. See, also, Editor's Note to "Monody on the Death of Chatterton," Poetical Works, p. 563.

[150] The Ode on the Departing Year.

[151] Œdipus.

[152] Poetical Works, p. 459.

[153] William and Joseph Strutt were the sons of Jedediah Strutt, of Derby. The eldest, William, was the father of Edward Strutt, created Lord Belper in 1856. Their sister, Elizabeth, who had married William Evans of Darley Hall, was at this time a widow. She had been struck by Coleridge's writings, or perhaps had heard him preach when he visited Derby on his Watchman tour, and was anxious to engage him as tutor to her children. The offer was actually made, but the relations on both sides intervened, and she was reluctantly compelled to withdraw her proposal. By way of consolation, she entertained Coleridge and his wife at Darley Hall, and before he left presented him with a handsome sum of money and a store of baby-linen, worth, if one may accept Coleridge's valuation, a matter of forty pounds. Thomas Poole and his Friends, i. 152-154; Estlin Letters, p. 13.

[154] Probably Jacob Bryant, 1715-1804, author of An Address to Dr. Priestley upon his Doctrine of Philosophical Necessity, 1780; Treatise on the Authenticity of the Scriptures, 1792; The Sentiments of Philo-Judæus concerning the Logos or Word of God, 1797, etc. Allibone's Dictionary, i. 270.

[155] "Ode to the Departing-Year," published in the Cambridge Intelligencer, December 24, 1796. The lines on the "Empress," to which Thelwall objected, are in the first epode:—

No more on Murder's lurid face
The insatiate Hag shall gloat with drunken eye.
Poetical Works, p. 79.

[156] Compare the well-known description of Dorothy Wordsworth, in a letter to Cottle of July, 1797: "W. and his exquisite sister are with me. She is a woman, indeed,—in mind I mean, and heart. Her information various. Her eye watchful in minutest observation of nature; and her taste a perfect electrometer. It bends, protrudes, and draws in, at subtlest beauties and most recondite faults."

Bennett's, or the gold leaf electroscope, is an instrument for "detecting the presence, and determining the kind of electricity in any body." Two narrow strips of gold leaf are attached to a metal rod, terminating in a small brass plate above, contained in a glass shade, and these under certain conditions of the application of positive and negative electricity diverge or collapse.

The gold leaf electroscope was invented by Abraham Bennett in 1786. Cottle's Early Recollections, i. 252; Ganot's Physics, 1870, p. 631.

[157] His tract On the Strength of the Existing Government (the Directory) of France, and the Necessity of supporting it, was published in 1796.

The translator, James Losh, described by Southey as "a provincial counsel," was at one time resident in Cumberland, and visited Coleridge at Greta Hall. At a later period he settled at Jesmond, Newcastle. His name occurs among the subscribers to The Friend. Letters from the Lake Poets, p. 453.

[158] Compare stanzas eight and nine of "The Mad Ox:"—

Old Lewis ('twas his evil day)
Stood trembling in his shoes;
The ox was his—what could he say?
His legs were stiffened with dismay,
The ox ran o'er him mid the fray,
And gave him his death's bruise.

The baited ox drove on (but here,
The Gospel scarce more true is,
My muse stops short in mid career—
Nay, gentle reader, do not sneer!
I could chuse but drop a tear,
A tear for good old Lewis!)
Poetical Works, p. 134.

[159] The probable date of this letter is Thursday, June 8, 1797. On Monday, June 5, Coleridge breakfasted with Dr. Toulmin, the Unitarian minister at Taunton, and on the evening of that or the next day he arrived on foot at Racedown, some forty miles distant. Mrs. Wordsworth, in a letter to Sara Coleridge, dated November 7, 1845, conveys her husband's recollections of this first visit in the following words: "Your father," she says, "came afterwards to visit us at Racedown, where I was living with my sister. We have both a distinct remembrance of his arrival. He did not keep to the high road, but leaped over a

high gate and bounded down the pathless field, by which he cut off an angle. We both retain the liveliest possible image of his appearance at that moment. My poor sister has just been speaking of it to me with much feeling and tenderness." A portion of this letter, of which I possess the original MS., was printed by Professor Knight in his Life of Wordsworth, i. 111.

[160] This passage, which for some reason Cottle chose to omit, seems to imply that the second edition of the poems had not appeared by the beginning of June.

[161]

... Such, O my earliest friend!
Thy lot, and such thy brothers too enjoy.
At distance did ye climb life's upland road,
Yet cheered and cheering: now fraternal love
Hath drawn you to one centre.
Poetical Works, p. 81, l. 9-14.

[162]

... and some most false,
False, and fair-foliaged as the Manchineel,
Have tempted me to slumber in their shade
E'en mid the storm; then breathing subtlest damp
Mixed their own venom with the rain from Heaven,
That I woke poisoned.
Poetical Works, p. 82, l. 25-30.

Compare Lamb's humorous reproach in a letter to Coleridge, September, 1797: "For myself I must spoil a little passage of Beaumont and Fletcher's to adapt it to my feelings:—

... I am prouder
That I was once your friend, tho' now forgot,
Than to have had another true to me.
"If you don't write to me now, as I told Lloyd, I shall get angry, and call you hard names— Manchineel, and I don't know what else."

Letters of Charles Lamb, i. 83.

[163] Charles Lamb's visit to the cottage of Nether Stowey lasted from Friday, July 7, to Friday, July 14, 1797.

[164] According to local tradition, the lime-tree bower was at the back of the cottage, but according to this letter it was in Poole's garden. From either spot the green ramparts of Stowey Castle and the "airy ridge" of Dowseborough are full in view.

[165] "He [Le Grice] and Favell ... wrote to the Duke of York, when they were at college, for commissions in the army. The Duke good-naturedly sent them." Autobiography of Leigh Hunt, p. 72.

[166] Possibly he alludes to his appointment as deputy-surgeon to the Second Royals, then stationed in Portugal.

His farewell letter to Coleridge (undated) has been preserved and will be read with interest.

Portsmouth.

My Beloved Friend,—Farewell! I shall never think of you but with tears of the tenderest affection. Our routes in life have been so opposite, that for a long time past there has not been that intercourse between us which our mutual affection would have otherwise occasioned. But at this serious moment, all your kindness and love for me press upon my memory with a weight of sensation I can scarcely endure.

....

You have heard of my destination, I suppose. I am going to Portugal to join the Second Royals, to which I have been appointed Deputy-Surgeon. What fate is in reserve for me I know not. I should be more indifferent to my future lot, if it were not for the hope of passing many pleasant hours, in times to come, in your society.

Adieu! my dearest fellow. My love to Mrs. C. Health and fraternity to young David.

Yours most affectionate,
R. Allen.

[167] A friend and fellow-collegian of Christopher Wordsworth at Trinity College, Cambridge. He was a member of the "Literary Society" to which Coleridge, C. Wordsworth, Le Grice, and others belonged. He afterwards became a sergeant-at-law. He was an intimate friend of H. Crabb Robinson. See H. C. Robinson's Diary, passim. See, too, Social Life at the English Universities, by Christopher Wordsworth, M. A., Fellow of Peterhouse, Cambridge, 1874, Appendix.

[168] Not, as has been supposed, Charles and Mary Lamb, but Wordsworth and his sister Dorothy. Mary Lamb was not and could not have been at that time one of the party. The version sent to Southey differs both from that printed in the Annual Anthology of 1800, and from a copy in a contemporary letter sent to C. Lloyd. It is interesting to note that the words, "My sister, and my friends," ll. 47 and 53, which gave place in the Anthology to the thrice-repeated, "My gentle-hearted Charles," appear, in a copy sent to Lloyd, as "My Sara and my friend." It was early days for him to address Dorothy Wordsworth as "My sister," but in forming friendships Coleridge did not "keep to the high road, but leaped over a gate and bounded" from acquaintance to intimacy. Poetical Works, p. 92. For version of "This Lime-Tree Bower my Prison," sent to C. Lloyd, see Ibid., Editor's Note, p. 591.

[169] "Elastic, I mean."—S. T. C.

[170] "The ferns that grow in moist places grow five or six together, and form a complete 'Prince of Wales's Feathers,'—that is, plumy."—S. T. C.

[171] "You remember I am a Berkleian."—S. T. C.

[172] "This Lime-Tree Bower," l. 38. Poetical Works, p. 93.

[173] "Osorio," Act V., Sc. 1, l. 39. Poetical Works, p. 507.

[174] Thelwall's visit brought Coleridge and Wordsworth into trouble. At the instance of a "titled Dogberry," Sir Philip Hale of Cannington, a government spy was sent to watch the movements of the supposed conspirators, and, a more serious matter, Mrs. St. Albyn, the owner of Alfoxden, severely censured her tenant for having sublet the house to Wordsworth. See letter of explanation and remonstrance from Poole to Mrs. St. Albyn, September 16, 1797. Thomas Poole and his Friends, i. 240. See, too, Cottle's Early Recollections, i. 319, and for apocryphal anecdotes about the spy, etc., Biographia Literaria, cap. x.

[175] Their proposal was to settle on Coleridge "an annuity for life of £150, to be regularly paid by us, no condition whatever being annexed to it." See letter of Josiah Wedgwood to Coleridge, dated January 10, 1798. Thomas Poole and his Friends, i. 258. An unpublished letter from Thelwall to Dr. Crompton dated Llyswen, March 3, 1798, contains one of several announcements of "his good fortune," made by Coleridge at the time to his numerous friends.

To Dr. Crompton, Eton House, Nr. Liverpool.

Llyswen, 3d March, 1798.

I am surprised you have not heard the particulars of Coleridge's good fortune. It is not a legacy, but a gift. The circumstances are thus expressed by himself in a letter of the 30th January: "I received an invitation from Shrewsbury to be the Unitarian minister, and at the same time an order for £100 from Thomas and Josiah Wedgwood. I accepted the former and returned the latter in a long letter explanatory of my motive, and went off to Shrewsbury, where they were on the point of electing me unanimously and with unusual marks of affection, where I received an offer from T. and J. Wedgwood of an annuity of £150 to be legally settled on me. Astonished, agitated, and feeling as I could not help feeling, I accepted the offer in the same worthy spirit, I hope, in which it was made, and this morning I have returned from Shrewsbury." This letter was written in a great hurry in Cottle's shop in Bristol, in answer to one which a friend of mine had left for him there, on his way from Llyswen to Gosport, and you will perceive that it has a dash of the obscure not uncommon to the rapid genius of C. Whether he did or did not accept the cure of Unitarian Souls, it is difficult from the account to make out. I suppose he did not, for I know his aversion to preachings God's holy word for hire, which is seconded not a little, I expect, by his repugnance to all regular routine and application. I also hope he did not, for I know he cannot preach very often without travelling from the pulpit to the Tower. Mount him but upon his darling hobby-horse, "the republic of God's own making," and away he goes like hey-go-mad, spattering and splashing through thick and thin and scattering more levelling sedition and constructive treason than poor Gilly or myself ever dreamt of. He promised to write to me again in a few days; but, though I answered his letter directly, I have not heard from him since.

[176] Count Benyowsky, or the Conspiracy of Kamtschatka, a Tragi-comedy. Translated from the German by the Rev. W. Render, teacher of the German Language in the University of Cambridge. Cambridge, 1798.

[177] Coleridge's copy of Monk Lewis' play is dated January 20, 1798.

[178] The following memoranda, presumably in Wordsworth's handwriting, have been scribbled on the outside sheet of the letter: "Tea—Thread fine—needles Silks—Strainer for starch—Mustard—Basil's shoes—Shoe horn.

"The sun's course is short, but clear and blue the sky."

[179] "Duplex nobis vinculum, et amicitiæ et similium junctarumque Camœnarum; quod utinam neque mors solvat, neque temporis longinquitas."

[180] The Task, Book V., "A Winter's Morning Walk."

[181] A later version of these lines is to be found at the close of the fourth book of "The Excursion." Works of Wordsworth, 1889, p. 467.

[182] In the series of letters to Dr. Estlin, contributed to the privately printed volumes of the Philobiblon Society, the editor, Mr. Henry A. Bright, dates this letter May (? 1797). A comparison with a second letter to Estlin, dated May 14, 1798 (Letter LXXXII.), with a letter to Poole, dated May 28, 1798 (Letter LXXXIV.), with a letter to Charles Lamb belonging to the spring of 1798 (Letter LXXXV.), and with an entry in Dorothy Wordsworth's journal for May 16, 1798, affords convincing proof that the date of the letter should be May, 1798.

The MS. note of November 10, 1810, to which a previous reference has been made, connects a serious quarrel with Lloyd, and consequent distress of mind, with the retirement to "the lonely farm-house," and a first recourse to opium. If, as the letters intimate, these events must be assigned to May, 1798, it follows that "Kubla Khan" was written at the same time, and not, as Coleridge maintained in the Preface of 1816, "in the summer of 1797."

It would, indeed, have been altogether miraculous if, before he had written a line of "Christabel," or "The Ancient Mariner," either in an actual dream, or a dreamlike reverie, it had been "given to him" to divine the enchanting images of "Kubla Khan," or attune his mysterious vision to consummate melody.

[183] Berkeley Coleridge, born May 14, 1798, died February 10, 1799.

[184] The original MS. of this letter, which was preserved by Coleridge, is, doubtless, a copy of that sent by post. Besides this, only three of Coleridge's letters to Lamb have been preserved,—the "religious letter" of 1796, a letter concerning the quarrel with Wordsworth, of May, 1812 [Letter CLXXXIV.], and one written in later life (undated, on the particulars of Hood's Odes to Great People).

[185] Charles Lloyd.

[186] The three sonnets of "Nehemiah Higginbottom" were published in the Monthly Magazine for November, 1797. Compare his letter to Cottle (E. R. i. 289) which Mr. Dykes Campbell takes to have been written at the same time.

"I sent to the Monthly Magazine, three mock sonnets in ridicule of my own Poems, and Charles Lloyd's and Charles Lamb's, etc., etc., exposing that affectation of unaffectedness, of jumping and misplaced accent, in commonplace epithets, flat lines forced into poetry by italics (signifying how well and mouthishly the author would read them), puny pathos, etc., etc. The instances were all taken from myself and Lloyd and Lamb. I signed them 'Nehemiah Higginbottom.' I hope they may do good to our young bards."

The publication of these sonnets in November, 1797, cannot, as Mr. Dykes Campbell points out (Poetical Works, p. 599), have been the immediate cause of the breach between Coleridge and Lamb which took place in the spring or early summer of 1798, but it seems that during the rise and progress of this quarrel the Sonnet on Simplicity was the occasion of bitter and angry words. As Lamb and Lloyd and Southey drew together, they drew away from Coleridge, and Southey, who had only been formally reconciled with his brother-in-law, seems to have regarded this sonnet as an ill-natured parody of his earlier poems. In a letter to Wynn, dated November 20, 1797, he says, "I am aware of the danger of studying simplicity of language," and he proceeds to quote some lines of blank verse to prove that he could employ the "grand style" when he chose.

A note from Coleridge to Southey, posted December 8, 1797, deals with the question, and would, if it had not been for Lloyd's "tittle-tattle," have convinced both Southey and Lamb that in the matter they were entirely mistaken.

. . . .

I am sorry, Southey! very sorry that I wrote or published those sonnets—but 'sorry' would be a tame word to express my feelings, if I had written them with the motives which you have attributed to me. I have not been in the habit of treating our separation with levity—nor ever since the first moment thought of it without deep emotion—and how could you apply to yourself a sonnet written to ridicule infantine simplicity, vulgar colloquialisms, and lady-like friendships? I have no conception, neither I believe could a passage in your writings have suggested to me or any man the notion of your 'plainting plaintively.' I am sorry that I wrote thus, because I am sorry to perceive a disposition in you to believe evil of me, of which your remark to Charles Lloyd was a painful instance. I say this to you, because I shall say it to no other being. I feel myself wounded and hurt and write as such. I believe in my letter to Lloyd I forgot to mention that the Editor of the Morning Post is called Stuart, and that he is the brother-in-law of Mackintosh. Yours sincerely,

S. T. Coleridge.

Thursday morning.
Post-mark, Dec. 8, 1797.

Mr. Southey, No. 23 East Street, Red Lion Square, London.

[187] Charles Lloyd's novel, Edmund Oliver, was published at Bristol in 1798. It is dedicated to "His friend Charles Lamb of the India House." He says in the Preface: "The incidents relative to the army were given me by an intimate friend who was himself eye-witness of one of them." The general resemblance between the events of Coleridge's earlier history and the story of Edmund Oliver is not very striking, but apart from the description of "his person" in the first letter of the second volume, which is close enough, a single sentence from Edmund Oliver's journal, i. 245, betrays the malignant nature of the attack. "I have at all times a strange dreaminess about me which makes me indifferent to the future, if I can by any means fill the present with sensations,—with that dreaminess I have gone on here from day to day; if at any time thought-troubled, I have swallowed some spirits, or had recourse to my laudanum." In the same letter, the account which Edmund Oliver gives of his sensations as a recruit in a regiment of light horse, and the vivid but repulsive picture which he draws of his squalid surroundings in "a pot-house in the Borough," leaves a like impression that Coleridge confided too much, and that Lloyd

remembered "not wisely but too well." How Coleridge regarded Lloyd's malfeasance may be guessed from one of his so-called epigrams.

TO ONE WHO PUBLISHED IN PRINT WHAT HAD BEEN INTRUSTED TO HIM BY MY FIRESIDE.

Two things hast thou made known to half the nation,
My secrets and my want of penetration:
For oh! far more than all which thou hast penned,
It shames me to have called a wretch, like thee, my friend!
Poetical Works, p. 448.

[188] In a letter dated November 1, 1798, Mrs. Coleridge acquaints her husband with the danger and the disfigurement from smallpox which had befallen her little Berkeley. "The dear child," she writes, "is getting strength every hour; but 'when you lost sight of land, and the faces of your children crossed you like a flash of lightning,' you saw that face for the last time."

[189] "Fears in Solitude, written in 1798, during the alarm of an invasion. To which are added, France, an Ode; and Frost at Midnight. By S. T. Coleridge. London: Printed for J. Johnson, in St. Paul's Churchyard. 1798."

[190] According to Burke's Peerage, Emanuel Scoope, second Viscount Howe, and father of the Admiral, "Our Lord Howe," married, in 1719, Mary Sophia, daughter of Baron Kielmansegge, Master of the Horse to George I. Coleridge's countess must have been a great-granddaughter of the baron. In her reply to this letter, dated December 13, 1798, Mrs. Coleridge writes: "I am very proud to hear that you are so forward in the language, and that you are so gay with the ladies. You may give my respects to them, and say that I am not at all jealous, for I know my dear Samuel in her affliction will not forget entirely his most affectionate wife, Sara Coleridge."

[191] The "Rev. Mr. Roskilly" had been curate-in-charge of the parish of Nether Stowey, and the occasion of the letter was his promotion to the Rectory of Kempsford in Gloucestershire. Mrs. S. T. Coleridge, in a late letter (probably 1843) to her sister, Mrs. Lovell, writes: "In March [1800] I and the child [Hartley] left him [S. T. C.] in London, and proceeded to Kempsford in Gloucestershire, the Rectory of Mr. Roskilly; remained there a month. Papa was to have joined us there, but did not." See Thomas Poole and his Friends, i. 25-27, and Letters from the Lake Poets, p. 6.

[192] In his letter of January 20, 1799, Josiah Wedgwood acknowledges the receipt of a letter dated November 29, 1798, but adds that an earlier letter from Hamburg had not come to hand. A third letter, dated Göttingen, May 21, 1799, was printed by Cottle in his Reminiscences, 1848, p. 425.

[193] Miss Meteyard, in her Group of Englishmen, 1871, p. 99, gives extracts from the account-current of Messrs. P. and O. Von Axen, the Hamburg agents of the Wedgwoods. According to her figures, Coleridge drew £125 from October 20 to March 29, 1799, and, "conjointly with Wordsworth," £106 10s. on July 8, 1799. Mr. Dykes Campbell, in a footnote to his Memoir, p. xliv., combats Miss Meteyard's assertion that these sums were advanced by the Wedgwoods to Coleridge and Wordsworth, and argues that Wordsworth merely drew on the Von Axens for sums already paid in from his own resources. Coleridge, he thinks, had only his annuity to look to, but probably anticipated his income. In a MS.

note-book of 1798-99, Coleridge inserted some concise but not very business-like entries as to expenditures and present resources, but says nothing as to receipts.

"March 25th, being Easter Monday, Chester and S. T. C., in a damn'd dirty hole in the Burg Strasse at Göttingen, possessed at that moment eleven Louis d'ors and two dollars. When the money is spent in common expenses S. T. Coleridge will owe Chester 5 pounds 12 shillings.

"Note.—From September 8 to April 8 I shall have spent £90, of which £15 was in Books; and Cloathes, mending and making, £10.

"May 10. We have 17 Louis d'or, of which, as far as I can at present calculate, 10 belong to Chester."

The most probable conclusion is that both Coleridge and Chester were fairly well supplied with money when they left England, and that the £178 10s. which Coleridge received from the Von Axens covered some portion of Chester's expenses in addition to his own. I may add that a recent collation of the autograph letter of Coleridge to Josiah Wedgwood dated May 21, 1799, Göttingen, with the published version in Cottle's Reminiscences, pp. 425-429, fully bears out Mr. Campbell's contention, that though Coleridge anticipated his annuity, he was not the recipient of large sums over and above what was guaranteed to him.

[194] A portion of this description of Ratzeburg is included in No. III. of Satyrane's Letters, originally published in No. 10 of The Friend, December 21, 1809.

[195] The following description of the frozen lake was thrown into a literary shape and published in No. 19 of The Friend, December 28, 1809, as "Christmas Indoors in North Germany."

[196] A letter from Mrs. Coleridge to her husband, dated March 25, 1799, followed Poole's letter of March 15. (Thomas Poole and his Friends, i. 290.) She writes:—

"My dearest Love,—I hope you will not attribute my long silence to want of affection. If you have received Mr. Poole's letter you will know the reason and acquit me. My darling infant left his wretched mother on the 10th of February, and though the leisure that followed was intolerable to me, yet I could not employ myself in reading or writing, or in any way that prevented my thoughts from resting on him. This parting was the severest trial that I have ever yet undergone, and I pray to God that I may never live to behold the death of another child. For, O my dear Samuel, it is a suffering beyond your conception! You will feel and lament the death of your child, but you will only recollect him a baby of fourteen weeks, but I am his mother and have carried him in my arms and have fed him at my bosom, and have watched over him by day and by night for nine months. I have seen him twice at the brink of the grave, but he has returned and recovered and smiled upon me like an angel,—and now I am lamenting that he is gone!"

In her old age, when her daughter was collecting materials for a life of her father, Mrs. Coleridge wrote on the back of the letter:—

"No secrets herein. I will not burn it for the sake of my sweet Berkeley."

[197] From "Osorio," Act V. Sc. 1. Poetical Works, p. 506.

[198] The following description of the Christmas-tree, and of Knecht Rupert, was originally published, almost verbatim, in No. 19 of the original issue of The Friend, December 28, 1809.

[199] First published in Annual Anthology of 1800, under the signature Cordomi. See Poetical Works, p. 146, and Editor's Note, p. 621.

[200] The men who rip the oak bark from the logs for tanning.

[201]

My dear babe,
Who capable of no articulate sound,
Mars all things with his imitative lisp,
How he would place his hand beside his ear,
His little hand, the small forefinger up,
And bid us listen.
—"The Nightingale, a Conversation Poem," written in April, 1798. Poetical Works, p. 133.

[202] Hutton Hall, near Penrith.

[203] First published in the Annual Anthology of 1800. See Poetical Works, p. 146, and Editor's Note, p. 621. According to Carlyon the lines were dictated by Coleridge and inscribed by one of the party in the "Stammbuch" of the Wernigerode Inn. Early Years, i. 66.

[204] Olaus Tychsen, 1734-1815, was "Professor of Oriental Tongues" at Rostock, in Mecklenburg-Schwerin.

[205] F. C. Achard, born in 1754, was author of an "Instruction for making sugar, molasses, and vinous spirit from Beet-root."

[206] The Coleridges were absent from Stowey for about a month. For the first fortnight they were guests of George Coleridge at Ottery. The latter part of the time was spent with the Southeys in their lodgings at Exeter. It was during this second visit that Coleridge accompanied Southey on a walking tour through part of Dartmoor and as far as Dartmouth.

[207] Coleridge took but few notes during this tour. In 1803 he retranscribed his fragmentary jottings and regrets that he possessed no more, "though we were at the interesting Bovey waterfall [Becky Fall], through that wild dell of ashes which leads to Ashburton, most like the approach to upper Matterdale." "I have," he adds, "at this moment very distinct visual impressions of the tour, namely of Torbay, the village of Paignton with the Castle." Southey was disappointed in South Devon, which he contrasts unfavourably with the North of Somersetshire, but for "the dell of ashes" he has a word of praise. Selections from Letters of Robert Southey, i. 84.

[208] Suwarrow, at the head of the Austro-Russian troops, defeated the French under Joubert at Novi near Alessandria, in North Italy, August 15, 1799.

[209] A temporary residence of Josiah Wedgwood, who had taken it on lease in order to be near his newly purchased property at Combe Florey, in Somersetshire. Meteyard's Group of Englishmen, 1871, p. 107.

[210] Southey's brother, a midshipman on board the Sylph gun-brig. A report had reached England that the Sylph had been captured and brought to Ferrol. Southey's Life and Correspondence, ii. 30.

[211] Marshal Massena defeated the Russians under Prince Korsikov at Zurich, September 25, 1799.

[212] William Jackson, organist of Exeter Cathedral, 1730-1803, a musical composer and artist. He published, among other works, The Four Ages with Essays, 1798. See letter of Southey to S. T. Coleridge, October 3, 1799, Southey's Life and Correspondence, ii. 26.

[213] John Codrington Warwick Bampfylde, second son of Richard Bampfylde, of Poltimore, was the author of Sixteen Sonnets, published in 1779. In the letter of October 3 (see above) Southey gives an interesting account of his eccentric habits and melancholy history. In a prefatory note to four of Bampfylde's sonnets, included by Southey in his Specimens of the Later English Poets, he explains how he came to possess the copies of some hitherto unpublished poems.

"Jackson of Exeter, a man whose various talents made all who knew him remember him with regret, designed to republish the little collection of Bampfylde's Sonnets, with what few of his pieces were still unedited.

"Those poems which are here first printed were transcribed from the originals in his possession."

"Bampfylde published his Sonnets at a very early age; they are some of the most original in our language. He died in a private mad-house, after twenty years' confinement." Specimens of the Later English Poets, 1808, iii. 434.

[214] "A sister of General McKinnon, who was killed at Ciudad Rodrigo." In the same letter to Coleridge (see above) Southey says that he looked up to her with more respect because the light of Buonaparte's countenance had shone upon her.

[215] Dr. Cookson, Canon of Windsor and Rector of Forncett, Norfolk. Dorothy Wordsworth passed much of her time under his roof before she finally threw in her lot with her brother William in 1795.

[216] The journal, or notes for a journal, of this first tour in the Lake Country, leaves a doubt whether Coleridge and Wordsworth slept at Keswick on Sunday, November 10, 1799, or whether they returned to Cockermouth. It is certain that they passed through Keswick again on Friday, November 15, as the following entry testifies:—

"1 mile and ½ from Keswick, a Druidical circle. On the right the road and Saddleback; on the left a fine but unwatered vale, walled by grassy hills and a fine black crag standing single at the terminus as sentry. Before me, that is, towards Keswick, the mountains stand, one behind the other, in orderly array, as if evoked by and attentive to the white-vested wizards." It was from almost the same point of view that, thirty years afterwards, his wife, on her journey south after her daughter's marriage, took a solemn farewell of the Vale of Keswick once so strange, but then so dear and so familiar.

[217] George Fricker, Mrs. Coleridge's younger brother.

[218] A gossiping account of the early history and writings of "Mr. Robert Southey" appeared in Public Characters for 1799-1800, a humble forerunner of Men of the Time, published by Richard Phillips, the founder of the Monthly Magazine, and afterwards knighted as a sheriff of the city of London. Possibly Coleridge was displeased at the mention of his name in connection with Pantisocracy, and still more by the following sentence: "The three young poetical friends, Lovel, Southey, and Coleridge, married three sisters. Southey is attached to domestic life, and, fortunately, was very happy in his matrimonial connection." It was Sir Richard Phillips, the "knight" of Coleridge's anecdote, who told Mrs. Barbauld that he would have given "nine guineas a sheet for the last hour and a half of his conversation." Letters, Conversations, etc., 1836, ii. 131, 132.

[219] "These various pieces were rearranged in three volumes under the title of Minor Poems, in 1815, with this motto, Nos hæc novimus esse nihil." Poetical Works of Robert Southey, 1837, ii., xii.

[220] Mary Hayes, a friend of Mary Wollstonecraft, whose opinions she advocated with great zeal, and whose death she witnessed. Among other works, she wrote a novel, Memoirs of Emma Courtney, and Female Biography, or Memoirs of Illustrious and Celebrated Women. Six volumes. London: R. Phillips. 1803.

[221] He used the same words in a letter to Poole dated December 31, 1799. Thomas Poole and his Friends, i. 1.

[222] "Essay on the New French Constitution," Essays on His Own Times, i. 183-189.

[223] The Ode appeared in the Morning Post, December 24, 1799. The stanzas in which the Duchess commemorated her passage over Mount St. Gothard appeared in the Morning Post, December 21. They were inscribed to her children, and it was the last stanza, in which she anticipates her return, which suggested to Coleridge the far-fetched conceit that maternal affection enabled the Duchess to overcome her aristocratic prejudices, and "hail Tell's chapel and the platform wild." It runs thus:—

Hope of my life! dear children of my heart!
That anxious heart to each fond feeling true,
To you still pants each pleasure to impart,
And soon—oh transport—reach its home and you.
From a transcript in my possession of which the opening lines are in the handwriting of Mrs. H. N. Coleridge.

[224] The libel of which Coleridge justly complained was contained in these words: "Since this time (that is, since leaving Cambridge) he has left his native country, commenced citizen of the world, left his poor children fatherless and his wife destitute. Ex his disce his friends Lamb and Southey." Biographia Literaria, 1817, vol. i. chapter i. p. 70, n.

[225] Mrs. Robinson ("Perdita") contributed two poems to the Annual Anthology of 1800, "Jasper" and "The Haunted Beach." The line which caught Coleridge's fancy, the first of the twelfth stanza, runs thus:—

"Pale Moon! thou Spectre of the Sky."
Annual Anthology, 1800, p. 168.

[226] St. Leon was published in 1799. William Godwin, his Friends and Contemporaries, i. 330.

[227] See "Mr. Coleridge's Report of Mr. Pitt's Speech in Parliament of February 17, 1800, On the continuance of the War with France." Morning Post, February 18, 1800; Essays on His Own Times, ii. 293. See, too, Mrs. H. N. Coleridge's note, and the report of the speech in The Times. Ibid. iii. 1009-1019. The original notes, which Coleridge took in pencil, have been preserved in one of his note-books. They consist, for the most part, of skeleton sentences and fragmentary jottings. How far Coleridge may have reconstructed Pitt's speech as he went along, it is impossible to say, but the speech as reported follows pretty closely the outlines in the note-book. The remarkable description of Buonaparte as the "child and champion of Jacobinism," which is not to be found in The Times report, appears in the notes as "the nursling and champion of Jacobinism," and, if these were the words which Pitt used, in this instance, Coleridge altered for the worse.

[228] "The Beguines I had looked upon as a religious establishment, and the only good one of its kind. When my brother was a prisoner at Brest, the sick and wounded were attended by nurses, and these women had made themselves greatly beloved and respected." Southey to Rickman, January 9, 1800. Life and Correspondence, ii. 46. It is well known that Southey advocated the establishment of Protestant orders of Sisters of Mercy.

[229] In a letter from Southey to Coleridge, dated February 15, 1800 (unpublished), he proposes the establishment of a Magazine with signed articles. But a "History of the Levelling Principle," which Coleridge had suggested as a joint work, he would only publish anonymously.

[230] See Letter from Southey to Coleridge, December 27, 1799. Life and Correspondence, ii. 35.

[231] "Concerning the French, I wish Bonaparte had staid in Egypt and that Robespierre had guilloteened Sieyès. These cursed complex governments are good for nothing, and will ever be in the hands of intriguers: the Jacobins were the men, and one house of representatives, lodging the executive in committees, the plain and common system of government. The cause of republicanism is over, and it is now only a struggle for dominion. There wants a Lycurgus after Robespierre, a man loved for his virtue, and bold and inflexible, who should have levelled the property of France, and then would the Republic have been immortal—and the world must have been revolutionized by example." From an unpublished letter from Southey to Coleridge, dated December 23, 1799.

[232] "Alas, poor human nature! Or rather, indeed, alas, poor Gallic nature! For Γραῖοι ἀεὶ μαῖδες the French are always children, and it is an infirmity of benevolence to wish, to dread, aught concerning them." S. T. C., Morning Post, December 31, 1797; Essays on His Own Times, i. 184.

[233] See Poetical Works, Appendix K, pp. 544, 545. Editor's Note, pp. 646-649.

[234]

"The winter Moon upon the sand
A silvery Carpet made,
And mark'd the sailor reach the land—
And mark'd his Murderer wash his hand
Where the green billows played!"
Annual Anthology, 1800: "The Haunted Beach," sixth stanza, p. 256.

[235] These letters, under the title of "Monopolists" and "Farmers," appeared in the Morning Post, October 3-9, 1800. Coleridge wrote the first of the series, and the introduction to No. III. of "Farmers," "In what manner they are affected by the War" Essays on His Own Times, ii. 413-450; Thomas Poole and his Friends, ii. 15, 16.

[236] It is impossible to explain this statement, which was repeated in a letter to Josiah Wedgwood, dated November 1, 1800. The printed "Christabel," even including the conclusion to Part II., makes only 677 lines, and the discarded portion, if it ever existed, has never come to light. See Mr. Dykes Campbell's valuable and exhaustive note on "Christabel," Poetical Works, pp. 601-607.

[237] A former title of "The Excursion."

[238] "Sunday night, half past ten, September 14, 1800, a boy born (Bracy).

"September 27, 1800. The child being very ill was baptized by the name of Derwent. The child, hour after hour, made a noise exactly like the creaking of a door which is being shut very slowly to prevent its creaking." (MS.) S. T. C.

My father's life was saved by his mother's devotion. "On the occasion here recorded," he writes, "I had eleven convulsion fits. At last my father took my mother gently out of the room, and told her that she must make up her mind to lose this child. By and by she heard the nurse lulling me, and said she would try once more to give me the breast." She did so; and from that time all went well, and the child recovered.

[239] Afterwards Sir Anthony, the distinguished surgeon, 1768-1840.

[240] According to Dr. Davy, the editor of Fragmentary Remains of Sir H. Davy, London, 1858, the reference is to the late Mr. James Thompson of Clitheroe.

[241] William, the elder brother of Raisley Calvert, who left Wordsworth a legacy of nine hundred pounds. In that mysterious poem, "Stanzas written in my Pocket Copy of Thomson's Castle of Indolence," it would seem that Wordsworth begins with a blended portrait of himself and Coleridge, and ends with a blended portrait of Coleridge and William Calvert. Mrs. Joshua Stanger (Mary Calvert) maintained that "the large gray eyes" and "low-hung lip" were certainly descriptive of Coleridge and could not apply to her father; but she admitted that, in other parts of the poem, Wordsworth may have had her father in his mind. Of this we may be sure, that neither Coleridge nor Wordsworth had "inventions rare," or displayed beetles under a microscope. It is evident that Hartley Coleridge, who said "that his father's character and habits are here [that is, in these stanzas] preserved in a livelier way than in anything that has been written about him," regarded the first and not the second half of the poem as a description of S. T. C. "The Last of the Calverts," Cornhill Magazine, May, 1890, pp. 494-520.

[242] On page 210 of vol. ii. of the second edition of the Lyrical Ballads (1800), there is a blank space. The omitted passage, fifteen lines in all, began with the words, "Though nought was left undone." Works of Wordsworth, p. 134, II. 4-18.

[243] During the preceding month Coleridge had busied himself with instituting a comparison between the philosophical systems of Locke and Descartes. Three letters of prodigious length, dated February 18, 24 (a double letter), and addressed to Josiah Wedgwood, embodied the result of his studies. They would serve, he thought, as a preliminary excursus to a larger work, and would convince the Wedgwoods that his wanderjahr had not been altogether misspent. Mr. Leslie Stephen, to whom this correspondence has been submitted, is good enough to allow me to print the following extract from a letter which he wrote at my request: "Coleridge writes as though he had as yet read no German philosophy. I knew that he began a serious study of Kant at Keswick; but I fancied that he had brought back some knowledge of Kant from Germany. This letter seems to prove the contrary. There is certainly none of the transcendentalism of the Schelling kind. One point is, that he still sticks to Hartley and to the Association doctrine, which he afterwards denounced so frequently. Thus he is dissatisfied with Locke, but has not broken with the philosophy generally supposed to be on the Locke line. In short, he seems to be at the point where a study of Kant would be ready to launch him in his later direction, but is not at all conscious of the change. When he wrote the Friend [1809-10] he had become a Kantian. Therefore we must, I think, date his conversion later than I should have supposed, and assume that it was the study of Kant just after this letter was written which brought about the change."

[244] Nothing is known of these lines beyond the fact that in 1816 Coleridge printed them as "Conclusion to Part II." of "Christabel." It is possible that they were intended to form part of a distinct poem in the metre of "Christabel," or, it may be, they are the sole survival of an attempted third part of the ballad itself. It is plain, however, that the picture is from the life, that "the little child, the limber elf," is the four-year-old Hartley, hardly as yet "fitting to unutterable thought, The breeze-like motion, and the self-born carol."

[245] George Hutchinson, the fourth son of John Hutchinson of Penrith, was at this time in occupation of land at Bishop's Middleham, the original home of the family. He migrated into Radnorshire in 1815, being then about the age of thirty-seven; but between that date and his leaving Bishop's Middleham he had resided for some time in Lincolnshire, at Scrivelsby, where he was engaged probably as agent on the estate of the "Champion." His first residence after migration was at New Radnor, where he married Margaret Roberts of Curnellan, but he subsequently removed into Herefordshire, where he resided in many places, latterly at Kingston. He died at his son's house, The Vinery, Hereford, in 1866. It would seem from a letter dated July 25, 1801 (Letter CXX.), that at this time Sarah Hutchinson kept house for her brother George, and that Mary (Mrs. Wordsworth) and Joanna Hutchinson lived with their elder brother Tom at Gallow Hill, in the parish of Brompton, near Scarborough. The register of Brompton Church records the marriage of William Wordsworth and Mary Hutchinson, on October 4, 1802; but in the notices of marriages in the Gentleman's Magazine, of October, 1802, the latter is described as "Miss Mary Hutchinson of Wykeham," an adjoining parish.

[From information kindly supplied to me by Mr. John Hutchinson, the keeper of the Library of the Middle Temple.]

[246] The historian William Roscoe (afterwards M. P. for Liverpool), and the physician James Currie, the editor and biographer of Burns, were at this time settled at Liverpool and on terms of intimacy with Dr. Peter Crompton of Eaton Hall.

[247] The Bristol merchant who lent the manor-house of Racedown to Wordsworth in 1795.

[248] In the well-known lines "On revisiting the Sea-shore," allusion is made to this "mild physician," who vainly dissuaded him from bathing in the open sea. Sea-bathing was at all times an irresistible pleasure to Coleridge, and he continued the practice, greatly to his benefit, down to a late period of his life and long after he had become a confirmed invalid. Poetical Works, p. 159.

[249] Francis Wrangham, whom Coleridge once described as "admirer of me and a pitier of my political principles" (Letter to Cottle [April], 1796), was his senior by a few years. On failing to obtain, it is said on account of his advanced political views, a fellowship at Trinity Hall, he started taking pupils at Cobham in Surrey in partnership with Basil Montagu. The scheme was of short duration, for Montagu deserted tuition for the bar, and Wrangham, early in life, was preferred to the benefices of Hemmanby and Folkton, in the neighborhood of Scarborough. He was afterwards appointed to a Canonry of York, to the Archdeaconry of Cleveland, and finally to a prebendal stall at Chester. He published a volume of Poems (London, 1795), in which are included Coleridge's Translation of the "Hendecasyllabi ad Bruntonam e Grantâ exituram," and some "Verses to Miss Brunton with the preceding Translation." He died in 1842. Poetical Works, p. 30. See, too, Editor's Note, p. 569; Reminiscences of Cambridge, by Henry Gunning, London, 1855, ii. 12 seq.

[250] "I took a first floor for him in King Street, Covent Garden, at my tailor's, Howell's, whose wife is a cheerful housewife of middle age, who I knew would nurse Coleridge as kindly as if he were her son." D. Stuart, Gent. Mag., May, 1838. See, too, Letters from the Lake Poets, p. 7.

[251] Captain Luff, for many years a resident at Patterdale, near Ulleswater, was held in esteem for the energy with which he procured the enrolment of large companies of volunteers. Wordsworth and Coleridge were frequent visitors at his house, For his account of the death of Charles Gough, on Helvellyn, and the fidelity of the famous spaniel, see Coleorton Letters, i. 97. Letters from the Lake Poets, p. 131.

[252] Ciceronis Epist. ad Fam. iv. 10.

[253] Ib. i. 2.

[254] The lines are taken, with some alterations, from a kind of l'envoy or epilogue which Bruno affixed to his long philosophical poem, Jordani Bruni Nolani de Innumerabilibus Immenso et Infigurabili; seu de Universo et Mundis libri octo. Francofurti, 1591, p. 654.

[255] John Hamilton Mortimer, 1741-1779. He painted King John granting Magna Charta, the Battle of Agincourt, the Conversion of the Britons, and other historical subjects.

[256] Drayton's Poly-Olbion, Song 22, 1-17.

[257] The Latin Iambics, in which Dean Ogle celebrated the little Blyth, which ran through his father's park at Kirkley, near Ponteland, deserve the highest praise; but Bowles's

translation is far from being execrable. He may not have caught the peculiar tones of the Northumbrian burn which awoke the memories of the scholarly Dean, but his irregular lines are not without their own pathos and melody. Bowles was a Winchester boy, and Dr. Newton Ogle, then Dean of Winchester, was one of his earliest patrons. It was from the Dean's son, his old schoolfellow, Lieutenant Ogle, that he claimed to have gathered the particulars of Coleridge's discovery at Reading and discharge from the army. "Poems of William Lisle Bowles," Galignani, 1829, p. 131; "The Late Mr. Coleridge a Common Soldier," Times, August 13, 1834.

[258] One of a series of falls made by the Dash Beck, which divides the parishes of Caldbeck and Skiddaw Forest, and flows into Bassenthwaite Lake.

The following minute description is from an entry in a note-book dated October 10, 1800:—

"The Dash itself is by no means equal to the Churnmilk (sic) at Eastdale (sic) or the Wytheburn Fall. This I wrote standing under and seeing the whole Dash; but when I went over and descended to the bottom, then I only saw the real Fall and the curve of the steep slope, and retracted. It is, indeed, so seen, a fine thing. It falls parallel with a fine black rock thirty feet, and is more shattered, more completely atomized and white, than any I have ever seen.... The Fall of the Dash is in a horse-shoe basin of its own, wildly peopled with small ashes standing out of the rocks. Crossed the beck close by the white pool, and stood on the other side in a complete spray-rain. Here it assumes, I think, a still finer appearance. You see the vast rugged net and angular points and upright cones of the black rock; the Fall assumes a variety and complexity, parts rushing in wheels, other parts perpendicular, some in white horse-tails, while towards the right edge of the black [rock] two or three leisurely fillets have escaped out of the turmoil."

[259] I have been unable to discover any trace of the MS. of this translation.

[260] The "Ode to Dejection," of which this is the earliest version, was composed on Sunday evening, April 4, and published six months later, in the Morning Post of October 4, 1802. It was reprinted in the Sibylline Leaves, 1817. A comparison of the Ode, as sent to Sotheby, with the first printed version (Poetical Works, Appendix G, pp. 522-524) shows that it underwent many changes before it was permitted to see the "light of common day" in the columns of the Morning Post. The Ode was begun some three weeks after Coleridge returned to Keswick, after an absence of four months. He had visited Southey in London, he had been a fellow guest with Tom Wedgwood for a month at Stowey, he had returned to London and attended Davy's lectures at the Royal Institution, and on his way home he had stayed for a fortnight with his friend T. Hutchinson, Wordsworth's brother-in-law, at Gallow Hill.

He left Gallow Hill "on March 13 in a violent storm of snow, wind, and rain," and must have reached Keswick on Sunday the 14th or Monday the 15th of March. On the following Friday he walked over to Dove Cottage, and once more found himself in the presence of his friends, and, once again, their presence and companionship drove him into song. The Ode is at once a confession and a contrast, a confession that he had fled from the conflict with his soul into the fastnesses of metaphysics, and a contrast of his own hopelessness with the glad assurance of inward peace and outward happiness which attended the pure and manly spirit of his friend.

But verse was what he had been wedded to,

And his own mind did like a tempest strong
Come thus to him, and drove the weary wight along.
A MS. note-book of 1801-2, which has helped to date his movements at the time, contains, among other hints and jottings, the following almost illegible fragment: "The larches in spring push out their separate bundles of ... into green brushes or pencils which ... small tassels;"—and with the note may be compared the following lines included in the version contained in the letter, but afterwards omitted:—

In this heartless mood,
To other thoughts by yonder throstle woo'd,
That pipes within the larch-tree, not unseen
The larch that pushes out in tassels green
Its bundled leafits—woo'd to mild delights,
By all the tender sounds and gentle sights
Of this sweet primrose-month, and vainly woo'd!
O dearest Poet, in this heartless mood—

Another jotting in the same note-book: "A Poem on the endeavour to emancipate the mind from day-dreams, with the different attempts and the vain ones," perhaps found expression in the lines which follow "My shaping spirit of Imagination," which appeared for the first time in print in Sibylline Leaves, 1817, but which, as Mr. Dykes Campbell has rightly divined, belonged to the original draft of the Ode. Poetical Works, p. 159. Appendix G, pp. 522-524. Editor's Note, pp. 626-628.

[261] "A lovely skye-canoe." Morning Post. The reference is to the Prologue to "Peter Bell." Compare stanza 22,

"My little vagrant Form of light,
My gay and beautiful Canoe."
Wordsworth's Poetical Works, p. 100.

[262] For Southey's reply, dated Bristol, August 4, 1802, see Life and Correspondence, ii. 189-192.

[263] The Right Hon. Isaac Corry, Chancellor of the Exchequer for Ireland, to whom Southey acted as secretary for a short time.

[264] "On Sunday, August 1st, ½ after 12, I had a shirt, cravat, 2 pairs of stockings, a little paper, and half dozen pens, a German book (Voss's Poems), and a little tea and sugar, with my night cap, packed up in my natty green oil-skin, neatly squared, and put into my net knapsack, and the knapsack on my back and the besom stick in my hand, which for want of a better, and in spite of Mrs. C. and Mary, who both raised their voices against it, especially as I left the besom scattered on the kitchen floor, off I sallied over the bridge, through the hop-field, through the Prospect Bridge, at Portinscale, so on by the tall birch that grows out of the centre of the huge oak, along into Newlands." MS. Journal of tour in the Lake District, August 1-9, 1802, sent in the form of a letter to the Wordsworths and transcribed by Miss Sarah Hutchinson.

[265] "The following month, September (1802), was marked by the birth of his first child, a daughter, named after her paternal grandmother, Margaret." Southey's Life and Correspondence, ii. 192.

[266] Southey's reply, which was not in the affirmative, has not been preserved. The joint-residence at Greta Hall began in September, 1803.

[267] Charles and Mary Lamb's visit to Greta Hall, which lasted three full weeks, must have extended from (about) August 12 to September 2, 1802. Letters of Charles Lamb, i. 180-184.

[268]

"Here melancholy, on the pale crags laid,
Might muse herself to sleep; or Fancy come,
Watching the mind with tender cozenage
And shaping things that are not."
"Coombe-Ellen, written in Radnorshire, September, 1798." "Poems of William Lisle Bowles," Galignani, p. 139. For "Melancholy, a Fragment," see Poetical Works, p. 34.

[269] I have not been able to verify this reference.

[270] "O my God! what enormous mountains there are close by me, and yet below the hill I stand on.... And here I am, lounded [i. e., sheltered],—so fully lounded,—that though the wind is strong and the clouds are hastening hither from the sea, and the whole air seaward has a lurid look, and we shall certainly have thunder,—yet here (but that I am hungered and provisionless), here I could be warm and wait, methinks, for to-morrow's sun—and on a nice stone table am I now at this moment writing to you—between 2 and 3 o'clock, as I guess. Surely the first letter ever written from the top of Sca Fell."

"After the thunder-storm I shouted out all your names in the sheep-fold—where echo came upon echo, and then Hartley and Derwent, and then I laughed and shouted Joanna. It leaves all the echoes I ever heard far, far behind, in number, distinctness and humanness of voice; and then, not to forget an old friend, I made them all say Dr. Dodd etc." MS. Journal, August 6, 1802. Compare Lamb's Latin letter of October 9, 1802:—

"Ista tua Carmina Chamouniana satis grandia esse mihi constat; sed hoc mihi nonnihil displicet, quod in iis illæ montium Grisosonum inter se responsiones totidem reboant anglicé, God, God, haud aliter atque temet audivi tuas [sic] montes Cumbrianas [sic] resonare docentes, Tod, Tod, nempe Doctorem infelicem: vocem certe haud Deum sonantem." Letters of Charles Lamb, i. 185. See, too, Canon Ainger's translation and note, ibid. p. 331. See, also, Southey's Letter to Grosvenor Bedford, January 9, 1804. Life and Correspondence, ii. 248.

[271] "The Spirit of Navigation and Discovery." "Bowles's Poetical Works," Galignani, p. 142.

[272] These lines form part of the poem addressed "To Matilda Betham. From a Stranger." The date of composition was September 9, 1802, the day before they were quoted in the letter to Sotheby. Poetical Works, p. 168.

[273] The "Hymn before Sunrise in the Vale of Chamouni" was first printed in the Morning Post, September 11, 1802. It was reprinted in the original issue of The Friend, No. xi. (October 16, 1809, pp. 174-176), and again in Sibylline Leaves, 1817. As De Quincey was the first to point out, Coleridge was indebted to the Swiss poetess, Frederica Brun, for the framework of the poem and for many admirable lines and images, but it was his solitary

walk on Scafell, and the consequent uplifting of spirit, which enabled him "to create the dry bones of the German outline into the fulness of life."

Coleridge will never lose his title of a Lake Poet, but of the ten years during which he was nominally resident in the Lake District, he was absent at least half the time. Of his greater poems there are but four, the second part of "Christabel," the "Dejection: an Ode," the "Picture," and the "Hymn before Sunrise," which take their colouring from the scenery of Westmoreland and Cumberland.

He was but twenty-six when he visited Ottery for the last time. It was in his thirty-fifth year that he bade farewell to Stowey and the Quantocks, and after he was turned forty he never saw Grasmere or Keswick again. Ill health and the res angusta domi are stern gaolers, but, if he had been so minded, he would have found a way to revisit the pleasant places in which he had passed his youth and early manhood. In truth, he was well content to be a dweller in "the depths of the huge city" or its outskirts, and like Lamb, he "could not live in Skiddaw." Poetical Works, p. 165, and Editor's Note, pp. 629, 630.

[274] Coleridge must have presumed on the ignorance of Sotheby and of his friends generally. He could hardly have passed out of Boyer's hands without having learned that Ἔστησε signifies, "He hath placed," not "He hath stood." But, like most people who have changed their opinions, he took an especial pride in proclaiming his unswerving allegiance to fixed principles. The initials S. T. C., Grecised and mistranslated, expressed this pleasing delusion, and the Greek, "Punic [sc. punnic] Greek," as he elsewhere calls it, might run the risk of detection.

[275] Parts III. and IV. of the "Three Graves"—were first published in The Friend, No. vi. Sept. 21, 1809. Parts I. and II. were published for the first time in The Poetical Works of Samuel Taylor Coleridge, Macmillan, 1893. The final version of this stanza (ll. 509-513) differs from that in the text. "A small blue sun" became "A tiny sun," and for "Ten thousand hairs of colour'd light" Coleridge substituted "Ten thousand hairs and threads of light." See Poetical Works, p. 92, and Editor's Note, pp. 589-591.

[276] The six essays to which he calls Estlin's attention are reprinted in Essays on His Own Times, ii. 478-585.

[277] The residence of Josiah Wedgwood.

[278] Paley's last work, "Natural Theology; or, Evidences of the Existence and Attributes of A Deity, collected from the Appearances of Nature," was published in 1802.

[279] For Southey's well known rejoinder to this "ebullience of schematism," see Life and Correspondence, ii. 220-223.

[280] Southey's correspondence contains numerous references to the historian Sharon Turner [1768-1847], and to William Owen, the translator of the Mabinogion and author of the Welsh Paradise Lost.

[281] It may be interesting to compare the following unpublished note from Coleridge's Scotch Journal with the well known passage in Dorothy Wordsworth's Journal of her tour in the Highlands (Memoir of Wordsworth, i. 235): "Next morning we went in the boat to the end of the lake, and so on by the old path to the Garrison to the Ferry House by Loch

Lomond, where now the Fall was in all its fury, and formed with the Ferry cottage, and the sweet Highland lass, a nice picture. The boat gone to the preaching we stayed all day in the comfortless hovel, comfortless, but the two little lassies did everything with such sweetness, and one of them, 14, with such native elegance. Oh! she was a divine creature! The sight of the boat, full of Highland men and women and children from the preaching, exquisitely fine. We soon reached E. Tarbet—all the while rain. Never, never let me forget that small herd-boy in his tartan-plaid, dim-seen on the hilly field, and long heard ere seen, a melancholy voice calling to his cattle! nor the beautiful harmony of the heath, and the dancing fern, and the ever-moving birches. That of itself enough to make Scotland visitable, its fields of heather giving a sort of shot silk finery in the apotheosis of finery. On Monday we went to Arrochar. Here I left W. and D. and returned myself to E. Tarbet, slept there, and now, Tuesday, Aug. 30, 1803, am to make my own way to Edinburgh."

Many years after he added the words: "O Esteese, that thou hadst from thy 22nd year indeed made thy own way and alone!"

[282]

A sweet and playful Highland girl,
As light and beauteous as a squirrel,
As beauteous and as wild!

Her dwelling was a lonely house,
A cottage in a heathy dell;
And she put on her gown of green
And left her mother at sixteen,
And followed Peter Bell.
Peter Bell, Part III.

[283] Margaret Southey, who was born in September, 1802, died in the latter part of August, 1803.

[284] The "Pains of Sleep" was published for the first time, together with "Christabel" and "Kubla Khan," in 1816. With the exception of the insertion of the remarkable lines 52-54, the first draft of the poem does not materially differ from the published version. A transcript of the same poem was sent to Poole in a letter dated October 3, 1803. Poetical Works, p. 170, and Editor's Note, pp. 631, 632.

[285] The Rev. Peter Elmsley, the well known scholar, who had been a school and college friend of Southey's, was at this time resident at Edinburgh. The Edinburgh Review had been founded the year before, and Elmsley was among the earliest contributors. His name frequently recurs in Southey's correspondence.

[286] Compare Southey's first impressions of Edinburgh, contained in a letter to Wynn, dated October 20, 1805: "You cross a valley (once a loch) by a high bridge, and the back of the old city appears on the edge of this depth—so vast, so irregular—with such an outline of roofs and chimneys, that it looks like the ruins of a giant's palace. I never saw anything so impressive as the first sight of this; there was a wild red sunset slanting along it." Selections from the Letters of R. Southey, i. 342.

[287] Compare Table Talk, for September 26, 1830, where a similar statement is made in almost the same words.

[288] The same sentence occurs in a letter to Sir G. Beaumont, dated September 22, 1803. Coleorton Letters, i. 6.

[289] The MS. of this letter was given to my father by the Rev. Dr. Wreford. I know nothing of the person to whom it was addressed, except that he was "Matthew Coates, Esq., of Bristol."

[290] Dr. Joseph Adams, the biographer of Hunter, who in 1816 recommended Coleridge to the care of Mr. James Gillman.

CXLIV. TO RICHARD SHARP.[1]

King's Arms, Kendal,
Sunday morning, January 15, 1804.

My dear Sir,—I give you thanks—and, that I may make the best of so poor and unsubstantial a return, permit me to say, that they are such thanks as can only come from a nature unworldly by constitution and by habit, and now rendered more than ever impressible by sudden restoration—resurrection I might say—from a long, long sick-bed. I had gone to Grasmere to take my farewell of William Wordsworth, his wife, and his sister, and thither your letters followed me. I was at Grasmere a whole month, so ill, as that till the last week I was unable to read your letters. Not that my inner being was disturbed; on the contrary, it seemed more than usually serene and self-sufficing; but the exceeding pain, of which I suffered every now and then, and the fearful distresses of my sleep, had taken away from me the connecting link of voluntary power, which continually combines that part of us by which we know ourselves to be, with that outward picture or hieroglyphic, by which we hold communion with our like—between the vital and the organic—or what Berkeley, I suppose, would call mind and its sensuous language. I had only just strength enough to smile gratefully on my kind nurses, who tended me with sister's and mother's love, and often, I well know, wept for me in their sleep, and watched for me even in their dreams. Oh, dear sir! it does a man's heart good, I will not say, to know such a family, but even to know that there is such a family. In spite of Wordsworth's occasional fits of hypochondriacal uncomfortableness,—from which, more or less, and at longer or shorter intervals, he has never been wholly free from his very childhood,—in spite of this hypochondriacal graft in his nature, as dear Wedgwood calls it, his is the happiest family I ever saw, and were it not in too great sympathy with my ill health—were I in good health, and their neighbour—I verily believe that the cottage in Grasmere Vale would be a proud sight for Philosophy. It is with no idle feeling of vanity that I speak of my importance to them; that it is I, rather than another, is almost an accident; but being so very happy within themselves they are too good, not the more, for that very reason, to want a friend and common object of love out of their household. I have met with several genuine Philologists, Philonoists, Physiophilists, keen hunters after knowledge and science; but truth and wisdom are higher names than these—and revering Davy, I am half angry with him for doing that which would make me laugh in another man—I mean, for prostituting and profaning the name of "Philosopher," "great Philosopher," "eminent Philosopher," etc., etc., etc., to every fellow who has made a lucky experiment, though the man should be Frenchified to the heart, and though the whole Seine, with all its filth and poison, flows in his veins and arteries.

Of our common friends, my dear sir, I flatter myself that you and I should agree in fixing on T. Wedgwood and on Wordsworth as genuine Philosophers—for I have often said (and no wonder, since not a day passes but the conviction of the truth of it is renewed in me, and with the conviction, the accompanying esteem and love), often have I said that T. Wedgwood's faults impress me with veneration for his moral and intellectual character more than almost any other man's virtues; for under circumstances like his, to have a fault only in that degree is, I doubt not, in the eye of God, to possess a high virtue. Who does not prize the Retreat of Moreau[2] more than all the straw-blaze of Bonaparte's victories? And then to make it (as Wedgwood really does) a sort of crime even to think of his faults by so many virtues retained, cultivated, and preserved in growth and blossom, in a climate—where now the gusts so rise and eddy, that deeply rooted must that be which is not snatched up and made a plaything of by them,—and, now, "the parching air burns frore."

W. Wordsworth does not excite that almost painfully profound moral admiration which the sense of the exceeding difficulty of a given virtue can alone call forth, and which therefore I feel exclusively towards T. Wedgwood; but, on the other hand, he is an object to be contemplated with greater complacency, because he both deserves to be, and is, a happy man; and a happy man, not from natural temperament, for therein lies his main obstacle, not by enjoyment of the good things of this world—for even to this day, from the first dawn of his manhood, he has purchased independence and leisure for great and good pursuits by austere frugality and daily self-denials; nor yet by an accidental confluence of amiable and happy-making friends and relatives, for every one near to his heart has been placed there by choice and after knowledge and deliberation; but he is a happy man, because he is a Philosopher, because he knows the intrinsic value of the different objects of human pursuit, and regulates his wishes in strict subordination to that knowledge; because he feels, and with a practical faith, the truth of that which you, more than once, my dear sir, have with equal good sense and kindness pressed upon me, that we can do but one thing well, and that therefore we must make a choice. He has made that choice from his early youth, has pursued and is pursuing it; and certainly no small part of his happiness is owing to this unity of interest and that homogeneity of character which is the natural consequence of it, and which that excellent man, the poet Sotheby, noticed to me as the characteristic of Wordsworth.

Wordsworth is a poet, a most original poet. He no more resembles Milton than Milton resembles Shakespeare—no more resembles Shakespeare than Shakespeare resembles Milton. He is himself and, I dare affirm that, he will hereafter be admitted as the first and greatest philosophical poet, the only man who has effected a complete and constant synthesis of thought and feeling and combined them with poetic forms, with the music of pleasurable passion, and with Imagination or the modifying power in that highest sense of the word, in which I have ventured to oppose it to Fancy, or the aggregating power—in that sense in which it is a dim analogue of creation—not all that we can believe, but all that we can conceive of creation.—Wordsworth is a poet, and I feel myself a better poet, in knowing how to honour him than in all my own poetic compositions, all I have done or hope to do; and I prophesy immortality to his "Recluse," as the first and finest philosophical poem, if only it be (as it undoubtedly will be) a faithful transcript of his own most august and innocent life, of his own habitual feelings and modes of seeing and hearing.—My dear sir! I began a letter with a heart, Heaven knows! how full of gratitude toward you—and I have flown off into a whole letter-full respecting Wedgwood and Wordsworth. Was it that my heart demanded an outlet for grateful feelings—for a long stream of them—and that I felt it would be oppressive to you if I wrote to you of yourself half of what I wished to write? Or was it that I knew I should be in sympathy with you, and that few subjects are more pleasing to you than a detail of the merits of two men, whom, I am sure, you esteem equally with myself—though accidents have thrown me, or rather Providence has placed me, in a closer connection with them, both as confidential friends and the one as my benefactor, and to whom I owe that my bed of sickness has not been in a house of want, unless I had bought the contrary at the price of my conscience by becoming a priest.

I leave this place this afternoon, having walked from Grasmere yesterday. I walked the nineteen miles through mud and drizzle, fog and stifling air, in four hours and thirty-five minutes, and was not in the least fatigued, so that you may see that my sickness has not much weakened me. Indeed, the suddenness and seeming perfectness of my recovery is really astonishing. In a single hour I have changed from a state that seemed next to death, swollen limbs, racking teeth, etc., to a state of elastic health, so that I have said, "If I have been dreaming, yet you, Wordsworth, have been awake." And Wordsworth has answered, "I could not expect any one to believe it who had not seen it." These changes have always been produced by sudden changes of the weather. Dry hot weather or dry frosty weather seem alike friendly to me, and my persuasion is strong as the life within me, that a year's residence in Madeira would renovate me. I shall spend two days in Liverpool, and hope to be in London, coach and coachman permitting, on Friday afternoon or Saturday at the furthest. And on this day week I look forward to the pleasure of thanking you personally, for I still hope to avail myself of your kind introductions. I mean to wait in London till a good vessel sails for Madeira; but of this when I see you.

Believe me, my dear sir, with grateful and affectionate thanks, your sincere friend,

S. T. Coleridge.

CXLV. TO THOMAS POOLE.

Kendal, Sunday, January 15, 1804.

My dear Poole,—My health is as the weather. That, for the last month, has been unusually bad, and so has my health. I go by the heavy coach this afternoon. I shall be at Liverpool tomorrow night. Tuesday, Wednesday, I shall stay there; not more certainly, for I have taken my place all the way to London, and this stay of two days is an indulgence and entered in the road-bill, so I expect to be in London on Friday evening about six o'clock, at the Saracen's Head, Snow Hill. Now my dearest friend! will you send a twopenny post letter directed, "Mr. Coleridge (Passenger in the Heavy Coach from Kendal and Liverpool), to be left at the bar, Saracen's Head, Snow Hill," informing me whether I can have a bed at your lodgings, or whether Mr. Rickman could let me have a bed for one or two nights,—for I have such a dread of sleeping at an Inn or Coffee house in London, that it quite unmans me to think of it. To love and to be beloved makes hothouse plants of us, dear Poole!

Though wretchedly ill, I have not yet been deserted by hope—less dejected than in any former illness—and my mind has been active, and not vaguely, but to that determinate purpose which has employed me the last three months, and I want only one fortnight steady reading to have got all my materials before me, and then I neither stir to the right nor to the left, so help me God! till the work is finished. Of its contents, the title will, in part, inform you, "Consolations and Comforts from the exercise and right application of the

Reason, the Imagination, the Moral Feelings, Addressed especially to those in sickness, adversity, or distress of mind, from speculative gloom,[3] etc."

I put that last phrase, though barbarous, for your information. I have puzzled for hours together, and could never hit off a phrase to express that idea, that is, at once neat and terse, and yet good English. The whole plan of my literary life I have now laid down, and the exact order in which I shall execute it, if God vouchsafe me life and adequate health; and I have sober though confident expectations that I shall render a good account of what may have appeared to you and others, a distracting manifoldness in my objects and attainments. You are nobly employed,—most worthily of you. You are made to endear yourself to mankind as an immediate benefactor: I must throw my bread on the waters. You sow corn and I plant the olive. Different evils beset us. You shall give me advice, and I will advise you, to look steadily at everything, and to see it as it is—to be willing to see a thing to be evil, even though you see, at the same time, that it is for the present an irremediable evil; and not to overrate, either in the convictions of your intellect, or in the feelings of your heart, the Good, because it is present to you, and in your power—and, above all, not to be too hasty an admirer of the Rich, who seem disposed to do good with their wealth and influence, but to make your esteem strictly and severely proportionate to the worth of the Agent, not to the value of the Action, and to refer the latter wholly to the Eternal Wisdom and Goodness, to God, upon whom it wholly depends, and in whom alone it has a moral worth.

I love and honour you, Poole, for many things—scarcely for anything more than that, trusting firmly in the rectitude and simplicity of your own heart, and listening with faith to its revealing voice, you never suffered either my subtlety, or my eloquence, to proselytize you to the pernicious doctrine of Necessity.[4] All praise to the Great Being who has graciously enabled me to find my way out of that labyrinth-den of sophistry, and, I would fain believe, to bring with me a better clue than has hitherto been known, to enable others to do the same. I have convinced Southey and Wordsworth; and W., as you know, was, even to extravagance, a Necessitarian. Southey never believed and abhorred the Doctrine, yet thought the argument for it unanswerable by human reason. I have convinced both of them of the sophistry of the argument, and wherein the sophism consists, viz., that all have hitherto—both the Necessitarians and their antagonists—confounded two essentially different things under one name, and in consequence of this mistake, the victory has been always hollow, in favor of the Necessitarians.

God bless you, and

S. T. Coleridge.

P. S. If any letter come to your lodgings for me, of course you will take care of it.

CXLVI. TO THE SAME.

[January 26, 1804.]

My dearest Poole,—I have called on Sir James Mackintosh,[5] who offered me his endeavours to procure me a place under him in India, of which endeavour he would not for a moment doubt the success; and assured me on his Honour, on his Soul!! (N. B. his

Honour!!) (N. B. his Soul!!) that he was sincere. Lillibullero ahoo! ahoo! ahoo! Good morning, Sir James!

I next called on Davy, who seems more and more determined to mould himself upon the Age, in order to make the Age mould itself upon him. Into this language at least I could have translated his conversation. Oh, it is a dangerous business this bowing of the head in the Temple of Rimmon; and such men I aptly christen Theo-mammonists, that is, those who at once worship God and Mammon. However, God grant better things of so noble a work of His! And, as I once before said, may that Serpent, the World, climb around the club which supports him, and be the symbol of healing; even as in Tooke's "Pantheon,"[6] you may see the thing done to your eyes in the picture of Esculapius. Well! now for business. I shall leave the note among the schedules. They will wonder, plain, sober people! what damn'd madcap has got among them; or rather I will put it under the letter just arrived for you, that at least it may perhaps be under the Rose.[7]

Well, once again. I will try to get at it, but I am landing on a surfy shore, and am always driven back upon the open sea of various thoughts.

I dine with Davy at five o'clock this evening at the Prince of Wales's Coffee House, Leicester Square, an he can give us three hours of his company; and I beseech you do make a point and come. God bless you, and may His Grace be as a pair of brimstone gloves to guard against dirty diseases from such bad company as you are keeping—Rose[8] and Thomas Poole!—!!!

S. T. Coleridge.

T. Poole, Esq., Parliament Office.

[Note in Poole's handwriting: "Very interesting jeu d'esprit, but not sent."]

CXLVII. TO THE WORDSWORTHS.

Dunmow, Essex, Wednesday night, half past 11,
February 8, 1804.

My dearest Friends,—I must write, or I shall have delayed it till delay has made the thought painful as of a duty neglected. I had meant to have kept a sort of journal for you, but I have not been calm enough; and if I had kept it, I should not have time to transcribe, for nothing can exceed the bustle I have been in from the day of my arrival in town. The only incident of any extraordinary interest was a direful quarrel between Godwin and me,[9] in which, to use his own phrase (unless Lamb suggested it to him), I "thundered and lightened with frenzied eloquence" at him for near an hour and a half. It ended in a reconciliation next day; but the affair itself, and the ferocious spirit into which a plusquam sufficit of punch had betrayed me, has sunk deep into my heart. Few events in my life have grieved me more, though the fool's conduct richly merited a flogging, but not with a scourge of scorpions. I wrote to Mrs. Coleridge the next day, when my mind was full of it, and, when you go into Keswick, she will detail the matter, if you have nothing better to talk of. My health has greatly improved, and rich and precious wines (of several of which I had never before heard the names) agree admirably with me, and I fully believe, most dear William! they would with you. But still I am as faithful a barometer, and previously to, and during all falling weather, am as asthmatic and stomach-twitched as when with you. I am a perfect conjuror as to the state of the weather, and it is such that I detected myself in being somewhat flattered at finding the infallibility of my uncomfortable feelings, as to falling weather, either coming or come. What Sicily may do for me I cannot tell, but Dalton,[10] the Lecturer on Natural Philosophy at the R. Institution, a man devoted to Keswick, convinced me that there was five times the duration of falling weather at Keswick compared with the flat of midland counties, and more than twice the gross quantity of water fallen. I have as yet been able to do nothing for myself. My plans are to try to get such an introduction to the Captain of the war-ship that shall next sail for Malta, as to be taken as his friend (from Malta to Syracuse is but six hours passage in a spallanza). At Syracuse I shall meet with a hearty welcome from Mr. Lecky, the Consul, and I hope to be able to have a letter from Lord Nelson to the Convent of Benedictines at Catania to receive and lodge me for such time as I may choose to stay. Catania is a pleasant town, with pleasant, hospitable inhabitants, at the foot of Etna, though fifteen miles, alas! from the woody region. Greenough[11] has read me an admirable, because most minute, journal of his Sights, Doings, and Done-untos in Sicily.

As to money, I shall avail myself of £105, to be repaid to you on the first of January, 1805, and another £100, to be employed in paying the Life Assurance, the bills at Keswick, Mrs. Fricker, next half year; and if any remain, to buy me comforts for my voyage, etc., Dante and a dictionary. I shall borrow part from my brothers, and part from Stuart. I can live a year at Catania (for I have no plan or desire of travelling except up and down Etna) for £100, and the getting back I shall trust to chance.

O my dear, dear friends! if Sicily should become a British island,—as all the inhabitants intensely desire it to be,—and if the climate agreed with you as well as I doubt not it will with me,—and if it be as much cheaper than even Westmoreland, as Greenough reports, and if I could get a Vice-Consulship, of which I have little doubt, oh, what a dream of happiness could we not realize! But mortal life seems destined for no continuous happiness, save that which results from the exact performance of duty; and blessed are you, dear William! whose path of duty lies through vine-trellised elm-groves, through Love and Joy and Grandeur. "O for one hour of Dundee!"[12] How often shall I sigh, "Oh! for one hour of 'The Recluse'!"

I arrived at Dunmow on Tuesday, and shall stay till Tuesday morning. You will direct No. 116 Abingdon St., Westminster. I was not received here with mere kindness; I was welcomed almost as you welcomed me when first I visited you at Racedown. And their solicitude and attention is enough to effeminate one. Indeed, indeed, they are kind and good people; and old Lady Beaumont, now eighty-six, is a sort of miracle for beauty and clear understanding and cheerfulness. The house is an old house by a tan-yard, with nothing remarkable but its awkward passages. We talk by the long hours about you and Hartley, Derwent, Sara, and Johnnie; and few things, I am persuaded, would delight them more than to live near you. I wish you would write out a sheet of verses for them, and I almost promised for you that you should send that delicious poem on the Highland Girl at Inversnade. But of more importance, incomparably, is it, that Mary and Dorothy should begin to transcribe all William's MS. poems for me. Think what they will be to me in Sicily! They should be written in pages and lettered up in parcels not exceeding two ounces and a quarter each, including the seal, and three envelopes, one to the Speaker, under that, one to John Rickman, Esqre, and under that, one to me. (Terrible mischief has happened from foolish people of R.'s acquaintance neglecting the middle envelope, so that the Speaker, opening his letter, finds himself made a letter smuggler to Nicholas Noddy or some other unknown gentleman.) But I will send you the exact form. The weight is not of much importance, but better not exceed two ounces and a quarter. I will write again as soon as I hear from you. In the mean time, God bless you, dearest William, Dorothy, Mary, S., and my godchild.

S. T. Coleridge.

CXLVIII. TO HIS WIFE.

February 19, 1804.

"J. Tobin, Esqre.,[13] No. 17 Barnard's Inn, Holborn. For Mr. Coleridge." So, if you wish me to answer it by return of post: but if it be of no consequence, whether I receive it four hours sooner or four hours later, then direct "Mr. Lambe,[14] East India House, London."

I did not receive your last letter written on the "very, very windy and very cold Sunday night," till yesterday afternoon, owing to Poole's neglect and forgetfulness. But Poole is one of those men who have one good quality, namely, that they always do one thing at a time; but who likewise have one defect, that they can seldom think but of one thing at a time. For instance, if Poole is intent on his matter while he is speaking, he cannot give the least attention to his language or pronunciation, in consequence of which there is no one error in his dialect which he has ever got rid of. My mind is in general of the contrary make. I too often do nothing, in consequence of being impressed all at once (or so rapidly consecutively as to appear all at once) by a variety of impressions. If there are a dozen people at table I hear, and cannot help giving some attention to what each one says, even though there should be three or four talking at once. The detail of the Good and the Bad, of the two different makes of mind, would form a not uninteresting brace of essays in a Spectator or Guardian.

You will of course repay Southey instantly all the money you may have borrowed either for yourself or for Mr. Jackson,[15] and do not forget to remember that a share of the wine-bill belonged to me. Likewise when you pay Mr. Jackson, you will pay him just as if he had not had any money from you. Is it half a year? or a year and a half's rent that we owe him? Did we pay him up to July last? If we did, then, were I you, I would now pay him the whole year's rent up to July next, and tell him that you shall not want the twenty pounds which you have lent him till the beginning of May. Remember me to him in the most affectionate manner, and say how sincerely I condole with him on his sprain. Likewise, and as affectionately, remember me to Mrs. Wilson.

It gave me pain and a feeling of anxious concern on our own account, as well as Mr. Jackson's, to find him so distressed for money. I fear that he will be soon induced to sell the house.

Now for our darling Hartley. I am myself not at all anxious or uneasy respecting his habits of idleness; but I should be very unhappy if he were to go to the town school, unless there were any steady lad that Mr. Jackson knew and could rely on, who went to the same school regularly, and who would be easily induced by half-a-crown once in two or three months to take care of him, let him always sit by him, and to whom you should instruct the child to yield a certain degree of obedience. If this can be done (and you will read what I say to Mr. Jackson), I have no great objection to his going to school and making a fair trial of it. Oh, may God vouchsafe me health that he may go to school to his own father! I exceedingly wish that there were any one in Keswick who would give him a little instruction in the elements of drawing. I will go to-morrow and enquire for some very elementary book, if there be any, that proposes to teach it without the assistance of a drawing master, and which you might make him read to you instead of his other books. Sir G. Beaumont was very much pleased and interested by Hartley's promise of attachment to his darling Art. If I can find the book I will send it off instantly, together with the Spillĕkins (Spielchen, or Gamelet, I suppose), a German refinement of our Jack Straw. You or some one of your sisters will be so good as to play with Hartley, at first, that Derwent may learn it. Little Albert at Dr. Crompton's, and indeed all the children, are quite spillekin mad. It is certainly an excellent game to teach children steadiness of hand and quickness of eye, and a good opportunity to impress upon them the beauty of strict truth, when it is against their own interest, and to give them a pride in it, and habits of it,—for the slightest perceptible motion produced in any of the spillekins, except the one attempted to be crooked off the heap, destroys that turn, and there is a good deal of foresight executed in knowing when to give it a lusty pull, so as to move the spillekins under, if only you see that your adversary who will take advantage of this pull, will himself not succeed, and yet by his or the second pull put the spillekin easily in the power of the third pull.... I am now writing in No. 44 Upper Titchfield Street, where I have for the first time been breakfasting with A. Welles, who seems a kind, friendly man, and instead of recommending any more of his medicine to me, advises me to persevere in and expedite my voyage to a better climate, and has been very pressing with me to take up my home at his house. To-morrow I dine with Mr. Rickman at his own house; Wednesday I dine with him at Tobin's. I shall dine with Mr. Welles to-day, and thence by eight o'clock to the Royal Institution to the lecture.[16] On Thursday afternoon, two o'clock to the lecture, and Saturday night, eight o'clock to the lecture. On Friday, I spend the day with Davy certainly, and I hope with Mr. Sotheby likewise. To-morrow or Wednesday I expect to know certainly what my plans are to be, whither to go and when, and whether the intervening space will make it worth my while to go to Ottery, or whether I shall go back to Dunmow, and return with Sir George and Lady B. when they come to their house in Grosvenor Square. I cannot express to you how very, very affectionate the behaviour of these good people has been to me; and how they seem to love by anticipation those very few whom I love. If Southey would but permit me to copy that divine passage of his "Madoc,"[17] respecting the Harp of the Welsh Bard, and its imagined divinity, with the Two Savages, or any other detachable passage, or to transcribe his "Kehama," I will pledge myself that Sir George Beaumont and Lady B. will never suffer a single individual to hear or see a single line, you saying that it is to be kept sacred to them, and not to be seen by any one else.

[No signature.]

CXLIX. TO ROBERT SOUTHEY.

Rickman's Office, H. of Commons,
February 20, 1804, Monday noon.

Dear Southey,—The affair with Godwin began thus. We were talking of reviews, and bewailing their ill effects. I detailed my plan for a review, to occupy regularly the fourth side of an evening paper, etc., etc., adding that it had been a favourite scheme with me for two years past. Godwin very coolly observed that it was a plan which "no man who had a spark of honest pride" could join with. "No man, not the slave of the grossest egotism, could unite in," etc. Cool and civil! I asked whether he and most others did not already do what I proposed in prefaces. "Aye! in prefaces; that is quite a different thing." I then adverted to the extreme rudeness of the speech with regard to myself, and added that it was not only a very rough, but likewise a very mistaken opinion, for I was nearly if not quite sure that it had received the approbation both of you and of Wordsworth. "Yes, sir! just so! of Mr. Southey—just what I said," and so on mōrĕ Godwiniāno in language so ridiculously and exclusively appropriate to himself, that it would have made you merry. It was even as if he was looking into a sort of moral looking-glass, without knowing what it was, and, seeing his own very, very Godwinship, had by a merry conceit christened it in your name, not without some annexment of me and Wordsworth. I replied by laughing in the first place at the capricious nature of his nicety, that what was gross in folio should become double-refined in octavo foolscap or pickpocket quartos, blind slavish egotism in small pica, manly discriminating self-respect in double primer, modest as maiden's blushes between boards, or in calf-skin, and only not obscene in naked sheets. And then in a deep and somewhat sarcastic tone, tried to teach him to speak more reverentially of his betters, by stating what and who they were, by whom honoured, by whom depreciated. Well! this gust died away. I was going home to look over his Duncity; he begged me to stay till his return in half an hour. I, meaning to take nothing more the whole evening, took a crust of bread, and Mary Lamb made me a glass of punch of most deceitful strength. Instead of half an hour, Godwin stayed an hour and a half. In came his wife, Mrs. Fenwick,[18] and four young ladies, and just as Godwin returned, supper came in, and it was now useless to go (at supper I was rather a mirth-maker than merry). I was disgusted at heart with the grossness and vulgar insanocecity of this dim-headed prig of a philosophocide, when, after supper, his ill stars impelled him to renew the contest. I begged him not to goad me, for that I feared my feelings would not long remain in my power. He (to my wonder and indignation) persisted (I had not deciphered the cause), and then, as he well said, I did "thunder and lighten at him" with a vengeance for more than an hour and a half. Every effort of self-defence only made him more ridiculous. If I had been Truth in person, I could not have spoken more accurately; but it was Truth in a war-chariot, drawn by the three Furies, and the reins had slipped out of the goddess's hands!... Yet he did not absolutely give way till that stinging contrast which I drew between him as a man, as a writer, and a benefactor of society, and those of whom he had spoken so irreverently. In short, I suspect that I seldom, at any time and for so great a length of time, so continuously displayed so much power, and do hope and trust that never did I display one half the scorn and ferocity. The next morning, the moment when I awoke, O mercy! I did feel like a very wretch. I got up and immediately wrote and sent off by a porter, a letter, I dare affirm an affecting and eloquent letter to him, and since then have been working for him, for I was heart-smitten with the recollection that I had said all, all in the presence of his wife. But if I had known all I now know, I will not say that I should not have apologised, but most certainly I should not have made such an apology, for he confessed to Lamb that he should not have persisted in irritating me, but that Mrs. Godwin had twitted him for his prostration before me, as if he was afraid to say his life was his own in my presence. He admitted, too, that although he never to the very last suspected that I was tipsy, yet he saw clearly that something unusual ailed me, and that I had not been my natural self the whole evening. What a poor creature! To attack a man who had been so kind to him at the instigation of such a woman![19] And what a woman to instigate him to quarrel with me, who with as much power as any, and more than most of his acquaintances, had been perhaps the only one who had never made a butt of him—who had uniformly spoken respectfully to him. But it is past! And I trust will teach me wisdom in future.

I have undoubtedly suffered a great deal from a cowardice in not daring to repel unassimilating acquaintances who press forward upon my friendship; but I dare aver, that if the circumstances of each particular case were examined, they would prove on the whole honourable to me rather than otherwise. But I have had enough and done enough. Hereafter I shall show a different face, and calmly inform those who press upon me that my health, spirits, and occupation alike make it necessary for me to confine myself to the society of those with whom I have the nearest and highest connection. So help me God! I will hereafter be quite sure that I do really and in the whole of my heart esteem and like a man before I permit him to call me friend.

I am very anxious that you should go on with your "Madoc." If the thought had happened to suggest itself to you originally and with all these modifications and polypus tendrils with which it would have caught hold of your subject, I am afraid that you would not have made the first voyage as interesting at least as it ought to be, so as to preserve entire the fit proportion of interest. But go on!

I shall call on Longman as soon as I receive an answer from him to a note which I sent....

God bless you and

S. T. Coleridge.

P. S. I have just received Sara's four lines added to my brother George's letter, and cannot explain her not having received my letters. If I am not mistaken I have written three or four times: upon an average I have written to Greta Hall once every five days since I left Liverpool—if you will divide the letters, one to each five days. I will write to my brother immediately. I wrote to Sara from Dunmow; to you instantly on my return, and now again. I do not deserve to be scolded at present. I met G. Burnett the day before yesterday in Lincoln's Inn Fields, so nervous, so helpless with such opium-stupidly-wild eyes.

Oh, it made the place one calls the heart feel as it was going to ache.

CL. TO HIS WIFE.

Mr. J. C. Motley's, Thomas Street, Portsmouth,
Sunday, April 1, 1804.

My dear Sara,—I am waiting here with great anxiety for the arrival of the Speedwell. The Leviathan, Man of War, our convoy, has orders to sail with the first fair wind, and whatever wind can bring in the Speedwell will carry out the Leviathan, unless she have other orders than those generally known. I have left the Inn, and its crumena-mulga natio, and am only at the expense of a lodging at half a guinea a week, for I have all my meals at Mr. Motley's, to whom a letter from Stuart introduced me, and who has done most especial honour to the introduction. Indeed he could not well help, for Stuart in his letter called me his very, very particular friend, and that every attention would sink more into his heart than one offered to himself or his brother. Besides, you know it is no new thing for people to take sudden and hot likings to me. How different Sir G. B.! He disliked me at first. When I am in better spirits and less flurried I will transcribe his last letter. It breathed the very soul of calm and manly yet deep affection.

Hartley will receive his and Derwent's Spillekins with a letter from me by the first waggon that leaves London after Wednesday next.

My dear Sara! the mother, the attentive and excellent mother of my children must needs be always more than the word friend can express when applied to a woman. I pray you, use no word that you use with reluctance. Yet what we have been to each other, our understandings will not permit our hearts to forget! God knows, I weep tears of blood, but so it is! For I greatly esteem and honour you. Heaven knows if I can leave you really comfortable in your circumstances I shall meet Death with a face, which I feel at the moment I say it, it would rather shock than comfort you to imagine.

My health is indifferent. I am rather endurably unwell than tolerably well. I will write Southey to-morrow or next day, though Motley rides and drives me about sightseeing so as to leave me but little time. I am not sure that I shall see the Isle of Wight.

Write to Wordsworth. Inform him that I have received all and everything and will write him very soon, as soon as I can command spirits and time.... Motley can send off all letters to Malta under Government covers. You direct, therefore, at all times merely to me at Mr. J. C. Motley's, Portsmouth.

My very dear Sara, may God Almighty bless you and your affectionate

S. T. Coleridge.

I mourn for poor Mary.

CLI. TO ROBERT SOUTHEY.

Off Oporto and the coast of Portugal,
Monday noon, April 16, 1804.

My dear Southey,—I was thinking long before daylight this morning, that I ought, spite of toss and tumble and cruel rocking, to write a few letters in the course of this and the three following days; at the end of which, if the northwest wind still blows behind, we may hope to be at Gibraltar. I have two or three very unpleasant letters to write, and I was planning whether I should not begin with these, have them off my hands and thoughts, in short, whistle them down into the sea, and then take up the paper, etc., a whole man. When, lo! I heard the Captain above deck talking of Oporto, slipped on my greatcoat and went shoeless up to have a look. And a beautiful scene verily it was and is! The high land of Portugal, and the mountain land behind it, and behind that fair mountains with blue pyramids and cones. By the glass I could distinguish the larger buildings in Oporto, a scrambling city, part of it, seemingly, walls washed by the sea, part of it upon hills. At first view, it looked much like a vast brick kiln in a sandy, clayey country on a hot summer afternoon; seen more distinctly, it gave the nobler idea of a ruined city in a wilderness, its houses and streets lying low in ruins under its ruined walls, and a few temples and palaces standing untouched. But over all the sea between us and the land, short of a stone's throw on the left of the vessel, there is such a delicious warm olive green, almost yellow, on the water, and now it has taken in the vessel, and its boundary is a gunshot to my right, and one fine vessel exactly on its edge. This, though occasioned by the impurity of the nigh shore and the disemboguing rivers, forms a home scene; it is warm and landlike. The air is balmy and genial, and all that the fresh breeze can do can scarcely keep under its vernal warmth. The country round about Oporto seems darkly wooded; and in the distant gap far behind and below it on the curve of that high ridge forming a gap, I count seventeen conical and pyramidal summits; below that the high hills are saddlebacked. (In picturesque cant I ought to have said but below that, etc.) To me the saddleback is a pleasant form which it never would have occurred to me to christen by that name. Tents and marquees with little points and summits made by the tent-poles suggest a more striking likeness. Well! I need not say that the sight of the coast of Portugal made it impossible for me to write to any one before I had written to you—I now seeing for the first time a country you love so dearly. But you, perhaps, are not among my mountains! God Almighty grant that you may not. Yes! you are in London: all is well, and Hartley has a younger sister than tiny Sally. If it be so, call her Edith—Edith by itself—Edith. But somehow or other I would rather it were a boy, then let nothing, I conjure you, no false compliment to another, no false feeling indulged in yourself, deprive your eldest son of his father's name. Such was ever the manner of our forefathers, and there is a dignity, a self-respect, or an awful, preëminently self-referring event in the custom, that makes it well worthy of our imitation. I would have done [so], but that from my earliest years I have had a feeling of dislike and disgust connected with my own Christian name— such a vile short plumpness, such a dull abortive smartness in the first syllable, and this so harshly contrasted by the obscurity and indefiniteness of the syllabic vowel, and the feebleness of the uncovered liquid with which it ends, the wobble it makes, and struggling between a dis- and a tri-syllable, and the whole name sounding as if you were abeeceeing S. M. U. L. Altogether, it is, perhaps, the worst combination of which vowels and consonants are susceptible. While I am writing we are in 41° 10m. latitude, and are almost three leagues from land; at one time we were scarcely one league from it, and about a quarter of an hour ago, the whole country looked so very like the country from Hutton Moor to Saddleback and the adjoining part of Skiddaw.

I cannot help some anxious feelings respecting you, nor some superstitious twitches within, as if it were wrong at this distance to write so prospectively and with such particularization of that which is contingent, which may be all otherwise. But—God forbid! and, surely, hope is less ominous than fear. We set sail from St. Helier's, April 9th, Monday morning, having dropped down thither from Spithead on Sunday evening. We lost twenty-six hours of fair wind before our commodore gave the signal—our brig, a most excellent and first-rate sailor, but laden deep with heavy goods (eighty-four large cannon for Trieste in the hold), which makes it rock most cruelly. I can only—

Wed. April 18. I was going to say I can only compare it to a wench kept at home on some gay day to nurse a fretful infant and who, having long rocked it in vain, at length rocks it in spite.... But though the rough weather and the incessant rocking does not disease me, yet the damn'd rocking depresses one inconceivably, like hiccups or itching; it is troublesome and impertinent and forces you away from your thoughts like the presence and gossip of an old aunt, or long-staying visitor, to two lovers. Oh with what envy have I gazed at our commodore, the Leviathan of seventy-four guns, the majestic and beautiful creature sailing right before us, sometimes half a mile, oftener a furlong (for we are always first), with two or at most three topsails that just bisect the naked masts—as much naked mast above as below, upright, motionless as a church with its steeple, as though it moved by its will, as though its speed were spiritual, the being and essence without the body of motion, or as though the distance passed away by it and the objects of its pursuit hurried onward to it! In all other respects I cannot be better off, except perhaps the two passengers; the one a gay, worldly-minded fellow, not deficient in sense or judgment, but inert to everything except gain and eating; the other, a woman once housekeeper in General Fox's family, a creature with a horrible superfluity of envelope, a monopolist and patentee of flabby flesh, or rather fish. Indeed, she is at once fish, flesh, and fowl, though no chicken. But, ... to see the man eat and this Mrs. Carnosity talk about it! "I must have that little potato" (baked in grease under the meat), "it looks so smilingly at me." "Do cut me, if you please" (for she is so fat she cannot help herself), "that small bit, just there, sir! a leetle, tiny bit below if you please." "Well, I have brought plenty of pickles, I always think," etc. "I have always three or four jars of brandy cherries with me: for with boil'd rice now," etc., "for I always think," etc. And true enough, if it can be called thinking, she does always think upon some little damned article of eating that belongs to the housekeeper's cupboard's locker. And then her plaintive yawns, such a mixture of moan and petted child's dry cry, or try at a cry in them. And then she said to me this morning, "How unhappy, I always think, one always is, when there is nothing and nobody as one may say, about one to amuse one. It makes me so nervous." She eats, drinks, snores, and simply the being stupid, and silly, and vacant the learned body calls nervous. Shame on me for talking about her! The sun is setting so exactly behind my back that a ball from it would strike the stem of the vessel against which my back rests. But sunsets are not so beautiful, I think, at sea as on land. I am sitting at my desk, namely the rudder-case, on the duck coop, the ducks quacking at my legs. The chicken and duck coops run thus and so inclose on three sides the rudder-case. But now immediately that the sun has sunk, the sea runs high, and the vessel begins its old trick of rocking, which it had intermitted the whole day—the second intermission only since our voyage. Oh, how glad I was to see Cape Mondego, and then yesterday the Rock of Lisbon and the fine mountains at its interior extremity, which I conceived to be Cintra! Its outline from the sea is something like this

and just at A. where the fine stony M. begins, with a C. lying on its back, is a village or villages, and before we came abreast of this, we saw far inland, seemingly close by, several breasted peaks, two towers, and, by the glass, three, of a very large building, be it convent or palace. However, I knew you had seen all these places over and over again. The dome-shaped mountain or Cape Esperichel, between Lisbon and Cape St. Vincent, is one of the finest I ever saw; indeed all the mountains have a noble outline. We sail on at a wonderful rate, and considering that we are in convoy, shall have made a most lucky voyage to Gibraltar, if we are not becalmed and taken in the Gut; for we shall be there to-morrow afternoon if the wind hold, and have gone it in ten days. It is unlucky to prophesy good things, but if we have as good fortune in the Mediterranean, instead of nine or eleven weeks, we may reach Malta in a month or five weeks, including the week which we shall most probably stay at Gibraltar. I shall keep the letters open till we arrive there, simply put two strokes under the word "Gibraltar," and close up the letter, as I may gain thereby a fortnight's post. You will not expect to hear from me again till we get to Malta. I had hoped to have done something during my voyage; at all events, to have written some letters, etc. But what with the rains, the incessant rocking, and my consequent ill health or stupefaction, I have done little else than read through the Italian Grammar. I took out with me some of the finest wine and the oldest in the kingdom, some marvellous brandy, and rum twenty years old, and excepting a pint of wine, which I had mulled at two different times, and instantly ejected again, I have touched nothing but lemonade from the day we set sail to the present time. So very little does anything grow into a habit with me! This I should say to poor Tobin, who continued advising and advising to the last moment. O God, he is a good fellow, but this rage of advising and discussing character, and (as almost all men of strong habitual health have the trick of doing) of finding out the cause of everybody's ill health in some one malpractice or other. This, and the self-conceit and presumption necessarily generated by it, added to his own marvellous genius at utterly misunderstanding what he hears, and transposing words often in a manner that would be ludicrous if one did not suspect that his blindness had a share in producing it—all this renders him a sad mischief-maker, and with the best intentions, a manufacturer and propagator of calumnies. I had no notion of the extent of the mischief till I was last in town. I was low, even to sinking, when I was at the Inn. Stuart, best, kindest man to me! was with me, and Lamb, and Sir G. B.'s valet. But Tobin fastened upon me, and advised and reproved, and just before I stepped into the coach, reminded me of a debt of ten pounds which I had borrowed of him for another person, an intimate friend of his, on the condition that I was not to repay him till I could do it out of my own purse, not borrowing of another, and not embarrassing myself—in his very words, "till he wanted it more than I." I was calling to Stuart in order to pay the sum, but he stopped me with fervour, and, fully convinced that he did it only in the rage of admonition, I was vexed that it had angered me. Therefore say nothing of it, for really he is at bottom a good man.

I dare say nothing of home. I will write to Sara from Malta, the moment of my arrival, if I have not time to write from Gibraltar. One of you write to me by the regular post, "S. T. Coleridge, Esqre. Dr. Stoddart's, Malta:" the other to me at Mr. J. C. Motley's, Portsmouth, that I may see whether Motley was right or no, and which comes first.

God bless you all and

S. T. Coleridge.

Remember me kindly to Mr. Jackson, Mrs. Wilson, to the Calverts and Mrs. Wilkinson, to Mary Stamper, etc.

CLII. TO DANIEL STUART.

On board the Speedwell, at anchor in the Bay of Gibraltar,
Saturday night, April 21, 1804.

My dear Stuart,—We dropped anchor half a mile from the landing place of the Rock of Gibraltar on Thursday afternoon between four and five; a most prosperous voyage of eleven days....

Since we anchored I have passed nearly the whole of each day in scrambling about on the back of the rock, among the monkeys. I am a match for them in climbing, but in hops and flying leaps they beat me. You sometimes see thirty or forty together of these our poor relations, and you may be a month on the rock and go to the back every day and not see one. Oh, my dear friend! it is a most interesting place, this! A rock which thins as it rises up, so that you can sit a-straddle on almost any part of its summit, between two and three miles from north to south.

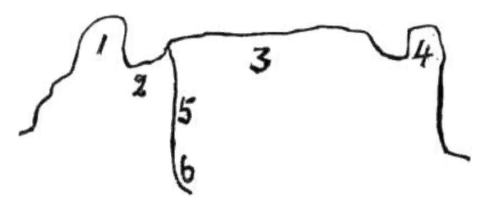

Rude as this line is, it gives you the outline of its appearance, from the sea close to it, tolerably accurately; only, in nature, it gives you very much the idea of a rude statue of a lion couchant, like that in the picture of the Lion and the Gnat, in the common spelling-books, or of some animal with a great dip in the neck. The lion's head [turns] towards the Spanish, his stiffened tail (4) to the African coast. At (5) a range of Moorish towers and wall begins; and at (6) the town begins, the Moorish wall running straight down by the side of it. Above the town, little gardens and neat small houses are scattered here and there, wherever they can force a bit of gardenable ground; and in these are poplars, with a profusion of geraniums and other flowers unknown to me; and their fences are most commonly that strange vegetable monster, the prickly aloe; its leaves resembling the head of a battledore, or the wooden wings of a church-cherub, and one leaf growing out of another. Under the Lion's Tail is Europa Point, which is full of gardens and pleasant trees; but the highest head of this mountain is a heap of rocks, with the palm-trees growing in vast quantities in their interstices, with many flowering weeds very often peeping out of the small holes or slits in the body of the rock, just as if they were growing in a bottle. To have left England only eleven days ago, with two flannel waistcoats on, and two others over them; with two flannel drawers under cloth pantaloons, and a thick pair of yarn stockings; to have had no temptation to lay any part of these aside during the whole voyage, and now to find myself in the heat of an English summer, among flowers, and seeking shade, and courting the sea-breezes; all the trees in rich foliage, and the corn knee-high, and so exquisitely green! and to find myself forced to retain only one flannel waistcoat, and roam about in a pair of silk stockings and nankeen pantaloons, is a delightful transition. How I shall bear the intensity of a Maltese or even a Sicilian summer I cannot guess; but if I get over it, I am confident, from what I have experienced the last four days, that their late autumn and winter will almost re-create me. I could fill a fresh sheet with the description of the singular faces, dresses, manners, etc., etc., of the Spaniards, Moors, Jews (who have here a peculiar dress resembling a college dress), Greeks, Italians, English, etc., that meet in the hot crowded streets of the town, or walk under the aspen poplars that form an Exchange in the very centre. But words would do nothing. I am sure that any young man who has a turn for character-painting might pass a year on the Rock with infinite advantage. A dozen plates by Hogarth from this town! We are told that we shall not sail to-morrow evening. The Leviathan leaves us and goes to join the fleet, and the Maidstone Frigate is to convoy us to

Malta. When you write, send one letter to me at Mr. J. C. Motley's, Portsmouth, and another by the post to me at Dr. Stoddart's,[20] Malta, that I may see which comes first. God grant that my present health may continue, and then my after-letters will be better worth the postage. But even this scrawl will not be unwelcome to you, since it tells you that I am safe, improving in my health, and ever, ever, my dear Stuart, with true affection, and willing gratitude, your sincere friend,

S. T. Coleridge.

In the diary of his voyage on the Speedwell Coleridge records at greater length and in a more impassioned strain his first impressions of Gibraltar. "Saturday, April 21st, went again on shore, walked up to the furthermost signal-house, the summit of that third and last segment of the mountain ridge which looks over the blue sea to Africa. The mountains around me did not anywhere arrange themselves strikingly, and few of their shapes were striking. One great pyramidal summit far above the rest, on the coast of Spain, and an uncouth form, an old Giant's Head and shoulders, looking in upon us from Africa far inland, were the most impressive; but the sea was so blue, calm, sunny, so majestic a lake where it is enshored by mountains, and, where it is not [enshored], having its indefiniteness the more felt from those huge mountain boundaries, which yet by their greatness prepared the mind for the sublimity of unbounded ocean—altogether it reposed in the brightness and quietness of the noon—majestic, for it was great with an inseparable character of unity, and, thus, the more touching to me who had looked from far loftier mountains over a far more manifold landscape, the fields and habitations of Englishmen, children of one family, one religion, and that my own, the same language and manners—by every hill, by every river some sweet name familiar to my ears, or, if first heard, remembered as soon as heard! But here, on this side of me, Spaniards, a degraded race that dishonour Christianity; on the other, Moors of many nations, wretches that dishonour human nature! If any one were near me and could tell me, 'that mountain yonder is called so and so, and at its foot runs such and such a river,' oh, with how blank an ear should I listen to sounds which probably my tongue could not repeat, and which I should be sure to forget, and take no pleasure in remembering! And the Rock itself, on which I stand (nearly the same in length as our Carrock, but not so high, nor one tenth as wide), what a complex Thing! At its feet mighty ramparts establishing themselves in the sea with their huge artillery, hollow trunks of iron where Death and Thunder sleep; the gardens in deep moats between lofty and massive walls; a town of all nations and all languages—close below me, on my left, fields and gardens and neat small mansions—poplars, cypresses, and willow-leaved aspens, with fences of prickly aloe—strange plant that does not seem to be alive, but to have been so, a thing fantastically carved in wood, and coloured—some hieroglyphic or temple ornament of undiscovered meaning. On my right and immediately with and around me white stone above stone, an irregular heap of marble rocks, with flowers growing out of the holes and fissures, and palmettoes everywhere ... beyond these an old Moorish tower, and then galleries and halls cut out by human labour out of the dense hard rock, with enormous cannon the apertures for which no eye could distinguish, from the sea or the land below them, from the nesting-holes of seafowl. On the north side, aside these, one absolutely perpendicular precipice, the absolute length of the Rock, at its highest a precipice of 1,450 feet—the whole eastern side an unmanageable mass of stones and weeds, save one place where a perpendicular precipice of stone slants suddenly off in a swelling slope of sand like the Screes on Wastwater. The other side of this rock 5,000 men in arms, and no less than 10,000 inhabitants—in this [side] sixty or seventy apes! What a multitude, an almost discordant complexity of associations! The Pillars of Hercules, Calpe, and Abyla, the realms of Masinissa, Jugurtha, and Syphax: Spain, Gibraltar: the Dey of Algiers, dusky Moor and black African, and others. Quiet it is to the eye, and to the heart, which in it will entrance itself in the present vision, and know nothing, feel nothing, but the abiding things of Nature, great, calm, majestic, and one! From the road I climbed up among the rocks, crushing the tansy, the strong smell of which the open air reconciled to me. I reached the 'striding edge,' where, as I sate, I fell into the above musing."

CLIII. TO HIS WIFE.

[Malta,] June, 1804.

[My dear Sara,]—[I wrote] to Southey from Gibraltar, directing you to open the letter in case Southey should be in town. You received it, I trust, and learnt from it that I had been pretty well, and that we had had a famous quick passage. At Gibraltar we stayed five days, and so lost our fair wind, and [during our] after-voyage to Malta [there] was [a] storm, that carried away our main yard, etc., long dead calms, every rope of the whole ship reflected in the bright, soft blue sea, and light winds, often varying every quarter of an hour, and more often against us than for us. We were the best sailing vessel in the whole convoy; but every day we had to lie by and wait for the laggards. This is very disheartening; likewise the frequent danger in light winds or calms, or in foggy weather of running foul of each other is another heavy inconvenience of convoy, and, in case of a deep calm in a narrow sea, as in the Gut of Gibraltar and in the Archipelago, etc., where calms are most common, a privateering or piratical row-boat might board you and make slaves of you under the very nose of the man-of-war, which would lie a lifeless hulk on the smooth water. For these row-boats, mounting from one to four or five guns, would instantly sink a man-of-war's boat, and one of them, last war, had very nearly made a British frigate strike. I mention these facts because it is a common notion that going under convoy you are "as snug as a bug in a rug." If I had gone without convoy on board the Speedwell, we should have reached Malta in twenty days from the day I left Portsmouth, but, however, we were congratulated on having had a very good passage for the time of the year, having been only forty days including our stay at Gibraltar; and if there be inconvenience in a convoy, I have reason to know and to be grateful for its advantages. The whole of the voyage from Gibraltar to Malta, excepting the four or five last days, I was wretchedly unwell.... The harbour at Valetta is narrow as the neck of a bottle in the entrance; but instantly opens out into a lake with tongues of land, capes, one little island, etc., etc., where the whole navy of England might lie as in a dock in the worst of weather. All around its banks, in the form of an amphitheatre, rise the magnificent houses of Valetta, and its two over-the-water towns, Burmola and Flavia (which are to Valetta what the Borough is to London). The houses are all lofty and built of fine white freestone, something like Bath, only still whiter and newer looking, yet the windows, from the prodigious thickness of the walls, being all out of sight, the whole appeared to me as Carthage to Æneas, a proud city, well nigh but not quite finished. I walked up a long street of good breadth, all a flight of stairs (no place for beast or carriage, each broad stair composed of a cement-sand of terra pozzolana, hard and smooth as the hardest pavement of smooth rock by the seaside and very like it). I soon found out Dr. Stoddart's house, which seemed a large pile of building. He was not at home, but I stayed for him, and in about two hours he came, and received me with an explosion of surprise and welcome—more fun than affection in the manner, but just as I wished it.... Yesterday and to-day I have been pretty well. In a hot climate, now that the glass is high as 80 in the shade, the healthiest persons are liable to fever on the least disagreement of food with the first passages, and my general health is, I would fain believe, better on the whole.... I will try the most scrupulous regimen of diet and exercise; and I rejoice to find that the heat, great as it is, does not at all annoy me. In about a fortnight I shall probably take a trip into Sicily, and spend the next two or three months in some cooler and less dreary place, and return in September. For eight months in the year the climate of Malta is delightful, but a drearier place eye never saw. No stream in the whole island, only one place of springs, which are conveyed by aqueducts and supply the island with about one third of its water; the other two thirds they depend for upon the rain. And the reservoirs under the houses, walls, etc., to preserve the rain are stupendous! The tops of all the houses are flat, and covered with that smooth, hard composition, and on these and everywhere where rain can fall are channels and pipes to conduct it to the reservoirs. Malta is about twenty miles by twelve—a mere rock of freestone. In digging out this they find large quantities of vegetable soil. They separate it, and with the stones they build their houses and garden and field walls, all of an enormous thickness. The fields are seldom so much as half an acre one above another in that form, so that everything grows as in huge garden pots. The whole island looks like one monstrous fortification. Nothing green meets your eye—one dreary, grey-white,—and all the country towns from the retirement and invisibility of the windows look like towns burnt out and desolate. Yet the fertility is marvellous. You almost see things grow, and the population is, I suppose, unexampled. The town of Valetta itself contains about one hundred and ten streets, all at right angles to each other, each having from twelve to fifty houses; but many of them very steep—a few staired all across, and almost all, in some part or other, if not the whole, having the footway on each side so staired. The houses lofty, all looking new. The good houses are built with a court in the centre, and the rooms large and lofty, from sixteen to twenty feet high, and walls enormously thick, all necessary for coolness. The fortifications of Valetta are endless. When I first walked about them, I was struck all of a heap with their strangeness, and when I came to understand a little of their purpose, I was overwhelmed with wonder. Such vast masses—bulky mountain-breasted heights; gardens with pomegranate trees—the prickly pears in the fosses, and the caper (the most beautiful of flowers) growing profusely in the interstices of the high walls and on the battlements. The Maltese are a dark, light-limbed people. Of the women five tenths are ugly; of the remainder, four fifths would be ordinary but that they look so quaint, and one tenth, perhaps, may be called quaint-pretty. The prettiest resemble pretty Jewesses in England. They are the noisiest race[21] under heaven, and Valetta the noisiest place. The sudden shot-up, explosive bellows-cries you ever heard in London would give you the faintest idea of it. Even when you pass by a fruit stall the fellow will put his hand like a speaking trumpet to his mouth and shoot such a thunderbolt of sound full at you. Then the endless jangling of those cursed bells, etc. Sir Alexander Ball and General Valette (the civil and military commanders) have been marvellously attentive—Sir A. B. even friendly and confidential to me.

Poor Mrs. Stoddart was brought to bed of a little girl on the 24th of May, and it died on Tuesday, June 5th. On the night of its birth, poor little lamb! I had such a lively vision of my little Sara, that it brought on a sort of hysterical fit on me. O merciful God! how I tremble at the thought of letters from England. I should be most miserable without them, and yet I shall receive them as a sentence of death! So terribly has fear got the upper hand in my habitual feelings, from my long destitution of hope and joy.

Hartley, Derwent, my sweet children! a father's blessing on you! With tears and clasped hands I bless you. Oh, I must write no more of this. I have been haunted by the thought that I have lost a box of books containing Shakespeare (Stockdale's), the four or five first volumes of the "British Poets," Young's "Syllabus" (a red paper book), Condillac's "Logic," "Thornton on Public Credit," etc. Be sure you inform me whether or no I did take these books from Keswick. I will write to Southey by the next opportunity. You recollect that I went away without knowing the result of Edith's confinement; not a day in which I do not think of it.

My love to dear Southey, and remember me to Mr. Jackson, and Mrs. Wilson with the kindest words, and to Mary Stamper. My kind remembrances to Mr. and Mrs. Wilkinson, and to the Calverts. How is your sister Mary in her spirits? My wishes and prayers attend her. I am anxious to hear about poor George and shall write about him to Portsmouth in the course of a week, for by that time a convoy will be going to England as we expect. I hope that in the course of three weeks or a month I may be able to give a more promising account of my health. As it is, I have reason to be satisfied. The effect of years cannot be done away in a few weeks. I am tranquil and resigned, and, even if I should not bring back health, I shall at least bring back experience, and suffer with patience and in silence. Again and again God bless you, my dear Sara! Let me know everything of your health, etc., etc. Oh, the letters are on the sea for me, and what tidings may they not bring to me!

S. T. Coleridge.

Single sheet. Per Germania a Londra. An. 1804.

CLIV. TO DANIEL STUART.

Syracuse,[22] October 22, 1804.

My dear Stuart,—I have written you a long letter this morning by way of Messina, and from other causes am so done up and brain weary that I must put you to the expense of this as almost a blank, except that you will be pleased to observe my attention to business in having written two letters of advice, as well as transmitted first and second of exchange for £50 which I have drawn upon you, payable to order of Dr. Stoddart at usance. I shall want no more for my return. I shall stay a month at Messina, and in that time visit Naples. Supposing the letter of this morning to miss, I ought to repeat to you that I leave the publication of the Pacquet,[23] which is waiting for convoy at Malta for you, to your own opinion. If the information appear new or valuable to you, and the letters themselves entertaining, etc., publish them; only do not sell the copyright of more than the right of two editions to the bookseller. He will not give more, or much more for the copyright of the whole.

May God bless you! I am, and shall be as long as I exist, your truly grateful and affectionate friend,

S. T. Coleridge.

CLV. TO ROBERT SOUTHEY.

Sat. morning, 4 o'clock. Treasury, Malta.
February 2, 1805.

Dear Southey,—A Privateer is to leave this Port to-day at noon for Gibraltar, and, it chancing that an officer of rank takes his passage in her, Sir A. Ball trusts his dispatches with due precaution to this unusual mode of conveyance, and I must enclose a letter to you in the government parcel. I pray that the lead attached to it will not be ominous of its tardy voyage, much less of its making a diving tour whither the spirit of Shakespeare went, under the name of the Dreaming Clarence.[24] Certain it is that I awoke about some half hour ago from so vivid a dream that the work of sleep had completely destroyed all sleepiness. I got up, went to my office-room, rekindled the wood-fire for the purpose of writing to you, having been so employed from morn till eve in writing public letters, some as long as memorials, from the hour that this opportunity was first announced to me, that for once in my life, at least, I can with strict truth affirm that I have had no time to write to you, if by time be understood the moments of life in which our powers are alive. I am well—at least, till within the last fortnight I was perfectly so, till the news of the sale of my blessed house played "the foe intestine" with me. But of that hereafter.

My dear Southey![25] the longer I live, and the more I see, know, and think, the more deeply do I seem to know and feel your goodness; and why, at this distance, may I not allow myself to utter forth my whole thought by adding your greatness? "Thy kingdom come" will have been a petition already granted, when in the minds and hearts of all men both words mean the same; or (to shake off a state of feeling deeper than may be serviceable to me) when gulielmosartorially speaking (i. e. William "Taylorice") the latter word shall have become an incurable synonym, a lumberly duplicate, thrown into the kennel of the Lethe-lapping Chronos Anubioeides,[26] as a carriony, bare-ribbed tautology. Oh me! it will not do! You, my children, the Wordsworths, are at Keswick and Grasmere, and I am at Malta, and it is a silly hypocrisy to pretend to joke when I am heavy at heart. By the accident of the sale of a dead Colonel's effects, who arrived in this healing climate too late to be healed, I procured the perusal of the second volume of the "Annual Review." I was suddenly and strangely affected by the marked attention which you had paid to my few hints, by the insertion of my joke on Booker; but more, far more than all, by the affection for me which peeped forth in that "William Brown of Ottery." I knew you stopped before and after you had written the words. But I am to speak of your reviews in general. I am confident, for I have carefully reperused almost the whole volume, and what I knew or detected to be yours I have read over and over again, with as much care and as little warping of partiality as if it had been a manuscript of my own going to the press—I can say confidently that in my best judgment they are models of good sense and correct style; of high and honest feeling intermingled with a sort of wit which (I now translate as truly, though not as verbally, as I can, the sense of an observation which a literary Venetian, who resides here as the editor of a political journal, made to me after having read your reviews of Clarke's "Maritime Discoveries") unites that happy turn of words, which is the essence of French wit, with those comic picture-making combinations of fancy that characterises the old wit of old England. If I can find time to copy off what in the hurry of the moment I wrote on loose papers that cannot be made up into a letter without subjecting you to an expense wholly disproportionate to their value, I shall prove to you that I have been watchful in marking what appeared to me false, or better-not, or better-otherwise, parts, no less than what I felt to be excellent. It is enough to say at present, that seldom in my course of reading have I been more deeply impressed than by the sense of the diffused good they were likely to effect. At the same time I could not help feeling to how many false and pernicious principles, both in taste and in politics, they were likely, by their excellence, to give a non-natural circulation. W. Taylor grows worse and worse. As to his political dogmata concerning Egypt, etc., God forgive him! He knows not what he does! But as to his spawn about Milton and Tasso—nay, Heaven forbid it should be spawn, it is pure toad-spit, not as toad-spit is, but as it is vulgarly believed to be. (See, too, his Article in the "Critical Review.") Now for your feelings respecting "Madoc." I regard them as all nerve and stomach-work, you having too recently quitted the business. Genius, too, has its intoxication, which, however divine, leaves its headaches and its nauseas. Of the very best of the few bad, good, and indifferent things, I have had the same sensations. Concerning the immediate chryso-poetic powers of "Madoc" I can only fear somewhat and hope somewhat. Midas and Apollo are as little cronies as Marsyas and Apollo. But of its great and lasting effects on your fame, if I doubted, I should then doubt all things in which I had hitherto had firm faith. Neither am I without cheerful belief respecting its ultimate effects on your worldly fortune. O dear Southey! when I see this booby with his ten pound a day as Mr. Commissary X., and that thorough-rogue two doors off him with his fifteen pound a day as Mr. General Paymaster Y. Z., it stirs up a little bile from the liver and gives my poor stomach a pinch, when I hear you talk of having to look forward to an £100 or £150. But cheerily! what do we complain of? would we be either of these men? Oh, had I domestic happiness, and an assurance only of the health I now possess continuing to me in England, what a blessed creature should I be, though I found it necessary to feed me and mine on roast potatoes for two days in each week in order to make ends meet, and to awake my beloved with a kiss on the first of every January. "Well, my best darling! we owe nobody a farthing! and I have you, my children, two or three friends, and a thousand books!" I have written very lately to Mrs. Coleridge. If my letter reaches her, as I have quoted in it a part of yours of Oct. 19th, she will wonder that I took no notice of the house and the Bellygerent. From Mrs. C. I have received no letter by the last convoy. In truth I am and have reason to be ashamed to own to what a diseased excess my sensibility has worsened into. I was so agitated by the receipt of letters, that I did not bring myself to open them for two or three days, half-dreaming that from there being no letter from Mrs. C. some one of the children had died, or that she herself had been ill, or—for so help me God! most ill-starred as our marriage has been, there is perhaps nothing that would so frightfully affect me as any change respecting her health or life; and, when I had read about a third of your letter, I walked up and down and then out, and much business intervening, I wrote to her before I had read the remainder, or my other letters. I grieve exceedingly at the event, and my having foreseen it does not diminish the shock. My dear study! and that house in which such persons have been! where my Hartley has made his first love-commune with Nature, to belong to White. Oh, how could Mr. Jackson have the heart to do it! As to the climate, I am fully convinced that to an invalid all parts of England are so much alike, that no disadvantages on that score can overbalance any marked advantages from other causes. Mr. J. well knows that but for my absolute confidence in him I should have taken the house for a long lease—but, poor man! I am rather to soothe than to reproach him. When will he ever again have loving friends and housemates like to us? And dear good Mrs. Wilson! Surely Mrs. Coleridge must have written to me, though no letter has arrived. Now for myself. I am most anxiously expecting the arrival of Mr. Chapman from Smyrna, who is (by the last ministry if that should hold valid) appointed successor to Mr. Macaulay, as Public Secretary of Malta, the second in rank to the Governor. Mr. M., an old man of eighty, died on the 18th of last month, calm as a sleeping baby, in a tremendous thunder-and-lightning storm. In the interim, I am and some fifty times a day subscribe myself, Segretario Pubblico dell' Isole di Malta, Gozo, e delle loro dipendenze. I live in a perfect palace and have all my meals with the Governor; but my profits will be much less than if I had employed my time and efforts in my own literary pursuits. However, I gain new insights and if (as I doubt not I shall) I return having expended nothing, having paid all my prior debts as well as interim expense (of the which debts I consider the £100 borrowed by me from Sotheby on the firm of W. Wordsworth, the heaviest), with health, and some additional knowledge both in things and languages, I surely shall not have lost a year. My intention is, assuredly, to leave this place at the farthest in the latter end of this month, whether by the convoy, or overland by Trieste, Vienna, Berlin, Embden, and Denmark, but I must be guided by circumstances. At all events, it will be well if a letter should be left for me at the "Courier" office in London, by the first of May, informing me of all which it is necessary for me to know. But of one thing I am most anxious, namely, that my assurance money should be paid. I pray you, look to that. You will have heard long before this letter reaches you that the French fleet have escaped from Toulon. I have no heart for politics, else I could tell you how for the last nine months I have been working in memorials concerning Egypt, Sicily, and the coast of Africa. Could France ever possess these, she would be, in a far grander sense than the Roman, an Empire of the World. And what would remain to England? England; and that which our miserable diplomatists affect now to despise, now to consider as a misfortune, our language and institutions in America. France is blest by nature, for in possessing Africa she would have a magnificent outlet for her population as near her own coasts as Ireland to ours; an America that must forever be an integral part of the mother-country. Egypt is eager for France—only eager, far more eager for G. Britain. The universal cry there (I have seen translations of twenty, at least, mercantile letters in the Court of Admiralty here (in which I have made a speech with a wig and gown, a true Jack of all Trades), all stating that the vox populi) is English, English, if we can! but Hats at all events! (Hats means Europeans in contradistinction to Turbans.) God bless you, Southey! I wish earnestly to kiss your child. And all whom you love, I love, as far as I can, for your sake.

For England. Per Inghilterra.
Robert Southey, Esqre, Greta Hall, Keswick, Cumberland.

CLVI. TO DANIEL STUART.

Favoured by Captain Maxwell of the Artillery.—N. B., an amiable mild man, who is prepared to give you any information.

Malta, April 20, 1805.

Dear Stuart,—The above is a duplicate, or rather a sex or septem-plicate of an order sent off within three weeks after my draft on you had been given by me; and very anxious I have been, knowing that all or almost all of my letters have failed. It seems like a judgment on me. Formerly, when I had the sure means of conveying letters, I neglected my duty through indolence or procrastination. For the last year, when, having all my heart, all my hope in England, I found no other gratification than that of writing to Wordsworth and his family, his wife, sister, and wife's sister; to Southey, to you, to T. Wedgwood, Sir. G. Beaumont, etc. Indeed, I have been supererogatory in some instances—but an evil destiny has dogged them—one large and (forgive my vanity!) rather important set of letters to you on Sicily and Egypt were destroyed at Gibraltar among the papers of a most excellent man, Major Adye, to whom I had entrusted them on his departure from Sicily, and who died of the Plague four days after his arrival at Gibraltar. But still was I afflicted (shame on me! even to violent weeping) when all my many, many letters were thrown overboard from the Arrow, the Acheron, and a merchant vessel, to all which I had entrusted them; the last through my own over care. For I delivered them to the captain with great pomp of seriousness, in my official character as Public Secretary of the Islands.[27] He took them, and considering them as public papers, on being close chased and expecting to be boarded, threw them overboard; and he, however, escaped, steering for Africa, and returned to Malta. But regrets are idle things.

In my letter, which will accompany this, I have detailed my health and all that relates to me. In case, however, that letter should not arrive, I will simply say, that till within the last two months or ten weeks my health had improved to the utmost of my hopes, though not without some intrusions of sickness; but latterly the loss of my letters to England, the almost entire non-arrival of letters from England, not a single one from Mrs. Coleridge or

Southey or you; and only one from the Wordsworths, and that dated September, 1804! my consequent heart-saddening anxieties, and still, still more, the depths which Captain John Wordsworth's death[28] sunk into my heart, and which I heard abruptly, and in the very painfullest way possible in a public company—all these joined to my disappointment in my expectation of returning to England by this convoy, and the quantity and variety of my public occupations from eight o'clock in the morning to five in the afternoon, having besides the most anxious duty of writing public letters and memorials which belongs to my talents rather than to my pro-tempore office; these and some other causes that I cannot mention relative to my affairs in England have produced a sad change indeed on my health; but, however, I hope all will be well.... It is my present intention to return home over-land by Naples, Ancona, Trieste, etc., on or about the second of next month.

The gentleman who will deliver this to you is Captain Maxwell of the Royal Artillery, a well-informed and very amiable countryman of yours. He will give you any information you wish concerning Malta. An intelligent friend of his, an officer of sense and science, has entrusted to him an essay on Lampedusa,[29] which I have advised him to publish in a newspaper, leaving it to the Editor to divide it. It may, perhaps, need a little softening, but it is an accurate and well-reasoned memorial. He only wishes to give it publicity, and to have not only his name concealed, but every circumstance that could lead to a suspicion. If after reading it you approve of it, you would greatly oblige him by giving it a place in the "Courier." He is a sensible, independent man. For all else to my other letter.—I am, dear Stuart, with faithful recollections, your much obliged and truly grateful friend and servant,

S. T. Coleridge.

April 20, 1805.

CLVII. TO HIS WIFE.

Malta, July 21, 1805.

Dear Sara,—The Niger is ordered off for Gibraltar at a moment's warning, and the Hall is crowded with officers and merchants whose oaths I am to take, and accompts to sign. I will not, however, suffer it to go without a line, and including a draft for £110—another opportunity will offer in a week or ten days, and I will enclose a duplicate in a letter at large. Now for the most important articles. My health had greatly improved; but latterly it has been very, very bad, in great measure owing to dejection of spirits, my letters having failed, the greater part of those to me, and almost all mine homeward.... My letters and the duplicates of them, written with so much care and minuteness to Sir George Beaumont—those to Wedgwood, to the Wordsworths, to Southey, Major Adye's sudden death, and then the loss of the two frigates, the capture of a merchant's privateer, all have seemed to spite. No one not absent on a dreary island, so many leagues of sea from England, can conceive the effect of these accidents on the spirit and inmost soul. So help me Heaven! they have nearly broken my heart. And, added to this, I have been hoping and expecting to get away for England for five months past, and Mr. Chapman not arriving, Sir Alexander's importunities have always overpowered me, though my gloom has increased at each disappointment. I am determined, however, to go in less than a month. My office, as Public Secretary, the next civil dignitary to the Governor, is a very, very busy one, and not to involve myself in the responsibility of the Treasurer I have but half the salary. I oftentimes subscribe my name 150 times a day, S. T. Coleridge, Pub. Sec. to H. M. Civ. Commissr, or (if in Italian) Seg. Pub. del Commiss' Regio, and administer half as many oaths—besides which I have the public memorials to write, and, worse than all, constant matters of arbitration. Sir A. Ball is indeed exceedingly kind to me. The officers will be impatient. I would I could write a more cheerful account of my health; all I can say is that I am better than I have been, and that I was very much better before so many circumstances of dejection happened. I should overset myself completely, if I ventured to mention a single name. How deeply I love, O God! it is agony at morning and evening.

S. T. Coleridge.

P. S. On being abruptly told by Lady Ball of John Wordsworth's fate, I attempted to stagger out of the room (the great saloon of the Palace with fifty people present), and before I could reach the door fell down on the ground in a convulsive hysteric fit. I was confined to my room for a fortnight after; and now I am afraid to open a letter, and I never dare ask a question of any new-comer. The night before last I was much affected by the sudden entrance of poor Reynell (our inmate at Stowey);[30] more of him in my next. May God Almighty bless you and—

(Signed with seal, ΕΣΤΗΣΕ.)

For England.
Mrs. Coleridge, Keswick, Cumberland.

Postmark, Sept. 8, 1805.

CLVIII. TO WASHINGTON ALLSTON.

Direct to me at Mr. Degens, Leghorn. God bless you!

Tuesday, June 17, 1806.[31]

My dear Allston,—No want of affection has occasioned my silence. Day after day I expected Mr. Wallis. Benvenuti received me with almost insulting coldness, not even asking me to sit down; neither could I, by any enquiry, find that he ever returned my call, and even in answer to a very polite note enquiring for letters, sent a verbal message, that there was one, and that I might call for it. However, within the last seven or eight days he has called and made his amende honourable; he says he forgot the name of my inn, and called at two or three in vain. Whoo! I did not tell him that within five days I sent him a note in which the inn was mentioned, and that he sent me a message in consequence, and yet never called for ten days afterwards. However, yester-evening the truth came out. He had been bored by letters of recommendation, and till he received a letter from Mr. —— looked upon me as a bore—which, however, he might and ought to have got rid of in a more gentlemanly manner. Nothing more was necessary than the day after my arrival to have sent his card by his servant. But I forgive him from my heart. It should, however, be a lesson to Mr. Wallis, to whom, and for whom, he gives letters of recommendation.

I have been dangerously ill for the last fortnight, and unwell enough, Heaven knows, previously; about ten days ago, on rising from my bed, I had a manifest stroke of palsy along my right side and right arm. My head felt like another man's head, so dead was it, that I seemed to know it only by my left hand, and a strange sense of numbness....

Enough of it, continual vexations and preyings upon the spirit—I gave life to my children,[32] and they have repeatedly given it to me; for, by the Maker of all things, but for them I would try my chance. But they pluck out the wing-feathers from the mind. I have not entirely recovered the sense of my side or hand, but have recovered the use. I am harassed by local and partial fevers. This day, at noon, we set off for Leghorn;[33] all passage through the Italian States and Germany is little other than impossible for an Englishman, and Heaven knows whether Leghorn may not be blockaded. However, we go thither, and shall go to England in an American ship. Inform Mr. Wallis of this, and urge him to make his way—assure him of my anxious thoughts and fervent wishes respecting him and of my love for T——, and his family. Tell Mr. Migliorus [?] that I should have written him long ago but for my ill health; and will not fail to do it on my arrival at Pisa— from thence, too, I will write a letter to you, for this I do not consider as a letter. Nothing can surpass Mr. Russell's[34] kindness and tender-heartedness to me, and his understanding is far superior to what it appears on first acquaintance. I will write likewise to Mr. Wallis and conjure him not to leave Amelia. I have heard in Leghorn a sad, sad character of one of those whom you called acquaintance, but who call you their dear friend.

My dear Allston, somewhat from increasing age, but more from calamity and intense fra[ternal affections], my heart is not open to more than kind, good wishes in general. To you, and to you alone, since I left England, I have felt more, and had I not known the Wordsworths, should have esteemed and loved you first and most; and, as it is, next to them I love and honour you. Heaven knows, a part of such a wreck as my head and heart is scarcely worth your acceptance.

S. T. Coleridge.

CLIX. TO DANIEL STUART.

Bell Inn, Friday Street,
Monday morning, August 18, 1806.

My dear Sir,—I arrived here from Stangate Creek last night, a little after ten, and have found myself so unusually better ever since I leaped on land yester-afternoon, that I am glad that neither my strength nor spirits enabled me to write to you on my arrival in Quarantine on the eleventh. Both the captain and my fellow-passengers were seriously alarmed for my life; and indeed such have been my unremitting sufferings from pain, sleeplessness, loathing of food, and spirits wholly despondent, that no motive on earth short of an awful duty would ever prevail on me to take any sea-voyage likely to be longer than three or four days. I had rather starve in a hovel, and, if life through disease become worthless, will choose a Roman death. It is true I was very low before I embarked.... To have been working so hard for eighteen months in a business I detested; to have been flattered, and to have flattered myself that I should, on striking the balance, have paid all my debts and maintained both myself and family during my exile out of my savings and earnings, including my travels through Germany, through which I had to the very last hoped to have passed, and found myself!—but enough! I cannot charge my conscience with a single extravagance, nor even my judgment with any other imprudences than that of suffering one good and great man to overpersuade me from month to month to a delay which was gnawing away my very vitals, and in being duped in disobedience to my first feelings and previous ideas by another diplomatic Minister.... A gentleman offered to take me without expense to Rome, which I accepted with the full intention of staying only a fortnight, and then returning to Naples to pass the winter.... I left everything but a good suit of clothes and my shirts, etc., all my letters of credit, manuscripts, etc. I had not been ten days in Rome before the French torrent rolled down on Naples. All return was impossible, and all transmission of papers not only insecure, but being English and many of them political, highly dangerous both to the sender and sendee.... But this is only a fragment of a chapter of contents, and I am too much agitated to write the details, but will call on you as soon as my two or three remaining [guineas] shall have put a decent hat upon my head and shoes upon my feet. I am literally afraid, even to cowardice, to ask for any person or of any person. Including the Quarantine we had fifty-five days of shipboard, working up against head-winds, rotting and sweating in calms, or running under hard gales with the dead lights secured. From the captain and my fellow-passenger I received every possible tenderness, only when I was very ill they laid their wise heads together, and the latter in a letter to his father begged him to inform my family that I had arrived, and he trusted that they would soon see me in better health and spirits than when I had quitted them; a letter which must have alarmed if they saw into it, and wounded if they did not. I was not informed of it till this morning. God bless you, my dear sir! I have yet cheerful hopes that Heaven will not suffer me to die degraded by any other debts than those which it ever has been, and ever will be, my joy and pride still to pay and still to owe; those of a truly grateful heart, and to you among the first of those to whom they are due.

S. T. Coleridge.

CHAPTER VIII
HOME AND NO HOME
1806-1807

CLX. TO DANIEL STUART.

Monday, (?) September 15, 1806.

My dear Stuart,—I arrived in town safe, but so tired by the next evening, that I went to bed at nine and slept till past twelve on Sunday. I cannot keep off my mind from the last subject we were talking about; though I have brought my notions concerning it to hang so well on the balance that I have in my own judgment few doubts as to the relative weight of the arguments persuasive and dissuasive. But of this "face to face." I sleep at the "Courier" office, and shall institute and carry on the inquiry into the characters of Mr. Pitt and Mr. Fox, and having carried it to the Treaty of Amiens, or rather to the recommencement of the War, I propose to give a full and severe Critique of the "Enquiry into the State of the Nation," taking it for granted that this work does, on the whole, contain Mr. Fox's latest political creed; and this for the purpose of answering the "Morning Chronicle"(!) assertions, that Mr. Fox was the greatest and wisest statesman; that Mr. Pitt was no statesman. I shall endeavour to show that both were undeserving of that high character; but that Mr. Pitt was the better; that the evils which befell him were undoubtedly produced in great measure by blunders and wickedness on the Continent which it was almost impossible to foresee; while the effects of Mr. Fox's measures must in and of themselves produce calamity and degradation.

To confess the truth, I am by no means pleased with Mr. Street's character of Mr. Fox as a speaker and man of intellect. As a piece of panegyric, it falls woefully short of the Article in the "Morning Chronicle" in style and selection of thoughts, and runs at least equally far beyond the bounds of truth. Persons who write in a hurry are very liable to contract a sort of snipt, convulsive style, that moves forward by short repeated pushes, with iso-chronous asthmatic pants, "He—He—He—He—," or the like, beginning a dozen short sentences, each making a period. In this way a man can get rid of all that happens at any one time to be in his memory, with very little choice in the arrangement and no expenditure of logic in the connection. However, it is the matter more than the manner that displeased me, for fear that what I shall write for to-morrow's "Courier" may involve a kind of contradiction. To one outrageous passage I persuaded him to add a note of amendment, as it was too late to alter the Article itself. It was impossible for me, seeing him satisfied with the Article himself, to say more than that he appeared to me to have exceeded in eulogy. But beyond doubt in the political position occupied by the "Courier," with so little danger of being anticipated by the other papers in anything which it ought to say, except some obvious points which being common to all the papers can give credit to none, it would have been better to have announced his death, and simply led the way for an after disquisition by a sort of shy disclosure with an appearance of suppression of the spirit with which it could be conducted.

There are letters at the Post Office, Margate, for me. Be so good as to send them to me, directed to the "Courier" office. I think of going to Mr. Smith's[35] to-morrow, or not at all. Whether Mr. Fox's death[36] will keep Mr. S. in town, or call him there, I do not know. At all events I shall return by the time of your arrival.

May God bless you! I am ever, my dear sir, as your obliged, so your affectionately grateful friend,

S. T. Coleridge.

CLXI. TO HIS WIFE.

September 16, [1806.]

My dear Sara,—I had determined on my arrival in town to write to you at full, the moment I could settle my affairs and speak decisively of myself. Unfortunately Mr. Stuart was at Margate, and what with my journey to and fro, day has passed on after day, Heaven knows, counted by me in sickness of heart. I am now obliged to return to Parndon to Mr. W. Smith's, at whose house Mr. and Mrs. Clarkson are, and where I spent three or four days a fortnight ago. The reason at present is that Lord Howick has sent a very polite message to me through Mr. Smith, expressing his desire to make my acquaintance. To this I have many objections which I want to discuss with Mr. S., and at all events I had rather go with him to his Lordship's than by myself. Likewise I have had application from the R. Institution for a course of lectures, which I am much disposed to accept, both for money and reputation. In short, I must stay in town till Friday sen'night; for Mr. Stuart returns to town on Monday next, and he relies on my being there for a very interesting private concern of his own, in which he needs both my counsel and assistance. But on Friday sen'night, please God, I shall quit town, and trust to be at Keswick on Monday, Sept. 29th. If I finally accept the lectures, I must return by the middle of November, but propose to take you and Hartley with me, as we may be sure of rooms either in Mr. Stuart's house at Knightsbridge, or in the Strand. My purpose is to divide my time steadily between my reflections moral and political, grounded on information obtained during two years' residence in Italy and the Mediterranean, and the lectures on the "Principles common to all the Fine Arts." It is a terrible misfortune that so many important papers are not in my power, and that I must wait for Stoddart's care and alertness, which, I am sorry to say, is not to be relied on. However, it is well that they are not in Paris.

My heart aches so cruelly that I do not dare trust myself to the writing of any tenderness either to you, my dear, or to our dear children. Be assured, I feel with deep though sad affection toward you, and hold your character in general in more than mere esteem—in reverence.... I do not gather strength so fast as I had expected; but this I attribute to my very great anxiety. I am indeed very feeble, but after fifty-five days of such horrors, following the dreary heart-wasting of a year and more, it is a wonder that I am as I am. I sent you from Malta £110, and a duplicate in a second letter. If you have not received it, the triplicate is either at Malta or on its way from thence. I had sent another £100, but by Elliot's villainous treatment of me[37] was obliged to recall it. But these are trifles.

Mr. Clarkson is come, and is about to take me down to Parndon (Mr. S.'s country seat in Essex, about twenty miles from town). I shall return by Sunday or Monday, and my address, "S. T. Coleridge, Esqre, No. 348 Strand, London."

My grateful love to Southey, and blessing on his little one. And may God Almighty preserve you, my dear! and your faithful, though long absent husband,

S. T. Coleridge.

CLXII. TO THE SAME.

[Farmhouse near Coleorton,]
December 25, 1806.

My dear Sara,—By my letter from Derby you will have been satisfied of our safety so far. We had, however, been grossly deceived as to the equi-distance of Derby and Loughborough. The expense was nearly double. Still, however, I was in such torture and my boils bled, throbbed, and stabbed so con furia, that perhaps I have no reason for regret. At Coleorton we found them dining, Sunday, ½ past one o'clock. To-day is Xmas day. Of course we were welcomed with an uproar of sincere joy: and Hartley hung suspended between the ladies for a long minute. The children, too, jubilated at Hartley's arrival. He has behaved very well indeed—only that when he could get out of the coach at dinner, I was obliged to be in incessant watch to prevent him from rambling off into the fields. He twice ran into a field, and to the further end of it, and once after the dinner was on table, I was out five minutes seeking him in great alarm, and found him at the further end of a wet meadow, on the marge of a river. After dinner, fearful of losing our places by the window (of the long coach), I ordered him to go into the coach and sit in the place where he was before, and I would follow. In about five minutes I followed. No Hartley! Halloing—in vain! At length, where should I discover him! In the same meadow, only at a greater distance, and close down on the very edge of the water. I was angry from downright fright! And what, think you, was Cataphract's excuse! "It was a misunderstanding, Father! I thought, you see, that you bid me go to the very same place, in the meadow where I was." I told him that he had interpreted the text by the suggestions of the flesh, not the inspiration of the spirit; and his Wish the naughty father of the baseborn Thought. However, saving and excepting his passion for field truantry, and his hatred of confinement [in which his fancy at least—

Doth sing a doleful song about green fields;
How sweet it were in woods and wild savannas;
To hunt for food and be a naked man
And wander up and down at liberty!],[38]
he is a very good and sweet child, of strict honour and truth, from which he never deviates except in the form of sophism when he sports his logical false dice in the game of excuses. This, however, is the mere effect of his activity of thought, and his aiming at being clever and ingenious. He is exceedingly amiable toward children. All here love him most dearly: and your namesake takes upon her all the duties of his mother and darling friend, with all the mother's love and fondness. He is very fond of her; but it is very pretty to hear how, without any one set declaration of his attachment to Mrs. Wilson and Mr. Jackson, his love for them continually breaks out—so many things remind him of them, and in the coach he talked to the strangers of them just as if everybody must know Mr. J. and Mrs. W. His letter is only half written; so cannot go to-day. We all wish you a merry Christmas and many following ones. Concerning the London Lectures, we are to discuss it, William and I, this evening, and I shall write you at full the day after to-morrow. To-morrow there is no post, but this letter I mean merely as bearer of the tidings of our safe arrival. I am better than usual. Hartley has coughed a little every morning since he left Greta Hall; but only such a little cough as you heard from him at the door. He is in high health. All the children have the hooping cough; but in an exceedingly mild degree. Neither Sarah Hutchinson nor I ever remember to have had it. Hartley is made to keep at a distance from them, and only to play with Johnny in the open air. I found my spice-megs; but many papers I miss.

The post boy waits.

My love to Mrs. Lovell, to Southey and Edith, and believe me anxiously and for ever,

Your sincere friend
S. T. Coleridge.

CLXIII. TO HARTLEY COLERIDGE, ÆTAT. X.[39]

April 3, 1807.

My dear Boy,—In all human beings good and bad qualities are not only found together, side by side, as it were, but they actually tend to produce each other; at least they must be considered as twins of a common parent, and the amiable propensities too often sustain and foster their unhandsome sisters. (For the old Romans personified virtues and vices both as women.) This is a sufficient proof that mere natural qualities, however pleasing and delightful, must not be deemed virtues until they are broken in and yoked to the plough of Reason. Now to apply this to your own case—I could equally apply it to myself—but you know yourself more accurately than you can know me, and will therefore understand my argument better when the facts on which it is built exist in your own consciousness. You are by nature very kind and forgiving, and wholly free from revenge and sullenness; you are likewise gifted with a very active and self-gratifying fancy, and such a high tide and flood of pleasurable feelings, that all unpleasant and painful thoughts and events are hurried away upon it, and neither remain in the surface of your memory nor sink to the bottom of your heart. So far all seems right and matter of thanksgiving to your Maker; and so all really is so, and will be so, if you exert your reason and free will. But on the other hand the very same disposition makes you less impressible both to the censure of your anxious friends and to the whispers of your conscience. Nothing that gives you pain dwells long enough upon your mind to do you any good, just as in some diseases the medicines pass so quickly through the stomach and bowels as to be able to exert none of their healing qualities. In like manner, this power which you possess of shoving aside all disagreeable reflections, or losing them in a labyrinth of day-dreams, which saves you from some present pain, has, on the other hand, interwoven with your nature habits of procrastination, which, unless you correct them in time (and it will require all your best exertions to do it effectually), must lead you into lasting unhappiness.

You are now going with me (if God have not ordered it otherwise) into Devonshire to visit your Uncle G. Coleridge. He is a very good man and very kind; but his notions of right and of propriety are very strict, and he is, therefore, exceedingly shocked by any gross deviations from what is right and proper. I take, therefore, this means of warning you against those bad habits, which I and all your friends here have noticed in you; and, be assured, I am not writing in anger, but on the contrary with great love, and a comfortable hope that your behaviour at Ottery will be such as to do yourself and me and your dear mother credit.

First, then, I conjure you never to do anything of any kind when out of sight which you would not do in my presence. What is a frail and faulty father on earth compared with God, your heavenly Father? But God is always present. Specially, never pick at or snatch up anything, eatable or not. I know it is only an idle, foolish trick; but your Ottery relations would consider you as a little thief; and in the Church Catechism picking and stealing are both put together as two sorts of the same vice, "And keep my hands from picking and stealing." And besides, it is a dirty trick; and people of weak stomachs would turn sick at a dish which a young filth-paw had been fingering.

Next, when you have done wrong acknowledge it at once, like a man. Excuses may show your ingenuity, but they make your honesty suspected. And a grain of honesty is better than a pound of wit. We may admire a man for his cleverness; but we love and esteem him only for his goodness; and a strict attachment to truth, and to the whole truth, with openness and frankness and simplicity is at once the foundation stone of all goodness, and no small part of the superstructure. Lastly, do what you have to do at once, and put it out of hand. No procrastination; no self-delusion; no "I am sure I can say it, I need not learn it again," etc., which sures are such very unsure folks that nine times out of ten their sureships break their word and disappoint you.

Among the lesser faults I beg you to endeavour to remember not to stand between the half-opened door, either while you are speaking, or spoken to. But come in or go out, and always speak and listen with the door shut. Likewise, not to speak so loud, or abruptly, and never to interrupt your elders while they are speaking, and not to talk at all during meals. I pray you, keep this letter, and read it over every two or three days.

Take but a little trouble with yourself, and every one will be delighted with you, and try to gratify you in all your reasonable wishes. And, above all, you will be at peace with yourself, and a double blessing to me, who am, my dear, my very dear Hartley, most anxiously, your fond father,

S. T. Coleridge.

P. S. I have not spoken about your mad passions and frantic looks and pout-mouthing; because I trust that is all over.

Hartley Coleridge, Coleorton, Leicestershire.

CLXIV. TO SIR H. DAVY.

September 11, 1807.

... Yet how very few are there whom I esteem and (pardon me for this seeming deviation from the language of friendship) admire equally with yourself. It is indeed, and has long been, my settled persuasion, that of all men known to me I could not justly equal any one to you, combining in one view powers of intellect, and the steady moral exertion of them to the production of direct and indirect good; and if I give you pain, my heart bears witness that I inflicted a greater on myself,—nor should I have written such words, if the chief feeling that mixed with and followed them had not been that of shame and self-reproach, for having profited neither by your general example nor your frequent and immediate incentives. Neither would I have oppressed you at all with this melancholy statement, but that for some days past I have found myself so much better in body and mind, as to cheer me at times with the thought that this most morbid and oppressive weight is gradually lifting up, and my will acquiring some degree of strength and power of reaction.

....

I have, however, received such manifest benefit from horse exercise, and gradual abandonment of fermented and total abstinence from spirituous liquors, and by being alone with Poole, and the renewal of old times, by wandering about among my dear old walks of Quantock and Alfoxden, that I have seriously set about composition, with a view to ascertain whether I can conscientiously undertake what I so very much wish, a series of Lectures at the Royal Institution. I trust I need not assure you how much I feel your kindness, and let me add, that I consider the application as an act of great and unmerited condescension on the part of the managers as may have consented to it. After having discussed the subject with Poole, he entirely agrees with me, that the former plan suggested by me is invidious in itself, unless I disguised my real opinions; as far as I should deliver my sentiments respecting the arts, [it] would require references and illustrations not suitable to a public lecture room; and, finally, that I ought not to reckon upon spirits enough to seek about for books of Italian prints, etc. And that, after all, the general and most philosophical principles, I might naturally introduce into lectures on a more confined plan—namely, the principles of poetry, conveyed and illustrated in a series of lectures. 1. On the genius and writings of Shakespeare, relatively to his predecessors and contemporaries, so as to determine not only his merits and defects, and the proportion that each must bear to the whole, but what of his merits and defects belong to his age, as being found in contemporaries of genius, and what belonged to himself. 2. On Spenser, including the metrical romances, and Chaucer, though the character of the latter as a manner-painter I shall have so far anticipated in distinguishing it from, and comparing it with, Shakespeare. 3. Milton. 4. Dryden and Pope, including the origin and after history of poetry of witty logic. 5. On Modern Poetry and its characteristics, with no introduction of any particular names. In the course of these I shall have said all I know, the whole result of many years' continued reflection on the subjects of taste, imagination, fancy, passion, the source of our pleasures in the fine arts, in the antithetical balance-loving nature of man, and the connexion of such pleasures with moral excellence. The advantage of this plan to myself is, that I have all my materials ready, and can rapidly reduce them into form (for this is my solemn determination, not to give a single lecture till I have in fair writing at least one half of the whole course), for as to trusting anything to immediate effort, I shrink from it as from guilt, and guilt in me it would be. In short, I should have no objection at once to pledge myself to the immediate preparation of these lectures, but that I am so surrounded by embarrassments....

For God's sake enter into my true motive for this wearing detail; it would torture me if it had any other effect than to impress on you my desire and hope to accord with your plan, and my incapability of making any final promise till the end of this month.

S. T. Coleridge.

CHAPTER IX
PUBLIC LECTURER
1807-1808

CLXV. TO THE MORGAN FAMILY.

Hatchett's Hotel, Piccadilly, Monday evening,
[November 23, 1807.]

My dear Friends,—I arrived here in safety this morning between seven and eight, coach-stunned, and with a cold in my head; but I had dozed away the whole night with fewer disturbances than I had reason to expect, in that sort of whether-you-will-or-no slumber brought upon me by the movements of the vehicle, which I attribute to the easiness of the mail. About one o'clock I moaned and started, and then took a wing of the fowl and the rum, and it operated as a preventive for the after time. If very, very affectionate thoughts, wishes, recollections, anticipations, can score instead of grace before and after meat, mine was a very religious meal, for in this sense my inmost heart prayed before, after, and during. After breakfast, on attempting to clean and dress myself from crown to sole, I found myself quite unfit for anything, and my legs were painful, or rather my feet, and nothing but an horizontal position would remove the feeling. So I got into bed, and did not get up again till Mr. Stuart called at my chamber, past three. I have seen no one else, and therefore must defer all intelligence concerning my lectures, etc., to a second letter, which you will receive in a few days, God willing, with the D'Espriella, etc. When I was leaving you, one of the little alleviations which I looked forward to, was that I could write with less embarrassment than I could utter in your presence the many feelings of grateful affection and most affectionate esteem toward you, that pressed upon my heart almost, as at times it seemed, with a bodily weight. But I suppose it is yet too short a time since I left you—you are scarcely out of my eyes yet, dear Mrs. M. and Charlotte! To-morrow I shall go about the portraits. I have not looked at the profile since, nor shall I till it is framed. An absence of four or five days will be a better test how far it is a likeness. For a day or two, farewell, my dear friends! I bless you all three fervently, and shall, I trust, as long as I am

S. T. Coleridge.

I shall take up my lodgings at the "Courier" office, where there is a nice suite of rooms for me and a quiet bedroom without expense. My address therefore, "Squire Coleridge," or "S. T. Coleridge, Esq: 'Courier' Office, Strand,"—unless you are in a sensible mood, and then you will write Mr. Coleridge, if it were only in compassion to that poor, unfortunate exile, from the covers of letters at least, despised MR.

Mr. Jno. Jas. Morgan,
St. James's Square, Bristol.

CLXVI. TO ROBERT SOUTHEY.

[Postmark, December 14, 1807.]

My dear Southey,—I have been confined to my bedroom, and, with exceptions of a few hours each night, to my bed for near a week past—having once ventured out, and suffered in consequence. My complaint a low bilious fever. Whether contagion or sympathy, I know not, but I had it hanging about me from the time I was with Davy. It went off, however, by a journey which I took with Stuart, to Bristol, in a cold frosty air. Soon after my return Mr. Ridout informed me from Drs. Babbington and Bailly, that Davy was not only ill, but his life precarious, his recovery doubtful. And to this day no distinct symptom of safety has appeared, though to-day he is better. I cannot express what I have suffered. Good heaven! in the very springtide of his honour—his? his country's! the world's! after discoveries more intellectual, more ennobling, and impowering human nature than Newton's! But he must not die! I am so much better that I shall go out to-morrow, if I awake no worse than I go to sleep. Be so good as to tell Mrs. Coleridge that I will write to her either Tuesday or Wednesday, and to Hartley and Derwent, with whose letters I was much both amused and affected. I was with Hartley and Mrs. Wilson and Mr. Jackson in spirit at their meeting. Howel's bill I have paid, tell Mrs. C. (for this is what she will be most anxious about), and that I had no other debt at all weighing upon me, either prudentially or from sense of propriety or delicacy, till the one I shall mention, after better subjects, in the tail of this letter.

I very thoroughly admired your letter to W. Scott,[40] concerning the "Edinburgh Review." The feeling and the resolve are what any one knowing you half as well as I must have anticipated, in any case where you had room for ten minutes thinking, and relatively to any person, with regard to whom old affection and belief of injury and unworthy conduct had made none of those mixtures, which people the brains of the best men—none but good men having the component drugs, or at least the drugs in that state of composition—but it is admirably expressed—if I had meant only well expressed, I should have said, "and it is well expressed,"—but, to my feeling, it is an unusual specimen of honourable feeling supporting itself by sound sense and conveyed with simplicity, dignity, and a warmth evidently under the complete control of the understanding. I am a fair judge as to such a sentence, for from morbid wretchedness of mind I have been in a far, far greater excess, indifferent about what is said, or written, or supposed, concerning me or my compositions, than W. can have been ever supposed to be interested respecting his—and the "Edinburgh Review" I have not seen for years, and never more than four or five numbers. As to reviewing W.'s poems, my sole objection would rest on the time of the publication of the "Annual Review." Davy's illness has put off the commencement of my Lectures to the middle of January. They are to consist of at least twenty lectures, and the subject of modern poetry occupies at least three or four. Now I do not care in how many forms my sentiments are printed: if only I do not defraud my hirers, by causing my lectures to be anticipated. I would not review them at all, unless I can do it systematically, and with the whole strength of my mind. And, when I do, I shall express my convictions of the faults and defects of the poems and system, as plainly as of the excellencies. It has been my constant reply to those who have charged me with bigotry, etc.,—"While you can perceive no excellencies, it is my duty to appear conscious of no defects, because, even though I should agree with you in the instances, I should only confirm you in what I deem a pernicious error, as our principle of disapprobation must necessarily be different." In my Lectures I shall speak out, of Rogers, Campbell, yourself (that is "Madoc" and "Thalaba;" for I shall speak only of poems, not of poets), and Wordsworth, as plainly as of Milton, Dryden, Pope, etc.... I did not overhugely admire the "Lay of the Last Minstrel," but saw no likeness whatever to the "Christabel," much less any improper resemblance.

I heard by accident that Dr. Stoddart had arrived a few days ago, and wrote him a letter expostulating with him for his unkindness in having detained for years my books and MSS., and stating the great loss it had been to me (a loss not easy to be calculated. I have as witnesses T. Poole and Squire Acland[41] (who calls me infallible Prophet), that from the information contained in them, though I could not dare trust my recollection sufficiently for the proofs, I foretold distinctly every event that has happened of importance, with one which has not yet happened, the evacuation of Sicily). This, however, of course, I did not write to Dr. S., but simply requested he would send me my chests. In return I received yesterday an abusive letter confirming what I suspected, that he is writing a book himself. In this he conjures up an indefinite debt, customs, and some old affair before I went to Malta, amounting to more than fifty pounds (the customs twenty-five pounds, all of which I should have had remitted, if he had sent them according to his promise), and informing me that when I send a person properly documented to settle this account, that person may then take away my goods. This I shall do to-morrow, though without the least pledge that I shall receive all that I left.... This will prevent my sending Mrs. C. any money for three weeks, I mean exclusive of the [annuity of] £150 which, assure her, is, and for the future will remain, sacred to her. By Wallis' attitude to Allston I lost thirty pounds in customs, by my brother's refusal[42] all the expenses up and down of my family. So it has been a baddish year; but I am not disquieted.

S. T. C.

Poor Godwin is going to the dogs. He has a tragedy[43] to come out on Wednesday. I will write again to you in a few days. After my Lectures I would willingly undertake any Review with you, because I shall then have given my Code. I omit other parts of your letter, not that they interested me less, but because I have no room, and am too much exhausted to take up a second sheet. God bless you. My kisses to your little ones, and love to your wife. The only vindictive idea I have to Dr. S. is the anticipation of showing his letter to Sir Alexander Ball!! The folly of sinning against our first and pure impressions! It is the sin against our own ghost at least!

CLXVII. TO MRS. MORGAN.

348, Strand, Friday morning, January 25, 1808.

Dear and honoured Mary,—Having had you continually, I may almost say, present to me in my dreams, and always appearing as a compassionate comforter therein, appearing in shape as your own dear self, most innocent and full of love, I feel a strong impulse to address a letter to you by name, though it equally respects all my three friends. If it had been told me on that evening when dear Morgan was asleep in the parlour, and you and beloved Caroletta asleep at opposite corners of the sopha in the drawing-room, of which I occupied the centre in a state of blessed half-unconsciousness as a drowsy guardian of your slumbers; if it had been then told me that in less than a fortnight the time should come when I should not wish to be with you, or wish you to be with me, I should have out with one of Caroletta's harmless "condemn its" (commonly pronounced "damn it"), "that's no truth!" And yet since on Friday evening, my lecture having made an impression far beyond its worth or my expectation, I have been in such a state of wretchedness, confined to my bed, in such almost continued pain ... that I have been content to see no one but the unlovable old woman, as feeling that I should only receive a momently succession of pangs from the presence of those who, giving no pleasure, would make my wretchedness appear almost unnatural, even as if the fire should cease to be warm. Who would not rather shiver on an ice mount than freeze before the fire which had used to spread comfort through his fibres and thoughts of social joy through his imagination? Yet even this, yet even from this feeling that your society would be an agony, oh I know, I feel how I love you, my dear sisters and friends.

I have been obliged, of course, to put off my lecture of to-day; a most painful necessity, for I disappoint some hundreds! I have sent for Abernethy, who has restored Mr. De Quincey to health! Could I have foreseen my present state I would have stayed at Bristol and taken lodgings at Clifton in order to be within the power of being seen by you, without being a domestic nuisance, for still, still I feel the comfortlessness of seeing no face, hearing no voice, feeling no hand that is dear, though conscious that the pang would outweigh the solace.

When finished, let the two dresses, etc., be sent to me; but if my illness should have a completed conclusion, of me as well as of itself, and there seems to be a distinct inflammation of the mesentery,—then let them be sent to Grasmere for Mrs. Wordsworth and Miss Hutchinson,—gay dresses, indeed, for a mourning.

I write in great pain, but yet I deem, whatever become of me, that it will hereafter be a soothing thought to you that in sickness or in health, in hope or in despondency, I have thought of you with love and esteem and gratitude.

My dear Mary! dear Charlotte! May Heaven bless you! With such a wife and such a sister, my friend is already blest! May Heaven give him health and elastic spirits to enjoy these and all other blessings! Once more bless you, bless you. Ah! who is there to bless

S. T. Coleridge?

P. S. Sunday Night. I do not know when this letter was written—probably Thursday morning, not Wednesday, as I have said in my letter to John. I have opened this by means of the steam of a tea-kettle, merely to say that I have, I know not how or where, lost the pretty shirt-pin Charlotte gave me. I promise her solemnly never to accept one from any other, and never to wear one hereafter as long as I live, so that the sense of its real absence shall make a sort of imaginary presence to me. I am more vexed at the accident than I ought to be; but had it been either of your locks of hair or her profile (which must be by force and association your profile too, and a far more efficacious one than that done for you, which had no other merit than that of having no likeness at all, and this certainly is a sort of negative advantage) I should have fretted myself into superstition and been haunted with it as by an omen. Of the lady and her poetical daughter I had never before heard even the name. Oh these are shadows! and all my literary admirers and flatterers, as well as despisers and calumniators, pass over my heart as the images of clouds over dull sea. So far from being retained, they are scarcely made visible there. But I love you, dear ladies! substantially, and pray do write at least a line in Morgan's letter, if neither will write me a whole one, to comfort me by the assurance that you remember me with esteem and some affection. Most affectionately have you and Charlotte treated me, and most gratefully do I remember it. Good-night, good-night!

To be read after the other.

Mrs. Morgan,
St. James's Square, Bristol.

CLXVIII. TO FRANCIS JEFFREY.

348 Strand, May 23, 1808.

Dear Sir,—Without knowing me you have been, perhaps rather unwarrantably, severe on my morals and understanding, inasmuch as you have, I understand,—for I have not seen the Reviews,—frequently introduced my name when I had never brought any publication within your court. With one slight exception, a shilling pamphlet[44] that never obtained the least notice, I have not published anything with my name, or known to be mine, for thirteen years. Surely I might quote against you the complaint of Job as to those who brought against him "the iniquities of his youth." What harm have I ever done you, dear sir, by act or word? If you knew me, you would yourself smile at some of the charges, which, I am told, you have fastened on me. Most assuredly, you have mistaken my sentiments, alike in morality, politics, and—what is called—metaphysics, and, I would fain hope, that if you knew me, you would not have ascribed self-opinion and arrogance to me. But, be this as it may, I write to you now merely to intreat—for the sake of mankind—an honourable review of Mr. Clarkson's "History of the Abolition of the Slave Trade."[45] I know the man, and if you knew him you, I am sure, would revere him, and your reverence of him, as an agent, would almost supersede all judgment of him as a mere literary man. It would be presumptuous in me to offer to write the review of his work. Yet I should be glad were I permitted to submit to you the many thoughts which occurred to me during its perusal. Be assured, that with the greatest respect for your talents—as far as I can judge of them from the few numbers of the "Edinburgh Review" which I have had the opportunity of reading—and every kind thought respecting your motives,

I am, dear sir, your ob. humb. ser't,
S. T. Coleridge.

—— Jeffray (sic), Esq.,
to the care of Mr. Constable, Bookseller, Edingburgh (sic).

CLXIX. TO THE SAME.

[Postmark] Bury St. Edmunds,
July 20, 1808.

Dear Sir,—Not having been gratified by a letter from you, I have feared that the freedom with which I opened out my opinions may have given you offence. Be assured, it was most alien from my intention. The purport of what I wrote was simply this—that severe and long-continued bodily disease exacerbated by disappointment in the great hope of my Life had rendered me insensible to blame and praise, even to a faulty degree, unless they proceeded from the one or two who love me. The entrance-passage to my heart is choked up with heavy lumber, and I am thus barricadoed against attacks, which, doubtless, I should otherwise have felt as keenly as most men. Instead of censuring a certain quantum of irritability respecting the reception of published composition, I rather envy it—it becomes ludicrous then only, when it is disavowed, and the opposite temper pretended to. The ass's skin is almost scourge-proof—while the elephant thrills under the movements of every fly that runs over it. But though notoriously almost a zealot in behalf of my friend's poetic reputation, yet I can leave it with cheerful confidence to the fair working of his own powers. I have known many, very many instances of contempt changed into admiration of his genius; but I neither know nor have heard of a single person, who having been or having become his admirer had ceased to be so. For it is honourable to us all that our kind affections, the attractions and elective affinities of our nature, are of more permanent agency than those passions which repel and dissever. From this cause we may explain the final growth of honest fame, and its tenacity of life. Whenever the struggle of controversy ceases, we think no more of works which give us no pleasure and apply our satire and scorn to some new object, and thus the field is left entire to friends and partisans.

But the case of Mr. Clarkson appeared to me altogether different. I do not hold his fame dear because he is my friend; but I sought and cultivated his acquaintance, because a long and sober enquiry had assured me, that he had been, in an awful sense of the word, a benefactor of mankind: and this from the purest motives unalloyed by the fears and hopes of selfish superstition—and not with that feverish power which fanatics acquire by crowding together, but in the native strength of his own moral impulses. He, if ever human being did it, listened exclusively to his conscience, and obeyed its voice at the price of all his youth and manhood, at the price of his health, his private fortune, and the fairest prospects of honourable ambition. Such a man I cannot regard as a mere author. I cannot read or criticise such a work as a mere literary production. The opinions publicly expressed and circulated concerning it must of necessity in the author's feelings be entwined with the cause itself, and with his own character as a man, to which that of the historian is only an accidental accession. Were it the pride of authorship alone that was in danger of being fretted, I should have remained as passive in this instance as in that of my most particular friend, to whom I am bound by ties more close and of longer standing than those which connect me personally with Mr. Clarkson. But I know that any sarcasms or ridicule would deeply wound his feelings, as a veteran warrior in a noble contest, feelings that claim the reverence of all good men.

The Review was sent, addressed to you, by the post of yester-evening. There is not a sentence, not a word in it, which I should not have written, had I never seen the author.

I am myself about to bring out two works—one a small pamphlet[46]—the second of considerable size—it is a rifacciamento, a very free translation with large additions, etc., etc., of the masterly work for which poor Palm was murdered.

I hope to be in the North, at Keswick, in the course of a week or eight days. I shall be happy to hear from you on this or any other occasion.

Yours, dear sir, sincerely,

S. T. Coleridge.

CHAPTER X
GRASMERE AND THE FRIEND
1808-1810

CLXX. TO DANIEL STUART.

[December 9, 1808.]

My dear Stuart,—Scarcely when listening to count the hour, have I been more perplexed by the "Inopem me copia fecit" of the London church clocks, than by the press of what I have to say to you. I must do one at a time. Briefly, a very happy change[47] has taken place in my health and spirits and mental activity since I placed myself under the care and inspection of a physician, and I dare say with confident hope, "Judge me from the 1st January, 1809."

I send you the Prospectus, and intreat you to do me all the good you can; which like the Lord's Prayer is Thanksgiving in the disguise of petition. If you think that it should be advertized in any way, or if Mr. Street can do anything for me—but I know you will do what you can.

I have received promises of contribution from many tall fellows with big names in the world of Scribes, and count even Pharisees (two or three Bishops) in my list of patrons. But whether I shall have 50, 100, 500, or 1,000 subscribers I am not able even to conjecture. All must depend on the zeal of my friends, on which I fear I have thrown more water than oil—but some like the Greek fire burn beneath the wave!

Wordsworth has nearly finished a series of most masterly Essays[48] on the Affairs of Portugal and Spain, and by my advice he will first send them to you that if they suit the "Courier" they may be inserted.

I have not heard from Savage, but I suppose that he has printed a thousand of these Prospectuses, and you may have any number from him. He lives hard by some of the streets in Covent Garden which I do not remember, but a note to Mr. Savage, R. Institution, Albemarle Street, will find him.

May God Almighty bless you! I feel that I shall yet live, to give proof of what is deep within me towards you.

S. T. Coleridge.

CLXXI. TO FRANCIS JEFFREY.

Grasmere, December 14, 1808.

Dear Sir,—The only thing in which I have been able to detect any degree of hypochrondriasis in my feelings is the reading and answering of letters, and in this instance I have been at times so wofully under its domination as to have left every letter received lie unopened for weeks together, all the while thoroughly ashamed of the weakness and yet without power to get rid of it. This, however, has not been the case of late, and I was never yet so careless as knowingly to suffer a letter relating to money to remain unanswered by the next post in my power. I, therefore, on reading your very kind letter of 8 Dec. conclude that one letter from you during my movements from Grasmere, now to Keswick, now to Bratha and Elleray, and now to Kendal, has been mislayed.

As I considered your insertion of the review of Mr. Clarkson's as an act of personal kindness and attention to the request of one a stranger to you except by name, the thought of any pecuniary remuneration never once occurred to me; and had it been written at your request I should have thought twenty guineas a somewhat extravagant price whether I considered the quantity or quality of the communication. As to the alterations, your character and interest, as the known Editor of the Review, are pledged for a general consistency of principle in the different articles with each other, and you had every possible right to alter or omit ad libitum, unless a special condition had been insisted on of aut totum aut nihil. As the writer, therefore, I neither thought nor cared about the alterations; as a general reader, I differed with you as [to] the scale of merit relatively to Mr. Wilberforce, whose services I deem to have been overrated, not, perhaps, so much absolutely as by comparison. At all events, some following passages should have been omitted, as they are in blank contradiction to the paragraph inserted, and betrayed a co-presence of two writers in one article. As to the longer paragraph, Wordsworth thinks you on the true side; and Clarkson himself that you were not far from the truth. As to my own opinion, I believed what I wrote, and deduced my belief from all the facts pro and con, with which Mr. Clarkson's conversation have furnished [me]; but such is my detestation of that pernicious Minister,[49] such my contempt of the cowardice and fatuity of his measures, and my horror at the yet unended train of their direful consequences, that, if obedience to truth could ever be painful to me, this would have been. I acted well in writing what on the whole I believed the more probable, and I was pleased that you acted equally well in altering it according to your convictions.

I had hoped to have furnished a letter of more interesting contents to you, but an honest gentleman in London having taken a great fancy to two thirds of the possible profits of my literary labours without a shadow of a claim, and having over-hurried the business through overweening of my simplicity and carelessness, has occasioned me some perplexity and a great deal of trouble and letter-writing. I will write, however, again to you my first leisure evening, whether I hear from you or no in the interim.

I trust you have received my scrawl with the prospectus[50] and feel sincerely thankful to you for your kindness on the arrival of the prospectuses, prior to your receipt of the letter which was meant to have announced them. But our post here is very irregular as well as circuitous—but three times a week—and then, too, we have to walk more than two miles for the chance of finding letters. This you will be so good as to take into account whenever my answers do not arrive at the time they might have been expected from places in general. I remain, dear sir, with kind and respectful feeling, your obliged,

S. T. Coleridge.

I entirely coincide in your dislike of "speculative gloom"—it is illogical as well as barbarous, and almost as bad as "picturesque eye." I do not know how I came to pass it; for when I first wrote it, I undermarked it, not as the expression, but as a remembrancer of some better that did not immediately occur to me. "Year-long absences" I think doubtful—had any one objected to it, I should have altered it; but it would not much offend me in the writings of another. But to "moral impulses" I see at present no objections, nor does any other phrase suggest itself to me which would have expressed my meaning. That there is a semblance of presumptuousness in the manner I exceedingly regret, if so it be—my heart bears me witness that the feeling had no place there. Yet I need not say to you that it is impossible to succeed in such a work unless at the commencement of it there be a quickening and throb in the pulse of hope; and what if a blush from inward modesty disguise itself on these occasions, and the hectic of unusual self-assertion increase the appearance of that excess which it in reality resists and modifies? It will amuse you to be informed that from two correspondents, both of them men of great literary celebrity, I have received reproof for a supposed affectation of humility in the style of the prospectus. In my own consciousness I was guilty of neither. Yet surely to advance as a teacher, and in the very act to declare yourself inferior to those whom you propose to teach, is incongruous; and must disgust a pure mind by its evident hypocrisy.

CLXXII. TO THOMAS WILKINSON.[51]

Grasmere, December 31, 1808.

Dear Sir,—I thank you for your exertions in my behalf, and—which more deeply interests me—for the openness with which you have communicated your doubts and apprehensions. So much, indeed, am I interested, that I cannot lay down my head on my pillow in perfect tranquillity, without endeavoring to remove them. First, however, I must tell you that ... "The Friend" will not appear at the time conditionally announced. There are, besides, great difficulties at the Stamp Office concerning it. But the particulars I will detail when we meet. Myself, with William Wordsworth and the family, are glad that we are so soon to see you. Now then for what is so near my heart. Only a certain number of prospectuses were printed at Kendal, and sent to acquaintances. The much larger number, which were to have been printed at London, have not been printed. When they are, you will see in the article, noted in this copy, that I neither intend to omit, nor from any fear of offence have scrupled to announce my intention of treating, the subject of religion. I had supposed that the words "speculative gloom" would have conveyed this intention. I had inserted another article, which I was induced to omit, from the fear of exciting doubts and queries. This was: On the transition of natural religion into revelation, or the principle of internal guidance: and the grounds of the possibility of the connection of spiritual revelation with historic events; that is, its manifestation in the world of the senses. This meant as a preliminary—leaving, as already performed by others, the proof of the reality of this connection in the particular fact of Christianity. Herein I wished to prove only that true philosophy rather leads to Christianity, than contained anything preclusive of it, and therefore adopted the phrase used in the definition of philosophy in general: namely, The science which answers the question of things actual, how they are possible? Thus the laws of gravitation illustrate the possibility of the motion of the heavenly bodies, the action of the lever, etc.; the reality of which was already known. I mention this, because the argument assigned which induced me to omit it in a prospectus was, that by making a distinction between revelation in itself (i. e. a principle of internal supernatural guidance), and the same revelation conjoined with the power of external manifestation by supernatural works, would proclaim me to be a Quaker, and "The Friend" as intended to propagate peculiar and sectarian principles. Think then, dear Friend! what my regret was at finding that you had taken it for granted that I denied the existence of an internal monitor! I trust I am neither of Paul, or of Apollos, or of Cephas; but of Christ. Yet I feel reverential gratitude toward those who have conveyed the spirit of Christ to my heart and understanding so as to afford light to the latter and vital warmth to the former. Such gratitude I owe and feel toward W. Penn. Take his Preface to G. Fox's Journal, and his Letter to his Son,—if they contain a faithful statement of genuine

Christianity according to your faith, I am one with you. I subscribe to each and all of the principles therein laid down; and by them I propose to try, and endeavour to justify, the charge made by me (my conscience bears me witness) in the spirit of entire love against some passages of the journals of later Friends. Oh—and it is a groan of earnest aspiration! a strong wish of bitter tears and bitter self-dissatisfaction,—Oh that in all things, in self-subjugation, unwearied beneficence, and unfeigned listening and obedience to the Voice within, I were as like the evangelic John Woolman, as I know myself to be in the belief of the existence and the sovran authority of that Voice! When we meet, I will endeavour to be wholly known to you as I am, in principle at least.

A few words more. Unsuspicious of the possibility of misunderstanding, I had inserted in this prospectus Dress and Dancing among the fine Arts, the principles common to which I was to develope. Now surely anything common to Dress or Dancing with Architecture, Gardening, and Poetry could contain nothing to alarm any man who is not alarmed by Gardening, Poetry, etc., and secondly, principles common to Poetry, Music, etc., etc., could hardly be founded in the ridiculous hopping up and down in a modern ball-room, or the washes, paints, and patches of a fine lady's toilet. It is well known how much I admired Thomas Clarkson's Chapter on Dancing. The truth is, that I referred to the drapery and ornamental decoration of Painting, Statuary, and the Greek Spectacles; and to the scientific dancing of the ancient Greeks, the business of a life confined to a small class, and placed under the direction of particular magistrates. My object was to prove the truth of the principles by shewing that even dress and dancing, when the ingenuity and caprice of man had elaborated them into Fine Arts, were bottomed in the same principles. But desirous even to avoid suspicion, the passage will be omitted in the future prospectuses. Farewell! till we meet.

S. T. Coleridge. See P. S.

P. S. Do you not know enough of the world to be convinced that by declaring myself a warm defender of the Established Church against all sectarians, or even by attacking Quakerism in particular as a sect hateful to the bigots of the day from its rejection of priesthood and outward sacraments, I should gain twenty subscribers to one? It shocks me even to think that so mean a motive could be supposed to influence me. I say aloud everywhere, that in the essentials of their faith I believe as the Quakers do, and so I make enemies of the Church, of the Calvinists, and even of the Unitarians. Again, I declare my dissatisfaction with several points both of notion and of practice among the present Quakers—I dare not conceal my convictions—and therefore receive little good opinion even from those, with whom I most accord. But Truth is sacred.

CLXXIII. TO THOMAS POOLE.

Grasmere, Kendal, February 3, 1809.

My dearest Poole,—For once in my life I shall have been blamed by you for silence, indolence, and procrastination without reason. Even now I write this letter on a speculation, for I am to take it with me to-morrow to Kendal, and if I can bring the proposed printer and publisher to final terms, to put it into the post. It would be a tiresome job were I to detail to you all the vexations, hindrances, scoundrelisms, disappointments, and pros and cons that, without the least fault or remissness on my part, have rendered it impracticable to publish "The Friend" till the first week of March. The whole, however, is now settled, provided that Pennington (a worthy old bookseller and printer of Kendal, but a genius and mightily indifferent about the affairs of this life, both from that cause and from age, and from being as rich as he wishes) will become, as he has almost promised, the printer and publisher.[52]

"The Friend" will be stamped as a newspaper and under the Newspaper Act, which will take 3½d. from each shilling, but enable the essay to pass into all parts and corners of the Empire without expense or trouble. It will be so published as to appear in London every Saturday morning, and be sent off from the Kendal post to every part of the Kingdom by the Thursday morning's post. I hope that Mr. Stuart will have the prospectuses printed by this time,—at all events, within a day or two after your receipt of this letter you will receive a parcel of them. The money is to be paid to the bookseller, the agent, in the next town, once in twenty weeks, where there are several subscribers in the same vicinity; otherwise, [it] must be remitted to me direct. This is the ugliest part of the business: but there is no getting over it without a most villainous diminution of my profits. You will, I know, exert yourself to procure me as many names as you can, for if it succeeds, it will almost make me.

Among my subscribers I have Mr. Canning and Sturges Bourne, and Mr. W. Rose, of whose moral odour your nose, I believe, has had competent experience. The first prospectus I receive, I shall send with letters to Lord Egmont and Lady E. Percival, and to Mr. Acland.

You will probably have seen two of Wordsworth's Essays in the "Courier," signed "G." The two last columns of the second, excepting the concluding paragraph, were written all but a few sentences by me.[53] An accident in London delayed the publication ten days. The whole, therefore, is now publishing as a pamphlet, and I believe with a more comprehensive title.

I cannot say whether I was—indeed, both I and W. W.—more pleased or affected by the whole of your last letter; it came from a very pure and warm heart through the moulds of a clear and strong brain. But I have not now time to write on these concerns. For my opinions, feelings, hopes, and apprehensions, I can safely refer you to Wordsworth's pamphlet. The minister's conduct hitherto is easily defined. A great deal too much because not half enough. Two essays of my own on this most lofty theme,—what we are entitled to hope, what compelled to fear concerning the Spanish nation, by the light of history and psychological knowledge, you will soon see in the "Courier." Poor Wardle![54] I fear lest his zeal may have made him confound that degree of evidence which is sufficient to convince an unprejudiced private company with that which will satisfy an unwilling numerous assembly of factious and corrupt judges. As to the truth of the charges, I have little doubt, knowing myself similar facts.

O dear Poole! Beddoes' departure[55] has taken more hope out of my life than any former event except perhaps T. Wedgwood's. That did indeed pull very hard at me; never a week, seldom two days have passed in which the recollection has not made me sad or thoughtful. Beddoes' seems to pull yet harder, because it combines with the former, because it is the second, and because I have not been in the habit of connecting such a weight of despondency with my attachment to him as with my love of my revered and dear benefactor. Poor Beddoes! he was good and beneficent to all men, but to me he was, moreover, affectionate and loving, and latterly his sufferings had opened out his being to a delicacy, a tenderness, a moral beauty, and unlocked the source of sensibility as with a key from heaven.

My own health is more regular than formerly, for I am severely temperate and take nothing that has not been pronounced medically unavoidable; yet my sufferings are often great, and I am rarely indeed wholly without pain or sensations more oppressive than definite pain. But my mind, and what is far better, my will is active. I must leave a short space to add at Kendal after all is settled.

My beloved and honoured friend! may God preserve you and your obliged, and affectionately grateful,

S. T. Coleridge.

My dearest Poole,—Old Mr. Pennington has ultimately declined the printing and publishing; indeed, he is about to decline business altogether. There is no other in this country capable of doing the work, and to printing and publishing in London there are gigantic objections. What think you of a press at Grasmere? I will write when I get home. Oh, if you knew what a warmth of unusual feeling, what a genial air of new and living hope breathed upon me as I read that casual sentence in your letter, seeming to imply a chance we have of seeing you at Grasmere! I assure you that the whole family, Mrs. Wordsworth and her all-amiable sister, not with less warmth than W. W. and Dorothy, were made cheerful and wore a more holiday look the whole day after. Oh, do, do come!

CLXXIV. TO DANIEL STUART.

Posted March 31, 1809.

My dear Friend,—I have been severely indisposed, knocked up indeed, with a complaint of a contagious nature called the Mumps;[56] preceded by most distressing low spirits, or rather absence of all spirits; and accompanied with deafness and stupefying perpetual echo in the ear. But it is going off. Little John Wordsworth was attacked with it last year when I was in London, and from the stupor with which it suffuses the eyes and look, it was cruelly mistaken for water on the brain. It has been brought here a second time by some miners, and is a disease with little danger and no remedy.

I attributed your silence to its right cause, and I assure you when I was at Penrith and Kendal it was very pleasant to me to hear how universally the conduct of the "Courier" was extolled; indeed, you have behaved most nobly, and it is impossible but that you must have had a great weight in the displacing of that prime grievance of grievances. Among many reflections that kept crowding on my mind during the trial,[57] this was perhaps the chief— What if, after a long, long reign, some titled sycophant should whisper to Majesty, "By what means do your Ministers manage the Legislature?" "By the distribution of patronage, according to the influence of individuals who claim it." "Do this yourself, or by your own family, and you become independent of parties, and your Ministers are your servants. The Army under a favourite son, the Church with a wife, etc., etc." Good heavens! the very essence of the Constitution is unmoulded, and the venerable motto of our liberty, "The king can do no wrong," becomes nonsense and blasphemy. As soon as ever my mind is a little at ease, I will put together the fragments I have written on this subject, and if Wordsworth have not anticipated me, add to it some thoughts on the effect of the military principle. We owe something to Whitbread for his quenching at the first smell a possible fire. How is it possible that a man apparently so honest can talk and think as he does respecting France, peace, and Buonaparte?...

On Thursday Wordsworth, Southey, and myself, with the printer and publisher, go to Appleby to sign and seal, which paper, etc., will of course be immediately dispatched to London. I doubt not but that the £60 will be now paid at the "Courier" office in a few days; and as soon as you will let me know whether the stamped paper is to be paid for necessarily in ready money, or with what credit, I shall instantly write to some of my friends to advance me what is absolutely necessary. I can only say I am ready and eager to commence, and that I earnestly hope to see "The Friend" advertised shortly for the first of May. As to the Paper, how and from whom, and what and in what quantity, I must again leave to your judgment, and recommend to your affection for me. I have reason to believe that I shall commence with 500 names.

I write from Keswick. Mrs. Southey was delivered yester-morning of a girl.[58] I forgot to say, that I have been obliged to purchase, and have paid for, a font of types of small pica, the same with the London Prospectus, from Wilsons of Glasgow. I was assured they would cost only from £25 to £28, instead of which, £38 odd.

God bless you and

S. T. Coleridge.

CLXXV. TO THE SAME.

Grasmere, Kendal, June 13, 1809.

Dear Stuart,—I left Penrith Monday noon, and, prevented by the heavy rain from crossing Grisedale Tarn (near the summit of Helvellyn, and our most perilous and difficult Alpine Pass), the same day I slept at Luff's, and crossed it yester-morning, and arrived here by breakfast time. I was sadly grieved at Wordsworth's account of your late sorrows and troubles....

I cannot adequately express how much I am concerned lest anything I wrote in my last letter (though God knows under the influence of no one feeling which you would not wish me to have) should chance to have given you any additional unpleasantness, however small. Would that I had worthier means than words and professions of proving to you what my heart is....

I rise every morning at five, and work three hours before breakfast, either in letter-writing or serious composition....

I take for granted that more than the poor £60 has been expended in the paper I have received. But I have written to Mr. Clarkson to see what can be done; for it would be a sad thing to give it all up now I am going on so well merely for want of means to provide the first twenty weeks paper. My present stock will not quite suffice for three numbers. I printed 620 of No. 1, and 650 of No. 2, and so many more are called for that I shall be forced to reprint both as soon as I hear from Clarkson. The proof sheet of No. 3 goes back to-day, and with it the copy of No. 4, so that henceforth we shall be secure of regularity; indeed it was not all my fault before, but the printer's inexperience and the multitude of errors, though from a very decent copy, which took him a full day and more in correcting. I had altered my plan for the Introductory Essays after my arrival at Penrith, which cost me exceeding trouble; but the numbers to come are in a very superior style of polish and easy intelligibility. The only thing at present which I am under the necessity of applying to you for respects Clement. It may be his interest to sell "The Friend" at his shop, and a certain number will always be sent; but I am quite in the dark as to what profits he expects. Surely not book-profits for a newspaper that can circulate by the post? And it is certainly neither my interest, nor that of the regular purchasers of "The Friend," to have it bought at a shop, instead of receiving it as a franked letter. All I want to know is his terms, for I have quite a horror of booksellers, whose mode of carrying on trade in London is absolute rapacity....

On this ruinous plan poor Southey has been toiling for years, with an industry honourable to human nature, and must starve upon it were it not for the more profitable employment of reviewing; a task unworthy of him, or even of a man with not one half of his honour and honesty.

I have just read Wordsworth's pamphlet, and more than fear that your friendly expectations of its sale and influence have been too sanguine. Had I not known the author I would willingly have travelled from St. Michael's Mount to Johnny Groat's House on a pilgrimage to see and reverence him. But from the public I am apprehensive, first, that it will be impossible to rekindle an exhausted interest respecting the Cintra Convention, and therefore that the long porch may prevent readers from entering the Temple. Secondly, that, partly from Wordsworth's own style, which represents the chain of his thoughts and the movements of his heart, admirably for me and a few others, but I fear does not possess the more profitable excellence of translating these down into that style which might easily convey them to the understandings of common readers, and partly from Mr. De Quincey's strange and most mistaken system of punctuation—(The periods are often alarmingly long, perforce of their construction, but De Quincey's punctuation has made several of them immeasurable, and perplexed half the rest. Never was a stranger whim than the notion that , ; : and . could be made logical symbols, expressing all the diversities of logical connection)—but, lastly, I fear that readers, even of judgement, may complain of a want of shade and background; that it is all foreground, all in hot tints; that the first note is pitched at the height of the instrument, and never suffered to sink; that such depth of feeling is so incorporated with depth of thought, that the attention is kept throughout at its utmost strain and stretch; and—but this for my own feeling. I could not help feeling that a considerable part is almost a self-robbery from some great philosophical poem, of which it would form an appropriate part, and be fitlier attuned to the high dogmatic eloquence, the oracular [tone] of impassioned blank verse. In short, cold readers, conceited of their supposed judgement, on the score of their possessing nothing else, and for that reason only, taking for granted that they must have judgement, will abuse the book as positive, violent, and "in a mad passion;" and readers of sense and feeling will have no other dread, than that the Work (if it should die) would die of a plethora of the highest qualities of combined philosophic and poetic genius. The Apple Pie they may say is made all of Quinces. I much admired our young friend's note on Sir John Moore and his despatch;[59] it was excellently arranged and urged. I have had no opportunity, as yet, to speak a word to Wordsworth himself about it; I wrote to you as usual in full confidence.

I shall not be a little anxious to have your opinion of my third number. Lord Lonsdale blames me for excluding party politics and the events of the day from my plan. I exclude both the one and the other, only as far as they are merely party, i. e. personal and temporal interests, or merely events of To-day, that are defunct in the To-morrow. I flatter myself that I have been the first, who will have given a calm, disinterested account of our Constitution as it really is and how it is so, and that I have, more radically than has been done before, shown the unstable and boggy grounds on which all systematic reformers hitherto have stood. But be assured that I shall give up this opinion with joy, and consider a truer view of the question a more than recompense for the necessity of retracting what I have written.

God bless you! Do, pray, let me hear from you, though only three lines.

S. T. Coleridge.

CLXXVI. TO THOMAS POOLE.

October 9, 1809.

My dear Poole,—I received yours late last night, and sincerely thank you for the contents. The whole shall be arranged as you have recommended. Yet if I know my own wishes, I would far rather you had refused me, and said you should have an opportunity in a few days of explaining your motives in person, for oh, the autumn is divine here. You never beheld, I will answer for it, such combinations of exquisite beauty with sufficient grandeur of elevation, even in Switzerland. Besides, I sorely want to talk with you on many points.

All the defects you have mentioned I am perfectly aware of, and am anxiously endeavouring to avoid. There is too often an entortillage in the sentences and even in the thought (which nothing can justify), and, always almost, a stately piling up of story on story in one architectural period, which is not suited to a periodical essay or to essays at all (Lord Bacon, whose style mine more nearly resembles than any other, in his greater works, thought Seneca a better model for his Essays), but least of all suited to the present illogical age, which has, in imitation of the French, rejected all the cements of language, so that a popular book is now a mere bag of marbles, that is, aphorisms and epigrams on one subject. But be assured that the numbers will improve; indeed, I hope that if the dire stoppage have not prevented it, you will have seen proof of improvement already in the seventh and eighth numbers,—still more in the ninth, tenth, eleventh, twelfth, thirteenth, fourteenth, and fifteenth numbers. Strange! but the "Three Graves" is the only thing I have yet heard generally praised and inquired after!! Remember how many different guests I have at my Round Table. I groan beneath the Errata, but I am thirty miles cross-post from my printer and publisher, and Southey, who has been my corrector, has been strangely oscitant, or, which I believe is sometimes the case, has not understood the sentences, and thought they might have a meaning for me though they had not for him. There was one direful one,[60] No. 5, p. 80, lines 3 and 4. Read,—"its functions being to take up the passive affections of the senses into distinct thoughts and judgements, according to its own essential forms, formæ formantes in the language of Lord Bacon in contradistinction to the formæ formatæ."

My greatest difficulty will be to avoid that grievous defect of running one number into another, I not being present at the printing. To really cut down or stretch out every subject to the Procrustes-Bed of sixteen pages is not possible without a sacrifice of my whole plan, but most often I will divide them polypus-wise, so that the first half should get itself a new tail of its own, and the latter a new head, and always take care to leave off at a paragraph. With my best endeavours I am baffled in respect of making one Essay fill one number. The tenth number is, W. thinks, the most interesting, "On the Errors of both Parties," or "Extremes Meet;" and, do what I would, it stretched to seven or eight pages more; but I have endeavoured to take your advice in toto, and shall announce to the public that, with the exception of my volume of Political Essays and State Memorials, and some technical works of Logic and Grammar, I shall consider "The Friend" as both the reservoir and the living fountain of all my mind, that is, of both my powers and my attainments, and shall therefore publish all my poems in "The Friend," as occasion rises. I shall begin with the "Fears in Solitude," and the "Ode on France," which will fill up the remainder of No. 11; so that my next Essay on vulgar Errors concerning Taxation, in which I have alluded to a conversation with you, will just fill No. 12 by itself.

I have been much affected by your efforts respecting poor Blake. Cannot you with propriety give me that narrative? But, above all, if you have no particular objection, no very particular and insurmountable reason against it, do, do let me have that divine narrative of John Walford,[61] which of itself stamps you a poet of the first class in the pathetic, and the painting of poetry so very rarely combined.

As to politics, I am sad at the very best. Two cabinet ministers duelling on Cabinet measures like drunken Irishmen. O heaven, Poole! this is wringing the dregs in order to drink the last drops of degradation. Such base insensibility to the awfulness of their situation and the majesty of the country! As soon as I can get them transcribed, I will send you some most interesting letters from the ablest soldier I ever met with (extra aide-de-camp to Sir J. Moore, and shot through the body at Flushing, but still alive); they will serve as a key to more than one woe-trumpet in the Apocalypse of national calamity. But the truth is, that to combine a government every way fitted as ours is for quiet, justice, freedom, and commercial activity at home, with the conditions of raising up that individual greatness, and of securing in every department the very man for the very place, which are requisite for maintaining the safety of our Empire and the Majesty of our power abroad, is a state-riddle which yet remains to be solved. I have thought myself as well employed as a private citizen can be, in drawing off well-intentioned patriots from the wrong scent and pointing out what the true evils are and why, and the exceeding difficulty of removing them without hazarding worse.... I was asked for a motto for a market clock. I uttered the following literally, without a moment's premeditation:—

What now, O man! thou dost or mean'st to do
Will help to give thee peace, or make thee rue,
When hovering o'er the Dot this hand shall tell
The moment that secures thee Heaven or Hell.[62]

May God bless you! My kindest remembrances to Mr. Chubb, and to Ward. Pray remember me when you write to your sister and Mr. King. Oh, but Poole! do stretch a point and come. If the F. rises to a 1,000 I will frank you. Do come; never will you have layed out money better.

CLXXVII. TO ROBERT SOUTHEY.

December, 1809.

My dear Southey,—I suspect you have misunderstood me, and applied to the Maltese Regiment what I said of the Corsican Rangers. Both are bad enough, but of the former I know little, of course, as I was away from Malta before the regiment had left the island. But in the Essays (2 or 3) which I am now writing on Sir A. Ball, I shall mention it as an exemplification among many others of his foresight. It was a job, I have no doubt, merely to get General Valette a lucrative regiment; but G. V. is dead, and it was not such a job as that of the Corsican Rangers, which can be made appear glaring. The long and short of the story is, that the men were four fifths married, would have fought as well as the best, at home and behind their own walls, but could not be expected to fight abroad, where they had no interest. Besides, it was cruel, shameful to take 1,500 men as soldiers for any part of our enormous Empire, out of a population, man, woman, and child, not at that time more than 100,000. There were two Maltese Militia Regiments officered by their own Maltese nobility—these against the entreaties and tears of the men and officers (I myself saw them weeping), against the remonstrances and memorial (written by myself) of Sir A. B., were melted into one large one, officered by English officers, and a general affront given to the island, because General Valette had great friends at the War Office, Duke of York, etc.! This is the whole, but do not either expose yourself or me to judicial inquiries. It is one thing to know a thing, and another to be able to prove it in a law court. This remark applies to the damnable treatment of the prisoners of war at Malta.

I should have thought your facts, with which I am familiar, a confirmation of Miss Schöning.[63] Be that as it may, take my word for it, that in substance the story is as certain as that Dr. Dodd was hung. To mention one proof only, Von Hess,[64] the celebrated historian of Hamburg, and, since Lessing, the best German prosist, went himself to Nuremberg, examined into the facts officially and personally, and it was on him that I relied, though if you knew the government of Nuremberg, you would see that the first account could not have been published as it was, if it had not been too notorious even for concealment to be hoped for. After I left Germany, Von Hess had a public controversy that threatened to become a Diet concern with the magistrates of Nuremberg, for some other bitter charges against them. I have their defence of themselves, but they do not even attempt to deny the fact of Harlin and Schöning. But, indeed, Southey! it is almost as bad as if I could have mistaken e converso Patch's trial for a novel.

Your remark on the voice is most just, but that was my purpose. Not only so, but the whole passage was inserted, and intertruded after the rest was written, reluctante amanuensi meâ, in order to unrealize it even at the expense of disnaturalizing it. Lady B. therefore pleased me by saying, "never was the golden tint of the poet more judiciously employed," etc. For this reason, too, I introduced the simile of the leaf, etc., etc. I not only thought the "voice" part out of place, but in bad taste per se.

May God bless you all.

S. T. Coleridge.

CLXXVIII. TO THOMAS POOLE.

Grasmere, Kendal, January 28, 1810.

My dear Friend,—My "mantraps and spring guns in this garden" have hitherto existed only in the painted board, in terrorem. Of course, I have received and thank you for both your letters. What Wordsworth may do I do not know, but I think it highly probable that I shall settle in or near London. Of the fate of "The Friend" I remain in the same ignorance nearly as at the publication of the 20th November. It would make you sick were I to waste my paper by detailing the numerous instances of meanness in the mode of payment and discontinuance, especially among the Quakers. So just was the answer I once made in the presence of some "Friends" to the query: What is genuine Quakerism? Answer, The antithesis of the present Quakers. I have received this evening together with yours, one as a specimen. (N. B. Three days after the publication of the 21st Number, and sixteen days after the publication of the "Supernumerary" [number of "The Friend," January 11, 1810], a bill upon a postmaster, an order of discontinuance, and information that any others that may come will not be paid for, as if I had been gifted with prophecy. And this precious epistle directed, "To Thomas Coleridge, of Grazemar"! And yet this Mr. —— would think himself libelled, if he were called a dishonest man.)... We will take for granted that "The Friend" can be continued. On this supposition I have lately studied "The Spectator," and with increasing pleasure and admiration. Yet it must be evident to you that there is a class of thoughts and feelings, and these, too, the most important, even practically, which it would be impossible to convey in the manner of Addison, and which, if Addison had possessed, he would not have been Addison. Read, for instance, Milton's prose tracts, and only try to conceive them translated into the style of "The Spectator," or the finest part of Wordsworth's pamphlet. It would be less absurd to wish that the serious Odes of Horace had been written in the same style as his Satires and Epistles. Consider, too, the very different objects of "The Friend," and of "The Spectator," and above all do not forget, that these are awful times! that the love of reading as a refined pleasure, weaning the mind from grosser enjoyments, which it was one of "The Spectator's" chief objects to awaken, has by that work, and those that followed (Connoisseur, World, Mirror, etc.), but still more, by Newspapers, Magazines, and Novels, been carried into excess: and "The Spectator" itself has innocently contributed to the general taste for unconnected writing, just as if "Reading made easy" should act to give men an aversion to words of more than two syllables, instead of drawing them through those words into the power of reading books in general. In the present age, whatever flatters the mind in its ignorance of its ignorance, tends to aggravate that ignorance, and, I apprehend, does on the whole do more harm than good. Have you read the debate on the Address? What a melancholy picture of the intellectual feebleness of the country! So much on the one side of the question. On the other (1) I will, preparatory to writing on any chosen subject, consider whether it can be treated popularly, and with that lightness and variety of illustration which form the charms of "The Spectator." If it can, I will do my best. If not, next, whether yet there may not be furnished by the results of such an Essay thoughts and truths that may be so treated, and form a second Essay. (2) I shall always, besides this, have at least one number in four of rational entertainment, such as "Satyrane's Letters," as instructive as I can, but yet making entertainment the chief object in my own mind. But, lastly, in the Supplement of "The Friend" I shall endeavour to include whatever of higher and more abstruse meditation may be needed as the foundations of all the work after it; and the difference between those who will read and master that Supplement, and those who decline the toil, will be simply this, that what to the former will be demonstrated conclusions, the latter must start from as from postulates, and (to all whose minds have not been sophisticated by a half-philosophy) axioms. For no two things, that are yet different, can be in closer harmony than the deductions of a profound philosophy, and the dictates of plain common sense. Whatever tenets are obscure in the one, and requiring the greatest powers of abstraction to reconcile, are the same which are held in manifest contradiction by the common sense, and yet held and firmly believed, without sacrificing A to —A, or —A to A.... After this work I shall endeavour to pitch my note to the idea of a common, well-educated, thoughtful man, of ordinary talents; and the exceptions to this rule shall not form more than one fifth of the work. If with all this it will not do, well! And well it will be, in its noblest sense: for I shall have done my best. Of parentheses I may be too fond, and will be on my guard in this respect. But I am certain that no work of impassioned and eloquent reasoning ever did or could subsist without them. They are the drama of reason, and present the thought growing, instead of a mere Hortus siccus. The aversion to them is one of the numberless symptoms of a feeble Frenchified Public. One other observation: I have reason to hope for contributions from strangers. Some from you I rely on, and these will give a variety which is highly desirable—so much so, that it would weigh with me even to the admission of many things from unknown correspondents, though but little above mediocrity, if they were proportionately short, and on subjects which I should not myself treat....

May God bless you, and your affectionate

S. T. Coleridge.

CHAPTER XI
A JOURNALIST, A LECTURER, A PLAYWRIGHT
1810-1813

CLXXIX. TO HIS WIFE.

Spring, 1810.

My dear Love,—I understand that Mr. De Quincey is going to Keswick to-morrow; though between ourselves he is as great a to-morrower to the full as your poor husband, and without his excuses of anxiety from latent disease and external pressure.

Now as Lieutenant Southey is with you, I fear that you could not find a bed for me if I came in on Monday or Tuesday. I not only am desirous to be with you and Sara for a while, but it would be of great importance to me to be within a post of Penrith for the next fortnight or three weeks. How long Mr. De Quincey may stay I cannot guess. He (Miss Wordsworth says) talks of a week, but Lloyd of a month! However, put yourself to no violence of inconvenience, only be sure to write to me (N. B.—to me) by the carrier to-morrow.

I am middling, but the state of my spirit of itself requires a change of scene. Catherine W. [the Wordsworths' little daughter] has not recovered the use of her arm, etc., but is evidently recovering it, and in all other respects in better health than before,—indeed, so much better as to confirm my former opinion that nature was weak in her, and can more easily supply vital power for two thirds of her nervous system than for the whole.

May God bless you, my dear! and

S. T. Coleridge.

Hartley looks and behaves all that the fondest parent could wish. He is really handsome; at least as handsome as a face so original and intellectual can be. And Derwent is "a nice little fellow," and no lack-wit either. I read to Hartley out of the German a series of very masterly arguments concerning the startling gross improbabilities of Esther (fourteen improbabilities are stated). It really surprised me, the acuteness and steadiness of judgment with which he answered more than half, weakened many, and at last determined that two only were not to be got over. I then read for myself and afterwards to him Eichhorn's solution of the fourteen, and the coincidences were surprising. Indeed, Eichhorn, after a lame attempt, was obliged to give up the two which H. had declared as desperate.

CLXXX. TO THE MORGANS.

December 21, "1810."

My dear Friends,—I am at present at Brown's Coffee House, Mitre Court, Fleet Street. My objects are to settle something by which I can secure a certain sum weekly, sufficient for lodging, maintenance, and physician's fees, and in the mean time to look out for a suitable place near Gray's Inn. My immediate plan is not to trouble myself further about any introduction to Abernethy, but to write a plain, honest, and full account of my state, its history, causes, and occasions, and to send it to him with two or three pounds enclosed, and asking him to take me under his further care. If I have raised the money for the enclosure, this I shall do to-morrow. For, indeed, it is not only useless but unkind and ungrateful to you and all who love me, to trifle on any longer, depressing your spirits, and, spite of myself, gradually alienating your esteem and chilling your affection toward me. As soon as I have heard from Abernethy, I will walk over to you, and spend a few days before I enter into my lodging, and on my dread ordeal—as some kind-hearted Catholics have taught, that the soul is carried slowly along close by the walls of Paradise on its way to Purgatory, and permitted to breathe in some snatches of blissful airs, in order to strengthen its endurance during its fiery trial by the foretaste of what awaits it at the conclusion and final gaol-delivery.

I pray you, therefore, send me immediately all my books and papers with such of my linen as may be clean, in my box, by the errand cart, directed—"Mr. Coleridge, Brown's Coffee House, Mitre Court, Fleet Street." A couple of nails and a rope will sufficiently secure the box.

Dear, dear Mary! Dearest Charlotte! I entreat you to believe me, that if at any time my manner toward you has appeared unlike myself, this has arisen wholly either from a sense of self-dissatisfaction or from apprehension of having given you offence; for at no time and on no occasion did I ever see or imagine anything in your behaviour which did not awaken the purest and most affectionate esteem, and (if I do not grossly deceive myself) the sincerest gratitude. Indeed, indeed, my affection is both deep and strong toward you, and such too that I am proud of it.

"And looking towards the Heaven that bends above you,
Full oft I bless the lot that made me love you!"
Again and again and for ever may God bless you, and love you.

S. T. Coleridge.

J. J. Morgan, Esq., No. 7, Portland Place, Hammersmith.

CLXXXI. TO W. GODWIN.

March 15, 1811.

My dear Godwin,—I receive twice the pleasure from my recovery that it would have otherwise afforded, as it enables me to accept your kind invitation, which in this instance I might with perfect propriety and manliness thank you for, as an honour done to me. To sit at the same table with Grattan, who would not think it a memorable honour, a red letter day in the almanac of his life? No one certainly who is in any degree worthy of it. Rather than not be in the same room, I could be well content to wait at the table at which I was not permitted to sit, and this not merely for Grattan's undoubted great talents, and still less from any entire accordance with his political opinions, but because his great talents are the tools and vehicles of his genius, and all his speeches are attested by that constant accompaniment of true genius, a certain moral bearing, a moral dignity. His love of liberty has no snatch of the mob in it.

Assure Mrs. Godwin of my anxious wishes respecting her health. The scholar Salernitanus[65] says:—

"Si tibi deficiant medici, medici tibi fiant
Hæc tria: mens hilaris, requies, moderata diæta."
The regulated diet she already has, and now she must contrive to call in the two other doctors. God bless you.

S. T. Coleridge.

CLXXXII. TO DANIEL STUART.

Tuesday, June 4, 1811.

Dear Stuart,—I brought your umbrella in with me yester-morning, but, having forgotten it at leaving Portland Place, sent the coachman back for it, who brought what appeared to me not the same. On returning, however, with it, I could find no other, and it is certainly as good or better, but looks to me as if it were not equally new, and as if it had far more silk in it. I will, however, leave it at Brompton, and if by any inexplicable circumstance it should not prove the same, you must be content with the substitute. The family at Portland Place caught at my doubts as to the identity of it. I had hoped to have seen you this morning, it being a leisurely time in respect of fresh tidings, to have submitted to you two Essays,[66] one on the Catholic Question, and the other on Parliamentary Reform, addressed as a letter (from a correspondent) to the noblemen and members of Parliament who had associated for this purpose. The former does not exceed two columns; the latter is somewhat longer. But after the middle of this month it is probable that the Paper will be more open to a series of Articles on less momentary, though still contemporary, interests. Mr. Street seems highly pleased with what I have written this morning on the battle[67] of the 16th (May), though I apprehend the whole cannot be inserted. I am as I ought to be, most cautious and shy in recommending anything; otherwise, I should have requested Mr. Street to give insertion to the paragraphs respecting Holland, and the nature of Buonaparte's resources, ending with the necessity of ever re-fuelling the moral feelings of the people, as to the monstrosity of the giant fiend that menaces them; [with an] allusion to Judge Grose's opinion[68] on Drakard[69] before the occasion had passed away from the public memory. So, too, if the Duke's return is to be discussed at all, the Article should be published before Lord Milton's motion.[70] For though in a complex and widely controverted question, where hundreds rush into the field of combat, it is wise to defer it till the Debates in Parliament have shown what the arguments are on which most stress is laid by men in common, as in the Bullion Dispute; yet, generally, it is a great honour to the London papers, that for one argument they borrow from the parliamentary speakers, the latter borrow two from them, at all events are anticipated by them. But the true prudential rule is, to defer only when any effect of freshness or novelty is impracticable; but in most other cases to consider freshness of effect as the point which belongs to a Newspaper and distinguishes it from a library book; the former being the Zenith, and the latter the Nadir, with a number of intermediate degrees, occupied by pamphlets, magazines, reviews, satirical and occasional poems, etc., etc. Besides, in a daily newspaper, with advertisements proportioned to its sale, what is deferred must, four times in five, be extinguished. A newspaper is a market for flowers and vegetables, rather than a granary or conservatory; and the drawer of its editor, a common burial ground, not a catacomb for embalmed mummies, in which the defunct are preserved to serve in after times as medicines for the living. To turn from the Paper to myself, as candidate for the place of auxiliary to it. I drew, with Mr. Street's consent and order, ten pounds, which I shall repay during the week as soon as I can see Mr. Monkhouse of Budge Row, who has collected that sum for me. This, therefore, I put wholly aside, and indeed expect to replace it with Mr. Green to-morrow morning. Besides this I have had five pounds from Mr. Green,[71] chiefly for the purposes of coach hire. All at once I could not venture to walk in the heat and other accidents of weather from Hammersmith to the Office; but hereafter I intend, if I continue here, to return on foot, which will reduce my coach hire for the week from eighteen shillings to nine shillings. But to walk in, I know, would take off all the blossom and fresh fruits of my spirits. I trust that I need not say, how pleasant it would be to me, if it were in my power to consider everything I could do for the "Courier," as a mere return for the pecuniary, as well as other obligations I am under to you; in short as working off old scores. But you know how I am situated; and that by the daily labour of the brain I must acquire the daily demands of the other parts of the body. And it now becomes necessary that I should form some settled system for my support in London, and of course know what my weekly or monthly means may be. Respecting the "Courier," I consider you not merely as a private friend, but as the Co-proprietor of a large concern, in which it is your duty to regulate yourself with relation to the interests of that concern, and of your partner in it; and so take for granted, and, indeed, wish no other, than that you and he should weigh whether or no I can be of any material use to a Paper already so flourishing, and an Evening Paper. For, all mock humility out of the question (and when I write to you, every other sort of insincerity), I see that such services as I might be able to afford, would be more important to a rising than to a risen Paper; to a morning, perhaps, more than to an evening one. You will however decide, after the experience hitherto afforded, and modifying it by the temporary circumstances of debates, press of foreign news, etc.; how far I can be of actual use by my attendance, in order to help in the things of the day, as are the paragraphs, which I have for the most part hitherto been called [upon] to contribute; and, by my efforts, to sustain the literary character of the Paper, by large articles, on open days, and [at] more leisure times.

My dear Stuart! knowing the foolish mental cowardice with which I slink off from all pecuniary subjects, and the particular weight I must feel from the sense of existing obligations to you, you will be convinced that my only motive is the desire of settling with others such a plan for myself, as may, by setting my mind at rest, enable me to realize whatever powers I possess, to as much satisfaction to those who employ them, and to my own sense of duty, as possible. If Mr. Street should think that the "Courier" does not require any auxiliary, I shall then rely on your kindness, for putting me in the way of some other paper, the principles of which are sufficiently in accordance with my own; for while cabbage stalks rot on dung hills, I will never write what, or for what, I do not think right. All that prudence can justify is not to write what at certain times one may yet think. God bless you and

S. T. Coleridge.

CLXXXIII. TO SIR G. BEAUMONT.

J. J. Morgan's, Esq., 7, Portland Place, Hammersmith,
Saturday morning, December 7, 1811.

Dear Sir George,—On Wednesday night I slept in town in order to have a mask[72] taken, from which, or rather with which, Allston means to model a bust of me. I did not, therefore, receive your letter and the enclosed till Thursday night, eleven o'clock, on my return from the lecture; and early on Friday morning, I was roused from my first sleep by an agony of toothache, which continued almost without intermission the whole day, and has left my head and the whole of my trunk, "not a man but a bruise."[73] What can I say more, my dear Sir George, than that I deeply feel the proof of your continued friendship, and pray from my inmost soul that more perseverance in efforts of duty may render me more worthy of your kindness than I at present am? Ingratitude, like all crimes that are at the same time vices—bad as malady, and worse as symptom—is of so detestable a nature that an honest man will mourn in silence under real injuries, [rather] than hazard the very suspicion of it, and will be slow to avail himself of Lord Bacon's remark[74] (much as he may admire its profundity),—"Crimen ingrati animi, quod magnis ingeniis haud raro objicitur, sæpius nil aliud est quam perspicacia quædam in causam beneficii collati." Yet that man has assuredly tenfold reason to be grateful who can be so, both head and heart, who, at once served and honoured, knows himself more delighted by the motive that influenced his friend than by the benefit received by himself; were it only perhaps for this cause—that the consciousness of always repaying the former in kind takes away all regret that he is incapable of returning the latter.

Mr. Dawe, Royal Associate, who plastered my face for me, says that he never saw so excellent a mask, and so unaffected by any expression of pain or uneasiness. On Tuesday, at the farthest, a cast will be finished, which I was vain enough to desire to be packed up and sent to Dunmow. With it you will find a chalk drawing of my face,[75] which I think far more like than any former attempt, excepting Allston's full-length portrait of me,[76] which, with all his casts, etc., two or three valuable works of the Venetian school, and his Jason—almost finished, and on which he had employed eighteen months without intermission—are lying at Leghorn, with no chance of procuring them. There will likewise be an epistolary essay for Lady Beaumont on the subject of religion in reference to my own faith; it was too long to send by the post.

Dawe is engaged on a picture (the figures about four feet) from my poem of Love.

She leaned beside the armed man,
The statue of the armed knight;
She stood and listened to my harp
Amid the lingering light.
His dying words—but when I reached, etc.
All impulses of soul and sense, etc.
His sketch is very beautiful, and has more expression than I ever found in his former productions—excepting, indeed, his Imogen.

Allston is hard at work on a large Scripture piece—the dead man recalled to life by touching the bones of the Prophet. He models every figure. Dawe, who was delighted with the Cupid and Psyche, seemed quite astonished at the facility and exquisiteness with which Allston modelled. Canova at Rome expressed himself to me in very warm terms of admiration on the same subject. He means to exhibit but two or at the most three pictures, all poetical or history painting, in part by my advice. It seemed to me impolitic to appear to be trying in half a dozen ways, as if his mind had not yet discovered its main current. The longer I live the more deeply am I convinced of the high importance, as a symptom, of the love of beauty in a young painter. It is neither honourable to a young man's heart or head to attach himself year after year to old or deformed objects, comparatively too so easy, especially if bad drawing and worse colouring leaves the spectator's imagination at lawless liberty, and he cries out, "How very like!" just as he would at a coal in the centre of the fire, or at a frost-figure on a window pane. It is on this, added to his quiet unenvious spirit, to his lofty feelings concerning his art, and to the religious purity of his moral character, that I chiefly rest my hopes of Allston's future fame. His best productions seem to please him principally because he sees and has learnt something which enables him to promise himself, "I shall do better in my next."

I have not been at the "Courier" office for some months past. I detest writing politics, even on the right side, and when I discovered that the "Courier" was not the independent paper I had been led to believe, and had myself over and over again asserted, I wrote no more for it. Greatly, indeed, do I prefer the present Ministers to the leaders of any other party, but indiscriminate support of any class of men I dare not give, especially when there is so easy and honourable an alternative as not to write politics at all, which, henceforth, nothing but blank necessity shall compel me to do. I will write for the Permanent, or not at all. "The Comet" therefore I have never seen or heard of it, yet most true it is that I myself have composed some verses on the comet, but I am quite certain that no one ever saw them, for the best of all reasons, that my own brain is the only substance on which they have been recorded. I will, however, consign them to paper, and send them to you with the "Courier" poem as soon as I can procure it, for the curiosity of the thing....

My most affectionate respects to Lady Beaumont, and believe me, dear Sir George, with heartfelt regard,

Your obliged and grateful friend,
S. T. Coleridge.

P. S. Were you in town, I should be very sorry, indeed, to see you in Fetter Lane.[77] The lectures were meant for the young men of the City. Several of my friends join to take notes, and if I can correct what they can shape out of them into any tolerable form, I will send them to you. On Monday I lecture on "Love and the Female Character as displayed by Shakespeare." Good Dr. Bell is in town. He came from Keswick, all delight with my little Sara, and quite enchanted with Southey. Some flights of admiration in the form of questions to me ("Did you ever see anything so finely conceived? so profoundly thought? as this passage in his review on the Methodists? or on the Education?" etc.) embarrassed me in a very ridiculous way; and, I verily believe, that my odd way of hesitating left on Bell's mind some shade of a suspicion, as if I did not like to hear my friend so highly extolled. Half a dozen words from Southey would have precluded this, without diminution to his own fame—I mean, in conversation with Dr. Bell.

CLXXXIV. TO J. J. MORGAN.

Keswick,[78] Sunday, February 28, 1812.

My dear Morgan,—I stayed a day in Kendal in order to collect the reprint of "The Friend," and reached Keswick on Tuesday last before dinner, having taken Hartley and Derwent with me from Ambleside. Of course the first evening was devoted Laribus domesticis, to Southey and his and my children. My own are all the fondest father could pray for; and little Sara does honour to her mother's anxieties, reads French tolerably, and Italian fluently, and I was astonished at her acquaintance with her native language. The word "hostile" occurring in what she read to me, I asked her what "hostile" meant? and she answered at once, "Why! inimical; only that 'inimical' is more often used for things and measures and not, as 'hostile' is, to persons and nations." If I had dared, I should have urged Mrs. C. to let me take her to London for four or five months, and return with Southey, but I feared it might be inconvenient to you, and I knew it would be presumptuous in me to bring her to you. But she is such a sweet-tempered, meek, blue-eyed fairy and so affectionate, trustworthy, and really serviceable! Derwent is the self-same, fond, small, Samuel Taylor Coleridge as ever. When I went for them from Mr. Dawes,[79] he came in dancing for joy, while Hartley turned pale[80] and trembled all over,—then after he had taken some cold water, instantly asked me some questions about the connection of the Greek with the Latin, which latter he has just begun to learn. Poor Derwent, who has by no means strong health (having inherited his poor father's tenderness of bowels and stomach, and consequently capriciousness of animal spirits), has complained to me (having no other possible grievance) "that Mr. Dawes does not love him, because he can't help crying when he is scolded, and because he ain't such a genius as Hartley—and that though Hartley should have done the same thing, yet all the others are punished, and Mr. Dawes only looks at Hartley and never scolds him, and that all the boys think it very unfair—he is a genius." This was uttered in low spirits and a tenderness brought on by my petting, for he adores his brother. Indeed, God be praised, they all love each other. I was delighted that Derwent, of his own accord, asked me about little Miss Brent that used to play with him at Mr. and Mrs. Morgan's, adding that he had almost forgot what sort of a lady she was, "only she was littler,—less I mean—(this was said hastily and laughing at his blunder) than Mama." A gentleman who took a third of the chaise with me from Ambleside, and whom I found a well-informed and thinking man, said after two hours' knowledge of us, that the two boys united would be a perfect representation of myself.

I trust I need not say that I should have written on the second day if nothing had happened; but from the dreadful dampness of the house, worse than it was in the rudest state when I first lived in it, and the weather, too, all storm and rain, I caught a violent cold which almost blinded me by inflammation of both my eyes, and for three days bore all the symptoms of an ague or intermittent fever. Knowing I had no time to lose, I took the most Herculean remedies, among others a solution of arsenic, and am now as well as when I left you, and see no reason to fear a relapse. I passed through Grasmere; but did not call on Wordsworth. I hear from Mrs. C. that he treats the affair as a trifle, and only wonders at my resenting it, and that Dorothy Wordsworth before my arrival expressed her confident hope that I should come to them at once! I who "for years past had been an absolute nuisance in the family." This illness has thrown me behindhand; so that I cannot quit Keswick till the end of the week. On Friday I shall return by way of Ambleside, probably spend a day with Charles Lloyd.... It will not surprise you that the statements respecting me and Montagu and Wordsworth have been grossly perverted: and yet, spite of all this, there is not a friend of Wordsworth's, I understand, who does not severely blame him, though they execrate the Montagus yet more heavily. But the tenth part of the truth is not known. Would you believe it possible that Wordsworth himself stated my wearing powder as a proof positive that I never could have suffered any pain of mind from the affair, and that it was all pretence!! God forgive him! At Liverpool I shall either give lectures, if I can secure a hundred pounds for them, or return immediately to you. At all events, I shall not remain there beyond a fortnight, so that I shall be with you before you have changed houses. Mrs. Coleridge seems quite satisfied with my plans, and abundantly convinced of my obligations to your and Mary's kindness to me. Nothing (she said) but the circumstance of my residing with you could reconcile her to my living in London. Southey is the semper idem. It is impossible for a good heart not to esteem and to love him; but yet the love is one fourth, the esteem all the remainder. His children are, 1. Edith, seven years; 2. Herbert, five; 3. Bertha, four; 4. Catharine, a year and a half.

I had hoped to have heard from you by this time. I wrote from Slough, from Liverpool, and from Kendal. Why need I send my kindest love to Mary and Charlotte? I would not return if I had a doubt that they believed me to be in the very inmost of my being their and your affectionate and grateful and constant friend,

S. T. Coleridge.

CLXXXV. TO HIS WIFE.

71, Berners Street, Tuesday, April 21, 1812.

My dear Love,—Everything is going on so very well, so much beyond my expectation, that I will not revert to anything unpleasant to damp good news with. The last receipt for the insurance is now before me, the date the 4th of May. Be assured that before April is past, you shall receive both receipts, this and the one for the present year, in a frank.

In the first place, my health, spirits, and disposition to activity have continued such since my arrival in town, that every one has been struck with the change, and the Morgans say they had never before seen me myself. I feel myself an altered man, and dare promise you that you shall never have to complain of, or to apprehend, my not opening and reading your letters. Ever since I have been in town, I have never taken any stimulus of any kind, till the moment of my getting into bed, except a glass of British white wine after dinner, and from three to four glasses of port, when I have dined out. Secondly, my lectures have been taken up most warmly and zealously by Sir Thomas Bernard,[81] Sir George Beaumont, Mr. Sotheby, etc., and in a few days, I trust that you will be agreeably surprised with the mode in which Sir T. B. hopes and will use his best exertions to have them announced. Thirdly, Gale and Curtis are in high spirits and confident respecting the sale of "The Friend,"[82] and the call for a second edition, after the complemental numbers have been printed, and not less so respecting the success of the other work, the Propædia (or Propaideia) Cyclica, and are desirous to have the terms properly ratified, and signed as soon as possible. Nothing intervenes to overgloom my mind, but the sad state of health of Mr. Morgan, a more faithful and zealous friend than whom no man ever possessed. Thank God! my safe arrival, the improvement of my health and spirits, and my smiling prospects have already exerted a favourable influence on him. Yet I dare not disguise from myself that there is cause for alarm to those who love and value him. But do not allude to this subject in your letters, for to be thought ill or to have his state of health spoken of, agitates and depresses him.

As soon as ever I have settled the lecture room, which perhaps will be Willis's in Hanover Square, the price of which is at present ten guineas a time, I will the very first thing pay the insurance and send off a parcel of books for Hartley, Derwent, and dear Sara, whom I kissed seven times in the shape of her pretty letterlet.

My poor darling Derwent! I shall be most anxious to receive a letter from you, or from himself, about him.

In giving my love to Mrs. Lovell, tell her that I have not since the day after my arrival been able to go into the city, my business having employed me wholly either in writing or in traversing the West End of the town. I dined with Lady Beaumont and her sister on Saturday, for Sir George was engaged to Sir T. Bernard. He however came and sat with us to the very last moment, and I dine with him to-day, and Allston is to be of the party. The bust and the picture from Genevieve are at the Royal Academy, and already are talked of. Dawe and I will be of mutual service to each other. As soon as the pictures are settled, that is, in the first week of May, he means to treat himself with a fortnight's relaxation at the Lakes. He is a very modest man, his manners not over polished, and his worst point is that he is (at least, I have found him so) a fearful questionist, whenever he thinks he can pick up any information, or ideas, poetical, historical, topographical, or artistical, that he can make bear on his profession. But he is sincere, friendly, strictly moral in every respect, I firmly believe even to innocence, and in point of cheerful indefatigableness of industry, in regularity, and temperance—in short, in a glad, yet quiet, devotion of his whole being to the art he has made choice of, he is the only man I ever knew who goes near to rival Southey— gentlemanly address, person, physiognomy, knowledge, learning, and genius being of course wholly excluded from the comparison. God knows my heart! and that it is my full belief and conviction, that taking all together, there does not exist the man who could without flattery or delusion be called Southey's equal. It is quite delightful to hear how he is spoken of by all good people. Dawe will doubtless take him. Were S. and I rich men, we would have ourselves and all of you, short and tall, in one family picture. Pray receive Dawe as a friend. I called on Murray, who complained that by Dr. Bell's delays and irresolutions and scruples, the book "On the Origin,"[83] etc., instead of 3,000 in three weeks, which he has no doubt would have been the sale had it been brought out at the fit time, will not now sell 300. I told him that I believed otherwise, but much would depend on the circumstance whether temper or prudence would have most influence on the Athenian critic and his friend Brougham. If, as I hoped, the former, and the work should be reviewed in the "Edinburgh Review," if they took up the gauntlet thrown at them, then there was no doubt but that a strong tide of sale would set in. Though verily this gauntlet was of weighty metal, though of polished steel, and being thrown at rather than down, it was challenging a man to fight by a blow that threatened to brain him. I have seen Dr. Bell and shall dine with him at Sir T. Bernard's on Monday next. The venerable Bishop of Durham[84] has sent me a very kind message, that though he cannot himself appear in a hired lecture room, yet he will be not only my subscriber but use his best influence with his acquaintance. I am very anxious that my books should be sent forward as soon as possible. They may be sent at three different times, with a week's intervention. But there is one, scarcely a book, but a collection of loose sheets tied up together at Grasmere, which I want immediately, and, if possible, would have sent up by the coach from Kendal or Penrith. It is a German Romance with some name beginning with an A, followed by "oder Die Glückliche Inseln." It makes two volumes, but several of the sheets are missing, at least were so when I put them together. If sent off immediately, it would be of serious benefit to me in my lectures. Miss Hutchinson knows them, and will probably recollect the sheets I allude to, and these are what I especially want.

One pair only of breeches were in the parcel, and I am sadly off for stockings, but the white and under ones I can buy here cheap, but if young Mr. White could procure half a dozen or even a dozen pair of black silk made as stout and weighty as possible, I would not mind giving seventeen shillings per pair, if only they can be relied on, which one cannot do in London. A double knock. I meant to read over your letter again, lest I should have forgot anything. If I have, I will answer it in my next.

God bless you and your affectionate husband,

S. T. Coleridge.

Has Southey read "Childe Harold"? All the world is talking of it. I have not, but from what I hear it is exactly on the plan that I myself had not only conceived six years ago, but have the whole scheme drawn out in one of my old memorandum books. My dear Edith, and my dear Moon![85] Though I have scarce room to write it, yet I love you very much.

CLXXXVI. TO THE SAME.

71, Berners Street, April 24, 1812.

My dear Sara,—Give my kind love to Southey, and inform him that I have, egomet his ipsis meis oculis, seen Nobs, alive, well, and in full fleece; that after the death of Dr. Samuel Dove,[86] of Doncaster, who did not survive the loss of his faithful wife, Mrs. Dorothy Dove, more than eleven months, Nobs was disposed of by his executors to Longman and Clements, Musical Instrument Manufacturers, whose grand pianoforte hearses he now draws in the streets of London. The carter was astonished at the enthusiasm with which I intreated him to stop for half a minute, and the embrace I gave to Nobs, who evidently understood me, and wistfully with such a sad expression in his eye, seemed to say, "Ah, my kind old master, Doctor Daniel, and ah! my mild mistress, his dear duteous Dolly Dove, my gratitude lies deeper than my obligation; it is not merely skin-deep! Ah, what I have been! Oh, what I am! his naked, neighing, night-wandering, new-skinned, nibbling, noblenursling, Nobs!"

His legs and hoofs are more than half sheepified, and his fleece richer than one ever sees in the Leicester breed, but not so fine as might have been the case had the merino cross been introduced before the surprising accident and more surprising remedy took place. More surprising I say, because the first happened to St. Bartholomew (for there were skinners even in the days of St. Bartholomew), but the other never before there was no Dr. Daniel Dove. I trust that Southey will now not hesitate to record and transmit to posterity so remarkable a fact. I am delighted, for now malice itself will not dare to attribute the story to my invention. If I can procure the money, I will attempt to purchase Nobs, and send him down to Keswick by short journeys for Herbert and Derwent to ride upon, provided you can get the field next us.

I have not been able to procure a frank, but I daresay you will be glad to receive the enclosed receipt even with the drawback of postage.

Everything, my dear, goes on as prosperously as you could yourself wish. Sir T. Bernard has taken Willis's Rooms, King Street, St. James's, for me, at only four guineas a week, fires, benches, etc., included, and I expect the lectures to commence on the first Tuesday in May. But at the present moment I need both the advice and the aid of Southey. The "Friends" have arrived in town. I am at work on the Supplemental Numbers, and it is of the last importance that they should be brought out as quickly as possible during the flush and fresh breeze of my popularity; but this I cannot do without knowing whether Mr. Wordsworth will transmit to me the two finishing Essays on Epitaphs.[87] It is, I know and feel, a very delicate business; yet I wish Southey would immediately write to Wordsworth and urge him to send them by the coach, either to J. J. Morgan, Esq., 71, Berners Street, or to Messrs. Gale and Curtis, Booksellers, Paternoster Row, with as little delay as possible, or if he decline it, that Southey should apprize me as soon as possible.

S. T. Coleridge.

The Morgans desire to be kindly remembered, and Charlotte Brent (tell Derwent) hopes he has not forgot his old playfellow.

CLXXXVII. TO CHARLES LAMB.

May 2, 1812.

My dear Charles,—I should almost deserve what I have suffered, if I refused even to put my life in hazard in defence of my own honour and veracity, and in satisfaction of the honour of a friend. I say honour, in the latter instance, singly, because I never felt as a matter of serious complaint, what was stated to have been said (for this, though painfully aggravated, was yet substantially true)—but by whom it was said, and to whom, and how and when. Grievously unseasonable therefore as it is, that I should again be overtaken and hurried back by the surge, just as I had begun to feel the firm ground under my feet—just as I had flattered myself, and given reason to my hospitable friends to flatter themselves, that I had regained tranquillity, and had become quite myself—at the time, too, when every thought should be given to my lectures, on the success or failure of my efforts in which no small part of my reputation and future prospects will depend—yet if Wordsworth, upon reflection, adheres to the plan proposed, I will not draw back. It is right, however, that I should state one or two things. First, that it has been my constant desire that evil should not propagate evil—or the unhappy accident become the means of spreading dissension. (2) That I never quarrelled with Mr. Montagu—say rather, for that is the real truth, that Mr. Montagu never was, or appeared to be, a man with whom I could, without self-contempt, allow myself to quarrel—and lastly, that in the present business there are but three possible cases—either (1) Mr. Wordsworth said what I solemnly aver that I most distinctly recollect Mr. Montagu's representing him as having said, and which I understood, not merely as great unkindness and even cruelty, but as an intentional means of putting an end to our long friendship, or to the terms at least, under which it had for so long a period subsisted—or (2), Mr. Montagu has grossly misrepresented Wordsworth, and most cruelly and wantonly injured me—or (3), I have wantonly invented and deliberately persevered in atrocious falsehoods, which place me in the same relation to Mr. Montagu as (in the second case) Mr. Montagu would stand in to me. If, therefore, Mr. Montagu declares to my face that he did not say what I solemnly aver that he did—what must be the consequence, unless I am a more abject coward than I have hitherto suspected, I need not say. Be the consequences what they may, however, I will not shrink from doing my duty; but previously to the meeting I should very much wish to transmit to Wordsworth a statement which I long ago began, with the intention of sending it to Mrs. Wordsworth's sister,—but desisted in consequence of understanding that she had already decided the matter against me. My reason for wishing this is that I think it right that Wordsworth should know, and have the means of ascertaining, some conversations which yet I could not publicly bring forward without hazarding great disquiet in a family known (though slightly) to Wordsworth—(2) Because common humanity would embarrass me in stating before a man what I and others think of his wife—and lastly, certain other points which my own delicacy and that due to Wordsworth himself and his family, preclude from being talked of. For Wordsworth ought not to forget that, whatever influence old associations may have on his mind respecting Montagu, yet that I never respected or liked him—for if I had ever in a common degree done so, I should have quarrelled with him long before we arrived in London. Yet all these facts ought to be known—because supposing Montagu to affirm what I am led to suppose he has—then nothing remains but the comparative probability of our two accounts, and for this the state of my feelings towards Wordsworth and his family, my opinion of Mr. and

Mrs. Montagu, and my previous intention not to lodge with them in town, are important documents as far as they do not rely on my own present assertions. Woe is me, that a friendship of fifteen years should come to this! and such a friendship, in which I call God Almighty to be my witness, as I ever thought it no more than my duty, so did I ever feel a readiness to prefer him to myself, yea, even if life and outward reputation itself had been the pledge required. But this is now vain talking. Be it, however, remembered that I have never wandered beyond the one single complaint, that I had been cruelly and unkindly treated—that I made no charge against my friend's veracity, even in respect to his charges against me—that I have explained the circumstance to those only who had already more or less perfectly become acquainted with our difference, or were certain to hear of it from others, and that except on this one point, no word of reproach, or even of subtraction from his good name, as a good man, or from his merits as a great man, ever escaped me. May God bless you, my dear Charles.

S. T. Coleridge.

CLXXXVIII. TO WILLIAM WORDSWORTH.

71, Berners Street. Monday, May 4, 1812.

I will divide my statement, which I will endeavour to send you to-morrow, into two parts, in separate letters. The latter, commencing from the Sunday night, 28 October, 1810, that is, that on which the communication was made to me, and which will contain my solemn avowal of what was said by Mr. and Mrs. Montagu, you will make what use of you please— but the former I write to you, and in confidence—yet only as far as to your own heart it shall appear evident, that in desiring it I am actuated by no wish to shrink personally from any test, not involving an acknowledgement of my own degradation, and so become a false witness against myself, but only by delicacy towards the feelings of others, and the dread of spreading the curse of dissension. But, Wordsworth! the very message you sent by Lamb and which Lamb did not deliver to me from the anxiety not to add fuel to the flame, sufficiently proves what I had learnt on my first arrival at Keswick, and which alone prevented my going to Grasmere—namely, that you had prejudged the case. As soon as I was informed that you had denied having used certain expressions, I did not hesitate a moment (nor was it in my power to do so) to give you my fullest faith, and approve to my own consciousness the truth of my declaration, that I should have felt it as a blessing, though my life had the same instant been hazarded as the pledge, could I with firm conviction have given Montagu the lie, at the conclusion of his story, even as, at the very first sentence, I exclaimed—"Impossible! It is impossible!" The expressions denied were indeed only the most offensive part to the feelings—but at the same time I learnt that you did not hesitate instantly to express your conviction that Montagu never said those words and that I had invented them—or (to use your own words) "had forgotten myself." Grievously indeed, if I know aught of my nature, must I have forgotten both myself and common honesty, could I have been villain enough to have invented and persevered in such atrocious falsehoods. Your message was that "if I declined an explanation, you begged I would no longer continue to talk about the affair." When, Wordsworth, did I ever decline an explanation? From you I expected one, and had a right to expect it—for let Montagu have added what he may, still that which remained was most unkind and what I had little deserved from you, who might by a single question have learnt from me that I never made up my mind to lodge with Montagu and had tacitly acquiesced in it at Keswick to tranquillise Mrs. Coleridge, to whom Mrs. Montagu had made the earnest professions of watching and nursing me, and for whom this and her extreme repugnance to my original, and much wiser, resolution of going to Edinburgh and placing myself in the house, and under the constant eye, of some medical man, were the sole grounds of her assent that I should leave the North at all. Yet at least a score of times have I begun to write a detailed account, to Wales[88] and afterwards to Grasmere, and gave it up from excess of agitation,—till finally I learnt that all of your family had decided against me unheard—and that [you begged] I would no longer talk about it. If, Wordsworth, you had but done me the common justice of asking those with whom I have been most intimate and confidential since my first arrival in Town in Oct., 1810, you would have received other negative or positive proofs how little I needed the admonition or deserve the sarcasm. Talk about it? O God! it has been talked about! and that it had, was the sole occasion of my disclosing it even to Mary Lamb, the first person who heard of it from me and that not voluntarily—but that morning a friend met me, and communicated what so agitated me that then having previously meant to call at Lamb's I was compelled to do so from faintness and universal trembling, in order to sit down. Even to her I did not intend to mention it; but alarmed by the wildness and paleness of my countenance and agitation I had no power to conceal, she entreated me to tell her what was the matter. In the first attempt to speak, my feelings overpowered me; an agony of weeping followed, and then, alarmed at my own imprudence and conscious of the possible effect on her health and mind if I left her in that state of suspense, I brought out convulsively some such words as—"Wordsworth, Wordsworth has given me up. He has no hope of me—I have been an absolute nuisance[89] in his family"—and when long weeping had relieved me, and I was able to relate the occurrence connectedly, she can bear witness for me that, disgraceful as it was that I should be made the topic of vulgar gossip, yet that "had the whole and ten times more been proclaimed by a speaking-trumpet from the chimneys, I should have smiled at it—or indulged indignation only as far as it excited me to pleasurable activity—but that you had said it, this and this only, was the sting! the scorpion-tooth!" Mr. Morgan and afterwards his wife and her sister were made acquainted with the whole case—and why? Not merely that I owed it to their ardent friendship, which has continued to be mainly my comfort and my only support, but because they had already heard of it, in part—because a most intimate and dear friend of Mr. and Mrs. Montagu's had urged Mr. Morgan to call at the Montagus in order to be put on his guard against me. He came to me instantly, told me that I had enemies at work against my character, and pressed me to leave the hotel and to come home with him—with whom I have been ever since, with the exception of a few intervals when, from the bitter consciousness of my own infirmities and increasing irregularity of temper, I took lodgings, against his will, and was always by his zealous friendship brought back again. If it be allowed to call any one on earth Saviour, Morgan and his family have been my Saviours, body and soul. For my moral will was, and I fear is, so weakened relatively to my duties to myself, that I cannot act, as I ought to do, except under the influencing knowledge of its effects on those I love and believe myself loved by. To him likewise I explained the affair; but neither from him or his family has one word ever escaped me concerning it. Last autumn Mr. and Mrs. Southey came to town, and at Mr. Ray's at Richmond, as we were walking alone in the garden, the subject was introduced, and it became my duty to state the whole affair to them, even as the means of transmitting it to you. With these exceptions I do not remember ever to have made any one my confidant—though in two or three instances I have alluded to the suspension of our familiar intercourse without explanation, but even here only where I knew or fully believed the persons to have already heard of it. Such was Mrs. Clarkson, who wrote to me in consequence of one sentence in a letter to her; yet even to her I entered into no detail, and disclosed nothing that was not necessary to my own defence in not continuing my former correspondence. In short, the one only thing which I have to blame in myself was that in my first letter to Sir G. Beaumont I had concluded with a desponding remark allusive to the breach between us, not in the slightest degree suspecting that he was ignorant of it. In the letters, which followed, I was compelled to say more (though I never detailed the words which had been uttered to me) in consequence of Lady Beaumont's expressed apprehension and alarm lest in the advertisement for my lectures the sentence "concerning the Living Poets" contained an intention on my part to attack your literary merits. The very thought, that I could be imagined capable of feeling vindictively toward you at all, much more of gratifying the passion in so despicable as well as detestable manner, agitated me. I sent her Ladyship the verses composed after your recitation of the great Poem at Coleorton, and desired her to judge whether it was possible that a man, who had written that poem, could be capable of such an act, and in a letter to Sir G. B., anxious to remove from his mind the assumption that I had been agitated by the disclosure of any till then unknown actions of mine or parts of conduct, I endeavoured to impress him with the real truth that not the facts disclosed, but the manner and time and the person by whom and the person to whom they had been disclosed, formed the whole ground of the breach. And writing in great agitation I once again used the same words which had venially burst from me the moment Montagu had ended his account. "And this is cruel! this is base!" I did not reflect on it till it was irrevocable—and for that one word, the only word of positive reproach that ever escaped from me, I feel sorrow—and assure you, that there is no permanent feeling in my heart which corresponds to it. Talk about it? Those who have seen me and been with me, day by day, for so many many months could have told you, how anxiously every allusion to the subject was avoided—and with abundant reason—for immediate and palpable derangement of body as well as spirits regularly followed it. Besides, had there not existed in your mind—let me rather say, if ever there had existed any portion of esteem and regard for me since the autumn of 1810, would it have been possible that your quick and powerful judgement could have overlooked the gross improbability, that I should first invent and then scatter abroad for talk at public tables the phrases which (Mr. Robinson yesterday informed me) Mr. Sharon Turner was indelicate enough to trumpet abroad at Longman's table? I at least will call on Mr. Sharon and demand his authority. It is my full conviction, that in no one of the hundred tables at which any particulars of our breach have been mentioned, could the authority be traced back to those who had received the account from myself.

It seemed unnatural to me, nay, it was unnatural to me to write to you or to any of your family with a cold exclusion of the feelings which almost overpower me even at this moment, and I therefore write this preparatory letter to disburthen my heart, as it were, before I sit down to detail my recollections simply, and unmixed with the anguish which, spite of my best efforts, accompany them.

But one thing more, the last complaint that you will hear from me, perhaps. When without my knowledge dear Mary Lamb, just then on the very verge of a relapse, wrote to Grasmere, was it kind or even humane to have returned such an answer, as Lamb deemed it unadvisable to shew me; but which I learnt from the only other person, who saw the answer, amounted in substance to a sneer on my reported high spirits and my wearing powder? When and to whom did I ever make a merit of my sufferings? Is it consistent now to charge me with going about complaining to everybody, and now with my high spirits? Was I to carry a gloomy face into every society? or ought I not rather to be grateful that in the natural activity of my intellect God had given me a counteracting principle to the intensity of my feelings, and a means of escaping from a part of the pressure? But for this I had been driven mad, and yet for how many months was there a continual brooding and going on of the one gnawing recollection behind the curtain of my outward being, even when I was most exerting myself, and exerting myself more in order the more to benumb it! I might have truly said with Desdemona:—

"I am not merry, but I do beguile
The Thing I am, by seeming otherwise."

And as to the powder, it was first put in to prevent my taking cold after my hair had been thinned, and I was advised to continue it till I became wholly grey, as in its then state it looked as if I had dirty powder in my hair, and even when known to be only the everywhere-mixed-grey, yet contrasting with a face even younger than my real age it gave a queer and contradictory character to my whole appearance. Whatever be the result of this long-delayed explanation, I have loved you and yours too long and too deeply to have it in my own power to cease to do so.

S. T. Coleridge.

CLXXXIX. TO DANIEL STUART.

May 8, 1812.

My dear Stuart,—I send you seven or eight tickets,[90] entreating you, if pre-engagements or your health does not preclude it, to bring a group with you; as many ladies as possible; but gentlemen if you cannot muster ladies—for else I shall not only have been left in the lurch as to the actual receipts by my great patrons (the five hundred half-promised are likely to shrink below fifty) but shall absolutely make a ridiculous appearance. The tickets are transferable. If you can find occasion for more, pray send for them to me, as (what it really will be) a favour done to myself.

I am anxious to see you, and to learn how far Bath has improved or (to use a fashionable slang phrase) disimproved your health.

Sir James and Lady Mackintosh are I hear at Bath Hotel, Jermyn Street. Do you think it will be taken amiss if I enclosed two or three tickets and cards with my respectful congratulations on his safe return.[91] I abhor the doing anything that could be even interpreted into servility, and yet feel increasingly the necessity of not neglecting the courtesies of life....

God bless you, my dear sir, and your obliged and affectionate friend,

S. T. Coleridge.

P. S. Mr. Morgan has left his card for you.

CXC. TO WILLIAM WORDSWORTH.

71, Berners Street,
Monday afternoon, 3 o'clock, May 11, 1812.

My dear Wordsworth,—I declare before God Almighty that at no time, even in my sorest affliction, did even the possibility occur to me of ever doubting your word. I never ceased for a moment to have faith in you, to love and revere you; though I was unable to explain an unkindness, which seemed anomalous in your character. Doubtless it would have been better, wiser, and more worthy of my relation to you, had I immediately written to you a full account of what had happened—especially as the person's language concerning your family was such as nothing but the wild general counter-panegyric of the same person almost in the same breath of yourself—as a converser, etc.,—could have justified me in not resenting to the uttermost....[92] All these, added to what I mentioned in my letter to you, may not justify, but yet must palliate, the only offence I ever committed against you in deed or word or thought—that is, the not writing to you and trusting instead to our common friends. Since I left you my pocket books have been my only full confidants,[93]—and though instructed by prudence to write so as to be intelligible to no being on earth but yourself and your family, they for eighteen months together would furnish proof that in anguish or induration I yet never ceased both to honour and love you.

S. T. Coleridge.

I need not say, of course, that your presence at the Lectures, or anywhere else, will be gratifying to me.

CXCI. TO ROBERT SOUTHEY.

[May 12, 1812.]

My dear Southey,—The awful event of yester-afternoon has forced me to defer my Lectures to Tuesday, the 19th, by advice of all my patrons. The same thought struck us all at the same moment, so that our letters might be said to meet each other. I write now to urge you, if it be in your power, to give one day or two of your time to write something in your impressive way on that theme which no one I meet seems to feel as they ought to do,—which, I find scarcely any but ourselves estimate according to its true gigantic magnitude—I mean the sinking down of Jacobinism below the middle and tolerably educated classes into the readers and all-swallowing auditors in tap-rooms, etc.; and the [political sentiments in the] "Statesman," "Examiner," etc. I have ascertained that throughout the great manufacturing counties, Whitbread's, Burdett's, and Waithman's speeches and the leading articles of the "Statesman" and "Examiner" are printed in ballad [shape] and sold at a halfpenny or a penny each. I was turned numb, and then sick, and then into a convulsive state of weeping on the first tidings—just as if Perceval[94] had been my near and personal friend. But good God! the atrocious sentiments universal among the populace, and even the lower order of householders. On my return from the "Courier," where I had been to offer my services if I could do anything for them on this occasion, I was faint from the heat and much walking, and took that opportunity of going into the tap-room of a large public house frequented about one o'clock by the lower orders. It was really shocking, nothing but exultation! Burdett's health drank with a clatter of pots and a sentiment given to at least fifty men and women—"May Burdett soon be the man to have sway over us!" These were the very words. "This is but the beginning." "More of these damned scoundrels must go the same way, and then poor people may live." "Every man might maintain his family decent and comfortable, if the money were not picked out of our pockets by these damned placemen." "God is above the devil, I say, and down to Hell with him and all his brood, the Ministers, men of Parliament fellows." "They won't hear Burdett; no! he is a Christian man and speaks for the poor," etc., etc. I do not think I have altered a word.

My love to Sara, and I have received everything right. The plate will go as desired, and among it a present to Sariola and Edith from good old Mr. Brent, who had great delight in hearing them talked of. It was wholly the old gentleman's own thought. Bless them both!

The affair between Wordsworth and me seems settled, much against my first expectation from the message I received from him and his refusal to open a letter from me. I have not yet seen him, but an explanation has taken place. I sent by Robinson an attested, avowed statement of what Mr. and Mrs. Montagu told me, and Wordsworth has sent me an unequivocal denial of the whole in spirit and of the most offensive passages in letter as well as spirit, and I instantly informed him that were ten thousand Montagus to swear against it, I should take his word, not ostensibly only, but with inward faith!

To-morrow I will write out the passage from "Apuleius," and send the letter to Rickman. It is seldom that want of leisure can be fairly stated as an excuse for not writing; but really for the last ten days I can honestly do it, if you will but allow a due portion to agitated feelings. The subscription is languid indeed compared with the expectations. Sir T. Bernard almost pledged himself for my success. However, he has done his best, and so has Lady Beaumont, who herself procured me near thirty names. I should have done better by myself for the present, but in the future perhaps it will be better as it is.

CXCII. TO WILLIAM WORDSWORTH.[95]

71, Berners Street,
Monday noon, December 7, 1812.

Write? My dear Friend! Oh that it were in my power to be with you myself instead of my letter. The Lectures I could give up; but the rehearsal of my Play commences this week, and upon this depends my best hopes of leaving town after Christmas, and living among you as long as I live. Strange, strange are the coincidences of things! Yesterday Martha Fricker dined here, and after tea I had asked question after question respecting your children, first one, then the other; but, more than all, concerning Thomas, till at length Mrs. Morgan said, "What ails you, Coleridge? Why don't you talk about Hartley, Derwent, and Sara?" And not two hours ago (for the whole family were late from bed) I was asked what was the matter with my eyes? I told the fact, that I had awoke three times during the night and morning, and at each time found my face and part of the pillow wet with tears. "Were you dreaming of the Wordsworths?" she asked.—"Of the children?" I said, "No! not so much of them, but of Mrs. W. and Miss Hutchinson, and yourself and sister."

Mrs. Morgan and her sister are come in, and I have been relieved by tears. The sharp, sharp pang at the heart needed it, when they reminded me of my words the very yester-night: "It is not possible that I should do otherwise than love Wordsworth's children, all of them; but Tom is nearest my heart—I so often have him before my eyes, sitting on the little stool by my side, while I was writing my essays; and how quiet and happy the affectionate little fellow would be if he could but touch one, and now and then be looked at."

O dearest friend! what comfort can I afford you? What comfort ought I not to afford, who have given you so much pain? Sympathy deep, of my whole being.... In grief, and in joy, in the anguish of perplexity, and in the fulness and overflow of confidence, it has been ever what it is! There is a sense of the word, Love, in which I never felt it but to you and one of your household! I am distant from you some hundred miles, but glad I am that I am no longer distant in spirit, and have faith, that as it has happened but once, so it never can happen again. An awful truth it seems to me, and prophetic of our future, as well as declarative of our present real nature, that one mere thought, one feeling of suspicion, jealousy, or resentment can remove two human beings farther from each other than winds or seas can separate their bodies.

The words "religious fortitude" occasion me to add that my faith in our progressive nature, and in all the doctrinal facts of Christianity, is become habitual in my understanding, no less than in my feelings. More cheering illustrations of our survival I have never received, than from the recent study of the instincts of animals, their clear heterogeneity from the reason and moral essence of man and yet the beautiful analogy. Especially, on the death of children, and of the mind in childhood, altogether, many thoughts have accumulated, from which I hope to derive consolation from that most oppressive feeling which hurries in upon the first anguish of such tidings as I have received; the sense of uncertainty, the fear of enjoyment, the pale and deathy gleam thrown over the countenances of the living, whom we love.... But this is bad comforting. Your own virtues, your own love itself, must give it. Mr. De Quincey has left town, and will by this time have arrived at Grasmere. On Sunday last I gave him a letter for you; but he (I have heard) did not leave town till Thursday night, by what accidents prevented I know not. In the oppression of spirits under which I wrote that letter, I did not make it clear that it was only Mr. Josiah's half of the annuity[96] that was withdrawn from me. My answer, of course, breathed nothing but gratitude for the past.

I will write in a few days again to you. To-morrow is my lecture night, "On the human causes of the spread of Christianity, and its effects after the establishment of Christendom." Dear Mary! dear Dorothy! dearest Sara! Oh, be assured, no thought relative to myself has half the influence in inspiring the wish and effort to appear and to act what I always in my will and heart have been, as the knowledge that few things could more console you than to see me healthy, and worthy of myself! Again and again, my dearest Wordsworth!!! I am affectionately and truly yours,

S. T. Coleridge.

CXCIII. TO HIS WIFE.

Wednesday afternoon [January 20,] 18[13].

My dear Sara,—Hitherto the "Remorse" has met with unexampled applause, but whether it will continue to fill the house, that is quite another question, and of this, my friends are, in my opinion, far, far too sanguine. I have disposed not of the copyright but of edition by edition to Mr. Pople, on terms advantageous to me as an author and honourable to him as a publisher. The expenses of printing and paper (at the trade-price) advertising, etc., are to be deducted from the total produce, and the net profits to be divided into three equal parts, of which Pople is to have one, and I the other two. And at any future time, I may publish it in any volume of my poems collectively. Mr. Arnold (the manager) has just left me. He called to urge me to exert myself a little with regard to the daily press, and brought with him "The Times"[97] of Monday as a specimen of the infernal lies of which a newspaper scribe can be capable. Not only is not one sentence in it true; but every one is in the direct face of a palpable truth. The misrepresentations must have been wilful. I must now, therefore, write to "The Times," and if Walter refuses to insert, I will then, recording the circumstance, publish it in the "Morning Post," "Morning Chronicle," and "The Courier." The dirty malice of Antony Pasquin[98] in the "Morning Herald" is below notice. This, however, will explain to you why the shortness of this letter, the main business of which is to desire you to draw upon Brent and Co., No. 103 Bishopsgate Street Within, for an hundred pounds, at a month's date from the drawing, or, if that be objected to, for three weeks, only let me know which. In the course of a month I have no hesitation in promising you another hundred, and I hope likewise before Midsummer, if God grant me life, to repay you whatever you have expended for the children.

My wishes and purposes concerning Hartley and Derwent I will communicate as soon as this bustle and endless rat-a-tat-tat at our door is somewhat over. I concluded my Lectures last night most triumphantly, with loud, long, and enthusiastic applauses at my entrance, and ditto in yet fuller chorus as, and for some minutes after I had retired. It was lucky that (as I never once thought of the Lecture till I had entered the Lecture Box), the two last were the most impressive and really the best. I suppose that no dramatic author ever had so large a number of unsolicited, unknown yet predetermined plauditors in the theatre, as I had on Saturday night. One of the malignant papers asserted that I had collected all the saints from Mile End turnpike to Tyburn Bar. With so many warm friends, it is impossible, in the present state of human nature, that I should not have many unprovoked and unknown enemies. You will have heard that on my entering the box on Saturday night, I was discovered by the pit, and that they all turned their faces towards our box, and gave a treble cheer of claps.

I mention these things because it will please Southey to hear that there is a large number of persons in London who hail with enthusiasm my prospect of the stage's being purified and rendered classical. My success, if I succeed (of which I assure you I entertain doubts in my opinion well founded, both from the want of a prominent actor for Ordonio, and from the want of vulgar pathos in the play itself—nay, there is not enough even of true dramatic pathos), but if I succeed, I succeed for others as well as myself....

S. T. Coleridge.

P. S. I pray you, my dear Sara! do take on yourself the charge of instantly sending off by the waggon Mr. Sotheby's folio edition of all Petrarch's Works, which I left at Grasmere. (I am ashamed to meet Sotheby till I have returned it.) At the same time my quarto MS. Book with the German Musical Play in it,[99] and the two folio volumes of the Greek Poets may go. For I want them hourly and I must try to imitate W. Scott in making hay while the sun shines.

Kisses and heartfelt loves for my sweet Sara, and scarce less for dear little Herbert and Edith.

CXCIV. TO ROBERT SOUTHEY.

71, Berners Street, Tuesday, February 8, 1813.

My dear Southey,—It is seldom that a man can with literal truth apologise for delay in writing; but for the last three weeks I have had more upon my hands and spirits than my health was equal to.

The first copy I can procure of the second edition (of the play) I will do my best to get franked to you. You will, I hope, think it much improved as a poem. Dr. Bell, who is all kindness and goodness, came to me in no small bustle this morning in consequence of "a censure passed on the 'Remorse' by a man of great talents, both in prose and verse, who was impartial, and thought highly of the work on the whole." What was it, think you? There were many unequal lines in the Play, but which he did not choose to specify. Dr. Bell would not mention the critic's name, but was very earnest with me to procure some indifferent person of good sense to read it over, by way of spectacles to an author's own dim judgement. Soon after he left me I discovered that the critic was Gifford, who had said good-naturedly that I ought to be whipt for leaving so many weak and slovenly lines in so fine a poem. What the lines were he would not say and I do not care. Inequalities have every poem, even an Epic—much more a Dramatic Poem must have and ought to have. The question is, are they in their own place dissonances? If so I am the last man to stickle for them, who am nicknamed in the Green Room the "anomalous author," from my utter indifference or prompt facility in sanctioning every omission that was suggested. That paragraph in the "Quarterly Review"[100] respecting me, as ridiculed in "Rejected Addresses," was surely unworthy of a man of sense like Gifford. What reason could he have to suppose me a man so childishly irritable as to be provoked by a trifle so contemptible? If he had, how could he think it a parody at all? But the noise which the "Rejected Addresses" made, the notice taken of Smith the author by Lord Holland, Byron, etc., give a melancholy confirmation of my assertion in "The Friend" that "we worship the vilest reptile if only the brainless head be expiated by the sting of personal malignity in the tail." I wish I could procure for you the "Examiner" and Drakard's London Paper. They were forced to affect admiration of the Tragedy, but yet abuse me they must, and so comes the old infamous crambe bis millies cocta of the "sentimentalities, puerilities, whinings, and meannesses, both of style and thought," in my former writings, but without (which is worth notice both in these gentlemen and in all our former Zoili), without one single quotation or reference in proof or exemplification. No wonder! for excepting the "Three Graves," which was announced as not meant for poetry, and the poem on the Tethered Ass, with the motto Sermoni propriora,[101] and which, like your "Dancing Bear," might be called a ludicro-splenetic copy of verses, with the diction purposely appropriate, they might (as at the first appearance of my poems they did) find, indeed, all the opposite vices. But if it had not been for the Preface to W.'s "Lyrical Ballads," they would never themselves have dreamt of affected simplicity and meanness of thought and diction. This slang has gone on for fourteen or fifteen years against us, and really deserves to be exposed. As far as my judgement goes, the two best qualities of the tragedy are, first, the simplicity and unity of the plot, in respect of that which, of all the unities, is the only one founded on good sense—the presence of a one all-pervading, all-combining Principle. By Remorse I mean the anguish and disquietude arising from the self-contradiction introduced into the soul by guilt, a feeling which is good or bad according as the will makes use of it. This is expressed in the lines chosen as the motto:—

Remorse is as the heart in which it grows:
If that be gentle, it drops balmy dews
Of true repentance; but if proud and gloomy,
It is a poison tree that, pierced to the inmost,
Weeps only tears of poison!
Act i. sc. 1.

And Remorse is everywhere distinguished from virtuous penitence. To excite a sanative remorse Alvar returns, the Passion is put in motion at Ordonio's first entrance by the appearance of Isidore's wife, etc.; it is carried still higher by the narration of Isidore, Act ii. sc. 1; higher still by the interview with the supposed wizard; and to its acme by the

Incantation Scene and Picture. Now, then, we are to see its effects and to exemplify the second part of the motto, "but if proud and gloomy, It is a poison tree," etc. Ordonio, too proud to look steadily into himself, catches a false scent, plans the murder of Isidore and the poisoning of the Sorcerer, perpetrates the one, and, attempting the other, is driven by Remorse and the discovery of Alvar to a temporary distraction; and, finally, falling a victim to the only crime that had been realized, by the hand of Alhadra, breathes his last in a pang of pride: "O couldst thou forget me!" As from a circumference to a centre, every ray in the tragedy converges to Ordonio. Spite of wretched acting, the passage told wonderfully in which, as in a struggle between two unequal Panathlists or wrestlers, the weaker had for a moment got uppermost, and Ordonio, with unfeigned love, and genuine repentance, says, "I will kneel to thee, my Brother! Forgive me, Alvar!" till the Pride, like the bottom-swell on our lake, gusts up again in "Curse me with forgiveness!" The second good quality is, I think, the variety of metres according as the speeches are merely transitive, or narrative, or passionate, or (as in the Incantation) deliberate and formal poetry. It is true they are all, or almost all, Iambic blank verse, but under that form there are five or six perfectly distinct metres. As to the outcry that the "Remorse" is not pathetic (meaning such pathos as convulses in "Isabella" or "The Gamester") the answer is easy. True! the poet never meant that it should be. It is as pathetic as the "Hamlet" or the "Julius Cæsar." He woo'd the feelings of the audience, as my wretched epilogue said:—

With no too real Woes that make you groan
(At home-bred, kindred grief, perhaps your own),
Yet with no image compensate the mind,
Nor leave one joy for memory behind.

As to my thefts from the "Wallenstein," they came on compulsion from the necessity of haste, and do not lie on my conscience, being partly thefts from myself, and because I gave Schiller twenty for one I have taken, and in the mean time I hope they will lie snug. "The obscurest Haunt of all our mountains,"[102] I did not recognize as Wordsworth till after the play was all printed. I must write again to-morrow on other subjects.

The House was crowded again last night, and the Manager told me that they lost £200 by suspending it on [the] Saturday night that Jack Bannister came out.

(No signature.)

CXCV. TO THOMAS POOLE.

February 13, 1813.

Dear Poole,—Love so deep and so domesticated with the whole being, as mine was to you, can never cease to be. To quote the best and sweetest lines I ever wrote:[103]—

Alas! they had been Friends in Youth!
But whisp'ring Tongues can poison Truth;
And Constancy lives in Realms above;
And Life is thorny; and Youth is vain;
And to be wroth with one we love
Doth work, like Madness, in the Brain!
And so it chanced (as I divine)
With Roland and Sir Leoline.

Each spake words of high Disdain
And Insult to his heart's best Brother:
They parted—ne'er to meet again!
But never either found another
To free the hollow Heart from Paining—
They stood aloof, the Scars remaining,
Like Cliffs, which had been rent asunder,
A dreary Sea now flows between!—
But neither Frost, nor Heat, nor Thunder,
Shall wholly do away, I ween,
The marks of that which once hath been!

Stung as I have been with your unkindness to me, in my sore adversity, yet the receipt of your two heart-engendered lines was sweeter than an unexpected strain of sweetest music, or, in humbler phrase, it was the only pleasurable sensation which the success of the "Remorse" has given me. I have read of, or perhaps only imagined, a punishment in Arabia, in which the culprit was so bricked up as to be unable to turn his eyes to the right or the left, while in front was placed a high heap of barren sand glittering under the vertical sun. Some slight analogue of this, I have myself suffered from the mere unusualness of having my attention forcibly directed to a subject which permitted neither sequence of imagery, or series of reasoning. No grocer's apprentice, after his first month's permitted riot, was ever sicker of figs and raisins than I of hearing about the "Remorse." The endless rat-a-tat-tat at our black-and-blue-bruised door, and my three master-fiends, proof sheets, letters (for I have a raging epistolophobia), and worse than these—invitations to large dinners, which I cannot refuse without offence and imputation of pride, or accept without disturbance of temper the day before, and a sick, aching stomach for two days after, so that my spirits quite sink under it.

From what I myself saw, and from what an intelligent friend, more solicitous about it than myself, has told me, the "Remorse" has succeeded in spite of bad scenes, execrable acting, and newspaper calumny. In my compliments to the actors, I endeavoured (such is the lot of this world, in which our best qualities tilt against each other, ex. gr., our good nature against our veracity) to make a lie edge round the truth as nearly as possible. Poor Rae (why poor? for Ordonio has almost made his fortune) did the best in his power, and is a good man ... a moral and affectionate husband and father. But nature has denied him person and all volume and depth of voice; so that the blundering coxcomb Elliston, by mere dint of voice and self-conceit, out-dazzled him. It has been a good thing for the theatre. They will get £8,000 or £10,000, and I shall get more than all my literary labours put together; nay, thrice as much, subtracting my heavy losses in the "Watchman" and "Friend,"—£400 including the copyright.

You will have heard that, previous to the acceptance of "Remorse," Mr. Jos. Wedgwood had withdrawn from his share of the annuity![104] Well, yes, it is well!—for I can now be sure that I loved him, revered him, and was grateful to him from no selfish feeling. For equally (and may these words be my final condemnation at the last awful day, if I speak not the whole truth), equally do I at this moment love him, and with the same reverential gratitude! To Mr. Thomas Wedgwood I felt, doubtless, love; but it was mingled with fear, and constant apprehension of his too exquisite taste in morals. But Josiah! Oh, I ever did, and ever shall, love him, as a being so beautifully balanced in mind and heart deserves to be!

'Tis well, too, because it has given me the strongest impulse, the most imperious motive I have experienced, to prove to him that his past munificence has not been wasted!

You perhaps may likewise have heard (in the Whispering Gallery of the World) of the year-long difference between me and Wordsworth (compared with the sufferings of which all the former afflictions of my life were less than flea-bites), occasioned (in great part) by the wicked folly of the arch-fool Montagu.

A reconciliation has taken place, but the feeling, which I had previous to that moment, when the (three-fourth) calumny burst, like a thunderstorm from a blue sky, on my soul, after fifteen years of such religious, almost superstitious idolatry and self-sacrifice. Oh, no! no! that, I fear, never can return. All outward actions, all inward wishes, all thoughts and admirations will be the same—are the same, but—aye, there remains an immedicable But. Had W. said (what he acknowledges to have said) to you, I should have thought it unkind, and have had a right to say, "Why, why am I, whose whole being has been like a glass beehive before you for five years, why do I hear this from a third person for the first time?" But to such ... as Montagu! just when W. himself had forewarned me! Oh! it cut me to the heart's core.

S. T. Coleridge.

CHAPTER XII
A MELANCHOLY EXILE
1813-1815

CXCVI. TO DANIEL STUART.

September 25, 1813.

Dear Stuart,—I forgot to ask you by what address a letter would best reach you! Whether Kilburn House, Kilburn? I shall therefore send it, or leave it at the "Courier" office. I found Southey so chevaux-de-frized and pallisadoed by preëngagements that I could not reach at him till Sunday sennight, that is, Sunday, October 3, when, if convenient, we should be happy to wait on you. Southey will be in town till Monday evening, and you have his brother's address, should you wish to write to him (Dr. Southey,[105] 28, Little Queen Anne Street, Cavendish Square).

A curious paragraph in the "Morning Chronicle" of this morning, asserting with its usual comfortable anti-patriotism the determination of the Emperor of Austria to persevere in the terms[106] offered to his son-in-law, in his frenzy of power, even though he should be beaten to the dust. Methinks there ought to be good authority before a journalist dares prophesy folly and knavery in union of our Imperial Ally. An excellent article ought to be written on this subject. In the same paper there is what I should have called a masterly essay on the causes of the downfall of the Comic Drama, if I was not perplexed by the distinct recollection of having conversed the greater part of it at Lamb's. I wish you would read it, and tell me what you think; for I seem to remember a conversation with you in which you asserted the very contrary; that comic genius was the thing wanting, and not comic subjects—that the watering places, or rather the characters presented at them, had never been adequately managed, etc.

Might I request you to present my best respects to Mrs. Stuart as those of an old acquaintance of yours, and, as far as I am myself conscious of, at all times with hearty affection, your sincere friend,

S. T. Coleridge.

P. S. There are some half dozen more books of mine left at the "Courier" office, Ben Jonson and sundry German volumes. As I am compelled to sell my library,[107] you would oblige me by ordering the porter to take them to 19, London Street, Fitzroy Square; whom I will remunerate for his trouble. I should not take this liberty, but that I had in vain written to Mr. Street, requesting the same favour, which in his hurry of business I do not wonder that he forgot.

CXCVII. TO JOSEPH COTTLE.[108]

April 26, 1814.

You have poured oil in the raw and festering wound of an old friend's conscience, Cottle! but it is oil of vitriol! I but barely glanced at the middle of the first page of your letter, and have seen no more of it—not from resentment (God forbid!), but from the state of my bodily and mental sufferings, that scarcely permitted human fortitude to let in a new visitor of affliction.

The object of my present reply is to state the case just as it is. First, that for ten years the anguish of my spirit has been indescribable, the sense of my danger staring, but the consciousness of my guilt worse, far worse than all. I have prayed, with drops of agony on my brow, trembling not only before the justice of my Maker, but even before the mercy of my Redeemer. "I gave thee so many talents, what hast thou done with them?" Secondly, overwhelmed as I am with a sense of my direful infirmity, I have never attempted to disguise or conceal the cause. On the contrary, not only to friends have I stated the whole case with tears and the very bitterness of shame, but in two instances I have warned young men, mere acquaintances, who had spoken of having taken laudanum, of the direful consequences, by an awful exposition of the tremendous effects on myself.

Thirdly, though before God I cannot lift up my eyelids, and only do not despair of His mercy, because to despair would be adding crime to crime, yet to my fellow-men I may say that I was seduced into the accursed habit ignorantly. I had been almost bed-ridden for many months with swellings in my knees. In a medical journal, I unhappily met with an account of a cure performed in a similar case (or what appeared to me so), by rubbing in of laudanum, at the same time taking a given dose internally. It acted like a charm, like a miracle! I recovered the use of my limbs, of my appetite, of my spirits, and this continued for near a fortnight. At length the unusual stimulus subsided, the complaint returned, the supposed remedy was recurred to—but I cannot go through the dreary history.

Suffice it to say, that effects were produced which acted on me by terror and cowardice, of pain and sudden death, not (so help me God!) by any temptation of pleasure, or expectation, or desire of exciting pleasurable sensations. On the very contrary, Mrs. Morgan and her sister will bear witness, so far as to say, that the longer I abstained the higher my spirits were, the keener my enjoyment—till the moment, the direful moment, arrived when my pulse began to fluctuate, my heart to palpitate, and such a dreadful falling abroad, as it were, of my whole frame, such intolerable restlessness, and incipient bewilderment, that in the last of my several attempts to abandon the dire poison, I exclaimed in agony, which I now repeat in seriousness and solemnity, "I am too poor to hazard this." Had I but a few hundred pounds, but £200—half to send to Mrs. Coleridge, and half to place myself in a private madhouse, where I could procure nothing but what a physician thought proper, and where a medical attendant could be constantly with me for two or three months (in less than that time life or death would be determined), then there might be hope. Now there is none!! O God! how willingly would I place myself under Dr. Fox, in his establishment; for my case is a species of madness, only that it is a derangement, an utter impotence of the volition, and not of the intellectual faculties. You bid me rouse myself: go bid a man paralytic in both arms, to rub them briskly together, and that will cure him. "Alas!" he would reply, "that I cannot move my arms is my complaint and my misery."

May God bless you, and your affectionate, but most afflicted,

S. T. Coleridge.
CXCVIII. TO THE SAME.

Friday, May 27, 1814.

My dear Cottle,—Gladness be with you, for your convalescence, and equally so, at the hope which has sustained and tranquillised you through your imminent peril. Far otherwise is, and hath been, my state; yet I too am grateful; yet I cannot rejoice. I feel, with an intensity unfathomable by words, my utter nothingness, impotence, and worthlessness, in and for myself. I have learned what a sin is, against an infinite imperishable being, such as is the soul of man!

I have had more than a glimpse of what is meant by death and outer darkness, and the worm that dieth not—and that all the hell of the reprobate is no more inconsistent with the love of God, than the blindness of one who has occasioned loathsome and guilty diseases, to eat out his eyes, is inconsistent with the light of the sun. But the consolations, at least, the sensible sweetness of hope, I do not possess. On the contrary, the temptation which I have constantly to fight up against is a fear, that if annihilation and the possibility of heaven were offered to my choice, I should choose the former.

This is, perhaps, in part, a constitutional idiosyncrasy, for when a mere boy I wrote these lines:—

O, what a wonder seems the fear of death,
Seeing how gladly we all sink to sleep,
Babes, children, youths, and men,
Night following night, for three-score years and ten![109]
And in my early manhood, in lines descriptive of a gloomy solitude, I disguised my own sensations in the following words:—

Here wisdom might abide, and here remorse!
Here, too, the woe-worn man, who, weak in soul,
And of this busy human heart aweary,
Worships the spirit of unconscious life
In tree or wild-flower. Gentle lunatic!

If so he might not wholly cease to be,
He would far rather not be what he is;
But would be something that he knows not of,
In woods or waters, or among the rocks.[110]

My main comfort, therefore, consists in what the divines call the faith of adherence, and no spiritual effort appears to benefit me so much as the one earnest, importunate, and often for hours, momently repeated prayers: "I believe! Lord, help my unbelief! Give me faith, but as a mustard seed, and I shall remove this mountain! Faith! faith! faith! I believe. Oh, give me faith! Oh, for my Redeemer's sake, give me faith in my Redeemer."

In all this I justify God, for I was accustomed to oppose the preaching of the terrors of the gospel, and to represent it as debasing virtue by the admixture of slavish selfishness.

I now see that what is spiritual can only be spiritually apprehended. Comprehended it cannot.

Mr. Eden gave you a too flattering account of me. It is true, I am restored as much beyond my expectations almost as my deserts; but I am exceedingly weak. I need for myself solace and refocillation of animal spirits, instead of being in a condition of offering it to others. Yet as soon as I may see you, I will call upon you.

S. T. Coleridge.

CXCIX. TO CHARLES MATHEWS.

2, Queen's Square, Bristol, May 30, 1814.

Dear Sir,—Unusual as this liberty may be, yet as it is a friendly one, you will pardon it, especially from one who has had already some connection with the stage, and may have more. But I was so highly gratified with my feast of this night, that I feel a sort of restless impulse to tell you what I felt and thought.

Imprimis, I grieved that you had such miserable materials to deal with as Colman's Solomon Grundy,[111] a character which in and of itself (Mathews and his Variations ad libitum put out of the question) contains no one element of genuine comedy, no, nor even of fun or drollery. The play is assuredly the very sediment, the dregs of a noble cask of wine; for such was, yes, in many instances was and has been, and in many more might have been, Colman's dramatic genius.

A genius Colman is by nature. What he is not, or has not been, is all of his own making. In my humble opinion, he possessed the elements of dramatic power in a far higher degree than Sheridan: or which of the two, think you, should pronounce with the deeper sigh of self-reproach, "Fuimus Troes! and what might we not have been?"

But I leave this to proceed to the really astonishing effect of your duplicate of Cook in Sir Archy McSarcasm.[112] To say that in some of your higher notes your voice was rather thinner, rather less substance and thick body than poor Cook's, would be merely to say that A. B. is not exactly A. A. But, on the whole, it was almost illusion, and so very excellent, that if I were intimate with you, I should get angry and abuse you for not forming for yourself some original and important character. The man who could so impersonate Sir

Archy McSarcasm might do anything in profound Comedy (that is, that which gives us the passions of men and their endless modifications and influences on thought, gestures, etc., modified in their turn by circumstances of rank, relations, nationality, etc., instead of mere transitory manners; in short, the inmost man represented on the superficies, instead of the superficies merely representing itself). But you will forgive a stranger for a suggestion? I cannot but think that it would answer for your still increasing fame if you were either previously to, or as an occasional diversification of Sir Archy, to study and give that one most incomparable monologue of Sir Pertinax McSycophant,[113] where he gives his son the history of his rise and progress in the world. Being in its essence a soliloquy with all the advantages of a dialogue, it would be a most happy introduction to Sir Archy McSarcasm, which, I doubt not, will call forth with good reason the Covent Garden Manager's thanks to you next season.

I once had the presumption to address this advice to an actor on the London stage: "Think, in order that you may be able to observe! Observe, in order that you may have materials to think upon! And thirdly, keep awake ever the habit of instantly embodying and realising the results of the two; but always think!"

A great actor, comic or tragic, is not to be a mere copy, a fac simile, or but an imitation, of Nature. Now an imitation differs from a copy in this, that it of necessity implies and demands difference, whereas a copy aims at identity. What a marble peach on a mantelpiece, that you take up deluded and put down with pettish disgust, is, compared with a fruit-piece of Vanhuyser's, even such is a mere copy of nature compared with a true histrionic imitation. A good actor is Pygmalion's Statue, a work of exquisite art, animated and gifted with motion; but still art, still a species of poetry.

Not the least advantage which an actor gains by having secured a high reputation is this, that those who sincerely admire him may dare tell him the truth at times, and thus, if he have sensible friends, secure his progressive improvement; in other words, keep him thinking. For without thinking, nothing consummate can be effected.

Accept this, dear sir, as it is meant, a small testimony of the high gratification I have received from you and of the respectful and sincere kind wishes with which I am

Your obedient
S. T. Coleridge.

—— Mathews, Esq., to be left at the Bristol Theatre.

CC. TO JOSIAH WADE.

Bristol, June 26, 1814.

Dear Sir,—For I am unworthy to call any good man friend—much less you, whose hospitality and love I have abused; accept, however, my intreaties for your forgiveness, and for your prayers.

Conceive a poor miserable wretch, who for many years has been attempting to beat off pain, by a constant recurrence to the vice that reproduces it. Conceive a spirit in hell, employed in tracing out for others the road to that heaven, from which his crimes exclude him! In short, conceive whatever is most wretched, helpless, and hopeless, and you will form as tolerable a notion of my state, as it is possible for a good man to have.

I used to think the text in St. James that "he who offended in one point, offends in all," very harsh; but I now feel the awful, the tremendous truth of it. In the one crime of opium, what crime have I not made myself guilty of!—Ingratitude to my Maker! and to my benefactors—injustice! and unnatural cruelty to my poor children!—self-contempt for my repeated promise—breach, nay, too often, actual falsehood!

After my death, I earnestly entreat, that a full and unqualified narration of my wretchedness, and of its guilty cause, may be made public, that at least some little good may be effected by the direful example.

May God Almighty bless you, and have mercy on your still affectionate, and in his heart, grateful

S. T. Coleridge.

CCI. TO JOHN MURRAY.

Josiah Wade's, Esq., 2, Queen's Square, Bristol,
August 23, 1814.

Dear Sir,—I have heard, from my friend Mr. Charles Lamb, writing by desire of Mr. Robinson, that you wish to have the justly-celebrated "Faust"[114] of Goethe translated, and that some one or other of my partial friends have induced you to consider me as the man most likely to execute the work adequately, those excepted, of course, whose higher power (established by the solid and satisfactory ordeal of the wide and rapid sale of their works) it might seem profanation to employ in any other manner than in the development of their own intellectual organisation. I return my thanks to the recommender, whoever he be, and no less to you for your flattering faith in the recommendation; and thinking, as I do, that among many volumes of praiseworthy German poems, the "Louisa" of Voss, and the "Faust" of Goethe, are the two, if not the only ones, that are emphatically original in their conception, and characteristic of a new and peculiar sort of thinking and imagining, I should not be averse from exerting my best efforts in an attempt to import whatever is importable of either or of both into our own language.

But let me not be suspected of a presumption of which I am not consciously guilty, if I say that I feel two difficulties: one arising from long disuse of versification, added to what I know, better than the most hostile critic could inform me, of my comparative weakness; and the other, that any work in Poetry strikes me with more than common awe, as proposed for realization by myself, because from long habits of meditation on language, as the symbolical medium of the connection of Thought with Thought, and of Thought as affected and modified by Passion and Emotion, I should spend days in avoiding what I deemed faults, though with the full fore-knowledge that their admission would not have offended perhaps three of all my readers, and might be deemed Beauties by 300—if so many there were; and this not out of any respect for the Public (i. e. the persons who might happen to purchase and look over the Book), but from a hobby-horsical, superstitious regard to my own feelings and sense of duty. Language is the Sacred Fire in this Temple of Humanity, and the Muses are its especial and vestal Priestesses. Though I cannot prevent the vile drugs and counterfeit Frankincense, which render its flame at once pitchy, glowing, and unsteady, I would yet be no voluntary accomplice in the Sacrilege. With the commencement of a Public, commences the degradation of the Good and the Beautiful—both fade and retire before the accidentally Agreeable. "Othello" becomes a hollow lip-worship; and the "Castle Spectre" or any more peccant thing of Froth, Noise, and Impermanence, that may have overbillowed it on the restless sea of curiosity, is the true Prayer of the Praise and Admiration.

I thought it right to state to you these opinions of mine, that you might know that I think the Translation of the "Faust" a task demanding (from me, I mean) no ordinary efforts—and why? This—that it is painful, very painful, and even odious to me, to attempt anything of a literary nature, with any motive of pecuniary advantage; but that I bow to the all-wise Providence, which has made me a poor man, and therefore compelled me by other duties inspiring feelings, to bring even my Intellect to the Market. And the finale is this. I should like to attempt the Translation. If you will mention your terms, at once and irrevocably (for I am an idiot at bargaining, and shrink from the very thought), I will return an answer by the next Post, whether in my present circumstances, I can or cannot undertake it. If I do, I will do it immediately; but I must have all Goethe's works, which I cannot procure in Bristol; for to give the "Faust" without a preliminary critical Essay would be worse than nothing, as far as regards the Public. If you were to ask me as a friend whether I think it would suit the General Taste, I should reply that I cannot calculate on caprice and accident (for instance, some fashionable man or review happening to take it up favourably), but that otherwise my fears would be stronger than my hopes. Men of genius will admire it, of necessity. Those must, who think deepest and most imaginatively. Then "Louisa" would delight all of good hearts.

I remain, dear sir, with every respect,

S. T. Coleridge.

CCII. TO DANIEL STUART.

Mr. Smith's, Ashley, Box, near Bath,
September 12, 1814.

My dear Sir,—I wrote some time ago to Mr. Smith, earnestly requesting your address, and entreating him to inform you of the dreadful state in which I was, when your kind letter must have arrived, during your stay at Bath.... But let me not complain. I ought to be and I trust I am, grateful for what I am, having escaped with my intellectual powers, if less elastic, yet not less vigorous, and with ampler and far more solid materials to exert them on. We know nothing even of ourselves, till we know ourselves to be as nothing (a solemn truth, spite of point and antithesis, in which the thought has chanced to word itself)! From this word of truth which the sore discipline of a sick bed has compacted into an indwelling reality, from this article, formerly, of speculative belief, but which [circumstances] have actualised into practical faith, I have learned to counteract calumny by self-reproach, and not only to rejoice (as indeed from natural disposition, from the very constitution of my heart, I should have done at all periods of my life) at the temporal prosperity, and increased and increasing reputation of my old fellow-labourers in philosophical, political, and poetical literature, but to bear their neglect, and even their detraction, as if I had done nothing at all, when it would have asked no very violent strain of recollection for one or two of them to have considered, whether some part of their most successful somethings were not among the nothings of my intellectual no-doings. But all strange things are less strange than the sense of intellectual obligations. Seldom do I ever see a Review, yet almost as often as that seldomness permits have I smiled at finding myself attacked in strains of thought which would never have occurred to the writer, had he not directly or indirectly learned them from myself. This is among the salutary effects, even of the dawn of actual religion on the mind, that we begin to reflect on our duties to God and to ourselves as permanent beings, and not to flatter ourselves by a superficial auditing of our negative duties to our neighbours, or mere acts in transitu to the transitory. I have too sad an account to settle between myself that is and has been, and myself that can not cease to be, to allow me a single complaint that, for all my labours in behalf of truth against the Jacobin party, then against military despotism abroad, against weakness and despondency and faction and factious goodiness at home, I have never received from those in power even a verbal acknowledgment; though by mere reference to dates, it might be proved that no small number of fine speeches in the House of Commons, and elsewhere, originated, directly or indirectly, in my Essays and conversations.[115] I dare assert, that the science of reasoning and judging concerning the productions of literature, the characters and measures of public men, and the events of nations, by a systematic subsumption of them, under Principles, deduced from the nature of man, and that of prophesying concerning the future (in contradiction to the hopes or fears of the majority) by a careful cross-examination of some period, the most analogous in past history, as learnt from contemporary authorities, and the proportioning of the ultimate event to the likenesses as modified or counteracted by the differences, was as good as unknown in the public prints, before the year 1795-96. Earl Darnley, on the appearance of my letters in the "Courier" concerning the Spaniards,[116] bluntly asked me, whether I had lost my senses, and quoted Lord Grenville at me. If you should happen to cast your eye over my character of Pitt,[117] my two letters to Fox, my Essays on the French Empire under Buonaparte, compared with the Roman, under the first Emperors; that on the probability of the restoration of the Bourbons, and those on Ireland, and Catholic Emancipation (which last unfortunately remain for the greater part in manuscript, Mr. Street not relishing them), and should add to them my Essays in "The Friend" on Taxation, and the supposed effects of war on our commercial prosperity; those on international law in defence of our siege of Copenhagen; and if you had before you the long letter which I wrote to Sir G. Beaumont in 1806,[118] concerning the inevitableness of a war with America, and the specific dangers of that war, if not provided against by specific pre-arrangements; with a list of their Frigates, so called, with their size, number, and weight of metal, the characters of their commanders, and the proportion suspected of British seamen.—I have luckily a copy of it, a rare accident with me.—I dare amuse myself, I say, with the belief, that by far the better half of all these, would read to you now, as history. And what have I got for all this? What for my first daring to blow the trumpet of sound philosophy against the Lancastrian faction? The answer is not complex. Unthanked, and left worse than defenceless, by the friends of the Government and the Establishment, to be undermined or outraged by all the malice, hatred, and calumny of its enemies; and to think and toil, with a patent for all the abuse, and a transfer to others of all the honours. In the "Quarterly" Review of the "Remorse" (delayed till it could by no possibility be of the least service to me, and the compliments in which are as senseless and silly as the censures; every fault ascribed to it, being either no improbability at all, or from the very essence and end of the drama no dramatic improbability, without noticing any one of the real faults, and there are many glaring, and one or two deadly sins in the tragedy)—in this Review, I am abused, and insolently reproved as a man, with reference to my supposed private habits, for not publishing. Would to heaven I never had! To this very moment I am embarrassed and tormented, in consequence of the non-payment of the subscribers to "The Friend." But I could rebut the charge; and not merely say, but prove, that there is not a man in England, whose thoughts, images, words, and erudition have been published in larger quantities than mine; though I must admit, not by, or for, myself. Believe me, if I felt any pain from these things, I should not make this exposé; for it is constitutional with me, to shrink from all talk or communication of what gnaws within me. And, if I felt any real anger, I should not do what I fully intend to do, publish two long satires, in Drydenic verse, entitled "Puff and Slander."[119] But I seem to myself to have endured the hootings and peltings, and "Go up bald head" (2 Kings, ch. ii. vs. 23, 24) quite long enough; and shall therefore send forth my two she-bears, to tear in pieces the most obnoxious of these ragged children in intellect; and to scare the rest of these mischievous little mud-larks back to their crevice-nests, and lurking holes. While those who know me best, spite of my many infirmities, love me best, I am determined, henceforward, to treat my unprovoked enemies in the spirit of the Tiberian adage, Oderint modo timeant.

And now, having for the very first time in my whole life opened out my whole feelings and thoughts concerning my past fates and fortunes, I will draw anew on your patience, by a detail of my present operations. My medical friend is so well satisfied of my convalescence, and that nothing now remains, but to superinduce positive health on a system from which disease and its removable causes have been driven out, that he has not merely consented to, but advised my leaving Bristol, for some rural retirement. I could indeed pursue nothing uninterruptedly in that city. Accordingly, I am now joint tenant with Mr. Morgan, of a sweet little cottage, at Ashley, half a mile from Box, on the Bath road. I breakfast every morning before nine; work till one, and walk or read till three. Thence, till tea-time, chat or read some lounge book, or correct what I have written. From six to eight work again; from eight till bed-time, play whist, or the little mock billiard called bagatelle, and then sup, and go to bed. My morning hours, as the longest and most important division, I keep sacred to my most important Work,[120] which is printing at Bristol; two of my friends having taken upon themselves the risk. It is so long since I have conversed with you, that I cannot say, whether the subject will, or will not be interesting to you. The title is "Christianity, the one true Philosophy; or, Five Treatises on the Logos, or Communicative Intelligence, natural, human, and divine." To which is prefixed a prefatory Essay, on the laws and limits of toleration and liberality, illustrated by fragments of auto-biography. The first Treatise—Logos Propaidenticos, or the Science of systematic thinking in ordinary life. The second—Logos Architectonicus, or an attempt to apply the constructive or Mathematical process to Metaphysics and Natural Theology. The third—Ὁ Λόγος ὁ θεάνθρωπος (the divine logos incarnate)—a full commentary on the Gospel of St. John, in development of St. Paul's doctrine of preaching Christ alone, and Him crucified. The fourth—on Spinoza and Spinozism, with a life of B. Spinoza. This entitled Logos Agonistes. The fifth and last, Logos Alogos (i. e., Logos Illogicus), or on modern Unitarianism, its causes and effects. The whole will be comprised in two portly octavos, and the second treatise will be the only one which will, and from the nature of the subject must, be unintelligible to the great majority even of well educated readers. The purpose of the whole is a philosophical defence of the Articles of the Church, as far as they respect doctrine, as points of faith. If originality be any merit, this Work will have that, at all events, from the first page to the last.

The evenings I have employed in composing a series of Essays on the principles of Genial Criticism concerning the fine Arts, especially those of Statuary and Painting;[121] and of these four in title, but six or more in size, have been published in "Felix Farley's Bristol Journal;" a strange plan for such a publication; but my motive was originally to serve poor Allston, who is now exhibiting his pictures at Bristol. Oh! dear sir! do pray if you have the power or opportunity use your influence with "The Sun," not to continue that accursed system of calumny and detraction against Allston. The articles, by whomever written, were a disgrace to human nature, and, to my positive knowledge, argued only less ignorance than malignity. Mr. Allston has been cruelly used. Good God! what did I not hear Sir George Beaumont say, with my own ears! Nay, he wrote to me after repeated examination of Allston's great picture, declaring himself a complete convert to all my opinions of Allston's paramount genius as a historical painter. What did I not hear Mr. West say? After a full hour's examination of the picture, he pointed out one thing he thought out of harmony (and which against my earnest desire Allston altered and had reason to repent sorely) and then said, "I have shot my bolt. It is as near perfection as a picture can be!"...

But to return to my Essays. I shall publish no more in Bristol. What they could do, they have done. But I have carefully corrected and polished those already published, and shall carry them on to sixteen or twenty, containing animated descriptions of all the best pictures of the great masters in England, with characteristics of the great masters from Giotto to Correggio. The first three Essays were of necessity more austere; for till it could be determined what beauty was; whether it was beauty merely because it pleased, or pleased because it was beauty, it would have been as absurd to talk of general principles of taste, as of tastes. Now will this series, purified from all accidental, local, or personal references, tint or serve the "Courier" in the present dearth? I have no hesitation in declaring them the best compositions I have ever written, I could regularly supply two Essays a week, and one political Essay. Be so good as to speak to Mr. Street.[122] I could send him up eight or ten at once.

Make my best respects to Mrs. Stuart. I shall be very anxious to hear from you.

Your affectionate and grateful friend,

S. T. Coleridge.

CCIII. TO THE SAME.

"October 30, 1814."

Dear Stuart,—After I had finished the third letter,[123] I thought it the best I had ever written; but, on re-perusal, I perfectly agree with you. It is misty, and like most misty compositions, laborious,—what the Italians call faticoso. I except the two last paragraphs ("In this guise my Lord," to—"aversabitur"). These I still like. Yet what I wanted to say is very important, because it strikes at the root of all legislative Jacobinism. The view which our laws take of robbery, and even murder, not as guilt of which God alone is presumed to be the Judge, but as crimes depriving the King of one of his subjects, rendering dangerous and abating the value of the King's Highways, etc., may suggest some notion of my meaning. Jack, Tom, and Harry have no existence in the eye of the law, except as included in some form or other of the permanent property of the realm. Just as, on the other hand, Religion has nothing to do with Ranks, Estates, or Offices; but exerts itself wholly on what is personal, viz., our souls, consciences, and the morality of our actions, as opposed to mere legality. Ranks, Estates, Offices, etc., were made for persons! exclaims Major Cartwright[124] and his partizans. Yes, I reply, as far as the divine administration is concerned, but human jurisprudence, wisely aware of its own weakness, and sensible how incommensurate its powers are with so vast an object as the well-being of individuals, as individuals, reverses the position, and knows nothing of persons, other than as properties, officiaries, subjects. The preambles of our old statutes concerning aliens (as foreign merchants) and Jews, are all so many illustrations of my principle; the strongest instance of opposition to which, and therefore characteristic of the present age, was the attempt to legislate for animals by Lord Erskine;[125] that is, not merely interfering with persons as persons; or with what are called by moralists the imperfect duties (a very obscure phrase for obligations of conscience, not capable of being realized (perfecta) by legal penalties), but extending personality to things.

In saying this, I mean only to designate the general spirit of human law. Every principle, on its application to practice, must be limited and modified by circumstances; our reason by our common sense. Still, however, the principle is most important, as aim, rule, and guide. Guided by this spirit, our ancestors repealed the Puritan Law, by which adultery was to be punished with death, and brought it back to a civil damage. So, too, actions for seduction. Not that the Judge or Legislator did not feel the guilt of such crimes, but that the Law knows nothing about guilt. So, in the Exchequer, common debts are sued for on the plea that the creditor is less able to pay our Lord the King, etc., etc. Now, contrast with this, the preamble to the first French Constitution, and I think my meaning will become more intelligible; that the pretence of considering persons not states, happiness not property, always has ended, and always will end, in making a new state, or corporation, infinitely more oppressive than the former; and in which the real freedom of persons is as much less, as the things interfered with are more numerous, and more minute. Compare the duties, exacted from a United Irishman by the Confederacy, with those required of him by the law of the land. This, I think, not ill expressed, in the two last periods of the fourth paragraph. "Thus in order to sacrifice … confederation."

Of course I immediately recognised your hand in the Article concerning the "Edinburgh Review," and much pleased I was with it; and equally so in finding, from your letter, that we had so completely coincided in our feelings, concerning that wicked Lord Nelson Article.[126] If there be one thing on earth that can outrage an honest man's feelings, it is the assumption of austere morality for the purposes of personal slander. And the gross ingratitude of the attack! In the name of God what have we to do with Lord Nelson's mistresses, or domestic quarrels? Sir A. Ball, himself exemplary in this respect, told me of his own personal knowledge Lady Nelson was enough to drive any man wild.... She had no sympathy with his acute sensibilities, and his alienation was effected, though not shown, before he knew Lady Hamilton, by being heart starved, still more than by being teased and tormented by her sullenness. Observe that Sir A. Ball detested Lady Hamilton. To the same enthusiastic sensibilities which made a fool of him with regard to his Emma, his country owed the victories of the Nile, Copenhagen, and Trafalgar, and the heroic spirit of all the officers reared under him.

When I was at Bowood there was a plan suggested between Bowles and myself, to engage among the cleverest literary characters of our knowledge, six or eight, each of whom was to engage to take some one subject of those into which the "Edinburgh Review" might be aptly divided; as Science, Classical Knowledge, Style, Taste, Philosophy, Political Economy, Morals, Religion, and Patriotism; to state the number of Essays he could write and the time at which he would deliver each; and so go through the whole of the "Review":—to be published in the first instance in the "Courier" during the Recess of Parliament. We thought of Southey, Wordsworth, Crowe, Crabbe, Wollaston; and Bowles thought he could answer for several single Articles from persons of the highest rank in the Church and our two Universities. Such a plan, adequately executed, seven or eight years ago, would have gone near to blow up this Magazine of Mischief.

As to Ridgeway[127] and the Essays, I have not only no objection to my name being given, but I should prefer it. I have just as much right to call myself dramatically an Irish Protestant, when writing in the character of one, as Swift had to call himself a draper.[128] I have waded through as mischievous a Work, as two huge quartos, very dull, can be, by a Mr. Edward Wakefield, called an Account of Ireland. Of all scribblers these agricultural quarto-mongers are the vilest. I thought of making the affairs of Ireland, in toto, chiefly however with reference to the Catholic Question, a new series, and of republishing in the Appendix to the eight letters to Mr. Justice Fletcher, Lord Clare's (then Chancellor Fitzgibbon's) admirable speech, worthy of Demosthenes, of which a copy was brought me over from Dublin by Rickman, and given to Lamb. It was never printed in England, nor is it to be procured. I never met with a person who had heard of it. Except that one main point is omitted (and it is remarkable that the poet Edmund Spenser in his Dialogue on Ireland[129] is the only writer who has urged this point), viz., the forcing upon savages the laws of a comparatively civilised people, instead of adopting measures gradually to render them susceptible of those laws, this speech might be deservedly called the philosophy of the past and present history of Ireland. It makes me smile to observe, how all the mediocre men exult in a Ministry that have been so successful without any overpowering talent of eloquence, etc. It is true that a series of gigantic events like those of the last eighteen months, will lift up any cock-boat to the skies upon their billows; but no less true that, sooner or later, parliamentary talent will be found absolutely requisite for an English Ministry.

With sincere regard and esteem, your obliged

S. T. Coleridge.

CCIV. TO JOHN KENYON.[130]

Mr. B. Morgan's, Bath, November 3 [1814].

My dear Sir,—At Binn's, Cheap Street, I found Jeremy Taylor's "Dissuasive from Popery," in the largest and only complete edition of his Polemical Tracts. Mr. Binns had no objection to the paragraphs being transcribed any morning or evening at his house, and I put in a piece of paper with the words at which the transcript should begin and with which end—p. 450, l. 5, to p. 451, l. 31, I believe. But indeed I am ashamed, rather I feel awkward and uncomfortable at obtruding on you so long a task, much longer than I had imagined. I don't like to use any words that might give you unpleasure, but I cannot help fearing that, like a child spoilt by your and Mrs. Kenyon's great indulgence, I may have been betrayed into presuming on it more than I ought. Indeed, my dear sir! I do feel very keenly how exceeding kind you and Mrs. K. have been to me. It makes this scrawl of mine look dim in a way that was less uncommon with me formerly than it has been for the last eight or ten years.

But to return, or turn off, to the good old Bishop. It would be worth your while to read Taylor's "Letter on Original Sin," and what follows. I compare it to an old statue of Janus, with one of the faces, that which looks towards his opponents, the controversial phiz in highest preservation,—the force of a mighty one, all power, all life,—the face of a God rushing on to battle, and, in the same moment, enjoying at once both contest and triumph; the other, that which should have been the countenance that looks toward his followers, that with which he substitutes his own opinion, all weather eaten, dim, useless, a Ghost in marble, such as you may have seen represented in many of Piranesi's astounding engravings from Rome and the Campus Martius. Jer. Taylor's discursive intellect dazzle-darkened his intuition. The principle of becoming all things to all men, if by any means he might save any, with him as with Burke, thickened the protecting epidermis of the tact-nerve of truth into something like a callus. But take him all in all, such a miraculous combination of erudition, broad, deep, and omnigenous; of logic subtle as well as acute, and as robust as agile; of psychological insight, so fine yet so secure! of public prudence and practical sageness that one ray of creative Faith would have lit up and transfigured into wisdom, and of genuine imagination, with its streaming face unifying all at one moment like that of the setting sun when through an interspace of blue sky no larger than itself, it emerges from the cloud to sink behind the mountain, but a face seen only at starts, when some breeze from the higher air scatters, for a moment, the cloud of butterfly fancies, which flutter around him like a morning-garment of ten thousand colours—(now how shall I get out of this sentence? the tail is too big to be taken up into the coiler's mouth)—well, as I was saying, I believe such a complete man hardly shall we meet again.

May God bless you and yours!

Your obliged
S. T. Coleridge.

P. S. My address after Tuesday will be (God permitting) Mr. Page's, Surgeon, Calne.

J. Kenyon, Esq., 9, Argyle Street.

CCV. TO LADY BEAUMONT.

April 3, 1815.

Dear Madam,—Should your Ladyship still have among your papers those lines of mine to Mr. Wordsworth after his recitation of the poem on the growth of his own spirit,[131] which you honoured by wishing to take a copy, you would oblige me by enclosing them for me, addressed—"Mr. Coleridge, Calne, Wilts." Of "The Excursion," excluding the tale of the ruined cottage, which I have ever thought the finest poem in our language, comparing it with any of the same or similar length, I can truly say that one half the number of its beauties would make all the beauties of all his contemporary poets collectively mount to the balance:—but yet—the fault may be in my own mind—I do not think, I did not feel, it equal to the work on the growth of his own spirit. As proofs meet me in every part of "The Excursion" that the poet's genius has not flagged, I have sometimes fancied that, having by the conjoint operation of his own experiences, feelings, and reason, himself convinced himself of truths, which the generality of persons have either taken for granted from their infancy, or, at least, adopted in early life, he has attached all their own depth and weight to doctrines and words, which come almost as truisms or commonplaces to others. From this state of mind, in which I was comparing Wordsworth with himself, I was roused by the infamous "Edinburgh" review of the poem. If ever guilt lay on a writer's head, and if malignity, slander, hypocrisy, and self-contradictory baseness can constitute guilt, I dare openly, and openly (please God!) I will, impeach the writer of that article of it. These are awful times—a dream of dreams! To be a prophet is, and ever has been, an unthankful office. At the Illumination for the Peace I furnished a design for a friend's transparency—a vulture, with the head of Napoleon, chained to a rock, and Britannia bending down, with one hand stretching out the wing of the vulture, and with the other clipping it with shears, on the one blade of which was written Nelson, on the other Wellington. The motto—

We've fought for peace, and conquer'd it at last;
The ravening Vulture's leg is fetter'd fast.
Britons, rejoice! and yet be wary too!
The chain may break, the clipt wing sprout anew.[132]

And since I have conversed with those who first returned from France, I have weekly expected the event. Napoleon's object at present is to embarrass the Allies, and to cool the enthusiasm of their subjects. The latter he unfortunately will be too successful in. In London, my Lady, it is scarcely possible to distinguish the opinions of the people from the ravings and railings of the mob; but in country towns we must be blind not to see the real state of the popular mind. I do not know whether your Ladyship read my letters to Judge Fletcher. I can assure you it is no exaggerated picture of the predominance of Jacobinism. In this small town of Calne five hundred volunteers were raised in the last war. I am persuaded that five could not be raised now. A considerable landowner, and a man of great observation, said to me last week, "A famine, sir, could scarce have produced more evil than the Corn Bill[133] has done under the present circumstances." I speak nothing of the Bill itself, except that, after the closest attention and the most sedulous inquiry after facts from landowners, farmers, stewards, millers, and bakers, I am convinced that both opponents and advocates were in extremes, and that an evil produced by many causes was by many remedies to have been cured, not by the universal elixir of one sweeping law.

My poems will be put to press by the middle of June. A number adequate to one volume are already in the hands of my friends at Bristol, under conditions that they are to be published at all events, even though I should not add another volume, which I never had so little reason to doubt. Within the last two days I have composed three poems, containing 500 lines in the whole.

Mr. and Mrs. Morgan present their respective compliments to your Ladyship and Sir George.

I remain, my Lady, your Ladyship's obliged humble servant,

S. T. Coleridge.

CCVI. TO WILLIAM WORDSWORTH.

Calne, May 30, 1815.

My honoured Friend,—On my return from Devizes, whither I had gone to procure some vaccine matter (the small-pox having appeared in Calne, and Mrs. Morgan's sister believing herself never to have had it), I found your letter: and I will answer it immediately, though to answer it as I could wish to do would require more recollection and arrangement of thought than is always to be commanded on the instant. But I dare not trust my own habit of procrastination, and, do what I would, it would be impossible in a single letter to give more than general convictions. But, even after a tenth or twentieth letter, I should still be disquieted as knowing how poor a substitute must letters be for a vivâ voce examination of a work with its author, line by line. It is most uncomfortable from many, many causes, to express anything but sympathy, and gratulation to an absent friend, to whom for the more substantial third of a life we have been habituated to look up: especially where a love, though increased by many and different influences, yet begun and throve and knit its joints in the perception of his superiority. It is not in written words, but by the hundred modifications that looks make and tone, and denial of the full sense of the very words used, that one can reconcile the struggle between sincerity and diffidence, between the persuasion that I am in the right, and that as deep though not so vivid conviction, that it may be the positiveness of ignorance rather than the certainty of insight. Then come the human frailties, the dread of giving pain, or exciting suspicions of alteration and dyspathy, in short, the almost inevitable insincerities between imperfect beings, however sincerely attached to each other. It is hard (and I am Protestant enough to doubt whether it is right) to confess the whole truth (even of one's self, human nature scarce endures it, even to one's self), but to me it is still harder to do this of and to a revered friend.

But to your letter. First, I had never determined to print the lines addressed to you. I lent them to Lady Beaumont on her promise that they should be copied, and returned; and not knowing of any copy in my own possession, I sent for them, because I was making a MS. collection of all my poems—publishable and unpublishable—and still more perhaps for the handwriting of the only perfect copy, that entrusted to her ladyship. Most assuredly, I never once thought of printing them without having consulted you, and since I lit on the first rude draught, and corrected it as well as I could, I wanted no additional reason for its not being published in my lifetime than its personality respecting myself. After the opinions I had given publicly, in the preference of "Lycidas" (moral no less than poetical) to Cowley's Monody, I could not have printed it consistently. It is for the biographer, not the poet, to give the accidents of individual life. Whatever is not representative, generic, may be indeed most poetically expressed, but is not poetry. Otherwise, I confess, your prudential reasons would not have weighed with me, except as far as my name might haply injure your reputation, for there is nothing in the lines, as far as your powers are concerned, which I have not as fully expressed elsewhere; and I hold it a miserable cowardice to withhold a deliberate opinion only because the man is alive.

Secondly, for "The Excursion," I feared that had I been silent concerning "The Excursion," Lady Beaumont would have drawn some strange inference; and yet I had scarcely sent off the letter before I repented that I had not run that risk rather than have approach to disparage communicated to you by a third person. But what did my criticism amount to, reduced to its full and naked sense? This, that comparatively with the former poem, "The Excursion," as far as it was new to me, had disappointed my expectations; that the excellencies were so many and of so high a class that it was impossible to attribute the inferiority, if any such really existed, to any flagging of the writer's own genius—and that I conjectured that it might have been occasioned by the influence of self-established convictions having given to certain thoughts and expressions a depth and force which they had not for readers in general. In order, therefore, to explain the disappointment, I must recall to your mind what my expectations were: and, as these again were founded on the supposition that (in whatever order it might be published) the poem on the growth of your own mind was as the ground plot and the roots, out of which "The Recluse" was to have sprung up as the tree, as far as [there was] the same sap in both, I expected them, doubtless, to have formed one complete whole; but in matter, form, and product to be different, each not only a distinct but a different work. In the first I had found "themes by thee first sung aright,"

Of smiles spontaneous and mysterious fears
(The first-born they of reason and twin-birth)
Of tides obedient to external force,

And currents self-determin'd, as might seem,
Or by some central breath; of moments awful,
Now in thy inner life, and now abroad,
When power stream'd from thee, and thy soul received
The light reflected as a light bestowed;
Of fancies fair, and milder hours of youth,
Hyblæan murmurs of poetic thought
Industrious in its joy, in vales and glens
Native or outland, lakes and famous hills!
Or on the lonely highroad, when the stars
Were rising; or by secret mountain streams,
The guides and the companions of thy way;
Of more than fancy—of the social sense
Distending wide, and man beloved as man,
Where France in all her towns lay vibrating,
Ev'n as a bark becalm'd beneath the burst
Of Heaven's immediate thunder, when no cloud
Is visible, or shadow on the main!
For Thou wert there, thy own brows garlanded,
Amid the tremor of a realm aglow,
Amid a mighty nation jubilant,
When from the general heart of human kind
Hope sprang forth, like a full-born Deity!
Of that dear Hope afflicted, and amaz'd,
So homeward summon'd! thenceforth calm and sure
From the dread watch-tower of man's absolute self,
With light unwaning on her eyes, to look
Far on! herself a glory to behold,
The Angel of the vision! Then (last strain)
Of duty, chosen laws controlling choice,
Action and Joy! An Orphic song indeed,
A song divine of high and passionate truths,
To their own music chaunted!

Indeed, through the whole of that Poem, με Αὖρα τις εἰσ ἔπνευσε μουσικωτάτη. This I considered as "The Excursion;"[134] and the second, as "The Recluse" I had (from what I had at different times gathered from your conversation on the Place [Grasmere]) anticipated as commencing with you set down and settled in an abiding home, and that with the description of that home you were to begin a philosophical poem, the result and fruits of a spirit so framed and so disciplined as had been told in the former.

Whatever in Lucretius is poetry is not philosophical, whatever is philosophical is not poetry; and in the very pride of confident hope I looked forward to "The Recluse" as the first and only true philosophical poem in existence. Of course, I expected the colours, music, imaginative life, and passion of poetry; but the matter and arrangement of philosophy; not doubting from the advantages of the subject that the totality of a system was not only capable of being harmonised with, but even calculated to aid, the unity (beginning, middle, and end) of a poem. Thus, whatever the length of the work might be, still it was a determinate length; of the subjects announced, each would have its own appointed place, and, excluding repetitions, each would relieve and rise in interest above the other. I supposed you first to have meditated the faculties of man in the abstract, in their correspondence with his sphere of action, and, first in the feeling, touch, and taste, then in the eye, and last in the ear,—to have laid a solid and immovable foundation for the edifice by removing the sandy sophisms of Locke, and the mechanic dogmatists, and demonstrating that the senses were living growths and developments of the mind and spirit, in a much juster as well as higher sense, than the mind can be said to be formed by the senses. Next, I understood that you would take the human race in the concrete, have exploded the absurd notion of Pope's "Essay on Man," Darwin, and all the countless believers even (strange to say) among Christians of man's having progressed from an ourang-outang state—so contrary to all history, to all religion, nay, to all possibility—to have affirmed a Fall in some sense, as a fact, the possibility of which cannot be understood from the nature of the will, but the reality of which is attested by experience and conscience. Fallen men contemplated in the different ages of the world, and in the different states—savage, barbarous, civilised, the lonely cot, or borderer's wigwam, the village, the manufacturing town, seaport, city, universities, and, not disguising the sore evils under which the whole creation groans, to point out, however, a manifest scheme of redemption, of reconciliation from this enmity with Nature—what are the obstacles, the Antichrist that must be and already is—and to conclude by a grand didactic swell on the necessary identity of a true philosophy with true religion, agreeing in the results and differing only as the analytic and synthetic process, as discursive from intuitive, the former chiefly useful as perfecting the latter; in short, the necessity of a general revolution in the modes of developing and disciplining the human mind by the substitution of life and intelligence (considered in its different powers from the plant up to that state in which the difference of degree becomes a new kind (man, self-consciousness), but yet not by essential opposition) for the philosophy of mechanism, which, in everything that is most worthy of the human intellect, strikes Death, and cheats itself by mistaking clear images for distinct conceptions, and which idly demands conceptions where intuitions alone are possible or adequate to the majesty of the Truth. In short, facts elevated into theory—theory into laws—and laws into living and intelligent powers—true idealism necessarily perfecting itself in realism, and realism refining itself into idealism.

Such or something like this was the plan I had supposed that you were engaged on. Your own words will therefore explain my feelings, viz., that your object "was not to convey recondite, or refined truths, but to place commonplace truths in an interesting point of view." Now this I suppose to have been in your two volumes of poems, as far as was desirable or possible, without an insight into the whole truth. How can common truths be made permanently interesting but by being bottomed on our common nature? It is only by the profoundest insight into numbers and quantity that a sublimity and even religious wonder become attached to the simplest operations of arithmetic, the most evident properties of the circle or triangle. I have only to finish a preface, which I shall have done in two, or, at farthest, three days; and I will then, dismissing all comparison either with the poem on the growth of your own support, or with the imagined plan of "The Recluse," state fairly my main objections to "The Excursion" as it is. But it would have been alike unjust both to you and to myself, if I had led you to suppose that any disappointment I may have felt arose wholly or chiefly from the passages I do not like, or from the poem considered irrelatively.

Allston lives at 8, Buckingham Place, Fitzroy Square. He has lost his wife, and been most unkindly treated and most unfortunate. I hope you will call on him. Good God! to think of such a grub as Dawe with more than he can do, and such a genius as Allston without a single patron!

God bless you! I am, and never have been other than your most affectionate

S. T. Coleridge.

Mr. and Mrs. Morgan desire to be affectionately remembered to you, and they would be highly gratified if you could make a little tour and spend a short time at Calne. There is an admirable collection of pictures at Corsham. Bowles left Bremhill (two miles from us, where he has a perfect paradise of a place) for town yesterday morning.

CCVII. TO THE REV. W. MONEY.[135]

Calne, Wednesday, 1815.

Dear Sir,—I have seldom made a greater sacrifice and gratification to prudence than in the determination most reluctantly formed, that the state of my health, which requires hourly regimen, joined with the uncertain state of the weather and the perilous consequences of my taking cold in the existing weakness of the viscera, renders it improper for me to hazard a night away from my home. No pleasure, however intellectual (and to all but intellectual pleasures I have long been dead, for surely the staving off of pain is no pleasure), could repay me even for the chance of being again unwell in any house but my own. I have a great, a gigantic effort to make, and I will go through with it or die. Gross have been the calumnies concerning me; but enough remains of truth to enforce the necessity of considering all other things as unimportant compared with the necessity of living them down. This letter is, of course, sacred to yourself, and a pledge of the high respect I entertain for your moral being; for you need not the feelings of friendship to feel as a friend toward every fellow Christian.

To turn to another subject, Mr. Bowles, I understand, is about to publish, at least is composing a reply to some answer to the "Velvet Cushion."[136] I have seen neither work. But this I will venture to say, that if the respondents in favour of the Church take upon them to justify in the most absolute sense, as if Scripture were the subject of the controversy, every minute part of our admirable Liturgy, and liturgical and sacramental services, they will only furnish new triumph to ungenerous adversaries.

The Church of England has in the Articles solemnly declared that all Churches are fallible—and in another, to assert its absolute immaculateness, sounds to me a mere contradiction. No! I would first overthrow what can be fairly and to all men intelligibly overthrown in the adversaries' objections (and of this kind the instances are as twenty to one). For the remainder I would talk like a special pleader, and from the defensive pass to the offensive, and then prove from St. Paul (for of the practice of the early Church even in its purest state, before the reign of Constantine, our opponents make no account) that errors in a Church that neither directly or indirectly injure morals or oppugn salvation are exercises for mutual charity, not excuses for schism. In short, is there or is there [not] such a condemnable thing as schism? In the proof of consequences of the affirmative lies, in my humble opinion, the complete confutation of the (so-called) Evangelical Dissenters.

I shall be most happy to converse with you on the subject. If Mr. Bowles were not employed on it, I should have had no objection to have reduced my many thoughts to order and have published them; but this might now seem invidious and like rivalry.

Present my best respects to Mrs. Money, and be so good as to make the fitting apologies for me to Mr. T. Methuen,[137] the man wise of heart! But an apology already exists for me in his own mind.

I remain, dear sir, respectfully your obliged

S. T. Coleridge.

Wednesday, Calne.

P. S. I have opened this letter to add, that the greater number, if not the whole, of the arguments used apply only to the ministers, not to the members of the Established Church. Some one of our eminent divines refused even to take the pastoral office, I believe, on account of the Funeral Service and the Absolution of the Sick; but still it remains to justify schism from Church-Membership.

To the Rev. W. Money, Whetham.

CHAPTER XIII
NEW LIFE AND NEW FRIENDS
1816-1821

With Coleridge's name and memory must ever be associated the names of James and Anne Gillman. It was beneath the shelter of their friendly roof that he spent the last eighteen years of his life, and it was to their wise and loving care that the comparative fruitfulness and well-being of those years were due. They thought themselves honoured by his presence, and he repaid their devotion with unbounded love and gratitude. Friendship and loving-kindness followed Coleridge all the days of his life. What did he not owe to Poole, to Southey for his noble protection of his family, to the Morgans for their long-tried faithfulness and devotion to himself? But to the Gillmans he owed the "crown of his cup and garnish of his dish," a welcome which lasted till the day of his death. Doubtless there were chords in his nature which were struck for the first time by these good people, and in their presence and by their help he was a new man. But, for all that, their patience must have been inexhaustible, their loyalty unimpeachable, their love indestructible. Such friendship is rare and beautiful, and merits a most honourable remembrance.

CCVIII. TO JAMES GILLMAN.

42, Norfolk Street, Strand,
Saturday noon, [April 13, 1816.]

My dear Sir,—The very first half hour I was with you convinced me that I should owe my reception into your family exclusively to motives not less flattering to me than honourable to yourself. I trust we shall ever in matters of intellect be reciprocally serviceable to each other. Men of sense generally come to the same conclusion; but they are likely to contribute to each other's exchangement of view, in proportion to the distance or even opposition of the points from which they set out. Travel and the strange variety of situations and employments on which chance has thrown me, in the course of my life, might have made me a mere man of observation, if pain and sorrow and self-miscomplacence had not forced my mind in on itself, and so formed habits of meditation. It is now as much my nature to evolve the fact from the law, as that of a practical man to deduce the law from the fact.

With respect to pecuniary remuneration,[138] allow me to say, I must not at least be suffered to make any addition to your family expenses—though I cannot offer anything that would be in any way adequate to my sense of the service; for that, indeed, there could not be a compensation, as it must be returned in kind, by esteem and grateful affection.

And now of myself. My ever wakeful reason, and the keenness of my moral feelings, will secure you from all unpleasant circumstances connected with me, save only one, viz., the evasion of a specific madness. You will never hear anything but truth from me:—prior habits render it out of my power to tell an untruth, but unless carefully observed, I dare not promise that I should not, with regard to this detested poison, be capable of acting one. No sixty hours have yet passed without my having taken laudanum, though for the last week [in] comparatively trifling doses. I have full belief that your anxiety need not be extended beyond the first week, and for the first week I shall not, I must not, be permitted to leave your house, unless with you. Delicately or indelicately, this must be done, and both the servants and the assistant must receive absolute commands from you. The stimulus of conversation suspends the terror that haunts my mind; but when I am alone, the horrors I have suffered from laudanum, the degradation, the blighted utility, almost overwhelm me. If (as I feel for the first time a soothing confidence it will prove) I should leave you restored to my moral and bodily health, it is not myself only that will love and honour you; every friend I have (and thank God! in spite of this wretched vice, I have many and warm ones, who were friends of my youth and have never deserted me) will thank you with reverence. I have taken no notice of your kind apologies. If I could not be comfortable in your house, and with your family, I should deserve to be miserable. If you could make it convenient I should wish to be with you by Monday evening, as it would prevent the necessity of taking fresh lodgings in town.

With respectful compliments to Mrs. Gillman and her sister, I remain, dear sir, your much obliged

S. T. Coleridge.

CCIX. TO DANIEL STUART.

James Gillman's, Esq., Surgeon, Highgate,
Wednesday, May 8, 1816.

My dear Stuart,—Since you left me I have been reflecting a good deal on the subject of the Catholic Question, and somewhat on the "Courier" in general. With all my weight of faults (and no one is less likely to underrate them than myself) a tendency to be influenced by selfish motives in my friendships, or even in the cultivation of my acquaintances, will not, I am sure, be by you placed among them. When we first knew each other, it was perhaps the most interesting period of both our lives, at the very turn of the flood; and I can never cease to reflect with affectionate delight on the steadiness and independence of your conduct and principles; and how, for so many years, with little assistance from others, and with one main guide, a sympathising tact for the real sense, feeling, and impulses of the respectable part of the English nation, you went on so auspiciously, and likewise so effectively. It is far, very far, from being a hyperbole to affirm, that you did more against the French scheme of Continental domination, than the Duke of Wellington has done; or rather Wellington could neither have been supplied by the Ministers, nor the Ministers supported by the Nation, but for the tone first given, and then constantly kept up, by the plain, unministerial, anti-opposition, anti-jacobin, anti-gallican, anti-Napoleonic spirit of your writings, aided by the colloquial style, and evident good sense, in which as acting on an immense mass of knowledge of existing men and existing circumstances, you are superior to any man I ever met with in my lifetime. Indeed you are the only human being of whom I can say, with severe truth, that I never conversed with you for an hour, without rememberable instruction. And with the same simplicity I dare affirm my belief, that my greater knowledge of man has been useful to you; though from the nature of things, not so useful, as your knowledge of men has been to me. Now with such convictions, my dear Stuart, how is it possible that I can look back on the conduct of the "Courier," from the period of the Duke of York's restoration, without some pain? You cannot be seriously offended or affronted with me, if in this deep confidence, and in a letter which, or its contents, can meet no eye but your own, I venture to declare that, though since then much has been done, very much of high utility to the country by and under Mr. Street, yet the "Courier" itself has gradually lost that sanctifying spirit which was the life of its life, and without which even the best and soundest principles lose half their effect on the human mind. I mean, the faith in the faith of the person or paper which brings them forward. They are attributed to the accident of their happening to be for such a side or such a party. In short there is no longer any root in the paper, out of which all the various branches and fruits and even fluttering leaves are seen or believed to grow. But it is the old tree barked round above the root, though the circular decortication is so small, and so neatly filled up and coloured as to be scarcely visible but in its total effects. Excellent fruits still at times hang on the boughs, but they are tied on by threads and hairs.

In all this I am well aware that you are no otherwise to blame, than in permitting what, without disturbance to your health and tranquillity, you could not perhaps have prevented, or effectively modified. But the whole plan of Street's seems to me to have been motiveless from the beginning, or at least affected by the grossest miscalculations in respect even of pecuniary interest. For had the paper maintained and asserted not only its independence but its appearance of it, it is true that Mr. Street might not have had Mr. Croker to dine with him, or received as many nods or shakes of the hand from Lord this, or that, but it is at least equally true, that the Ministry would have been far more effectually served, and that (I speak now from facts) both paper and its conductor would have been held by the adherents of Ministers in far higher respect. And after all, Ministers do not love newspapers in their hearts; not even those that support them. Indeed it seems epidemic among Parliament men in general, to affect to look down upon and to despise newspapers to which they owe 999/1000 their influence and character—and at least three fifths of their knowledge and phraseology. Enough! Burn this letter and forgive the writer for the purity and affectionateness of his motive.

With regard to the Catholic Question, if I write I must be allowed to express the truth and the whole truth concerning the imprudent avowal of Lord Castlereagh that it was not to be a government question. On this condition I will write immediately a tract on the question which to the best of my knowledge will be about from 120 to 140 octavo pages; but so contrived that Mr. Street may find no difficulty in dividing it into ten or twenty essays, or leading paragraphs. In my scheme I have carefully excluded every approximation to metaphysical reasoning; and set aside every thought which cannot be brought under one or the other of three heads—1. Plain evident sense. 2. Historical documental facts. 3. Existing circumstances, character, etc., of Ireland in relation to Great Britain, and to its own interests, and those of its various classes of proprietors. I shall not deliver it till it is wholly finished, and if you and Mr. Street think that such a work delivered entire will be worth fifty pounds to the paper, I will begin it immediately. Let me either see or hear from you as soon as possible. Cannot Mr. Street send me some one or other of the daily papers, without expense to you, after he has done with them? Kind respects to Mrs. Stuart.

Your affectionate and obliged friend,
S. T. Coleridge.

CCX. TO THE SAME.

Monday, May 13, 1816.

Dear Stuart,—It is among the feeblenesses of our nature, that we are often, to a certain degree, acted on by stories, gravely asserted, of which we yet do most religiously disbelieve every syllable, nay, which perhaps we know to be false. The truth is that images and thoughts possess a power in, and of themselves, independent of that act of the judgment or understanding by which we affirm or deny the existence of a reality correspondent to them.

Such is the ordinary state of the mind in dreams. It is not strictly accurate to say that we believe our dreams to be actual while we are dreaming. We neither believe it, nor disbelieve it. With the will the comparing power is suspended, and without the comparing power, any act of judgment, whether affirmation or denial, is impossible. The forms and thoughts act merely by their own inherent power, and the strong feelings at times apparently connected with them are, in point of fact, bodily sensations which are the causes or occasions of the images; not (as when we are awake) the effects of them. Add to this a voluntary lending of the will to this suspension of one of its own operations (that is, that of comparison and consequent decision concerning the reality of any sensuous impression) and you have the true theory of stage illusion, equally distant from the absurd notion of the French critics, who ground their principles on the presumption of an absolute delusion, and of Dr. Johnson who would persuade us that our judgments are as broad awake during the most masterly representation of the deepest scenes of Othello, as a philosopher would be during the exhibition of a magic lanthorn with Punch and Joan and Pull Devil, Pull Baker, etc., on its painted slides. Now as extremes always meet, this dogma of our dramatic critic and soporific irenist would lead, by inevitable consequences, to that very doctrine of the unities maintained by the French Belle Lettrists, which it was the object of his strangely overrated, contradictory, and most illogical preface to Shakespeare to overthrow.

Thus, instead of troubling you with the idle assertions that have been most authoritatively uttered, concerning your being under bond and seal to the present Ministry, which I know to be (monosyllabically speaking) a lie, and which formed, I guess, part of the impulse which occasioned my last letter, I have given you a theory which, as far as I know, is new, and which I am quite sure is most important as the ground and fundamental principle of all philosophic and of all common-sense criticisms concerning the drama and the theatre.

To put off, however, the Jack-the-Giant-Killer-seven-leagued boots, with which I am apt to run away from the main purpose of what I had to write, I owe it to myself and the truth to observe, that there was as much at least of partiality as of grief and inculpation in my remarks on the spirit of the "Courier;" and that with all its faults, I prefer it greatly to any other paper, even without reference to its being the best and most effective vehicle of what I deem most necessary and urgent truths. Be assured there was no occasion to let me know, that with regard to the proposed disquisition you were interested as a patriot and a protestant, not as a proprietor of the particular paper. Such too, Heaven knows, is my sole object! for as to the money that it may be thought worth according to the number and value of the essays, I regard it merely as enabling me to devote a given portion of time and effort to this subject, rather than to any one of the many others by which I might procure the same remuneration. From this hour I sit down to it tooth and nail, and shall not turn to the left or right till I have finished it. When I have reached the half-way house I will transmit the MSS. to you, that I may, without the necessity of dis- or re-arranging the work, be able to adopt any suggestions of yours, whether they should be additive, alterative, or emendative. One question only I have to consult you concerning—viz., the form which would be the most attractive of notice; simply essays? or letters addressed to Lord Liverpool for instance, on the supposition that he remains firm to the Perceval principle on this blind, blundering, and feverous scheme?

Mr. and Mrs. Gillman will be most happy to see you to share in a family dinner, and spend the evening with us; and if you will come early, I can show you some most delicious walks. You will like Mr. Gillman. He is a man of strong, fervid, and agile intellect, with such a master passion for truth, that his most abstracted verities assume a character of veracity. And his wife, it will be impossible not to respect, if a balance and harmony of powers and qualities, unified and spiritualized by a native feminine fineness of character, render womanhood amiable and respectable. In serious truth I have much reason to be most grateful for the choice and chance which has placed me under their hospitable roof. I have no doubt that Mr. Gillman as friend and as physician will succeed in restoring me to my natural self.

My kind respects to Mrs. Stuart. I long to see the little one.

Your obliged and sincere friend,

S. T. Coleridge.

CCXI. TO JOHN MURRAY.

Highgate, February 27, 1817.

My dear Sir,—I had a visit from Mr. Morgan yester-afternoon, and trouble you with these lines in consequence of his communications. When I stated to you the circumstances respecting the volumes of mine that have been so long printed, and the embarrassment into which the blunder of the printer had entangled me, with the sinking down of my health that made it so perplexing for me to remedy it, I did it under the belief that you were yourself very little disposed to the publication of the "Zapolya"[139] as a separate work—unless it had, in some shape or other, been brought out at the Theatre. Of this I seemed to have less and less chance. What had been declared an indispensable part, and of all the play, the most theatrical as well as dramatic, by Lord Byron, was ridiculed and thrown out of all question by Mr. Douglas Kinnaird, with no other explanation vouchsafed but that Lord Byron knew nothing about the matter—and, besides that, was in the habit of overrating my performances. These were not the words, but these words contain the purport of what he said. Meantime what Mr. D. Kinnaird most warmly approved, Mr. Harris had previously declared would convulse a house with laughter, and damn the piece beyond any possibility of a further hearing. Still I was disposed in my distressed circumstances of means, health, and spirits, to have tried the plan suggested by Mr. D. Kinnaird of turning the "Zapolya" into a melodrama by the omission of the first act. But Mr. K. was, with Lord Byron, dropped from the sub-committee, and I knew no one to whom I could apply. Mr. Dibdin, who had promised to befriend me, was likewise removed from the stage-managership. Mr. Rae did indeed promise to give me a few hours of his time repeatedly, and from my former acquaintance with him, as the Ordonio of the "Remorse," I had some reason to be wounded by his neglect. Indeed, at Drury Lane, no one knows to whom any effective application is to be made. Mr. Kinnaird had engaged to look over the "Zapolya" with me, and appointed the time. I went accordingly and passed the whole of the fore-dinner day with him—in what? In hearing an opera of his own, and returned as wise as I came. Much is talked of the advantages of a managership of noblemen, but as far as I have seen and experienced, an author has no cause to congratulate himself on the change, either in the taste, courtesy, or reliability of his judges. Desponding concerning this (and finding that every publication with my name would be persecuted by pre-determination by the one guiding party, that I had no support to expect from the other, and that the thicker and closer the cloud of misfortunes gathered round me, the more actively and remorselessly were the poisoned arrows of wanton enmity shot through it), I sincerely believed that it would be neither to your advantage or mine that the "Zapolya" should be published singly. It appeared, at that time, that the annexing to it a collection of all my poems would enable the work to be brought out without delay,—and I therefore applied to you, offering either to repay the money received for it, or to work it out by furnishing you with miscellaneous matter for the "Quarterly," or by sitting down to the "Rabbinical Tales"[140] as soon as ever the works now in the press were put out of my hand, that is, as far as the copy was concerned. Your answer impressed me with your full assent to the plan. Nay, however mortifying it might in ordinary circumstances have been to an author's vanity, it was not so to me, that the "Zapolya" was a work of which you had no objection to be rid. But, if I misunderstood you, let me now be better informed, and whatever you wish shall be done. I have never knowingly or intentionally been guilty of a dishonourable transaction, but have in all things that respect my neighbour been more sinned against than sinning. Much less would I hazard the appearance of an equivocal conduct at present when I feel that I am sinking into the grave, with fainter and fainter hopes of achieving that which, God knows my inmost heart! is the sole motive for the wish to live—namely, that of preparing for the press the results of twenty-five years hard study and almost constant meditation. Reputation has no charm for me, except as a preventive of starving. Abuse and ridicule are all which I could expect for myself, if the six volumes were published which would comprise the sum total of my convictions; but, most thoroughly satisfied both of their truth and of the vital importance of these truths, convinced that of all systems that have ever been prescribed, this has the least of mysticism, the very object throughout from the first page to the last being to reconcile the dictates of common sense with the conclusions of scientific reasoning—it would assuredly be like a sudden gleam of sunshine falling on the face of a dying man, if I left the world with a knowledge that the work would have a chance of being read in better times. But of all men in the way of business, my dear sir! I should be most reluctant to give you any just cause of reproaching my integrity; because I know and feel, and have at all times and to all persons who had any literary concerns with me, acknowledged that you have acted with a friendly kindness towards me,—and if Mr. Gifford have taken a prejudice against me or my writings, I never imputed it as blame to you. Let me then know what you wish me to do, and I will do it. I ought to add, that in yielding to the proposal of annexing the "Zapolya" to the volume of poetry, provided I could procure your assent, I expressly stipulated that if, in any shape or modification, it should be represented on the stage, the copyright of it in that form would be reserved for your refusal or acceptance, and, in like manner the "Christabel" when completed, and the "Rabbinical Tales." The second "Lay Sermon" (a most unfortunate name) will appear, I trust, next week.

I remain, my dear sir, with respect and regard, your obliged

S. T. Coleridge.

P. S. I have not seen either the "Edinburgh"[141] or the "Quarterly" last Reviews. The article against me in the former was, I am assured, written by Hazlitt. Now what can I think of Mr. Jeffrey, who knows nothing personally of me but my hospitable attentions to him, and from whom I heard nothing but very high seasoned compliments, and who yet can avail himself of such an instrument of his most unprovoked malignity towards me, an inoffensive man in distress and sickness? As soon as I have read the article (and the loan of the book is promised me), I shall make up my mind whether or not to address a letter, publicly to Mr. Jeffrey, or, in the form of an appeal, to the public, concerning his proved predetermined malice.

Mr. Murray, Bookseller, Albemarle Street, Piccadilly.

CCXII. TO ROBERT SOUTHEY.

[May, 1817.]

Dear Southey,—Mr. Ludwig Tieck[142] has continued to express so anxious a wish to see you, as one man of genius sees another, that he will not lose even the slight chance of possibility that you may not have quitted Paris when he arrives there. I have only therefore (should this letter be delivered to you by Mr. Tieck) to tell you—first, that Mr. Tieck is the gentleman who was so kind to me at Rome; secondly, that he is a good man, emphatically, without taint of moral or religious infidelity; thirdly, that as a poet, critic, and moralist, he stands (in reputation) next to Goethe (and I believe that this reputation will be fame); lastly, it will interest you with Bristol, Keswick, and Grasmere associations, that Mr. Tieck has had to run, and has run, as nearly the same career in Germany as yourself and Wordsworth and (by the spray of being known to be intimate with you)

Yours sincerely,
S. T. Coleridge.

P. S. Should this meet you, for God's sake, do let me know of your arrival in London; it is so very important that I should see you.

R. Southey, Esq.
Honoured by Mr. Ludwig Tieck.

CCXIII. to H. C. Robinson.[143]

June, 1817.

My dear Robinson,—I shall never forgive you if you do not try to make some arrangement to bring Mr. L. Tieck and yourself up to Highgate very soon. The day, the dinner-hour, you may appoint yourself; but what I most wish would be, either that Mr. Tieck would come in the first stage, so as either to walk or to be driven in Mr. Gillman's gig to Caen Wood, and its delicious groves and alleys (the finest in England, a grand cathedral aisle of giant lime-trees, Pope's favourite composition walk when with the old Earl, a brother-rogue of yours in the law line), or else to come up to dinner, sleep here, and return (if then return he must) in the afternoon four o'clock stage the day after. I should be most happy to make him and that admirable man, Mr. Frere,[144] acquainted—their pursuits have been so similar—and to convince Mr. Tieck that he is the man among us in whom taste at its maximum has vitalized itself into productive power. [For] genius, you need only show him the incomparable translation annexed to Southey's "Cid" (which, by the bye, would perhaps give Mr. Tieck the most favourable impression of Southey's own powers); and I would finish the work off by Mr. Frere's "Aristophanes." In such goodness, too, as both my Mr. Frere (the Right Hon. J. H. Frere), and his brother George (the lawyer in Brunswick Square), live, move, and have their being, there is genius.

I have read two pages of "Lalla Rookh," or whatever it is called. Merciful Heaven! I dare read no more, that I may be able to answer at once to any questions, "I have but just looked at the work." O Robinson! if I could, or if I dared, act and feel as Moore and his set do, what havoc could I not make amongst their crockery-ware! Why, there are not three lines together without some adulteration of common English, and the ever-recurring blunder of using the possessive case, "compassion's tears," etc., for the preposition "of"—a blunder of which I have found no instances earlier than Dryden's slovenly verses written for the trade. The rule is, that the case 's is always personal; either it marks a person, or a personification, or the relique of some proverbial personification, as "Who for their belly's sake," in "Lycidas." But for A to weep the tears of B puts me in mind of the exquisite passage in Rabelais where Pantagruel gives the page his cup, and begs him to go down into the courtyard, and curse and swear for him about half an hour or so.

God bless you!

S. T. Coleridge.

CCXIV. TO THOMAS POOLE.

[July 22, 1817.]

My dear Poole,—It was a great comfort to me to meet and part from you as I did at Mr. Purkis's:[145] for, methinks, every true friendship that does not go with us to heaven, must needs be an obstacle to our own going thither,—to one of the parties, at all events.

I entreat your acceptance of a corrected copy of my "Sibylline Leaves" and "Literary Life;" and so wildly have they been printed, that a corrected copy is of some value to those to whom the works themselves are of any. I would that the misprinting had been the worst of the delusions and ill-usage, to which my credulity exposed me, from the said printer. After repeated promises that he took the printing, etc., merely to serve me as an old schoolfellow, and that he should charge "one sixpence profit," he charged paper, which I myself ordered for him at the paper-mill, at twenty-five to twenty-six shillings per ream, at thirty-five shillings, and, exclusive of this, his bill was £80 beyond the sum assigned by two eminent London printers as the price at which they would be willing to print the same quantity. And yet even this is among the minima of his Bristol honesty.

Fenner,[146] or rather his religious factotum, the Rev. T. Curtis, ci-devant bookseller, and whose affected retirement from business is a humbug, having got out of me a scheme for an Encyclopædia, which is the admiration of all the Trade, flatter themselves that they can carry it on by themselves. They refused to realise their promise to advance me £300 on the pledge of my works (a proposal of their own) unless I would leave Highgate and live at Camberwell. I took the advice of such friends as I had the opportunity of consulting immediately, and after taking into consideration the engagement into which I had entered, it was their unanimous opinion that their breach of their promise was a very fortunate circumstance, that it could not have been kept without the entire sacrifice of all my powers, and, above all, of my health—in short, that I could not in all human probability survive the first year. Mr. Frere yesterday advised me strenuously to finish the "Christabel," to keep the third volume of "The Friend" within a certain fathom of metaphysical depth, but within that to make it as elevated as the subjects required, and finally to devote myself industriously to the Works I had planned, alternating a poem with a prose volume, and, unterrified by reviews on the immediate sale, to remain confident that I should in some way or other be enabled to live in comfort, above all, not to write any more in any newspaper. He told me both Mr. Canning and Lord Liverpool had spoken in very high terms of me, and advised me to send a copy of all my works with a letter of some weight and length to the Marquis of[Wellesley. He offered me all his interest with regard to Derwent,[147] if he was sent to Cambridge. "It is a point" (these were his words) "on which I should feel myself authorised not merely to ask but to require and importune."

Hartley has been with me for the last month. He is very much improved; and, if I could see him more systematic in his studies and in the employment of his time, I should have little to complain of in him or to wish for. He is very desirous to visit the place of his infancy, poor fellow! And I am very desirous, if it were practicable, that he should be in the neighbourhood, as it were, of his uncles, so that there might be a probability of one or the other inviting him to spend a few weeks of his vacation at Ottery. His cousins[148] (the sons of my brothers James and George) are very good and affectionate to him; and it is a great comfort to me to see the chasm of the first generation closing and healing up in the second. From the state of your sister-in-law's health, when I last saw you, and the probable results of it, I cannot tell how your household is situated. Otherwise, I should venture to entreat of you, that you would give poor Hartley an invitation to pass a fortnight or three weeks with you this vacation.[149]

The object of the third volume of my "Friend," which will be wholly fresh matter, is briefly this,—that morality without religion is as senseless a scheme as religion without morality; that religion not revealed is a contradiction in terms, and an historical nonentity; that religion is not revealed unless the sacred books containing it are interpreted in the obvious and literal sense of the word, and that, thus interpreted, the doctrines of the Bible are in strict harmony with the Liturgy and Articles of our Established Church.

May God Almighty bless you, my dear Friend! and your obliged and affectionately grateful

S. T. Coleridge.

CCXV. TO H. F. CARY.[150]

Little Hampton, October [29], 1817.

I regret, dear sir! that a slave to the worst of tyrants (outward tyrants, at least), the booksellers, I have not been able to read more than two books and passages here and there of the other, of your translation of Dante. You will not suspect me of the worthlessness of exceeding my real opinion, but like a good Christian will make even modesty give way to charity, though I say, that in the severity and learned simplicity of the diction, and in the peculiar character of the Blank Verse, it has transcended what I should have thought possible without the Terza Rima. In itself, the metre is, compared with any English poem of one quarter the length, the most varied and harmonious to my ear of any since Milton, and yet the effect is so Dantesque that to those who should compare it only with other English poems, it would, I doubt not, have the same effect as the Terza Rima has compared with other Italian metres. I would that my literary influence were enough to secure the knowledge of the work for the true lovers of poetry in general.[151] But how came it that you had it published in so too unostentatious a form? For a second or third edition, the form has its conveniences; but for the first, in the present state of English society, quod non arrogas tibi, non habes. If you have any other works, poems, or poemata, by you, printed or MSS., you would gratify me by sending them to me. In the mean time, accept in the spirit in which it is offered, this trifling testimonial of my respect from, dear sir,

Yours truly, S. T. Coleridge.

CCXVI. TO THE SAME.

Little Hampton, Sussex, November 6, 1817.

My dear Sir,—I thank you for your kind and valued present, and equally for the kind letter that accompanied it. What I expressed concerning your translation, I did not say lightly or without examination: and I know enough of myself to be confident that any feeling of personal partiality would rather lead me to doubts and dissatisfactions respecting a particular work in proportion as it might possibly occasion me to overrate the man. For example, if, indeed, I do estimate too highly what I deem the characteristic excellencies of Wordsworth's poems, it results from a congeniality of taste without a congeniality in the productive power; but to the faults and defects I have been far more alive than his detractors, even from the first publication of the "Lyrical Ballads," though for a long course of years my opinions were sacred to his own ear. Since my last, I have read over your translation, and have carefully compared it with my distinctest recollections of every specimen of blank verse I am familiar with that can be called epic, narrative, or descriptive, excluding only the dramatic, declamatory, and lyrical—with Cowper, Armstrong, Southey, Wordsworth, Landor (the author of "Gebir"), and with all of my own that fell within comparisons as above defined, especially the passage from 287 to 292, "Sibylline Leaves,"[152]—and I find no other alteration in my judgement but an additional confidence in it. I still affirm that, to my ear and to my judgement, both your metre and your rhythm have in a far greater degree than I know any instance of, the variety of Milton without any mere Miltonisms, that (wherein I in the passage referred to have chiefly failed) the verse has this variety without any loss of continuity, and that this is the excellence of the work considered as a translation of Dante—that it gives the reader a similar feeling of wandering and wandering, onward and onward. Of the diction, I can only say that it is Dantesque even in that in which the Florentine must be preferred to our English giant—namely, that it is not only pure language, but pure English. The language differs from that of a mother or a well-bred lady who had read little but her Bible, and a few good books, only as far as the thoughts and things to be expressed require learned words from a learned poet! Perhaps I may be thought to appreciate this merit too highly; but you have seen what I have said in defence of this in the "Literary Life." By the bye, there is no Publisher's name mentioned in the title-page. Should I place any number of copies for you with Gale and Curtis, or at Murray's?

Believe me, that it will be both a pleasure and a relief to my mind should you bring with you any MSS. that you can yourself make it so as to read them to me.

Mrs. Gillman hopes, that, if choice or chance should lead you and yours near Highgate, you will not deprive us of the opportunity of introducing you to my excellent friend Mr. Gillman, and of shewing by our gladness how much we are, my dear sir, yours and Mrs. Cary's sincere respecters, and I beg you will accept an expression of particular esteem from your old lecturer,

S. T. Coleridge.

P. S. I return the "Prometheus" and the "Persæ" with thanks. I hope the Cambridge Professor will go through the remaining plays of Æschylus. They are delightful editions.

CCXVII. TO J. H. GREEN.[153]

Highgate, Friday morning, November 14, 1817.

Dear Sir,—I arrived at Highgate from Little Hampton yester-night: and the most interesting tidings I heard, were of your return and of your great kindness ... I can only say that I will call in Lincoln's Inn Fields the first day I am able to come to town—but should your occupation suffer you to take me in any of your rides for exercise or relaxation, need I say with what gladness I should welcome you? Our dinner-hour is four: but alterable without inconvenience to earlier or later. As soon as I have finished my present slave-work I shall write at large to Mr. Tieck. Be pleased to present my respectful regards to Mrs. Green, and believe me, dear sir, with marked esteem,

Your obliged
S. T. Coleridge.

CCXVIII. TO THE SAME.

[December 13, 1817.]

My dear Sir,—I thank you for the transcript. The lecture[154] went off beyond my expectations; and in several parts, where the thoughts were the same, more happily expressed extempore than in the Essay on the Science of Method[155] for the "Encyclopædia Metropolitana." However, you shall receive the first correct copy of the latter that I can procure. I would that I could present it to you, as it was written; though I am not inclined to quarrel with the judgment and prudence of omission, as far as the public are concerned. Be assured, I shall not fail to avail myself of your kind invitation, and that time passes happily with me under your roof, receiving and returning. Be pleased to make my best respects to Mrs. Green, and I beg her acceptance of the "Hebrew Dirge" with my free translation,[156] of which I will, as soon as it is printed, send her the music, viz. the original melody, and Bishop's additional music. Of this I am convinced, that a dozen of such "very pretty," and "so sweet," and "how smooth," "well, that is charming" compositions would gain me more admiration with the English public than twice the number of poems twice as good as the "Ancient Mariner," the "Christabel," the "Destiny of Nations," or the "Ode to the Departing Year."

My own opinion of the German philosophers does not greatly differ from yours; much in several of them is unintelligible to me, and more unsatisfactory. But I make a division. I reject Kant's stoic principle, as false, unnatural, and even immoral, where in his "Kritik der praktischen Vernunft,"[157] he treats the affections as indifferent ($\dot{\alpha}\delta\iota\dot{\alpha}\varphi o\rho\alpha$) in ethics, and would persuade us that a man who disliking, and without any feeling of love for virtue, yet acted virtuously, because and only because his duty, is more worthy of our esteem, than the man whose affections were aidant to and congruous with his conscience. For it would imply little less than that things not the objects of the moral will or under its control were yet indispensable to its due practical direction. In other words, it would subvert his own system. Likewise, his remarks on prayer in his "Religion innerhalb der reinen Vernunft," are crass, nay vulgar and as superficial even in psychology as they are low in taste. But with these exceptions, I reverence Immanuel Kant with my whole heart and soul, and believe him to be the only philosopher, for all men who have the power of thinking. I cannot conceive the liberal pursuit or profession, in which the service derived from a patient study of his works would not be incalculably great, both as cathartic, tonic, and directly nutritious.

Fichte in his moral system is but a caricature of Kant's, or rather, he is a Zeno, with the cowl, rope, and sackcloth of a Carthusian monk. His metaphysics have gone by; but he hath merit of having prepared the ground for, and laid the first stone of, the dynamic philosophy by the substitution of Act for Thing, Der einführen Actionen statt der Dinge an sich. Of the Natur-philosophen, as far as physical dynamics are concerned and as opposed to the mechanic corpuscular system, I think very highly of some parts of their system, as being sound and scientific—metaphysics of Quality, not less evident to my reason than the metaphysics of Quantity, that is, Geometry, etc.; of the rest and larger part, as tentative, experimental, and highly useful to a chemist, zoologist, and physiologist, as unfettering the mind, exciting its inventive powers. But I must be understood as confining these observations to the works of Schelling and H. Steffens. Of Schelling's Theology and Theanthroposophy, the telescopic stars and nebulæ are too many for my "grasp of eye." (N. B. The catachresis is Dryden's, not mine.) In short, I am half inclined to believe that both he and his friend Francis Baader are but half in earnest, and paint the veil to hide not the face but the want of one.[158] Schelling is too ambitious, too eager to be the Grand Seignior of the allein-selig Philosophie to be altogether a trustworthy philosopher. But he is a man of great genius; and, however unsatisfied with his conclusions, one cannot read him without being either whetted or improved. Of the others, saving Jacobi, who is a rhapsodist, excellent in sentences all in small capitals, I know either nothing, or too little to form a judgement. As my opinions were formed before I was acquainted with the schools of Fichte and Schelling, so do they remain independent of them, though I con- and pro-fess great obligations to them in the development of my thoughts, and yet seem to feel that I should have been more useful had I been left to evolve them myself without knowledge of their coincidence. I do not very much like the Sternbald[159] of our friend; it is too like an imitation of Heinse's "Ardinghello,"[160] and if the scene in the Painter's Garden at Rome is less licentious than the correspondent abomination in the former work, it is likewise duller.

I have but merely looked into Jean Paul's "Vorschule der Aisthetik,"[161] but I found one sentence almost word for word the same as one written by myself in a fragment of an Essay on the Supernatural[162] many years ago, viz. that the presence of a ghost is the terror, not what he does, a principle which Southey, too, overlooks in his "Thalaba" and "Kehama."

But I must conclude. Believe me, dear sir, with unfeigned regard and esteem, your obliged

S. T. Coleridge.

I expect my eldest son, Hartley Coleridge, to-day from Oxford.

CCXIX. TO CHARLES AUGUSTUS TULK.[163]

Highgate, Thursday evening, 1818.

Dear Sir,—As an innocent female often blushes not at any image which had risen in her own mind, but from a confused apprehension of some x y z that might be attributed to her by others, so did I feel uncomfortable at the odd coincidence of my commending to you the late Swedenborgian advertisement. But when I came home I simply asked Mrs. G. if she remembered my having read to her such an address. She instantly replied not only in the affirmative, but mentioned the circumstance of my having expressed a sort of half-inclination, half-intention of addressing a letter to the chairman mentioning my receipt of a book of which I highly approved, and requesting him to transmit my acknowledgments, if, as was probable, the author was known to him or any of the gentlemen with him. I asked her then if she had herself read the advertisement? "Yes, and I carried it to Mr. Gillman, saying how much you had been pleased with the style and the freedom from the sectarian spirit." "And do you recollect the name of the Chairman?" "No! why, bless me! could it be Mr. Tulk?" Very nearly the same conversation took place with Mr. Gillman afterwards. I can readily account for the fact in myself; for first I never recollect any persons by their names, and have fallen into some laughable perplexities by this specific catalepsy of memory, such as accepting an invitation in the streets from a face perfectly familiar to me, and being afterwards unable to attach the name and habitat thereto; and secondly, that the impression made by a conversation that appeared to me altogether accidental and by your voice and person had been completed before I heard your name; and lastly, the more habitual thinking is to any one, the larger share has the relation of cause and effect in producing recognition. But it is strange that neither Mrs. or Mr. Gillman should have recollected the name, though probably the accidentality of having made your acquaintance, and its being at Little Hampton, and associated with our having at the same time and by a similar accidental rencontre become acquainted with the Rev. Mr. Cary and his family, overlaid any former relique of a man's name in Mrs. G. as well as myself.

I return you Blake's poesies,[164] metrical and graphic, with thanks. With this and the book, I have sent a rude scrawl as to the order in which I was pleased by the several poems.

With respectful compliments to Mrs. Tulk, I remain, dear sir, your obliged

S. T. Coleridge.

Thursday evening, Highgate.

Blake's Poems.—I begin with my dyspathies that I may forget them, and have uninterrupted space for loves and sympathies. Title-page and the following emblem contain all the faults of the drawings with as few beauties as could be in the compositions of a man who was capable of such faults and such beauties. The faulty despotism in symbols amounting in the title-page to the μισητὸν, and occasionally, irregular unmodified lines of the inanimate, sometimes as the effect of rigidity and sometimes of exossation like a wet tendon. So likewise the ambiguity of the drapery. Is it a garment or the body incised and scored out? The lumpness (the effect of vinegar on an egg) in the upper one of the two prostrate figures in the title-page, and the straight line down the waistcoat of pinky goldbeaters' skin in the next drawing, with the I don't-know-whatness of the countenance, as if the mouth had been formed by the habit of placing the tongue not contemptuously, but stupidly, between the lower gums and the lower jaw—these are the only repulsive faults I have noticed. The figure, however, of the second leaf, abstracted from the expression of the countenance given it by something about the mouth, and the interspace from the lower lip to the chin, is such as only a master learned in his art could produce.

N. B. I signifies "It gave me great pleasure." ⨍, "Still greater." H, "And greater still," Θ, "In the highest degree." O, "In the lowest."

Shepherd, I; Spring, I (last stanza, ⨍); Holy Thursday, H; Laughing Song, ⨍; Nurse's Song, I; The Divine Image, Θ; The Lamb, ⨍; The little black Boy, Θ yea Θ+Θ; Infant Joy, H (N. B. For the three last lines I should write, "When wilt thou smile," or "O smile, O smile! I'll sing the while." For a babe two days old does not, cannot smile, and innocence and the very truth of Nature must go together. Infancy is too holy a thing to be ornamented). "The Echoing Green," I, (the figures †, and of the second leaf, ††); "The Cradle Song," I; "The School Boy," ††; Night, ʘ; "On another's Sorrow," I; "A Dream," ?; "The little boy lost," I (the drawing, †); "The little boy found," I; "The Blossom," O; "The Chimney Sweeper," O; "The Voice of the Ancient Bard," O.

Introduction, †; Earth's Answer, †; Infant Sorrow, I; "The Clod and the Pebble," I; "The Garden of Love," †; "The Fly," I; "The Tyger," †; "A little boy lost," †; "Holy Thursday," I; [p. 13, O; "Nurse's Song," O?]; "The little girl lost and found" (the ornaments most exquisite! the poem, I); "Chimney Sweeper in the Snow," O; "To Tirzah, and the Poison Tree," I—and yet O; "A little Girl lost," O. (I would have had it omitted, not for the want of innocence in the poem, but from the too probable want of it in many readers.) "London," I; "The Sick Rose," I; "The little Vagabond," O. Though I cannot approve altogether of this last poem, and have been inclined to think that the error which is most likely to beset the scholars of Emanuel Swedenborg is that of utterly demerging the tremendous incompatibilities with an evil will that arise out of the essential Holiness of the abysmal A-seity[165] in the love of the Eternal Person, and thus giving temptation to weak minds to sink this love itself into Good Nature, yet still I disapprove the mood of mind in this wild poem so much less than I do the servile blind-worm, wrap-rascal scurf-coat of fear of the modern Saint (whose whole being is a lie, to themselves as well as to their brethren), that I should laugh with good conscience in watching a Saint of the new stamp, one of the first stars of our eleemosynary advertisements, groaning in wind-pipe! and with the whites of his eyes upraised at the audacity of this poem! Anything rather than this degradation I of Humanity, and therein of the Incarnate Divinity!

S. T. C.

O means that I am perplexed and have no opinion.

I, with which how can we utter "Our Father"?

CCXX. TO J. H. GREEN.

Spring Garden Coffee House, [May 2, 1818.]

My dear Sir,—Having been detained here till the present hour, and under requisition for Monday morning early, I have decided on not returning to Highgate in the interim. I propose, therefore, to have the pleasure of passing the fore-dinner hours, from eleven o'clock to-morrow morning, with you in Lincoln's Inn Square, unless I should hear from you to the contrary.

The Cotton-children Bill[166] (an odd irony to children bred up in cotton!) which has passed the House of Commons, would not, I suspect, have been discussed at all in the House of Lords, but have been quietly assented to, had it not afforded that Scotch coxcomb, the plebeian Earl of Lauderdale,[167] too tempting an occasion for displaying his muddy three inch depths in the gutter (? Guttur) of his Political Economy. Whether some half-score of rich capitalists are to be prevented from suborning suicide and perpetuating infanticide and soul-murder is, forsooth, the most perplexing question which has ever called forth his determining faculties, accustomed as they are well known to have been, to grappling with difficulties. In short, he wants to make a speech almost as much as I do to have a release signed by conscience from the duty of making or anticipating answers to such speeches.

O when the heart is deaf and blind, how blear
The lynx's eye! how dull the mould-warp's ear!
Verily the World is mighty! and for all but the few the orb of Truth labours under eclipse from the shadow of the world!

With kind respects to Mrs. Green, believe me, my dear sir, with sincere and affectionate esteem,

Yours,
S. T. Coleridge.

CCXXI. TO MRS. GILLMAN.

J. Green's, Esq., St. Lawrence, nr. Maldon,
Wednesday, July 19, 1818.

My very dear Sister and Friend,—The distance from the post and the extraordinary thinness of population in this district (especially of men and women of letters) which affords only two days in the seven for sending to or receiving from Maldon, are the sole causes of your not hearing oftener from me. The cross roads from Margretting Street to the very house are excellent, and through the first gate we drove up between two large gardens, that on the right a flower and fruit garden not without kitchenery, and that on the left, a kitchen garden not without fruits and flowers, and both in a perfect blaze of roses. Yet so capricious is our, at least my, nature, that I feel I do not receive the fifth part of the delight from this miscellany of Flora, flowers at every step, as from the economized glasses and flower-pots at Highgate so tended and worshipped by me, and each the gift of some kind friend or courteous neighbour. I actually make up a flower-pot every night, in order to imitate my Highgate pleasures. The country road is very beautiful. About a quarter of a mile from the garden, all the way through beautiful fields in blossom, we come to a wood, full of birds and not uncharmed by the nightingales, and which the old workman, to please his mistress, has romanticised with, I dare say, fifty seats and honeysuckle bowers and green arches made by twisting the branches of the trees across the paths. The view from the hilly field above the wood commanding the arm of the sea, and ending in the open sea, reminded me very much of the prospects from Stowey and Alfoxden, in Somersetshire. The cottagers seem to be and are in possession of plenty of comfort. Poverty I have seen no marks of, nor of the least servility, though they are courteous and respectful. We have abundance of cream. The Farm must, I should think, be a valuable estate; and the parents are anxious to leave it as complete as possible for Joseph, their only child (for it is Mrs. J. Green's sisters that we have seen—G. himself has no sister). There is no society hereabouts. I like it the better therefore. The clergyman, a young man, is lost in a gloomy vulgar Calvinism, will read no book but the Bible, converse on nothing but the state of the soul, or rather he will not converse at all, but visit each house once in two months, when he prays and admonishes, and gives a lecture every evening at his own rooms. On being invited to dine with us, the sad and modest youth returned for answer, that if Mr. Green and I should be here when he visited the house, he should have no objection to enter into the state of our souls with us, and if in the mean time we desired any instruction from him, we might attend at his daily evening lecture! Election, Reprobation, Children of the Devil, and all such flowers of rhetoric, and flour of brimstone, form his discourses both in church and parlour. But my folly in not filling the snuff canister is a subject of far more serious and awful regret with me, than the not being in the way of being thus led by the nose of this Pseudo-Evangelist. Nothing but Scotch; and that five miles off. O Anne! it was cruel in you not to have calculated the monstrous disproportion between the huge necessities of my nostrils, or rather of my thumb and forefinger, and that vile little vial three fourths empty of snuff! The flat of my thumb, yea, the nail of my forefinger is not only clean; it is white! white as the pale flag of famine![168]

Now for my health.... Ludicrous as it may seem, yet it is no joke for me, that from the marshiness of these sea marshes, and the number of unnecessary fish ponds and other stagnancies immediately around the house, the gnats are a very plague of Egypt, and suspicious, with good reason, of an erysipelatous tendency, I am anxious concerning the effects of the irritation produced by these canorous visitants. While awake (and two thirds of last night I was kept awake by their bites and trumpetings) I can so far command myself as to check the intolerable itching by a weak mixture of goulard and rosewater; but in my sleep I scratch myself as if old Scratch had lent me his best set of claws. This is the only drawback from my comforts here, for nothing can be kinder or more cordial than my treatment. I like Mrs. J. Green better and better; but feel that in twenty years it would never be above or beyond liking. She is good-natured, lively, innocent, but without a soothingness, or something I do not know what that is tender. As to my return, I do not think it will be possible, without great unkindness, to be with you before Tuesday evening or Wednesday, calculating wholly by the progress of the manuscript; and we have been hard at it. Do not take it as words, of course, when I say and solemnly assure you, that if I followed my own wishes, I should leave this place on Saturday morning: for I feel more and more that I can be well off nowhere away from you and Gillman. May God bless him! For a dear friend he is and has been to be. Remember me affectionately to the Milnes and Betsy, if they are at Highgate. Love to James. Kisses for the Fish of Five Waters,[169] none of which are stagnant, and I hope that Mary, Dinah, and Lucy are well, and that Mary is quite recovered. Again and again and again, God bless you, my most dear friends; for I am, and ever trust to remain, more than can be expressed, my dear Anne! your affectionate, obliged, and grateful

S. T. Coleridge.

P. S. Not to put Essex after Maldon.

CCXXII. TO W. COLLINS, ESQ., A. R. A.

Highgate, December, 1818.

My dear Sir,—I at once comply with, and thank you for, your request to have some prospectuses. God knows I have so few friends, that it would be unpardonable in me not to feel proportionably grateful towards those few who think the time not wasted in which they interest themselves in my behalf. There is an old Latin adage, Vis videri pauper, et pauper es! Poor you profess yourself to be, and poor therefore you are, and will remain. The prosperous feel only with the prosperous, and if you subtract from the whole sum of their feeling for all the gratifications of vanity, and all their calculations of lending to the Lord, both of which are best answered by confessing the superfluity of their superfluities on advertised and advertisable distress, or on such cases as are known to be in all respects their inferior, you will have, I fear, but a scanty remainder. All this is too true; but then, what is that man to do whom no distress can bribe to swindle or deceive? who cannot reply as Theophilus Cibber did to his father, Colley Cibber, who, seeing him in a rich suit of clothes whispered to him as he passed, "The! The! I pity thee!" "Pity me! pity my tailor!"

Spite of the decided approbation which my plan of delivering lectures has received from several judicious and highly respectable individuals, it is still too histrionic, too much like a retail dealer in instruction and pastime, not to be depressing. If the duty of living were not far more awful to my conscience than life itself is agreeable to my feelings, I should sink under it. But, getting nothing by my publications, which I have not the power of making estimable by the public without loss of self-estimation, what can I do? The few who have won the present age, while they have secured the praise of posterity, as Sir Walter Scott, Mr. Southey, Lord Byron, etc., have been in happier circumstances. And lecturing is the only means by which I can enable myself to go on at all with the great philosophical work to which the best and most genial hours of the last twenty years of my life have been devoted. Poetry is out of the question. The attempt would only hurry me into that sphere of acute feelings from which abstruse research, the mother of self-oblivion, presents an asylum. Yet sometimes, spite of myself, I cannot help bursting out into the affecting exclamation of our Spenser (his "wine" and "ivy garland" interpreted as competence and joyous circumstances):—

"Thou kenn'st not, Percy, how the rhyme should cage!
Oh, if my temples were bedewed with wine,
And girt with garlands of wild ivy-twine,
How I could rear the Muse on stately stage!
And teach her tread aloft in buskin fine,
With queen'd Bellona in her equipage!
But ah, my courage cools ere it be warm!"[170]

But God's will be done. To feel the full force of the Christian religion it is, perhaps, necessary for many tempers that they should first be made to feel, experimentally, the hollowness of human friendship, the presumptuous emptiness of human hopes. I find more substantial comfort now in pious George Herbert's "Temple," which I used to read to amuse myself with his quaintness, in short, only to laugh at, than in all the poetry since the poems of Milton. If you have not read Herbert, I can recommend the book to you confidently. The poem entitled "The Flower" is especially affecting; and, to me, such a phrase as "and relish versing" expresses a sincerity, a reality, which I would unwillingly exchange for the more dignified "and once more love the Muse," etc. And so, with many other of Herbert's homely phrases.

We are all anxious to hear from, and of, our excellent transatlantic friend.[171] I need not repeat that your company, with or without our friend Leslie,[172] will gratify

Your sincere
S. T. Coleridge.

CCXXIII. TO THOMAS ALLSOP.

The origin of Coleridge's friendship with Thomas Allsop, a young city merchant, dates from the first lecture which he delivered at Flower de Luce Court, January 27, 1818. A letter from Allsop containing a "judicious suggestion" with regard to the subject advertised, "The Dark Ages of Europe," was handed to the lecturer, who could not avail himself of the hint on this occasion, but promised to do so before the close of the series. Personal intercourse does not seem to have taken place till a year later, but from 1819 to 1826 Coleridge and Allsop were close and intimate friends. In 1825 the correspondence seems to have dropped, but I am not aware that then or afterwards there was any breach of friendship. In 1836 Allsop published the letters which he had received from Coleridge. Partly on account of the personal allusions which some of the letters contain, and partly because it would seem that Coleridge expressed himself to his young disciple with some freedom on matters of religious opinion, the publication of these letters was regarded by Coleridge's friends as an act of mala fides. Allsop was kindness itself to Coleridge, but, no doubt, the allusions to friends and children, which were of a painful and private nature, ought, during their lifetime at least, to have been omitted. The originals of many of these letters were presented by the Allsop family to the late Emperor of Brazil, an enthusiastic student and admirer of Coleridge.[173]

December 2, 1818.

My dear Sir,—I cannot express how kind I felt your letter. Would to Heaven I had had many with feelings like yours, "accustomed to express themselves warmly and (as far as the word is applicable to you, even) enthusiastically." But, alas! during the prime manhood of my intellect I had nothing but cold water thrown on my efforts. I speak not now of my systematic and most unprovoked maligners. On them I have retorted only by pity and by prayer. These may have, and doubtless have, joined with the frivolity of "the reading public" in checking and almost in preventing the sale of my works; and so far have done injury to my purse. Me they have not injured. But I have loved with enthusiastic self-oblivion those who have been so well pleased that I should, year after year, flow with a hundred nameless rills into their main stream, that they could find nothing but cold praise and effective discouragement of every attempt of mine to roll onward in a distinct current of my own; who admitted that the "Ancient Mariner," the "Christabel," the "Remorse," and some pages of "The Friend" were not without merit, but were abundantly anxious to acquit their judgements of any blindness to the very numerous defects. Yet they knew that to praise, as mere praise, I was characteristically, almost constitutionally, indifferent. In sympathy alone I found at once nourishment and stimulus; and for sympathy alone did my heart crave. They knew, too, how long and faithfully I had acted on the maxim, never to admit the faults of a work of genius to those who denied or were incapable of feeling and understanding the beauties; not from wilful partiality, but as well knowing that in saying truth I should, to such critics, convey falsehood. If, in one instance, in my literary life, I have appeared to deviate from this rule, first, it was not till the fame of the writer (which I had been for fourteen years successively toiling like a second Ali to build up) had been established; and, secondly and chiefly, with the purpose and, I may safely add, with the effect of rescuing the necessary task from malignant defamers, and in order to set forth the excellences and the trifling proportion which the defects bore to the excellences. But this, my dear sir, is a mistake to which affectionate natures are liable, though I do not remember to have ever seen it noticed, the mistaking those who are desirous and well-pleased to be loved by you, for those who love you. Add, as a mere general cause, the fact that I neither am nor ever have been of any party. What wonder, then, if I am left to decide which has been my worse enemy,—the broad, predetermined abuse of the "Edinburgh Review," etc., or the cold and brief compliments, with the warm regrets of the "Quarterly"? After all, however, I have now but one sorrow relative to the ill success of my literary toils (and toils they have been, though not undelightful toils), and this arises wholly from the almost insurmountable difficulties which the anxieties of to-day oppose to my completion of the great work, the form and materials of which it has been the employment of the best and most genial hours of the last twenty years to mature and collect.

If I could but have a tolerably numerous audience to my first, or first and second Lectures on the History of Philosophy,[174] I should entertain a strong hope of success, because I know that these lectures will be found by far the most interesting and entertaining of any that I have yet delivered, independent of the more permanent interests of rememberable instruction. Few and unimportant would the errors of men be, if they did but know, first, what they themselves meant; and, secondly, what the words mean by which they attempt to convey their meaning; and I can conceive no subject so well fitted to exemplify the mode and the importance of these two points as the History of Philosophy, treated as in the scheme of these lectures. Trusting that I shall shortly have the pleasure of seeing you here,

I remain, my dear sir, yours most sincerely,
S. T. Coleridge.

CCXXIV. TO J. H. GREEN.

[Postmark, January 16, 1819.]

My dear Green,—I forgot both at the Lecture Room and at Mr. Phillips's to beg you to leave out for me Goethe's "Zur Farbenlehre." It is for a passage in the preface in which he compares Plato with Aristotle, etc., as far as I recollect, in a spirited manner. The books are at your service again, after the lecture. Either Mr. Cary or some messenger will call for them to-morrow! I piously resolve on Tuesday to put my books in some order, but at all events to select yours and send all of them that I do not want (and I do not recollect any that I do, unless perhaps the little volume edited by Tieck of his friend's composition), back to you. I am more and more delighted with Chantrey. The little of his conversation which I enjoyed ex pede Herculem, left me no doubt of the power of his insight. Light, manlihood, simplicity, wholeness. These are the entelechy of Phidian Genius; and who but must see these in Chantrey's solar face, and in all his manners? Item: I am bewitched with your wife's portrait. So very like and yet so ideal a portrait I never remember to have seen. But as Mr. Phillips[175] said: "Why, sir! she was a sweet subject, sir! That's a great thing."

As to my own, I can form no judgment. In its present state, the eyes appear too large, too globose, and their colour must be made lighter, and I thought that the face, exclusive of the forehead, was stronger, more energetic than mine seems to be when I catch it in the glass, and therefore the forehead and brow less so—not in themselves, but in consequence of the proportion. But of course I can form no notion of what my face and look may be when I am animated in friendly conversation. My kind and respectful remembrances to your Mother, and believe me, most affectionately,

Your obliged friend,
S. T. Coleridge.

CCXXV. TO JAMES GILLMAN.

[Ramsgate, Postmark, August 20, 1819.]

My dear Friend,—Whether from the mere intensity of the heat, and the restless, almost sleepless, nights in consequence, or from incautious exposure to draughts; or whether simply the change of air and the sea bath was repairing the intestinal canal (and bad indeed must the road be which is not better than a road a-mending, a hint which our revolutionary reformers would do well to attend to) or from whatever cause, I have been miserably unwell for the last three days—but last night passed a tolerably good night, and, finding myself convalescent this morning, I bathed, and now am still better, having had a glorious tumble in the waves, though the water is still not cold enough for my liking. The weather, however, is evidently on the change, and we have now a succession of flying April showers, and needle rains. My bath is about a mile and a quarter from the Lime Grove, a wearisome travail by the deep crumbly sands, but a very pleasant breezy walk along the top of the cliff, from which you descend through a deep steep lane cut through the chalk rocks. The tide comes up to the end of the lane, and washes the cliff, but a little before or a little after high-tide there are nice clean seats of rock with foot-baths, and then an expanse of sand, greater than I need; and exactly a hundred of my strides from the end of the lane there is a good, roomy, arched cavern, with an oven or cupboard in it, where one's clothes may be put free from the sand.... I find that I can write no more if I am to send this by the to-day's post. Pray, if you can with any sort of propriety, do come down to me—to us, I suppose I ought to say. We are all as should be Βυτ μονστρουσλι φορμαλ....

God bless you and
S. T. C.

CCXXVI. TO MRS. ADERS. [?][176]

[Highgate, October 28, 1819.]

Dear Madam,—I wish from my very heart that you could teach me to express my obligations to you with half the grace and delicacy with which you confer them! But not to the Giver does the evening cloud indicate the rich lights, which it has received and transmits and yet retains. For other eyes it must glow: and what it cannot return it will strive to represent, the poor proxy of the gracious orb which is departing. I would that the simile were less accurate throughout, and with those of Homer's lost its likeness as it approached to its conclusion! This, I fear, is somewhat too selfish; but we cannot have attachment without fear or grief.

"We cannot choose—
But weep to have what we so dread to lose,"
says Nature's child, our best Shakespeare; and that Humanity cannot grieve without a portion of selfishness, Nature herself says. To take up my allegoric strain with a slight variation, even in the fairest shews and liveliest demonstrations of grateful and affectionate leave-taking from a generous friend or disinterested patron or benefactor, we are like evening rainbows, that at once shine and weep, things made up of reflected splendour and our own tears.[177]

To meet, to know, t' esteem—and then to part,
Forms the sad tale of many a genial heart.[178]

The storm[179] now louring and muttering in our political atmosphere might of itself almost forbid me to regret your leaving England. For I have no apprehension of any serious or extensive danger to property or to the coercive powers of the Law. Both reason and history preclude the fear of any revolution, where none of the constituent states of a nation are arrayed against the others. The risk is still less in Great Britain where property is so widely diffused and so closely interlinked and co-organized. But I dare not promise as much for personal safety. The struggle may be short, the event certain; yet the mischief in the interim appalling!

May my Fears,
My filial fears, be vain! and may the vaunts
And menace of the vengeful enemy
Pass like the gust, that roared and died away
In the distant tree: which heard, and only heard
In this low dell, bow'd not the delicate grass.[180]
I confess that I read the poem from which these lines are extracted ("Fears in Solitude") and now cite them with far other than an author's feelings; those, I trust, of a patriot, I am sure, those of a Christian.

You will not, I know, fail to assure Miss Harding[181] of the kind feelings and wishes with which I accompany her; but my sense of the last boon, which I owe to her, I shall convey, my dear madam! by hands less likely to make extenuating comments on my words than your tongue or hand. Before I subscribe my name, I must tell you that had my wish been the chooser and had taken a month to deliberate on the choice, I could not have received a keepsake so in all respects gratifying to me, as the exquisite impressions of cameo's and intaglio's.[182] First, it enables me to entertain and gratify so many friends, my own and Mr. and Mrs. Gillman's; secondly, every little gem is associated with my recollections, or more or less recalls the images and persons seen and met with during my own stay in the Mediterranean and Italy; thirdly, they stand in the same connection with the places of your past and future sojourn, and therefore, lastly, supply me with the means and the occasion of expressing to others more strongly, perhaps, but not more warmly or sincerely than I now do to yourself, with how much respect and regard I remain, dear madam,

Your obliged friend and servant,
S. T. Coleridge.

Saturday, 28th Octr. 1819. On the 20th of this month completed my 49th year.

CCXXVII. TO J. H. GREEN.

January 14, 1820.

My dear Green,—Charles Lamb has just written to inform me that he and his sister will pay me their New Year's visit on Sunday next, and may perhaps bring a friend to see me, though certainly not to dine, and hopes I may not be engaged. I must therefore defer our philosophical intercommune till the Sunday after; but if you have no more pleasant way of passing the ante-prandial or, still better, the day including prandial and post-prandial, I trust that it will be no anti-philosophical expenditure of time, and I need not say an addition to the pleasure of all this household. I should like, too, to arrange some plan of going with you to Covent Garden Theatre, to see Miss Wensley, the new actress, whose father (a merchant of Bristol, at whose house I had once been, but whom the capricious Nymph of Trade has unhorsed from his seat) has called on me, a compound of the Oratorical, the Histrionic, and the Exquisite! All the dull colours in the colour-shop at the sign of the Bluecoat Boy would not suffice to neutralize the glare of his Colorit into any tolerably fair likeness that would not be scouted as Caricature! Gillman will give you a slight sketch of him. Since I saw you, we have dined and spent the night (for it was near one when we broke up) at Mathews', and heard and saw his forthcoming "At Home." There were present, besides G. and myself, Mrs. and young Mathews, and Mr. and Mrs. Chisholm, James Smith of Rej. Add. notoriety, and the author of (all the trash of) Mathews' Entertainment, for the good parts are his own, (What a pity that you dare not offer a word of friendly sensible advice to such men as M., but you may be certain that it will be useless to them and attributed to envy or some vile selfish object in the adviser!) Mr. Dubois,[183] the author of "Vaurien," "Old Nic," "My Pocket Book," and a notable share of the theatrical puffs and slanders of the periodical press; and, lastly, Mr. Thomas Hill,[184] quondam drysalter of Thames Street, whom I remember twenty-five years ago with exactly the same look, person, and manners as now. Mathews calls him the Immutable. He is a seemingly always good-natured fellow who knows nothing and about everything, no person, and about and all about everybody—a complete parasite, in the old sense of a dinner-hunter, at the tables of all who entertain public men, authors, players, fiddlers, booksellers, etc., for more than thirty years. It was a pleasant evening, however.

Be so good as to remember the drawing from the Alchemy Book.

Mrs. Gillman desires her love to Mrs. Green; and we hope that the twin obstacles, ague and the boreal weather, to our seeing her here, will vanish at the same time. Mrs. G. bids me tell her that she grumbles at the doctors, her husband included, and is confident that her husband would have made a cure long ago. A faithful wife is a common blessing, I trust: but what a treasure to have a wife full of faith! By the bye, I have lit on some (ὡς ἔμοιγε δοκεῖ analogous) cases in which the nauseating plan, even for a short time, appears to have had a wonderful effect in breaking the chain of a morbid tendency; and the almost infallible specific of seasickness in curing an old ague is surely a confirmation as far as it goes.

Yours most affectionately,
S. T. Coleridge.

CCXXVIII. TO THE SAME.

[May 25, 1820.]

My dear Green,—I was greatly affected in finding how ill you had been, and long ere this should have let you know it, but that I have myself been in no usual degree unwell. I wish I could with truth underline the words have been, and in the hope of being able to do so it was that I delayed answering your note. Unless a speedy change for the better takes place, I should culpably deceive myself if I did not interpret my present state as a summons. God's will be done! I cannot pretend that I have not received countless warnings; and for my neglect and for the habits, and all the feebleness and wastings of the moral will which unfit the soul for spiritual ascent, and must sink it, of moral necessity, lower and lower, if it be essentially imperishable, my only ray of hope is this, that in my inmost heart, as far as my consciousness can sound its depths, I plead nothing but my utter and sinful helplessness and worthlessness on one side, and the infinite mercy and divine Humanity of our Creator and Redeemer crucified from the beginning of the world, on the other! I use no comparatives, nor indeed could I ever charitably interpret the penitential phrases ("I am the vilest of sinners, worse than the wickedest of my fellow-men," etc.) otherwise than as figures of speech, the whole purport of which is, "In relation to God I appear to myself the same as the very worst man, if such there be, would appear to an earthly tribunal." I mean no comparatives; for what have a man's permanent concerns to do with comparison? What avails it to a bird shattered and irremediably disorganized in one wing, that another bird is similarly conditioned in both wings? Or to a man in the last stage of ulcerated lungs, that his neighbour is liver-rotten as well as consumptive? Both find their equation, the birds as to flight, the men as to life. In o o o's there is no comparison.

My nephew, the Revd. W. Hart Coleridge, came and stayed here from Monday afternoon to Tuesday noon, in order to make Derwent's acquaintance, and brought with him by accident Marsh's Divinity Lecture, No 3rd, on the authenticity and credibility of the Books collected in the New Testament. As I could not sit with the party after tea, I took the pamphlet with me into my bedroom, and gave it an attentive perusal, knowing the Bishop's intimate acquaintance with the investigations of Eichhorn, Paulus, and their numerous scarcely less celebrated scholars, and myself familiar with the works of the Göttingen Professor (Eichhorn), the founder and head of the daring school. I saw or seemed to see more management in the Lecture than proof of thorough conviction. I supplied, however, from my own reasonings enough of what appeared wanting or doubtful in the Bishop's to justify the conclusion that the Gospel History beginning with the Baptism of John, and the Doctrines contained in the fourth Gospel, and in the Epistles, truly represent the assertions of the Apostles and the faith of the Christian Church during the first century; that there exists no tenable or even tolerable ground for doubting the authenticity of the Books ascribed to John the Evangelist, to Mark, to Luke, and to Paul; nor the authority of Matthew and the author of the Epistle to the Hebrews; and lastly, that a man need only have common sense and a good heart to be assured that these Apostles and Apostolic men wrote nothing but what they themselves believed. And yet I have no hesitation in avowing that many an argument derived from the nature of man, nay, that many a strong though only speculative probability, pierces deeper, pushes more home, and clings more pressingly to my mind than the whole sum of merely external evidence, the fact of Christianity itself alone excepted. Nay, I feel that the external evidence derives a great and lively accession of force, for my mind, from my previous speculative convictions or presumptions; but that I cannot find that the latter are at all strengthened or made more or less probable to me by the former. Besides, as to the external evidence I make up my mind once for all, and merely as evidence think no more about it; but those facts or reflections thereon which tend to change belief into insight, can never lose their effect, any more than the distinctive sensations of disease, compared with a more perceived correspondence of symptoms with the diagnostics of a medical book.

I was led to this remark by reflecting on the awful importance of the physiological question (so generally decided one way by the late most popular writers on insanity), Does the efficient cause of disease and disordered action, and, collectively, of pain and perishing, lie entirely in the organs, and then, reawakening the active principle in me, depart—that all pain and disease would be removed, and I should stand in the same state as I stood in previous to all sickness, etc., to the admission of any disturbing forces into my nature? Or, on the contrary, would such a repaired Organismus be no fit organ for my life, as if, for instance, a worn lock with an equally worn key—[the key] might no longer fit the lock. The repaired organs might from intimate in-correspondence be the causes of torture and madness. A system of materialism, in which organisation stands first, whether compared by Nature, or God and Life, etc., as its results (even as the sound is the result of a bell), such a system would, doubtless, remove great part of the terrors which the soul makes out of itself; but then it removes the soul too, or rather precludes it. And a supposition of coexistence, without any wechselwirkung, it is not in our power to adopt in good earnest; or, if we did, it would answer no purpose. For which of the two, soul or body, am I to call "I"? Again, a soul separate from the body, and yet entirely passive to it, would be so like a drum playing a tattoo on the drummer, that one cannot build any hope on it. If then the organisation be primarily the result, and only by reaction a cause, it would be well to consider what the cases are in this life, in which the restoration of the organisation removes disease. Is the organisation ever restored, except as continually reproduced? And in the remaining number are they not cases into which the soul never entered as a conscious or rather a moral conscionable agent? The regular reproduction of scars, marks, etc., the increased susceptibility of disease in an organ, after a perfect apparent restoration to healthy structure in action; the insusceptibility in other cases, as in the variolous—these and many others are fruitful subjects, and even imperfect as the induction may be, and must be in our present degree of knowledge, we might yet deduce that a suicide, under the domination of disorderly passions and erroneous principles, plays a desperately hazardous game, and that the chance is, he may re-house himself in a worse hogshead, with the nails and spikes driven inward—or, sinking below the organising power, be employed fruitlessly in a horrid appetite of re-skinning himself, after he had succeeded in fleaing his life and leaving all its sensibilities bare to the incursive powers without even the cortex of a nerve to shield them? Would it not follow, too, from these considerations, that a redemptive power must be necessary if immortality be true, and man be a disordered being? And that no power can be redemptive which does not at the same time act in the ground of the life as one with the ground, that is, must act in my will and not merely on my will; and yet extrinsically, as an outward power, that is, as that which outward Nature is to the organisation, viz. the causa correspondens et conditio perpetua ab extra? Under these views, I cannot read the Sixth Chapter of St. John without great emotion. The Redeemer cannot be merely God, unless we adopt Pantheism, that is, deny the existence of a God; and yet God he must be, for whatever is less than God, may act on, but cannot act in, the will of another. Christ must become man, but he cannot become us, except as far as we become him, and this we cannot do but by assimilation; and assimilation is a vital real act, not a notional or merely intellective one. There are phenomena, which are phenomena relatively to our present five senses, and these Christ forbids us to understand as his meaning, and, collectively, they are entitled the Flesh that perishes. But does it follow that there are no other phenomena? or that these media of manifestation might not stand to a spiritual world and to our enduring life in the same relation as our visible mass of body stands to the world of the senses, and to the sensations correspondent to, and excited by, the stimulants of that world. Lastly, would not the sum of the latter phenomena (the spiritual) be appropriately named, the Flesh and Blood of the divine Humanity? If faith be a mere apperception, eine blösse Wahrnehmung, this, I grant, is senseless. For it is evident, that the assimilation in question is to be carried on by faith. But if faith be an energy, a positive act, and that too an act of intensest power, why should it necessarily differ in toto genere from any other act, ex. gr. from that of the animal life in the stomach? It will be found easier to laugh or stare at the question than to prove its irrationability. Enough for the present. I had been told that Dr. Leach[185] was a Lawrencian, a materialist, and I know not what. I met him at Mr. Abernethy's, and with sincere delight I found him the very contrary in every respect. Except yourself, I have never met so enlarged or so bold a love of truth in an English physiologist. The few minutes of conversation that I had the power of enjoying have left a strong wish in my mind to see more of him.

Give my kind love to Mrs. Green. Mr. and Mrs. Gillman are anxious to see you. I assure you they were very much affected by the account of your health. Young Allsop behaves more like a dutiful and anxious son than an acquaintance. He came up yester-night at ten o'clock, and left the house at eight this morning, in order to urge me to go to some sea-bathing place, if it was thought at all advisable.

Derwent goes on in every respect to my satisfaction and comfort.

Again and again, God bless you and your sincerely affectionate friend,

S. T. Coleridge.

CCXXIX. TO CHARLES AUGUSTUS TULK.

February 12, 1821.

My dear Sir,—"They say, Coleridge! that you are a Swedenborgian!" "Would to God," I replied fervently, "that they were anything." I was writing a brief essay on the prospects of a country where it has become the mind of the nation to appreciate the evil of public acts and measures by their next consequences or immediate occasions, while the principle violated, or that a principle is thereby violated, is either wholly dropped out of the consideration, or is introduced but as a garnish or ornamental commonplace in the peroration of a speech! The deep interest was present to my thoughts of that distinction between the Reason, as the source of principles, the true celestial influx and porta Dei in hominem æternum, and the Understanding; with the clearness of the proof, by which this distinction is evinced, viz. that vital or zoo-organic power, instinct, and understanding fall all three under the same definition in genere, and the very additions by which the definition is applied from the first to the second, and from the second to the third, are themselves expressive of degrees only, and in degree only deniable of the preceding. (Ex. gr. 1. Reflect on the selective power exercised by the stomach of the caterpillar on the undigested miscellany of food, and, 2, the same power exercised by the caterpillar on the outward plants, and you will see the order of the conceptions.) 1. Vital Power = the power by which means are adapted to proximate ends. 2. Instinct = the power which adapts means to proximate ends. 3. Understanding = the power which adapts means to proximate ends according to varying circumstances. May I not safely challenge any man to peruse Huber's "Treatise on Ants," and yet deny their claim to be included in the last definition. But try to apply the same definition, with any extension of degree, to the reason, the absurdity will flash upon the conviction. First, in reason there is and can be no degree. Deus introit aut non introit. Secondly, in reason there are no means nor ends, reason itself being one with the ultimate end, of which it is the manifestation. Thirdly, reason has no concern with things (that is, the impermanent flux of particulars), but with the permanent Relations; and is to be defined even in its lowest or theoretical attribute, as the power which enables man to draw necessary and universal conclusions from particular facts or forms, ex. gr. from any three-cornered thing, that the two sides of a triangle are and must be greater than the third. From the understanding to the reason, there is no continuous ascent possible; it is a metabasis εἰς ἄλλο γένος even as from the air to the light. The true essential peculiarity of the human understanding consists in its capability of being irradiated by the reason, in its recipiency; and even this is given to it by the presence of a higher power than itself. What then must be the fate of a nation that substitutes Locke for logic, and Paley for morality, and one or the other for polity and theology, according to the predominance of Whig or Tory predilection. Slavery, or a commotion is at hand! But if the gentry and clerisy (including all the learned and educated) do this, then the nation does it, or a commotion is at hand. Acephalum enim, aurâ quamvis et calore vitali potiatur, morientem rectius dicimus, quam quod vivit. With these thoughts was I occupied when I received your very kind and most acceptable present, and the results I must defer to the next post. With best regards to Mrs. Tulk,

Believe me, in the brief interval, your obliged and grateful

S. T. Coleridge.

C. A. Tulk, Esq., M. P., Regency Park.

CHAPTER XIV
THE PHILOSOPHER AND DIVINE
1822-1832

CCXXX. TO JOHN MURRAY.

Highgate, January 18, 1822.

Dear Sir,—If not with the works, you are doubtless familiar with the name of that "wonderful man" (for such, says Doddridge, I must deliberately call him), Archbishop Leighton. It would not be easy to point out another name, which the eminent of all parties, Catholic and Protestant, Episcopal and Presbyterian, Whigs and Tories, have been so unanimous in extolling. "There is a spirit in Archbishop Leighton I never met with in any human writings; nor can I read many lines in them without impressions which I could wish always to retain," observes a dignitary of our Establishment and F. R. S. eminent in his day both as a philosopher and a divine. In fact, it would make no small addition to the size of the volume, if, as was the fashion in editing the classics, we should collect the eulogies on his writings passed by bishops only and church divines, from Burnet to Porteus. That this confluence of favourable opinions is not without good cause, my own experience convinces me. For at a time when I had read but a small portion of the Archbishop's principal work, when I was altogether ignorant of its celebrity, much more of the peculiar character attributed to his writings (that of making and leaving a deep impression on readers of all classes), I remember saying to Mr. Southey[186] "that in the Apostolic Epistles I heard the last hour of Inspiration striking, and in Arch. Leighton's commentary the lingering vibration of the sound." Perspicuous, I had almost said transparent, his style is elegant by the mere compulsion of the thoughts and feelings, and in despite, as it were, of the writer's wish to the contrary. Profound as his conceptions often are, and numerous as the passages are, where the most athletic thinker will find himself tracing a rich vein from the surface downward, and leave off with an unknown depth for to-morrow's delving—yet there is this quality peculiar to Leighton, unless we add Shakespeare—that there is always a scum on the very surface which the simplest may understand, if they have head and heart to understand anything. The same or nearly the same excellence characterizes his eloquence. Leighton had by nature a quick and pregnant fancy, and the august objects of his habitual contemplation, and their remoteness from the outward senses, his constant endeavour to see or to bring all things under some point of unity, but, above all, the rare and vital union of head and heart, of light and love, in his own character,—all these working conjointly could not fail to form and nourish in him the higher power, and more akin to reason, the power, I mean, of imagination. And yet in his freest and most figurative passages there is a subduedness, a self-checking timidity in his colouring, a sobering silver-grey tone over all; and an experienced eye may easily see where and in how many instances Leighton has substituted neutral tints for a strong light or a bold relief—by this sacrifice, however, of particular effects, giving an increased permanence to the impression of the whole, and wonderfully facilitating its soft and quiet illapse into the very recesses of our convictions. Leighton's happiest ornaments of style are made to appear as efforts on the part of the author to express himself less ornamentally, more plainly.

Since the late alarm respecting Church Calvinism and Calvinistic Methodism (a cry of Fire! Fire! in consequence of a red glare on one or two of the windows, from a bonfire of straw and stubble in the church-yard, while the dry rot of virtual Socinianism is snugly at work in the beams and joists of the venerable edifice) I have heard of certain gentle doubts and questions as to the Archbishop's perfect orthodoxy—some small speck in the diamond which had escaped the quick eye of all former theological jewellers from Bishop Burnet to the outrageously anti-Methodistic Warburton. But on what grounds I cannot even conjecture, unless it be, that the Christianity which Leighton teaches contains the doctrines peculiar to the Gospel as well as the truths common to it with the (so-called) light of nature or natural religion, that he dissuades students and the generality of Christians from all attempts at explaining the mysteries of faith by notional and metaphysical speculations, and rather by a heavenly life and temper to obtain a closer view of these truths, the full light and knowledge of which it is in Heaven only that we shall possess. He further advises them in speaking of these truths to proper scripture language; but since something more than this had been made necessary by the restless spirit of dispute, to take this "something more" in the sound precise terms of the Liturgy and Articles of the Established Church. Enthusiasm? Fanaticism? Had I to recommend an antidote, I declare on my conscience that above all others it should be Leighton. And as to Calvinism, L.'s exposition of the scriptural sense of election ought to have prevented the very [suspicion of its presence]. You will long ago, I fear, have [been asking yourself], To what does all this tend? Briefly then, I feel strongly persuaded, perhaps because I strongly wish it, that the Beauties of Archbishop Leighton, selected and methodized, with a (better) Life of the Author, that is, a biographical and critical introduction as Preface, and Notes, would make not only a useful but an interesting Pocket Volume. "Beauties" in general are objectionable works—injurious to the original author, as disorganizing his productions, pulling to pieces the well-wrought crown of his glory to pick out the shining stones, and injurious to the reader, by indulging the taste for unconnected, and for that reason unretained single thoughts, till it fares with him as with the old gentleman at Edinburgh, who eat six kittywakes by way of whetting his appetite— "whereas" (said he) "it proved quite the contrary: I never sat down to a dinner with so little." But Leighton's principal work, that which fills two volumes and a half of the four, being a commentary on St. Peter's Epistles, verse by verse, and varying, of course, in subject, etc., with almost every paragraph, the volume, I propose, would not only bring together his finest passages, but these being afterwards arranged on a principle wholly independent of the accidental place of each in the original volumes, and guided by their relative bearings, it would give a connection or at least a propriety of sequency, that was before of necessity wanting. It may be worth noticing, that the editions, both the one in three, and the other in four volumes, are most grievously misprinted and otherwise disfigured. Should you be disposed to think this worthy your attention, I would even send you the proof transcribed, sheet by sheet, as it should be printed, though doubtless by sacrificing one copy of Leighton's works, it might be effected by references to volume, page, and line, I having first carefully corrected the copy. Or, should you think another more likely to execute the plan better, or that another name would better promote its sale, I should by no means resent the preference, nor feel any mortification for which, the having occasioned the existence of such a work, tastefully selected and judiciously arranged, would not be sufficient compensation for,

Dear sir, your obliged
S. T. Coleridge.

CCXXXI. TO JAMES GILLMAN.

October 28, 1822.

Dear Friend,—Words, I know, are not wanted between you and me. But there are occasions so awful, there may be instances and manifestations so affecting, and drawing up with them so long a train from behind, so many folds of recollection, as they come onward on one's mind, that it seems but a mere act of justice to one's self, a debt we owe to the dignity of our moral nature, to give them some record—a relief, which the spirit of man asks and demands to contemplate in some outward symbol of what it is inwardly solemnizing. I am still too much under the cloud of past misgivings;[187] too much of the stun and stupor from the recent peals and thunder-crash still remains to permit me to anticipate other than by wishes and prayers what the effect of your unweariable kindness may be on poor Hartley's mind and conduct. I pray fervently, and I feel a cheerful trust that I do not pray in vain, that on my own mind and spring of action it will be proved not to have been wasted. I do inwardly believe that I shall yet do something to thank you, my dear Gillman, in the way in which you would wish to be thanked, by doing myself honour.

Mrs. Gillman has been determined by your letter, and the heavenly weather, and moral certainty of the continuance of bathing-weather at least, to accept her sister's offer of coming into Ramsgate and to take a house, for a fortnight certain, at a guinea a week, in the buildings next to Wellington Crescent, and having a certain modicum and segment of sea-peep. You remember the house (the end one) with a balcony at the window, almost in a line with the Duke of W. ... in wood, lignum vitæ, like as life. I had thought of keeping my present bedroom at 10s. 6d. a week, but on consulting Mrs. Rogers, she did not think that this would satisfy the etiquette of the world, though the two houses are on different cliffs; and I felt so confident of the effect of the bathing and Ramsgate transparent water, the sands, the pier, etc., that as there was no alternative but of giving up the bathing (for Mrs. G. would not stay by herself, partly, if not chiefly, because she feared I might add more to your anxiety than your comfort in your bachelor state and with only Bessy of Beccles) or having Jane, I voted for the latter, and will do my very best to keep her in good humour and good spirits.

Dear Friend, and Brother of my Soul, God only knows how truly and in the depth you are loved and prized by your affectionate friend,

S. T. Coleridge.

CCXXXII. TO MISS BRENT.[188]

July 7, 1823.

My dear Charlotte,—I have been many times in town within the last three or four weeks; but with one exception, when I was driven in and back by Mr. Gillman to hear the present idol of the world of fashion, the Revd. Mr. Irving, the super-Ciceronian, ultra-Demosthenic pulpiteer of the Scotch Chapel in Cross Street, Hatton Garden, I have been always at the West End of the town, and mostly dancing attendance on a proud bookseller, and I fear to little purpose—weary enough of my existence, God knows! and yet not a tittle the more disposed to better it at the price of apostacy or suppression of the truth. If I could but once get off the two works, on which I rely for the proof that I have not lived in vain, and had those off my mind, I could then maintain myself well enough by writing for the purpose of what I got by it; but it is an anguish I cannot look in the face, to abandon just as it is completed the work of such intense and long-continued labour; and if I cannot make an agreement with Murray, I must try Colbourn, and if with neither, owing to the loud calumny of the "Edinburgh," and the silent but more injurious detraction of the "Quarterly Review," I must try to get them published by subscription. But of this when we meet. I write at present and to you as the less busy sister, to beg you will be so good as to send me the volume of Southey's "Brazil," which I am now in particular want of, by the Highgate Stage that sets off just before Middle Row. "Mr. Coleridge, or J. Gillman, Esq. (either will do), Highgate."

My kind love to Mary. I have little doubt that I shall see you in the course of next week.

Do you think of taking rooms out of the smoke during this summer for any time?

God bless you, my dear Charlotte, and your affectionate

S. T. Coleridge.

CCXXXIII. TO THE REV. EDWARD COLERIDGE.[189]

Highgate, July 23, 1823.

My dear Edward,—From Carlisle to Keswick there are several routes possible, and neither of these without some attraction. The choice, however, lies between two; which to prefer, I find it hard to decide, and if, as on the whole I am disposed to do, I advise the former, it is not from thinking the other of inferior interest. On the contrary, if your laking were comprised between Carlisle and Keswick, I should not hesitate to recommend the latter in preference, but because the first will bring you soonest to Keswick, where Mr. Southey still is, having, as your cousin Sara writes me, deferred his journey to town, on account of his book on "The Church," which has outgrown its intended dimensions; and because the sort of "scenery" (to use that slang word best confined to the creeking Daubenies of the Theatre) on the latter route, is what you will have abundant opportunities of seeing with the one leg of your compass fixed at Keswick.

First then, you may go from Carlisle to Rose Castle, and spend an hour in seeing that and its circumferency; and from thence to Caldbeck, its waterfalls and faery caldrons, with the Pulpit and Clerk's Desk Rocks, over which the Cata-, or rather Kitten-ract, flings itself, and the cavern to the right of the fall, as you front it; and from Caldbeck to the foot of Bassenthwaite, when you are in the vale of Keswick and not many miles from Greta Hall. The second route is from Carlisle to Penrith (a road of little or no interest), but from Carlisle you would go to Lowther (Earl of Lonsdale's seat and magnificent grounds), the village of Lowther, Hawes Water, and from Hawes Water you might pass over the mountains into Ulleswater, and when there, you might go round the head of the lake (that is, Patterdale), and, if on foot and strong enough and the weather is fine, pass over Helvellyn, and so get into the high road between Grasmere and Keswick, or, passing lower down on the lake, cross over by Graystock, or with a guide or manual instructions, over the fells so as to come out at or not far from Threlkeld, which is but three or four miles from Keswick. At least in good weather there is, I believe, a tolerably equitible (that is, horse or pony-tolerating) track. But at Patterdale you would receive the best direction. There is an inn at Patterdale where you might sleep, so as to make one day of it from Penrith to the Lake Head, viâ Lowther and Hawes Water; and thence to Keswick would take good part of a second. There is one consideration in favour of this plan, that from Carlisle to Penrith, or even to Lowther, you might go by the coach, and I question whether you could reach Greta

Hall by the Caldbeck Route in one day when at Keswick. When at Keswick, I would advise you to go to Wastdale through Borrowdale, and if you could return by Crummock and through the vale of Newlands, the inverted arch of which (on the A<u>B</u> (A B) of which I once saw the two legs of a rich rainbow so as to form with the arch a perfect circle) faces Greta Hall, you will have seen the very pith and marrow of the Lakes, especially as your route to Chester or Liverpool will take you that heavenly road through Thirlmere, Grasmere, Rydal (where you will, of course, pay your respects to Mr. Wordsworth), Ambleside, and the striking half of Windermere.

God bless you! Pray take care of yourself, were it only that you know how fearful and anxious your father and Fanny[190] are respecting your chest and lungs, in case of cold or over-exertion.

I have heard from Sara and from Mr. Watson (a friend of mine who has just come from the North) a very comfortable account of Hartley.

Believe me, dear Edward, with every kind wish, your affectionate uncle and sincere friend,

[S. T. Coleridge.]

P. S. Your query respecting the poem I can only answer by a Nescio. Irving (the Scotch preacher, so blackguarded in the "John Bull" of last Sunday), certainly the greatest orator I ever heard (N. B. I make and mean the same distinction between oratory and eloquence as between the mouth + the windpipe and the brain + heart), is, however, a man of great simplicity, of overflowing affections, and enthusiastically in earnest; and I have reason to believe, deeply regrets his conjunction of Southey with Byron, as far as the men (and not the poems) are in question.

CCXXXIV. TO J. H. GREEN.

Grove, Highgate, February 15, 1824.

I mentioned to you, I believe, Basil Montagu's kind endeavour to have an associateship of the Royal Society of Literature (a yearly £100 versus a yearly essay) conferred on me. I knew nothing of the particulars till this morning, or rather till within this hour, when I received a list of names (electors) from Mr. Montagu, with advice to write to such and such and such—while he, and he, and he had promised "for us"—in short, a regular canvass, or rather sackcloth with the ashes on it pulled out of the dust holes, moistened with cabbage-water, and other culinary excretions of the same kidney. Of course, I jibbed and with proper (if not equa; yet) mulanimity returned for answer—that what a man's friends did sub rosâ, and what one friend might say to another in favour of an individual, was one thing—what a man did in his own name and person was another—and that I would not, could not, solicit a single vote. I should think it an affrontive interference with a decision, in which there ought to be neither ground or motive, but the elector's own judgement, and conscience, and all for what? It is hard if, in the same time as I could produce an essay of the sort required, I could not get the same sum by compiling a school-book.

However, I fear, that having allowed my name, at Montagu's instance, to be proposed, which it was by a Mr. Jerdan (N. B. Neither the one sub cubili, nor that in Palestine; but the

Jerdan of Michael's Grove, Brompton, No. 1), I cannot now withdraw my name without appearing to trifle with my friends, and without hurting Montagu—so I must submit to the probability of being black-balled as the penalty of having given my assent before I had ascertained the conditions. So I have decided to let the thing take its own course. But as Montagu wishes to have Mr. Chantrey's vote for us, if you see and feel no objection (an objectiuncula will be quite sufficient), you will perhaps write him a line to state the circumstances. It comes on on Thursday next.

I look forward with a feel of regeneration to the Sundays.

My best and most affectionate respects to Mrs. J. Green, and to your dear and excellent mother if she be with you.

And till we meet, may God bless you and your obliged and sincere friend,

S. T. Coleridge.

CCXXXV. TO THE SAME.

Ædes Nemorosæ, apud Portm Altam,
May 19, 1824.

Mr. S. T. Coleridge, F. R. S. L., R. A., H. M., P. S. B., etc., etc., has the honour of avowing the high gratification he will receive should any answer from him be thought "to oblige Lincoln's Inn Fields." When he reflects indeed on their many and cogent claims on his admiration and gratitude, what a Fund of Literature they contain, what a Royal Society, what Royal Associates—not to speak of those as yet in the egg of futurity, the unhatched Decemvirate and Spes Altera Phœbi! What a royal College, where philosophy and eloquence unite to display their fresh and vernal green! what a conjunction of the Fine Arts with the Sciences, Law and Physique, Glossurgery and Chirurgery! when he remembers that if the Titanic Roc should take up the Great Pyramid in his beak, and drop the same with due skill, the L. I. F. would fit as cup to ball, bone to bone; though if S. T. C. might dare advise so great and rare a bird, the precious transport should be let fall point downwards, and thus prevent the adulteration of their intellectual splendours with "the light of common day," while a duplicate of the Elysium below might be reared on its ample base in mid air— (ah! if a duplicate of No. 22 could be found)!—when S. T. C. ponders on these proud merits, what is there he would not do to "oblige Lincoln's Inn Fields"? In vain does Gillman talk of a stop being put thereto! Between oblige and Lincoln's Inn Fields continuity alone can intervene for the heart's eye of their obliged and counter-obliging

S. T. Coleridge,

who, with his friends Mr. and Mrs. G., will, etc., on June 3rd.

J. H. Green, Esq., 22, Lincoln's Inn Fields.

CCXXXVI. TO JAMES GILLMAN.

Ramsgate, November 2, 1824.

My dear Friend,—That so much longer an interval has passed between this and my last letter you will not, I am sure, attribute to any correspondent interval of oblivion. I do not, indeed, think that any two hours of any one day, taken at sixteen, have elapsed in which you, past or future, or myself in connection with you, were not for a longer or shorter space my uppermost thought. But the two days following James's safe arrival by the coach I was so depressively unwell, so unremittingly restless, etc., and so exhausted by a teasing cough, and by two of these bad nights that make me moan out, "O for a sleep for sleep itself to rest in!" that I was quite disqualified for writing. And since then, I have been waiting for the Murrays to take a parcel with them, who were to have gone on Monday morning. But again not hearing from them, and remembering your injunction not to mind postage, I have resolved that no more time shall pass on and should have written to-day, even though Mrs. Gillman had not been dreaming about you last night, and about some letter, etc. Upon my seriousness, I do declare that I cannot make out certain dream-devils or damned souls that play pranks with me, whenever by the operation of a cathartic pill or from the want of one, a ci-devant dinner in its metempsychosis is struggling in the lower intestines. I cannot comprehend how any thoughts, the offspring or product of my own reflection, conscience, or fancy, could be translated into such images, and agents and actions, and am half-tempted (N. B. between sleeping and waking) to regard with some favour Swedenborg's assertion that certain foul spirits of the lowest order are attracted by the precious ex-viands, whose conversation the soul half appropriates to itself, and which they contrive to whisper into the sensorium. The Honourable Emanuel has repeatedly caught them in the fact, in that part of the spiritual world corresponding to the guts in the world of bodies, and driven them away. I do not pass this Gospel; but upon my honour it is no bad apocrypha. I am at present in my best sort and state of health, bathed yesterday, and again this morning in spite of the rain, and in so deep a bath, that having thrown myself forward from the first step of the machine ladder, and only taken two strokes after my re-immersion, I had at least ten strokes to take before I got into my depth again, so that it is no false alarm when those who cannot swim are warned that a person may be drowned a very few yards from the machine. I returned to fetch out our ladies to see the huge lengthy Columbus, with the two steam vessels,[191] before and behind, the former to tow, and the latter to, God knows what. By aid of a good glass, we saw it "quite stink," as the poor woman said, the people on board, etc. It is 310 feet long, and 50 wide, and looks exactly like a Brobdingnag punt, and on our return we had (from Mrs. Jones) the "Morning Herald," with Fauntleroy's trial, which (if he be not a treble-damned liar) completely bears out my assertion that nothing short of a miracle could acquit the partners of virtual accompliceship; this on my old principle, that the absence of what ought to have been present is all but equivalent to the presence of what ought to have been absent. Qui non prohibet quod prohibere potest et debet, facit.

Sir Alexander Johnston[192] has payed me great attention. There is a Lady Johnston not unlike Miss Sara Hutchinson in face and mouth, only that she is taller. Sir A. himself is a fine gentlemanly man, young-looking for his age, and with exception of one not easily describable motion of his head that makes him look as if he had been accustomed to have a pen behind his ear, a sort of "Torney's" clerk look, he might remind you of J. Hookham Frere. He is a sensible well-informed man, specious in no bad sense of the word, but (I guess) not much depth. In all probability, you will see him. We have talked a good deal together about you and me, and me and you, in consequence of occasion given. Sir A. is one of the leading men in our Royal Society of Literature, and beyond doubt, a man of influence in town. I am apt to forget superfluities, but a voice from above asks, "if I have said that we begin to be anxious to hear from you." But probably before you can sit down to answer this, you will have received another, and, I flatter myself, more amusing, at least pleasure-giving Scripture from me. (N. B. "Coleridge's Scriptures"—a new title.)

[No signature.]

CCXXXVII. TO THE REV. H. F. CARY.

Highgate, Monday, December 14, 1824.

My dear Friend,—The gentleman, Mr. Gabriel Rossetti,[193] whose letter to you I enclose, is a friend of my friend, Mr. J. H. Frere, with whom he lived in habits of intimacy at Malta and Naples. He seems to me what from Mr. Frere's high opinion of him I should have confidently anticipated, a gentleman, a scholar, and a man of talents. The nature of his request you will learn from the letter, namely, a perusal of his Manuscript on the spirit of Dante and the mechanism and interpretation of the "Divina Commedia," of which he believes himself to have the filum Ariadneum in his hand, and a frank opinion of the merits of his labours. My dear friend! I know by experience what is asked in this twofold request, and that the weight increases in proportion to the kindness and sensibility and the shrinking from the infliction of pain of the person on whom it is enjoined. The name of Mr. John Hookham Frere would alone have sufficed to make me undertake this office, had the request been directed to myself. It would have been my duty. But I would not, knowing your temper and habits and avocations, have sought to engage you, or even have put you to the discomfort of excusing yourself had I not been strongly impressed by Mr. Rossetti's manners and conversation with the belief that the interests of literature are concerned, and that Mr. Rossetti has a claim on all the services which the sons of the Muses, and more particularly the cultivators of ancient Italian Literature, and most particularly Dante's "English Duplicate and Re-incarnation" can render him. If your health and other duties allow your accession to this request (for the recommendation of the work to the booksellers is quite a secondary consideration, of minor importance in Mr. Rossetti's estimation, and I have, besides, explained to him how very limited our influence is), you will be so good as to let me hear from you, and where and when Mr. Rossetti might wait on you. He will be happy to attend you at Chiswick. He understands English, and, he speaking Italian and I our own language, we had no difficulty in keeping up an animated conversation.

Make mine and all our cordial remembrances to Mrs. Cary, and believe me, dear friend, with perfect esteem and most affectionate regard, yours,

S. T. Coleridge.

P. S. Both Mrs. G. and myself have returned much benefited by our sea-sojourn. Mr. Rossetti has, I find, an additional merit in good men's thoughts. He is a poet who has been driven into exile for the high morale of his writings. For even general sentiments breathing the spirit of nobler times are treasons in the present Neapolitan and Holy Alliance Codes! Wretches!! I dare even pray against them, even with Davidian bitterness. Do not forget to let me have an answer to this, if possible, by next day's post.

CCXXXVIII. TO WILLIAM WORDSWORTH.

Monday Night, ? 1824 ? 1829.

Dear Wordsworth,—Three whole days the going through the first book cost me, though only to find fault. But I cannot find fault, in pen and ink, without thinking over and over again, and without some sort of an attempt to suggest the alteration; and, in so doing, how soon an hour is gone! so many half seconds up to half minutes are lost in leaning back in one's chair, and looking up, in the bodily act of contracting the muscles of the brow and forehead, and unconsciously attending to the sensation. Had I the MS. with me for five or six months, so as to amuse myself off and on, without any solicitude as to a given day, and, could I be persuaded that if as well done as the nature of the thing (viz., a translation of Virgil,[194] in English) renders possible, it would not raise but simply sustain your well-merited fame for pure diction, where what is not idiom is never other than logically correct, I doubt not that the irregularities could be removed. But I am haunted by the apprehension that I am not feeling or thinking in the same spirit with you, at one time, and at another too much in the spirit of your writings. Since Milton, I know of no poet with so many felicities and unforgettable lines and stanzas as you. And to read, therefore, page after page without a single brilliant note, depresses me, and I grow peevish with you for having wasted your time on a work so much below you, that you cannot stoop and take. Finally, my conviction is, that you undertake an impossibility, and that there is no medium between a prose version and one on the avowed principle of compensation in the widest sense, that is, manner, genius, total effect. I confine myself to Virgil when I say this.

I must now set to work with all my powers and thoughts to my Leighton,[195] and then to my logic, and then to my opus maximum! if indeed it shall please God to spare me so long, which I have had too many warnings of late (more than my nearest friends know of) not to doubt. My kind love to Dorothy.

S. T. Coleridge.

CCXXXIX. TO JOHN TAYLOR COLERIDGE.

Grove, Highgate, Friday, April 8, 1825.

My dear Nephew,—I need not tell you that no attention in my power to offer shall be wanting to Dr. Reich. As a foreigner and a man of letters he might claim this in his own right; and that he came from you would have ensured it, even though he had been a Frenchman. But that he is a German, and that you think him a worthy and deserving man, and that his lot, like my own, has been cast on the bleak north side of the mountain, make me reflect with pain on the little influence I possess, and the all but zero of my direct means, to serve or to assist him. The prejudices excited against me by Jeffrey, combining with the mistaken notion of my German Metaphysics to which (I am told) some passages in some biographical gossip book about Lord Byron[196] have given fresh currency, have rendered my authority with the Trade worse than nothing. Of the three schemes of philosophy, Kant's, Fichte's, and Schelling's (as diverse each from the other as those of Aristotle, Zeno, and Plotinus, though all crushed together under the name Kantean Philosophy in the English talk) I should find it difficult to select the one from which I differed the most, though perfectly easy to determine which of the three men I hold in highest honour. And Immanuel Kant I assuredly do value most highly; not, however, as a metaphysician, but as a logician who has completed and systematised what Lord Bacon had boldly designed and loosely sketched out in the Miscellany of Aphorisms, his Novum Organum. In Kant's "Critique of the Pure Reason" there is more than one fundamental error; but the main fault lies in the title-page, which to the manifold advantage of the work might be exchanged for "An Inquisition respecting the Constitution and Limits of the Human Understanding." I can not only honestly assert, but I can satisfactorily prove by reference to writings (Letters, Marginal Notes, and those in books that have never been in my possession since I first left England for Hamburgh, etc.) that all the elements, the differentials, as the algebraists say, of my present opinions existed for me before I had even seen a book of German Metaphysics, later than Wolf and Leibnitz, or could have read it, if I had. But what will this avail? A High German Transcendentalist I must be content to remain, and a young American painter, Leslie (pupil and friend of a very dear friend of mine, Allston), to whom I have been in the habit for ten years and more of shewing as cordial regards as I could to a near relation, has, I find, introduced a portrait of me in a picture from Sir W. Scott's "Antiquary," as Dr. Duster Swivil, or whatever his name is.[197] Still, however, I will make any attempt to serve Dr. Reich, which he may point out and which, I am not sure, would dis-serve him! I do not, of course, know what command he has over the English language. If he wrote it fluently, I should think that it would answer to any one of our great publishers to engage him in the translation of the best and cheapest Natural History in existence, viz., Okens, in three thick octavo volumes, containing the inorganic world, and the animals from the Πρωτόζωα and animalcula of Infusions, to man. The Botany was not published two years ago. Whether it is now I do not know. There is one thin quarto of plates. It is by far the most entertaining as well as instructive book of the kind I ever saw; and with a few notes and the omission (or castigation) of one or two of Oken's adventurous whimsies, would be a valuable addition to our English literature. So much for this.

I will not disguise from you, my dearest nephew, that the first certain information of your having taken the "Quarterly"[198] gave me a pain, which it required all my confidence in the soundness of your judgement to counteract. I had long before by conversation with experienced barristers got rid of all apprehension of its being likely to injure you professionally. My fears were directed to the invidiousness of the situation, it being the notion of publishers that without satire and sarcasm no review can obtain or keep up a sale. Perhaps pride had some concern in it. For myself I have none, probably because I had time out of mind given it up as a lost cause, given myself over, I mean, a predestined author, though without a drop of true author blood in my veins. But a pride in and for the name of my father's house I have, and those with whom I live know that it is never more than a dog-sleep, and apt to start up on the slight alarms. Now, though very sillily, I felt pain at the notion of any comparisons being drawn between you (to whom with your sister my heart pulls the strongest) and Mr. Gifford, even though they should be [to] your advantage; and still more, the thought that ... Murray should be or hold himself entitled to have and express an opinion on the subject. The insolence of one of his proposals to me, viz., that he would publish an edition of my Poems, on the condition that a gentleman in his confidence (Mr. Milman![199] I understand) was to select, and make such omissions and corrections as should be thought advisable—this, which offered to myself excited only a smile in which there was nothing sardonic, might very possibly have rendered me sorer and more sensitive when I boded even an infinitesimal ejusdem farinæ in connection with you.

But henceforward I shall look at the thing in a sunnier mood. Mr. Frere is strongly impressed with the importance and even dignity of the trust, and on the power you have of gradually giving a steadier and manlier tone to the feelings and principles of the higher classes. But I hope very soon to converse with you on this subject, as soon as I have finished my Essay for the Literary Society, (in which I flatter myself I have thrown some light on the passages in Herodotus respecting the derivation of the Greek Mythology from Egypt, and in what respect that paragraph respecting Homer and Hesiod is to be understood), and have, likewise, got my "Aids to Reflection" out of the Press. But I have more to do for the necessities of the day, and which are Nos non nobis, than I can well manage so as to go on with my own works, though I work from morning to night, as far as my health admits and the loss of my friendly amanuensis. For the slowness with which I get on with the pen in my own hand contrasts most strangely with the rapidity with which I dictate. Your kind letter of invitation did not reach me, but there was one which I ought to have answered long ago, which came while I was at Ramsgate. We have had a continued succession of illness in our family here, at one time six persons confined to their beds. I have been sadly afraid that we should lose Mrs. Gillman, who would be a loss indeed to the whole neighbourhood, young and old. But she seems, thank God! to recover strength, though slowly. As I hope to write again in a few days with my book, I shall now desire my cordial regards to Mrs. J. Coleridge, and with my affectionate love to the little ones.

With the warmest interest of affection and esteem, I am, my dear John, your sincere friend,

S. T. Coleridge.

J. T. Coleridge, Esq., 65, Torrington Square.

CCXL. TO THE REV. EDWARD COLERIDGE.

May 19, 1825.

My very dear Nephew,—You have left me under a painful and yet genial feeling of regret, that my lot in life has hitherto so much estranged me from the children of the sons of my father, that venerable countenance and name which form my earliest recollections and make them religious. It is not in my power to express adequately so as to convey it to others what a revolution has taken place in my mind since I have seen your sister, and John, and Henry, and lastly yourself. Yet revolution is not the word I want. It is rather the sudden evolution of a seed that had sunk too deep for the warmth and exciting air to reach, but which a casual spade had turned up and brought close to the surface, and I now know the meaning as well as feel the truth of the Scottish proverb, Blood is thicker than water.

My book will be out on Monday next, and Mr. Hessey hopes that he shall be able to have a copy ready for me by to-morrow afternoon, so that I may present it to the Bishop of London, whom (at his own request Lady B. tells me) with his angel-faced wife and Miss Howley[200] I am to meet at Sir George's to-morrow at six o'clock. There are many on whose sincerity and goodness of heart I can rely. There are several in whose judgement and knowledge of the world I have greater trust than in my own. And among these few John Coleridge ranks foremost. It was, therefore, an indescribable comfort to me to hear from him, that the first draft of my "Aids to Reflection," that is, all he had yet seen, had delighted him beyond measure. I can with severest truth declare that half a score flaming panegyrical reviews in as many works of periodical criticism would not have given me half the pleasure, nor one quarter the satisfaction.

I dine D. V. on Saturday next in Torrington Square, when doubtless we shall drink your health with appropriate adjuncts. Yesterday I had to inflict an hour and twenty-five minutes' essay full of Greek and superannuated Metaphysics on the ears of the Royal Society of Literature, the subject being the Prometheus of Æschylus deciphered in proof and as instance of the connection of the Greek Drama with the Mysteries.[201] "Douce take it" (as Charles Lamb says in his Superannuated Man) if I did not feel remorseful pity for my audience all the time. For, at the very best, it was a thing to be read, not to read. God bless you or I shall be too late for the post.

Your affectionate uncle,
S. T. Coleridge.

P. S. I went yesterday to the Exhibition, and hastily "thrid" the labyrinth of the dense huddle, for the sole purpose of seeing our Bishop's portrait.[202] My own by the same artist is very much better, though even in this the smile is exaggerated. But Fanny and your mother were in raptures with it while they too seemed very cold in their praise of William's.

CCXLI. TO DANIEL STUART.

Postmark, July 9, 1825.

My dear Sir,—The bad weather had so far damped my expectations, that, though I regretted, I did not feel any disappointment at your not coming. And yet I hope you will remember our Highgate Thursday conversation evenings on your return to town; because, if you come once, I flatter myself, you will afterwards be no unfrequent visitor.

At least, I have never been at any of the town conversazioni, literary, or artistical, in which the conversation has been more miscellaneous without degenerating into pinches, a pinch of this, and a pinch of that, without the least connection between the subjects, and with as little interest. You will like Irving as a companion and a converser even more than you admire him as a preacher. He has a vigorous and (what is always pleasant) a growing mind, and his character is manly throughout. There is one thing, too, that I cannot help considering as a recommendation to our evenings, that, in addition to a few ladies and pretty lasses, we have seldom more than five or six in company, and these generally of as many professions or pursuits. A few weeks ago we had present, two painters, two poets, one divine, an eminent chemist and naturalist, a major, a naval captain and voyager, a physician, a colonial chief justice, a barrister, and a baronet; and this was the most numerous meeting we ever had.

It would more than gratify me to know from you, what the impressions are which my "Aids to Reflection" make on your judgment. The conviction respecting the character of the times expressed in the comment on Aph. vi., page 147, contains the aim and object of the whole book. I venture to direct your notice particularly to the note, page 204 to 207, to the note to page 218, and to the sentences respecting common sense in the last twelve lines of page 252, and the conclusion, page 377.

Lady Beaumont writes me that the Bishop of London has expressed a most favourable opinion of the book; and Blanco White was sufficiently struck with it, as immediately to purchase all my works that are in print, and has procured from Sir George Beaumont an introduction to me. It is well I should have some one to speak for it, for I am unluckily ill off ... and you will easily see what a chance a poor book of mine has in these days.

Such has been the influence of the "Edinburgh Review" that in all Edinburgh not a single copy of Wordsworth's works or of any part of them could be procured a few months ago. The only copy Irving saw in Scotland belonged to a poor weaver at Paisley, who prized them next to his Bible, and had all the Lyrical Ballads by heart—a fact which would cut Jeffrey's conscience to the bone, if he had any. I give you my honour that Jeffrey himself told me that he was himself an enthusiastic admirer of Wordsworth's poetry, but it was necessary that a Review should have a character.

Forgive this egotism, and be pleased to remember me kindly and with my best respects to Mrs. Stuart, and with every cordial wish and prayer for you and yours, be assured that I am your obliged and affectionate friend,

S. T. Coleridge.

Friday, July 8, 1825.

CCXLII. TO JAMES GILLMAN.

[8 Plains of Waterloo, Ramsgate,]
October 10, 1825.

My dear Friend,—It is a flat'ning thought that the more we have seen, the less we have to say. In youth and early manhood the mind and nature are, as it were, two rival artists both potent magicians, and engaged, like the King's daughter and the rebel genii in the Arabian Nights' Entertainments, in sharp conflict of conjuration, each having for its object to turn the other into canvas to paint on, clay to mould, or cabinet to contain. For a while the mind seems to have the better in the contest, and makes of Nature what it likes, takes her lichens and weather-stains for types and printers' ink, and prints maps and facsimiles of Arabic and Sanscrit MSS. on her rocks; composes country dances on her moonshiny ripples, fandangos on her waves, and waltzes on her eddy-pools, transforms her summer gales into harps and harpers, lovers' sighs and sighing lovers, and her winter blasts into Pindaric Odes, Christabels, and Ancient Mariners set to music by Beethoven, and in the insolence of triumph conjures her clouds into whales and walruses with palanquins on their backs, and chases the dodging stars in a sky-hunt! But alas! alas! that Nature is a wary wily long-breathed old witch, tough-lived as a turtle and divisible as the polyp, repullulative in a thousand snips and cuttings, integra et in toto. She is sure to get the better of Lady Mind in the long run and to take her revenge too; transforms our to-day into a canvas dead-coloured to receive the dull, featureless portrait of yesterday: not alone turns the mimic mind, the ci-devant sculptress with all her kaleidoscopic freaks and symmetries! into clay, but leaves it such a clay to cast dumps or bullets in; and lastly (to end with that which suggested the beginning) she mocks the mind with its own metaphor, metamorphosing the memory into a lignum vitæ escritoire to keep unpaid bills and dun's letters in, with outlines that had never been filled up, MSS. that never went further than the title-pages, and proof sheets, and foul copies of Watchmen, Friends, Aids to Reflection, and other stationary wares that have kissed the publishers' shelf with all the tender intimacy of inosculation! Finis! and what is all this about? Why, verily, my dear friend! the thought forced itself on me, as I was beginning to put down the first sentence of this letter, how impossible it would have been fifteen or even ten years ago for me to have travelled and voyaged by land, river, and sea a hundred and twenty miles with fire and water blending their souls for my propulsion, as if I had been riding on a centaur with a sopha for a saddle, and yet to have nothing more to tell of it than that we had a very fine day and ran aside the steps in Ramsgate Pier at half-past four exactly, all having been well except poor Harriet, who during the middle third of the voyage fell into a reflecting melancholy.... She looked pathetic, but I cannot affirm that I observed anything sympathetic in the countenances of her fellow-passengers, which drew forth a sigh from me and a sage remark how many of our virtues originate in the fear of death, and that while we flatter ourselves that we are melting in Christian sensibility over the sorrows of our human brethren and sisteren, we are in fact, though perhaps unconsciously, moved at the prospect of our own end. For who ever sincerely pities seasickness, toothache, or a fit of the gout in a lusty good liver of fifty?

What have I to say? We have received the snuff, for which I thank your providential memory.... To Margate, and saw the caverns, as likewise smelt the same, called on Mr. Bailey, and got the Novum Organum. In my hurry, I scrambled up the Blackwood instead of a volume of Giovanni Battista Vico, which I left on the table in my room, and forgot my sponge and sponge-bag of oiled silk. But perhaps when I sit down to work, I may have to request something to be sent, which may come with them. I therefore defer it till then....

God bless you, my dear friend! You will soon hear again from

S. T. Coleridge.

CCXLIII. TO THE REV. EDWARD COLERIDGE.

December 9, 1825.

My dear Edward,—I write merely to tell you, that I have secured Charles Lamb and Mr. Irving to meet you, and wait only to learn the day for the endeavour to induce Mr. Blanco White to join us. Will you present Mr. and Mrs. Gillman's regards to your brothers Henry and John, and that they would be most happy if both or either would be induced to accompany you?

I have had a very interesting conversation with Irving this evening on the present condition of the Scottish Church, the spiritual life of which, yea, the very core he describes as in a state of ossification. The greater part of the Scottish clergy, he complains, have lost the unction of their own church without acquiring the erudition and accomplishments of ours. Their sermons are all dry theological arguing and disputing, lifeless, pulseless,—a rushlight in a fleshless skull.

My kindest love to your sister, and kisses, prayers, and blessings for the little one.

[S. T. Coleridge.]

Thursday midnight.

I almost despair of John's coming; but do persuade Henry if you can. I quite long to see him again.

CCXLIV. TO MRS. GILLMAN.

May 3, 1827.

My dear Friend,—I received and acknowledge your this morning's present both as plant and symbol, and with appropriate thanks and correspondent feeling. The rose is the pride of summer, the delight and the beauty of our gardens; the eglantine, the honeysuckle, and the jasmine, if not so bright or so ambrosial, are less transient, creep nearer to us, clothe our walls, twine over our porch, and haply peep in at our chamber window, with the crested wren or linnet within the tufts wishing good morning to us. Lastly the geranium passes the door, and in its hundred varieties imitating now this now that leaf, odour, blossom of the garden, still steadily retains its own staid character, its own sober and refreshing hue and fragrance. It deserves to be the inmate of the house, and with due attention and tenderness will live through the winter grave yet cheerful, as an old family friend, that makes up for the departure of gayer visitors, in the leafless season. But none of these are the myrtle![203] In none of these, nor in all collectively, will the myrtle find a substitute. All together and joining with them all the aroma, the spices, and the balsams of the hot-house, yet would they be a sad exchange for the myrtle! Oh, precious in its sweetness is the rich innocence of its snow-white blossoms! And dear are they in the remembrance; but these may pass with the season, and while the myrtle plant, our own myrtle plant remains unchanged, its blossoms are remembered the more to endear the faithful bearer; yea, they survive invisibly in every more than fragrant leaf. As the flashing strains of the nightingale to the yearning murmurs of the dove, so the myrtle to the rose! He who has once possessed and prized a genuine myrtle will rather remember it under the cypress tree than seek to forget it among the rose bushes of a paradise.

God bless you, my dearest friend, and be assured that if death do not suspend memory and consciousness, death itself will not deprive you of a faithful participator in all your hopes and fears, affections and solicitudes, in your unalterable

S. T. Coleridge.

CCXLV. TO THE REV. GEORGE MAY COLERIDGE.

Monday, January 14, 1828.

My dear Nephew,—An interview with your cousin Henry on Saturday and a note received from him last night had enabled me in some measure to prepare my mind for the awful and humanly afflicting contents of your letter, and I rose to the receiving of it from earnest suplication to "the Father of Mercies and God of all Comfort"—that He would be strong in the weakness of His faithful servant, and his effectual helper in the last conflict. My first impulse on reading your letter was to set off immediately, but on a re-perusal, I doubt whether I shall not better comply with your suggestion by waiting for your next. Assuredly, if God permit I will not forego the claim, which my heart and conscience justify me in making, to be one among the mourners who ever truly loved and honoured your father.

Allow me, my dear nephew, in the swelling grief of my heart to say, that if ever man morning and evening and in the watches of the night had earnestly intreated through his Lord and Mediator, that God would shew him his sins and their sinfulness, I, for the last ten years at least of my life, have done so! But, in vain, have I tried to recall any one moment since my quitting the University, or any one occasion, in which I have either thought, felt, spoken, or intentionally acted of or in relation to my brother, otherwise than as one who loved in him father and brother in one, and who independent of the fraternal relation and the remembrance of his manifold goodness and kindness to me from boyhood to early manhood should have chosen him above all I had known as the friend of my inmost soul. Never have man's feeling and character been more cruelly misrepresented than mine. Before God have I sinned, and I have not hidden my offences before him; but He too knows that the belief of my brother's alienation and the grief that I was a stranger in the house of my second father has been the secret wound that to this hour never closed or healed up. Yes, my dear nephew! I do grieve, and at this moment I have to struggle hard in order to keep my spirit in tranquillity, as one who has long since referred his cause to God, through the grief at my little communication with my family. Had it been otherwise, I might have been able to shew myself, my whole self, for evil and for good to my brother, and often have said to myself, "How fearful an attribute to sinful man is Omniscience!" and yet have I earnestly wished, oh, how many times! that my brother could have seen my inmost heart, with every thought and every frailty. But his reward is nigh: in the light and love of his Lord and Saviour he will soon be all light and love, and I too shall have his prayers before the throne. May the Almighty and the Spirit the Comforter dwell in your and your mother's spirit. I must conclude. Only, if I come and it should please God that your dear father shall be still awaiting his Redeemer's final call, I shall be perfectly satisfied in all things to be directed by you and your mother, who will judge best whether the knowledge of my arrival though without seeing him would or would not be a satisfaction, would or would not be a disturbance to him.

Your affectionate uncle,
S. T. Coleridge.

Grove, Highgate.
Rev. George May Coleridge,
Warden House, Ottery St. Mary, Devon.

CCXLVI. TO GEORGE DYER.[204]

June 6, 1828.

My dear long known, and long loved friend,—Be assured that neither Mr. Irving nor any other person, high or low, gentle or simple, stands higher in my esteem or bears a name endeared to me by more interesting recollections and associations than yourself; and if gentle man or gentle woman, taking too literally the partial portraiture of a friend, has a mind to see the old lion in his sealed cavern, no more potent "Open, Sesame, Open" will be found than an introduction from George Dyer, my elder brother under many titles— brother Blue, brother Grecian, brother Cantab, brother Poet, and last best form of fraternity, a man who has never in his long life, by tongue or pen, uttered what he did not believe to be the truth (from any motive) or concealed what he did conceive to be such from other motives than those of tenderness for the feelings of others, and a conscientious fear lest what was truly said might be falsely interpreted,—in all these points I dare claim brotherhood with my old friend (not omitting grey hairs, which are venerable), but in one point, the long toilsome life of inexhaustible, unsleeping benevolence and beneficence, that slept only when there was no form or semblance of sentient life to awaken it, George Dyer must stand alone! He may have a few second cousins, but no full brother.

Now, with regard to your friends, I shall be happy to see them on any day they may find to suit their or your convenience, from twelve (I am not ordinarily visible before, or if the outward man were forced to make his appearance, yet from sundry bodily infirmities, my soul would present herself with unwashed face) till four, that is, after Monday next,—we having at present a servant ill in bed, you must perforce be content with a sandwich lunch or a glass of wine.

But if you could make it suit you to take your tea, an early tea, at or before six o'clock, and spend the evening, a long evening, with us on Thursday next, Mr. and Mrs. Gillman will be most happy to see you and Mrs. Dyer, with your friends, and you will probably meet some old friend of yours. On Thursday evening, indeed, at any time, between half-past five and eleven, you may be sure of finding us at home, and with a very fair chance of Basil Montagu taking you and Mrs. Dyer back in his coach.

I have long owed you a letter, and should have long since honestly paid my debt; but we have had a house of sickness. My own health, too, has been very crazy and out of repair, and I have had so much work accumulated on me that I have been like an overtired man roused from insufficient sleep, who sits on his bedside with one stocking on and the other in his hand, doing nothing, and thinking what a deal he has to do.

But I am ever, sick or well, weary or lively, my dear Dyer, your sincere and affectionate friend,

S. T. Coleridge.

CCXLVII. TO GEORGE CATTERMOLE.[205]

Grove, Highgate, Thursday, August 14, 1828.

My dear Sir,—I have but this moment received yours of the 13th, and though there are but ten minutes in my power, if I am to avail myself of this day's post, I will rather send you a very brief than not an immediate answer. I shall be much gratified by standing beside the baptismal font as one of the sponsors of the little pilgrim at his inauguration into the rights and duties of Immortality, and he shall not want my prayers, nor aught else that shall be within my power, to assist him in becoming that of which the Great Sponsor who brought light and immortality into the world has declared him an emblem.

There are one or two points of character belonging to me, so, at least, I believe and trust, which I would gladly communicate with the name,—earnest love of Truth for its own sake, and steadfast convictions grounded on faith, not fear, that the religion into which I was baptised is the Truth, without which all other knowledge ceases to merit the appellation. As to other things, which yet I most sincerely wish for him, a more promising augury might be derived from other individuals of the Coleridge race.

Any day, that you and your dear wife (to whom present my kindest remembrances and congratulations) shall find convenient, will suit me, if only you will be so good as to give me two or three days' knowledge of it.

Believe me, my dear sir, with sincere respect and regard,

Your obliged
S. T. Coleridge.

P. S. I returned from my seven weeks' Continental tour with Mr. Wordsworth and his daughter this day last week. We saw the Rhine as high up as Bingen, Holland, and the Netherlands.

CCXLVIII. TO J. H. GREEN.

Grove, Highgate, June 1, 1830.

My dear Friend,—Do you happen among your acquaintances and connections to know any one who knows any one who knows Sir Francis Freeling of the Post Office sufficiently to be authorised to speak a recommendatory word to him? Our Harriet,[206] whose love and willing-mindedness to me-ward during my long chain of bodily miserablenesses render it my duty no less than my inclination to shew to her that I am not insensible of her humbly affectionate attentions, has applied to me in behalf of her brother, a young man who can have an excellent character, from Lord Wynford and others, for sobriety, integrity, and discretion, and who is exceedingly ambitious to get the situation of a postman or deliverer of letters to the General Post Office. Perhaps, before I see you next, you will be so good as to tumble over the names of your acquaintances, and if any connection of Sir Francis' should turn up, to tell me, and if it be right and proper, to make my request and its motive.

Dr. Chalmers with his daughter and his very pleasing wife honoured me with a call this morning, and spent an hour with me, which the good doctor declared on parting to have been "a refreshment" such as he had not enjoyed for a long season.[207] N. B.—There were no sandwiches; only Mrs. Aders was present, who is most certainly a bonne bouche for both eye and ear, and who looks as bright and sunshine-showery as if nothing had ever ailed her. The main topic of our discourse was Mr. Irving and his unlucky phantasms and phantis(ms). I was on the point of telling Dr. Chalmers, but fortunately recollected there were ladies and Scotch ladies present, that, while other Scotchmen were content with brimstone for the itch, Irving had a rank itch for brimstone, new-sublimated by addition of fire. God bless you and your

Ever obliged and affectionate friend,
S. T. Coleridge.

30 May? or 1 June? at all events.
Monday night, 11 o'clock.

P. S.—Kind remembrances to Mrs. Green. I continue pretty well, on the whole, considering, save the soreness across the base of my chest.

CCXLIX. TO THOMAS POOLE.

1830.

My dear Poole,—Mr. Stutfield Junr.[208] has been so kind as to inform me of his father's purposed journey to Stowey, and to give me this opportunity of writing; though in fact I have little pleasant to say, except that I am advancing regularly and steadily towards the completion of my Opus Magnum on Revelation and Christianity, the Reservoir of my reflections and reading for twenty-five years past, and in health not painfully worse. I do not know, however, that I should have troubled you with a letter merely to convey this piece of information, but I have a great favour to request of you; that is, that, supposing you to have still in your possession the two letters of the biography of my own childhood which I wrote at Stowey for you, and a copy of the letter from Germany containing the account of my journey to the Harz and my ascent of Mount Brocken, you would have them transcribed, and send me the transcript addressed to me, James Gillman's Esq., Highgate, London.

O that riches would but make wings for me instead of for itself, and I would fly to the seashore at Porlock and Lynmouth, making a good halt at dear, ever fondly remembered Stowey, of which, believe me, your image and the feelings and associations connected therewith constitute four fifths, to, my dear Poole,

Your obliged and affectionate friend,
S. T. Coleridge.

CCL. TO MRS. GILLMAN.

1830.

Dear Mrs. Gillman,—Wife of the friend who has been more than a brother to me, and who have month after month, yea, hour after hour, for how many successive years, united in yourself the affections and offices of an anxious friend and tender sister to me-ward!

May the Father of Mercies, the God of Health and all Salvation, be your reward for your great and constant love and loving-kindness to me, abiding with you and within you, as the Spirit of guidance, support, and consolation! And may his Grace and gracious Providence bless James and Henry for your sake, and make them a blessing to you and their father! And though weighed down by a heavy presentiment respecting my own sojourn here, I not only hope but have a steadfast faith that God will be your reward, because your love to me from first to last has begun in, and been caused by, what appeared to you a translucence of the love of the good, the true, and the beautiful from within me,—as a relic of glory gleaming through the turbid shrine of my mortal imperfections and infirmities, as a Light of Life seen within "the body of this Death,"—because in loving me you loved our Heavenly Father reflected in the gifts and influences of His Holy Spirit!

S. T. Coleridge.

CCLI. TO J. H. GREEN.

December 15, 1831.

My dear Friend,—It is at least a fair moiety of the gratification I feel, that it will give you so much pleasure to hear from me, that I tacked about on Monday, continued in smooth water during the whole day, and with exceptions of about an hour's muttering, as if a storm was coming, had a comfortable night. I was still better on Tuesday, and had no relapse yesterday. I have so repeatedly given and suffered disappointment, that I cannot even communicate this gleam of convalescence without a little fluttering distinctly felt at my heart, and a sort of cloud-shadow of dejection flitting over me. God knows with what aims, motives, and aspirations I pray for an interval of ease and competent strength! One of my present wishes is to form a better nomenclature or terminology. I have long felt the exceeding inconvenience of the many different meanings of the term objective,—sometimes equivalent to apparent or sensible, sometimes in opposition to it,—ex. gr. "The objectivity is the rain drops and the reflected light, the iris, is but an appearance." Thus, sometimes it means real and sometimes unreal, and the worst is, that it forms an obstacle to the fixation of the great truth, that the perfect reality is predicable only where actual and real are terms of identity, that is, where there is no potential being, and that this alone is absolute reality; and further, of that most fundamental truth, that the ground of all reality, the objective no less than of the subjective, is the Absolute Subject. How to get out of the difficulty I do not know, save that some other term must be used as the antithet to phenomenal, perhaps noumenal.

James Gillman has passed an unusually strict and long examination for ordination with great credit, and was selected by the bishop to read the lessons in the service. The parents are, of course, delighted, and now, my dear friend, with affectionate remembrances to Mrs. Green, may God bless you and

S. T. Coleridge.

CCLII. TO HENRY NELSON COLERIDGE.[209]

The Grove, February 24, 1832.

My dear Nephew, and by a higher tie, Son, I thank God I have this day been favoured with such a mitigation of the disease as amounts to a reprieve, and have had ease enough of sensation to be able to think of what you said to me from Lockhart, and the result is a wish that you should—that is, if it appears right to you, and you have no objection of feeling—write for me to Professor Wilson, offering the Essays, and the motives for the wish to have them republished, with the authority (if there be no breach of confidence) of Mr. Lockhart. I cannot with propriety offer them to Fraser, having for a series of years received "Blackwood's Magazine" as a free gift to me, until I have made the offer to Blackwood. Of course, my whole and only object is the desire to see them put into the possibility of becoming useful. But, oh! this is a faint desire, my dear Henry, compared with that of seeing a fair abstract of the principles I have advanced respecting the National Church and its revenue, and the National Clerisy as a coördinate of the State, in the minor and antithetic sense of the term State!

I almost despair of the Conservative Party, too truly, I fear, and most ominously, self-designated Tories, and of course half-truthmen! One main omission both of senators and writers has been, ὡς ἔμοιγε δοκεῖ, that they have forgotten to level the axe of their argument at the root, the true root, yea, trunk of the delusion, by pointing out the true nature and operation and modus operandi of the taxes in the first instance, and then and not till then the utter groundlessness, the absurdity of the presumption that any House of Commons formed otherwise, and consisting of other men of other ranks, other views or with other interests, than the present has been for the last twenty years at least, would or could (from any imaginable cause) have a deeper interest or a stronger desire to diminish the taxes, as far as the abolition of this or that tax would increase the ability to pay the remainder. For what are taxes but one of the forms of circulation? Some a nation must have, or it is no nation. But he that takes ninepence from me instead of a shilling, but at the same time and by this very act prevents sixpence from coming into my pocket,—am I to thank him? Yet such are the only thanks that Mr. Hume and the Country Squires, his cowardly back-clapping flatterers, can fairly claim. In my opinion, Hume is an incomparably more mischievous being than O'Connell and the gang of agitators. They are mere symptomatic and significative effects, the roars of the inwardly agitated mass of the popular sea. But Hume is a fermenting virus. But I must end my scrawl. God bless my dear Sara. Give my love to Mrs. C. and kiss the baby for

S. T. Coleridge.

H. N. Coleridge, Esq., 1, New Court, Lincoln's Inn.

CCLIII. TO MISS LAWRENCE.[210]

March 22, 1832.

My dear Miss Lawrence,—You and dear, dear Mrs. Crompton are among the few sunshiny images that endear my past life to me, and I never think of you without heartfelt esteem, without affection, and a yearning of my better being toward you. I have for more than eighteen months been on the brink of the grave, the object of my wishes, and only not of my prayers, because I commit myself, poor dark creature, to an Omniscient and All-merciful, in whom are the issues of life and death,—content, yea, most thankful, if only His Grace will preserve within me the blessed faith that He is and is a God that heareth prayers, abundant in forgiveness, and therefore to be feared, no fate, no God as imagined by the Unitarians, a sort of, I know not what law-giving Law of Gravitation, to whom prayer would be as idle as to the law of gravity, if an undermined wall were falling upon me; but "a God that made the eye, and therefore shall He not see? who made the ear, and shall He not hear?" who made the heart of man to love Him, and shall He not love the creature whose ultimate end is to love Him?—a God who seeketh that which was lost, who calleth back that which had gone astray; who calleth through His own Name; Word, Son, from everlasting the Way and the Truth; and who became man that for poor fallen mankind he might be (not merely announced but be) the Resurrection and the Life,—"Come unto me, all ye that are weary and heavy-laden, and I will give you rest!" Oh, my dear Miss Lawrence! prize above all earthly things the faith. I trust that no sophistry of shallow infra-socinians has quenched it within you,—that God is a God that heareth prayers. If varied learning, if the assiduous cultivation of the reasoning powers, if an accurate and minute acquaintance with all the arguments of controversial writers; if an intimacy with the doctrines of the

Unitarians, which can only be obtained by one who for a year or two in his early life had been a convert to them, yea, a zealous and by themselves deemed powerful supporter of their opinions; lastly, if the utter absence of any imaginable worldly interest that could sway or warp the mind and affections,—if all these combined can give any weight or authority to the opinion of a fellow-creature, they will give weight to my adjuration, sent from my sickbed to you in kind love. O trust, O trust, in your Redeemer! in the coeternal Word, the Only-begotten, the living Name of the Eternal I AM, Jehovah, Jesus!

I shall endeavour to see Mr. Hamilton.[211] I doubt not his scientific attainments. I have had proofs of his taste and feeling as a poet, but believe me, my dear Miss Lawrence! that, should the cloud of distemper pass from over me, there needs no other passport to a cordial welcome from me than a line from you importing that he or she possesses your esteem and regard, and that you wish I should shew attention to them. I cannot make out your address, which I read "The Grange;" but where that is I know not, and fear that the Post Office may be as ignorant as myself. I must therefore delay the direction of my letter till I see Mr. Hamilton; but in all places, and independent of place, I am, my dear Miss Lawrence, with most affectionate recollections,

Your friend,
S. T. Coleridge.

Miss S. Lawrence, The Grange, nr. Liverpool.

CCLIV. TO THE REV. H. F. CARY.

Grove, Highgate, April 22, 1832.

My dear Friend,—For I am sure by my love for you that you love me too well to have suffered my very rude and uncourteous vehemence of contradiction and reclamation respecting your advocacy of the Catilinarian Reform Bill, when we were last together, to have cooled, much less alienated your kindness; even though the interim had not been a weary, weary time of groaning and life-loathing for me. But I hope that this fearful night-storm is subsiding, as you will have heard from Mr. Green or dear Charles Lamb. I write now to say, that if God, who in His Fatherly compassion and through His love wherewith He hath beheld and loved me in Christ, in whom alone He can love the world, hath worked almost a miracle of grace in and for me by a sudden emancipation from a thirty-three years' fearful slavery,[212] if God's goodness should in time and so far perfect my convalescence as that I should be capable of resuming my literary labours, I have a thought by way of a light prelude, a sort of unstiffening of my long dormant joints and muscles, to give a reprint as nearly as possible, except in quality of the paper, a facsimile of John Asgill's tracts with a life and copious notes,[213] to which I would affix Pastilla et Marginalia. See my MSS. notes, blank leaf and marginal, on Southey's "Life of Wesley," and sundry other works. Now can you direct me to any source of information respecting John Asgill, a prince darling of mine, the most honest of all Whigs, whom at the close of Queen Anne's reign the scoundrelly Jacobite Tories twice expelled from Parliament, under the pretext of his incomparable, or only-with-Rabelais-to-be-compared argument against the base and cowardly custom of ever dying? And this tract is a very treasure, and never more usable as a medicine for our clergy, at least all such as the Bishop of London, Archbishops of Canterbury and of Dublin, the Paleyans and Mageeites,[214] any one or all of whom I would defy to answer a single paragraph of Asgill's tract, or unloose a single link from the chain of logic. I have no biographical dictionary, and never saw one but in a little sort of one-volume thing. If you can help me in this, do. I give my kindest love to Mrs. Cary.

Yours, with unutterable and unuttered love and regard, in all (but as to the accursed Reform Bill! that mendacium ingens to its own preamble (to which no human being can be more friendly than I am), that huge tapeworm lie of some threescore and ten yards) entire sympathy of heart and soul,

Your affectionate
S. T. Coleridge.

CCLV. TO JOHN PEIRSE KENNARD.[215]

Grove, Highgate, August 13, 1832.

My dear Sir,—Your letter has announced to me a loss too great, too awful, for common grief, or any of its ordinary forms and outlets. For more than an hour after, I remained in a state which I can only describe as a state of deepest mental silence, neither prayer nor thanksgiving, but a prostration of absolute faith, as if the Omnipresent were present to me by a more special intuition, passing all sense and all understanding. Whether Death be but the cloudy Bridge to the Life beyond, and Adam Steinmetz has been wafted over it without suspension, or with an immediate resumption of self-conscious existence, or whether his Life be hidden in God, in the eternal only-begotten, the Pleroma of all Beings and the Habitation both of the Retained and the Retrieved, therein in a blessed and most divine Slumber to grow and evolve into the perfected Spirit,—for sleep is the appointed season of all growth here below, and God's ordinances in the earthly may shadow out his ways in the Heavenly,—in either case our friend is in God and with God. Were it possible for me even to think otherwise,[216] the very grass in the fields would turn black before my eyes, and nature appear as a skeleton fantastically mossed over beneath the weeping vault of a charnel house!

Deeply am I persuaded that for every man born on earth there is an appointed task, some remedial process in the soul known only to the Omniscient; and, this through divine grace fulfilled, the sole question is whether it be needful or expedient for the church that he should still remain: for the individual himself "to depart and to be with Christ" must needs be great gain. And of my dear, my filial friend, we may with a strong and most consoling assurance affirm that he was eminently one

Who, being innocent, did even for that cause
Bestir him in good deeds!
Wise Virgin He, and wakeful kept his Lamp
Aye trimm'd and full; and thus thro' grace he liv'd
In this bad World as in a place of Tombs,
And touch'd not the Pollutions of the Dead.

And yet in Christ only did he build a hope. Yea, he blessed the emptiness that made him capable of his Lord's fullness, gloried in the blindness that was a receptive of his Master's light, and in the nakedness that asked to be cloathed with the wedding-garment of his Redeemer's Righteousness. Therefore say I unto you, my young friend, Rejoice! and again I say, Rejoice!

The effect of the event communicated in your letter has been that of awe and sadness on our whole household. Mrs. Gillman mourns as for a son, but with that grief which is felt for a departed saint. Even the servants felt as if an especially loved and honoured member of the family had been suddenly taken away. When I announced the sad tidings to Harriet, an almost unalphabeted but very sensible woman, the tears swelled in her eyes, and she exclaimed, "Ah sir! how many a Thursday night, after Mr. Steinmetz was gone, and I had opened the door for him, I have said to them below, 'That dear young man is too amiable to live. God will soon have him back.'" These were her very words. Nor were my own anticipations of his recall less distinct or less frequent. Not once or twice only, after he had shaken hands with me on leaving us, I have turned round with the tear on my cheek, and whispered to Mrs. Gillman, "Alas! there is Death in that dear hand."[217]

My dear sir! if our society can afford any comfort to you, as that of so dear a friend of Adam Steinmetz cannot but be to us, I beseech you in my own name, and am intreated by Mr. and Mrs. Gillman to invite you, to be his representative for us, and to take his place in our circle. And I must further request that you do not confine yourself to any particular evening of the week (for which there is now no reason), but that you consult your own convenience and opportunities of leisure. At whatever hour he comes, the fraternal friend of Adam Steinmetz will ever be dear and most welcome to

S. T. Coleridge.

CHAPTER XV
THE BEGINNING OF THE END
1833-1834

CCLVI. TO J. H. GREEN.

Sunday night, April 8, 1833.

It is seldom, my dearest friend, that I find myself differing from you in judgements of any sort. It is more than seldom that I am left in doubt and query on any judgement of yours of a practical nature, for on the good ground of some sixteen or more years' experience I feel a take-for-granted faith in the dips and pointings of the needle in every decision of your total mind. But in the instance you spoke of this afternoon, viz., your persistent rebuttal of the Temperance Society Man's Request, though I do not feel sure that you are not in the right, yet I do feel as if I should have been more delighted and more satisfied if you had intimated your compliance with it. I feel that in this case I should have had no doubt; but that my mind would have leapt forwards with content, like a key to a loadstone.

Assuredly you might, at least you would, have a very promising chance of effecting considerable good, and you might have commenced your address with your own remark of the superfluity of any light of information afforded to an habitual dram-drinker respecting the unutterable evil and misery of his thraldom. As wisely give a physiological lecture to convince a man of the pain of burns, while he is lying with his head on the bars of the fire-grate, instead of snatching him off. But in stating this, you might most effectingly and preventively for others describe the misery of that condition in which the impulse waxes as the motive wanes. (Mem. There is a striking passage in my "Friend" on this subject,[218] and a no less striking one in a schoolboy theme of mine[219] now in Gillman's possession, and in my own hand, written when I was fourteen, with the simile of the treacherous current of the Maelstrom.) But this might give occasion for the suggestion of one new charitable institution, under authority of a legislative act, namely, a Maison de Santé (what do the French call it?) for lunacy and idiocy of the will, in which, with the full consent of, or at the direct instance of the patient himself, and with the concurrence of his friends, such a person under the certificate of a physician might be placed under medical and moral coercion. I am convinced that London would furnish a hundred volunteers in as many days from the gin-shops, who would swallow their glass of poison in order to get courage to present themselves to the hospital in question. And a similar institution might exist for a higher class of will-maniacs or impotents. Had such a house of health been in existence, I know who would have entered himself as a patient some five and twenty years ago.

Second class. To the persons still capable of self-cure; and lastly, to the young who have only begun, and not yet begun—[add to this] the urgency of connecting the Temperance Society with the Christian churches of all denominations,—the classes known to each other, and deriving strength from religion. This is a beautiful part, or might have been made so, of the Wesleyan Church.

These are but raw hints, but unless the mercy of God should remove me from my sufferings earlier than I dare hope or pray for, we will talk the subject over again; as well as the reason why spirits in any form as such are so much more dangerous, morally and in relation to the forming a habit, than beer or wine. Item: if a government were truly fraternal, a healthsome and sound beer would be made universal; aye, and for the lower half of the middle classes wine might be imported, good and generous, from sixpence to eightpence per quart.

God bless you and your ever affectionate

S. T. Coleridge.

CCLVII. TO MRS. ADERS.[220]

[1833.]

My dear Mrs. Aders,—By my illness or oversight I have occasioned a very sweet vignette to have been made in vain—except for its own beauty. Had I sent you the lines that were to be written on the upright tomb, you and our excellent Miss Denman would have, first, seen the dimension requisite for letters of a distinctly visible and legible size; and secondly, that the homely, plain Church-yard Christian verses would not be in keeping with a Muse (though a lovelier I never wooed), nor with a lyre or harp or laurel, or aught else Parnassian and allegorical. A rude old yew-tree, or a mountain ash, with a grave or two, or any other characteristic of a village rude church-yard,—such a hint of a landscape was all I meant; but if any figure, rather that of an elderly man

Thoughtful, with quiet tears upon his cheek.
(Tombless Epitaph. See "Sibylline Leaves.")

But I send the lines, and you and Miss Denman will form your own opinion.

Is one of Wyville's proofs of my face worth Mr. Aders' acceptance? I wrote under the one I sent to Henry Coleridge the line from Ovid, with the translation, thus:

S. T. Coleridge, ætat. suæ 63.

Not / handsome / was / but / was / eloquent /
"Non formosus erat, sed erat facundus Ulysses."
Translation.

"In truth, he's no Beauty!" cry'd Moll, Poll, and Tab;
But they all of them own'd He'd the gift of the Gab.
My best love to Mr. Aders, and believe that as I have been, so I ever remain your affectionate and trusty friend,

S. T. Coleridge.

P. S. I like the tombstone very much.

The lines when printed would probably have on the preceding page the advertisement—

Epitaph on a Poet little known, yet better known by the Initials of his Name than by the Name itself.

S. T. C.
Stop, Christian Passer-by! Stop, Child of God!
And read with gentle heart. Beneath this sod
A Poet lies: or that, which once seem'd He.
O lift one thought in prayer for S. T. C.
That He, who many a year with toilsome breath
Found Death in Life, may here find Life in Death.
Mercy for Praise—to be forgiven for Fame
He ask'd, and hoped thro' Christ. DO THOU the Same.

CCLVIII. TO JOHN STERLING.[221]

Grove, Highgate, October 30, 1833.

My dear Sir,—I very much regret that I am not to see you again for so many months. Many a fond dream have I amused myself with, of your residing near me or in the same house, and of preparing, with your and Mr. Green's assistance, my whole system for the press, as far as it exists in writing in any systematic form; that is, beginning with the Propyleum, On the power and use of Words, comprising Logic, as the canons of Conclusion, as the criterion of Premises, and lastly as the discipline and evolution of Ideas (and then the Methodus et Epochee, or the Disquisition on God, Nature, and Man), the two first grand divisions of which, from the Ens super Ens to the Fall, or from God to Hades, and then from Chaos to the commencement of living organization, containing the whole scheme of the Dynamic Philosophy, and the deduction of the Powers and Forces, are complete; as is likewise a third, composed for the greater part by Mr. Green, on the "Application of the Ideas, as the Transcendents of the Truths, Duties, Affections, etc., in the Human Mind." If I could once publish these (but, alas! even these could not be compressed in less than three octavo volumes), I should then have no objection to print my MS. papers on "Positive Theology, from Adam to Abraham, to Moses, the Prophets, Christ and Christendom." But this is a dream! I am, however, very seriously disposed to employ the next two months in preparing for the press a metrical translation (if I find it practicable) of the Apocalypse, with an introduction on the "Use and Interpretation of Scriptures." I am encouraged to this by finding how much of original remains in my views after I have subtracted all I have in common with Eichhorn and Heinrichs. I write now to remind you, or to beg you to recall to my memory the name of the more recent work (Lobeck?) which you mentioned to me, and whether you can procure it for me, or rather the loan of it. Likewise, whether you know of any German translation and commentary on Daniel, that is thought highly of? I find Gesenius' version exceedingly interesting, and look forward to the Commentaries with delight. You mentioned some works on the numerical Cabbala, the Gematria (I think) they call it. But I must not scribble away your patience, and after I have heard from you from Cambridge I will try to write to you more to the purpose (for I did not begin this scrawl till the hour had passed that ought to have found me in bed).

With sincere regard, your obliged friend,
S. T. Coleridge.

CCLIX. TO MISS ELIZA NIXON.[222]

July 9, 1834.

My dear Eliza,—The three volumes of Miss Edgeworth's "Helen" ought to have been sent in to you last night, and are marked as having been so sent. And indeed, knowing how much noise this work was making and the great interest it had excited, I should not have been so selfish as to have retained them on my own account. But Mrs. Gillman is very anxious that I should read it, and has made me promise to write my remarks on it, and such reflections as the contents may suggest, which, in awe of the precisians of the Book Society, I shall put down on separate paper. The young people were so eager to read it, that with my slow and interrupted style of reading, it would have been cruel not to give them the priority. Mrs. Gillman flatters me that you and your sisters will think a copy of my remarks some compensation for the delay.

God bless you, my dear young friend. You, I know, will be gratified to learn, and in my own writing, the still timid but still strengthening and brightening dawn of convalescence with the last eight days.

S. T. Coleridge.

July 9, 1834.

The two volumes[223] that I send you are making a rumour, and are highly and I believe justly extolled. They are written by a friend of mine,[224] a remarkably handsome young man whom you may have seen on one of our latest Thursday evening conversazioni. I have not yet read them, but keep them till I send in "Helen," and longer, if you should not have finished them.

CCLX. TO ADAM STEINMETZ KENNARD.

Grove, Highgate, July 13, 1834.

My dear Godchild,—I offer up the same fervent prayer for you now as I did kneeling before the altar when you were baptized into Christ, and solemnly received as a living member of His spiritual body, the church. Years must pass before you will be able to read with an understanding heart what I now write. But I trust that the all-gracious God, the Father of our Lord Jesus Christ, the Father of mercies, who by His only-begotten Son (all mercies in one sovereign mercy!) has redeemed you from evil ground, and willed you to be born out of darkness, but into light; out of death, but into life; out of sin, but into righteousness; even into "the Lord our righteousness,"—I trust that He will graciously hear the prayers of your dear parents, and be with you as the spirit of health and growth, in body and in mind. My dear godchild, you received from Christ's minister at the baptismal font, as your Christian name, the name of a most dear friend of your father's, and who was to me even as a son,—the late Adam Steinmetz, whose fervent aspirations and paramount aim, even from early youth, was to be a Christian in thought, word, and deed; in will, mind, and affections. I, too, your godfather, have known what the enjoyment and advantages of this life are, and what the more refined pleasures which learning and intellectual power can give; I now, on the eve of my departure, declare to you, and earnestly pray that you may hereafter live and act on the conviction, that health is a great blessing; competence, obtained by honourable industry, a great blessing; and a great blessing it is, to have kind, faithful, and loving friends and relatives; but that the greatest of all blessings, as it is the most ennobling of all privileges, is to be indeed a Christian. But I have been likewise, through a large portion of my later life, a sufferer, sorely affected with bodily pains, languor, and manifold infirmities; and for the last three or four years have, with few and brief intervals, been confined to a sick-room, and at this moment, in great weakness and heaviness, write from a sickbed, hopeless of recovery, yet without prospect of a speedy removal. And I thus, on the brink of the grave, solemnly bear witness to you, that the Almighty Redeemer, most gracious in His promises to them that truly seek Him, is faithful to perform what He has promised; and has reserved, under all pains and infirmities, the peace that passeth all understanding, with the supporting assurance of a reconciled God, who will not withdraw His spirit from me in the conflict, and in His own time will deliver me from the evil one. Oh, my dear godchild! eminently blessed are they who begin early to seek, fear, and love their God, trusting wholly in the righteousness and mediation of their Lord, Redeemer, Saviour, and everlasting High Priest, Jesus Christ. Oh, preserve this as a legacy and bequest from your unseen godfather and friend,

S. T. Coleridge.

FOOTNOTES:

[1] Richard Sharp, 1759-1835, known as "Conversation Sharp," a banker, Member of Parliament, and distinguished critic. He was a friend of Wordsworth's, and on intimate terms with Coleridge and Southey. Life of W. Wordsworth, i. 377; Letters of R. Southey, i. 279, et passim.

[2] Jean Victor Moreau, 1763-1813. The "retreat" took place in October, 1796, after his defeat of the Archduke Charles at Neresheim, in the preceding August. Biographical Dictionary.

[3] This phrase reappears in the first issue (1808) of the Prospectus of The Friend. Jeffrey, to whom the Prospectus was submitted, objected to the wording, and it was changed, in the first instance, to "mental gloom" and finally to "dejection of mind." See letter to F. Jeffrey, December 14, 1808, published in the Illustrated London News, June 10, 1893. Letter CLXXI.

[4] See concluding paragraph of Introductory Address of Conciones ad Populum (February, 1795); The Friend, Section I., Essay xvi.; Coleridge's Works, 1853, ii. 307. For recantation of Necessitarianism, see footnote (1797) to lines "To a Friend, together with an Unfinished Poem." Poetical Works, p. 38.

[5] Stuart is responsible for a story that Coleridge's dislike and distrust of the "fellow from Aberdeen," the hero of The Two Round Spaces on a Tombstone, dated from a visit to the Wedgwoods at Cote House, when Mackintosh outtalked and outshone his fellow protégé, and drove him in dudgeon from the party. But in 1838, when he contributed his articles to the Gentleman's Magazine, Stuart had forgotten much and looked at all things from a different point of view. For instance, he says that the verses attacking Mackintosh were never published, whereas they appeared in the Morning Post of December 4, 1800. A more probable explanation is that Stuart, who was not on good terms with his brother-in-law, was in the habit of confiding his grievances, and that Coleridge, more suo, espoused his friend's cause with unnecessary vehemence. Gentleman's Magazine, May, 1838, p. 485.

[6] The Pantheon. By Andrew Tooke. Revised, etc., for the use of schools. London: 1791.

"Tooke was a prodigious favourite with us (at Christ's Hospital). I see before me, as vividly now as ever, his Mars and Apollo, his Venus and Aurora—the Mars coming on furiously in his car; Apollo, with his radiant head, in the midst of shades and fountains; Aurora with hers, a golden dawn; and Venus, very handsome, we thought, and not looking too modest in 'a slight cymar.'" Autobiography of Leigh Hunt, p. 75.

[7] See note infra.

[8] George Rose, 1744-1818, statesman and political writer. He had recently brought in a bill which "authorised the sending to all the Parish Overseers in the country a paper of questions on the condition of the poor." Poole, at the instance of John Rickman, secretary to Speaker Abbot, was at this time engaged at Westminster in drawing up an abstract of the various returns which had been made in accordance with Sir George Rose's bill. See Letter from T. Poole to T. Wedgwood, dated September 14, 1803. Cottle's Reminiscences, pp. 477, 478; Thomas Poole and his Friends, ii. 107-114.

[9] See Letter to Southey of February 20, 1804. Letter CXLIX.

[10] John Dalton, 1766-1844, chemist and meteorologist. He published his researches on the atomic theory, which he had begun in 1803, in his New System of Chemical Philosophy, in 1808. Biographical Dictionary.

[11] His old fellow-student at Göttingen.

[12]

"O for a single hour of that Dundee,
Who on that day the word of onset gave."
"In the Pass of Killicranky." Wordsworth's Poetical Works, 1889, p. 201.

[13] John Tobin the dramatist (or possibly his brother James), with whom Coleridge spent the last weeks of his stay in London, before he left for Portsmouth on the 27th of March, on his way to Malta.

[14] The misspelling, which was intentional, was an intimation to Lamb that the letter was not to be opened.

[15] A retired carrier, the owner of Greta Hall, who occupied "the smaller of the two houses inter-connected under one roof." He was godfather to Hartley Coleridge, and left him a legacy of fifty pounds. Mrs. Wilson, the "Wilsy" of Hartley's childhood, was Jackson's housekeeper. Memoir and Letters of Sara Coleridge, 1873, i. 13.

[16] Coleridge had already attended Davy's Lectures at the Royal Institution in 1802, and, possibly, in 1803. It is probable that allusions in his correspondence to Davy's Lectures gave rise to the mistaken supposition that he delivered public lectures in London before 1808.

[17]

"He said, and, gliding like a snake,
Where Caradoc lay sleeping made his way.
Sweetly slept he, and pleasant were his dreams
Of Britain, and the blue-eyed maid he loved.
The Azteca stood over him; he knew
His victim, and the power of vengeance gave
Malignant joy. 'Once hast thou 'scaped my arm:
But what shall save thee now?' the Tyger thought,
Exulting; and he raised his spear to strike.
That instant, o'er the Briton's unseen harp
The gale of morning past, and swept its strings
Into so sweet a harmony, that sure
It seem'd no earthly tone. The savage man
Suspends his stroke; he looks astonished round;
No human hand is near: ... and hark! again
The aërial music swells and dies away.
Then first the heart of Tlalala felt fear:
He thought that some protecting spirit watch'd
Beside the Stranger, and, abash'd, withdrew."
"Madoc in Aztlan," Book XI. Southey's Poetical Works, 1838, v. 274, 275.

[18] Mrs. E. Fenwick, author of Secrecy, a novel (1799); a friend of Godwin's first wife, Mary Wollstonecraft. William Godwin, by C. Kegan Paul, i. 282, 283. See, also, Lamb's Letters (ed. Ainger), i. 331; and Lamb's essays, "Two Races of Men," and "Newspapers Thirty-five Years ago."

[19] Lamb's "bad baby"—"a disgusting woman who wears green spectacles." Letters, passim.

[20] Afterwards Sir John Stoddart, Chief Justice of Malta, 1826-39.

[21] A note dated "Treasury, July 20th, 1805," gives vent to his feelings on this point. "Saturday morning ½ past nine o'clock, and soon I shall have to brace up my hearing in toto, (for I hear in my brain—I hear, that is, I have an immediate and peculiar feeling instantly co-adunated with the sense of external sound = (exactly) to that which is experienced when one makes a wry face, and putting one's right hand palm-wise to the right ear, and the left palm pressing hard on the forehead, one says to a bawler, 'For mercy's sake, man! don't split the drum of one's ear'—sensations analogous to this of various degrees of pain, even to a strange sort of uneasy pleasure. I am obnoxious to pure sound and therefore was saying—[N. B. Tho' I ramble, I always come back to sense—the sense alive, tho' sometimes a limb of syntax broken]—was saying that I hear in my brain, and still more hear in my stomach). For this ubiquity, almost (for I might safely add my toes—one or two, at least—and my knees) for this ubiquity of the Tympanum auditorium I am now to wind up my courage, for in a few seconds that accursed Reveille, the horrible crash and persevering malignant torture of the Pare-de-Drum, will attack me, like a party of yelling, drunken North American Indians attacking a crazy fort with a tired garrison, out of an ambush. The noisiness of the Maltese everybody must notice; but I have observed uniformly among them such utter impassiveness to the action of sounds as that I am fearful that the verum will be scarcely verisimile. I have heard screams of the most frightful kind, as of children run over by a cart, and running to the window I have seen two children in a parlour opposite to me (naked, except a kerchief tied round the waist) screaming in their horrid fiendiness—for fun! three adults in the room perfectly unannoyed, and this suffered to continue for twenty minutes, or as long as their lungs enabled them. But it goes thro' everything, their street-cries, their priests, their advocates, their very pigs yell rather than squeak, or both together, rather, as if they were the true descendants of some half-dozen of the swine into which the Devils went, recovered by the Royal Humane Society. The dogs all night long would draw curses on them, but that the Maltese cats—it surpasses description, for he who has only heard caterwauling on English roofs can have no idea of a cat-serenade in Malta. In England it has often a close and painful resemblance to the distressful cries of young children, but in Malta it is identical with the wide range of screams uttered by imps while they are dragging each other into hotter and still hotter pools of brimstone and fire. It is the discord of Torment and of Rage and of Hate, of paroxysms of Revenge, and every note grumbles away into Despair."

[22] The first Sicilian tour extended from the middle of August to the 7th of November, 1804. Two or three days, August 19-21, were spent in the neighbourhood of Etna. He slept at Nicolosi and visited the Hospice of St. Nicola dell' Arena. It is unlikely that he reached the actual summit, but two ascents were made, probably to the limit of the wooded region. A few days later, August 24, he reached Syracuse, where he was hospitably entertained by H. M. Consul G. F. Lecky. The notes which he took of his visit to Etna are fragmentary and imperfect, but the description of Syracuse and its surroundings occupies many pages of his note-book. Under the heading, "Timoleon's, Oct. 18, 1804, Wednesday, noon," he

writes: "The Gaza and Tree at Tremiglia. Rocks with cactus, pendulous branches, seed-pods black at the same time with the orange-yellow flower, and little daisy-like tufts of silky hair.... Timoleon's villa, supposed to be in the field above the present house, from which you ascend to fifty stairs. Grand view of the harbour and sea, over that tongue of land which forms the anti-Ortygian embracing arm of the harbour, the point of Plemmyrium where Alcibiades and Nicias landed. I left the aqueduct and walked ascendingly to some ruined cottages, beside a delve, with straight limestone walls of rock, on which there played the shadows of the fig-tree and the olive. I was on part of Epipolæ, and a glorious view indeed! Before me a neck of stony common and fields—Ortygia, the open sea and the ships, and the circular harbour which it embraces, and the sea over that again. To my right that large extent of plain, green, rich, finely wooded; the fields so divided and enclosed that you, as it were, knew at the first view that they are all hedged and enclosed, and yet no hedges nor enclosings obtrude themselves—an effect of the vast number of trees of the same sort. On my left, stony fields, two harbours, Magnisi and its sand isle, and Augusta, and Etna, whose smoke mingles with the clouds even as they rise from the crater.... Still as I walk the lizard gliding darts along the road, and immerges himself under a stone, and the grasshopper leaps and tumbles awkwardly before me."

It must have been in anticipation of this visit to Sicily, or after some communication with Coleridge, that Wordsworth, after alluding to his friend's abode,—

"Where Etna over hill and valley casts
His shadow stretching towards Syracuse,
The city of Timoleon,"
gives utterance to that unusual outburst of feeling:—

"Oh! wrap him in your shades, ye giant woods,
On Etna's side; and thou, O flowery field
Of Enna! is there not some nook of thine,
From the first play-time of the infant world
Kept sacred to restorative delight,
When from afar invoked by anxious love?"
Wordsworth's Poetical Works, 1889, "The Prelude," Book XI. p. 319.

[23] A short treatise entitled Observations on Egypt, which is extant in MS., may have been among the papers sent to Stuart with a view to publication.

[24] Shakespeare, Richard III., Act I. Scene 4.

[25] He had, perhaps, something more than a suspicion that Southey disliked these protestations. In the letter of friendly remonstrance (February, 1804), which Southey wrote to him after the affair with Godwin, he admits that he may be "too intolerant of these phrases," but, indeed, he adds, "when they are true, they may be excused, and when they are not, there is no excuse for them." Life and Correspondence, ii. 266.

[26] Cynocephalus, Dog-visaged. Compare Milton's "Hymn on the Nativity:"—

"The brutish gods of Nile as fast,
Isis and Orus and the dog Anubis haste."

[27] A printed slip, cut off from some public document, has been preserved in one of Coleridge's note-books. It runs thus: "Segreteria del Governo li 29 Gennajo 1805. Samuel

T. Coleridge Seg. Pub. del. Commis. Regio. G. N. Zammit Pro segretario." His actual period of office extended from January 18 to September 6, 1805.

[28] John Wordsworth, the poet's younger brother, the original of Leonard in "The Brothers," and of "The Happy Warrior," was drowned off the Bill of Portland, February 5, 1805. In a letter to Sir G. Beaumont, dated February 11, 1805, Wordsworth writes: "I can say nothing higher of my ever-dear brother than that he was worthy of his sister, who is now weeping beside me, and of the friendship of Coleridge; meek, affectionate, silently enthusiastic, loving all quiet things, and a poet in everything but words." "We have had no tidings of Coleridge. I tremble for the moment when he is to hear of my brother's death; it will distress him to the heart, and his poor body cannot bear sorrow. He loved my brother, and he knows how we at Grasmere loved him." The report of the wreck of the Earl of Abergavenny and of the loss of her captain did not reach Malta till the 31st of March. It was a Sunday, and Coleridge, who had been sent for to the Palace, first heard the news from Lady Ball. His emotion at the time, and, perhaps, a petition to be excused from his duties brought from her the next day "a kindly letter of apology." "Your strong feelings," she writes, "are too great for your health. I hope that you will soon recover your spirits." But Coleridge took the trouble to heart. It was the first death in the inner circle of his friends; it meant a heavy sorrow to those whom he best loved, and it seemed to confirm the haunting presentiment that death would once more visit his family during his absence from home. Ten days later he writes (in a note-book): "O dear John Wordsworth! What joy at Grasmere that you were made Captain of the Abergavenny! now it was next to certain that you would in a few years settle in your native hills, and be verily one of the concern. Then came your share in the brilliant action at Linois. I was at Grasmere in spirit only! but in spirit I was one of the rejoicers ... and all these were but decoys of death! Well, but a nobler feeling than these vain regrets would become the friend of the man whose last words were, 'I have done my duty! let her go!' Let us do our duty; all else is a dream—life and death alike a dream! This short sentence would comprise, I believe, the sum of all profound philosophy, of ethics and metaphysics, and conjointly from Plato to Fichte. S. T. C."

[29] An island midway between Malta and Tunis, ceded by Naples to Don Fernandez in 1802.

[30] A description of the cottage at Stowey and its inmates, contained in a letter written by Mr. Richard Reynell (in August, 1797) to his sister at Thorveston, was published in the Illustrated London News, April 22, 1893.

[31] Coleridge left Rome with his friend Mr. Russell on Sunday, May 18, 1806. He had received, so he tells us in the Biographia Literaria, a secret warning from the Pope that Napoleon, whose animosity had been roused by articles in the Morning Post, had ordered his arrest. A similar statement is made in a footnote to a title-page of a proposed reprint of newspaper articles (an anticipation of Essays on His Own Times), which was drawn up in 1817. "My essays," he writes, "in the Morning Post, during the peace of Amiens, brought my life into jeopardy when I was at Rome. An order for my arrest came from Paris to Rome at twelve at night—by the Pope's goodness I was off by one—and the arrest of all the English took place at six." In a letter to his brother George, which he wrote about six months after he returned to England, he says that he was warned to leave Rome, but does not enter into particulars. It is a well-known fact that Napoleon read the leading articles in the Morning Post, and deeply resented their tone and spirit, but whether Coleridge was rightly informed that an order for his arrest had come from Paris, or whether he was warned that, if with other Englishmen he should be arrested, his connection with the Morning Post would come to light, must remain doubtful. Coleridge's Works, 1853, iii. 309.

[32] An entry in a note-book, dated June 7, 1806, expresses this at greater length: "O my children! whether, and which of you are dead, whether any and which among you are alive I know not, and were a letter to arrive this moment from Keswick I fear that I should be unable to open it, so deep and black is my despair. O my children! My children! I gave you life once, unconscious of the life I was giving, and you as unconsciously have given life to me." A fortnight later, he ends a similar outburst of despair with a cry for deliverance:—

Come, come thou bleak December wind,
And blow the dry leaves from the tree!
Flash, like a love-thought thro' me, Death!
And take a life that wearies me.

[33] It is difficult to trace his movements during his last week in Italy. He reached Leghorn on Saturday, June 7. Thence he made his way to Florence and returned to Pisa on a Thursday, probably Thursday, June 19, the date of this letter. On Sunday, June 22, he was still at Pisa, but, I take it, on the eve of setting sail for England. Fifty-five days later, August 17, he leaped on shore at Stangate Creek. His account of Pisa is highly characteristic. "Of the hanging Tower," he writes, "the Duomo, the Cemetery, the Baptistery, I shall say nothing, except that being all together they form a wild mass, especially by moonlight, when the hanging Tower has something of a supernatural look; but what interested me with a deeper interest were the two hospitals, one for men, one for women," etc., and these he proceeds to describe. Nevertheless he must have paid more attention to the treasures of Pisan art than his note implies, for many years after in a Lecture on the History of Philosophy, delivered January 19, 1819, he describes minutely and vividly the "Triumph of Death," the great fresco in the Campo Santo at Pisa, which was formerly assigned to Oreagna, but is now, I believe, attributed to Ambrogio and Pietro Lorenzetti. MS. Journal; MS. Report of Lecture.

[34] Mr. Russell was an artist, an Exeter man, whom Coleridge met in Rome. They were fellow-travellers in Italy, and returned together to England.

[35] William Smith, M. P. for Norwich, who lived at Parndon House, near Harlow, in Essex. It was in a great measure through his advice and interest that Coleridge obtained his Lectureship at the Royal Institution. Ten years later (1817), on the occasion of the surreptitious publication of Wat Tyler, Mr. Smith, who was a staunch liberal, denounced the Laureate as a "renegade," and Coleridge with something of his old vigour gave battle on behalf of his brother-in-law in the pages of The Courier. Essays on His Own Times, iii. 939-950.

[36] Charles James Fox died on September 13, 1806.

[37] An unpublished letter from Sir Alexander Ball to His Excellency H. Elliot, Esq. (Minister at the Court of Naples), strongly recommends Coleridge to his favourable notice and consideration. Nothing that Coleridge ever said in favour of "Ball" exceeds what Sir Alexander says of Coleridge, but the Minister, whose hands must have been pretty full at the time, failed to be impressed, and withheld his patronage.

[38] "The Foster-Mother's Tale," Poetical Works, 1893, p. 83.

[39] Hartley Coleridge, now in his eleventh year, was under his father's sole care from the end of December, 1806, to May, 1807. The first three months were spent in the farmhouse near Coleorton, which Sir G. Beaumont had lent to the Wordsworths, and it must have

been when that visit was drawing to a close that this letter was written for Hartley's benefit. The remaining five or six weeks were passed in the company of the Wordsworths at Basil Montagu's house in London. Then it was that Hartley saw his first play, and was taken by Wordsworth and Walter Scott to the Tower. "The bard's economy," says Hartley, "would not allow us to visit the Jewel Office, but Mr. Scott, then no anactolater, took an evident pride in showing me the claymores and bucklers taken from the Loyalists at Culloden." Whilst he was at Coleorton, Hartley was painted by Sir David Wilkie. It is the portrait of a child "whose fancies from afar are brought," but the Hartley of this letter is better represented by the grimacing boy in Wilkie's "Blind Fiddler," for which, I have been told, he sat as a model. Poems of Hartley Coleridge, 1851, i. ccxxii.

[40] Scott had proposed to Southey that he should use his influence with Jeffrey to get him placed on the staff of the Edinburgh Review. Southey declined the offer alike on the score of political divergence from the editor, and disapproval of "that sort of bitterness [in criticism] which tends directly to wound a man in his feelings, and injure him in his fame and fortune." Life and Correspondence, iii. 124-128. See, too, Lockhart's Life of Sir Walter Scott, 1837, ii. 130.

[41] Sir John Acland. The property is now in the possession of a descendant in the female line, Sir Alexander Hood, of Fairfield, Dodington.

[42] To receive him and his family at Ottery as had been originally proposed. George Coleridge disapproved of his brother's intended separation from his wife, and declined to countenance it in any way whatever.

[43] Faulkner: a Tragedy, 1807-1808, 8vo.

[44] I presume that the reference is to the Conciones ad Populum, published at Bristol, November 16, 1795.

[45] Coleridge's article on Clarkson's History of the Abolition of the Slave Trade was published in the Edinburgh Review, July, 1808. It has never been reprinted. Samuel Taylor Coleridge, by J. Dykes Campbell, London, 1894, p. 168; Letters from the Lake Poets, p. 180; Allsop's Letters, 1836, ii. 112.

[46] Of this pamphlet or the translation of Palm's Deutschland in seiner tiefsten Erniedrigung, I know nothing. The author, John Philip Palm, a Nuremberg bookseller, was shot August 26, 1806, in consequence of the publication of the work, which reflected unfavorably on the conduct and career of Napoleon.

[47] Compare his letter to Poole, dated December 4, 1808. "Begin to count my life, as a friend of yours, from 1st January, 1809;" and a letter to Davy, of December, 1808, in which he speaks of a change for the better in health and habits. Thomas Poole and his Friends, ii. 227; Fragmentary Remains of Sir H. Davy, p. 101.

[48] The Convention of Cintra was signed August 30, 1808. Wordsworth's Essays were begun in the following November. "For the sake of immediate and general circulation I determined (when I had made a considerable progress in the manuscript) to print it in different portions in one of the daily newspapers. Accordingly two portions of it were printed, in the months of December and January, in the Courier. An accidental loss of several sheets of the manuscript delayed the continuance of the publication in that manner till the close of the Christmas holidays; and this plan of publication was given up."

Advertisement to Wordsworth's pamphlet on the Convention of Cintra, May 20, 1809: Letters from the Lake Poets, p. 385.

[49] "In the place of some just eulogiums due to Mr. Pitt was substituted some abuse and detraction." Allsop's Letters, 1836, ii. 112.

[50] A preliminary prospectus of The Friend was printed at Kendal and submitted to Jeffrey and a few others. A copy of this "first edition" is in my possession, and it is interesting to notice that Coleridge has directed his amanuensis, Miss Hutchinson, to amend certain offending phrases in accordance with Jeffrey's suggestions. "Speculative gloom" and "year-long absences" he gives up, but, as the postscript intimates, "moral impulses" he has the hardihood to retain. See The Friend's Quarterly Examiner for July, 1893, art. "S. T. Coleridge on Quaker Principles;" and Athenæum for September 16, 1893, art. "Coleridge on Quaker Principles."

[51] Thomas Wilkinson, of Yanwath, near Penrith, was a member of the Society of Friends. He owned and tilled a small estate on the banks of the Emont, which he laid out and ornamented "after the manner of Shenstone at his Leasowes." As a friend and neighbour of the Clarksons and of Lord Lonsdale he was well known to Wordsworth, who, greatly daring, wrote in his honour his lines "To the Spade of a Friend (an Agriculturist)."

Alas! for the poor Prospectus! "Speculative gloom" and "year-long absence" had been sacrificed to Jeffrey, and now "Architecture, Dress, Dancing, Gardening, Music, Poetry, and Painting" were erased in obedience to Wilkinson. Most of these articles, however, "Architecture, Dress," etc., reappeared in a second edition of the Prospectus, attached to the second number of The Friend, but Dancing, "Greek statuesque dancing," on which Coleridge might have discoursed at some length, was gone forever. Wordsworth's Works, p. 211 (Fenwick Note); The Friend's Quarterly Examiner, July, 1893; Records of a Quaker Family, by Anne Ogden Boyce, London, 1889, pp. 30, 31, 55.

[52] The original draft of the prospectus of The Friend, which was issued in the late autumn of 1808, was printed at Kendal by W. Pennington. Certain alterations were suggested by Jeffrey and others (Southey in a letter to Rickman dated January 18, 1809, complains that Coleridge had "carried a prospectus wet from the pen to the publisher, without consulting anybody"), and a fresh batch of prospectuses was printed in London. A third variant attached to the first number of the weekly issue, June 1, 1809, was printed by Brown, a bookseller and stationer at Penrith, who, on Mr. Pennington's refusal, undertook to print and publish The Friend. Some curious letters which passed between Coleridge and his printer, together with the MS. of The Friend, in the handwriting of Miss Sarah Hutchinson, are preserved in the Forster Library at the South Kensington Museum. Letters from the Lake Poets, pp. 85-188; Selections from the Letters of R. Southey, ii. 120.

[53] Compare letters to Stuart (December), 1808. "You will long ere this have received Wordsworth's second Essay, etc., rewritten by me, and in some parts recomposed." Letters from the Lake Poets, p. 101.

[54] Colonel Wardle, who led the attack in the House of Commons against the Duke of York, with regard to the undue influence in military appointments of the notorious Mrs. Clarke.

[55] Coleridge's friendship with Dr. Beddoes dated from 1795-96, and was associated with his happier days. It is possible that the recent amendment in health and spirits was due to

advice and sympathy which he had met with in response to a confession made in writing to his old Bristol friend. His death, which took place on the 24th of December, 1808, would rob Coleridge of a newly-found support, and would "take out of his life" the hope of self-conquest. The letter implies that he had recently heard from or conversed with Beddoes.

[56] Compare letter from Southey to J. N. White dated April 21, 1809. "A ridiculous disorder called the Mumps has nearly gone through the house, and visited me on its way—a thing which puts one more out of humour than out of health; but my neck has now regained its elasticity, and I have left off the extra swathings which yesterday buried my chin, after the fashion of fops a few years ago." Selections from the Letters of R. Southey, ii, 135, 136.

[57] The Parliamentary investigation of the charges and allegations with regard to the military patronage of the Duke of York.

[58] Bertha Southey, afterwards Mrs. Herbert Hill, was born March 27, 1809.

[59] "The Appendix (to the pamphlet On the Convention of Cintra), a portion of the work which Mr. Wordsworth regarded as executed in a masterly manner, was drawn up by Mr. De Quincey, who revised the proofs of the whole." Memoirs of Wordsworth, i. 384.

[60] In Southey's copy of the reprint of the stamped sheets of The Friend the passage runs thus: "However this may be, the Understanding or regulative faculty is manifestly distinct from Life and Sensation, its function being to take up the passive affections of the sense into distinct Thoughts and Judgements, according to its own essential forms. These forms, however," etc. The Friend, No. 5, Thursday, September 14, 1809, p. 79, n.

[61] For extracts from Poole's narrative of John Walford, see Thomas Poole and his Friends, ii. 235-237. Wordsworth endeavoured to put the narrative into verse, but was dissatisfied with the result. His lines have never been published.

[62] H. N. Coleridge included these lines, as they appear in a note-book, among the Omniana of 1809-1816. They are headed incorrectly, "Inscription on a Clock in Cheapside." The MS. is not very legible, but there can be no doubt that Coleridge wrote, "On a clock in a market place (proposed)." Table Talk, etc., 1884, p. 401; Poetical Works, p. 181.

[63] The story of Maria Eleanora Schöning appeared in No. 13 of The Friend, Thursday, November 16, 1809, pp. 194-208. It was reprinted as the "Second Landing Place" in the revised edition of The Friend, published in 1818. The somewhat laboured description of the heroine's voice, which displeased Southey, and the beautiful illustration of the "withered leaf" were allowed to remain unaltered, and appear in every edition. Coleridge's Works, 1853, ii. 312-326.

[64] Jonas Lewis von Hess, 1766-1823. He was a friend and pupil of Kant, and author of A History of Hamburg.

[65] John of Milan, who flourished 1100 a. d., was the author of Medicina Salernitana. He also composed "versibus Leoninis," a poem entitled Flos Medicinæ. Hoffmann's Lexicon Universale, art. "Salernum."

[66] Three letters on the Catholic Question appeared in the Courier, September 3, 21, and 26, 1811. Essays on His Own Times, iii. 891-896, 920-932.

[67] The Battle of Albuera. Articles on the battle appeared in the Courier on June 5 and 8, 1811. Essays on His Own Times, iii. 802-805.

[68] "That a Judge should have regarded as an aggravation of a libel on the British Army, the writer's having written against Buonaparte, is an act so monstrous," etc. "Buonaparte," Courier, June 29, 1811; Essays on His Own Times, iii. 818.

[69] John Drakard, the printer of the Stamford News, was convicted at Lincoln, May 25, 1811, of the publication of an article against flogging in the army, and sentenced to a fine and imprisonment.

[70] Lord Milton, one of the members for Yorkshire, brought forward a motion on June 6, 1811, against the reappointment of the Duke of York as Commander-in-Chief.

[71] Clerk of the Courier. Letter to Gentleman's Magazine, June, 1838, p. 586.

[72] Many years after the date of this letter, Dr. Spurzheim took a life-mask of Coleridge's face, and used it as a model for a bust which originally belonged to H. N. Coleridge, and is now in the Library at Heath's Court, Ottery St. Mary. Another bust of Coleridge, very similar to Spurzheim's, belonged to my father, and is still in the possession of the family. I have been told that it was taken from a death-mask, but as Mr. Hamo Thornycroft, who designed the bust for Westminster Abbey, pointed out to me, it abounds in anatomical defects. In a letter which Henry Coleridge wrote to his father, Colonel Coleridge, on the day of his uncle's death, he says that a death-mask had been taken of the poet's features. Whether this served as a model for a posthumous bust, or not, I am unable to say. In the curious and valuable article on death-masks which Mr. Laurence Hutton contributed to the October number of Harper's Magazine, for 1892, he gives a fac-simile of a death-mask which was said to be that of S, T. Coleridge. At the time that I wrote to him on the subject, I had not seen Henry Coleridge's letter, but I came to the conclusion that this sad memorial of death was genuine. The "glorious forehead" is there, but the look has passed away, and the "rest is silence." With regard to Allston's bust of Coleridge, which was exhibited at the Royal Academy in 1812, I possess no information. See Harper's Magazine, October, 1892, pp. 782, 783.

[73] A favourite quip. Apropos of the bed on which he slept at Trinity College, Cambridge, in June, 1833, he remarks, "Truly I lay down at night a man, and awoke in the morning a bruise." Table Talk, etc., Bell & Co., 1884, p. 231, note.

[74] "Crimen ingrati animi nil aliud est quam perspicacia quædam in causam collati beneficii." De Augmentis Scientiarum, cap. iii. 15. If this is the passage which Coleridge is quoting, he has inserted some words of his own. The Works of Bacon, 1711, i. 183.

[75] A crayon sketch of Coleridge, drawn by George Dawe, R. A., is now in existence at Heath Court. The figure, which is turned sideways, the face looking up, the legs crossed, is that of a man in early middle life, somewhat too portly for his years. An engraving of the sketch forms the frontispiece to Lloyd's History of Highgate. It was, in the late Lord Coleridge's opinion, a most characteristic likeness of his great-uncle. A time came when, for some reason, Coleridge held Dawe in but light esteem. I possess a card of invitation to his

funeral, which took place at St. Paul's Cathedral, on October 27, 1829. It is endorsed thus:—

"I really would have attended the Grub's Canonization in St. Paul's, under the impression that it would gratify his sister, Mrs. Wright; but Mr. G. interposed a conditional but sufficiently decorous negative. 'No! Unless you wish to follow his Grubship still further down.' So I pleaded ill health. But the very Thursday morning I went to Town to see my daughter, for the first time, as Mrs. Henry Coleridge, in Gower Street, and, odd enough, the stage was stopped by the Pompous Funeral of the unchangeable and predestinated Grub, and I extemporised:—

As Grub Dawe pass'd beneath the Hearse's Lid,
On which a large RESURGAM met the eye,
Col, who well knew the Grub, cried, Lord forbid!
I trust, he's only telling us a lie!
S. T. Coleridge."

Dawe, it may be remembered, is immortalised by Lamb in his amusing Recollections of a Late Royal Academician.

[76] This portrait, begun at Rome, was not finished when Coleridge left. It is now in the possession of Allston's niece, Miss Charlotte Dana, of Boston, Mass., U. S. A. The portrait by Allston, now in the National Portrait Gallery, was taken at Bristol in 1814. Samuel Taylor Coleridge, a Narrative, by J. Dykes Campbell, 1894, p. 150, footnote 5.

[77] The lectures were delivered at the rooms of "The London Philosophical Society, Scotch Corporation Hall, Crane Court, Fleet Street (entrance from Fetter Lane)." Of the lecture on "Love and the Female Character," which was delivered on December 9, 1811, H. C. Robinson writes: "Accompanied Mrs. Rough to Coleridge's seventh and incomparably best Lecture. He declaimed with great eloquence about love, without wandering from his subject, Romeo and Juliet." Among the friends who took notes were John Payne Collier, and a Mr. Tomalin. Coleridge's Lectures on Shakespeare, London, 1856, p. viii.; H. C. Robinson's Diary, ii. 348, MS. notes by J. Tomalin.

[78] The visit to Greta Hall, the last he ever paid to the Lake Country, lasted about a month, from February 23 to March 26. On his journey southward he remained in Penrith for a little over a fortnight, rejoining the Morgans towards the middle of April.

[79] The Reverend John Dawes, who kept a day-school at Ambleside. Hartley and Derwent Coleridge, Robert Jameson, Owen Lloyd and his three brothers (sons of Charles Lloyd), and the late Edward Jefferies, afterwards Curate and Rector of Grasmere, were among his pupils. In the Memoir of Hartley Coleridge, his brother Derwent describes at some length the character of his "worthy master," and adds: "We were among his earliest scholars, and deeming it, as he said, an honour to be entrusted with the education of Mr. Coleridge's sons, he refused, first for the elder, and afterwards for the younger brother, any pecuniary remuneration." Poems of Hartley Coleridge, 1851, i. liii.

[80] In an unpublished letter from Mrs. Coleridge to Poole, dated October 30, 1812, she tells her old friend that when "the boys" perceived that their father did not intend to turn aside to visit the Wordsworths at the Rectory opposite Grasmere Church, they turned pale and were visibly affected. No doubt they knew all about the quarrel and were mightily concerned, but their agitation was a reflex of the grief and passion "writ large" in their

father's face. One can imagine with what ecstasy of self-torture he would pass through Grasmere and leave Wordsworth unvisited.

[81] Sir Thomas Bernard, 1750-1818, the well-known philanthropist and promoter of national education, was one of the founders of the Royal Institution.

[82] It is probable that during his stay at Penrith he recovered a number of unbound sheets of the reprint of The Friend. His proposal to Gale and Curtis must have been to conclude the unfinished narrative of the life of Sir Alexander Ball, and to publish the whole as a complete work. A printed slip cut out of a page of publishers' advertisements and forwarded to "H. N. Coleridge, Esq., from W. Pickering," contains the following announcement:—

"Mr. Coleridge's Friend, of which twenty-eight Numbers are published, may now be had, in one Volume, royal 8vo. boards, of Mess. Gale and Curtis, Paternoster Row. And Mr. C. intends to complete the Work, in from eight to ten similar sheets to the foregoing, which will be published together in one part, sewed. The Subscribers to the former part can obtain them through their regular Booksellers. Only 300 copies remain of the 28 numbers, and their being printed on unstamped paper will account to the Subscribers for the difference of price. 23, Paternoster Row, London, 1st February, 1812."

[83] The full title of this work was The Origin, Nature and Object of the New System of Education. Southey's Life of Dr. Bell, ii. 409.

[84] The Honourable and Right Reverend John Shute Barrington, 1734-1826, sixth son of the first Lord Barrington, was successively Bishop of Llandaff, Salisbury, and Durham. He was a warm supporter of the Madras system of education. It was no doubt Dr. Bell who helped to interest the Bishop in Coleridge's Lectures.

[85] Herbert Southey, known in the family as "Dog-Lunus," and "Lunus," and "The Moon." Letters of R. Southey, ii. 399.

[86] Readers of The Doctor will not be at a loss to understand the significance of the references to Dr. Daniel Dove and his horse Nobs. According to Cuthbert Southey, the actual composition of the book began in 1813, but the date of this letter (April, 1812) shows that the myth or legend of the "Doctor," and his iron-grey, which had taken shape certainly as early as 1805, was fully developed in the spring of 1812, when Coleridge paid his last visit to Greta Hall. It was not till the winter of 1833-1834, that the first two volumes of The Doctor appeared in print, and, as they were published anonymously, they were, probably, by persons familiar with his contribution to Blackwood and the London Magazine, attributed to Hartley Coleridge. "No clue to the author has reached me," wrote Southey to his friend Wynne. "As for Hartley Coleridge, I wish it were his, but am certain that it is not. He is quite clever enough to have written it—quite odd enough, but his opinions are desperately radical, and he is the last person in the world to disguise them. One report was that his father had assisted him; there is not a page in the book, wise or foolish, which the latter could have written, neither his wisdom nor his folly are of that kind." There had been a time when Southey would have expressed himself differently, but in 1834 dissociation from Coleridge had become a matter alike of habit and of principle. Southey's Life and Correspondence, ii. 355, vi. 225-229; Letters of R. Southey, iv. 373.

[87] The first of the series of "Essays upon Epitaphs" was published in No. 25 of the original issue of The Friend (Feb. 22, 1810), and republished by Wordsworth in the notes to

The Excursion, 1814. "Two other portions of the 'Series,' of which the Bishop of Lincoln gives an outline and some extracts in the Memoirs (i. 434-445), were published in full in Prose Works of Wordsworth, 1876, ii. 41-75." Life of W. Wordsworth, ii. 152; Poetical Works of Wordsworth, Bibliography, p. 907.

[88] To Miss Sarah Hutchinson, then living in Wales.

[89] That Wordsworth ever used these words, or commissioned Montagu to repeat them to Coleridge, is in itself improbable and was solemnly denied by Wordsworth himself. But Wordsworth did not deny that with the best motives and in a kindly spirit he took Montagu into his confidence and put him on his guard, that he professed "to have no hope" of his old friend, and that with regard to Coleridge's "habits" he might have described them as a "nuisance" in his family. It was all meant for the best, but much evil and misery might have been avoided if Wordsworth had warned Coleridge that if he should make his home under Montagu's roof he could not keep silence, or, better still, if he had kept silence and left Montagu to fight his own battles. The cruel words which Montagu put into Wordsworth's mouth or Coleridge in his agitation and resentment put into Montagu's, were but the salt which the sufferer rubbed into his own wound. The time, the manner, and the person combined to aggravate his misery and dismay. Judgment had been delivered against him in absentiâ, and the judge was none other than his own "familiar friend." Henry Crabb Robinson's Diary, May 3-10, 1812, first published in Life of W. Wordsworth, ii. 168, 187.

[90] The tickets were numbered and signed by the lecturer. Printed cards which were issued by way of advertisement contained the following announcement:—

"Lectures on the Drama.

"Mr. Coleridge proposes to give a series of Lectures on the Drama of the Greek, French, English and Spanish stage, chiefly with Reference to the Works of Shakespeare, at Willis's Rooms, King Street, St. James's, on the Tuesdays and Fridays in May and June at Three o'clock precisely. The Course will contain Six Lectures, at One Guinea. The Tickets Transferable. An Account is opened at Mess. Ransom Morland & Co., Bankers, Pall Mall, in the names of Sir G. Beaumont, Bart., Sir T. Bernard, Bart., W. Sotheby, Esq., where Subscriptions will be received, and Tickets issued. The First Lecture on Tuesday, the 12th of May.—S. T. C., 71, Berners St."

For an account of the first four lectures, see H. C. Robinson's Diary, i. 385-388.

[91] From Bombay.

[92] I have followed Professor Knight in omitting a passage in which "he gives a lengthened list of circumstances which seemed to justify misunderstanding." The alleged facts throw no light on the relations between Coleridge and Wordsworth.

[93] The cryptogram which Coleridge invented for his own use was based on the arbitrary selection of letters of the Greek as equivalents to letters of the English alphabet. The vowels were represented by English letters, by the various points, and by algebraic symbols. An expert would probably decipher nine tenths of these memoranda at a glance, but here and there the words symbolised are themselves anagrams of Greek, Latin, and German words, and, in a few instances, the clue is hard to seek.

[94] The Right Honourable Spencer Perceval was shot by a man named Bellingham, in the lobby of the House of Commons, May 11, 1812.

[95] The occasion of this letter was the death of Wordsworth's son, Thomas, which took place December 1, 1812. It would seem, as Professor Knight intimates, that the letter was not altogether acceptable to the Wordsworths, and that "no immediate reply was sent to Coleridge." We have it, on the authority of Mr. Clarkson, that when Wordsworth and Dorothy did write, in the spring of the following year, inviting him to Grasmere, their letters remained unanswered, and that when the news came that Coleridge was about to leave London for the seaside, a fresh wound was inflicted, and fresh offence taken. As Mr. Dykes Campbell has pointed out, the consequences of this second rupture were fatal to Coleridge's peace of mind and to his well-being generally. The brief spell of success and prosperity which attended the representation of "Remorse" inspired him for a few weeks with unnatural courage, but as the "pale unwarming light of Hope" died away, he was left to face the world and himself as best or as worst he could. Of the months which intervened between March and September, 1813, there is no record, and we can only guess that he remained with his kind and patient hosts, the Morgans, sick in body and broken-hearted. Life of W. Wordsworth, ii. 182; Samuel Taylor Coleridge, a Narrative, by J. Dykes Campbell, 1894, pp. 193-197.

[96] See Letter CXCV., p. 611, note 2.

[97] The notice of "Remorse" in The Times, though it condemned the play as a whole, was not altogether uncomplimentary, and would be accepted at the present day by the majority of critics as just and fair. It was, no doubt, the didactic and patronising tone adopted towards the author which excited Coleridge's indignation. "We speak," writes the reviewer, "with restraint and unwillingly of the defects of a work which must have cost its author so much labour. We are peculiarly reluctant to touch the anxieties of a man," etc. The notice in the Morning Post was friendly and flattering in the highest degree. The preface to Osorio, London, 1873, contains selections of press notices of "Remorse," and other interesting matter. See, too, Poetical Works, Editor's Note on "Remorse," pp. 649-651.

[98] John Williams, described by Macaulay as "a filthy and malignant baboon," who wrote under the pseudonym of "Anthony Pasquin," emigrated to America early in this century. In 1804 he published a work in Boston, and there is, apparently, no reason to suppose that he subsequently returned to England. Either Coleridge was in error or he uses the term generally for a scurrilous critic.

[99] This note-book must have passed out of Coleridge's possession in his lifetime, for it is not among those which were bequeathed to Joseph Henry Green, and subsequently passed into the hands of my father. The two folio volumes of the Greek Poets were in my father's library, and are now in my possession.

[100] "Mr. Colridge (sic) will not, we fear, be as much entertained as we were with his 'Playhouse Musings,' which begin with characteristic pathos and simplicity, and put us much in mind of the affecting story of old Poulter's mare."

[101] The motto "Sermoni propriora," translated by Lamb "properer for a sermon," was prefixed to "Reflections on having left a Place of Retirement." The lines "To a Young Ass" were originally published in the Morning Chronicle, December 30, 1794, under the heading, "Address to a Young Jack Ass, and its tethered Mother. In Familiar Verse." Poetical Works,

pp. 35, 36, Appendix C, p. 477. See, too, Biographia Literaria, Coleridge's Works, 1853, iii. 161.

[102] The words, "Obscurest Haunt of all our mountains," are to be found in the first act of "Remorse," lines 115, 116. Their counterpart in Wordsworth's poems occurs in "The Brothers," l. 140. ("It is the loneliest place of all these hills.") "De minimis non curat lex," especially when there is a plea to be advanced, or a charge to be defended. Poetical Works, p. 362; Works of Wordsworth, p. 127.

[103] Many theories have been hazarded with regard to the broken friendship commemorated in these lines. My own impression is that Coleridge, if he had anything personal in his mind, and we may be sure that he had, was looking back on his early friendship with Southey and the bitter quarrel which began over the collapse of pantisocracy, and was never healed till the summer of 1799. In the late autumn of 1800, when the second part of "Christabel" was written, Southey was absent in Portugal, and the thought of all that had come and gone between him and his "heart's best brother" inspired this outburst of affection and regret.

[104] The annuity of £150 for life, which Josiah Wedgwood, on his own and his brother Thomas' behalf, offered to Coleridge in January, 1798. The letter expressly states that it is "an annuity for life of £150 to be regularly paid by us, no condition whatsoever being annexed to it." "We mean," he adds, "the annuity to be independent of everything but the wreck of our fortune." It is extraordinary that a man of probity should have taken advantage of the fact that the annuity, as had been proposed, was not secured by law, and should have struck this blow, not so much at Coleridge, as at his wife and children, for whom the annuity was reserved. It is hardly likely that a man of business forgot the terms of his own offer, or that he could have imagined that Coleridge was no longer in need of support. Either in some fit of penitence or of passion Coleridge offered to release him, or once again "whispering tongues had poisoned truth," and some one had represented to Wedgwood that the money was doing more harm than good. But a bond is a bond, and it is hard to see, unless the act and deed were Coleridge's, how Wedgwood can escape blame. Thomas Poole and his Friends, i. 257-259.

[105] Dr. Southey, the poet's younger brother Henry, and Daniel Stuart were afterwards neighbours in Harley Street. A close intimacy and lifelong friendship arose between the two families.

[106] Treaty of Vienna, October 9, 1809.

[107] This could only have been carried out in part. A large portion of the books which Coleridge possessed at his death consisted of those which he had purchased during his travels in Germany in 1799, and in Italy in 1805-1806.

[108] The publication by Cottle, in 1837, of this and the following letter, and still more of that to Josiah Wade of June 26, 1814 (Letter CC.), was deeply resented by Coleridge's three children and by all his friends. In the preface to his Early Recollections Cottle defends himself on the plea that in the interests of truth these confessions should be revealed, and urges that Coleridge's own demand that after his death "a full and unqualified narrative of my wretchedness and its guilty cause may be made public," not only justified but called for his action in the matter. The law of copyright in the letters of parents and remoter ancestors was less clearly defined at that time than it is at present, and Coleridge's literary executors contented themselves with recording their protest in the strongest possible terms. In 1848,

when Cottle reprinted his Early Recollections, together with some additional matter, under the title of Reminiscences of S. T. Coleridge, etc., he was able to quote Southey as an advocate, though, possibly, a reluctant advocate, for publication. There can be no question that neither Coleridge's request nor Southey's sanction gave Cottle any right to wound the feelings of the living or to expose the frailties and remorse of the dead. The letters, which have been public property for nearly sixty years, are included in these volumes because they have a natural and proper place in any collection of Coleridge's Letters which claims to be, in any sense, representative of his correspondence at large.

[109] At whatever time these lines may have been written, they were not printed till 1829, when they were prefixed to the "Monody on the Death of Chatterton." Poetical Works, p. 61; Editor's Note, pp. 562, 563.

[110] "The Picture; or The Lover's Resolution," lines 17-25. Poetical Works, p. 162.

[111] Solomon Grundy is a character, played by Fawcett, in George Colman the younger's piece, Who wants a Guinea? produced at Covent Garden, 1804-1805.

[112] A character in Macklin's play, Love à la Mode.

[113] A character in Macklin's play, A Man of the World.

[114] It is needless to say that Coleridge never even attempted a translation of Faust. Whether there were initial difficulties with regard to procuring the "whole of Goethe's works," and other books of reference, or whether his heart failed him when he began to study the work with a view to translation, the arrangement with Murray fell through. A statement in the Table Talk for February 16, 1833, that the task was abandoned on moral grounds, that he could not bring himself to familiarise the English public with "language, much of which was," he thought, "vulgar, licentious, and blasphemous," is not borne out by the tone of his letters to Murray, of July 29, August 31, 1814. No doubt the spirit of Faust, alike with regard to theology and morality, would at all times have been distasteful to him, but with regard to what actually took place, he deceived himself in supposing that the feelings and scruples of old age would have prevailed in middle life. Memoirs of John Murray, i. 297 et seq.

[115] "The thoughts of Coleridge, even during the whirl of passing events, discovered their hidden springs, and poured forth, in an obscure style, and to an unheeding age, the great moral truths which were then being proclaimed in characters of fire to mankind." Alison's History of Europe, ix. 3 (ninth edition).

[116] The eight "Letters on the Spaniards," which Coleridge contributed to the Courier in December, January, 1809-10, are reprinted in Essays on His Own Times, ii. 593-676.

[117] The character of Pitt appeared in the Morning Post, March 19, 1800; the letters to Fox, on November 4, 9, 1802; the Essays on the French Empire, etc., September 21, 25, and October 2, 1802; the Essay on the restoration of the Bourbons, October, 1802. They are reprinted in the second volume of Essays on His Own Times.

Six Letters to Judge Fletcher on Catholic Emancipation, which appeared at irregular intervals in the Courier, September-December, 1814, are reprinted in Essays on His Own Times, iii. 677-733.

The Essay on Taxation forms the seventh Essay of Section the First, on the Principles of Political Knowledge. The Friend; Coleridge's Works, Harper & Brothers, 1853, ii. 208-222.

[118] Neither the original nor the transcript of this letter has, to my knowledge, been preserved.

[119] He reverts to this "turning of the worm" in a letter to Morgan dated January 5, 1818. He threatened to attack publishers and printers in "a vigorous and harmonious satire" to be called "Puff and Slander." I am inclined to think that the remarkable verses entitled "A Character," which were first printed in 1834, were an accomplished instalment of "these two long satires." Letter in British Museum. MSS. Addit. 25612. Samuel Taylor Coleridge, a Narrative by J. Dykes Campbell, p. 234, note; Poetical Works, pp. 195, 642.

[120] A work which should contain all knowledge and proclaim all philosophy had been Coleridge's dream from the beginning, and, as no such work was ever produced, it may be said to have been his dream to the end. And yet it was something more than a dream. Besides innumerable fragments of metaphysical and theological speculation which have passed into my hands, he actually did compose and dictate two large quarto volumes on formal logic, which are extant. "Something more than a volume," a portentous introduction to his magnum opus, was dictated to his amanuensis and disciple, J. H. Green, and is now in my possession. A commentary on the Gospels and some of the Epistles, of which the original MS. is extant, and of which I possess a transcription, was an accomplished fact. I say nothing of the actual or relative value of this unpublished matter, but it should be put on record that it exists, that much labour, ill-judged perhaps, and ineffectual labour, was expended on the outworks of the fortresses, and that the walls and bastions are standing to the present day.

[121] The appearance of these "Essays on the Fine Arts" was announced in the Bristol Journal of August 6, 1814. They were reprinted in 1837 by Cottle, in his Early Recollections, ii. 201-240, and by Thomas Ashe in 1885, in his Miscellanies, Æsthetic and Literary, pp. 5-35. Coleridge himself "set a high value" on these essays. See Table Talk of January 1, 1834.

[122] The working editor of the Courier.

[123] The third letter to Judge Fletcher on Ireland was published in the Courier, October 21, 1814. It is reprinted in Essays on His Own Times, iii. 690-697.

[124] John Cartwright, 1740-1824, known as Major Cartwright, was an ardent parliamentary reformer and an advocate of universal suffrage. He refused to fight against the United States and wrote Letters on American Independence (1774).

[125] Lord Erskine's Bill for the Prevention of Cruelty to Animals was brought forward in the House of Lords May 15, 1809, and was passed without a division. The Bill was read a second time in the House of Commons but was rejected on going into committee, the opposition being led by Windham in a speech of considerable ability.

By "imperfect" duties Coleridge probably means "duties of imperfect obligation."

[126] This article, a review of "The Letters of Lord Nelson to Lady Hamilton; with a Supplement of Interesting Letters by Distinguished Personages. 2 vols. 8vo. Lovewell and Co. London. 1814," appeared in No. xxi. of The Quarterly Review, for April, 1814. The

attack is mainly directed against Lady Hamilton, but Nelson, with every pretence of reluctance and of general admiration, is also censured on moral grounds, and his letters are held up to ridicule.

[127] A partner in the publishing firm of Ridgeway and Symonds. Letters of R. Southey, iii. 65.

[128] The reference is to Swift's famous "Drapier" Letters. Swift wrote in the assumed character of a draper, and dated his letters "From my shop in St. Francis Street," but why he adopted the French instead of the English spelling of the word does not seem to have been satisfactorily explained. Notes and Queries, III. Series, x. 55.

[129] The View of the State of Ireland, first published in 1633.

[130] John Kenyon, 1783-1856, a poet and philanthropist. He settled at Woodlands near Stowey in 1802, and became acquainted with Poole and Poole's friends. He was on especially intimate terms with Southey, who writes of him (January 11, 1827) to his still older friend Wynne, as "one of the very best and pleasantest men whom I have ever known, one whom every one likes at first sight, and likes better the longer he is known." With Coleridge himself the tie was less close, but he was, I know, a most kind friend to the poet's wife during those anxious years, 1814-1819, when her children were growing up, and she had little else to depend upon but Southey's generous protection and the moiety of the Wedgwood annuity. Kenyon's friendship with the Brownings belongs to a later chapter of literary history.

[131] Poetical Works, p. 176; Appendix H, pp. 525, 526.

[132] Poetical Works, p. 450.

[133] In 1815 an act was brought in by Mr. Robinson (afterwards Lord Ripon) and passed, permitting the importation of corn when the price of home-grown wheat reached 80s. a quarter. During the spring of the year, January-March, while the bill was being discussed, bread-riots took place in London and Westminster.

[134] It would seem that Coleridge had either overlooked or declined to put faith in Wordsworth's Apology for The Excursion, which appeared in the Preface to the First Edition of 1814. He was, of course, familiar with the "poem on the growth of your mind," the hitherto unnamed and unpublished Prelude, and he must have been at least equally familiar with the earlier books of The Excursion. Why then was he disappointed with the poem as a whole, and what had he looked for at Wordsworth's hands? Not, it would seem, for an "ante-chapel," but for the sanctuary itself. He had been stirred to the depths by the recitation of The Prelude at Coleorton, and in his lines "To a Gentleman," which he quotes in this letter, he recapitulates the arguments of the poem. This he considered was The Excursion, "an Orphic song indeed"! and as he listened the melody sank into his soul. But that was but an exordium, a "prelusive strain" to The Recluse, which might indeed include the Grasmere fragment, the story of Margaret and so forth, but which in the form of poetry would convey the substance of divine philosophy. He had looked for a second Milton who would put Lucretius to a double shame, for a "philosophic poem," which would justify anew "the ways of God to men;" and in lieu of this pageant of the imagination there was Wordsworth prolific of moral discourse, of scenic and personal narrative—a prophet indeed, but "unmindful of the heavenly Vision."

[135] The Rev. William Money, a descendant of John Kyrle, the "Man of Ross," eulogised alike by Pope and Coleridge, was at this time in possession of the family seat of Whetham, a few miles distant from Calne, in Wiltshire. Coleridge was often a guest at his house.

[136] A controversial work on the inspiration of Scripture. A thin thread of narrative runs through the dissertation. It was the work of the Rev. J. W. Cunningham, Vicar of Harrow, and was published in 1813.

[137] The Hon. and Rev. T. A. Methuen, Rector of All Cannings, was the son of Paul Methuen, Esq., M. P., afterward Lord Methuen of Corsham House. He contributed some reminiscences of Coleridge at this period to the Christian Observer of 1845. Samuel Taylor Coleridge, a Narrative, by J. Dykes Campbell, 1894, p. 208.

[138] The annual payments for board and lodging, which were made at first, for some time before Coleridge's death fell into abeyance. The approximate amount of the debt so incurred, and the circumstances under which it began to accumulate, are alike unknown to me. The fact that such a debt existed was, I believe, a secret jealously guarded by his generous hosts, but as, with the best intentions, statements have been made to the effect that there was no pecuniary obligation on Coleridge's part, it is right that the truth should be known. On the other hand, it is only fair to Coleridge's memory to put it on record that this debt of honour was a sore trouble to him, and that he met it as best he could. We know, for instance, on his own authority, that the profits of the three volume edition of his poems, published in 1828, were made over to Mr. Gillman.

[139] Zapolya: A Christmas Tale, in two Parts, was published by Rest Fenner late in 1817. A year before, after the first part had been rejected by the Drury Lane Committee, Coleridge arranged with Murray to publish both parts as a poem, and received an advance of £50 on the MS. He had, it seems, applied to Murray to be released from this engagement, and on the strength of an ambiguous reply, offered the work to the publishers of Sybilline Leaves. From letters to Murray, dated March 26 and March 29, 1817, it is evident that the £50 advanced on A Christmas Tale was repaid. In acknowledging the receipt of the sum, Murray seems to have generously omitted all mention of a similar advance on "a play then in composition." In his letter of March 29, Coleridge speaks of this second debt, which does not appear to have been paid. Samuel Taylor Coleridge, a Narrative, by J. Dykes Campbell, p. 223; Memoirs of John Murray, i. 301-306.

[140] Murray had offered Coleridge two hundred guineas for "a small volume of specimens of Rabbinical Wisdom," but owing to pressure of work the project was abandoned. "Specimens of Rabbinical Wisdom selected from the Mishna" had already appeared in the original issue of The Friend (Nos. x., xi.), and these, with the assistance of his friend Hyman Hurwitz, Master of the Hebrew Academy at Highgate, he intended to supplement and expand into a volume. Samuel Taylor Coleridge, a Narrative, by J. Dykes Campbell, p. 224 and note.

[141] Apart from internal evidence, there is nothing to prove that this article, a review of "Christabel," which appeared in the Edinburgh Review, December, 1816, was written by Hazlitt. It led, however, to the insertion of a footnote in the first volume of the Biographia Literaria, in which Coleridge accused Jeffrey of personal and ungenerous animosity against himself, and reminded him of hospitality shown to him at Keswick, and of the complacent and flattering language which he had employed on that occasion. Not content with commissioning Hazlitt to review the book, Jeffrey appended a long footnote signed with his initials, in which he indignantly repudiates the charge of personal animus, and makes bitter

fun of Coleridge's susceptibility to flattery, and of his boasted hospitality. Southey had offered him a cup of coffee, and Coleridge had dined with him at the inn. Voila tout. Both footnotes are good reading. Biographia Literaria, ed. 1817, i. 52 note; Edinburgh Review, December, 1817.

[142] Two letters from Tieck to Coleridge have been preserved, a very long one, dated February 20, 1818, in which he discusses a scheme for bringing out his works in England, and asks Coleridge if he has succeeded in finding a publisher for him, and the following note, written sixteen years later, to introduce the German painter, Herr von Vogelstein. I am indebted to my cousin, Miss Edith Coleridge, for a translation of both letters.

Dresden, April 30, 1834.

I hope that my dear and honoured friend Coleridge still remembers me. To me those delightful hours at Highgate remain unforgettable. I have seen your friend Robinson, once here in Dresden, but you—At that time I believed that I should come again to England—and in such hopes we grow old and wear away.

My kindest remembrances to your excellent hosts at Highgate. It is with especial emotion that I look again and again at the Anatomy of Melancholy [a present from Mr. Gillman], as well as the Lay Sermons, Christabel, and the Biographia Literaria. Herr von Vogelstein, one of the most esteemed historical painters of Germany, brings you this letter from your loving

Ludwig Tieck.

[143] Henry Crabb Robinson, whose admirable diaries, first published in 1869, may, it is hoped, be reëdited and published in full, died at the age of ninety-one in 1867. He was a constant guest at my father's house in Chelsea during my boyhood. I have, too, a distinct remembrance of his walking over Loughrigg from Rydal Mount, where he was staying with Mrs. Wordsworth, and visiting my parents at High Close, between Grasmere and Langdale, then and now the property of Mr. Wheatley Balme. This must have been in 1857, when he was past eighty years of age. My impression is that his conversation consisted, for the most part, of anecdotes concerning Wieland and Schiller and Goethe. Of Wordsworth and Coleridge he must have had much to say, but his words, as was natural, fell on the unheeding ears of a child.

[144] The Right Hon. John Hookham Frere, 1769-1846, now better known as the translator of Aristophanes than as statesman or diplomatist, was a warm friend to Coleridge in his later years. He figures in the later memoranda and correspondence as ὁ καλοκάγαθος, the ideal Christian gentleman.

[145] Samuel Purkis, of Brentford, tanner and man of letters, was an early friend of Poole's, and through him became acquainted with Coleridge and Sir Humphry Davy. When Coleridge went up to London in June, 1798, to stay with the Wedgwoods at Stoke House, in the village of Cobham, he stayed a night at Brentford on the way. In a letter to Poole of the same date, he thus describes his host: "Purkis is a gentleman, with the free and cordial and interesting manners of the man of literature. His colloquial diction is uncommonly pleasing, his information various, his own mind elegant and acute." Thomas Poole and his Friends, i. 271, et passim.

[146] For an account of Coleridge's relations with his publishers, Fenner and Curtis, see *Samuel Taylor Coleridge, a Narrative*, by J. Dykes Campbell, p. 227. See, too, *Lippincott's Mag.* for June, 1870, art. "Some Unpublished Correspondence of S. T. Coleridge," and Brandl's *Samuel Taylor Coleridge and the Romantic School*, 1887, pp. 351-353.

[147] J. H. Frere was, I believe, one of those who assisted Coleridge to send his younger son to Cambridge.

[148] John Taylor Coleridge (better known as Mr. Justice Coleridge), and George May Coleridge, Vicar of St. Mary Church, Devon, and Prebendary of Wells. Another cousin who befriended Hartley, when he was an undergraduate at Merton, and again later when he was living with the Montagus, in London, was William Hart Coleridge, afterward Bishop of Barbados. The poet's own testimony to the good work of his nephews should be set against Allsop's foolish and uncalled for attack on "the Bishop and the Judge." *Letters, etc., of S. T. Coleridge*, 1836, i. 225, note.

[149] Poole's reply to this letter, dated July 31, 1817, contained an invitation to Hartley to come to Nether Stowey. Mrs. Sandford tells us that it was believed that "the young man spent more than one vacation at Stowey, where he was well-known and very popular, though the young ladies of the place either themselves called him the Black Dwarf, or cherished a conviction that that was his nickname at Oxford." *Thomas Poole and his Friends*, ii. 256-258.

[150] The Rev. H. F. Cary, 1772-1844, the well-known translator of the Divina Commedia. His son and biographer, the Rev. Henry Cary, gives the following account of his father's first introduction to Coleridge, which took place at Littlehampton in the autumn of 1817:—

"It was our custom to walk on the sands and read Homer aloud, a practice adopted partly for the sake of the sea-breezes.... For several consecutive days Coleridge crossed us in our walk. The sound of the Greek, and especially the expressive countenance of the tutor, attracted his notice; so one day, as we met, he placed himself directly in my father's way and thus accosted him: 'Sir, yours is a face I should know. I am Samuel Taylor Coleridge.'" *Memoir of H. F. Cary*, ii. 18.

[151] It appears, however, that he underrated his position as a critic. A quotation from Cary's Dante, and a eulogistic mention of the work generally, in a lecture on Dante, delivered by Coleridge at Flower-de-Luce Court, on February 27, 1818, led, so his son says, to the immediate sale of a thousand copies, and notices "reëchoing Coleridge's praises" in the Edinburgh and Quarterly Reviews. *Memoir of H. F. Cary*, ii. 28.

[152] From the *Destiny of Nations*.

[153] Joseph Henry Green, 1791-1863, an eminent surgeon and anatomist. In his own profession he won distinction as lecturer and operator, and as the author of the *Dissector's Manual*, and some pamphlets on medical reform and education. He was twice, 1849-50 and 1858-59, President of the College of Surgeons. His acquaintance with Coleridge, which began in 1817, was destined to influence his whole career. It was his custom for many years to pass two afternoons of the week at Highgate, and on these occasions as amanuensis and collaborateur, he helped to lay the foundations of the Magnum Opus. Coleridge appointed him his literary executor, and bequeathed to him a mass of unpublished MSS. which it was hoped he would reduce to order and publish as a connected system of philosophy. Two addresses which he delivered, as Hunterian Orations in 1841 and 1847, on "Vital

Dynamics" and "Mental Dynamics," were published in his lifetime, and after his death two volumes entitled Spiritual Philosophy, founded on the Teaching of S. T. Coleridge, were issued, together with a memoir, by his friend and former pupil, Sir John Simon.

His fame has suffered eclipse owing in great measure to his chivalrous if unsuccessful attempt to do honour to Coleridge. But he deserves to stand alone. Members of his own profession not versed in polar logic looked up to his "great and noble intellect" with pride and delight, and by those who were honoured by his intimacy he was held in love and reverence. To Coleridge he was a friend indeed, bringing with him balms more soothing than "poppy or mandragora," the healing waters of Faith and Hope. Spiritual Philosophy, by J. H. Green; Memoir of the author's life, i.-lix.

[154] This must have been the impromptu lecture "On the Growth of the Individual Mind," delivered at the rooms of the London Philosophical Society. According to Gillman, who details the circumstances under which the address was given, but does not supply the date, the lecturer began with an "apologetic preface": "The lecture I am about to give this evening is purely extempore. Should you find a nominative case looking out for a verb—or a fatherless verb for a nominative case, you must excuse it. It is purely extempore, though I have thought and read much on this subject." Life of Coleridge, pp. 354-357.

[155] The "Essay on the Science of Method" was finished in December, 1817, and printed in the following January. Samuel Taylor Coleridge, a Narrative, by J. Dykes Campbell, 1894, p. 232.

[156] The Hebrew text and Coleridge's translation were published in the form of a pamphlet, and sold by "T. Boosey, 4 Old Broad Street, 1817." The full title was "Israel's Lament. Translation of a Hebrew dirge, chaunted in the Great Synagogue, St. James' Place, Aldgate, on the day of the Funeral of her Royal Highness the Princess Charlotte. By Hyman Hurwitz, Master of the Hebrew Academy, Highgate, 1817."

The translation is below Coleridge at his worst. The "Harp of Quantock" must, indeed, have required stringing before such a line as "For England's Lady is laid low" could have escaped the file, or "worn her" be permitted to rhyme with "mourner"! Poetical Works, p. 187; Editor's Note, p. 638.

[157] The Kritik der praktischen Vernunft was published in 1797.

[158] This statement requires explanation. Franz Xavier von Baader, 1765-1841, was a mystic of the school of Jacob Böhme, and wrote in opposition to Schelling.

[159] Ludwig Tieck published his Sternbald's Wanderungen in 1798.

[160] Heinse's Ardinghello was published in 1787.

[161] Richter's Vorschule der Aisthetik was published in 1804 (3 vols.).

[162] See Table Talk for January 3 and May 1, 1823. See, also, The Friend, Essay iii. of the First Landing Place. Coleridge's Works, Harper & Brothers, 1853, ii. 134-137, and "Notes on Hamlet," Ibid. iv. 147-150.

[163] Charles Augustus Tulk, described by Mr. Campbell as "a man of fortune with an uncommon taste for philosophical speculation," was an eminent Swedenborgian, and

mainly instrumental in establishing the "New Church" in Great Britain. It was through Coleridge's intimacy with Mr. Tulk that his writings became known to the Swedenborgian community, and that his letters were read at their gatherings. I possess transcripts of twenty-five letters from Coleridge to Tulk, in many of which he details his theories of ontological speculation. The originals were sold and dispersed in 1882.

A note on Swedenborg's treatise, "De Cultu et Amore Dei," is printed in Notes Theological and Political, London, 1853, p. 110, but a long series of marginalia on the pages of the treatise, "De Cœlo et Inferno," of which a transcript has been made, remains unpublished.

For Coleridge's views on Swedenborgianism, see "Notes on Noble's Appeal," Literary Remains; Coleridge's Works, Harper & Brothers, 1853, v. 522-527.

[164] It may be supposed that it was Blake, the mystic and the spiritualist, that aroused Tulk's interest, and that, as an indirect consequence, the original edition of his poems, "engraved in writing-hand," was sent to Coleridge for his inspection and criticism. The Songs of Innocence were published in 1787, ten years before the Lyrical Ballads appeared, and more than thirty years before the date of this letter, but they were known only to a few. Lamb, writing in 1824, speaks of him as Robert Blake, and after praising in the highest terms his paintings and engravings, says that he has never read his poems, "which have been sold hitherto only in manuscript." It is strange that Coleridge should not have been familiar with them, for in 1812 Crabb Robinson, so he tells us, read them aloud to Wordsworth, who was "pleased with some of them, and considered Blake as having the elements of poetry, a thousand times more than either Byron or Scott." None, however, of these hearty and genuine admirers appear to have reflected that Blake had "gone back to nature," a while before Wordsworth or Coleridge turned their steps in that direction. Letters of Charles Lamb, 1886, ii. 104, 105, 324, 325; H. C. Robinson's Diary, i. 385.

[165] In the Aids to Reflection, at the close of a long comment on a passage in Field, Coleridge alludes to "discussions of the Greek Fathers, and of the Schoolmen on the obscure and abysmal subject of the divine A-seity, and the distinction between the θέλημα and the βουλή, that is, the Absolute Will as the universal ground of all being, and the election and purpose of God in the personal Idea, as Father." Coleridge's Works, 1853, i. 317.

[166] The bill in which Coleridge interested himself, and in favour of which he wrote two circulars which were printed and distributed, was introduced in the House of Commons by the first Sir Robert Peel. The object of the bill was to regulate the employment of children in cotton factories. A bill for prohibiting the employment of children under nine was passed in 1833, but it was not till 1844 that the late Lord Shaftesbury, then Lord Ashley, succeeded in passing the Ten Hours Bills. In a letter of May 3d to Crabb Robinson, Coleridge asks: "Can you furnish us with any other instances in which the legislature has interfered with what is ironically called 'Free Labour' (i. e. dared to prohibit soul-murder on the part of the rich, and self-slaughter on that of the poor!), or any dictum of our grave law authorities from Fortescue—to Eldon: for from the borough of Hell I wish to have no representatives." Henry Crabb Robinson's Diary, ii. 93-95.

[167] James Maitland, 1759-1839, eighth Earl of Lauderdale, belonged to the party of Charles James Fox, and, like Coleridge, opposed the first war with France, which began in 1793. In the ministry of "All the Talents" he held the Great Seal of Scotland. Coleridge calls

him plebeian because he inherited the peerage from a remote connection. He was the author of several treatises on finance and political economy.

[168] It was, I have been told by an eyewitness, Coleridge's habit to take a pinch of snuff, and whilst he was talking to rub it between his fingers. He wasted so much snuff in the process that the maid servant had directions to sweep up these literary remains and replace them in the canister.

[169] A pet name for the Gillmans' younger son, Henry.

[170] Coleridge was fond of quoting these lines as applicable to himself.

[171] Washington Allston.

[172] Charles Robert Leslie, historical painter, 1794-1859, was born of American parents, but studied art in London under Washington Allston. A pencil sketch, for which Coleridge sat to him in 1820, is in my possession. Mr. Hamo Thornycroft, R. A., after a careful inspection of other portraits and engravings of S. T. Coleridge, modelled the bust which now (thanks to American generosity) finds its place in Poets' Corner, mainly in accordance with this sketch.

[173] Letters, Conversations, and Recollections of S. T. Coleridge, London, 1836, i. 1-3.

[174] The Prospectus of the Lectures on the History of Philosophy was printed in Allsop's Letters, etc., as Letter xliv., November 26, 1818, but the announcement of the time and place has been omitted. A very rare copy of the original prospectus, which has been placed in my hands by Mrs. Henry Watson, gives the following details:—

"This course will be comprised in Fourteen Lectures, to commence on Monday evening, December 7, 1818, at eight o'clock, at the Crown and Anchor, Strand; and be continued on the following Mondays, with the intermission of Christmas week—Double Tickets, admitting a Lady and Gentleman, Three Guineas. Single Tickets, Two Guineas. Admission to a Single Lecture, Five Shillings. An Historical and Chronological Guide to the course will be printed."

A reporter was hired at the expense of Hookham Frere to take down the lectures in shorthand. A transcript, which I possess, contains numerous errors and omissions, but is interesting as affording proof of the conversational style of Coleridge's lectures. See, for further account of Lectures of 1819, Samuel Taylor Coleridge, a Narrative, by J. Dykes Campbell, pp. 238, 239.

[175] Thomas Phillips, R. A., 1770-1845, painted two portraits of Coleridge, one of which is in the possession of Mr. John Murray, and was engraved as the frontispiece of the first volume of the Table Talk; and the other in that of Mr. William Rennell Coleridge, of Salston, Ottery St. Mary. The late Lord Chief Justice used to say that the Salston picture was "the best presentation of the outward man." No doubt it recalled his great-uncle as he remembered him. It certainly bears a close resemblance to the portraits of Coleridge's brothers, Edward and George, and of other members of the family.

[176] My impression is that this letter was written to Mrs. Aders, the beautiful and accomplished daughter of the engraver Raphael Smith, but the address is wanting and I cannot speak with any certainty.

[177] Compare lines 16-20 of The Two Founts:—

"As on the driving cloud the shiny bow,
That gracious thing made up of tears and light."

The poem as a whole was composed in 1826, and, as I am assured by Mrs. Henry Watson (on the authority of her grandmother, Mrs. Gillman), addressed to Mrs. Aders; but the fifth and a preceding stanza, which Coleridge marked for interpolation, in an annotated copy of Poetical Works, 1828 (kindly lent me by Mrs. Watson), must have been written before that date, and were, as I gather from an insertion in a note-book, originally addressed to Mrs. Gillman. Poetical Works, p. 196. See, too, for unprinted stanza, Ibid. Editor's Note, p. 642.

[178] "To Two Sisters." Poetical Works, p. 179.

[179] The so-called "Manchester Massacre," nicknamed Peterloo, took place August 16, 1819. Towards the middle of October dangerous riots broke out at North Shields. Cries of "Blood for blood," "Manchester over again," were heard in the streets, and "so daring have the mob been that they actually threatened to burn or destroy the ships of war." Annual Register, October 15-23, 1819.

[180] "Fears in Solitude." Poetical Works, p. 127.

[181] Mrs. Gillman's sister.

[182] A collection of casts of antique gems, once, no doubt, the property of S. T. C., is now in the possession of Alexander Gillman, Esq., of Sussex Square, Brighton.

[183] Edward Dubois, satirist, 1775-1850, was the author of The Wreath, a Translation of Boccaccio's Decameron, 1804, and other works besides those mentioned in the text. Biographical Dictionary.

[184] A late note-book of the Highgate period contains the following doggerel:—

To the most veracious Anecdotist and
Small-Talk Man, Thomas Hill, Esq.

Tom Hill who laughs at cares and woes,
As nanci—nili—pili—
What is he like as I suppose?
Why to be sure, a Rose, a Rose.
At least no soul that Tom Hill knows,
Could e'er recall a Li-ly.
S. T. C.

"The first time," writes Miss Stuart, in a personal remembrance of Coleridge, headed "A Farewell, 1834," "I dined in company at my father's table, I sat between Coleridge and Mr. Hill (known as 'Little Tommy Hill') of the Adelphi, and Ezekiel then formed the theme of Coleridge's eloquence. I well remember his citing the chapter of the Dead Bones, and his sepulchral voice as he asked, 'Can these bones live?' Then, his observation that nothing in the range of human thought was more sublime than Ezekiel's reply, 'Lord, thou knowest,' in deepest humility, not presuming to doubt the omnipotence of the Most High." Letters from the Lake Poets, p. 322. See, too, Letters from Hill to Stuart, Ibid. p. 435.

[185] William Elford Leach, 1790-1836, a physician and naturalist, was at this time Curator of the Natural History Department at the British Museum.

By Lawrencian, Coleridge means a disciple of the eminent surgeon William Lawrence, whose "Lectures on the Physiology, Zoölogy, and Natural History of Man," which were delivered in 1816, are alluded to more than once in his "Theory of Life." "Theory of Life" in Miscellanies, Æsthetic and Literary, Bohn's Standard Library, pp. 377, 385.

[186] Included in the Omniana of 1809-1816. Table Talk, etc., Bell & Sons, 1884, p. 400.

[187] Compare a letter of Coleridge to Allsop, dated October 8, 1822, in which he details "the four griping and grasping sorrows, each of which seemed to have my very heart in its hands, compressing or wringing."

It was the publication of this particular letter, with its thinly-veiled allusions to Wordsworth, Southey, and to Coleridge's sons, which not only excited indignation against Allsop, but moved Southey to write a letter to Cottle. Letters, Conversation, etc., 1836, ii. 140-146.

[188] Compare "The Wanderer's Farewell to Two Sisters" (Mrs. Morgan and Miss Brent), 1807. Miss Brent made her home with her married sister, Mrs. J. J. Morgan, and during the years 1810-1815, when Coleridge lived under the Morgans' roof at Hammersmith, in London, and in the West of England, he received from these ladies the most affectionate care and attention, both in sickness and in health. Poetical Works, pp. 179, 180.

[189] The Reverend Edward Coleridge, 1800-1883, the sixth and youngest son of Colonel James Coleridge, was for many years a Master and afterwards a Fellow of Eton. He also held the College living of Mapledurham near Reading. He corresponded with his uncle, who was greatly attached to him, on philosophical and theological questions. It was to him that the "Confessions of an Enquiring Spirit" were originally addressed in the form of letters.

[190] Colonel Coleridge's only daughter, Frances Duke, was afterwards married to the Honourable Mr. Justice Patteson, a Judge of the Queen's Bench.

[191]

Like those trim skiffs, unknown of yore
On winding lake, or rivers wide,
That ask no aid of sail or oar,
That fear no spite of wind or tide.

"Youth and Age," ll. 12-15. Poetical Works, p. 191. A MS. copy of "Youth and Age" in my possession, of which the probable date is 1822, reads "boats" for "skiffs."

[192] Sir Alexander Johnston, 1775-1849, a learned orientalist. He was Advocate General (afterwards Chief Justice) of Ceylon, and had much to do with the reorganisation of the constitution of the island. He was one of the founders of the Royal Asiatic Society. Dict. of Nat. Biog. art. "Johnston, Sir Alexander."

[193] Gabriele Rossetti, 1783-1854, the father of Dante G. Rossetti, etc., first visited England as a political exile in 1824. In 1830 he was appointed Professor of the Italian language at King's College. He is best known as a commentator on Dante. He presented

Coleridge with a copy of his work, Dello Spirito Antipapale che Produsse la Riforma, and some of his verses in MS., which are in my possession.

[194] From the letter of Wordsworth to Lord Lonsdale, of February 5, 1819, it is plain that the translation of three books of the Æneid had been already completed at that date. Another letter written five years later, November 3, 1824, implies that the work had been put aside, and, after a long interval, reattempted. In the mean time a letter of Coleridge to Mrs. Allsop, of April 8, 1824, tells us that the three books had been sent to Coleridge and must have remained in his possession for some time. The MS. of this translation appears to have been lost, but "one of the books," Professor Knight tells us, was printed in the Philological Museum, at Cambridge, in 1832. Life of W. Wordsworth, ii. 296-303.

[195] Coleridge was at this time (1824) engaged in making a selection of choice passages from the works of Archbishop Leighton, which, together with his own comment and corollaries, were published as Aids to Reflection, in 1825. See Letter CCXXX.

[196] Conversations of Lord Byron, etc., by Captain Medwin.

[197] The frontispiece of the second volume of the Antiquary represents Dr. Dousterswivel digging for treasure in Misticot's grave. The resemblance to Coleridge is, perhaps, not wholly imaginary.

[198] John Taylor Coleridge was editor of the Quarterly Review for one year, 1825-1826. Southey's Life and Correspondence, v. 194, 201, 204, 239, etc.; Letters of Robert Southey, iii. 455, 473, 511, 514, etc.

[199] Henry Hart Milman, 1791-1868, afterwards celebrated as historian and divine (Dean of St. Paul's, 1849), was, at this time, distinguished chiefly as a poet. His Fall of Jerusalem was published in 1820. He was a contributor to the Quarterly Review.

[200] Afterward the wife of Sir George Beaumont, the artist's son and successor in the baronetcy.

[201] Almost the same sentence with regard to his address as Royal Associate occurs in a letter to his nephew, John Taylor Coleridge, of May 20, 1825. The "Essay on the Prometheus of Æschylus," which was printed in Literary Remains, was republished in Coleridge's Works, Harper & Brothers, 1853, iv. 344-365. See, also, Brandl's Life of Coleridge, p. 361.

[202] The portrait of William Hart Coleridge, Bishop of Barbadoes and the Leeward Islands, by Thomas Phillips, R. A., is now in the Hall of Christ Church, Oxford.

[203] A sprig of this myrtle (or was it a sprig of myrtle in a nosegay?) grew into a plant. At some time after Coleridge's death it passed into the hands of the late S. C. Hall, who presented it to the late Lord Coleridge. It now flourishes, in strong old age, in a protected nook outside the library at Heath's Court, Ottery St. Mary.

[204] George Dyer, 1755-1841, best remembered as the author of The History of the University of Cambridge, and a companion work on The Privileges of the University of Cambridge, began life as a Baptist minister, but settled in London as a man of letters in 1792. As a "brother-Grecian" he was introduced to Coleridge in 1794, in the early days of pantisocracy, and probably through him became intimate with Lamb and Southey. He

contributed "The Show, an English Eclogue," and other poems, to the Annual Anthology of 1799 and 1800. His poetry was a constant source of amused delight to Lamb and Coleridge. A pencil sketch of Dyer by Matilda Betham is in the British Museum. Letters of Charles Lamb, i. 125-128 et passim; Southey's Life and Correspondence, i. 218 et passim.

[205] George Cattermole, 1800-1868, to whose "peculiar gifts and powerful genius" Mr. Ruskin has borne testimony, was eminent as an architectural draughtsman and water-colour painter. With his marvellous illustrations of "Master Humphrey's Clock" all the world is familiar. Dict. of Nat. Biog. art. "George Cattermole." His brother Richard was Secretary of the Royal Society of Literature, of which Coleridge was appointed a Royal Associate in 1825. Copies of this and of other letters from Coleridge to Cattermole were kindly placed at my disposal by Mr. James M. Menzies of 24, Carlton Hill, St. John's Wood.

[206] Harriet Macklin, Coleridge's faithful attendant for the last seven or eight years of his life. On his deathbed he left a solemn request in writing that his family should make a due acknowledgment of her services. It was to her that Lamb, when he visited Highgate after Coleridge's death, made a present of five guineas.

[207] Dr. Chalmers represented the visit as having lasted three hours, and that during that "stricken" period he only got occasional glimpses of what the prophet "would be at." His little daughter, however, was so moved by the "mellifluous flow of discourse" that, when "the music ceased, her overwrought feelings found relief in tears." Samuel Taylor Coleridge, a Narrative, by J. Dykes Campbell, 1894, p. 260, footnote.

[208] A disciple and amanuensis, to whom, it is believed, he dictated two quarto volumes on "The History of Logic" and "The Elements of Logic," which originally belonged to Joseph Henry Green, and are now in the possession of Mr. C. A. Ward of Chingford Hatch. Samuel Taylor Coleridge, a Narrative, by J. Dykes Campbell, 1894, pp. 250, 251; Athenæum, July 1, 1893, art. "Coleridge's Logic."

[209] Henry Nelson Coleridge, 1798-1843, was the fifth son of Colonel James Coleridge of Heath's Court, Ottery St. Mary. His marriage with the poet's daughter took place on September 3, 1829. He was the author of Six Months in the West Indies, 1825, and an Introduction to the Study of the Greek Poets, 1830. He practised as a chancery barrister and won distinction in his profession. The later years of his life were devoted to the reëditing of his uncle's published works, and to throwing into a connected shape the literary as distinguished from the philosophical section of his unpublished MSS. The Table Talk, the best known of Coleridge's prose works, appeared in 1835. Four volumes of Literary Remains, including the "Lectures on Shakespeare and other Dramatists," were issued 1836-1839. The third edition of The Friend, 1837, the Confessions of an Inquiring Spirit, 1840, and the fifth edition of Aids to Reflection, 1843, followed in succession. The second edition of the Biographia Literaria, which "he had prepared in part," was published by his widow in 1847.

A close study of the original documents which were at my uncle's disposal enables me to bear testimony to his editorial skill, to his insight, his unwearied industry, his faithfulness. Of the charm of his appearance, and the brilliance of his conversation, I have heard those who knew him speak with enthusiasm. He died, from an affection of the spine, in January, 1843.

[210] This lady was for many years governess in the family of Dr. Crompton of Eaton Hall, near Liverpool. Memoirs and Letters of Sara Coleridge, London, 1873, i. 8 109-116.

[211] Sir William Rowan Hamilton, 1805-1865, the great mathematician, was at this time Professor of Astronomy at Dublin. He was afterwards appointed Astronomer Royal of Ireland. He was, as is well known, a man of culture and a poet; and it was partly to ascertain his views on scientific questions, and partly to interest him in his verses, that Hamilton was anxious to be made known to Coleridge. He had begun a correspondence with Wordsworth as early as 1827, and Wordsworth, on the occasion of his tour in Ireland in 1829, visited Hamilton at the Observatory. Miss Lawrence's introduction led to an interview, but a letter which Hamilton wrote to Coleridge in the spring of 1832 remained unanswered. In a second letter, dated February 3, 1833, he speaks of a "Lecture on Astronomy" which he forwards for Coleridge's acceptance, and also of "some love-poems to a lady to whom I am shortly to be married." The love-poems, eight sonnets, which are smoothly turned and are charming enough, have survived, but the lecture has disappeared. The interest of this remarkable letter lies in the double appeal to Coleridge as a scientific authority and a literary critic. Coleridge's reply, if reply there was, would be read with peculiar interest. In a letter to Mr. Aubrey de Vere, May 28, 1832, he thus records his impressions of Coleridge: "Coleridge is rather to be considered as a Faculty than as a Mind; and I did so consider him. I seemed rather to listen to an oracular voice, to be circumfused in a Divine ὀμφή, than—as in the presence of Wordsworth—to hold commune with an exalted man." Life of W. Wordsworth, iii. 157-174, 210, etc.

[212] He is referring to a final effort to give up the use of opium altogether. It is needless to say that, after a trial of some duration, the attempt was found to be impracticable. It has been strenuously denied, as though it had been falsely asserted, that under the Gillmans' care Coleridge overcame the habit of taking laudanum in more or less unusual quantities. Gillman, while he maintains that his patient in the use of narcotics satisfied the claims of duty, makes no such statement; and the confessions or outpourings from the later note-books which are included in the Life point to a different conclusion. That after his settlement at Highgate, in 1816, the habit was regulated and brought under control, and that this change for the better was due to the Gillmans' care and to his own ever-renewed efforts to be free, none can gainsay. There was a moral struggle, and into that "sore agony" it would be presumption to intrude; but to a moral victory Coleridge laid no claim. And, at the last, it was "mercy," not "praise," for which he pleaded.

[213] The notes on Asgill's Treatises were printed in the Literary Remains, Coleridge's Works, 1853, v. 545-550, and in Notes Theological and Political, London, 1853, pp. 103-109.

[214] Admirers of Dr. Magee, 1765-1831, who was successively Bishop of Raphoe, 1819, and Archbishop of Dublin, 1822. He was the author of Discourses on the Scriptural Doctrines of the Atonement. He was grandfather of the late Archbishop of York, better known as Bishop of Peterborough.

[215] I am indebted to Mr. John Henry Steinmetz, a younger brother of Coleridge's friend and ardent disciple, for a copy of this letter. It was addressed, he informs me, to his brother's friend, the late Mr. John Peirse Kennard, of Hordle Cliff, Hants, father of the late Sir John Coleridge Kennard, Bart., M. P. for Salisbury, and of Mr. Adam Steinmetz Kennard, of Crawley Court Hants, at whose baptism the poet was present, and to whom he addressed the well-known letter (Letter CCLX.), "To my Godchild, Adam Steinmetz Kennard."

[216] See Table Talk, August 14, 1832.

[217] So, too, of Keats. See Table Talk, etc., Bell & Sons. 1884, Talk for August 14, 1832. Table p. 179.

[218] "The sot would reject the poisoned cup, yet the trembling-hand with which he raises his daily or hourly draught to his lips has not left him ignorant that this, too, is altogether a poison." The Friend, Essay xiv.; Coleridge's Works, ii. 100.

[219] The motto of this theme, (January 19, 1794), of which I possess a transcript in Coleridge's handwriting, or perhaps the original copy, is—

Quid fas
Atque nefas tandem incipiunt sentire peractis
Criminibus.
The theme was selected by Boyer for insertion in his Liber Aureus of school exercises in prose and verse, now in the possession of James Boyer, Esq., of the Coopers' Company. The sentence to which Coleridge alludes ran thus: "As if we were in some great sea-vortex, every moment we perceive our ruin more clearly, every moment we are impelled towards it with greater force."

The essay was printed for the first time in the Illustrated London News, April 1, 1893.

[220] This letter, which is addressed in Coleridge's handwriting, "Mrs. Aders, favoured by H. Gillman," and endorsed in pencil, "S. T. C.'s letter for Miss Denman," refers to the new edition of his poetical works which Coleridge had begun to see through the press. Apparently he had intended that the "Epitaph" should be inscribed on the outline of a headstone, and that this should illustrate, by way of vignette, the last page of the volume.

[221] Of the exact date of Sterling's first visit to Highgate there is no record. It may, however, be taken for granted that his intimacy with Coleridge began in 1828, when he was in his twenty-third year, and continued until the autumn of 1833,—perhaps lasted until Coleridge's death. Unlike Maurice, and Maurice's disciple, Kingsley, Sterling outlived his early enthusiasm for Coleridge and his acceptance of his teaching. It may be said, indeed, that, thanks to the genius of his second master, Carlyle, he suggests both the reaction against and the rejection of Coleridge. Of that rejection Carlyle, in his Life of Sterling, made himself the mouth-piece. It is idle to say of that marvellous but disillusioning presentment that it is untruthful, or exaggerated, or unkind. It is a sketch from the life, and who can doubt that it is lifelike? But other eyes saw another Coleridge who held them entranced. To them he was the seer of the vision beautiful, the "priest of invisible rites behind the veil of the senses," and to their ears his voice was of one who brought good tidings of reconciliation and assurance. Many, too, who cared for none of these things, were attracted to the man. Like the wedding-guest in the Ancient Mariner, they stood still. No other, they felt, was so wise, so loveable. They, too, were eye-witnesses, and their portraiture has not been outpainted by Carlyle. Apart from any expression of opinion, it is worth while to note that Carlyle saw Coleridge for the last time in the spring of 1825, and that the Life of Sterling was composed more than a quarter of a century later. His opinion of the man had, indeed, changed but little, as the notes and letters of 1824-25 clearly testify, but his criticism of the writer was far less appreciative than it had been in Coleridge's lifetime. The following extracts from a letter of Sterling to Gillman, dated "Hurstmonceaux, October 9, 1834," are evidence that his feelings towards Coleridge were at that time those of a reverent disciple:—

"The Inscription [in Highgate Church] will forever be enough to put to shame the heartless vanity of a thousand such writers as the Opium Eater. As a portrait, or even as a hint for one, his papers seem to me worse than useless.

"If it is possible, I will certainly go to Highgate, and wait on Mrs. Gillman and yourself. I have travelled the road thither with keen and buoyant expectation, and returned with high and animating remembrances oftener than any other in England. Hereafter, too, it will not have lost its charm. There is not only all this world of recollection, but the dwelling of those who best knew and best loved his work." Life of Sterling, 1871, pp. 46-54; Samuel Taylor Coleridge, a Narrative, by J. Dykes Campbell, pp. 259-261; British Museum, add. MS. 34,225, f. 194.

[222] The following unpublished lines were addressed by Coleridge to this young lady, a neighbour, I presume, and friend of the Gillmans. They must be among the last he ever wrote:—

ELISA.
Translation of Claudian.

Dulcia dona mihi tu mittis semper Elisa!
Sweet gifts to me thou sendest always, Elisa!

Et quicquid mittis, Thura putare decet.
And whatever thou sendest, Sabean odours to think it it behoves me.
The whole adapted from an epigram of Claudius by substituting Thura for mella, the original distich being in return for a Present of Honey.

Imitation.
Sweet Gift! and always doth Eliza send
Sweet Gifts and full of fragrance to her Friend.
Enough for Him to know they come from Her,
Whate'er she sends is Frankincense and Myrrh.
Another on the same subject by S. T. C. himself:—

Semper, Eliza! mihi tu suaveolentia donas:
Nam quicquid donas, te redolere puto.
Literal translation: Always, Eliza! to me things of sweet odour thou presentest. For whatever thou presentest, I fancy redolent of thyself.

Whate'er thou giv'st, it still is sweet to me,
For still I find it redolent of thee!
[223] Philip Van Artevelde.

[224] Sir Henry Taylor.

Note from the Editor

Odin's Library Classics strives to bring you unedited and unabridged works of classical literature. As such, this is the complete and unabridged version of the original English text unless noted. In some instances, obvious typographical errors have been corrected. This is done to preserve the original text as much as possible. The English language has evolved since the writing and some of the words appear in their original form, or at least the most commonly used form at the time. This is done to protect the original intent of the author. If at any time you are unsure of the meaning of a word, please do your research on the etymology of that word. It is important to preserve the history of the English language.

Taylor Anderson

Printed in Poland
by Amazon Fulfillment
Poland Sp. z o.o., Wrocław